THE CENTRE POMPIDOU IN PARIS: CHRONICLES OF IDEAS, DESIGN, CONSTRUCTION, AND EVOLUTION (1968–2028)

In partnership with

Centre Pompidou

1968—1971

THE LIVE CENTRE OF INFORMATION

FROM POMPIDOU TO BEAUBOURG

BORIS HAMZEIAN

4

EARLY SKETCHES FOR THE CENTRE BEAUBOURG: A FLEXIBLE URBAN SYSTEM FOR INFORMATION

5

THE FINAL SUBMISSION: THE LIVE CENTRE OF INFORMATION

6

THE SELECTION PROCESS: THE GRAND AND PRESTIGIOUS GESTURE AND THE ARCHITECTURAL SIMPLICITY

<

ANNEXES

FOREWORD

>.1

PREFACE BY LAURENT LE BON

President of the Centre national d'art et de culture Georges Pompidou

Since its inauguration in 1977, the Centre Pompidou has been regarded as a unique place, both in its architecture and in its uses. Even so, it is astonishing that over the past forty years no major scientific research has been carried out on its architectural history, despite its many citations, descriptions, succinct analyses, and critiques it has been subject to. This dark age is henceforth a thing of the past thanks to the work of Boris Hamzeian, who has dedicated his PhD thesis–carried out at the Swiss Federal Institute of Technology in Lausanne (EPFL, or École Polytechnique fédérale de Lausanne)–to studying the genesis and construction of the Centre Pompidou.

Over a period of five years, the young architect Boris Hamzeian has taken on the role of a true historian. He has cross-referenced the available sources, public and private archival documents–both written and illustrated– as well as collected testimonies. He has benefited from the assistance of Centre Pompidou's teams: Jean-Philippe Bonilli, archivist, and Olivier Cinqualbre, curator of the architectural collection at the National Museum of Modern Art – Centre of Industrial Creation (Musée national d'art moderne – Centre de création industrielle). In particular, he has gained the trust of Richard Rogers and Renzo Piano, as well as of their associates from that time. In addition to the current curators of their respective archives within Rogers, Stirk, Harbour + Partners (now RSHP), Fondazione Renzo Piano, and the ARUP engineering studio. It fell upon him to write the history of the Centre Pompidou's construction–the entire duration of this adventure, all the twists and turns of this collective work, while keeping a suitable distance from his object of study. He did not allow himself to be overwhelmed by the exceptional character of this building which, for those of us who have had the pleasure of working there, never ceases to inspire awe.

Each decade, we have made a point of celebrating the anniversary of the Centre Pompidou's inauguration, the last time being in 2017 in the presence of Richard Rogers and Renzo Piano. It has also been important for us to celebrate their respective careers through retrospectives–firstly in 2000 for Renzo Piano on the occasion of the Centre Pompidou's reopening after a construction campaign, and then in 2007 for Richard Rogers on the occasion of the centre's 30th anniversary.

Today, as we approach its 50th anniversary, we can but rejoice that Boris Hamzeian's work be published, and that the Pompidou Centre be associated with it. This prospective publication caught the interest of Richard Rogers, and the project now benefits from the support of Fondazione Renzo Piano and the generosity of ARUP. Our own participation in this initiative has fallen naturally into place amidst the work of maintaining the memory and history for future generations, now that the building will be undergoing extensive construction works, and as those who witnessed and took part in its history are leaving us. We think, first and foremost, and with sadness, of Richard Rogers who left us at the end of 2021.

I would like to thank all those who have contributed to the success of this book, and above all its author, Boris Hamzeian.

>.2

INTRODUCTION BY ROBERTO GARGIANI

Emeritus Professor, École Politechnique Fédérale de Lausanne, EPFL

Right from the outset the construction of the Centre national d'art et de culture Georges Pompidou in the center of Paris was an event of signal importance for international architecture in the late sixties and the seventies. The creators of that exceptional masterpiece of the architecture of all time succeeded in embodying, in the work's technical systems, spaces, and public functioning, the radical impulses that lay behind the unrest rocking European society, with protests in the streets of Paris at the very moment the competition for the design of that new and experimental center for art and culture was launched. The Centre Pompidou was conceived by an international team of architects, engineers, and technicians, united in a cultural axis that ran from Britain to Italy under the banner of radical and neo-avant-garde movements and experimentalist impulses to discover the creative potential of technology. As designed by Ove Arup & Partners and by Richard Rogers, Renzo Piano, and Gianfranco Franchini, it assumed from the earliest phases of design the semblance of a piece of revolutionary social machinery to be installed in the heart of Paris. The design submitted to the competition concealed, under its festive Pop guise, its true nature as a political device rather than a place for the appreciation of contemporary art, which is what had been requested in its terms. The intent was for it to be used to broadcast information that would foster the genesis of an alternative collective and social consciousness, in the name of a planetwide pacifism. The architecture was identified with the structure and the plant to such an extent that what was finally presented, with no veils or rhetoric, was the essence of architecture's raison d'être. It is no coincidence that the Centre Pompidou emerged at the very moment in history at which this discipline was being called on to look again at its social and theoretical foundations. The result was a pure technological haven at the cutting edge of a primordial vital space. No work of architecture has ever dared cross that line again. It is a paradox of history that the device concocted by a group of British and Italian conspirators should have been accepted by the competition jury and judged by French president Georges Pompidou worthy of being built. The awkward beauty of the Centre Pompidou stems precisely from the political contradiction of a revolutionary project devised to counter the authority of a president who, in a surprise move, decided to make this project his own in order to celebrate himself. What went on in the discussions during the judging of the competition is therefore crucial to understanding the changes reflected in the significance of the British-Italian design. Greeted in accordance with the French tradition of grandiose works intended to mark, in Paris, an era and a regime, the Centre Pompidou would not escape the destiny that had characterized the other significant monument of the capital that shares with it the role of symbolic center of the various forms assumed by French power in civil history: the Louvre. The involvement of architects from outside France in their design is one of the traits shared by those two monuments offered to the capital as places for the celebration of a power that, however paradoxical it may seem, was similar in both cases in the structure of its political system and in its decision-making machinery, including that governing the erection of national monuments. It was a mechanism of construction that allowed the architects consulted by Jean-Baptiste Colbert to make the Louvre famous all over the world, with the virtuoso device of the reinforced stone used for its colonnade, and show to other nations the enlightened power of the Sun King. And it was a true piece of technological machinery, sophisticated in every component, that allowed the Pompidou presidency to fix its position at the head of the nation in collective French and international memory. Colbert had warned his architects and his artists that no one would be able to consider himself the creator of the Louvre. The work was to appear to have sprung from a transcendental will that could be identified with the king himself. When the competition for the Centre Pompidou commenced and the procedure for the selection of the design got underway, although the question of the authorship of the winning project no longer had the ideological traits indicated by Colbert, what did happen was sufficient to make that work an exceptional chapter in the history of the civil monuments of the 20th century—a work without an author.

To uncover the reasons it proved possible to produce the masterpiece that is the Centre Pompidou it was necessary to carry out the humble and painstaking work of research Boris Hamzeian has been doing for years in order to uncover all the documents that now allow us to gain a full understanding of that product of the French presidency and of a particular period in European society and politics. Many essays have been devoted to the Centre Pompidou over the years, from the moment of its inauguration onward, and by now constitute an enormous fund of texts. Only a few of them, however, were written on the basis of research in the archives, and even when they were it was always partial and perfunctory. While it is clear that truths are not preserved in archives (assuming they exist at all), it is still the case that in those archives there are documents which allow those who, like Hamzeian, know how to make use of them to reconstruct the sequence of events, the emergence of the idea, the succession of proposals, the roads gone down and then abandoned, the compromises accepted. Only in this way is it possible to give concrete expression to the visionary nature of the original idea and the progressive gestation of the work, day after day, in the workshop and on-site. In addition to the documents in the archives, the particular moment in history chosen by Hamzeian to look at the Centre Pompidou is such as to have allowed him to make direct contact with almost all of the numerous people who were involved in the design and

construction of the building, and thus to find himself standing on a threshold in time that is poised between current affairs and history. Although the literature devoted to the Centre Pompidou is extensive, no one prior to Hamzeian had carried out the research and conducted the interviews necessary to achieve a complete overview, to offer readers all the information they need to understand every aspect of that paradoxical work of architecture, at one and the same time dissenting and state-sponsored. There is no need to dwell on the "completeness" of the documentation gathered by Hamzeian. One need only to pick a page from the essay at random to be at once immersed, line after line, in committee reports, letters, notes, drawings, sketches, models, photographs, or accounts by the protagonists. We see Pompidou, his wife, architects, engineers, ministers, consultants, entrepreneurs, technicians, administrators, politicians, journalists, and critics pop in and out. We move continually from Paris to London to Genoa, taken on a journey through the story of the project. The approach Hamzeian follows in his treatment of the documents and testimonies pertains to a genre that can be traced back centuries, that of the chronicle, although in his case that chronicle adopts a "retroactive" perspective and thus creates such an effect of distancing that the chronicle becomes a critique of the methods usually applied by historians today. It is precisely in the way that he has reorganized those documents and accounts that the merits of Hamzeian's work lie. We might have expected a "brilliant" and "rhetorical" essay like many other writings on the Centre Pompidou, in which a few documents have been used as a pretext for critical interpretations that not infrequently reflect the fixations of the historian as "author." The value of this essay stems precisely from Hamzeian's inclination to privilege the document, whatever it may be, and to compose his text, document after document, guided by what constituted, in centuries past, the rule that time should be the basis of the "chronicle." Hamzeian has worked his way through the innumerable documents he has collected on the Centre Pompidou on the basis of what had been the fundamental principle of the chronicle, and has applied that principle to an organization by themes, different on each occasion, following what the progress of the retroactive chronicle suggested to be the most significant aspect at a particular moment in the history of the work. Hamzeian has placed at the disposal of us all an unprecedented amount of information that has often served to challenge, and sometimes even refute, certainties which had accumulated in the literature on the Centre Pompidou, repeated by author after author, turning the history into a story.
Many celebrated chapters in that story have been challenged by Hamzeian: that Jean Prouvé was from the outset the main supporter of the winning project; that the work had an author that has been identified increasingly over the years as a single architect; that only to Peter Rice went the merit for the choice of cast steel; not to mention Hamzeian's far from reassuring discoveries with regard to the imperfect execution of some essential components of the structure that were nevertheless installed without having been checked.
Just as there is not one author of the Centre Pompidou—for in the end Hamzeian's critical account leads to this conclusion—in writing the essay its author has kept himself as far as possible out of the picture, even offering us a glimpse, perhaps, of the unaccustomed profile of a historian to come.
Every time we see the Centre Pompidou and go into it, the building is able to get us to relive the social ideals that inspired the generation of its designers, and is able to instill in us once again the hope in a universal architecture of structure and plant alone, above and beyond any national character and any marker of identity. Today it is possible for us to have a clearer view of the aspiration that was embodied in the essence of a vital space with no more social hierarchies, that of the Centre Pompidou: to be the first cultural and political monument of a united Europe.

Renzo Piano, Richard Rogers, Gianfranco Franchini (from July 1971 on: Piano+Rogers Architects) and Ove Arup & Partners, Centre Beaubourg (from 1974 on: Centre national d'art et de culture Georges Pompidou), Paris, 1971-1977

1

FROM GEORGES POMPIDOU’S MONUMENT AT LES HALLES TO THE ART AND CULTURAL CENTER AT PLATEAU BEAUBOURG

1.1

A "MONUMENT EN HAUTEUR" AT LES HALLES FOR THE MINISTRY OF FINANCE

When we think about the origins of the Centre Beaubourg in Paris, known today as the Centre national d'art et de culture Georges Pompidou or simply Centre Pompidou, we are faced with a tangle of ideas and issues hard to unravel solely on the basis of the events that led between 1968 and 1971 to establishing the terms of the design competition for the art and culture center to be built on the plateau Beaubourg.[1] Some questions were topical at the end of the sixties but in certain cases it is necessary to go back to the years of Charles de Gaulle's presidency or those of the French Third and Fourth Republic: the crisis in contemporary architecture, in search of new languages of representation to put France back at the center of international debate; the problems, encountered for over a hundred years, establishing a museum of contemporary art, which first arose with the Musée du Luxembourg and were still unresolved at the time the Musée national d'art moderne (Mnam) was created in 1947, or the Centre national d'art contemporain (Cnac) in 1968; the acquisition since the end of the First World War of the greatest masterpieces of French avant-garde painting by foreign institutions; the center of gravity in contemporary art's creation and promotion shift from Paris to New York, Amsterdam, Stockholm, and Bern; the lack of a seat able to meet the new museological requirements that afflicted the Mnam, housed in the Palais de Tokyo, the Cnac, housed in the Hôtel Salomon de Rothschild, and the Centre de création industrielle (CCI), housed at the Pavilion de Marsan at the Palais du Louvre; the lack of a new kind of library, one that would no longer be confined to elitist centers of conservation devoted to the erudite but broadened in scope to serve as a recreational and information center open to all French citizens; the absence in France of centers, widespread in the English-speaking world, dedicated to industrial design, interior design, product design, and architecture; the impact, lastly, of the cultural upheaval of May 1968, a clear sign of the crisis in state patronage and the demonization of official culture and the museum, both seen as the emanation of a bourgeois and authoritarian culture from which it was necessary to break free.

A way out of this mishmash of open questions, unexpressed impulses, and unrealized plans was found in the promotion of artistic and architectural creativity backed by Georges Pompidou, leading light in the Gaullist Party, prime minister under the presidency of Charles de Gaulle and, from summer 1969, president of the French Republic.

So it was in Paris, between the prime minister's residence at the Hôtel de Matignon and the president's at the Élysée Palace, between autumn 1968 and autumn 1969, that the idea of the Centre Beaubourg in Paris was born.

This idea cannot be separated from the genuine and multifaceted passion for contemporary art that Pompidou and his wife Claude had shared since the end of the Second World War—a passion expressed in collecting art works, bringing them into contact with artists who would prove crucial to the story of the Centre Pompidou, from Op art pioneers such as Yaacov Agam and Victor Vasarely to leading exponents of postwar abstractionism such as Pierre Soulages and a versatile experimenter spanning the boundary between art and architecture of the caliber of Friedensreich Hundertwasser.[2] His love of art also gave Pompidou a particular feeling for architecture which found expression, on the one hand, in an appreciation of the modernist and monumental language of prominent architects such as Henry Bernard, Guillaume Gillet, Fernand Pouillon, and Bernard Zehrfuss and, on the other, in the intention to resort to this kind of architecture to renew the historic center and, in doing so, modernize Paris and France.[3] In contrast to the preservation of *vieilles pierres*, "old stones," desired by the more conservative fringes of French society, Pompidou felt the urgent need for a contemporary architectural effervescence that would reinvigorate French architecture in the international debate and, at the same time, delineate the "face of a nation."[4]

Il faut construire, "we must build," was the motto with which Pompidou exhorted the French from the pages of *Le Figaro Litteraire*.[5]

The opportunity to give concrete expression to his vision of architectural renewal presented itself in January 1968 when he was called on to appraise the shortlist of six projects the Société civile d'études pour l'aménagement des Halles de Paris (SEAH) had submitted to President de Gaulle for the redevelopment of the district of Les Halles in Paris.[6] The large models set up in a room at the Élysée Palace for a meeting attended by the highest-ranking members of the French government, including Pompidou, represented the last stage in a longstanding plan that in 1968 found concrete expression in the proposal to dismantle one of the great icons of the French tradition of metal and glass roofing: the pavilions built by Victor Baltard to a commission from Napoleon III to house the city markets. The idea was to replace them with a district of housing, hotels, public institutions, cultural buildings, and service activities laid out around the underground train station of the new Regional Express Network (RER).

The redevelopment scheme for the Les Halles district also comprised two of the institutions that would be included in the program of the future Centre Beaubourg: the Bibliothèque publique d'information (Bpi) that the administrator general of the Bibliothèque nationale de France Étienne Dennery and his associate Jean-Pierre Seguin planned to make up for the lack of a documentation center and public library in Paris at the time;[7] and the new Cnac—an institution whose creation Pompidou promoted between 1967 and 1968 with the aid of Henri Domerg, his brother-in-law and adviser on cultural matters who would act as the future president's guide all the way through the project of creating the Centre Beaubourg.[8]

At the time of the appraisal of the models for Les Halles, in a context in which Claude Charpentier's conservative approach contrasted with Louis Arretche's mimetic one and the distinctly monumental one set out in plans by Louis de Hoÿm de Marien and Jean Faugeron—this last favored by de Gaulle and the Minister of Cultural Affairs André Malraux—Pompidou's attention was focused neither on the cultural institutions that within a few years would become part of the Centre Beaubourg nor on the projects favored by the French authorities, as preferred by Domerg and Michel Bruguière, Pompidou's cabinet secretary with responsibility for all the dossiers related to Cultural Affairs and National Education.[9]

Instead Pompidou was concerned with the absence from the Les Halles project of the kind of modern, high-rise monumental architecture that he had encountered in recent works such as Bernard's Maison de la Radio, but that he may also have appreciated on his official trips to the United States, the sort of architecture that Pompidou felt was needed on the Paris skyline, as he would demonstrate a few years later with his justification of the skyscrapers which were going to go up in the Parisian district of La Défense.[10]

Whether we are talking about de Hoÿm de Marien's colossal rectangular plaza or the circular courtyard around which Faugeron's sculptural volumes were laid out, these proposals were the expression of a genre of overall monumental composition, appreciable only from above, through "spectacular [...] models" that in Pompidou's view gave no sense of the complex on a human scale.[11] Pompidou felt the need for a tall building, for a *monument en hauteur* ("high-rise monument"): a grand tower that would soar above the roofs of Paris.[12] The desire for this difference of scale is what induced him to oppose the *velum*, i.e., the height limit imposed by municipal authorities on buildings in the historic center which the participants in the Les Halles competition were obliged to respect. "Left to decide. Height. No towers? This makes me sad ([I am] opposed to the *velum*)" was Pompidou's comment.[13] The representative and symbolic role that Pompidou associated with his *monument en hauteur* was also underlined by the function assigned to the building, that of the new seat of the Ministry of Finance.[14] Pompidou associated the image of this grandiose monument with the idea of the financial power of the French state and with the more ambiguous one of the state control of taxes.

At the decisive meeting on January 26, 1968, Pompidou convinced de Gaulle to go ahead with an urban planning study to be followed up by specific and significant design studies aimed at creating an "architectural ensemble" of monumental character.[15] The idea of a *monument en hauteur* for the Ministry of Finance was taken up by de Gaulle, who at these meetings always stressed its iconic nature, capable of celebrating the Gaullist presidency in the future.[16] "The Ministry of Finance," declared de Gaulle, "must of necessity be erected in Les Halles as a monument that will symbolize the operation of renewal, just as royalty signed the Louvre and religion the cathedrals."[17]

It matters little that in the summer of 1968 the municipal authorities eliminated the Ministry of Finance from the Les Halles redevelopment project[18] and that in October of the same year the entire project took on the form of an underground forum intended to extend through a maze of tunnels and sunken buildings beneath the surface of the capital: the idea of the tall monument to French grandeur had lodged itself in Pompidou's mind and was destined to influence the idea of the Centre Beaubourg.

The Musée national d'art moderne–Mnam at Palais de Tokyo, Paris, 1969–1974.

Henry Bernard, Maison de la Radio, Paris, 1965.

Claude Charpentier, Competition proposal for the renovation of the Halles district, Paris, 1967.

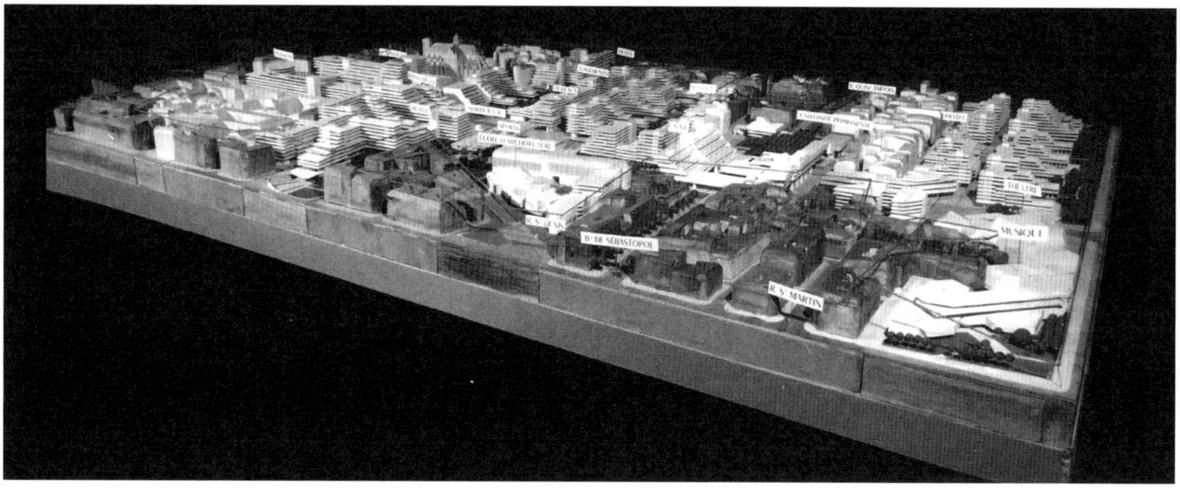

Louis Arretche, Competition proposal for the renovation of the Halles district, Paris, 1967.

Louis de Hoÿm de Marien, Competition proposal for the renovation of the Halles district, Paris, 1967.

Overleaf: Société anonyme d'économie mixte d'aménagement, de rénovation et de restauration du secteur des Halles–SEMAH and Atelier Parisien Urbanisme–APUR, Project for the new underground station of the RER line and the Forum des Halles, Paris, 1968.

Jean Faugeron, Competition proposal for the renovation of the Halles district, Paris, 1967.

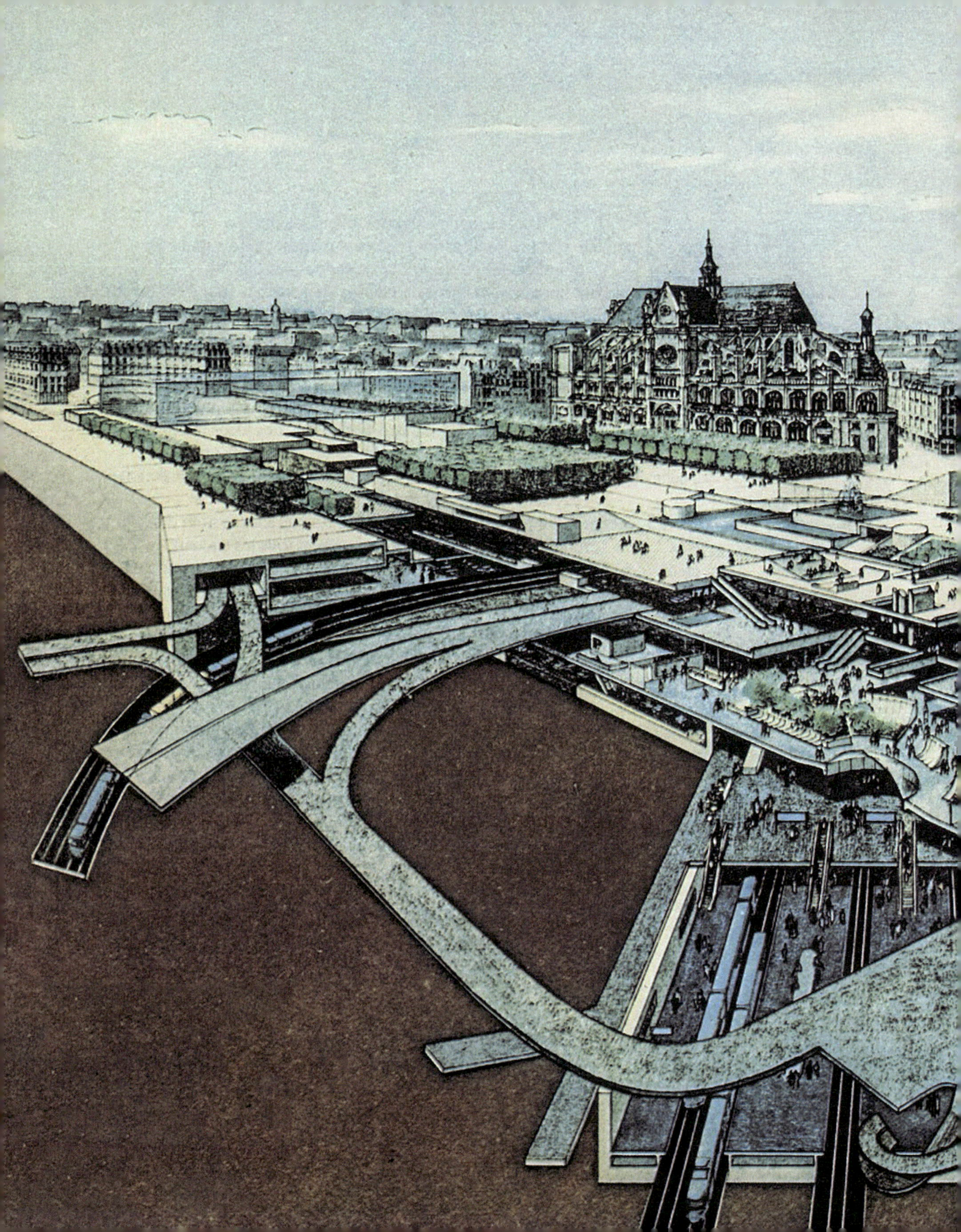

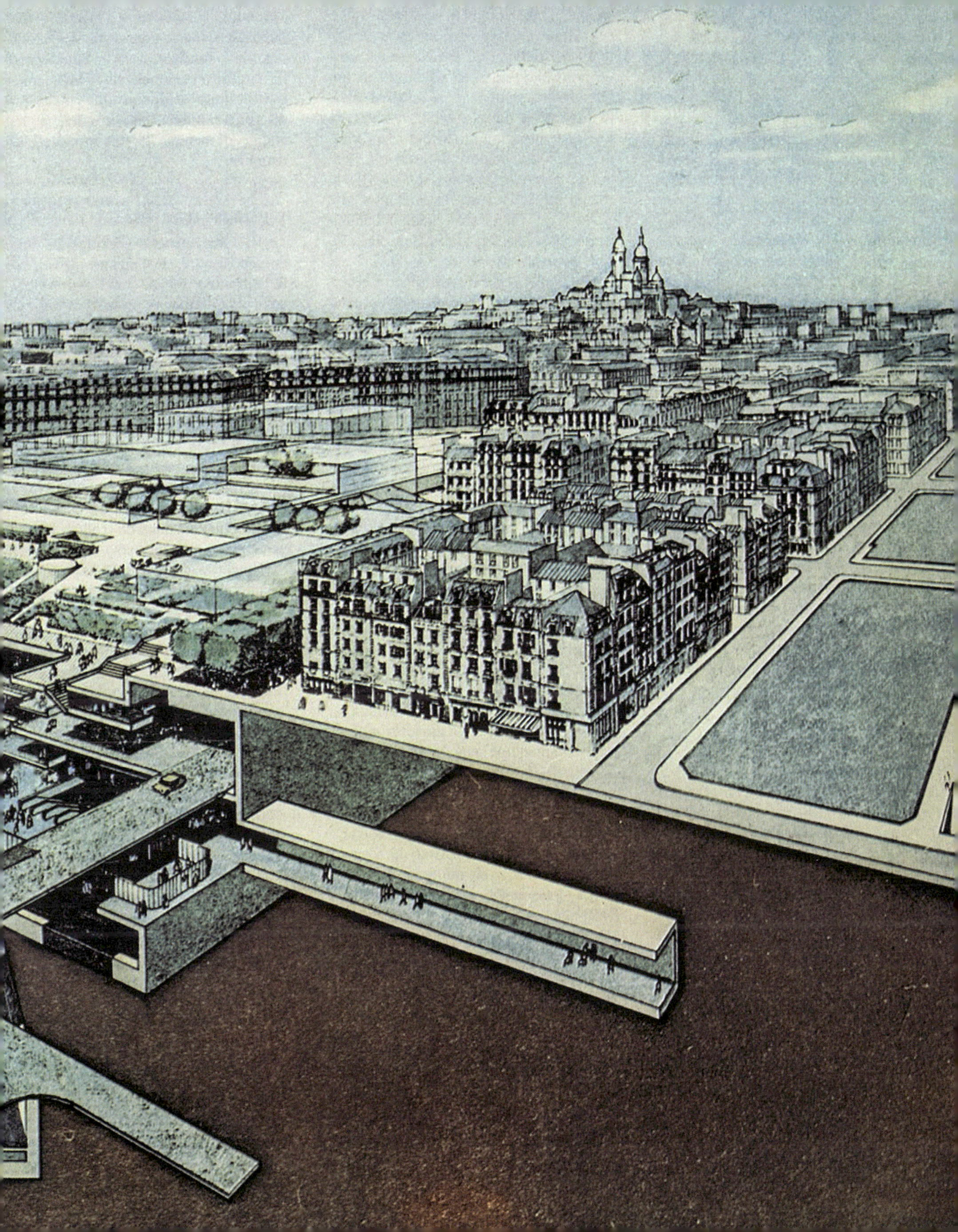

Société anonyme d'économie mixte d'aménagement, de rénovation et de restauration du secteur des Halles–SEMAH and Atelier Parisien Urbanisme–APUR, Project for the new underground station of the RER line and the Forum des Halles, diagram with sectors, Paris, 1968.

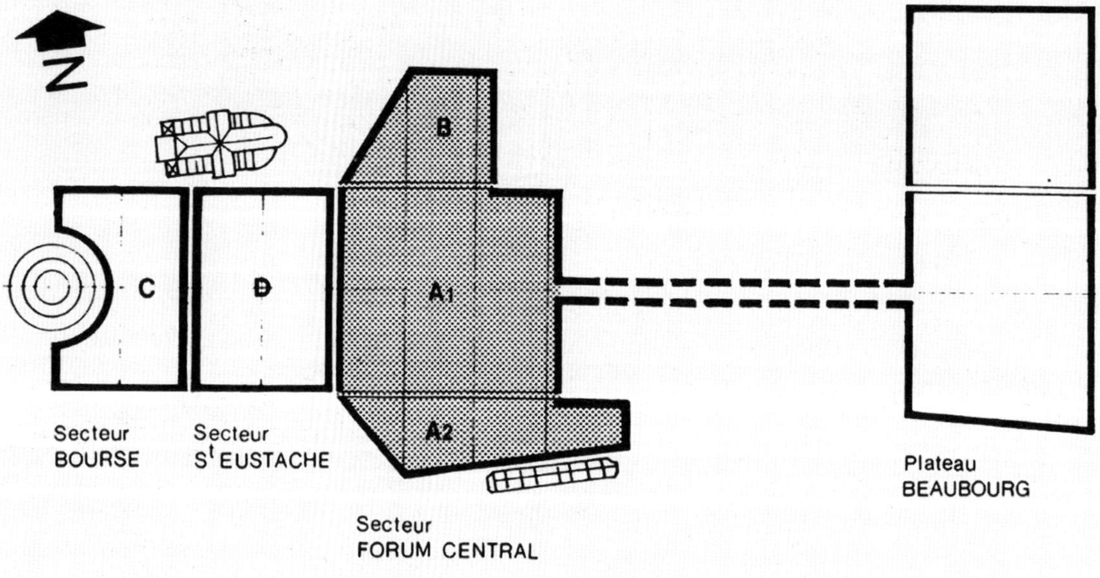

Société anonyme d'économie mixte d'aménagement, de rénovation et de restauration du secteur des Halles–SEMAH and Atelier Parisien Urbanisme–APUR, Project for the new underground station of the RER line and the Forum des Halles, diagram of the new underground road network, Paris, 1968.

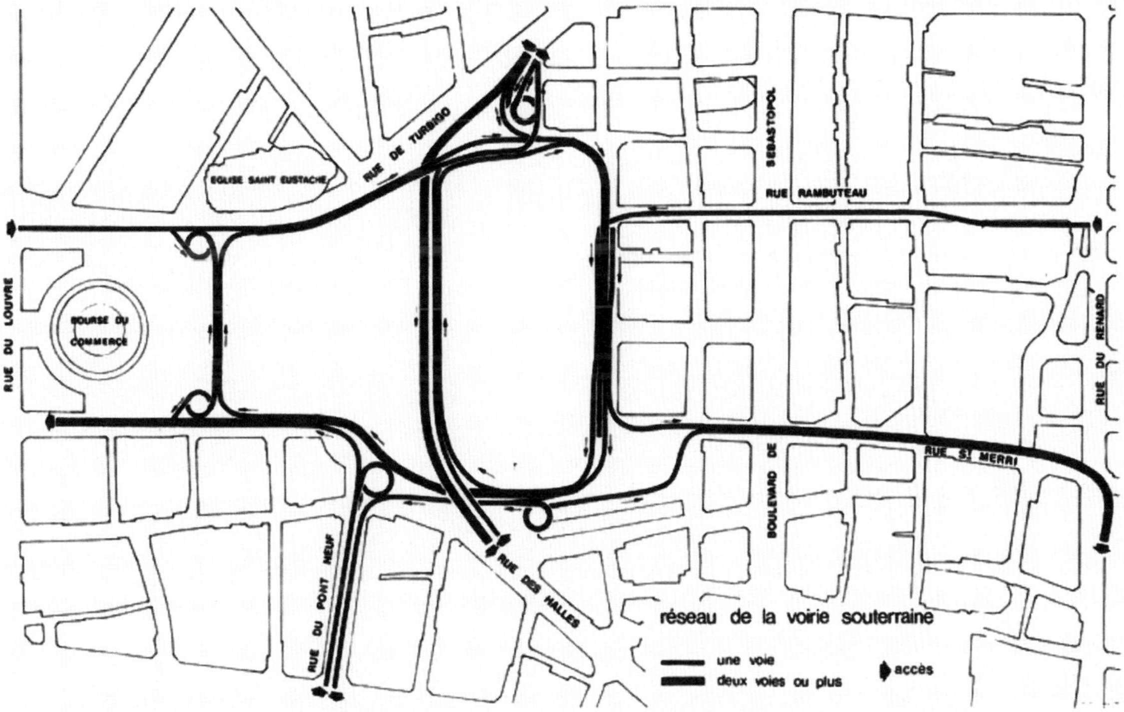

1.2

THE METAMORPHOSIS OF AN IDEA: "A MONUMENT TO CONTEMPORARY ART AND THOUGHT"

The idea of a monument to the glory of the nation and contemporary architectural design in the form of a tower to be erected in the heart of Paris came back into vogue between the summer and fall of 1969, when Pompidou, no longer prime minister but president of the French Republic, from an office in the Élysée Palace—furnished in the classical style but now decorated with works of contemporary art by Sonia Delaunay, Pierre Soulages and František Kupka—took charge of the Ministry of Cultural Affairs's principal dossiers, putting an end to the autonomy the ministry had won under Malraux. Between a series of initiatives aimed at reinvigorating French artistic creativity, such as the furnishing of some rooms of the Élysée Palace with the avant-garde pieces of the French designer Pierre Poulin and a decor conceived by Agam, the attempt to bring the composer and conductor Pierre Boulez back to France, and the entrusting of the curation of an exhibition of contemporary art to be staged at the Grand Palais to the director of the CCI François Mathey, Pompidou started to think once again about the need to promote contemporary French architecture. And so, at the end of November 1969, he drew up a letter for the new minister of Cultural Affairs Edmond Michelet in which he revived his idea of a "*monument en hauteur.*"[19]

In his desire for a monument that would no longer celebrate de Gaulle's presidency but his own, Pompidou did not pursue the idea of a seat for the Ministry of Finance. After the 1968 students' and workers' revolts against middle-class power the proposal to house in the presidential monument a financial institution that would be an emanation of that power had become unpopular, indeed unacceptable. So it was with culture, i.e., the sector with which he had linked his own public image, that Pompidou intended to associate his monument. Despite the lack of a precise plan, what Pompidou imagined at Les Halles was a monument "open to the present and to the future and dedicated in particular to contemporary art and thought."[20]

Despite confirming "the site of Les Halles" as the location for his monument, Pompidou was not looking precisely at the plateau des Halles, where the demolition of Baltard's pavilions, constantly deferred and much opposed by public opinion, rendered complicated any intervention in the short run. Determined to see the monument completed before the end of his mandate, he focused on the only part of the district of Les Halles free from construction and theoretically ready to be built on. The area in question was the plateau Beaubourg: rectangular in shape and measuring around 130 by 115 meters, it was situated between the Marais and Les Halles, to the east of the district of Les Halles but separated from Baltard's pavilions by the residential area of Sébastopol.[21]

The lack of a definite plan and of confirmation of the availability of the plateau Beaubourg by the municipal authorities, and the need to verify the economic feasibility of the project with the minister of finance Valéry Giscard d'Estaing, prompted Pompidou to wait before contacting Michelet and the Prefect of Paris Marcel Diebolt and write a "more precise letter" in view of an imminent "exhibition" of the project, coinciding in all likelihood with an interdepartmental meeting on December 11, 1969.

Pierre Paulin, Interior design of the private apartments of Georges and Claude Pompidou at the Élysée Palace, Paris, 1969–1974.

Yaacov Agam, Interior design of the private apartments of Georges and Claude Pompidou at the Élysée Palace, antechamber (also known as the Salon Agam), Paris, 1969–1974 (reconstructed at the Centre Pompidou of Paris).

Overleaf: The plateau Beaubourg before the beginning of the construction of the Centre Pompidou, Paris, 1971.

1.3

THE INCLUSION OF THE MUSÉE DU XXᴱ SIÈCLE AND THE BIBLIOTHÈQUE DES HALLES IN THE PRESIDENTIAL MONUMENT

While Pompidou and his collaborators outlined the nature of the monument, between late November and early December two projects drawn up during de Gaulle's presidency began to converge in these studies: the Musée du XXᵉ siècle and the Bibliothèque des Halles, destined to influence the future Centre Beaubourg to different degrees.

The still sketchy idea of a monument dedicated to contemporary art and thought induced Pompidou to make inquiries first of all about the Musée du XXᵉ siècle, one of the main projects developed under Malraux's direction to solve the crisis in the promotion of modern and contemporary art in France. The product of a program drawn up by the chief conservator of the Mnam, Jean Cassou, and his assistants, this project had been entrusted to Le Corbusier, who had seized the opportunity to try out his still unrealized proposal of a container for art, the *Musée à croissance illimité* or Museum of Unlimited Growth.[22] Cassou and Malraux intended to offer Paris an anti-monumental museum that would be economical, functional, and extendable over time: a large five-meter-high "shed"[23] based on the continual addition of modular units, called *cellules*,[24] around a central hall arranged in a squared spiral. In this structure that could be built out of modern materials and using a rapid and standardized process of construction,[25] Le Corbusier imagined a flexible space, reconfigurable to meet curators' needs, in which walls and fixed partitions were replaced by movable panels, "membranes" able to define a "wealth of automatic and interchangeable combinations of rooms."[26] Following Le Corbusier's death in 1965 the project ground to an abrupt halt and various attempts to revive it, even in different forms and locations, have come to nothing.

When Pompidou imagined his monument in 1969, his assistants and the technicians at the Ministry of Cultural Affairs immediately came up with the idea of making the presidential project, by now referred to as the "Monument des Halles," a sort of revival of the Musée du XXᵉ siècle project.[27] The decision to invoke this project at this stage in the development of the president's idea was still vague and, as would become clear in the following months, did not so much look to Le Corbusier's architectural solution as to the general principles of the design, from the idea of a functional and internally flexible and adaptable container to the intention to create a place where the historical collection of the Mnam and that of the new Cnac could be united.[28]

The case of the Bibliothèque des Halles is different. Paris City Council's construction approval for the library project at the plateau Beaubourg on July 11, 1969, revealed a profound link between this project and the presidential monument.[29] The studies for the realization of the library carried out by the administrator general of the Bibliothèque nationale de

France, Dennery, and his assistant, Seguin, were more advanced than those of the Musée du XXᵉ siècle and comprised a detailed program and an architectural design. The team called on to develop the idea of Pompidou's monument assimilated the library project and used it as a foundational model for the presidential project.

From 1965 to 1969 Seguin clarified this idea in a radical and advanced project organized around three main thematic planks: "reading," "information," and "animation."[30] The library imagined by Seguin took the form of a reading center where a nonspecialized public could have free access, without the mediation of librarians, to a collection of a million works on general culture and current affairs, including collections of photographs, constantly updated periodicals, microfilms, and other kinds of audiovisual material. The library also ought to have a documentary information center equipped with a pioneering computer providing access to catalogues, inventories, bibliographies, and other data-processing resources, drawing on both the library and other French documentation centers.[31] Unlike traditional French libraries, Seguin wanted to make his project a place for meeting and recreation as well, and one which could include exhibition rooms, a conference center, a cafeteria, a restaurant, and areas for conversation and relaxation.

Seguin's ideas were immediately translated into a series of design proposals made in 1967 by André Chatelin, chief architect of civilian buildings and national monuments for the French government. While these remained in the state of a preliminary study, they outlined the fundamental principles that would shape the design of the library and the philosophy of the Centre Beaubourg itself: the idea of a translucent volume enlivened by projections and terraces to shake off the image of an elitist treasure chest still associated with traditional French libraries; the intention to concentrate the main recreational activities on the ground floor so that this place would be able to suck in the crowd; and the idea of locating the majority of the storage facilities for the books on only one floor, in order to turn the rest of the building into a sequence of internally flexible platforms occupied by a "free and shifting mosaic of storage facilities with free access, tables for reading and areas for researchers."[32]

Among the proposals Chatelin drew up, those of a vertical character, including the project for the regeneration of Les Halles,[33] already foreshadowed the limitations of Pompidou's monument in the form of a tower, from the problems of scale resulting from the insertion of the volume in the low-rise fabric of the historic center to the complex system of circulation made necessary by the movement of visitors and products between the numerous floors of the building.

The failure of the competition for the regeneration of Les Halles and the assignment of the task of preparing the new urban "framework scheme" to the new public corporation set up in the place of SEAH, the Société anonyme d'économie mixte d'aménagement, de rénovation et de restauration du secteur des Halles, known as SEMAH, pushed the project for the Bibliothèque des Halles in the direction of its new location in the plateau Beaubourg.[34]

Like Pompidou, Seguin was aware that this site was occupied by a car park and could therefore be built on. Seguin was skeptical, if not uneasy, about the peripheral position of the site with respect to the core of the area slated for renewal, which remained the plateau des Halles.[35] It was precisely the distance from the plateau des Halles that made him think about a question which would prove crucial to the development of the definitive project of the library and then of the Centre Beaubourg itself, that of the links needed to connect the library to the plateau des Halles.

With the completion of the urban plan prepared by SEMAH and its preliminary approval by Prefect Diebolt and the Paris Council, work on the library entered a new phase. A detailed program was drawn up; a study trip to the United States and Canada was organized to analyze some state-of-the-art American libraries; and, finally, the job of creating the library was entrusted to Faugeron, i.e., the author of the project that Malraux and de Gaulle had favored in the failed competition for Les Halles.

In October 1969, over the course of three weeks and in the company of Chatelin and Faugeron, Seguin visited twenty-four American libraries, twenty-three in the United States and one in Canada, selected by the American Library Association and the Council for Library Resources, with the aim of identifying the most interesting and original examples among the American libraries built or designed over the previous fifteen years.[36]

From low-rise glass-and-steel containers like Ludwig Mies van der Rohe's Washington, DC, Public Library to institutions of a monumental character created through the serial repetition of concrete units like the Francis A. Countway Library of Medicine in Boston, Seguin obtained a clearer idea of a "functional architecture" based on the efficiency of its internal activities and the comfort of its occupants.[37] Not unlike what Le Corbusier had said about the museum—*Mais un Musée [...] c'est une fonction* ("But a Museum [...] is a function")—Seguin declared that "the library is first of all a service."[38] As a counterpoint to questions of a functional nature there were also aesthetic concerns and challenges to the very idea of monumentality, yet they remained subordinate to functionality, of which they constituted a sort of emanation, a harmonious formal expression.[39]

Seguin also visited works able to "provide lessons for the architecture of the library of Les Halles."[40] The buildings on the campus of the University of Illinois in Chicago designed by Skidmore Owings and Merrill (SOM) and the James V. Forrestal Building in Washington by Curtis & Davis, Fordyce and Hamby Associates, and Frank Grad & Sons presented to Seguin the same combination of internal flexibility and monumental container as he had admired in the American libraries. Ieoh Ming Pei and Henry N. Cobb's underground shopping mall on Place Ville Marie in Montreal offered a foretaste of the kind of subterranean citadel that SEMAH was working on beneath the plateau des Halles but that was soon going to become a fundamental feature of the design of his library in Paris. Other buildings, from Marcel Breuer's Whitney Museum to Frank Lloyd Wright's Guggenheim Museum in New York and the French Pavilion for the 1967 World's Fair in Montreal, designed by Faugeron himself,[41] showed Seguin the markedly monumental character that Seguin intended to curb but that Pompidou would stubbornly try to introduce during the development of the Centre Beaubourg project.

The conflict between monumentality and functionalism, fated to play a fundamental role throughout the story of the Centre Beaubourg, was already evident in the formulation of the project for the Bibliothèque des Halles and was reflected in Dennery and Seguin's choice, very likely the result of external pressure,[42] to entrust the project on the plateau Beaubourg not to Dennery but to Faugeron.[43]

After presenting Seguin with a series of proposals directly inspired by the projects of different people and in different styles, Faugeron went for a design that combined a sculptural and dynamic language based on the curved lines of his pavilion in Montreal with Seguin's functional concerns.

The importance Seguin assigned to the question of the connection of the library with the Forum des Halles led Faugeron to opt for a large urban void excavated below ground level and conceived as a labyrinth of platforms, escalators, underpasses, and even gardens laid out on several levels—a sort of citadel sunk in the bowels of Paris to connect the Forum des Halles and to create, in continuity with it, an underground complex not unlike the one he had seen in Montreal with Seguin.

In this subterranean citadel, between the underground levels and the ground floor, Faugeron placed a car park, a workshop for book restoration, a loading and unloading area, and storage facilities, along with a wide range of public spaces, from cafés and restaurants to a large entrance hall and a *salle d'actualité* where the latest issues of magazines and periodicals could be read.

To make sure that this citadel retained a monumental character, Faugeron inscribed it in an iconic circular bastion with a splayed profile like that of a funnel—yet another expression of the centripetal effect and the idea of a metropolitan magnet to attract the crowds that Seguin and Chatelin had imagined in the project sketched out two years earlier. At the center of this system of Wrightian circularity, Faugeron placed a circular building that was the expression and monument of this void: a series of concentric rings of increasing diameter set one on top of the other in an inverted cone. While on the outside this configuration defined an iconic and monumental volume, on the inside it generated a large central courtyard opening onto concentric terraces and covered at the top by a large domed skylight. Shaped in this way, the building revealed its direct derivation from the Guggenheim Museum he had visited with Seguin. Faugeron rejected the latter's opaque and monolithic envelope, however, something which Chatelin had objected to in the first variants of the design. The concrete shell conceived by Wright as a trailblazing support for works of art was transformed in Paris into a radiant and translucent surface for the illumination of the reading rooms and the storage facilities located on the upper rings of the library.[44]

The handling of the interiors was also faithful to Seguin's suggestions, with large spaces free of fixed partitions in which to freely lay out furnishings endowed with a curvilinear and aerodynamic expressionism reminiscent of an aesthetic language widespread in the American culture of the time.

In one of the early design studies, the aesthetics of the curved line were reinforced by the addition of a panoramic tower. While its function seems to have been that of a landmark to attract people to the library, its form was still uncertain, wavering between that of a slender column surmounted by a concentric platform that recalled the Space Needle in Seattle and that of a sculptural spire with a transparent envelope.

In December 1969 Seguin proposed to Pompidou combining the project of the Bibliothèque des Halles with the presidential monument to create "a large cultural ensemble of national and international significance" that would benefit from the proximity of the two institutions. Although there is no documentary record of Pompidou's view on this, the design of the Bibliothèque des Halles, shown to him between December and January,[45] must have made the potentialities of the plateau Beaubourg clear to the French president: creating routes running under the city to connect the intervention with the Forum des Halles; not necessarily having to construct a building covering the whole site; being able to model the site with reliefs and gardens intended for public use; making the plateau de La Reynie (a square-shaped open-air space located to the southwest of the plateau Beaubourg) a privileged point of observation from which to view and admire the library.

Le Corbusier and Pierre Jeanneret, Le Musée des artistes vivants (later known as the Musée à croissance illimité), 1931.

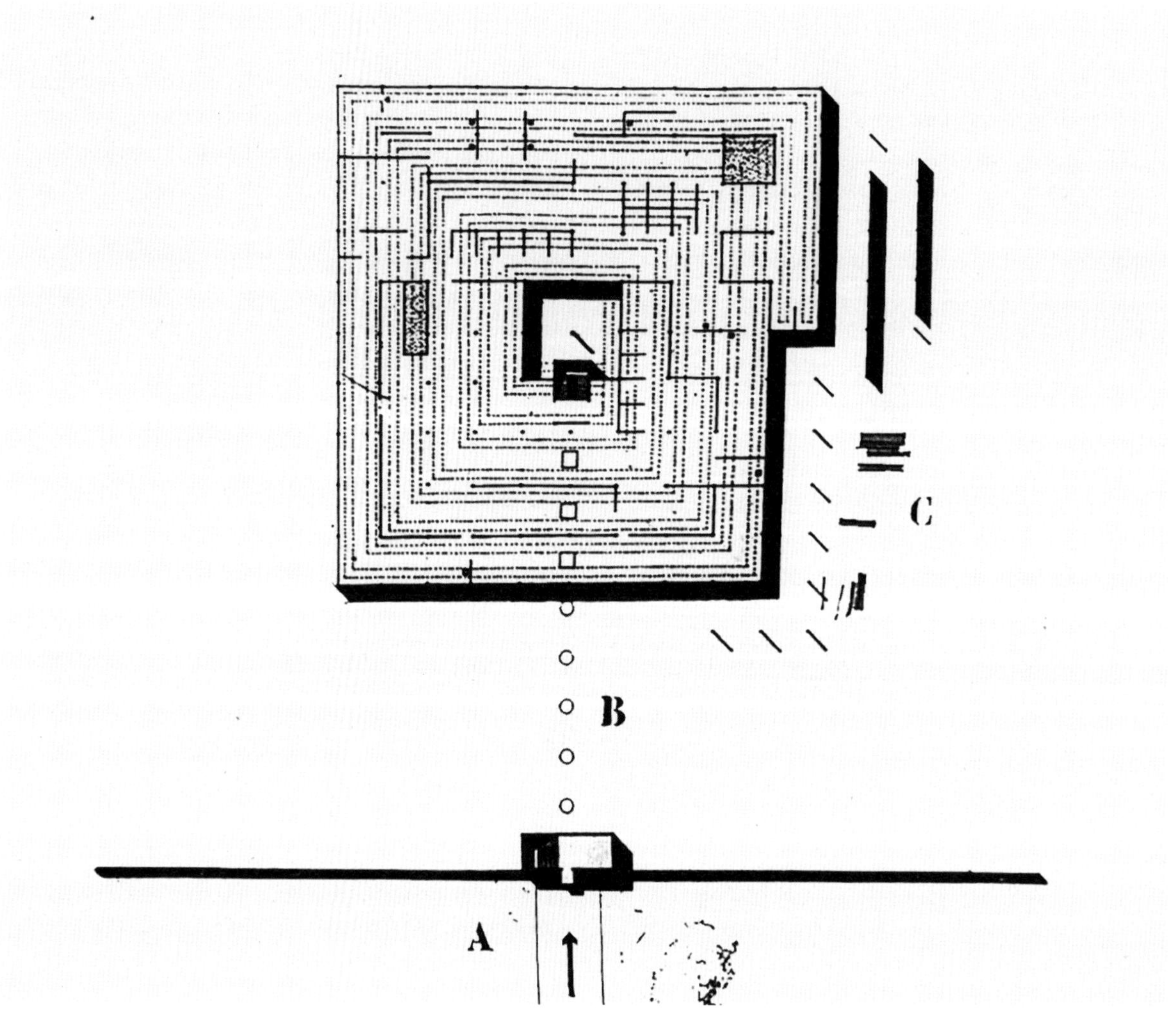

André Chatelin, Project for the Bibliothèque des Halles, preliminary studies (study n. 1), Paris, 1966–1967.

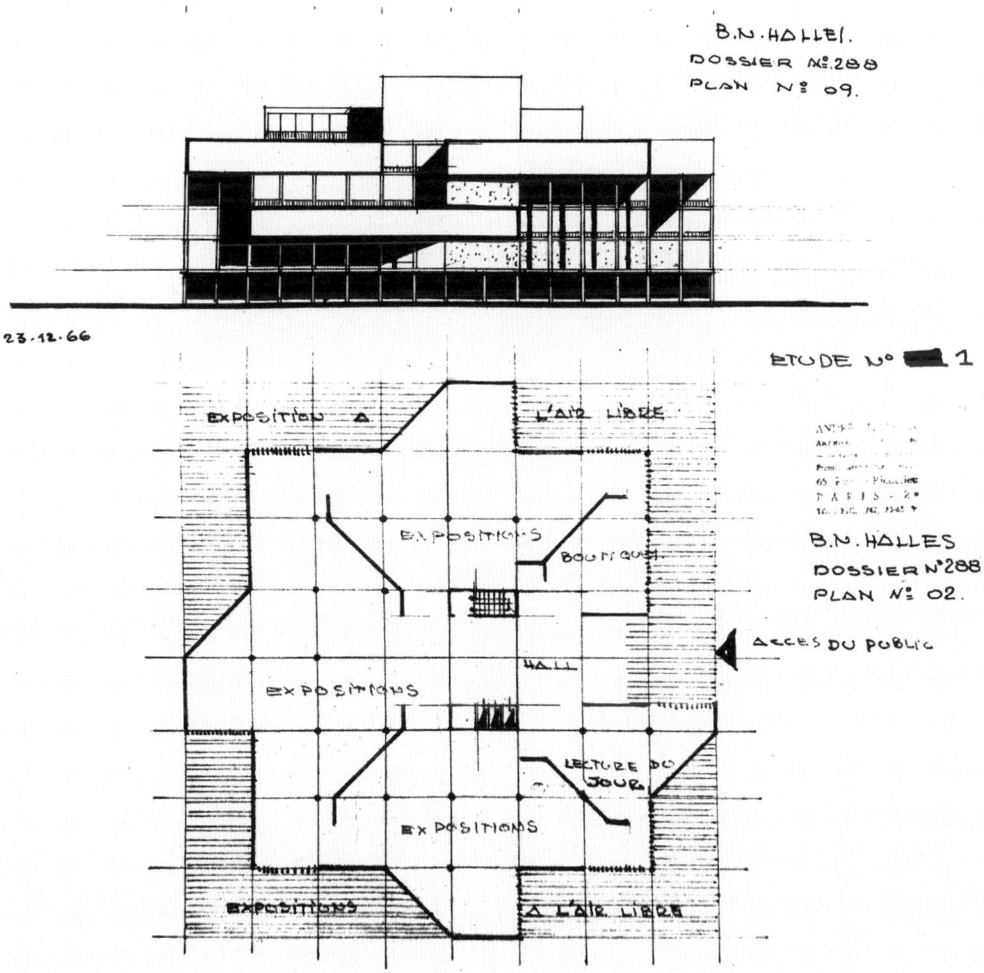

Jean Faugeron, French Pavilion at the Universal Exposition – Expo 67, Montreal, 1967.

Frank Lloyd Wright, Solomon Guggenheim Museum, New York, 1943–1959.

Jean Faugeron, Bibliothèque des Halles at plateau Beaubourg, preliminary study n° 1, Paris, 1969.

Jean Faugeron, Bibliothèque des Halles at plateau Beaubourg, preliminary study n° 3, Paris, 1969

Jean Faugeron, Bibliothèque des Halles at plateau Beaubourg, preliminary study n° 4, Paris, 1969.

Jean Faugeron, Bibliothèque des Halles at plateau Beaubourg, schematic design, Paris, 1969.

Jean Faugeron, Bibliothèque des Halles at plateau Beaubourg, preliminary study n° 6, Paris, 1969.

Jean Faugeron, Bibliothèque des Halles at plateau Beaubourg, schematic design, Paris, 1969.

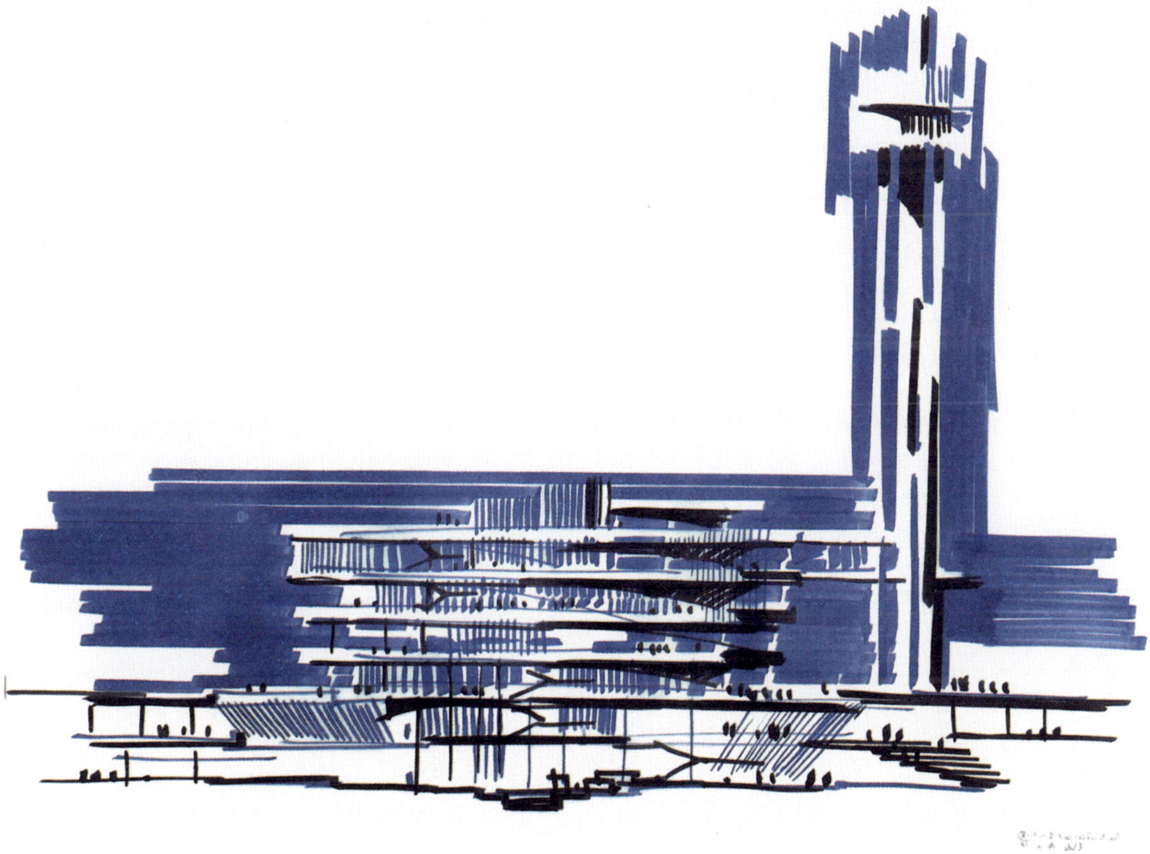

1.4

THE IDEA OF AN INTERNATIONAL JURY OF ARCHITECTS AND USERS TO CAPTURE THE YOUNG AVANT-GARDE GENERATION

The idea of the monument, destined to get tangled up with the projects for the Musée du XXe siècle and the Bibliothèque des Halles, was developed further between December 11 and 15, 1969, two dates that coincide respectively with the presentation of the project to ministers and the Prefect of Paris at a Select Council[46] and with the assignment of the project's feasibility studies to the minister of Cultural Affairs, Michelet.[47] The idea took shape of a cultural center of broad scope and with a complex program, which would comprise not only an "immense museum of painting and sculpture"[48] that would revive the plan for the Musée du XXe siècle, but also cultural institutions focusing on music, recording, and even cinema and theater.[49]

Faced with the existence of the Bibliothèque des Halles project, Pompidou became convinced of the need to include a library in his own project, but, given the complexity of Dennery and Seguin's library program and the contiguity with the "museum" to be included in his monument, contemplated the possibility of a simple library specializing in art.[50]

The wide range of activities now being included in the monument introduced a degree of uncertainty into its architectural translation. With the derogation of the limits on height imposed by the municipality in the historic center of Paris, Pompidou was suggesting a kind of vertical monumentality that harked back to the "steeple" and the "massive structure" imagined for Les Halles the previous year. Pompidou's insistence on the question of the height limit confirms his intention to free himself from the cultural and stylistic burden of the architectural heritage of the historic center and go instead for a new sort of architecture.

On the other hand, the multiplicity of institutions to be housed in the monument undermined the idea of a unitary high-rise building and steered the president toward a solution that could be achieved with the combination of a series of buildings, a "monumental ensemble," as he defined it, evoking a solution of which he did not seem fully convinced and from which he would dissociate himself over the following months.[51]

Pompidou was also looking for a formula for a prestigious competition to celebrate his presidential mandate and contemporary French architecture. "It will be a monument that, on the architectural level, will have to reflect our time."[52] Pompidou intended to resort to a progressive formula unusual among French public competitions: a competition open to all architects.[53] The hypothesis of widening the field to include foreign architects—"ought foreign architects to be allowed to compete?" he wondered in the letter to Michelet—should be seen as an opportunity for Pompidou to use a monument planned for the heart of Paris to insert French architectural culture into an international context.

That he was on the lookout for an innovative idea of architecture is confirmed by his intention to facilitate the participation of young talents lacking financial backing—"The competition should also be accessible to any talented architect, even if he is young and without financial means."[54]
This unprecedented opening is a hint that it was precisely the generation of architects who had received their training amidst the agitation of 1968 in France whom he saw as being able to offer him a truly trailblazing monument.
Pompidou imagined an international dimension for the jury, too. It would have to be composed of architects "of worldwide standing," but also of specialists in the institutions to be included in the project, whom he defined as *utilisateurs*, "users," giving the examples of a director of a modern art museum and a great musician—professional figures that not coincidentally corresponded to a couple of people received at the Élysée Palace in the previous weeks, the chief curator of the Mnam, Jean Leymarie, and the conductor Boulez. Again with the intention of reinvigorating the position of French architecture on the international scene, Pompidou leaned toward a jury consisting mostly of architects, hinting that the judges ought to give more weight to aesthetic, representative, and monumental factors than technological or functional ones. And yet it was the unexpected presence of a majority of *utilisateurs* among the members of the jury that was to play a decisive role in the choice of the winner of the competition.
Despite entrusting the feasibility study to Michelet and his assistants, Pompidou had no intention of delegating the decisive choices for a project he felt to be his own and in which he declared to Michelet his "personal interest." With the aid of Domerg and other advisers, Pompidou would follow the development of the project constantly and closely.

1.5

LOSTE'S VISION: FROM MUSÉE MONUMENT TO MUSÉE LABORATOIRE

As the news of the presidential idea of a monumental ensemble entered the public domain, prompting surprise but no particular hostility on the part of the French press and more hard-fought approval from the members of the Council of Paris,[55] Michelet entrusted a preliminary feasibility study of the president's project to two of his technical advisers, François Gresland and Sébastien Loste.

Although initially charged solely with contacting municipal authorities, within the space of a few weeks Loste, fortified by his previous role as de Gaulle's project manager for the Les Halles regeneration competition and his participation in the work of an interdepartmental committee for the promotion of reading by the public set up by Pompidou, made himself a central figure in the formulation of the presidential project, from the specification of its content to the organization of the competition and even the fine-tuning of the winning project.

A complicity developed between Loste and Pompidou that strengthened in December 1969, as is clear from a note from the president which ran: "It is Loste who oversees the study of the museum [at plateau Beaubourg]."[56]

On January 22, 1970, Loste drew up a preliminary study report on Pompidou's monumental ensemble with the aim of drawing attention to the unresolved questions of the project, from the nature of the building and the individual activities to its translation into architecture and all the way up to its inauguration and subsequent operation.[57]

Loste also invited Pompidou to give his views on the still undefined nature of the project, presenting several different possibilities to him, from a center focused specifically on the contemporary arts to a "cultural metropolis" including activities not necessarily connected with one another, on the model of the Maisons de la culture set up by Malraux in the French provinces in the sixties.

As well as on the nature of the individual activities to be comprised within the presidential project, Loste gave his opinion on its possible translation into architecture, calling on national and international models to support the exchange of views with Pompidou with concrete examples.

Loste was opposed to the idea of a massive building and leaned toward the complex that Pompidou called a monumental ensemble. From this perspective, he criticized the idea of "disproportionate monumentality," arguing that the museum understood as a "place to walk around" and a building of horizontal character did not fit with the idea of a vertical monument or with the "too-imposing proportions" of a grandiose building, suited, if at all, to industrial buildings or financial complexes. "Are we going to make the Parly 2 or the Maine Montparnasse of culture?" wrote Loste provocatively, referring to buildings that he saw as examples of the kind of

monumentality sought by the president.
Determined to dissuade Pompidou, Loste also criticized the work that might be used to counter his arguments about the incompatibility of a museum and a high-rise building, Wright's Guggenheim Museum with its ramp running in a continuous spiral to a height of thirty meters.
Loste leaned toward a monumental ensemble that could be obtained through the "addition" of buildings housing different activities and went so far as to suggest a model: Lincoln Center in New York, a complex devoted to music, dance, and the other performing arts designed by a team of American architects that included Philip Johnson, Eero Saarinen, and Gordon Bunshaft.[58]
Loste outlined a different sort of monumentality from the one imagined by Pompidou, a monumentality that was "not disproportionate" but still "remarkable" which he identified with the new seat of the Ministry of Foreign Affairs in Brasilia designed by Oscar Niemeyer in the form of a functionalist glass container caged in a monumental classical peristyle. In the choice of an example not unlike some of the buildings at Lincoln Center in its form and proportions, Loste was alluding to a kind of monumentality that would not clash with the functional and technological requirements of a museum but be in keeping with them.
With regard to the spaces that would be used to house temporary exhibitions, he mentioned the need for an "extremely supple structure" and "volumes" capable of the same mobility typical of the new art tendencies spreading in the sixties. Loste was calling for the kind of internal flexibility that would be suited precisely to the Bibliothèque des Halles and the Musée du XXe siècle.
Drawing in part on suggestions made by Domerg, Pompidou expressed his preference for a cultural center devoted to art but made up of a series of mutually independent institutions, two of which, the main ones, were now settled: on the one hand, a museum of modern art focused on forms of artistic expression from the period between 1900 and 1950 and able to house both temporary exhibitions and a permanent collection in order to make it a worthy successor to the Louvre; on the other, a public reading library that would revive Seguin's plan.
As for the architecture, while willing to accept the idea of a functional and flexible architecture for the interiors, Pompidou had no intention of renouncing a work of "grand proportions" and repeated his preference for a single high-rise building.
Writing to Loste that the supposed incompatibility between a monument and a museum was merely a question of internal division, Pompidou indicated that the content of the design would have to adapt itself to its aesthetic and monumental expression.
The conflict between Pompidou's and Loste's vi-

sions is confirmed by a report drawn up by the latter, which also included accounts of two journeys made between January and February 1970 to the Scandinavian countries and the United States for the study of new museums and a number of cultural centers.[59] With this document Loste tried once again to dissuade Pompidou from the idea of a vertical building, which he now described disparagingly as a monumental *"palais des arts."*

Insistently and with models to hand, Loste urged Pompidou toward a kind of architecture in which aesthetic value and functional efficiency could coexist rather than being mutually exclusive. In his notes he also included a radical and avant-garde museological model that he hinted reflected his personal idea of architecture. It was the "museum-laboratory" conceived by Pontus Hultén, the curator of the Moderna Museet in Stockholm, one of the new epicenters for the promotion of contemporary art.

And it is in reference to Hultén and his model of museum that the "supple structure" and internally flexible "volumes" of the president's project can be summed up: in the image of the "large fitted sheds" evoked by Hultén, immense shells of an industrial character containing spaces equipped with technological systems.[60]

Loste also specified the institutions that should be included in the project: a large museum of contemporary art in which to combine the two institutions of the Mnam and the newly established Cnac, the CCI, the Bibliotheque des Halles, finally given the name Bpi, and an unnamed film center, along with multipurpose facilities and spaces devoted to recreation and entertainment, including terraces, gardens, and a panoramic restaurant.

In giving his presidential approval on February 16, 1970,[61] Pompidou accepted a project that retained the content of the original idea but not its architecture. The victory of the *musée laboratoire* over the *musée monument* was confirmed by Loste's choice to baptize the project "Centre du plateau Beaubourg – Paris – Information et art contemporain – 1973," as if wishing to free the project of any aesthetic-monumental trappings in order to turn it into a popular antenna of culture.

The attraction to information that had guided Seguin and fascinated public opinion and the organizers of the competition for Les Halles became the main theme of the new "Centre du plateau Beaubourg." The project had now begun to reflect the latest developments in museology, echoing, among other things, the state-of-the-art information and technological center that Hultén was planning for his Moderna Museet in Stockholm.[62]

Although the nature of the new information center would only be made fully clear with the publication of the competition announcement in November 1970, the development of Pompidou's original idea between 1968 and 1969 reached a crucial junction that was, in some way, distant from what the president had at first had in mind. In the decision to accept ideas that differed from his own but to which he was not unsympathetic, Pompidou showed his deep sensitivity and farsightedness with regard to the new and groundbreaking.

Marcel Breuer, Whitney Museum, New York, 1966.

Jean Saubot et al., Operation Maine Montparnasse, Paris, 1960–1973.

1.6

LOMBARD'S "PROGRAMMATION": AN ADVANCED METHOD OF CONCERTED DESIGN

Having verified the feasibility of the presidential project, between January and February 1970 Loste gave the task of embarking on a thorough study of the contents of the Centre Beaubourg to François Lombard, at the time the foremost expert on planning in the field of architecture at the Ministry of Cultural Affairs. Drawing on the pioneering research into architectural planning he had studied during years of specialization in the United States, Lombard set out to make the Centre Beaubourg project a prototype for a kind of design based on an unprecedented degree of cooperation and consultation between the main players in the building process—uncommon in a context still dominated by the figure of the creative architect in the Beaux-Arts mold—and on the emergence of a professional figure, the so-called *programmateur* ("program planner") responsible for coordinating the entire construction process, from the formulation of the requirements of the *utilisateurs* in a program that would also include the aesthetic characteristics of the settings to management of the adaptation of the design to the program and supervision of the final inspection and maintenance of the building.

Defined between the spring and winter of 1970 in consultation with representatives of the institutions included in the Centre Beaubourg and American planning specialists, Lombard's program took on board Loste's ideas and many principles of the programs of the Musée du XXe siècle and Bibliothèque des Halles. Lombard's program would allow Pompidou and his aides to exercise unprecedented control over a project of the nature and scale of the Centre Beaubourg. The complexity of that program, confirmed in the successive versions drawn up during the fine-tuning of the winning design, was to have unexpected repercussions.

It would reduce the margin of freedom that Pompidou wanted to allow participants in the competition; during the development of the successful project, on the other hand, it would undermine the role of the architects and the engineers to the point of throwing the realization of the work itself into doubt.

François Lombard, Diagram of the programming operational process (“*programmation*”), 1970.

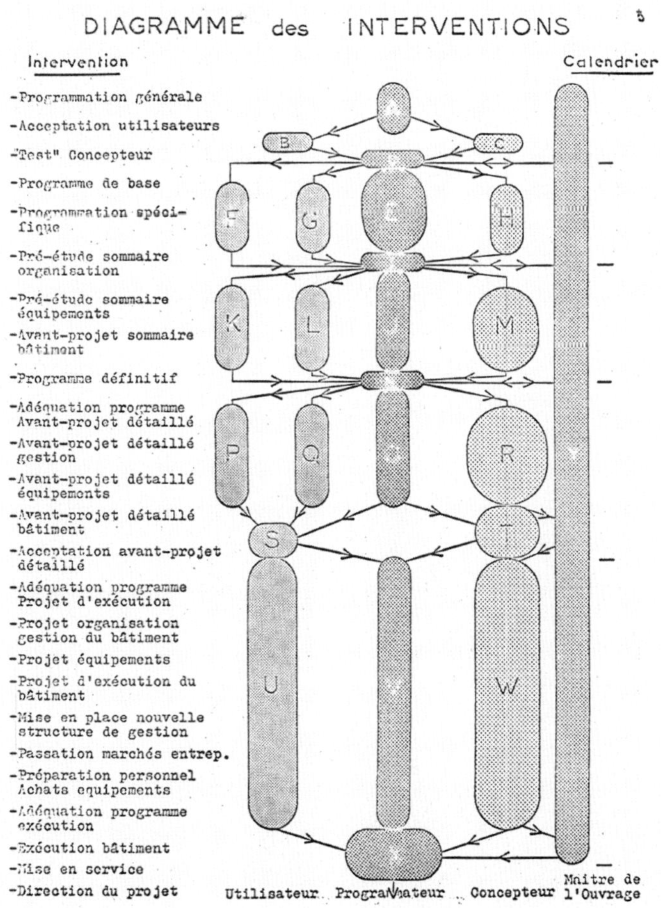

1.7

BORDAZ AND THE DELEGATION FOR THE REALIZATION OF THE CENTRE BEAUBOURG

With the arrival of Lombard, Loste's team was transformed into an institutional body of broader scope, the Délégation pour la réalisation du Centre Beaubourg, with the aim of completing the feasibility studies for the Centre and organizing the architectural competition for its design.

Pompidou did not put Loste in charge of the Délégation, although he would entrust him with coordinating the works as "Chargé de mission."

As Domerg suggested, what was needed for the role of the Délégation's director was someone able to negotiate between the different competences of its members and who possessed a certain amount of experience in administration as well as in the promotion of culture and contemporary art.

Initially Pompidou considered giving this post to Gaëtan Picon former Director general of arts and letters at the Minister of Cultural Affairs, who not only had tried unsuccessfully to build the museum of modern and contemporary art that Pompidou intended to include in the Centre Beaubourg, but in late December 1969 had contacted Pompidou to describe to him the fundamental characteristics of the museum that was to be made part of the president's monument.[63] Convinced by Domerg that Picon lacked the administrative and political qualities needed for the project, Pompidou opted for another candidate, Robert Bordaz, a French politician and member of the Council of State who had on his CV all the requisites imagined by Domerg: political and administrative experience (he had held the post of Director-general of the broadcaster Radiodiffusion-Télévision Française-RTS and been in charge of the withdrawal of French troops from Indochina); knowledge of the world of art and architecture; and a feeling for architecture in particular (he had been cabinet secretary to the minister of reconstruction and urban planning, Eugene-Claudius Petit, and coordinated the building of the French pavilions at the Moscow and Montreal Expos).[64]

For the other key Délégation functions, in addition to Lombard in the capacity of controller general, the engineer Robert Regard, as secretary-general, and Loste, as project leader, were picked to assist Bordaz in the performance of his duties.

1.8

THE FINAL JURY: CHALLENGING BALANCES AND A TROJAN HORSE

Following its official constitution and installation in the offices of the Ministry of Cultural Affairs at 3 rue de Valois, the Délégation devoted itself to formulation of the program, preparation of the architectural competition, studies of the project's urban integration, and, lastly, definition of the budget for the competition and the operations of the Délégation. Against the background of these works, which continued uninterrupted until the material staging of the competition in the rooms of the Grand Palais in Paris under the direction of the architect Pierre Molins, the Centre du plateau Beaubourg project, by now known as the Centre Beaubourg, was subject to a variety of pressures aimed at determining its nature. Loste continued to take an interest in the project and the same is true for Pompidou who, having dispensed with Michelet, established a direct relationship with the Délégation through Domerg and two other close aides, René Galy-Dejean and Eduard Balladur. In this phase a decisive role was also played by Mathey, director of the CCI, who through Jean Prouvé, one of the leading figures in the field of construction in metal and prefabrication, seized the opportunity of the Beaubourg competition to try to save the Baltard Pavilions from destruction. The first chance to influence the nature of the competition and the kind of structure that the Centre Beaubourg was going to become was provided by the constitution of the jury and the search for architects willing to take part in the competition. The responsibility fell to Loste, some experts from the Ministry of Cultural Affairs, and three advisors from two of the institutions that were going to be included in the Centre Beaubourg, Mathey of the CCI and Blaise Gautier and Germain Viatte of the Cnac. Following the drawing-up of a series of lists of jurors and possible competitors under the supervision of Mathey, a former member of the jury of the Grand prix international d'urbanisme et architecture organized in Cannes in 1969 with the participation of young exponents of the international avant-garde, and with advice from the director of the Department of Architecture of the Museum of Modern Art (MoMA) in New York, Arthur Drexler, Mathey and Loste came up with a selection of possible jurors that reflected Pompidou's original idea. Although Mathey suggested a diverse range of candidates, including engineers, artists, collectors, critics, and historians of art and architecture, Loste soon limited the jury to the two categories outlined by Pompidou in December 1969, that of architects and that of the so-called *utilisateurs*, i.e., representatives of the kinds of institution to be included in the Centre. The only figure from outside to this classification Mathey had included right from the first drafts and that he would succeed in getting onto the final jury was Prouvé. At the time of the constitution of the jury Mathey was engaged in an effort to prevent the destruction of the Baltard Pavilions, which between 1969 and 1970, while awaiting their dismantling, were used temporarily to house a series of cultural activities and institutions that included the CCI. Without knowing that the origins of the Centre lay in the high-rise monument of the Ministry of Finance at Les Halles and without even being aware of Seguin's desire to establish an underground link between the Forum des Halles and the building that was going to rise on the plateau Beaubourg, Mathey was nevertheless conscious of the fact that the Les Halles and Centre Beaubourg projects were linked on the basis of their location in the city and their being part of the grand operation of urban regeneration of the district. The idea that the Beaubourg competition could serve as a political and planning opportunity to save the Baltard Pavilions led Mathey to turn to Prouvé who, like him, was opposed to their destruction—so much so that the latter, together with Françoise Choay and Alicia and Hiéronim Listowski, had come up with a plan to install an art and cultural center in the pavilions, convinced as he was of their potential as a flexible and well-equipped infrastructure.[65] Unaware of the role of a sort of Trojan Horse that Prouvé intended to play on the Centre Beaubourg jury, Loste saw him as a figure who would bring balance, and it was with this in mind that on July 1, 1970, he included him in a proposal for the jury submitted to Pompidou.[66] Alongside him figured three architects and three *utilisateurs*, chosen individually for their experience in areas pertinent to the architectural design of the Centre or its program. The members of the first group were Johnson, picked for his experience in museums and libraries design, Leslie Martin, for the "insertion of a work of architecture into an urban setting," and Zehrfuss—the only French architect—for his "experience with large constructions."

The second group was made up of the curator of the Stedelijk Museum, Willem Sandberg, for his expertise in museum curating; the Director of the Bibliothèque Royale Albertine in Brussels, Herman Liebaers, for his experience in running libraries, and finally Picon who, described by Loste as "a person sensitive to the spirit that such a construction ought to have," was seen from this moment on as a figure close to the French president and an influential member of the jury. Even though it reflected both the international aspirations (four foreigners and three Frenchmen) and architectural orientation (Prouvé, while being a figure of balance, was nevertheless described by Loste as being close to the architects of the jury) indicated by Pompidou, the jury proposed by Loste was questioned by the president, who thought that "this jury is a bit 'classical.' There are no architects from Brazil, [...] no Japanese... I would prefer a list of architects chosen from among these 'moderns.'"[67] The adjective "classical" might be a reference to a genre of modern architecture that had established itself between the wars, which Pompidou would rather have seen replaced by a more avant-garde component coming out of Asia and the Americas. Pompidou's criticism may also have alluded to the rather advanced age of the members of the jury and the idea that precisely because of that age they would be incapable of grasping the contemporary tendencies to which Pompidou had referred in his first exchange with Michelet. At the end of July Loste and his colleagues in the Délégation submitted a new jury to the president, this time made up of nine members.[68] The architects Johnson and Prouvé (the latter now included in this category) were joined by the Englishman Denys Lasdun, the Dane Jørn Oberg Utzon, and the Frenchman Gérard Thurnauer; and to the *utilisateurs* Picon and Sandberg were added Frank Francis, director of the British Library in London, and Michel Laclotte, curator of the Department of Paintings at the Louvre. With the new jury Loste lowered the average age of the members and offered a greater open-mindedness in the positions expressed by the architects sitting on it: Utzon, with his affinity to the language of Wright and Aalto; Thurnauer, characterized by his use of curved lines; and Lasdun, with his prominent role in British Brutalism.[69] Although the jury was approved by Pompidou on July 28 and the Délégation contacted the candidates,[70] Lasdun and Thurnauer did not agree to participate, the former because of problems with the dates,[71] the latter owing to his personal aversion to the Centre Beaubourg project and the competition terms set out by the Délégation.[72] The search for substitutes for the jury kept the Délégation busy right through the month of September and focused on some of the names previously proposed by Mathey. As a replacement for Lasdun, Loste went along with Thurnauer's complaints about the lack of representation on the jury from Latin America and turned to Niemeyer, who was one of the greatest exponents of contemporary Brazilian architecture and had been mentioned by Loste to Pompidou, with the Ministry of Foreign Affairs building in Brasilia presented as an example of a sober and "not disproportionate" kind of monumentality.[73] The choice of Thurnauer's replacement proved more complicated. After the suggestion of André Wogenscky, one of Le Corbusier's closest collaborators and someone appreciated by the Délégation for his design of the Maison de la culture in Grenoble but opposed by Prouvé,[74] and of Henri-Pierre Maillard, a French architect admired for his research into the industrialization of the building process and component-based design, the Délégation, feeling the need for a well-known figure able to hold his own with Johnson and Niemeyer, opted for Émile Aillaud, exponent of a sort of monumental and plastic architecture that Pompidou was to defend in an interview published in *Le Monde* in 1972.[75] Although by the end of September the jury was complete and had received final approval and the names of its members had been communicated to the competitors,[76] on May 4, 1971, just a month before the beginning of the selection process, Utzon informed Bordaz of his inability to continue with the work of the jury for health reasons.[77]

Each of the suggestions made to solve the problem of Utzon's replacement proved immediately problematic. The candidature of the first person on the list of reserves, the librarian Liebaers, would have ensured a foreign majority on the jury but placed the architects in a minority; that of the second, the French architect Maillard, would have maintained the preponderance of architects on the jury but caused it to lose its international character; finally, that of a Scandinavian or at any rate foreign architect would have been able to reestablish the characteristics that the jury had had with Utzon but implied the introduction of a candidate not named in the competition announcement, with the risk of invalidating its legality. Despite Prouvé, Aillaud, and Picon preferring this last solution, the choice fell on Liebaers—a choice that would not be known to participants until the publication of the competition's results. In this way a jury was formed that, in addition to Johnson's charisma and Prouvé's strategies, had a majority of *utilisateurs*, who during the selection process would give unprecedented weight to the quality and intrinsic flexibility of the Centre's spaces.

Alicia and Hiéronim Listowski et al., Project for the reconversion of Victor Baltard's Pavilions Les Halles in an artistic and cultural center, Main hall featuring suspended information medias, Paris, 1966–1968.

Alicia and Hiéronim Listowski et al., Project for the reconversion of Victor Baltard's Pavilions Les Halles in an artistic and cultural center, free plan exhibition set up,Paris, 1966–1968

Overleaf: Alicia and Hiéronim Listowski et al., Project of a multipurpose center in the historical center of Paris, 1966–1968.

église St Eustache
Palais de la République
place ouverte
place couverte - Palais Populaire
rue St Honoré - prolongée
square des Innocents
place Ste Opportune
rue St Denis
rue à plusieurs niveaux - liaisons extérieures, accès, desserte,
stockage des véhicules
ancien boulevard de Sébastopol
rue Quincampoix
rue des Lombards
église St Merri

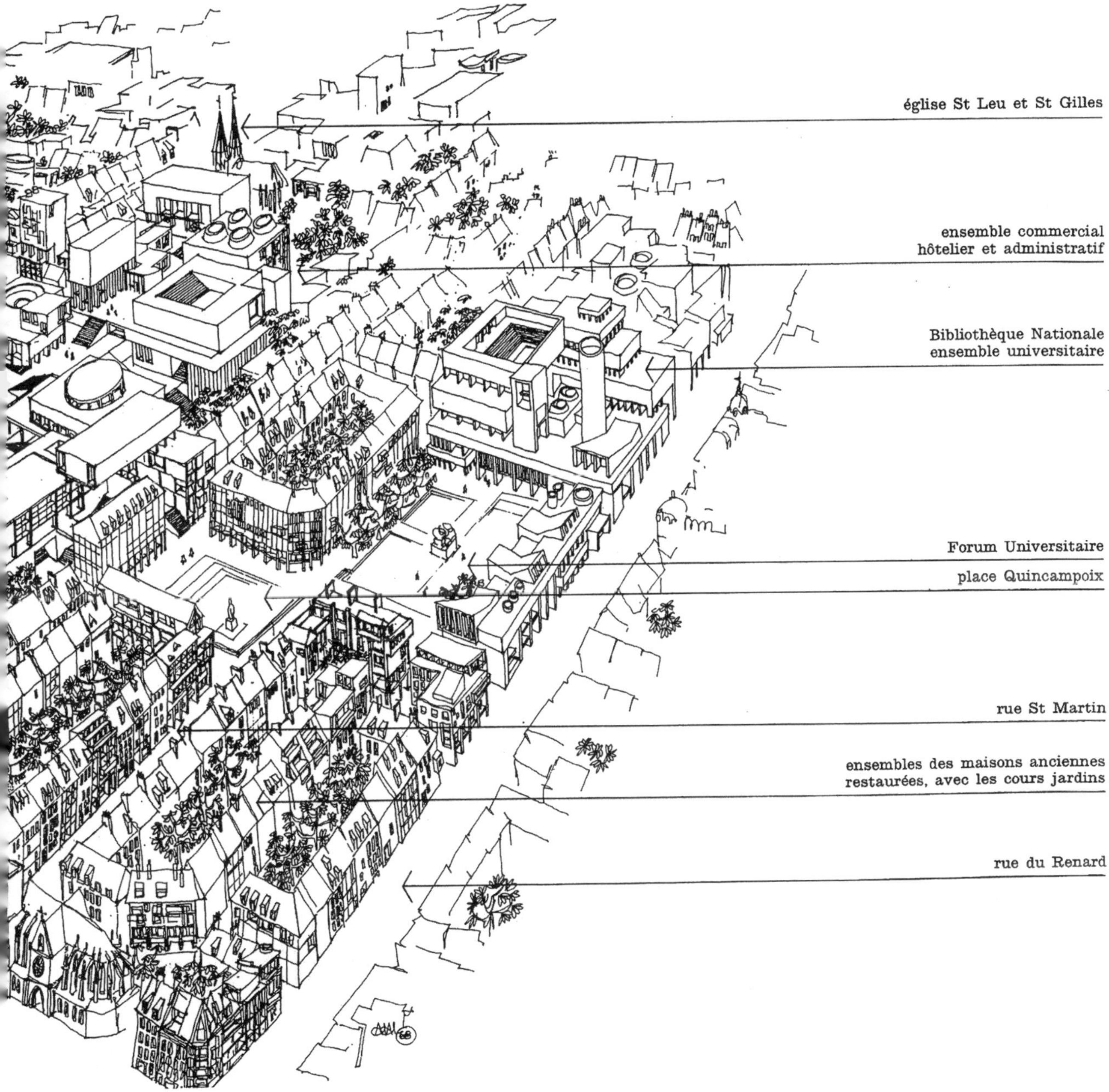
église St Leu et St Gilles
ensemble commercial
hôtelier et administratif
Bibliothèque Nationale
ensemble universitaire
Forum Universitaire
place Quincampoix
rue St Martin
ensembles des maisons anciennes
restaurées, avec les cours jardins
rue du Renard

1.9

PROUVÉ, JOHNSON AND POMPIDOU, THREE DIVERGENT VISIONS FOR ONE CENTER

Between the winter of 1970 and June 1971, i.e., over the months that preceded the start of the jury's deliberations at the Grand Palais, the Délégation focused on the material preparations for the competition on the building's premises and on an international promotional activity unprecendented that aimed to tap into avant-garde enthusiasm and tendencies all around the world and make the competition for the Centre Beaubourg the global and prestigious event Pompidou was looking for.

In this context Pompidou, Prouvé and Johnson increasingly established themselves as figures intent on exercising a significant influence on the results of the competition.

Elected chair of the jury (Picon was given the role of vice chair), Prouvé immediately undertook concrete initiatives to save the Baltard Pavilions.

At the very first jury meeting, held in Paris in November 1970, he persuaded his fellow jurors to sign an appeal addressed to the Élysée Palace requesting the preservation of the pavilions, even suggesting them as a structure compatible with the realization of the Centre Beaubourg's program ("The members of the jury even went so far as to say that these pavilions were exactly what the competition called for," was the comment that Domerg would report to the president).[78] One month later, in December, he unsuccessfully suggested "the great nave of the Grand Palais" as the place in which to carry out the competition selection process, and in so doing drew attention to a structure of the same kind as that of the Baltard Pavilions.[79] In the spring of 1971, at when the destruction of the Baltard Pavilions appeared imminent, Prouvé's strategy grew more complex. On the one hand he revised the judgment criteria outlined by the Délégation, eliminating any reference to the aesthetic-monumental evaluation that the Délégation had in the meantime inserted to comply with the wishes of the president. On the other, a few weeks prior to the beginning of the selection process, in June, Prouvé sent Pompidou a copy of his monograph on constructions in metal, *Une architecture par l'industrie*, to draw the president's attention to a kind of industrial construction that had originated with such large 19th-century structures as the Baltard Pavilions.[80]

These actions made it clear Prouvé's objective was no longer necessarily the preservation of the pavilions. It was turning into the no less ambitious one of steering the competition toward a kind of design that could emulate the intrinsic characteristics of those pavilions, from their internal flexibility to the refinement of the details of their structure. Prouvé would not only prove himself capable of discreetly deploying this strategy at the core of the jury's procedure but make it an out-and-out mission during the fine-tuning of the main project, succeeding in impressing on its structure a plastic and sculptural character on the level of the Baltard Pavilions.

For his part Pompidou persisted in his attempt to give his baby a monumental character and, in this phrase, let himself be guided by the world of contemporary art and two of its protagonists, Hans Hartung and Hundertwasser. Hartung introduced him to the works of the architect Marcel Breuer, one of the great masters of American Modernism whose designs including the recently completed Whitney Museum in New York.[81] Although in his discussions with the president on the nature of his monument, Loste had singled out the Whitney Museum as an internally flexible model but one whose aesthetics were not very convincing ("very convenient on the inside, but most unattractive," were his words), Pompidou must have been fascinated by Breuer's monumental style with his adroit use of raw concrete and stone.[82]

So with Bordaz acting as a go-between, he tried unsuccessfully to persuade Breuer to take part in the competition.[83]

If in the case of Breuer, Pompidou didn't obtain a candidature that would have been able to introduce a language he liked into the competition, in Hundertwasser's Pompidou came to formulate an idea for the design of his monument. In December 1970 Hundertwasser sent the Pompidous a series of manifestos based on the idea of a re-humanized and re-naturalized architecture through the right to self-construction, the revival of functionalist architecture with an artistic and liberating restoration based on what he called "creative molds" and on the location of gardens, lawns, meadows, and farms on the roofs of buildings to give back to nature the land that architecture had "killed" by constructing on it.[84]

Hundertwasser's sketched designs convinced Pompidou that, whatever its nature, the project chosen by the jury ought to be covered with trees and grass, and this was precisely the appearance that the winning project was destined to assume in its first phase of development in the fall of 1971. Whether Pompidou shared Hundertwasser's ideological premises or not, from this moment on Pompidou placed such trust in his own judgment that he expressed his views on questions of architecture from an artistic perspective which he felt to be his own. It is no accident that it was precisely through art and its protagonists, from Georges Braque to Jean Dubuffet to the exponents of avant-garde Op art, that Pompidou would constantly intervene on the appearance of the Centre Beaubourg in an attempt to turn it into a sort of artwork on an urban scale.

Right from his selection for the competition jury, Johnson too had begun to exercise a significance influence over the nature that the Centre was going to assume. His presence on the jury reflected a propensity for postwar modern American architecture, as had been made clear both by the interest Loste and the Ministry of Cultural Affairs had shown in Lincoln Center, in whose design Johnson had played a part, and by the fact that Seguin had turned to Johnson for advice on the Bibliothèque des Halles project. Johnson himself provided evidence of the Délégation's interest in American architecture when, a few weeks before the start of the competition and at Bordaz's request, he prepared for him a set of slides of "the main libraries and museums in the United States"—"recent ones" Johnson would stress—to be used to inform public opinion in the context of the exhibition of the results of the competition.[85] Also in the context of these meetings Johnson showed himself to be sensitive to Prouvé's concerns, and supported him in several initiatives, from the attempt to replace Utzon with another Scandinavian architect, or at least a foreign one, to the drafting of the appeal to save Baltard's pavilions. And yet in this phase Johnson's truly significant contribution to the future Centre lay in his criticism of the sketchy proposal of infrastructure integration between the plateau Beaubourg, the complex underground circuit planned at Les Halles, and the Paris road network.

The importance that Johnson, like Seguin, now attached to the question was such that he declared: "if the road scheme were retained and if I were consulted as a candidate, I would put the text of the competition straight in the garbage."[86]

Thanks to Johnson's forceful arguments and the support of the other jury members, convinced at once that the question was "the main point of the project," in the spring of 1971 Lombard, assisted by experts from SEMAH and the Prefecture of Paris, sent the participants a supplement to the competition notice that delved into just this question of the Centre's integration with the metropolitan infrastructure. Not coincidentally, just as had happened with Seguin and Faugeron, it was around the underground connection with the Forum des Halles and the links with the traffic flows beneath and above the surface of the city that the idea of the winning project of the competition would take shape.

Although the actions undertaken by Loste, Lombard, Prouvé, Johnson, and Pompidou suggest the emergence of different and in some ways still contradictory visions and desires, under Bordaz's direction the Délégation successfully concluded the preparations for staging an international public architecture competition that had no equal at the time and, in the words of Johnson and Sandberg, would be "the most important of the century."[87]

Victor Baltard, Pavilions Les Halles, Detail of the cast iron structure, Paris, 1970.

Overleaf: Friedensreich Hundertwasser, Sketches of the manifesto “Verwaldung der Städte” sent to Georges and Claude Pompidou, 1970.

Entwurf für ein

4 stöckiges Gemeindehaus
mit 5 WÄLDERN und Wiesen
übereinander.

Die Wohnungen hängen an der Unterseite der WÄLDER.

DIE Abwässer der Wohnungen werden *nicht* ins Ableitungsrohr sondern in den darunterliegenden Garten geleitet oder mit *Handpumpen* in den darüberliegenden. Die Scheisse und der Abfall werden mit Spezialgeräten die noch zu entwerfen sind halb-sterilisiert? in die grossen hängenden Gärten-Erdmassen eingegliedert. So ein Haus kann vielleicht Autark werden, d.h. von den eigenen Produkten leben.

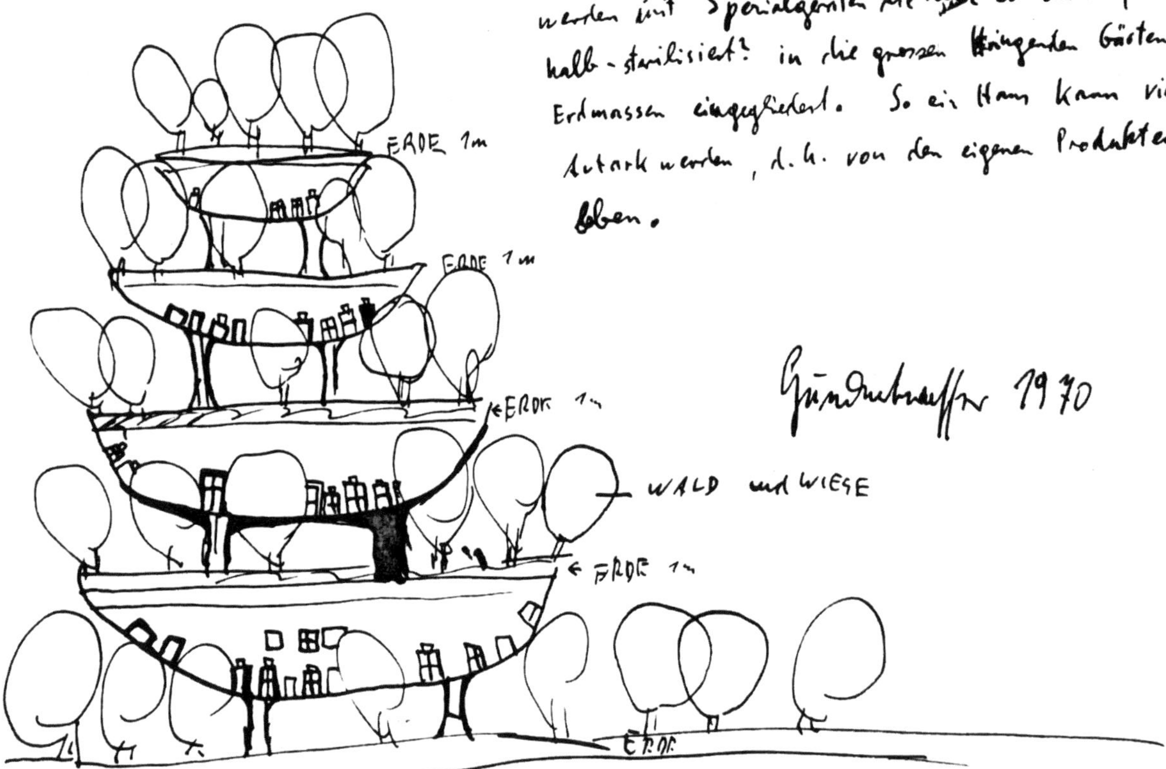

Hundertwasser 1970

Keine Kanalisation hier ist Grundwasser reiner

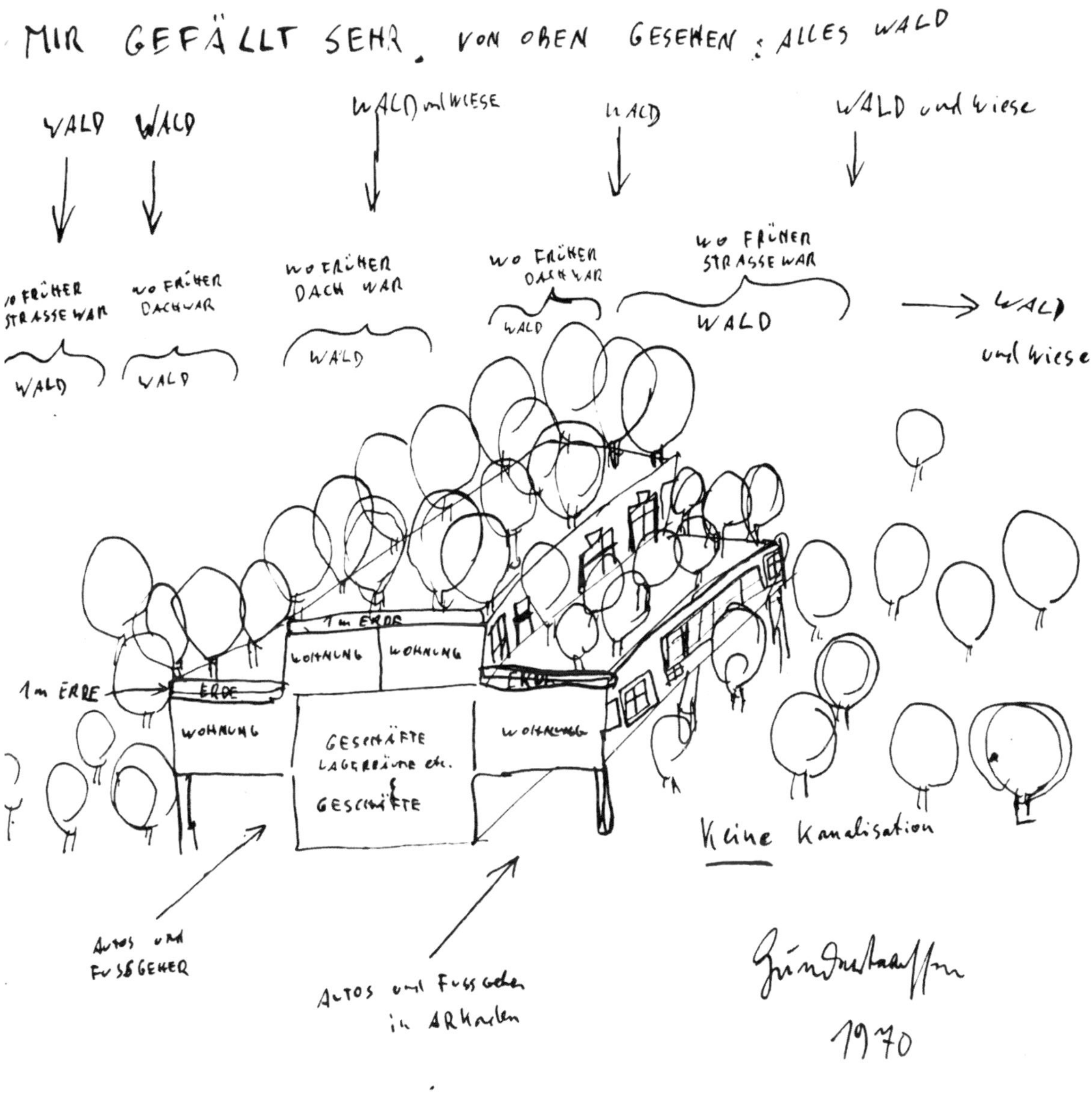

DETAIL EINES STRASSENZUGES IM SCHNITT

1 — This introduction to the work is a summary of four chapters of the author's PhD dissertation, written under the supervision of Roberto Gargiani and defended in October 2021 before a committee made up of Professors Bruno Marchand, Cuno Brullmann, Giovanni Galli, and Elena Cogato Lanza, with Renzo Piano, Gabriele Del Mese, and Shunji Ishida as reviewers of the work. Boris Hamzeian, Centre national d'art et de culture Georges Pompidou: Monument national e Live Centre of Information. Cronache di idea, progetto e fabbricazione, 1968-1977, École Polytechnique Fédérale de Lausanne-EPFL, Lausanne, 2021. For a more in-depth analysis of the themes dealt with here the reader is referred to the following chapters of the dissertation: 1. "La genesi del Centre Beaubourg, dal 'monument prestigieux' di Pompidou al 'musée laboratoire' di Loste," 39–66; 2. "La macchina concorsuale del Centre Beaubourg," 67–88; 3. "Il bando di concorso del Centre Beaubourg," 89–96; 4. "La promozione del concorso e la preparazione del processo di selezione al Grand Palais di Parigi," 97–108.

2 — Pompidou revealed his passion for art in an interview given to *Le Figaro litteraire* on September 1, 1966. On this occasion he spoke of his love for abstract painting, mentioning Robert and Sonia Delaunay, Piet Mondrian, František Kupka, Nicolas de Staël, Paul Klee, and Wols. He also expressed his admiration for the new generation of figurative painters, such as Martial Raysse. Michel Droit, "Entretien avec Georges Pompidou (Georges Pompidou répond à vingt questions sur les lettres, l'art et la culture," *Le Figaro littéraire*, no. 1063, September 1, 1966, 1. In an interview granted to *Paris Match* in 1968 he added the name of Arman. Pompidou's wife, Claude, spoke publicly of the couple's collecting in an interview published in a monograph devoted to the artistic and cultural sensibility of her dead husband. Claude Pompidou, "Georges Pompidou un président collectionneur," in *Hommage au Président Georges Pompidou, un homme de culture* (Paris: Artcurial, 1987), 15–31. The exchanges between the Pompidous and French and foreign protagonists of artistic creativity can also be traced in the innumerable meetings mentioned in Pompidou's engagement books, compiled by his secretary Madeleine Négrel and kept at the Institut Georges Pompidou in Paris. Négrel, Agendas de Georges Pompidou (années 1959–1974), IGP, n.p.

3 — "Besides, it is no longer a problem of construction but of architecture and it is not so much the public that has to be educated as architects. We have some great architects: Bernard, Gillet, Pouillon, Zehrfuss for example, but also many who are willing to build anything, anywhere." Droit, "Entretien avec Georges Pompidou (Georges Pompidou répond à vingt questions sur les lettres, l'art et la culture)," 1.

4 — "It is architecture, even more than landscape and scenery, which creates the face of a nation and on this point it is necessary for French architecture today to make a very great effort to take back the place that it had—it must be said—for some six centuries and that for several decades now we have too often let ourselves be beguiled by foreign architects." Georges Pompidou, "Extrait de l'allocution de Georges Pompidou à villagexpo, 30 septembre 1966," in Elise Capdevila, Jean-François Sirinelli, and Elisa Riera, *Georges Pompidou et la culture* (Paris: Peter Lang, 2011), 83–85: 84.

5 — Droit, "Entretien avec Georges Pompidou (Georges Pompidou répond à vingt questions sur les lettres, l'art et la culture," 1.

6 — The project leaders of the firms invited to take part in the competition for the redevelopment of the district of Les Halles were Claude Charpentier, Louis Arretche, Atelier d'Urbanisme et Architecture (AUA), Louis de Hoÿm de Marien, Michel Marot, and Jean Faugeron. For an analysis of the individual projects see Hamzeian, Centre national d'art et de culture Georges Pompidou: Monument national e Live Centre of Information. Cronache di idea, progetto e fabbricazione, 1968-1977, 46–47. See too Jean-Louis Violeau, Les *Halles. De la contre-culture aux cultures parallèles (1964–1984)* (Paris: Éditions B2, 2018).

7 — On the origins of the Bpi see: Jean-Pierre Seguin, *Comment est née la BPI: invention de la Médiathèque* (Paris: Centre Georges Pompidou, Bibliothèque publique d'information, 1987).

8 — Opened in 1968, the Cnac was based on a project drawn up by the Director-general of arts and letters Pierre Moinot and temporarily housed in the exhibition spaces of the Musées Nationaux (at the Mnam and the Galeries nationales du Grand Palais) and, later, the Hôtel Salomon de Rothschild, a large 19th-century townhouse situated in the eighth arrondissement of Paris. It was the culmination of a long-standing project on which not only Gaëtan Picon, Moinot's predecessor, had worked, but also François Mathey, curator of the Musée des Arts Décoratifs and then director of the CCI. For further information see: Boris Hamzeian, "La creazione del Centre national d'art contemporain," in Hamzeian, Centre national d'art et de culture Georges Pompidou: Monument national e Live Centre of Information, 42–45.

9 — On the subject of the suggestions made by Henri Domerg and Michel Bruguière to prepare Pompidou for the appraisal of the Les Halles projects see Michel Bruguière, Note pour le Premier Ministre (l'aménagement des Halles et le Ministère des Affaires Culturelles), January 19, 1968, AN, FHD, F 8, 1–4. On the preference of the French minister of Cultural Affairs André Malraux and his "entourage" for Jean Faugeron's project—"the only one" in Bruguière's view, "to mark a certain 'desire for grandeur' on the part of our generation" with its "very futuristic architecture" based on the use of curved lines—see Bruguière, Note pour le Premier Ministre, 1.

10 — On Pompidou's appreciation of skyscrapers see Jacques Michel, "Entretien avec Georges Pompidou (Le président de la République définit ses conceptions dans les domaines de l'art et de l'architecture)," *Le Monde*, October 17, 1972, 1, 12.

11 — "Prime Minister: 'I am in principle confused. The models are spectacular and do not make the decision easier (we see them from the sky). What will be the view of the man who is going to live or work in this neighborhood?'" Comité interministériel sur Paris, January 22, 1968, AN, FSL, F 100, 6.

12 — Comité interministériel sur Paris, 8–9.

13 — Henri Domerg, Untitled [handwritten notes on the interdepartmental meeting of January 22, 1968], January 22, 1968, AN, FHD, F 8, 1–2.

14 — "If there is anything," declared Pompidou, "that could be tall, a monument, it is the Ministry of Finance." Ibid.

15 — "General de Gaulle indicates that what is needed for Les Halles is something that stands out. We must make a bet and adopt a solution that will not be mediocre but significant, evident, substantial." Compte-rendu analytique du Conseil restreint du 26 janvier 1968 consacré à l'aménagement de Paris, January 26, 1968, AN, FSL, F 100, 8.

16 — Ibid.

17 — Compte-rendu analytique du Conseil restreint du 26 janvier 1968, 9.

18 — Although the City Council debate on the Les Halles redevelopment project was postponed until October 1968 owing to the student and worker revolt that broke out in the spring, René Capitant, elected president of the Permanent Commission on Les Halles, made the project guidelines clear that summer. "Regarding the Ministry of Finance, M. Capitant spoke without ambiguity: studies of this question 'only confirm,' he said, 'the contraindication given by our Council.' [...] Thus, once again, elected officials have expressed their opposition to the presence in Les Halles of the Ministry of Finance, whose imposing mass would pose delicate problems of architectural equilibrium and detract from the liveliness of the area," was the comment made by *Le Monde*. "Le transfert aux Halles du Ministère des finances. La commission permanente des élus souhaite que le gouvernement révise sa position," *Le Monde*, July 15, 1968.

19 —Georges Pompidou, Letter to the minister of Cultural Affairs Edmond Michelet [first version of November 28, 1969, not sent], November 28, 1969, AN, FHD, F 8. This letter constitutes the first document relating to the project known first as the Centre Beaubourg and then as the Centre national d'art et de culture Georges Pompidou. It is possible that Pompidou had been thinking about this project since July 17, when, in the presence of his adviser René Galy-Dejean, he asked for the model of the Les Halles project, which was at the origin of the Centre Beaubourg, to be installed in the Salon de Portraits of the Élysée Palace. Pompidou may also have discussed the project on October 25 when he received two French architects, Joseph Belmont and someone identified only as Jardin, at the Élysée Palace. Négrel, Agendas de Georges Pompidou (année 1969), n.p. That the primary aim of the monument was the reinvigoration of French architecture rather than contemporary art was made clear by Pompidou himself when he declared: "While the French of today can, in many respects, compare themselves to their elders without blushing, since the beginning of the century they have, it must be admitted, given too little luster to architecture. And we can only point, in Paris in particular, to the paucity of examples of such monuments, witnesses to an era, which have always been the mark of a nation's prestige. It is now time to fill this gap." Pompidou, Letter to the minister of Cultural Affairs Edmond Michelet.

20 — Ibid.

21 — Ibid.

22 — It has not been possible to trace the letter in which Malraux asked Le Corbusier to send him the documentation of the Musée à croissance illimité. What is known is that on December 10, 1962, Le Corbusier sent a "grid" of the design to Bernard Anthonioz, at the time project leader at the Ministry of Cultural Affairs, with an invitation to deliver the documentation "personally to M. Malraux." Le Corbusier, Letter to B. Anthonioz, December 10, 1962, AN, DGAL, F F21NC1314. In February 1963 Malraux invited Jean Cassou and his team to study the applicability of Le Corbusier's proposal to the Musée du XXe siècle. Maurice Besset, Musée à croissance illimité et Musée du XXe siècle, February 1962, AN,

DGAL, F F218294. The profound accord between the Musée à croissance illimité proposal and the preliminary program for the Musée du XXe siècle (which seems in fact to have been inspired by Le Corbusier's proposal) persuaded Cassou to confirm the compatibility of the two designs. Le Corbusier reduced the construction materials to a kit of just a few elements: posts and beams in concrete poured on site, modular floor slabs, and vertical, fixed, or movable infill panels. Christian Zervos, Le Corbusier, and Pierre Jeanneret, "Pour la création à Paris d'un musée des artistes vivants (II), réponse et projet d'aménagement et d'organisation," *Cahiers d'Art*, no. 1 (1931), 5–9.

23 — Zervos, Le Corbusier, and Jeanneret, "Pour la création à Paris d'un musée des artistes vivants," 8.

24 — Ibid.

25 — Le Corbusier envisaged a building/construction site that could be run by a single worker. "This," he asserted, "might also imply the permanent presence of a worker and his hod carrier, who alone could, from day to day, and over the years, build the whole museum, funded by donations or the widow's mite." Ibid.

26 — Ibid.

27 — After Le Corbusier's death, Director-general of arts and letters Moinot tried on several occasions to resurrect the project. First, he promoted the continuation of the project at La Défense, entrusting it to one of Le Corbusier's closest collaborators, André Wogenscky, and later considered inserting the Musée du XXe siècle into the plateau des Halles. Once this last plan had been rejected, the project was definitively abandoned, as the ministry's technicians told Domerg in December 1969. "It has been confirmed to me," wrote Domerg, "that the project for the Musée du XXe siècle which had been envisaged at La Défense has been abandoned. [...] It is likely that the monument at Les Halles would be considered a revival of this idea." Henri Domerg, Note pour Monsieur Jobert, December 10, 1969, AN, FHD, F 8.

28 — According to the notes made by Négrel, between December 3 and 6 Pompidou, accompanied by Domerg, received at the Élysée Palace the chief conservator of the Musée national d'art moderne Jean Leymarie and the director of the Department of Artistic Creation Anthonioz, who was also in charge of the CNAC. Négrel, Agendas de Pompidou (année 1969), IGP, n.p.

29 — According to the Bibliothèque des Halles program: "On July 11, 1969, the City Council took into consideration the development plan for the area of regeneration of the district of Les Halles and the elements that appear in the plan, including the library, located on the plateau Beaubourg." Jean-Pierre Seguin, Bibliothèque des Halles, December 1969, AN, FBPI, F 1, vol. I, 1.

30 — The program was drawn up in 1967. André Chatelin and Jean-Pierre Seguin, Bibliothèque des Halles (schéma des études présentés à M. Dennery, administrateur général de la B.N.F., January 23, 1967, AN, FBPI, F 1. The three thematic planks were reworked and translated into spatial requisites in the reports compiled between 1968 and 1969. Seguin, Bibliothèque des Halles.

31 — The idea of an "information" center to be inserted into the library had such an impact that the participants working on the cultural facilities program at Les Halles in the spring of 1967 turned it into a "Maison de l'information" (house of information). The idea of the Maison de l'information proved so popular with the Paris City Council and the public that Seguin turned directly to the prefect of Paris to obtain his support for the realization of the project. Seguin, Projet de lettre au préfet, February 1968, AN, FBPI, F 1.

32 — Chatelin and Seguin, Bibliothèque des Halles (schéma des études), 6. Seguin compared the interiors of the library with the transformable stage sets of "popular national theaters"—an image perfectly in keeping with the idea of transformability of the Musée du XXe siècle. Ibid.

33 — Chatelin and Seguin, Bibliothèque National Paris – Bibliothèque de Lecteur Publique dans le secteur de rénovation des anciennes Halles de Paris. Études n° 1 et 2 – (plans n° 288/1 à 18), January 15, 1967, AN, FBPI, F 1.

34 — Maurice Doublet, Letter to Étienne Dennery, December 23, 1968, AN, FBPI, F 1.

35 — "2: when will this construction begin?" Seguin asked himself, "does it depend on the site chosen? In Beaubourg, in 1968 [?], but in that case the library would not be at the center of the cultural complex and the necessary routes of access to this relatively remote area will undoubtedly be the last to be provided." Jean-Pierre Seguin, Letter to Étienne Dennery, n.d. [1967], AN, FBPI, F 1.

36 — The libraries visited by Seguin were: in Quebec, the Bibliothèque de l'Université Laval; in Boston, the Boston Public Library, and Francis A. Countway Library of Medicine; in Cambridge, the Massachusetts Institute of Technology Library, Harvard University Library, and Hilles Library; in New Haven, the Beinecker Rare Book and Manuscript Library; in New York, the New York Public Library, Mid-Manhattan Public Library, Library and Museum of Performing Arts at Lincoln Center, Queens Borough Public Library, and Brooklyn Public Library; in Washington, the Library of Congress and DC Public Library; in Bethesda, the National Library of Medicine; in Beltsville, the National Agricultural Library; in Chicago, the Chicago Public Library and John Crerar Library; in Detroit, the Detroit Public Library; in Buffalo, the Buffalo and Erie County Public Library. He also paid visits to the American Institute of Physics, the Donnel Library Center in New York, and the Council of Library Resources in Washington, where he met Sir Frank Francis, one of the future members of the Centre Beaubourg jury. He also met Philip Johnson, designer of the Boston Public Library as well as future jury member, like Francis, of the Beaubourg competition. Jean-Pierre Seguin, Bibliothèque Nationale – Bibliothèque des Halles. Voyage d'études au Canada et aux États-Unis, October 1969, AN, FBPI, F 3. According to Seguin, during his meeting with Johnson, the architect presented him the plans of his Boston Public Library and drew a "sketch" for Seguin's library based on what Johnson considered the fundamental idea of the project, "that of a library welcoming in all its parts." Seguin, *Comment est née la BPI*, 60.

37 — Seguin, *Comment est née la BPI*, 10.

38 — Le Corbusier, "Lettre Ouverte de Le Corbusier à M. le directeur général des Beaux-Arts. (datée 12 Janvier 1935)," *L'Architecture d'Aujourd'hui*, no. 11 (1934), 22–23: 23.

39 — In the program drawn up on his return from America Seguin wrote in this connection: "The Les Halles library is a service. The service comes before and overrides the monument. The monumental character should stem above all from a harmonious expression of the functional needs of the service. It will then necessarily be successful because it is suited to its purpose." Seguin, Bibliothèque des Halles, 1.

40 — Seguin, Bibliothèque des Halles, 42.

41 — The list provided by Seguin also included Lincoln Center in New York, the Museum of Modern Art in New York, and the Business and shopping center in Buffalo. Ibid., 42.

42 — Seguin, *Comment est née la BPI*.

43 — Faugeron's technical drawings and sketches for the Bibliothèque des Halles are now in the Archives nationales in Paris. AN, BDH, F 1.

44 — In some cases the library's envelope was represented with an alternation of stringcourses and modernist strip windows, in others it was defined by monumental brise-soleils consisting of metal slats arranged vertically to enclose the building in colossal metallic segments with an industrial and streamlined appearance.

45 — Pompidou's familiarity with Faugeron's project is attested by a note written by Domerg on January 9, 1970, that reads: "For the moment, we have elements like the report drawn up some time ago with a view to the design of the Museum of the 20th Century (which is not unrelated to what is under consideration today), the project—which you have seen—for the library." Henri Domerg, Note pour Monsieur the Président de la République. Travaux préparatoires concernant l'ensemble consacré à l'art contemporain, January 9, 1969, AN, FHD, F 10, 2. According to Seguin it was he who had contacted Claude Pompidou to ask her to show the president the Bibliothèque des Halles project. "So I personally took the liberty of writing to her, to inform her of the library project and to ask her to speak to the President about it. Later I learned that the idea had quickly gained his approval, and that he saw what impact the presence of these facilities would have on the numbers of people coming to the Center." Seguin, *Comment est née la BPI*.

46 — Among the participants at the meeting, in addition to Pompidou, there were ten state officials, including Prime Minister Jacques Chaban-Delmas, Michelet for Cultural Affairs, Olivier Guichard for National Education, Giscard d'Estaing for Economy and Finance, the Prefect of Paris, Diebolt, and the prefect of the Paris Region. "3rd / Museum of Contemporary Arts. It was decided that a museum of contemporary arts will be built on the plateau Beaubourg as part of the regeneration of Les Halles. It will be a monument that, on the architectural level, will have to reflect our time. The possibility of exceeding the *velum*, i.e. the ceiling on the height allowed in the sector, should be considered. The building could possibly house a public reading library," declare the minutes of the meeting. Présidence de la République, Relevé de décisions du Conseil Interministériel du Jeudi 11 décembre 1969 -15 heures 30 – Paris et Région Parisienne, December 11, 1969, AN, PM AP, F 2, n.p.

47 — Georges Pompidou, Letter to Edmond Michelet, December 15, 1969, AN, FHD, F 10.

48 — Pompidou, Letter to Michelet, 2.

49 — "[...] special facilities for music, recording and possibly film and theater research," were Pompidou's words. Ibid.

50 — The declarations of the Select Council of December 11 and those of the letter sent to Michelet concerning the inclusion of a library in the monument are

contradictory. In the first case the possibility was raised of including in it the Bibliothèque de lecture publique (BPI) and thus Dennery and Seguin's project ("The building could possibly house a public reading library."). Présidence de la République, Relevé de décisions du Conseil Interministériel du Jeudi 11 décembre. Pompidou favored a library specializing in art. "It would be desirable if it could also include a library, at the very least a library comprising all the works on the arts and their evolution in the present." Pompidou, Letter to Michelet, 2.

51 — "Following the decision taken by the Select Council on December 11 for the construction of a complex devoted to contemporary art on the site of the Plateau Beaubourg, I believe I ought to give you some details about the way I perceive the project" were Pompidou's words. Pompidou, Letter to Michelet, 1.

52 — Présidence de la République, Relevé de décisions du Conseil Interministériel du Jeudi 11 décembre, 1.

53 — Signs of the general skepticism concerning French competitions can be found in an article on the Beaubourg competition published in *Le Monde* in 1970: "This plan is going to have an exceptional procedure for France: it will be the subject of a competition and of an international one. To tell the truth, architects are wary of competitions in France. All too often, the results of such practices are known in advance in France from the makeup of the jury. And so many people refuse to participate, considering that they represent above all a waste of money and brainpower." Jaques Michel, "Une cité artistique et culturelle dans un seul édifice," *Le Monde*, 17 July 1970.

54 — Pompidou added: "The conditions for the organization of the competition must therefore provide, in ways still to be defined, the means for any architect whose project has been singled out to be paid for his work and his costs defrayed." Georges Pompidou, Letter to Edmond Michelet [handwritten version with corrections], December 8, 1969, AN, PGP, F 1073, 2.

55 — Étienne Mallet, "A fact-finding mission on the affair of La Villette has been set up – The museum of contemporary art desired by Mr. Pompidou has been favorably received," *Le Monde*, December 17, 1969. After a lively debate held on December 15, at the instigation of Prefect Diebolt and some members of the Union des républicains de progress and centrist political groupings, the Council voted in favor of the project. "Council of Paris. 4th ordinary session of 1969. Meeting on Monday, December 15, 1969 (Part 4: questions to the prefect of Paris: 1st from Messrs. Pierre Giraud, Astier, Seince, Chabrut, Pariggi, Salles and Luce on the conditions under which the decision to build a 20th-century museum on the site of the plateau Beaubourg was taken without the slightest consultation of the Council of Paris; 2nd from Mssrs. Charles Lederman, Pierre Mialet and Henri Carloni on the need to inform the Council of Paris on the Declarations regarding the installation of a museum of contemporary art at Les Halles and more specifically, it appears, at the site of the plateau Beaubourg; and on the consequences of this measure for all the decisions already taken by the Council of Paris, the competent authority)," *Bulletin Municipal officiel de la Ville de Paris*, vol. LXXXIX, 32, January 8, 1970, 1164.

56 — Georges Pompidou, Note manuscrite à M. Jobert (et M. Domerg), December 1969, AN, FHD, F 10.

57 — Sébastien Loste, Questions posées par le projet de monument consacré à l'art contemporain, January 22, 1970, AN, 574 AP, F 10, 2. Among the questions linked to the running of the future Centre Beaubourg were the funding of the project and the possibility of excluding the Centre from the National Museums system; the merging of the team responsible for the Centre national d'art contemporain with that of the Musée des arts décoratifs to form a high-level working group; the question of the future of the CNAC; preparation for the opening of the building; the inclusion in the Centre of activities able to create "as big an attraction as possible," such as a swimming pool or some other kind of sports facility; the inclusion in the Centre of public education activities; the broadcasting of some of the Centre's cultural activities through the setting up of a branch of the national radio and television corporation O.R.T.F. Loste, Questions posées par le projet de monument consacré à l'art contemporain, 7–8.

58 — Lincoln Center was also attracting the Ministry of Culture's attention, as is attested by the fact that Michelet had expressed his intention to send Loste to New York expressly to study this project as early as January 9.

59 — Sébastien Loste, Note à l'attention du Président de La République sur le Centre d'art moderne du plateau Beaubourg, February 14, 1970, AN, FHD, F 10.

60 — Loste declared: "We cannot, however, give the architect any other indication, with regard to the center of contemporary creativity, than the reflection of the director of one of the most important museums of modern art in the world, the one in Stockholm (Mr. Hulten) [...]. It seems that, given the impossibility of anticipating the architecture of a museum of modern art, it is necessary to provide space and tools, highly flexible premises, equipped with water, electricity, sound, etc., 'large fitted sheds.'" Loste, Note à l'attention du Président de La République sur le Centre d'art moderne, 11.

61 — Pompidou wrote in the introductory note to Loste's report: "It is possible to decide on these bases, but I think we need to look a bit longer at its 'development' and the extremely varied 'exhibitions' on the program. [But] the ideas are right." Henri Domerg, Note pour monsieur le Président de la République, February 16, 1970, AN, 574 AP, F 10.

62 — Hultén presented this project in Paris on the occasion of two meetings organized by UNESCO in October 1969 and April 1970 in the presence of two of the advisors who had helped Loste draw up the report on the "Centre du plateau Beaubourg," Leymarie and Mathey. Hultén summed up the project in four concentric "spheres" corresponding to the same number of functions centered on information: starting from the outside, a first sphere for "the collection of raw, unprocessed information, events and facts about the world today"; a second relating to the idea of a workshop where the public could process information independently; a third for information reworked by the museum for the staging of exhibitions and performances; the fourth, and innermost, sphere to house the historical memory of the museum and information in its physical form, from artworks to all the information that could be stored on an advanced computer. "Editorial," *Museum*, vol. 24, 1 ("Problems of the Museum of Contemporary Art in the West") (1972), 4–5; Pierre Gaudibert, Pontus Hultén, Michael Kustow *et al.*, "Exchange of Views of a Group of Experts," *Museum*, vol. 24, 1 (1972), 5–32: 13–14. On the same theme see Michael Kustow, "Profiles and Situations of Some Museums of Contemporary Art, *Museum*, vol. 24, 1 (1972), 43–44.

63 — Gaëtan Picon, Letter to Georges Pompidou, December 28, 1969, AN, FHD, F 10. Pompidou commented on his choice in an annotation made on a note from Domerg on July 15: "Gaëtan Picon must [be] the director!" Henri Domerg, Note pour Monsieur le Président de la République. État présent de la préparation du projet du plateau Beaubourg, July 15, 1970, AN, FHD, F 10, 1.

64 — Henri Domerg, Note pour Monsieur le Président de la République, July 16, 1970, AN, FHD, F 10.

65 — "A current—and quite logical—trend in the architectural design of public buildings is to make them multipurpose, as evolution in the occupation and use of locations is occurring very fast. So it would be necessary to design structures that provide unrestricted volumes into which technical equipment is integrated. The finest example of this concept is in Paris. It is Les Halles! Work on them began in 1851. They were opened in 1857. The large covered volumes requested by Napoleon III from the architect Baltard in opposition to a grandiose project of classical architecture were economically and masterfully built of metal and supplied with electricity and water. For more than a century this has worked. The structures are beautiful and in good condition. The volumes are immense and everything is possible in them. Napoleon III had said to the architect 'make me umbrellas,' preempting the architecture of the future. Do these exemplary buildings in Paris really have to be destroyed? If that happens, it will be necessary to be extraordinarily capable as well!" These are the words used by Prouvé in his essay "Les Halles," in Alicia & Hiéronim Listowski, Françoise Choay *et al.*, *Paris Demain. La ville en question, une proposition pour Paris* (Paris: Marcel Soucier Imprimeur, 1968), n.p.

66 — Sébastien Loste, Proposition pour un jury (plateau Beaubourg), July 1, 1970, AN, CNACGP, F 156.

67 — Domerg, Note pour Monsieur le Président de la République. Travaux préparatoires du Musée du plateau Beaubourg, July 15, 1970, AN, FHD, F 10.

68 — Sébastien Loste, Proposition pour le jury du concours international du plateau Beaubourg, July 27, 1970, AN, FHD, F 10. For the new proposal Loste turned to candidates who had already been considered by the Délégation but up until then had been regarded as only suitable to play the part of "substitutes," i.e., to be held in reserve.

69 — Loste tried to have a wide range of architectural styles represented on the jury in response to Pompidou's criticism. This fact is confirmed by Loste himself when he declared: "it is necessary to avoid this or that trend in modern architecture predominating on the jury, so that all have the same chance." Loste, Proposition pour le jury du concours international du plateau Beaubourg, July 27, 1970, 2.

70 — "OK on the new list," were Pompidou's words. Henri Domerg, Note pour Monsieur le Président de la République, July 28, 1970, AN, 574 AP, F 10, 1.

71 — "Lasdun has just refused, wishing to take part in the competition. We are therefore looking for another name to take Mr. Lasdun's place." Sébastien Loste, Note à l'attention de Monsieur Domerg. Jury du concours du plateau Beaubourg, September 11, 1970, AN, FHD, F 13, 2. Nonetheless, in a note dated September 21, Loste put down Lasdun's refusal to questions of scheduling.

Sébastien Loste, Note sur le jury du concours international (plateau Beaubourg), September 21, 1970, AN, FHD, F 13, 1.

72 — Gérard Thurnauer, Lettre adressée au directeur de l'Architecture Monsieur Danieul, September 4, 1970, AN, CNACGP, F 17.

73 — Loste, Questions posées par le projet du monument consacré à l'art contemporain, 2.

74 — As a note of September 10, 1970, shows, the Délégation initially agreed on Wogenscky's name. "One of the architects who had been approached to sit on the jury of the plateau Beaubourg Competition, Mr. Thurnauer, did not accept the proposal: he must therefore be replaced and we are thinking of Mr. Wogenscky, who in particular built the Maison de Culture in Grenoble." Henri Domerg, Note pour Monsieur le Président de la République, September 10, 1970, AN, FHD, F 10. In an annotation made on the same note Pompidou agreed to the nomination of Wogenscky with a curt "so be it." Ibid. From Loste's note of September 21 we learn that the appointment of Wogenscky was dropped following a fierce debate and Prouvé's hostility to his nomination. Loste, Note sur le jury du concours international (plateau Beaubourg), 2.

75 — After Wogenscky's exclusion, Loste described the debate within the Délégation as follows: the experts of the Department of Architecture at the Ministry of Cultural Affairs supported the appointment of Henri-Pierre Maillard, convinced of the need for a "younger architect whose future looks particularly promising." The future *utilisateurs* of the Centre, on the other hand, were more disposed to find a member "who is sufficiently well-known to stand alongside Philip Johnson or Utzon." Ibid.

76 — Sébastien Loste, Note pour le jury du plateau Beaubourg, September 23, 1970, AN, CNACGP, F 156.

77 — Jorn Utzon, Letter to Robert Bordaz, May 4, 1971, AN, CNACGP, F 17.

78 — Réunion du jury 4 novembre 1970 (aide-mémoire), November 5, 1970, AN, FHD, F 13, 3.

79 — Edouard Parker, Relevé des décisions prises lors de la réunion du 15 décembre 1970 concernant le règlement des candidatures pour le concours international, December 15, 1970, AN, CNACGP, F 78, 2.

80 — Pompidou wrote in his letter thanking Prouvé: "Dear sir, thank you for sending me the volume *Une architecture pour* [sic] *l'industrie*. This book illustrates a doctrine that is dear to you and deals with a problem of great importance to our world of today and tomorrow." Georges Pompidou, Letter to Jean Prouvé, June 1, 1971, BK, FJP, F PROU 26-28..

81 — On December 15, 1970, a few weeks before the beginning of the competition, Pompidou and his wife Claude invited to dinner Hans Hartung and his wife Anna-Eva Bergman, both of them known internationally for their abstract painting. Hans Hartung and Pompidou talked about Breuer, to whom, moreover, the artist had entrusted the design of a house-cum-studio in Antibes. Evidence of the interest that Breuer stirred in Pompidou is provided by Hartung's sending him, shortly after that dinner, two monographs on the American architect's work. Hans Hartung, Letter to Georges Pompidou, December 16, 1970, AN, FAP, Dossier Hartung.

82 — Loste, Note à l'attention du Président de la République sur le Centre d'Art Moderne du plateau Beaubourg, 15.

83 — Michel Jobert, Note pour monsieur Domerg, December 19, 1970, AN, 574 AP, F 10; Henri Domerg, Letter to Robert Bordaz, December 21, 1970, AN, 574 AP, F 10.

84 — Among the documents Pompidou received were a copy of one version of the *Verschimmelungsmanifest gegen den Rationalismus in der Architektur*, the manifesto for a new kind of architecture that the Austrian had developed over the course of the sixties, and *Verwaldung der Städte*, a manifesto presented in Venice around the time he sent the letter to the Pompidous. Ottilia Iten [Friedensreich Hundertwasser's assistant], Letter to Georges and Claude Pompidou, April 19, 1971, AN, FHD, F 18.

85 — Robert Bordaz, Letter to Philip Johnson, June 8, 1971, AN, CNACGP, F 78; Philip Johnson, Letter to Robert Bordaz, June 22, 1971, AN, CNACGP, F 78.

86 — Réunion du jury 4 novembre 1970 (aide-mémoire), November 5, 1970, AN, 574 AP, F 13.

87 — Réunion du jury 4 novembre 1970 (aide-mémoire), 3.

2

HAPPOLD AND THE QUEST FOR A COMPLEX CAST-STEEL STRUCTURE

2.1

THE QUESTION OF STEEL CASTING FOR THE DESIGN OF CUTTING-EDGE CIVIL STRUCTURES

When looking at the project that won the competition for the Centre Beaubourg, it seems only natural, almost automatic, to think of the collaboration between Richard Rogers and Renzo Piano and the development of a radical design whose forms and content were shaped by the conceptual approach of the neo-avant-gardes of the sixties. In reality the origin of this project lay in London, in the offices of the engineering firm Ove Arup & Partners.

In January 1971 Ted Happold—a civil engineer and a figure of great charisma who at the time was a junior partner and director of Structures division group 3 ("Structures 3")—was informed by Monica Schmoller,[1] his secretary at Ove Arup & Partners' head offices on Fitzroy Street, of the competition for the Centre Beaubourg recently announced in the *Royal Institute of British Architects Journal*.[2] Happold immediately decided to take part, encouraged by, among other things, the coincidence with two other competitions, one for a "New Parliamentary Building" in London and another for the new gallery of the Burrell Collection in Glasgow, on which, in his view, the majority of British architecture practices would be focusing, offering Ove Arup & Partners' possible entry in the Parisian competition a greater chance of success.[3] At an initial meeting with the engineers Gerry Clarke and Michael Barclay, administrative partners in Ove Arup,[4] Povl Ahm, one of Arup's senior partners, and the other Structures 3 engineers, the idea took shape of designing a steel structure in which to try out, among other things, the special technique of metal casting that had returned, in the fifties and sixties, to the forefront of engineering research for the new generation of oil platforms and nuclear power plants. This is a technique that had, around the same time, made its entry into the world of architecture through figures such as Frei Otto.[5]

The origin of this decision that would characterize the constructed work was twofold. It was influenced by Structures 3's established strategy of defining design themes to pursue in competitions based on an analysis of the competition announcement and the CV of each jury member.[6] Consequently, in the case of the Centre Beaubourg, the presence on the jury of Philip Johnson and Jean Prouvé, considered the key figures, oriented the engineers toward a metal building characterized by an imposing façade and extensive use of glass, on the model of Prouvé's prefabricated metal shells and the glazed envelopes of Johnson's Glass House and the Seagram Building, which he had designed with Ludwig Mies van der Rohe.[7] With this strategic approach came the desire to further the experimentation with complex metal structures Structures 3 had already embarked on at the time, albeit with still-limited expertise.[8]

In this context it is worth mentioning the large-span metal trusses designed in collaboration with the architect Trevor Dannatt; the tensile structures characterized by special cast joints developed with Otto and Rolf Gutbrod, like those of the hall for the International Hotel and Conference Centre in Mecca (1967–74); and a series of complex roofs inspired by Otto's designs, including the retractable tensile structure for the Chelsea Football Club stadium in London, conceived with Richard+Su Rogers Architects, a collaboration that was to prove crucial to the Centre Beaubourg's genesis.[9]

The choice of metal at the time was remote from any kind of nostalgia for the 19th-century cast-iron architecture of the French tradition, abandoned with few exceptions in the 20th century and, at the end of the sixties, even challenged, as can be deduced from the imminent demolition of one of its most significant emblems, Victor Baltard's pavilions at Les Halles in Paris.[10]

Among the steel structures and roofs on which Structures 3 could draw in the late sixties, Happold and his colleagues' interest was not directed toward horizontal trusses, but focused instead on experimental tensile structures with a complex geometry and on the design of their connections, for the creation of which architects and engineers, from Otto onward, had been bringing back the special technique of casting.

The tent-like roof of the International Hotel and Conference Centre in Mecca is a good example. Happold, together with his colleagues Peter Rice and Lennart Grut, developed a series of cast joints for the roofing of the conference hall and for the systems used to shade the terraces. Some specific aspects of the tensile structure pertain to these joints: the shaped steel flanges welded onto the structural masts and the special clamps located along and at the ends of the steel cables.[11] While they lacked the sculptural refinement of Otto's clamps, cast-steel joints were also used by Structures 3 in the tensile structure composed of steel cables and inflatable cushions commissioned by Michael Hirst in 1970 for a temporary circus in London.[12]

The theme of a large steel roof based on the use of cables and joints constitutes the point of contact between Happold and the Richard+Su Rogers Architects studio and the starting point for their collaboration at a time when its partners, Rogers and his wife Su, were imagining a roof that would be able to turn Chelsea Football Club stadium into a multifunctional center in the service of the community. Otto, unable to accept the Rogerses' invitation to participate in the project, recommended the Ove Arup & Partners engineering firm and its Structures 3 division, with which he had been working since 1967. From the collaboration between the Rogerses and Arup's Structures 3 engineers on Chelsea's stadium stemmed the design of a large, umbrella-shaped retractable roof composed of a tarpaulin able to slide over a structure composed of prestressed steel cables, not unlike the series of tensile structures for sports complexes, swimming pools, and skating rinks that Otto had developed over the course of the sixties.[13] Although the project remained in a preliminary state and would soon be abandoned, it is likely that right from the first discussions of the roof's design and its mechanical system, Rogers and Happold had thought of using special clamps and hinges of the sort employed in the Conference Hotel roof in Mecca and the Olympic Stadium in Munich.[14]

From the clamps adopted in Mecca to the joints of Hirst's circus, Structures 3's recourse to special joints cannot be separated from the use of cast steel, a technique destined to leave a mark on the whole story of the Centre Beaubourg. Following its abandonment after the 19th-century tradition of building bridges and large roofs out of cast iron ended, the casting technique found an application in the architectural field in the mechanical joints of space frame roofing and tensile structures with a complex geometry constructed after the World War II. Happold and Otto identified casting as a technique that would let them create shapes with curved lines that would stand out for their great strength and minimal weight; thus they were thinking about a joint that would allow cables to remain free to move and adapt to stresses on the structure.[15] "Details which breathe," is how Happold would describe Otto's cast joints in an article written with Rice and Grut at the time of the first discussions of the Paris competition.[16] The genesis and development of this steel joint in Otto's works was reflected in its significant definition as the "clamp of the future"—a declaration that would play a decisive role, even if in other forms, in the design of the Centre Beaubourg.[17]

Suggested by the collaboration with Otto, Structures 3's preference for cast elements was further reinforced by the collaborations with Kenzo Tange and his assistant at the URTEC studio, Koji Kamiya, on the tensile structure of the Kuwait Sports Center and the space frame structure of the visionary project for the Arctic City. According to Happold, it was on a trip to the Middle East in 1969, in the context of the work on the Kuwait Sports Center, that Happold and Kamiya discussed the potentialities of "engine block casting" and how it could be used at a structural level.[18] It is possible that on this occasion Kamiya had already spoken to Happold of the cast-steel "ball joints" used in the Theme Pavilion's space frame roof, designed with architect Asao Tomoo Fukuda and the engineer Yoshikatsu Tsuboi, under construction at the time for the 1970 Osaka Expo. The only evidence for this conjecture is an account from the nineties in which Happold traced the origin of the Centre Pompidou's special cast joints back to the discussions he had with Kamiya: "[In 1969 Kamiya and I] spent the rest of our time [...] talking about engine block castings—and how we would use the idea for structural joints. Kameya [*sic*] went off to use it for the joints of the space frame roof for Osaka and I took the idea back to use it on the structure for the Beaubourg competition."[19] And the Theme Pavilion project, from the configuration of its space frame to the fabrication of its cast-steel nodes and the various electronic and audiovisual systems located under its roof, was destined to become one of the crucial references for architects and engineers in the conception of the Centre Pompidou.

Equally crucial to Happold and his colleagues' inclination for complex metal structures and cast-steel nodes was the fact that Structures 3 could count on the scientific input of Ove Arup & Partners' R&D (Research and Development) division. This team of engineers had carried out preliminary research into the structural use of cast steel and a system for preventing the risk of fire in metal structures by filling them with treated water—two studies that Structures 3 would draw on in its entry for the Centre Beaubourg competition.

Right from Structures 3's earliest discussions of the possibility of using cast steel, it was clear that this issue would make this technique one of the most critical and challenging aspects of the Centre

Beaubourg project. The chemical impurities contained in cast steel, the complex procedure of casting molten steel in molds, the thermal stresses and phenomena of shrinkage during the phase of solidification; the complex processes of heat treatment and stress relief required to optimize the mechanical strength of the cast; the checks needed to ensure the absence of cracks: all this made cast steel a particularly complex and stimulating technique for engineers who, at the beginning of the seventies, wanted to use it in the field of construction.
From the stadium in Munich to the Theme Pavilion, Otto and Kamiya were resorting to cast steel for the joints of structural components, and this was the use that Happold intended to make of the technique for the Centre Beaubourg.

Richard+Su Rogers Architects and Ove Arup & Partners (Structures 3 Division), Project for a new stand for Chelsea Football Club stadium, London, 1969–1970.

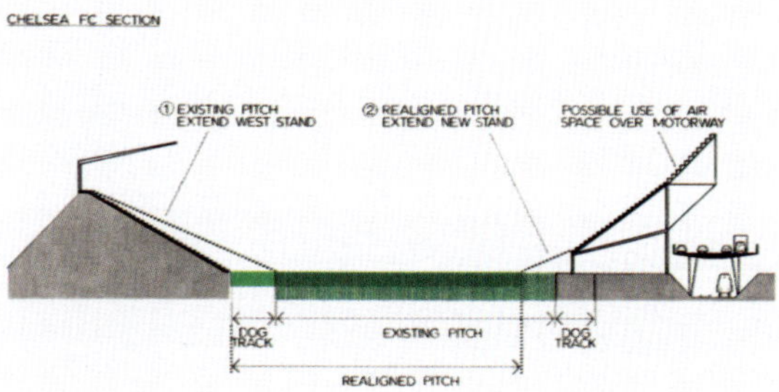

Richard+Su Rogers Architects and Ove Arup & Partners (Structures 3 Division), Project for a new stand for Chelsea Football Club stadium, London, 1969–1970.

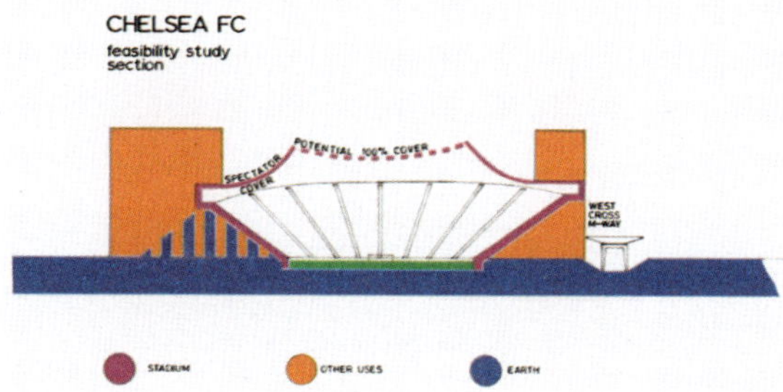

Frei Otto and Ove Arup & Partners (Structures 3 Division), Conference Centre and International Hotel, Mecca, 1967–1974.

Frei Otto et Ove Arup & Partners (Structures 3 Division), Conference Center and International Hotel, pole, clamps and cables of the tensostructure, Mecca, 1967–1974.

Frei Otto, Kenzo Tange, and Ove Arup & Partners (Division Structures 3), Arctic City, 1969–1970.

Frei Otto and Rolf Gutbrod, German Pavilion at Expo '67, tensile structure, detail, Montreal, 1965–1967.

Frei Otto, Kenzo Tange, and Ove Arup & Partners (Structures Division 3), Competition for the design of the Kuwait Sports Center, 1969–1970.

Kenzo Tange et al., Theme Pavilion for the Osaka World Expo, details of the Mero System metal roof with cast-steel ball joints, Osaka, 1970.

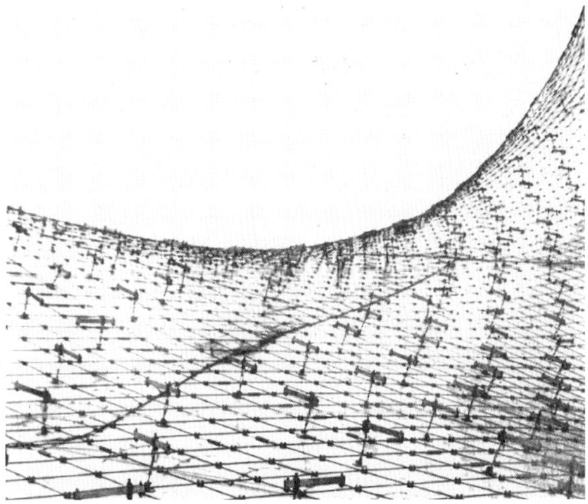

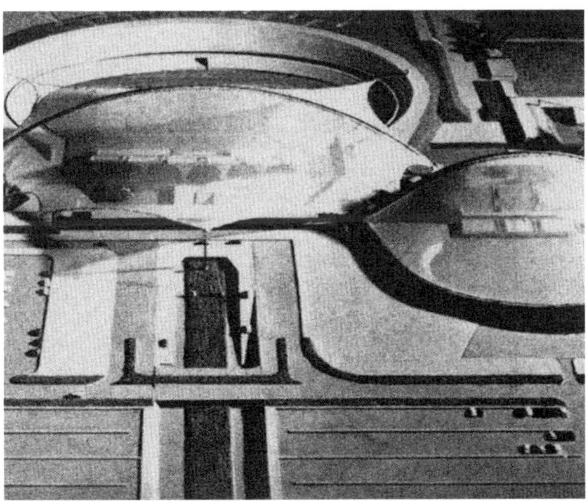

1 — Boris Hamzeian, Interview with John Morrison, July 27, 2017, Bath.

2 — "Memo. Competitions. Contemporary Arts Centre, Paris," *Royal Institute of British Architects Journal*, no. 2 (1971), 87.

3 — "Memo. Competitions. Parliamentary Building," *Royal Institute of British Architects Journal*, no. 9, 1970, 435; "Memo. Competitions. Burrell Collection," *Royal Institute of British Architects Journal*, no. 10 (1970), 487.

4 — According to Nathan Silver, Ted Happold would conduct lengthy discussions on the topic, consulting with Gerry Clarke and Michael Barclay. John Morrison confirmed this in 2017, pointing out that these were discussions that involved Povl Ahm as well as other Structures 3 colleagues. Nathan Silver, *The Making of Beaubourg: A Building Biography of the Centre Pompidou, Paris* (Cambridge MA: MIT Press, 1994), 14; Hamzeian, interview with Morrison.

5 — Silver outlined Happold's interest in Otto's casting joints and claims that Happold would have turned to steel early on for the Beaubourg competition. Morrison confirmed this in an interview when he stated: "Happold was looking for steel. He didn't want to go for concrete for that work. We were supposed to work with steel for the Beaubourg competition [...]." Hamzeian, interview with Morrison.

6 — "Ted [Happold] was always looking for competitions [...]. Ted was a great believer in competitions. He always said that it was not important to say how good you are. You had to prove that you were good. That was the purpose of the competition in his view. Another thing he used to say was that through competitions you could meet young up-and-coming architects who will come back, especially if you win. He thought that when you enter competitions you never tend to fall out. You all turn out to be friends." Hamzeian, interview with Morrison. See also: Derek Walker and Bill Addis, *Happold: The Confidence to Build* (London: Taylor & Francis, 1997), 55–74.

7 — "We went through the list of judges. There was Jean Prouvé. Happold said that he was a fine constructor for his metal furniture. The finest man in France for metal design and for prefabricated facades. He convinced us that our building had to be in metal and have a very good facade to catch his imagination. In regards to the American architect Philip Johnson. Happold pointed out that he was trained by Ludwig Mies van der Rohe. Happold spent a lot of time in America before the time of Structures 3, you know. I remember him mentioning the Seagram Building because he was very well aware that Johnson took part in the design of Seagram Building. Johnson also built his own house, the Glass House. That was a very famous work of architecture at the time." Hamzeian, Interview with Morrison.

8 — "When we started working with Rolf Gutbrod and Frei Otto on the Mecca project, we were moving into a field we had not worked in before [...]." Lennart Grut, Ted Happold, and Peter Rice, "Lennart Grut, Ted Happold and Peter Rice Discuss Frei Otto and his Work," *Architectural Design*, no. 3 (1971), 144-145, 150-154, 156..

9 — Happold became interested in Otto's tensile structures after visiting the Snow and Rocks Pavilion at the Swiss Regional Expo in Lausanne in 1964 and the German Pavilion at the Montreal Expo in 1967. The collaboration with Otto originated in the consultancy with Structures 3 for the Hotel and Conference Center in Mecca (1967–1974). This project was followed by other collaborations for roof structures realized in collaboration with Kenzo Tange, such as a project for the Kuwait Sports Center (1969–70) and a new urban settlement in the Arctic Circle (1971), dubbed Arctic City. The professional relationship established between Happold and Otto was confirmed by Happold's visits to the Institute for Lightweight Structures in Stuttgart. Happold's appreciation for Otto's tensile structures, experimental load testing on models and cast-steel node design are reported in Happold, Rice, and Grut's article in *Architectural Design*. See, too, Walker and Addis, *Happold: The Confidence to Build.*

10 — In France, and particularly in Paris, the only exceptions consist of some functionalist buildings built between 1900 and 1939, as well as Mies van der Rohe's projects and post-war towers with curtain walls. We can pick out George Chedanne's Immeuble Industriel (1905), Pierre Chareau and Bernard Bijvoet's Maison de verre (1931), Jean Balladur's office building (1958), Raymond Lopez's Caisse Centrale d'Allocation Familiale (1959), Édouard Albert and Serge Ketoff's Faculty of Sciences building (1965), Jean de Mailly and Prouvé's tower of the Nobel offices (1966), Paul Depont and Marcel Lods's Maison des sciences de l'homme (1968), and Claude Parent's Fondation Avicenne (formerly the Iranian Pavilion) (1968). It is also worth mentioning the experimental research into prefabrication and large spatial structures carried out by Jean Prouvé, Robert le Ricolais and Stéphane du Chateau. Hervé Martin, *Guide de l'architecture Moderne à Paris [Guide to Modern Architecture in Paris].* (Paris: Syros Alternatives, 1990), 20.

11 — Lennart Grut, "Trial Structure at Tours," *The Arup Journal*, no. 3 (1971), 14–15; Mickey Courtney, "Mecca Hotel and Conference Centre," *The Arup Journal*, no. 3 (1971), 12–14.

12 — Peter Rice, "Notes on the Design of Cable Roofs," *The Arup Journal*, no. 4 (1971), 9.

13 — The project is unpublished and to date the only documentary trace is a series of schematic drawings in RSHP (formerly Rogers Stirk Harbour + Partners) in London (part of the Rogers family's private archives), which do not allow us to understand the structural characteristics of the project. In addition to the fragmentary descriptions of the project provided by Bryan Appleyard and Silver, there is the testimony of John Young, collaborator with and later partner at Richard+Su Rogers Architects, who stated: "The Chelsea Football Club stadium certainly worked very much as a very good retractable roof. It could be opened or closed. Nowadays practically every new big stadium has its own retractable roof but then nobody used to do it. Very flexible space that was also able to be used by the local community, not just Chelsea Football Club. Again, these kinds of things happen nowadays in contemporary stadiums, but they were not happening back then." Boris Hamzeian, interview with John Young, July 25, 2017, Hayling Island. By the time of the Chelsea Football Club stadium project, Otto had already completed several retractable tensile structures for sports centers and swimming pools in Europe: the convertible roof of the Boulevard Carnot swimming pool in Paris (1966–1967), the Multimedia Stadium project (1967–1970), and the All-Weather Pool completed in Regensburg. Richard and Su Rogers' knowledge of these projects is confirmed by two slides of the Regensburg project showing the roof in its various configurations found in the RSHP Archives. Winfried Nerdinger et al., *Frei Otto, Complete Works: Lightweight Construction Natural Design* (Basel: Birkhäuser, 2009).

14 — Bryan Appleyard, *Richard Rogers: A Biography* (London: Faber & Faber, 1986).

15 — Ted Happold, Peter Rice and Lennart Grut described Otto's casting clamps in an article in *Architectural Design* devoted to his work. They stated: "T[ed Happold]: Another principle which is essential to the understanding of Frei's work is that he understands the need for flexibility in a cable net. His intuitive feeling has led him to develop details which breathe, that is details which can relax under excessive loads, vide Mecca Kafesses. He expects that the structure will require modifications during erections and has developed details which enable him to do this. However, these details are quite different from those traditionally used, e.g. turnbuckles in that they place the emphasis on getting the structure correct in the first place and adjustment, though possible, is a complex and difficult process. L[ennart Grut]: It is interesting to look at the various connections and clamps which Frei has designed for the clamps. These invariably have a great respect for the fragile cables." Otto himself described his clamps in the same article when he stated: "I only started to design clamps because the engineers could not. I am interested in a form with minimum material, to develop out of the function of the clamp. Less weight, a very good strength." Grut, Happold and Rice, "Lennart Grut, Ted Happold, and Peter Rice Discuss Frei Otto and his Work," 150.

16 — The importance that Happold and colleagues placed on Otto's clamps is confirmed by the choice to include a photo of some of Otto's clamps on a desk in Structures 3's office in the article. Grut, Happold, and Rice, "Lennart Grut, Ted Happold and Peter Rice Discuss Frei Otto and his Work," 137.

17 — *Ibid*, 151.

18 — Ted Happold, "Essential Engineer: A Book Review of An Engineer Imagines by Peter Rice," *RSA Journal*, 143, no. 5456 (1995), 86.

19 — Happold, "Essential Engineer," 85–86.

Applications of cast steel for civil construction after World War II: Frei Otto's "clamps of the future" and Kenzo Tange, Koji Kamiya, and Yoshikatsu Tsuboi, "ball joints," 1968–1972, 1969–1970.

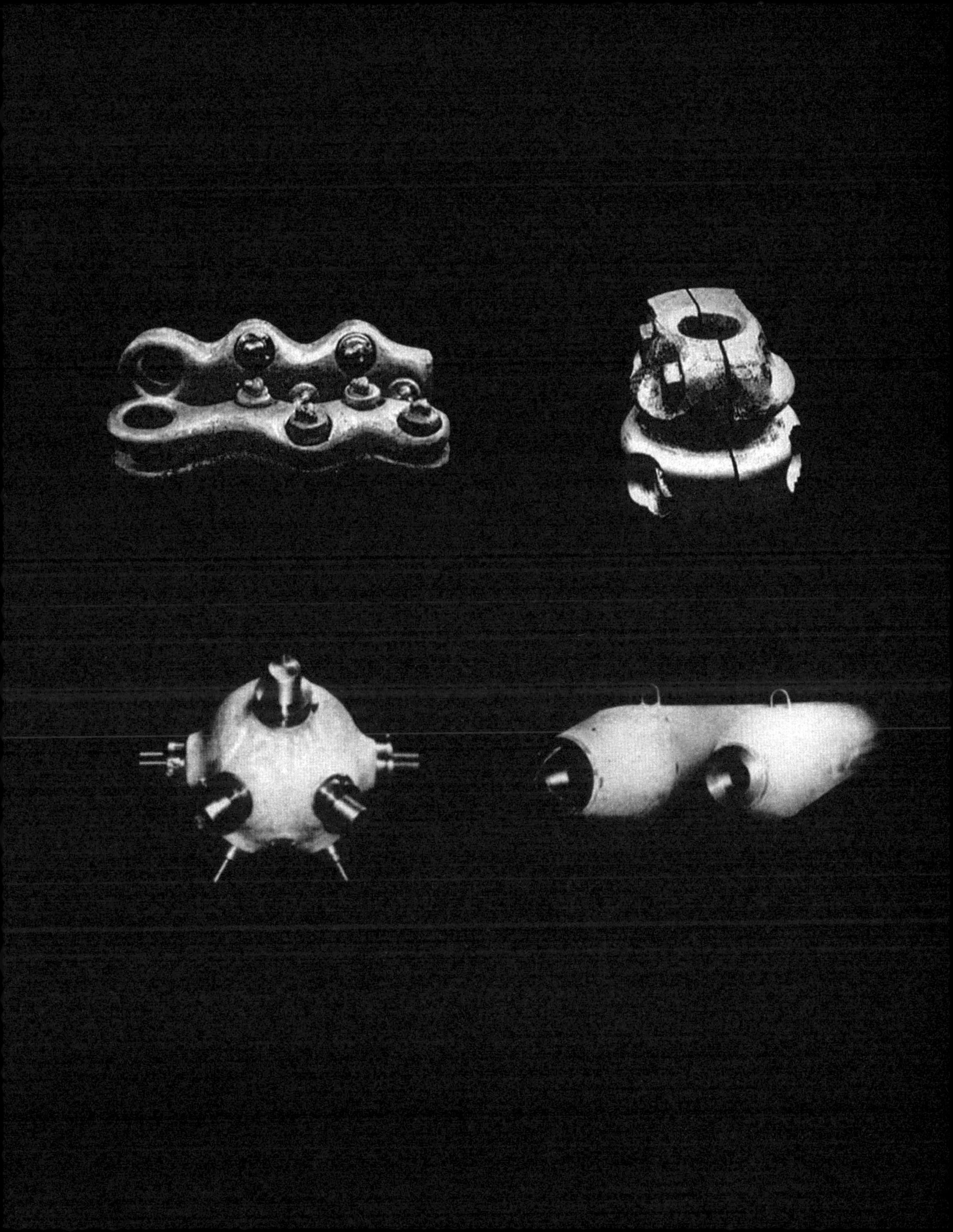

3

PIANO+ROGERS+ FRANCHINI= AN AVANT-GARDE SCHOOL SYSTEM FOR THE CITY'S RESTORATION

3.1

EARLY EXPERIMENTS ON INDUSTRIAL COMPONENTS, SHELLS, LIGHT ROOFS, AND URBAN INTEGRATION

At the moment Ted Happold and the Structures 3 engineers were wondering whether to take part in the Centre Beaubourg competition, Richard+Su Rogers Architects was going through a period of change and renewal in which the meeting between Richard Rogers and Renzo Piano played a crucial role.
At the time, Rogers and the other members of his practice had for some years been studying prefabricated shells that could be cheaply and rapidly assembled: conceived as containers for flexible spaces, adaptable to different uses, and laid out on a single level, they were the "general-purpose shells" of which Su Rogers spoke.[1]
Piano's experience acquired in pavilion and roof construction, fruit in part of a fertile exchange of ideas with some of the protagonists in the development of complex metal structures such as Zygmunt Stanislaw Makowski, Robert Le Ricolais, Richard Buckminster Fuller, Frei Otto, and Louis Kahn was to prove decisive in transforming these shells into envelopes of considerable size, able to house more than one level.
There were two principles guiding Richard+Su Rogers Architects' conception of the shell, from the first Zip-Up House prototype (1968) to its various versions in the Sweetheart Plastic (1969) and Universal Oil Products (1969–70) offices and the practice's own studio at 32 Aybrook Street in London: recourse to industrial materials and methods and explicit political and social connotations. For their production, from the configuration of the envelope to the design of the technical plant, the Rogerses looked to pioneers integrating industrial processes and materials into the world of construction and the building trade. The discovery of the Californian Case Study Houses and Jean Prouvé's prefabricated metal shells, the meeting with James Stirling,[2] the rediscovery of Pierre Chareau and Bernard Bijvoet's Maison de verre as a model for an alternative form of modern and functional architecture, and their fascination with the consumerist architecture of the Archigram group oriented the Rogerses toward a modular system based on low-cost components ("lightweight, component building") that were quick to assemble and easy to obtain, sourced from the land-, air-, and space-transport industries.[3] "We tried to use components already designed for other industries, for example [shipping] containers, aircrafts [*sic*] or caravan industries," were Su's words on the subject.[4]
Conceived as systems with a technological and industrial aesthetic, Richard+Su Rogers Architects' shells also represented a form of political and activist architecture that was intended to replace the metropolitan "concrete jungle," the "never-ending suburbia," and traditional types of building with a new approach called "environmental planning," refocused on the community and the expression of its

individual members.[5] The political and social component at the root of this vision of urban planning stemmed from Su's sociological background and her and Richard's fascination with the studies of Serge Chermayeff, whom they had gotten to know while studying at Yale University.[6] Political activism was not foreign to Richard. Probably originating with his participation in student demonstrations against the Vietnam War, Richard's political engagement matured through Su's links with a circle of politicians and intellectuals centered on the British Labour Party and his meeting with Ruthie Elias, an American-born designer he met at the end of the sixties and who went on to become his second wife.[7] It was from this political and social perspective that the Rogerses saw their shells as devices that could be reconfigured over time to meet the community's needs, as well as customized in their forms and materials and used to suit the desires of each community, and potentially of each individual. From the large range of extension and connection systems that Reyner Banham had dubbed "clip-on," (a name which the Rogerses often adopted), to devices for moving the entire unit, the degree of the shells' transformability and adaptability became the expression of a powerful effort at social redemption.

The space enclosed in the shell drew on the same ideology. Completely open and free from any obstruction—whether structure, plant, or partition—the uninterrupted and flexible setting designed by the Rogerses assumed the tones of a socialist manifesto, the spatial expression of a social promise of democracy and equality. With the objective of a genuine "freedom of choice," the shells gave individuals the possibility of self-determination through modification of their living environment.[8]

While Richard and Su Rogers set about the design of prefabricated containers, Piano, after finishing his education at the Department of Architecture of the University of Florence (1959–60) and the Polytechnic University of Milan (1961–65), turned his attention to the study of construction materials and new building methods.

In fact he started to work at the Polytechnic as an assistant to Marco Zanuso on the Stage Design: Morphological Treatment of Materials course.

At the same time, he devoted himself to designing buildings using prefabricated components, which led him to specialize in the design of lightweight roofing made of modular reinforced-polyester elements for a wide range of uses, from the carpentry workshop in Ceranesi (1965), numerous gas station canopies (1966–71), the open-plan residence in Garonne, or the office and workshop in Erzelli (1968–69).[9] This kind of structure—created with help from his brother Ermanno's Genoese building firm run and influenced by figures such as Prouvé and spatial-structures specialists of the caliber of Makowski (Director of the Space Structures Research Centre at Battersea College of Advanced Technology) and Le Ricolais (Director of a structural research laboratory at the University of Pennsylvania)—earned Piano a certain, even international, reputation in the field.[10] This is clear from his participation in the First International Conference on Space Structures at the University of Surrey in Guildford in 1966, along with Makowski and Le Ricolais, among others, and, three years later, a seminar at Delft University of Technology with Otto, another figure of reference for Piano in the field of tensile and double-curved shell structures.[11]

Piano's reputation in the space-structures sector led to important collaborations, first with Zanuso and then with Kahn, on the integration of prefabricated overhead lighting modules into the roofing of some Olivetti factories in Italy and the United States. Piano's standing is also demonstrated by the promotion of his research and designs.

He staged two exhibitions in London, the first in November 1967 at the Centre for Advanced Study of Science in Art run by Marcello Salvadori, an exponent of Op and kinetic art,[12] and the second in August 1969 at the Architectural Association School.[13] Between 1966 and 1971 he published numerous articles, ranging from contributions to technical journals such as *Materie plastiche ed elastomeri* and *Acciaio* to essays in major Italian and foreign architecture magazines such as *Domus*, *Casabella*, *Techniques et architecture*, *Architecture Association Quarterly*, and *Architectural Design*.

The latter, under the editorship of Monica Pidgeon, devoted a lengthy article to the young architect from Genoa.[14]

Despite playing a crucial role in his meeting and subsequent professional partnership with the Rogerses, the prefabrication was not the only subject in which Piano showed an interest at that time. His attention was also drawn to a series of questions and considerations that, while they did not as yet go beyond schematic designs or mere readings, were to find a unique and unprecedented synthesis in the origins of the Centre Beaubourg competition project, for which they became indispensable models.

One of these themes was his interest in the works which Banham would dub "megastructures" in 1975: structures created through the combination of gigantic servant blocks with prefabricated housing units or platforms for public and recreational activities. Piano's curiosity had been stirred by megastructure in his years at university, following his discovery of the huge residential structures conceived by Kenzo Tange for Tokyo Bay and the Japanese Metabolism Group's projects—Kenji Ekuan's Dwelling City, Arata Isozaki's bridge buildings for the Shinjuku Terminal, Kisho Kurokawa's vertical helictical structures in the Nihonbashi and Kanda districts in Tokyo, and Kiyonori Kikutake's cluster towers for Tokyo—as well as Tange's residential structures for the plan for the reconstruction of Skopje a few years later.[15] Piano continued to show an interest in this kind of colossal structure in the second half of the sixties. Its potentialities for a structured design of territory were revealed to him through the ideas of the Metabolist Group and of Guido Canella and Francesco Tentori, as well as a number of British governmental and urban planning agencies.[16]

He picked out and studied numerous examples published in the journals, including Archigram's Plug-In City, Yona Friedman's Ville spatiale, Arthur Quarmby's study for a tower building, Wolfgang Döring's design for a housing unit, Friedrich St. Florian's linear city, and Paul Maymont and Walter Jonas's huge structures, along with a number of educational megastructures such as the one designed by Alexis Josic, Georges Candilis, Shadrach Woods, and Manfred Schiedhelm for the Free University of Berlin or those conceived by the students at the Department of Architecture at the University of Florence.[17] He went deeper into the question of the prefabricated unit, leaning toward standardized and transportable modules and going so far as to imagine the use of shipping containers.[18]

He tried to use the concept of megastructure borrowed from the Metabolism Group, that of a permanent infrastructure combined with reconfigurable components, in his project for a housing complex in the Boschetto district of Genoa, which he imagined "as split into a primary structure and a secondary structure."

The former was "conceived as something constant and definitive" that could be described as "connection to the ground, support of the secondary, housing of the stairs, the elevators (mechanical systems of circulation in general) and the main ducts of the technical plant." The latter was "conceived as something variable, that could be functionally and physically altered to meet requirements" and could be described as the "functional definition of spaces fitted with container blocks, services, infill panels."[19]

Piano took an interest in interventions in the historical city as well. Introduced to the subject by Italo Gamberini's lectures at the course of Elements of Architecture and Survey of Monuments at the Department of Architecture in Florence and those at the course of Stylistic and Structural Characteristics of Monuments given by Ernesto Nathan Rogers at the Polytechnic University of Milan, Piano looked into it in the second half of the sixties through study of some significant essays published in architecture periodicals: the monographic feature "L'incontro fra antico e nuovo" in *Casabella* in 1967 in which Roberto Pane, Renato De Fusco, and others reflected on the outcome of the International Congress of Architects and Specialists in Historic Buildings held in Venice in 1964, which culminated in the drafting of the Venice Charter for the Conservation and Restoration of Monuments and Sites; and an issue of *The Architectural Review* in 1968 devoted to the question of housing and the environment to which William Cowburn, among others, had contributed.[20] Among the things Piano read, Pane presented a new sensibility with regard to the historical city, viewed as a heritage to be preserved as an "environmental whole" that went beyond a collection of "individual monuments"; De Fusco showed how urgent it was to find provisional and contemporary criteria by which to evaluate the insertion of modern architecture into the historical center; Cowburn urged the development of an integrated planning strategy—"[The inhabitants should] build their houses as an integral part of the fabric of their towns," were his words.[21] Piano's interest in this subject was not reflected in his design work until in 1969 he met Yoshinobu Ashihara, a Japanese architect with whom he collaborated on the Italian Industry Pavilion at the Osaka Expo and who had just published *Exterior Design in Architecture*,[22] a monograph devoted to the interpretation of public space as a form of "architecture without a roof." The best example would be the historical Italian city, "a centripetal space surrounded by walls," with its streets and piazzas described by Ashihara as "a way of life, a concept of living," a true extension of the home: "a living room for the city as a whole."[23] Ashihara's analysis of the piazza, using Siena's Piazza del Campo, portrayed in Yukio Futagawa's photographs, as a model, led him to call for a planning strategy that would include the design of public space, so it would come to be seen as genuine architectural space.[24]

Reading *Exterior Design in Architecture* encouraged Piano to develop his own design strategy based on the integration of public space, as reflected in two articles he published in *Architectural Design* and *L'Industria italiana per l'edilizia-LIPE* in 1970.[25] Here Piano outlined a critical analysis of the urban fabric that anticipated in some ways what Colin Rowe and Fred Koetter were to include in their 1975 book *Collage City*, contrasting the complex and organic character of medieval urban centers—the example cited in the article was, in fact, Siena—with the compartmentalized and fragmentary planning of the contemporary city. Piano wrote in *Architectural Design*: "We have moved from the traditional multifunctional structure (expressing a deep integration between social patterns and structures) to the monofunctional units which dot our current landscape."[26] From this radical reassessment of the design of public space, now stripped of its connective role and reduced to the "negative space" theorized by Ashihara, Piano envisaged a new form of integrated environmental planning that would encompass the design not just of buildings but also of

their related connective fabrics.[27]
To illustrate the article in *Architectural Design* Piano chose an aerial photograph of the Piazza del Campo in Siena. Rather than the one used in Ashihara's monograph, it was the picture that had accompanied Pane's *Casabella* article; reproduced alongside the aerial photo of the new districts of Rome taken from the same source, it confirmed Piano's interest in the historical city.
Something else that interested Piano right through the second half of the sixties was the question of schools and educational architecture in general. Since 1965 Piano had been collecting and analyzing dozens of designs for schools published in Italian and foreign architecture periodicals, from schools in England built by the Greater London County Council such as those in Richmond, Hampstead, Streatham, and Pimlico to advanced higher-education facilities such as Simon Fraser University in British Columbia, Canada, the Claremont Complex in Newcastle, or the linear megastructure built for Scarborough University, as well as recent schools or kindergartens built in Italy, Switzerland, Germany, and Scandinavia.[28] Annotations made to articles in his library show that, while focusing on prefabricated educational facilities characterized by well-lit, flexible, and adaptable internal spaces, Piano was also interested in more general and radical approaches aimed at putting the very concept of educational architecture on a new footing, as in a special spring, 1968, issue of *Architectural Design* entitled "What about Learning?" guest-edited by Cedric Price and in the feature "Campus Design" published by Piero Sartogo and Carlo Pelliccia in *Casabella* the same year. These articles revealed to Piano the extent to which the idea of a university for the masses and an educational system able to last an individual's lifetime (what Sartogo called "life-long learning"), together with new digital technologies based on the storage, production, and exchange of information, made it necessary to reconsider the university as an open structure, able to integrate itself into the city and absorb some of the latter's primary functions, from accommodation to recreation. "If, as we have already said, education is going to assume an emergent role along with political and economic power," wrote Sartogo, "the logical consequence will be the transformation of the campus into an open structure integrated into the urban fabric."[29] This integration found expression in a range of projects. An example is the Free University of Brussels—designed by Nizzoli Associati and the young Florentine group 1999 (later known as 9999)—with its "permanent education center" laid out along a metropolitan axis. Enclosed in a prismatic multistory volume with a reflective envelope, this project was turned into the focal point of a multifunctional structure that extended into the urban fabric with its lateral blocks. Another example of advanced educational facilities was the Free University of Berlin by Candilis and his colleagues, which renounced the assemblage of heterogeneous parts and imposing volumes in order to limit itself to a horizontal infrastructure open to evolution and made up of roads and viaducts, conceived to blend into the urban fabric and enclose in its mesh flexible shells not unlike those Piano designed in the sixties. Rogers and Piano would choose this as a reference model when they first formulated the idea for the Centre Beaubourg design.
The features in *Casabella* and *Architectural Design* presented Piano with some projects on a larger scale as well, in which the open and integrated educational facility took the form of a territorial network based on the exchange of information produced by its nodes. These were conceived as centers devoted to information storage and transmission, from the multi-towered "plant for the production of knowledge" Sartogo and Pelliccia imagined for their Megalopolis project to Peter Cook's Plug-In University Node with metal lattices topped by "brain-silos" and "broadcasting centers," and even to proposals in which the centers were mobile, as in the case of Cook's Ideas Circus campers or the multimedia systems Price created for his Atom Project.[30]
Prior to his professional association with the Rogerses and the conception of the Centre Beaubourg, Piano's ideas about a work integrated

into the historical fabric and a new kind of educational architecture found a synthesis in the pilot project for the Sestri Ponente-district municipalities in Genoa that

Piano developed in 1969 and published in the *Architectural Association Quarterly* the following year.[31] Here Piano imagined laying a series of "truly catalytic interventions, extremely flexible and adaptable in time" along the Via Aurelia, thereby creating an "organism capable of continual upgrading to [meet] the changing functional and circumstantial conditions of the city" and characterized by activities of the "most evident communal interest." In addition to offering leisure, sport, and commercial activities, Piano declared it should include "educational and communication facilities."[32]

Part of the project was rehabilitation of the historical center of Sestri Ponente through "a program for urban reconstruction by means of educational and leisure facilities," as Piano put it.[33] While it did not get beyond the draft stage, the project already laid down the guidelines for the sort of work the Rogerses and Piano would propose for the historical center of Paris a year later. It was a network for the meeting of the crowd made up of streets and squares, perhaps pedestrianized, and elevated roadways. The circulation system was designed to connect discrete renewal renovations, entailing the "salvaging of existing facilities" or the insertion of "new organisms with improved potential for change" composed of modular reinforced-polyester units or doubly curved shells similar to those proposed for the Milan Triennale.

In developing this project Piano was assisted by Gianfranco Franchini, one of the figures who was going to shape, together with Piano and Rogers, the idea for the design of the Centre Beaubourg. A fellow student of Piano's at the Polytechnic University of Milan and, like him, Zanuso's assistant on the Stage Design: Morphological Treatment of Materials course, Franchini began to take an interest in the second half of the sixties in some of the themes on which Piano was working at the time, from lightweight prefabricated structures to the relationship between form and structure and making the most of the historical built heritage.[34]

It was on the basis of research of this kind that Franchini joined the Renzo Piano Architetto practice in 1966. He worked alongside Piano on projects ranging from three-dimensional structures for sheds and gas station canopies to the study of reinforced-polyester "shell shape" prototypes, the staging of the exhibition *Changing Form in Architecture* at the 14th Milan Triennale, and, finally, the Sestri Ponente historic center regeneration project.

It is likely that Franchini played a central role in developing prototypes for educational facilities included in the Sestri Ponente project.

At the time he became a member of the practice, Franchini's CV included academic research into prefabrication, much of it centered on component sets for educational architecture, such as the School Construction Systems Development (SCSD) that Ezra Ehrenkrantz had recently been experimenting with in the United States.

In the light of Franchini's experience in the field of educational facilities, it is no surprise that in spring 1970 Piano chose to involve Franchini in the research that laid the foundations for the design of the Centre Beaubourg in Paris.

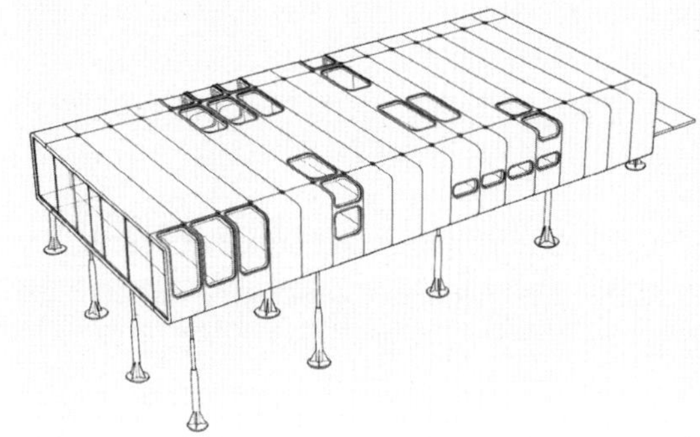

Richard+Su Rogers Architects, Zip-Up House (otherwise known as Dupont House), 1968–1971.

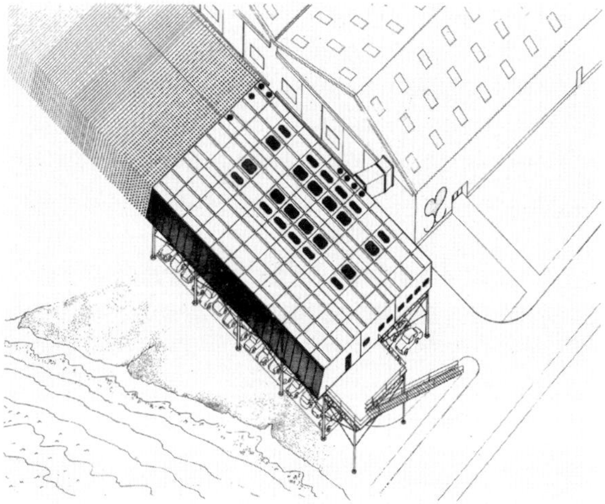

Richard+Su Rogers Architects (in collaboration with Hugh Chapman), Zip-Up Envelope Design for Sweetheart Plastic Company Office Extension, Gosport, 1969–1970.

Richard+Su Rogers Architects, Zip-Up Envelope Design for Universal Oil Products, Tadworth, 1970–1972.

Richard+Su Rogers Architects, Design Research Unit-DRU and Richard+Su Rogers (later Piano+Rogers Architects) offices at 32 Aybrook Street, London, 1969–1971.

Renzo Piano and Ermanno Piano costruzioni, Prototype of a roof with reinforced polyester modules at Erzelli, Genoa, 1965.

Renzo Piano Architetto, Mobile structure for the extraction of sulfur, Ceranesi, 1966.

Overleaf: Richard+Su Rogers Architects (in collaboration with Hugh Chapman), Zip-Up Envelope Design for Sweetheart Plastic Company Office Extension, interiors, Gosport, 1969-1970.

Renzo Piano Architetto and Marco Zanuso, Sheds for the Olivetti factory, Scarmagno, 1969.

Renzo Piano Architetto, Carpentry Workshop, Pomezia, 1965.

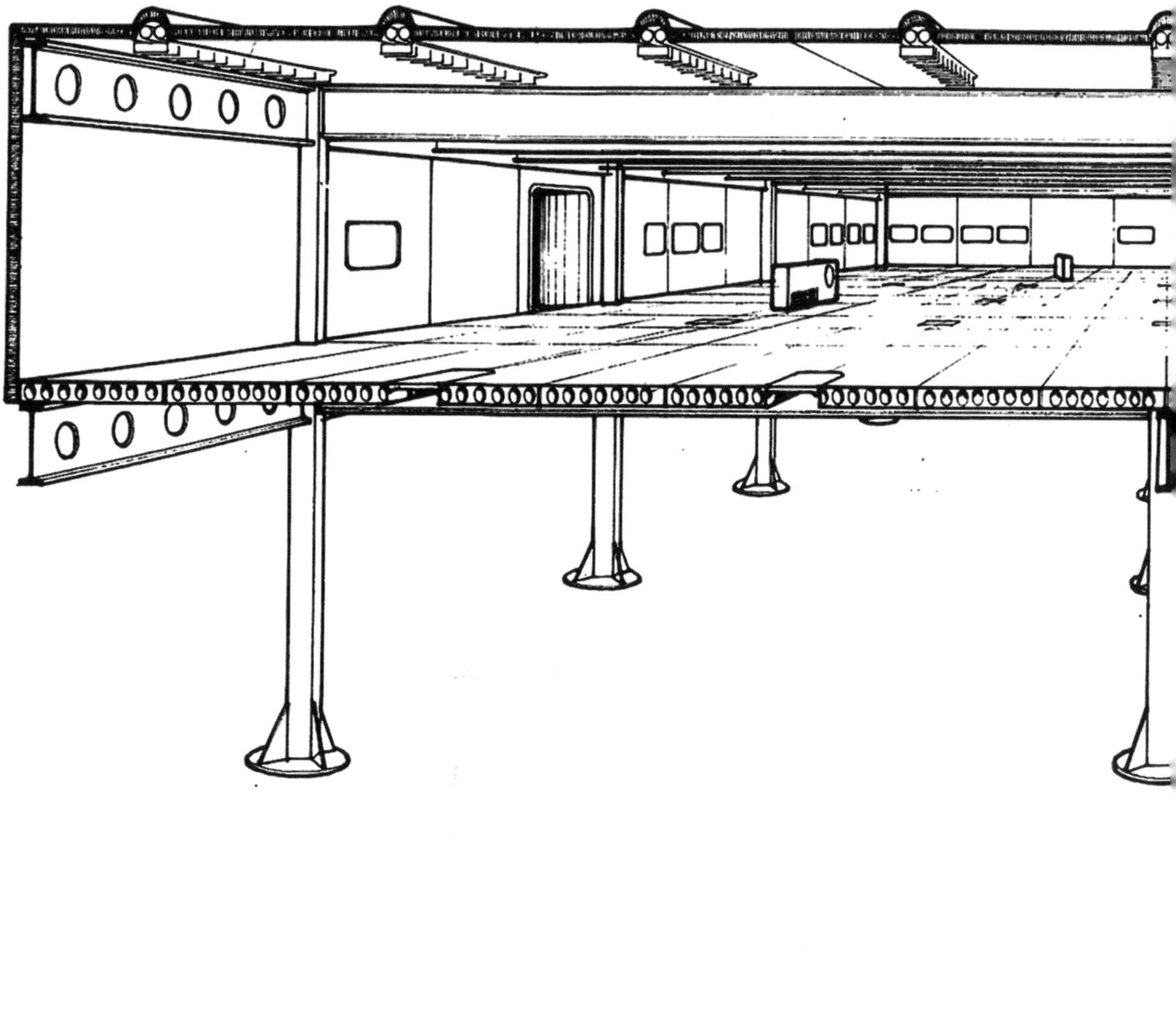

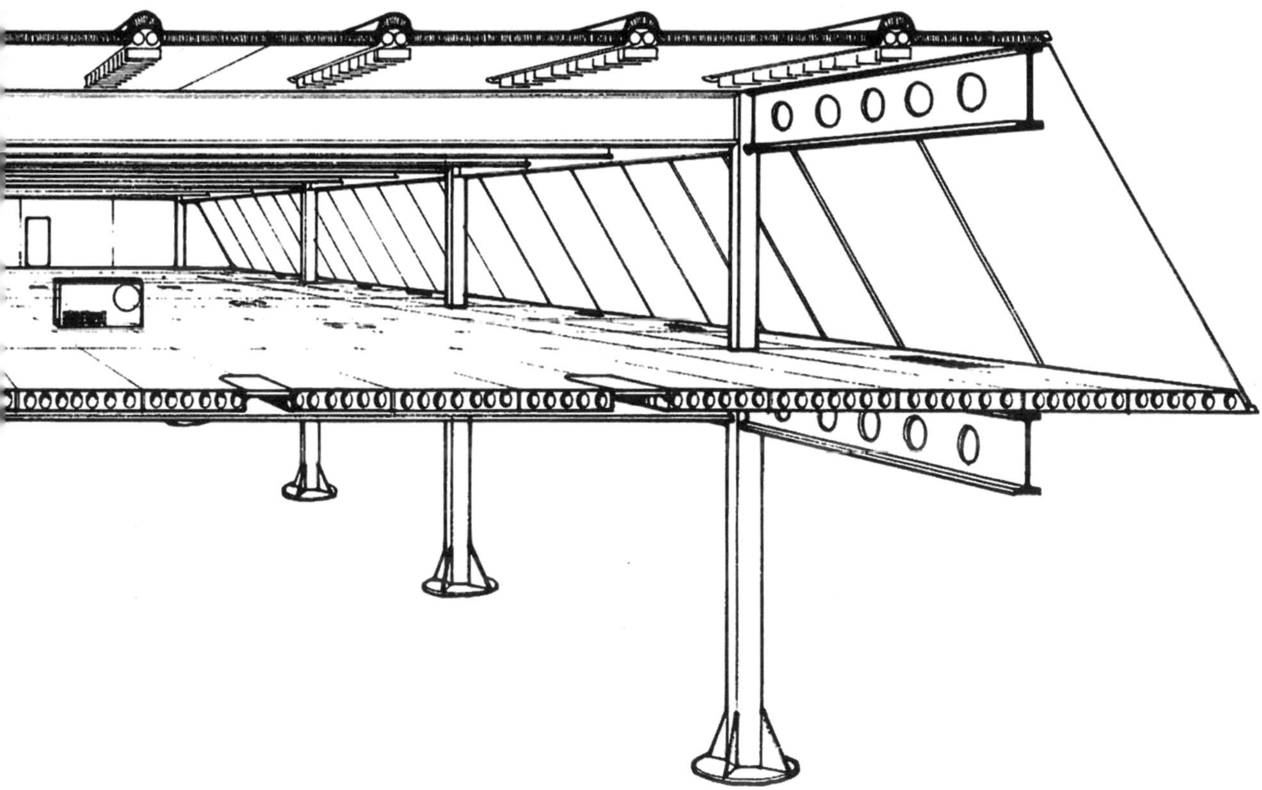

Renzo Piano, Photograph of a facade on rue La Pereuse made with panels designed by Jean Prouvé (shot from Piano's Parisian visit to Prouvé and his architecture), Paris, April 1966.

Renzo Piano, Photograph of a Square Mozart facade made with metallic panels designed by Jean Prouvé (shoot taken in the framework of a Parisian visit to Prouvé and his architecture), Paris, April 1966.

Renzo Piano, Photograph of a model of an office building (shoot taken in the framework of a Parisian visit to Prouvé and his architecture), Paris, April 1966.

Renzo Piano, Photograph of Jean Prouvé's studio at the Conservatoire national des arts et métiers, (shoot taken in the framework of a Parisian visit to Prouvé and his architecture), Paris, April 1966.

Articles annotated by Renzo Piano as part of the research on the "School System": Nizzoli Associati and group 1999 (later known as 9999), "La didactique permanente. Project for the Free University of Brussels" (*Casabella*, n° 349, 1970)

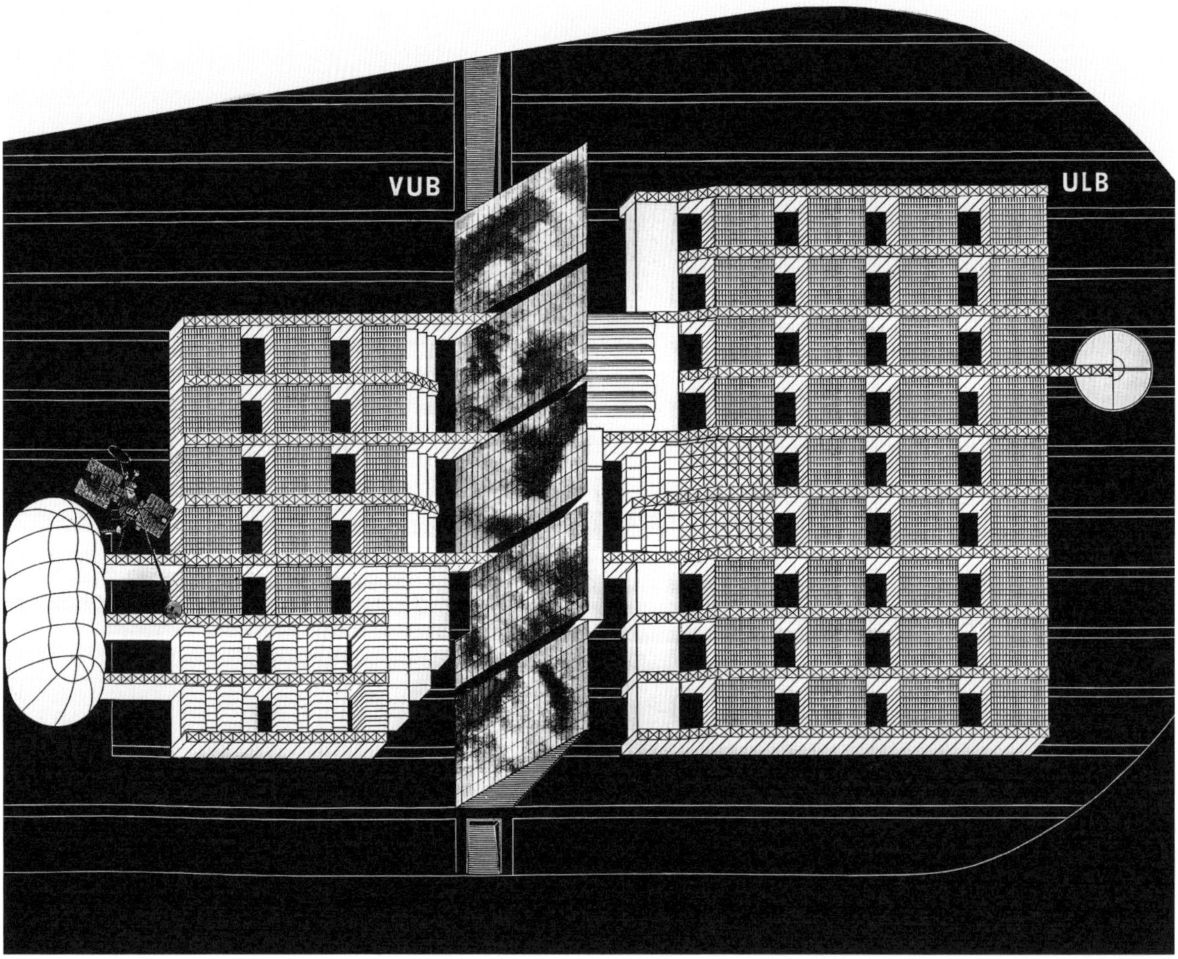

Articles annotated by Renzo Piano for the research on the "School System": Nizzoli Associati and group 1999 (later known as 9999), "La didattica permanente. Progetto per la Libera Università di Bruxelles" (*Casabella*, n° 349, 1970)

Overleaf: Articles annotated by Renzo Piano in the context of research on the "School System": L. M. Boschini, "Utopia come ipotesi di progetto" (*Casabella*, no. 305, 1966): the megastructure.

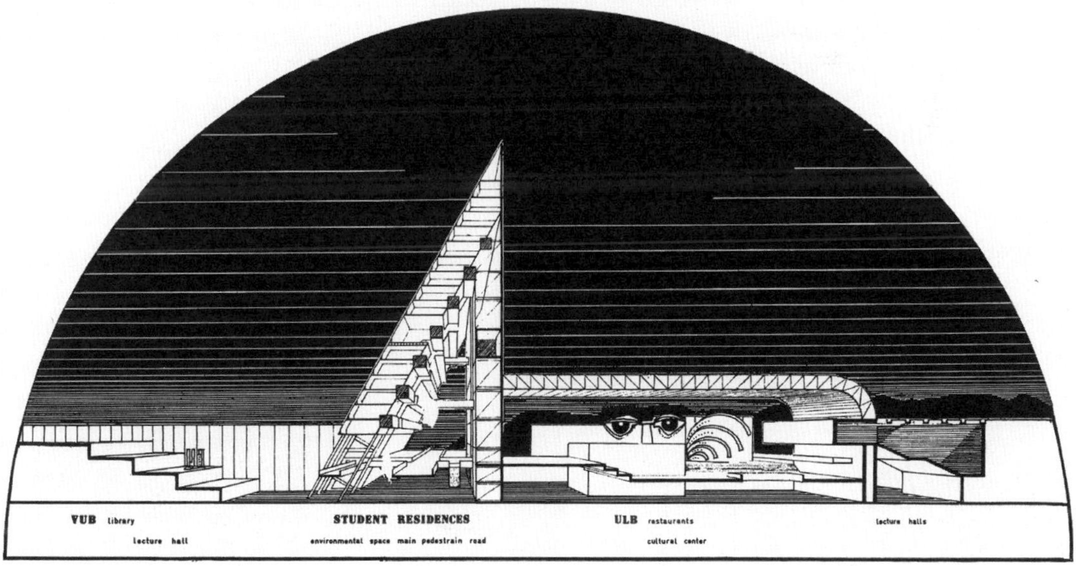

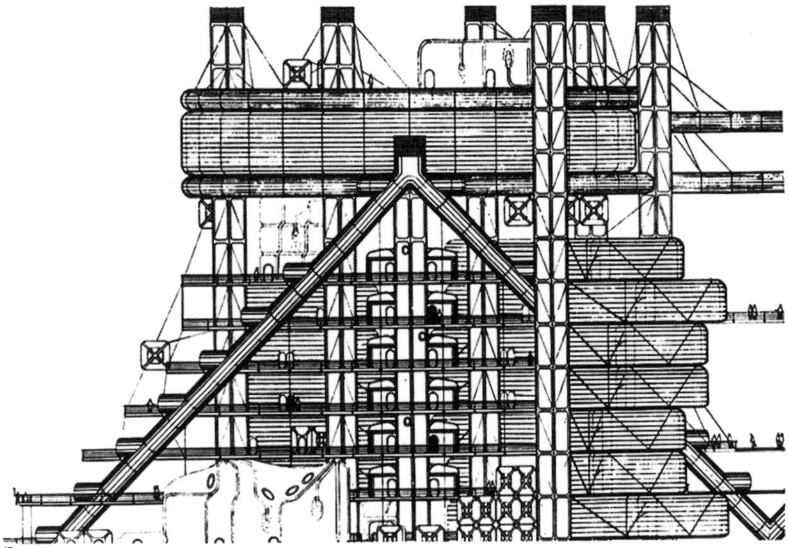

17

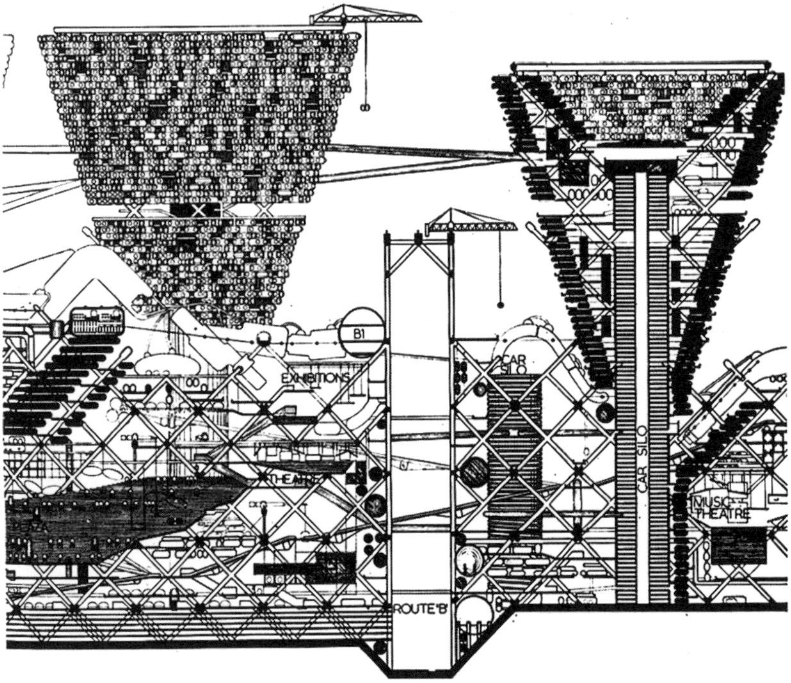
B1
EXHIBITIONS
CAR SILO
CAR SILO
THEATRE
MUSIC THEATRE
ROUTE 'B'

18

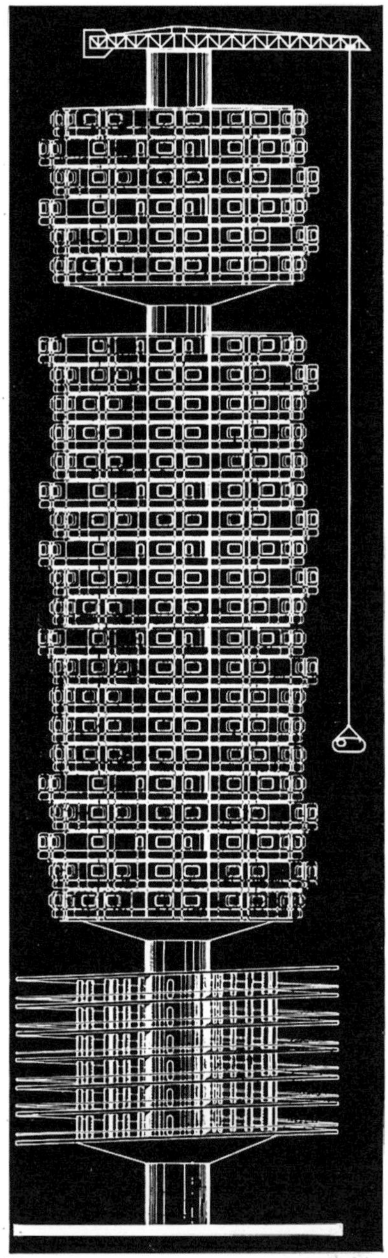

19

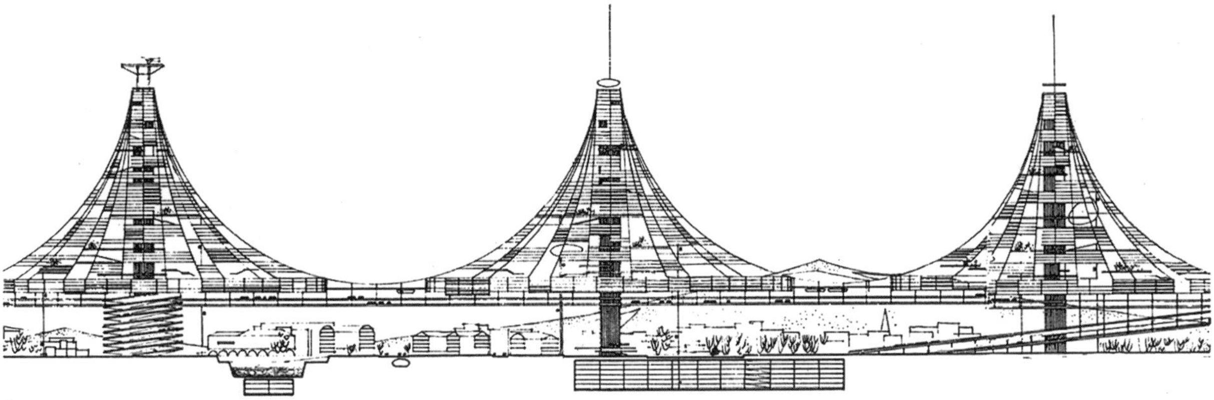

11

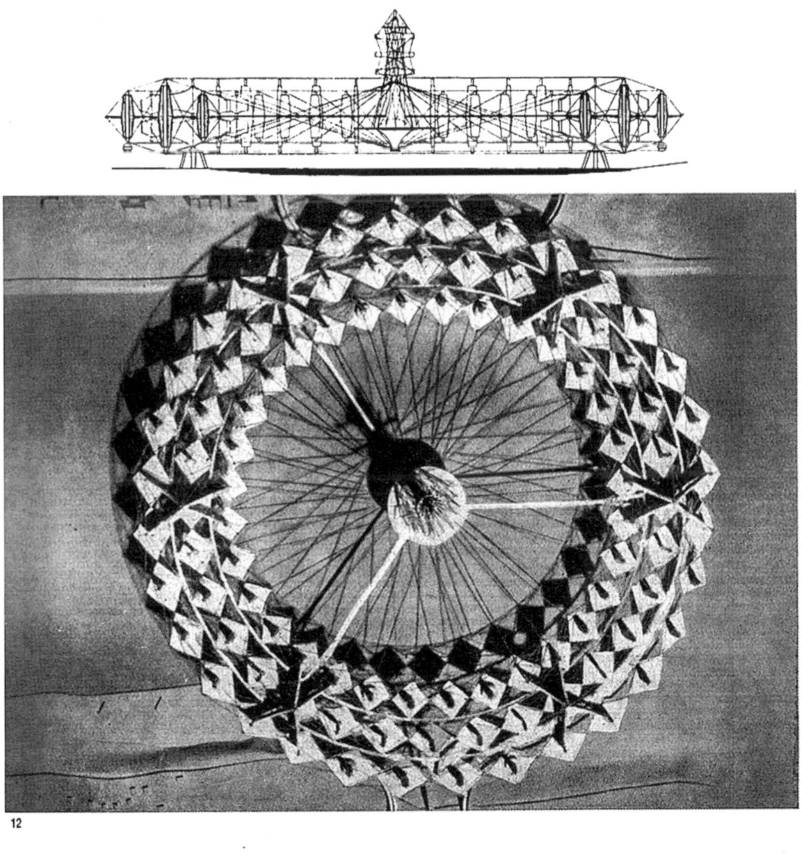

12

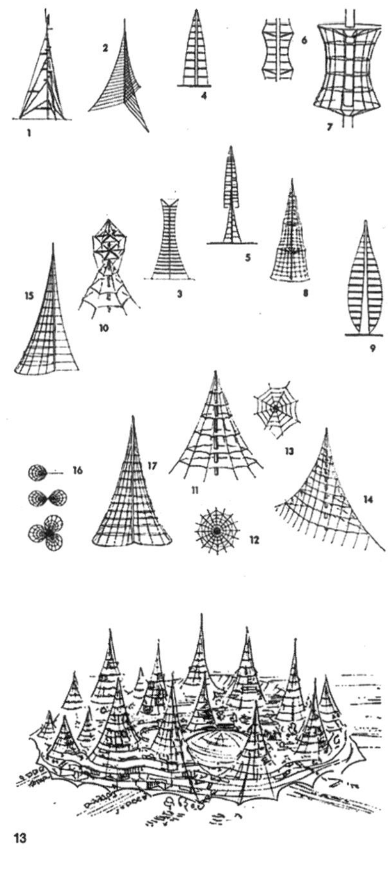

13

Articles annotated by Renzo Piano for the research on the "School System": L. M. Boschini, "Utopia come ipotesi di progetto" (*Casabella*, no. 305, 1966): the megastructure.

Articles annotated by Renzo Piano for the research on the "School System": Carlo Pelliccia and Piero Sartogo, "Campus Design, 1. Il passaggio da una struttura monofunzionale a una struttura educativa integrata" (*Casabella*, no. 322, 1968): the university megastructure.

14
K. Kikutake, Giappone: Move block, 1961. E' una città costruita su enormi zatteroni triangolari, al centro è un pilone di sostegno alto circa 300 metri, all'interno del quale sono i collegamenti verticali. Da questo pilone partono dalla base e dalla cima grossi cavi di acciaio che sono agganciati ai vertici del triangolo. Verticalmente al suolo sono collegate ai cavi dei sostegni, ai quali sono appese le cellule abitative, prodotte in serie come le automobili. Ogni triangolo può contenere da 10.000 a 30.000 persone.
15
P. Hausermann, Germania: proposta urbanistica, 1960. Le cellule sono ottenute da un blocco unico di plastica.
16
K. Kikutake, Giappone: la città galleggiante, 1961. Questa città propone dei grattacieli cilindrici formati da un sostegno centrale e da cellule costruite in serie, appese. Di questa città esistono due versioni: in una, questa, degli zatteroni sostengono i grattacieli; nell'altra i grattacieli, galleggiando come per solito fanno le bottiglie vuote, sostengono una piattaforma pedonale.
17|18|19
Gruppo Archigram, Gran Bretagna: proposte urbanistiche, 1963-1964. I principali esponenti di questo gruppo sono: P. Cook, D. Crompton, M. Webb, D. Green, W. Chalk, R. Herron.

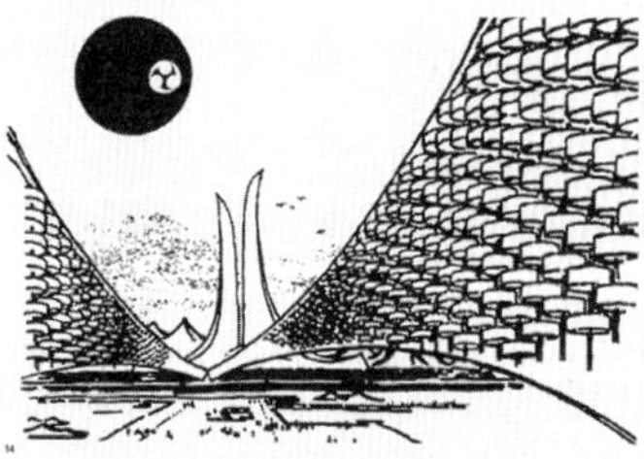

14

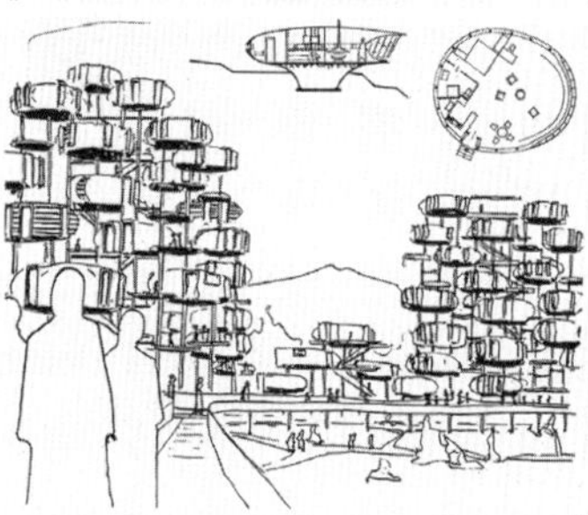

15

16

22

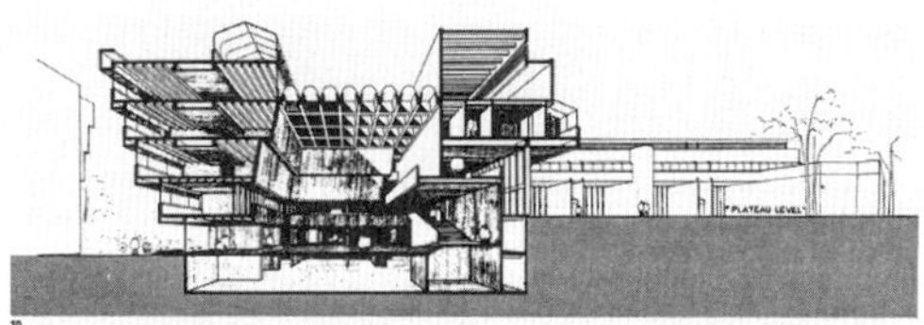

10

sociali, traslando l'identità dalla scala del dipartimento a quella dell'intera struttura.
Alla perdita d'identità del dipartimento corrisponde dunque un'identità ad una scala maggiore, quella collettiva, non più nella sede delle attività didattiche (dipartimento) ma nel sistema delle attività sociali.
Il sistema delle attività sociali assume configurazioni assai diverse nello Scarborough college e nella Università libera di Berlino: nel primo caso vi è un grande spazio comunitario che fa da drenaggio e raccoglie al centro in un « unicum architettonico » tutti i diversi livelli di vita comunitaria che si svolgono nei bracci. L'assunzione di un unico fuoco sociale conferisce una enorme rigidità al sistema ed è riscontrabile anche a livello figurale dove alla accidentalità ed articolazione, alle varie scale, della vita associativa lungo le strade pedonali che si snodano nei bracci, si contrappone la monumentalità, l'assialità del grande spazio centrale.
Nella Università libera di Berlino non c'è un unico fuoco, ma piuttosto una matrice per una pluralità di fuochi che variano in funzione del variare del contesto sociale.
La matrice assunta, la griglia delle strade interne pedonali, è di tipo geometrico e stabilisce un ordine gerarchico di organizzazione delle funzioni conferendo al tutto una sua precisa fisionomia; fisionomia che si configura attraverso l'uso e le attività che permeano la matrice.
Tale approccio pone un problema generale, quello di un rapporto tra forma e contesto, tra spazio e relazioni sociali. La mobilità dei rapporti sociali rende estremamente variabile tale rapporto.
Christopher Alexander nelle « Note sulla sintesi della forma » ci dà un'interessante interpretazione del fenomeno quando fa l'esempio del campo magnetico e della limatura di ferro: « ... Supponiamo di inventare una disposizione di limatura di ferro che sia stabile quando è posta in una certa posizione in un dato campo magnetico. E' chiaro che si può considerare questa ipotesi come un problema di progettazione. La limatura di ferro costituisce una forma, il campo magnetico il contesto. Anche in questo caso, possiamo giudicare facilmente la rispondenza della forma ponendola nel campo magnetico ed osservando se la limatura si muove sotto la sua influenza. Se non si muove, la forma è rispondente ».
Nei progetti (Università libera di Berlino) dove si punta maggiormente sul parametro delle relazioni sociali, proprio alla luce dell'esempio fatto, alla indeterminatezza di

11

23

Articles annotated by Renzo Piano belonging to his library: Roberto Pane et al., “L’incontro fra antico e nuovo” (*Casabella*, no. 314, 1967, p. 16).

Articles annotated by Renzo Piano belonging to his library: Roberto Pane et al., “L’incontro fra antico e nuovo” (*Casabella*, no. 314, 1967, p. 17).

1|2
Siena: piazza del Campo. Roma: nuovi quartieri.
Queste e le fotografie che seguono ad illustrazione del presente servizio, senza proporre riferimenti precisi alle indicazioni date dai partecipanti al dibattito sul patrimonio storico e il mondo moderno, possono tuttavia rappresentare adeguatamente il punto di applicazione delle gravi preoccupazioni che alimentano il tema del territorio storico, quando si vada alla ricerca di soluzioni ordinate per i nuovi problemi della città e dell'ambiente. Le immagini sono parte del ricchissimo censimento dei beni naturali ed artificiali del nostro paese e dei danni ad essi apportati, raccolto da R. Bazzoni e dai suoi collaboratori in occasione della mostra «Italia da salvare», allestita per conto dell'associazione «Italia nostra».

1

negare le complesse e specifiche esigenze culturali perché le considerano troppo scarsamente produttive e quindi anacronistiche. In sostanza, dunque, è la supina obbedienza a tali forze quella che induce gli architetti ad affermare che occorre ridurre la tutela degli ambienti a ciò che è veramente essenziale, quasi che tale richiesta non significasse implicitamente la negazione di quegli stessi valori che le moderne leggi intendono tutelare.
Intanto noi non possiamo limitarci a trasmettere un'eredità culturale senza qualificare ciò che trasmettiamo per la parte che ci riguarda. Se l'ambiente storico deve sussistere come una realtà viva, esso non potrà continuare ad essere tale a forza di provvedimenti di eccezione e di incrementi turistici. Se, in altre parole, la dissociazione che distingue l'attuale urbanistica diverrà un normale aspetto del futuro, se cioè un nuovo ambiente non sarà stato creato in senso umanamente positivo, nemmeno sarà possibile, a lungo andare, il sussistere degli ambienti storici. Essi saranno divenuti ormai privi di significato perché non più legati al nostro divenire; ed ovviamente la perdita non si limiterà alla mutilazione degli aspetti del passato poiché implicherà la scomparsa dei valori stessi di cui quegli ambienti sono testimonianza.
L'isolamento al quale vanno oggi riducendosi le opere di maggior significato, proprio a causa della progressiva scomparsa di quelle stratificazioni che storicamente le qualificavano, è la prova allarmante di questo processo di estraniazione che coinvolge l'uomo insieme con la memoria del suo passato.
Ora, se si ritiene che tale sia, e non possa non essere, l'immagine del mondo moderno, non è più possibile parlare di qualificazione e quindi di cultura; la parola «moderno», che tanti insistono ad usare solo in senso positivo, diventa allora sinonimo di «irresponsabilità». Poiché non si tratta di una diversa dimensione alla quale dobbiamo adeguare noi stessi, rinnovando il nostro comportamento e le nostre abitudini di vita, ma della rinuncia pura e semplice a qualsiasi dimensione; allo stesso modo con cui secondo una fatale coerenza, siamo indotti a rinunziare a qualsiasi futuro.
Del resto, non sembra possibile individuare le vere e più profonde cause dell'attuale disintegrazione dei valori ambientali senza risalire alle cause più generali della moderna crisi di civiltà. E' noto, ad esempio, che lo spreco del patrimonio d'arte e di natura fa tutt'uno con quello del patrimonio biologico; e non per nulla una delle voci più autorevoli della nostra comune società europea, quella del biologo Julian Huxley, si è spesso sollevata per affermare ragioni che tornano a pieno sostegno delle nostre attuali.
Nessuna proposta di pratici interventi potrà dunque aver valore per l'avvenire senza una piena consapevolezza di tali presupposti. Basta per questo rilevare come essa sia strettamente associata e subordinata agli sforzi che si vanno compiendo in gran parte del mondo al fine di scongiurare la minaccia più grave per l'avvenire dell'umanità: quella del pauroso e progressivo aumento della popolazione mondiale e quindi della progressiva, inevitabile rinunzia a qualsiasi sforzo di qualificazione. Per quanto non sembri immediatamente coerente, è certo che la tutela della eredità del passato — che è quanto dire l'aspirazione ad una continuità di cultura e di storia — sarà possibile solo se il più rigoroso controllo delle nascite sarà la legge di domani. Se ciò non accadrà, il caos dei nostri grattacieli di abitazione sarà presto considerato come una testimonianza di tempi ancora fiduciosi ed ingenui; né sarà più consentito agli architetti di tentare, come già essi vanno facendo, novità di giganteschi volumi e di sovrapposizioni, nella narcisistica illusione che un qualche velleitario formalismo possa rendere più tollerabile l'orrore della futura convivenza umana. Allora non vi sarà posto che nella totale obbedienza alla «ragione»; e finalmente, la scomparsa di miliardi di essere umani si imporrà come la sola condizione possibile per la sopravvivenza dell'umanità. Se poi, non piacendo questa apocalittica seppur logica conclusione, io dovessi sostituire ad essa una proposta immediata, insisterei sulla necessità che le nostre scuole di architettura si decidessero finalmente ad assumere, tra i loro compiti fondamentali, lo studio dei problemi che abbiamo enunciato (1).

R. Pane

1)
Relazione presentata al convegno sul tema «Passage de l'idée de monument isolé à l'idée d'ensemble historique et artistique», svoltosi a Bath tra il 3 e il 7 ottobre 1966, ad iniziativa del Consiglio d'Europa.

16

Antico e nuovo come valori

In sede operativa il problema del rapporto tra antico e nuovo non dovrebbe più presentare alcuna incognita. Conosciamo esattamente, in base ad attendibili previsioni, quale sarà lo stato dei centri storici e del paesaggio, continuando la presente evoluzione tecnologica. La previsione globale è confermata anche da approfondite indagini settoriali qual è, ad esempio, il rapporto Buchanan sul traffico.
In questo quadro del futuro tutte le indicazioni e i rimedi sono da considerare e valutare, tranne, forse, quello che si ispira al liberismo e ad una artisticità fuori luogo.
Liberistico, nel migliore dei casi, è il modo in cui si effettua tutta la produzione edilizia nazionale con i risultati che sappiamo, e liberistico è l'atteggiamento di alcuni architetti e critici italiani quando negano, per l'architettura da attuarsi nell'ambiente antico, ogni limitazione formale e volumetrica. Tale posizione, che nel suo radicalismo sembra rivoluzionaria e serve soprattutto a scuotere qualche soprintendente misoneista, risulta, nell'ormai maturo dibattito sul rapporto tra antico e nuovo, una tautologia. Conferma cioè con un crisma di cultura quanto già avviene nella pratica professionale per altri e ben noti motivi.
La polemica che essi conducono non è, come affermano, contro una teoria dell'ambientamento, coltivata forse in privato da qualcuno dei suddetti soprintendenti e non condivisa da alcuno studioso responsabile, ma contro alcune proposte d'ordine pratico, avanzate da una minoranza per limitare il danno all'ambiente antico. Non importa in questa sede entrare nel merito di tali proposte; esse valgono essenzialmente come testimonianza di un dissenso culturale che ha altre radici e non va identificato con il falso problema dell'ambientamento.
Inoltre vorrei rilevare che il suddetto dibattito, da circoscriversi ad un solo settore della grande trasformazione urbanistica in atto, non va posto tra due fittizie schiere di conservatori ed avanguardisti, e che è inutile ed ingenuo dire o far dire se l'una o l'altra parte abbia o meno spirito di simpatia per l'antico o per il nuovo, più per l'uno e meno per l'altro; per nostra fortuna la questione non sta in questi termini e, anche se lo fosse, nessuno, se non totalmente sprovveduto, confesserebbe le sue preferenze.
Eppure in questa malposta polemica, la cui soluzione sarebbe in gran parte attuata da una più efficiente politica urbanistica, esiste un problema di valutazione. Di una valutazione etico-estetica perché sono in discussione gli aspetti di una più civile convivenza connessi a quelli della cultura e dell'arte.
Ora, non è difficile riconoscere che tutti i quesiti inerenti al rapporto tra antico e nuovo, quali la legittimità o meno di costruire nell'ambiente antico, i suggerimenti per limitarne il danno, le decisioni da assumersi caso per caso, le scelte su quello che si debba vincolare, la definizione stessa di ambiente, rimarranno irrisolti fino a quando non saremo in grado di definirli ed inglobarli in una valutazione oggettiva o almeno concordata.
Che, nelle sue linee generali, il patrimonio storico-artistico-paesistico sia un valore, è fuori dubbio, come certamente, sempre in generale, è un valore l'architettura moderna e la sua cultura. Ma appena dobbiamo esprimere dei giudizi particolari, queste generiche ammissioni non sono più sufficienti. Non potendo da un lato conservare tutto, né dall'altro costruire tutto e dovunque, siamo costretti ad esaminare storicamente, ossia da una visuale di oggi, ciò che realmente vale (ossia serve a soddisfare le più ampie esigenze maggioritarie e minoritarie) e realmente è vivo, sia che appartenga all'antico sia che rientri nel nuovo. Abbiamo pertanto bisogno di principi per giudizi di valore.
Una prima relazione tra antico, nuovo e rispettive valutazioni si deduce dalla «Teoria della valutazione» di J. Dewey quando afferma: «In base alla continuità delle attività umane personali ed associate, la portata delle valutazioni presenti non può essere validamente stabilita fino a che esse non sono inserite e viste nella prospettiva dei passati eventi di valutazione con i quali sono continue. Senza ciò, la prospettiva futura, cioè le conseguenze delle presenti e nuove valutazioni, è indefinita». In altri termini, nel nostro caso, i nuovi valori dell'architettura, per essere definibili, dovrebbero porsi in continuità con quelli antichi, continuità che non escluderebbe il contrasto dialettico. Ma a questa esigenza di legame tra passato e presente, che si traduce in norme di comportamento, si oppongono numerose difficoltà prodotte da altrettante soluzioni particolari di continuità proprie alla vicenda dell'arte e dell'architettura moderna.
In una dimensione minore e con un ritmo più lento di quello attuale, il mondo antico formulava dei principi di valore cui si atteneva sino alla nascita dell'evento e delle personalità emergenti che sconvolgevano l'ordine delle cose imponendo diversi principi di valore.
Ad investire di valore le cose era il gusto, inteso come il denominatore comune della cultura del tempo; i criteri derivanti erano, oltre quelli formali, l'ordine, la simmetria, l'equilibrio, la

2

17

Articles annotated by Renzo Piano belonging to his library: Carlo Pelliccia and Piero Sartogo, “Campus Design, 5. Percorsi educativi individuali come alternativa alle istituzioni educative” (*Casabella*, no. 332, 1969): the Plug-In University Node by Peter Cook (Archigram).

Articles annotated by Renzo Piano belonging to his library: Carlo Pelliccia and Piero Sartogo, “Campus Design, 5. Percorsi educativi individuali come alternativa alle istituzioni educative ” (*Casabella*, no. 332, 1969, p. 14): the Ideas Circus by Peter Cook (Archigram).

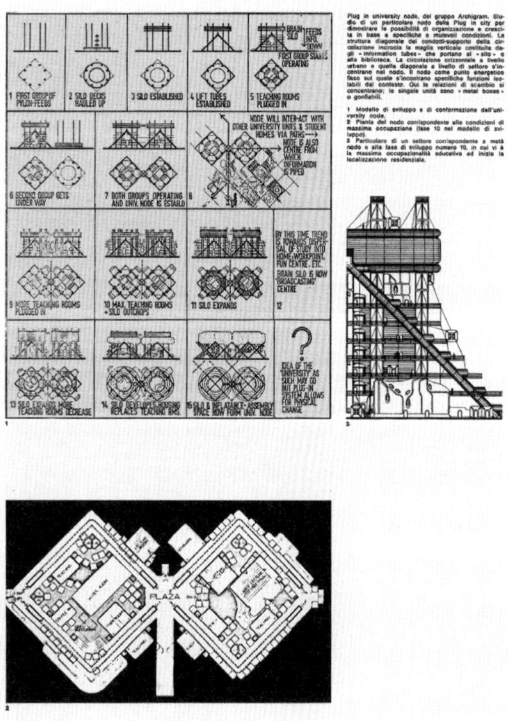

Plug in university node, del gruppo Archigram. Studio di un particolare nodo della Plug in city per dimostrare le possibilità di organizzazione e crescita in base a specifiche e mutevoli condizioni. La struttura diagonale dei condotti-supporto della circolazione incrocia la maglia verticale costituita dagli « information tubes » che portano al « silo » e alla biblioteca. La circolazione orizzontale a livello urbano e quella diagonale a livello di settore s'incontrano nel nodo. Il nodo come punto energetico fisso sul quale s'incontrano specifiche funzioni isolabili dal contesto. Qui le relazioni di scambio si concentrano; le singole unità sono « metal boxes » o gonfiabili.

1 Modello di sviluppo e di conformazione dell'university node.
2 Pianta del nodo corrispondente alle condizioni di massima occupazione (fase 10 nel modello di sviluppo).
3 Particolare di un settore corrispondente a metà nodo e alla fase di sviluppo numero 10, in cui vi è la massima occupazionalità educativa ed inizia la localizzazione residenziale.

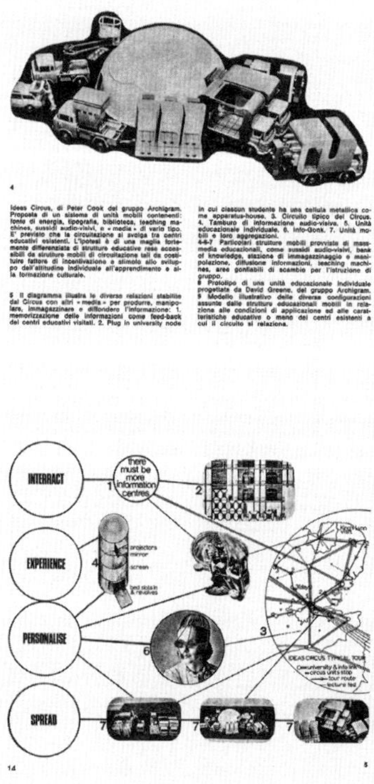

Ideas Circus, di Peter Cook del gruppo Archigram. Proposta di un sistema di unità mobili contenenti: fonte di energia, tipografia, biblioteca, teaching machines, sussidi audio-visivi, e « media » di vario tipo. E' previsto che la circuitazione si svolga tra centri educativi esistenti. L'ipotesi è di una maglia fortemente differenziata di strutture educative rese accessibili da strutture mobili di circuitazione tali da costituire fattore di incentivazione e stimolo allo sviluppo dell'attitudine individuale all'apprendimento e alla formazione culturale.

5 Il diagramma illustra le diverse relazioni stabilite dal Circus con altri « media » per produrre, manipolare, immagazzinare e diffondere l'informazione: 1. memorizzazione delle informazioni come feed-back dei centri educativi visitati. 2. Plug in university node in cui ciascun studente ha una cellula metallica come apparatus-house. 3. Circuito tipico del Circus. 4. Tamburo di informazione audio-visiva. 5. Unità educazionale individuale. 6. Info-Gonk. 7. Unità mobili e loro aggregazioni.
4-6-7 Particolari strutture mobili provviste di mass-media educazionali, come sussidi audio-visivi, bank of knowledge, stazione di immagazzinaggio e manipolazione, diffusione informazioni, teaching machines, aree gonfiabili di scambio per l'istruzione di gruppo.
8 Prototipo di una unità educazionale individuale progettata da David Greene, del gruppo Archigram.
9 Modello illustrativo delle diverse configurazioni assunte dalle strutture educazionali mobili in relazione alle condizioni di applicazione ed alle caratteristiche educative o meno dei centri esistenti a cui il circuito si relaziona.

plement the instructor's presentation. Obviously, depending on their manner of use, some devices may be either aids or media » (1).

Mass media

In relazione a questi strumenti di comunicazione e diffusione del sapere, le diverse tipologie che fanno capo all'organizzazione degli spazi per le attività didattico-scientifiche dovranno rispondere ai seguenti requisiti:
— spazi di scambio nei quali lo studente entra in contatto con i « media » e con il docente.
— Spazi di produzione, nei quali « media » in varie forme sono prodotti ed originati per soddisfare le necessità di particolari situazioni educazionali.
— Spazi per l'immagazzinaggio e la manipolazione in cui « media » in varie forme sono catalogati, ordinati e resi accessibili per l'apprendimento individuale e per lo sviluppo dell'istruzione di gruppo.
Risulta chiaro da ciò che le tipologie tradizionali relative alle funzioni che fanno capo all'organizzazione didattico-scientica risultano ampiamente obsolete: basti pensare alla consueta configurazione dell'aula scolastica dove la trasmissione dell'informazione tra docente e studente avviene entro i limiti della parola, al più amplificata, quando esistono già strumenti collaudati capaci di trasmettere simultaneamente l'informazione dall'uomo sulla terra a strumenti nel cosmo e viceversa.

Processi autoeducazionali

Si può ritenere che la tecnologia dell'istruzione si svilupperà nei prossimi anni verso la produzione sempre maggiore di materiali autoeducazionali largamente accessibili a tutti i livelli. Da ciò consegue che l'ipotesi, per la quale lo sviluppo dell'istituzione come tale appare chiuso dalle vie individuali all'istruzione, è resa plausibile dallo sviluppo tecnologico stesso, e dalle possibilità di recuperare la funzione educativa all'interno delle altre funzioni consolidate dell'habitat umano. Detta ipotesi rifiuta la concezione di una cultura « solo universitaria » come prodotto di una organizzazione autonoma, rispetto alle condizioni produttive della società.
Il vero significato non sta, quindi, nella moltiplicazione e diffusione di nuovi organismi educativi in cui i processi siano sotto il controllo istituzionale, ma piuttosto di apparati i cui processi educativi siano sotto il controllo dell'individuo. L'obiettivo è quello di una « generalizzazione » della istruzione a tutti i livelli della società in quanto strumento necessario a ciascun individuo per la piena coscienza delle proprie scelte e delle proprie azioni.
In linea generale l'educazione di massa è perseguita attraverso la circuitazione delle idee entro canali in cui i « mass-media educazionali » sono mobili o fissi. Mobili quando l'ipotesi è quella di una maglia differenziata di strutture educative e la circuitazione avviene non solo a livello dell'informazione, ma soprattutto degli individui che la personalizzano e la trasformano in esperienza. Fissi quando la maglia ipotizzata per le strutture educative tende all'omogeneità, all'uniformità nei vari livelli, e la circuitazione avviene attraverso una rete di comunicazioni capillare ed indifferenziata. C'è da aggiungere che, dando per scontata l'incidenza educazionale dei «mass-media», restano determinanti le condizioni dell'environment nella loro accezione sociologica, psicologica, percettiva, economica eccete-

Articles annotated by Renzo Piano belonging to his library: Carlo Pelliccia and Piero Sartogo, “Campus Design, 5. Percorsi educativi individuali come alternativa alle istituzioni educative” (*Casabella*, no. 332, 1969, p. 15): the Ideas Circus by Peter Cook (Archigram).

Renzo Piano Architetto, Project for the renovation of the Sestri Ponente city center, 1969–1970 (*Architectural Association Quarterly*, no. 3, 1970).

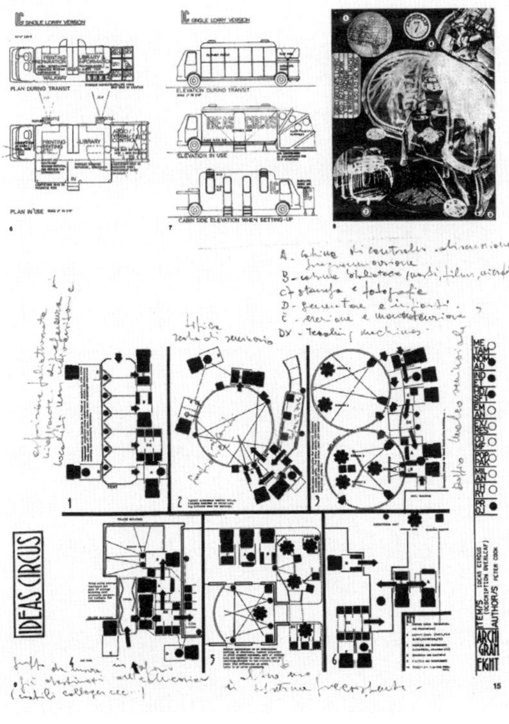

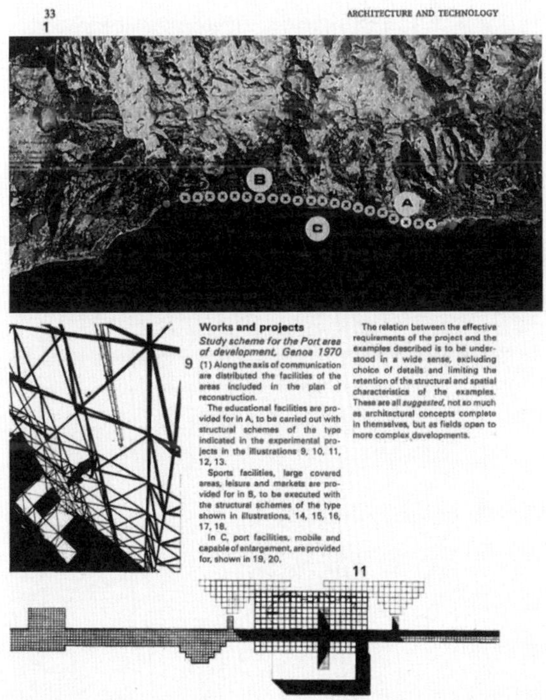

33 ARCHITECTURE AND TECHNOLOGY

1

Works and projects

Study scheme for the Port area of development, Genoa 1970

9 (1) Along the axis of communication are distributed the facilities of the areas included in the plan of reconstruction.

The educational facilities are provided for in A, to be carried out with structural schemes of the type indicated in the experimental projects in the illustrations 9, 10, 11, 12, 13.

Sports facilities, large covered areas, leisure and markets are provided for in B, to be executed with the structural schemes of the type shown in illustrations, 14, 15, 16, 17, 18.

In C, port facilities, mobile and capable of enlargement, are provided for, shown in 19, 20.

The relation between the effective requirements of the project and the examples described is to be understood in a wide sense, excluding choice of details and limiting the retention of the structural and spatial characteristics of the examples. These are all *suggested*, not so much as architectural concepts complete in themselves, but as fields open to more complex developments.

11

Renzo Piano Architetto, Project for the renovation of Sestri Ponente city center, prototype of a multi-functional platform with different equipment, Genoa, 1970.

Renzo Piano Architetto, Project for the renovation of Sestri Ponente city center, study model for the platform's interior equipement, 1970.

Renzo Piano Architetto, Project for the renovation of Sestri Ponente city center, study model for the insertion of the educational prototype in Sestri Ponente, detail with salvaging of existing facilities (W), new organisms with improved potential for change (Y), and new network for pedestrian communication and service connections (Z), Genoa, 1970.

Renzo Piano Architetto, Project for the renovation of Sestri Ponente city center, study model for the insertion of the educational prototype in Sestri Ponente, Genoa, 1970.

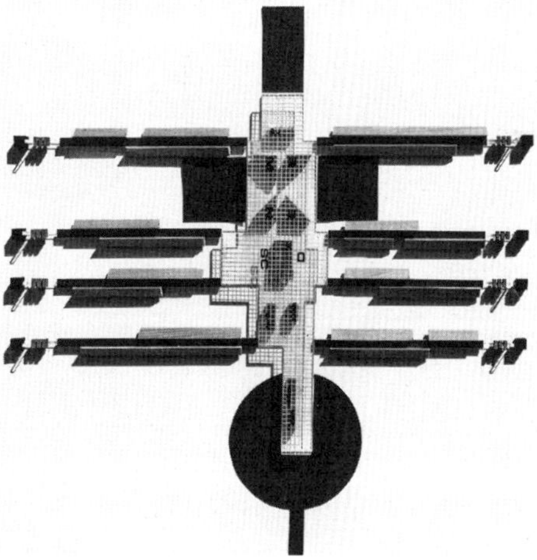

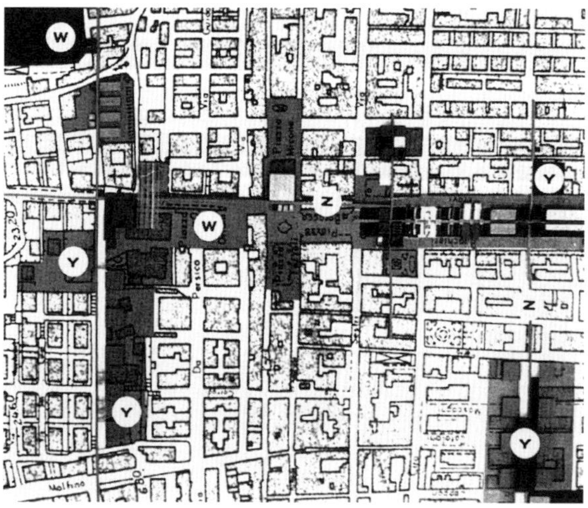

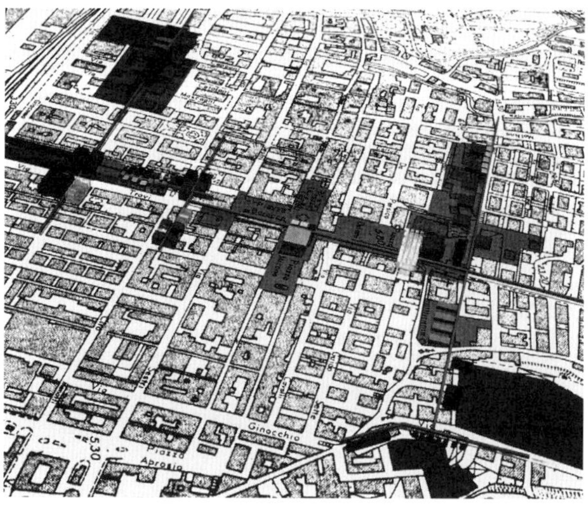

Gianfranco Franchini, Portfolio, Academic studies on the analysis of the architectural heritage of Western Liguria, 1970.

A2

Gianfranco Franchini, Portfolio, exercises on form in construction carried out with students of the Academy of Fine Arts in the course Elements of Architecture (1968-1969), 1970.

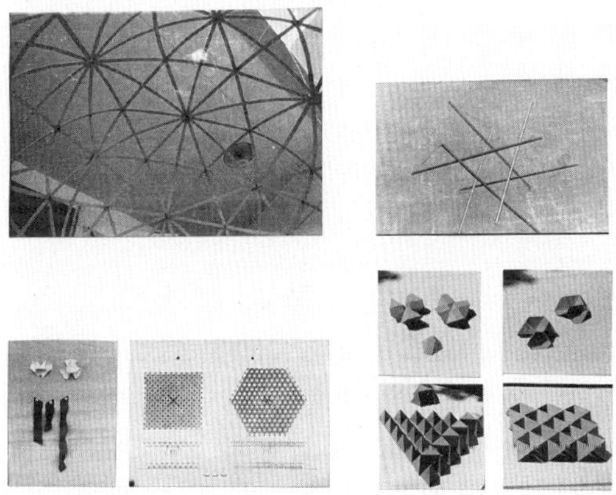

E15

Gianfranco Franchini, Portfolio, Analysis of the SCSD Building System by Ezra Ehrenkrantz prepared for the course Architectural Composition, structural details and assembly, 1970.

SCSD

Gianfranco Franchini, Portfolio, Analysis of the SCSD Building System by Ezra Ehrenkrantz prepared for the course Architectural Composition, components system, 1970.

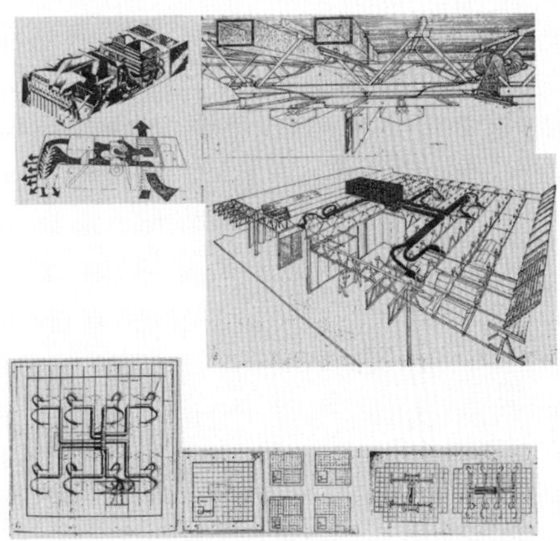

SCSD

3.2

THE HYPOTHESIS OF A COLLABORATION ON A PIONEERING SCHOOL SYSTEM

The origins of the professional practice that would develop the winning Centre Beaubourg competition project can be traced back to Piano's earliest visits to London, before he got to know the Rogerses.
It was probably in the spring of 1966 that the Genoese architect paid his first visit to the British capital, undertaken to show Makowski the results of his research in the field of plastic materials and the first modular reinforced-polyester roofing prototypes produced with the family company between 1964 and 1965.[35] In 1966 Piano presented these works to sector experts at the First International Conference on Space Structures, organized by Makowski, and, subsequently, showed them to the public thanks to the article Makowski published on Piano's experiments.[36] It is likely that on this first trip to London Piano took the opportunity to study some new towns founded since the last war, such as Harlow and Stevenage, a series of British schools built with prefabricated systems, a recent housing complex in Pimlico, and a public housing project under construction using the Wates system of modular prefabrication, as well as the celebrated Roehampton housing development conceived by London County Council.[37]
It was in London again, between 1967 and 1970, that Piano got involved in the British debate over contemporary architecture and awareness of his work began to spread.
Evidence for this comes both from the publication of his experiments in *Architectural Design* and *Architectural Association Quarterly* and from the staging of exhibitions at the Centre for Advanced Study of Science in Art and the Architectural Association.[38]
Despite the absence of any trace of their first meeting in the documents, it is probable that Rogers and Piano got to know one another in 1968, when Piano was in London to work with Salvadori and Franchini on the exhibition organized by the Centre for Advanced Study of Science in Art for the 14th Milan Triennale in 1968 entitled *Mutazioni della forma in architettura* ("Mutations of Form in Architecture").[39]
In 1969 Rogers and Piano established a relationship of trust and mutual esteem that led to their exchanging views on the projects on which each of them was working at the time (according to Rogers, Piano was "the best of the young generation of architects in Europe").[40]
In December of the same year, during a discussion of their respective projects and the publication of a series of articles on them, Piano spoke formally for the first time of the possibility of a collaboration between the two practices. "I hope that we can soon think about taking on some programs of work integrating our operating possibilities," were Piano's words.[41]

The idea of working with Piano was nothing unusual for Rogers and should be seen in the context of Richard+Su Rogers Architects' practice of establishing collaborations and working with consultants on projects that required specific expertise.[42]
Richard had set up a studio called Team 4 with Su, Yale classmate Norman Foster, and Foster's wife-to-be, Wendy Cheesman, in 1963; it remained active until 1967. He also worked with Mike Davies—a former Architectural Association student, follower of Archigram, and expert on inflatable materials—on the construction of inflatable industrial structures, and with Hugh Chapman, former Richard+Su Rogers Architects collaborator, on a prefabricated Zip-Up-series module for the Sweetheart Plastics offices in Gosport.[43] Another of Rogers's many collaborations was with Happold and Structures 3 on Chelsea Football Club's stadium in London.
On February 14 and 15, 1970, Piano took advantage of a brief stopover in London on his way to Japan to complete the Italian Industry Pavilion at the Osaka Expo; he proposed to Rogers a collaboration centered on the study of prototypes for educational facilities of the sort he had conceived with Franchini for the Sestri Ponente project.
In this hypothetical collaboration Piano saw the possibility of turning that project into a proper strategic study with a wide range of applications, a "school system" to be developed "in Italy and England."[44]
Although there is no documentary record of the content of the discussions between Rogers and Piano on February 14 and 15, the course of subsequent events shows that Rogers accepted Piano's proposal and was ready to start research on the school system with the participation of Su and his London practice.
Unable to devote himself to the project until his return from Japan at the end of March, Piano entrusted the preliminary studies to Franchini—a further confirmation of the role the latter played in the design of the educational prototype conceived in the Sestri Ponente district of Genoa.
In March, Franchini went to London, to the offices at 32 Aybrook Street, and with the Rogerses developed the school-system project. On the one hand, it took up the fundamental principles outlined in Sestri Ponente, those of the open plan, prefabrication, and urban renewal, and on the other, it integrated new technological, structural, and social concerns.[45]
First of all, Franchini added to the research into the literature that Piano had compiled over the previous months with publications that looked at the question of school design from a more general perspective, rather than at specific projects, and, in some cases, relied on open-ended solutions and component kits to be assembled to suit requirements.[46]
It is no coincidence that the term "system" was

used by Rogers to draw Piano's attention to an issue of *The Architectural Review* devoted to the theme of educational architecture in the fall of 1969.[47] The bibliographic research carried out at 32 Aybrook Street also allowed Piano, Rogers, and Franchini to investigate the new audiovisual, telecommunication, and computerized media available for use in education, something which Piano had already noted in several cutting-edge projects, including Cook's Ideas Circus, but that had not been applied in Sestri Ponente.[48] Probably at Rogers's suggestion, the research into the literature also tackled the question of the school from an important social perspective, orienting the project toward a system in the service of the community in the manner of the Rogerses' shells: "community school – i.e. neighborhood" were the terms Richard used in March to describe the school system.

Between the end of March and his return from Japan at the beginning of April, Piano translated Franchini and Rogers's research into a first architectural proposal: a floor space as free as possible of structural obstructions (a "deep plan"), hermetically sealed and supplied with a kit of components similar to the one Ehrenkrantz had just come up with for his SCSD.[49] Piano rejected the opaque and multilayered roof of this American model in favor of an original system of natural overhead illumination in the service of education. While Piano had not yet specified a technical solution, the hypothesis of an "insulating and translucent roofing material" mentioned in this phase already hinted at the conceptual and technological conflict between a translucent and radiant roof and structures and cumbersome technical systems whose bulk threatened to reduce the amount of light entering to a minimum.

Although at the beginning of April Piano and Rogers were working on a portfolio of their respective practices' works, to which they would give the title "Rogers+Piano," to accompany the research on schools, the intended collaboration abruptly ground to a halt owing to "major financial problems" Piano was experiencing and a substantial overhaul of the firm that entailed its transfer to a new location in Genoa, on Piazza della Vittoria.[50]

Although the school-system project would never be formally taken up again, its ideas crystallized in the minds of Piano, Rogers, and Franchini and were destined to come to the fore again at the time of their participation in the competition for the Centre Beaubourg in Paris.

Renzo Piano Architetto. Renzo Piano Architetto workshop at Erzelli, Genoa, 1969–1970.

3.3

THE ESTABLISHMENT OF PIANO+ROGERS ARCHITECTS

Given Piano's professional and personal crisis, at the end of June, Rogers invited Piano to move to London with his family and reopened the possibility of a collaboration with Richard+Su Rogers Architects. "Why don't you come and work in England? You can begin a collaboration with us at any moment, and I'm quite serious about this," he wrote in a letter of June 25.[51]

At this difficult junction in his career, however, Rogers set aside the school-system project, still at a preliminary stage and lacking a client, to focus on more concrete professional opportunities, ranging from the distribution to potential British clients of a "brochure" of the two practices' projects to the possibility of joint participation in a competition of ideas and the intention of finding Piano a teaching post at a university in London.

At the end of the summer, Rogers's initiative led to Piano being taken on at the Architectural Association, where, from the summer of 1970, he was given the role of tutor in a fifth-year Department of Tropical Studies course.[52]

Although he was able to create the necessary conditions for Piano's move to London, over the course of the summer of 1970 Rogers himself, like Piano a few months earlier, went through a period of major crisis that was connected with the separation from his wife Su and with the practice running out of commissions, as well as the end of the contract of collaboration with the Design Research Unit (DRU) that since 1967 had provided Richard+Su Rogers Architects with a fixed source of funding. It was against this background that Rogers revived and consolidated the idea of collaborating with Piano, starting to talk about it with his clients and colleagues. "Renzo Piano is about to come and live in England and I hope to join our partnership," wrote Rogers to the architecture critic Allan Temko and his wife Becky.[53]

From September to December of the same year Rogers went to the United States with his new partner, Ruthie Elias, to teach at Cornell University in Ithaca, from where he continued to oversee the work done at the studio in London.[54]

Notwithstanding his distance from the studio and the lack of an opportunity for collaboration on a concrete project, at the end of the summer Rogers invited Piano to transfer his activity to the offices at 32 Aybrook Street and presented to the director of the DRU, Misha Black, the idea of a "partnership between Piano and R+SR" that Richard and Su Rogers held could offer new professional opportunities for their practice.[55] The idea that Renzo might help to revive the fragile professional situation of the Richard+Su Rogers Architects practice was so deep-rooted in the Rogerses' mind that in October they came up for the first time with the idea of publishing news of the collaboration in the *Architects' Journal*.[56]

The lack of opportunities for new projects and perhaps Black's reaction meant that it was only at the time of Rogers's return to London in the spring of 1971 that the first concrete occasions for a collaboration with Piano arose.
These coincided with a series of commissions received by Richard+Su Rogers Architects, including some that preceded Piano's joining the practice and others from clients and consultants with whom Richard or Su were acquainted.
Although these occasions were not directly linked to the research into the school system, it was through these first commissions that Piano and Rogers took up again the fundamental principles that had underpinned that collaboration, from the breakdown of the architectural project into a system of modular and prefabricated elements to those of an internally flexible and unobstructed space and a means of rehabilitating the urban fabric.
The first of these opportunities was probably the design of a mobile hospital module for the Association for Rural Aid in Medicine (ARAM).
The collaboration, begun in 1969 and documented by an exchange of letters between Richard and Su and ARAM's director Dr. Lalla Iverson, was given concrete form between December 1970 and March 1971 with Piano's collaboration.[57] The phrase "Evolution of Idea – Renzo's [proposal]" written in pen and ink on a note relating to the preparation of a report confirms Piano's involvement in the project.[58] Also in December 1970 a meeting was held at the studio of Richard+Su Rogers Architects between Richard, Su, Piano, and some representatives of CIBA (ARL), a company specializing in synthetic adhesives used in the aeronautics industry with whom the Rogerses had already been in contact for the realization of experimental housing with a lightweight prefabricated structure.[59] It was precisely by presenting themselves to clients with the Genoese architect and showing them his work together with their own ("a slide show of work by Piano, Rogers") that the collaboration between Richard and Su Rogers and Piano started to assume a concrete and professional dimension ("It was felt that there were grounds for possible collaborations between CIBA and Piano, Rogers based on their mutual interest in the use of composite structures in the building industry"[60]). The decision to present themselves as two partners representing their respective practices—"Piano, Rogers could act as consultants to CIBA in this matter"—suggests that Rogers still saw the collaboration with Piano in terms of an association between two independent firms and in any case limited to experimental projects based on themes of common interest such as that of lightweight structures. It is precisely in this way that we can interpret the choice made between late 1970 and January 1971 to participate with Piano in the

design competition for the new home for the Burrell Collection in Glasgow (the notice was published in the *Royal Institute of British Architects Journal* in October 1970 and the deadline for the delivery of the plans was May 14, 1971).[61] The same is true for the inclusion of Piano in the project for a shopping mall and multistory parking garage in the Fitzroy Street/Burleigh Street district of Cambridge, on which Richard+Su Rogers Architects had been at work since 1969.[62]

That Rogers at this moment was thinking of the collaboration with Piano in terms of an informal and occasional association is attested by an article published on January 20 in *Architects' Journal*.[63] Notwithstanding Rogers's idea to publish the announcement of the partnership with Piano in the fall of 1970, the article in *Architects' Journal* presented the studio at 32 Aybrook Street as Richard+Su Rogers Architects and made no reference to Piano, absent both from the description of the practice and from the photograph of its members.

So it is likely that it was only Happold's invitation to participate with Ove Arup & Partners in the competition for the Centre Beaubourg in Paris and the discussions of the conditions of that participation which were held between February and March 1971 that provided the basis for a formal and structured partnership between Rogers and Piano—one capable, among other things, of bearing the risk of a new professional commitment such as that of the Beaubourg competition. Between March and April 1971, the idea of a new form of collaboration led to the founding of "Piano & Rogers, Architects," later known as Piano+Rogers Architects, a new firm in whose name Rogers and Piano began, in March 1971, to sign all projects under way, from the ARAM hospital module to the Fitzroy shopping mall.[64] The news of the establishment of the new practice was published only on April 7, 1971, in the *Architects' Journal*'s "announcements" section.[65] From this date on, the new practice worked in two locations, in London at 32 Aybrook Street, the studio of Richard+Su Rogers Architects, and in Genoa, at Piazza della Vittoria 15, the studio of Renzo Piano Architetto. The lack of any changes to the staff or internal hierarchy of either office—the members of the practices in London and Genoa would continue to report to Rogers and Piano respectively—shows that the nature of the collaboration was that of an association between two professional offices which remained essentially independent of one another.

In addition to Rogers and Su, the staff of the office at 32 Aybrook Street was made up of the architects Marco Goldschmied and John Young, associate members, and Pierre Botschi and John Doggart, along with the secretary, Sally Appleby, and a number of assistants and interns, including Dominic Michaelis, Andrew Holmes, Peter Flack, and Jan Kaplický.[66] The staff of the office in Genoa consisted, alongside Piano, of the engineer Flavio Marano, the surveyor Ottaviano Celadon, the draftsman Giorgio Fascioli, secretary Angela Sacco, and some external collaborators, including Franchini.[67]

The architects of the winning team of the competition for the realization of the Centre Beaubourg (from left to right: Richard Rogers, Renzo Piano, Su Rogers and Gianfranco Franchini), Paris, July 1971.

3.4

FLEXIBLE DEVICES FOR AN INTEGRATED AND DEMOCRATIC ENVIRONMENT

With the ARAM hospital module and Fitzroy shopping mall projects, the first two commissions carried out by the new professional entity of Piano+Rogers Architects, Rogers and Piano resumed the discussions of the school system they had commenced a year earlier. They went back to the idea of an architecture that could be broken down into a system, an industrial and prefabricated kit of parts to be used for the definition of a flexible and climate-controlled environment. The experience gained by Piano through building pavilions and roofs and through the exchange of ideas with Makowski, Le Ricolais, Buckminster Fuller, Otto, and Kahn would prove crucial in the transformation of these systems into envelopes of very large dimensions capable of housing several stories. Precisely for reasons of scale, Piano+Rogers Architects's first projects abandoned the envelopes of the Rogerses' shells and opted instead for the deep plan that Piano had suggested for the school system—a solution that would lead to a clash between the empty and undivided space of the shell and the question of the vertical elements of the structure. The ARAM hospital module and the Fitzroy shopping mall served to verify the compatibility of Piano+Rogers Architects' deep plan with complex programs and study its adaptability to systems with several floors, sometimes designed on the scale of the city and its preexisting structures. From the discussions that developed around the school system, Rogers and Piano also took the idea of making their project a device for the rehabilitation of the city and the district and, at the same time, a catalyst for the community, leading to an initial synthesis of the research that Piano and Rogers had conducted between Sestri Ponente and their school system.

The ARAM hospital module was Piano+Rogers Architects' first project. The project stemmed from research commissioned by ARAM into the design of an innovative hospital facility to be proposed as an alternative to traditional structures, seen as the products of an elitist domain for an "urban and white community" (the project was in fact intended for "non-white communities").[68] The objective was to configure a universal hospital structure that could be adapted to any setting, from the big city to the American suburbs to the rural centers of developing countries.[69] Not for nothing was it defined as a "module" and at the same time conceived of as a "tool for the community"[70] and system capable of generating new interactions with different places and new activities. "Catalyst" was another designation Rogers and Piano gave it.[71]

The need to respond to a complex program to be laid out on more than one floor was a crucial step in the design of the shell, leading to its transfiguration. The references to which the Piano+Rogers Architects practice looked were those of the designs for mobile and transportable structures of the sixties, from the aforementioned projects studied by Piano, such as Cook's Ideas Circus, to Price's celebrated Potteries Thinkbelt and the Medikit developed by Tony Dugdale, whom Rogers had gotten to know in the years he taught at the Architectural Association (1968–70). Rogers esteemed Dugdale highly enough to recommend him to the British embassy for participation in the 6th Paris Biennale in 1969 and then to share a teaching post at Cornell University with him between 1970 and 1971.[72]

In the ARAM module project, instead of a single shell, a series of reduced-size envelopes were each allocated to a function. Transportable like the equipment invented by Price for the Potteries Thinkbelt, Cook for the Ideas Circus, and Dugdale for the Medikit, they had different lifetimes (from ten to sixty years).[73] The decision to use the name "container" suggests that Rogers and Piano were evaluating the possibility of reusing shipping containers for some of these shells, thereby applying the research Piano had been carrying out for years. The containers were combined with a spatial structure that allowed the hospital functions to be laid out on two floors, but their points of support were not made clear. Although not yet specified, it is likely that this structure housed, from the earliest studies, services and technical plant, from the air-conditioning system to the power-supply generators.

From the combination of spatial structure and containers, Piano+Rogers Architects derived several variants in which the containers could be housed in a single envelope again, to be placed on or hitched to the spatial structure.[74] Finally, consideration was also given to the organization of spatial structures and unitary envelopes on three floors with a service tower at the side that turned the ARAM module into a building of Kahnian derivation[75]—a solution that Piano+Rogers Architects would also study in the project for the Centre Beaubourg.

The spaces' limited flexibility—resulting from the confinement of the functions to the containers, the presence of intermediate vertical supports needed for the unitary envelopes, or the passage of wiring and plumbing, which was still problematic—induced Piano+Rogers Architects to turn the spatial structure into an imposing system composed of two structural floors and four vertical lattices that transformed what could have been another prototype of the Rogerses shells into a genuine deep plan.[76]

The ARAM module structural floors, which were also supposed to house services and equipment for emergency use (electricity generators, inflatable units) and thus defined as "service floors," were organized on a mesh of trusses with a fifteen-meter span, and permitted the configuration of a main floor, in line with a solution based on the alternation of servant and served floors that Piano had appreciated in the skyscrapers designed by I. M. Pei and in Kahn's Richards Medical Research Laboratories and Salk Institute.[77] Thanks to the service floors, the main floor was made as open and flexible as that of the Zip-Up House, "to be planned in any number of ways" and "respond to new situations."[78] To stiffen the structure and obtain spaces with a smaller number of vertical supports, the architects and engineers connected the tops of the lattices and the perimeter of the horizontal structure with steel cables.[79] Each of the vertical lattices was equipped with a crane to facilitate the assembly of the module and allow the loading and unloading of objects.[80]

Conceived in this way, the structure of the ARAM module took on the iconic characteristics of flexible British megastructures, from Price's Fun Palace to Archigram's Plug-In City, and could be considered to derive directly from one of them, Dugdale's Learning Shed, from which it also took its structural configuration.

The envelope and the mechanical circulation were also influenced by the Rogerses' rhetoric of flexible and adaptable shells. For the envelope Piano+Rogers Architects resorted to modular sandwich panels similar to those used in the Zip-Up series; for the mechanical circulation they returned, instead, to servant towers reconfigurable over time, in the tradition of the mobile equipment that could be hitched onto the building which Banham had described as "clip-on architecture."[81]

With the ARAM module Piano+Rogers Architects adapted the shells' spatial and functional principles to a multistory system whose accent on structure came out of Piano's 1968 and 1970 experiments on pre-tension and the use of special components in the Erzelli workshop's roofing or in the series of three-dimensional portals, including one for a yacht club and another for the Italian Industry Pavilion at the Osaka Expo.[82]

Founded on the same principles of flexibility and adaptability, but entailing an unprecedented urban system for the movement and amusement of a metropolitan crowd, was the design of a shopping mall for the Fitzroy/Burleigh district in Cambridge—a commission on which work was begun by Richard+Su Rogers Architects in 1969 and then reformulated in a series of variants concluding in the one developed by Piano+Rogers Architects in April 1971.[83]

The project was part of a decongestion scheme for the historic center launched by Cambridge City Council in 1969 based on revitalizing the Burleigh/Fitzroy district through the insertion of a new commercial hub and a multistory parking garage.[84]

The location in historical Cambridge prompted Piano+Rogers Architects to transform the undifferentiated shells adaptable to any geographical and climatic setting into an urban system able to establish completely new synergies with the site. In this sense an awareness of the inherent qualities of the Fitzroy/Burleigh district was crucial—a value which Piano+Rogers Architects found not in the excellence of one particular building but in the aesthetic quality of the whole area, in an approach that reflected the integrated environmental planning Piano and Franchini had undertaken in Sestri Ponente and, together with the Rogerses, tried to apply to the school system.

Piano's appreciation of the historical context, moreover, chimed with Rogers's interest in British "townscapes," an interest stirred by urban planner Gordon Cullen, from whom, not coincidentally, the Rogerses commissioned a series of picturesque perspectives of the Fitzroy shopping mall project to be used to stress the project's harmonization with its setting.

Out of the recognition of the potentialities of the Burleigh/Fitzroy district and the council's request to separate vehicle and foot traffic through the creation of pedestrian areas came the idea of a community-oriented scheme able to preserve the local townscape, where people, insulated from urban chaos, could devote themselves to recreation and shopping.[85] These ideas led to the design of a pedestrian arcade, bounded by a curtain of buildings: a townscape obtained by integrating the majority of the existing buildings with a prefabricated multistory metal structure.[86]

It was still the central role of the system of movement that defined the organization of this hybrid building, with commercial activities on the ground floor opening onto the pedestrian walkway and a parking facility on the upper floors, separate from the commercial activities and the pedestrian traffic below, but connected with them by adaptable systems of mechanized circulation similar to those of the ARAM module. In its metropolitan vocation and recourse to a monumental tunnel vault of glass and steel, the pedestrian walkway took on the character of a Parisian *passage*, Crystal Palace, and Italian Risorgimento galleries. This urban system for the movement of the crowd included an open-air plaza with civic activities intended to create a social and community catalyst—"magnets" were, not coincidentally, the name that Piano+Rogers Architects gave to this and other community elements in the project.[87]

While a conservative approach and recourse to elements in a fairly traditional style distanced the project from the industrial and Archigramesque language of Richard+Su Rogers Architects' shells, flexibility and adaptability remained the spaces' organizational principles.[88] With the intention of making the project a "framework with built-in flexibility"[89] able "to provide the greatest freedom of choice before and after completion," Piano+Rogers Architects, just as they had done for the ARAM module, abandoned self-supporting shells in favor of the deep plan suggested by Piano to support as large a span as the one required for Cambridge. The result was a structure composed of metal floor slabs supported by a regular mesh of posts and beams with a twelve-meter span. "Deep plan" was, not coincidentally, the name utilized in the project report. In the choice of this inexpensive, standardized, and modular structural solution, the design of the Fitzroy shopping mall was an expression of the reduction of the building to an inhabitable infrastructure that was undetermined and open to change.[90] "The aim has been to define a system rather than design finite buildings and the framework offers the minimum organization necessary for the different disciplines."[91] The traditional organization of the space into galleries, corridors and rooms left the space in an open system: "[the structure] allocates zones, defines movement levels, activities, magnets, etc."[92]

Instead of a façade, Piano+Rogers Architects resorted to a modular system similar in configuration to the aluminum and polyurethane sandwich modules of the Zip-Up series and the ARAM module, but based on an insulating and translucent panel that had not previously appeared in Piano+Rogers Architects' research.[93] Although in the Fitzroy shopping mall project its name is not mentioned and its characteristics are limited to its transparence,[94] when the module would be taken up again for the design of the new home of the Burrell Collection in Glasgow and then for the Centre Beaubourg, Piano+Rogers Architects would explore its reflective and even its artistic potentialities, making it an original element.

With the Fitzroy shopping mall project, Rogers and Piano brought to a new degree of synthesis the social orientation and technological and industrial rhetoric that had emerged in their preceding designs, conceiving a flexible industrial container able to react to the context and turn itself into an urban and community system.

Piano+Rogers Architects, Project of a hospital module for ARAM (Association of Rural Aid in Medicine), meeting sketch, December 14, 1970.

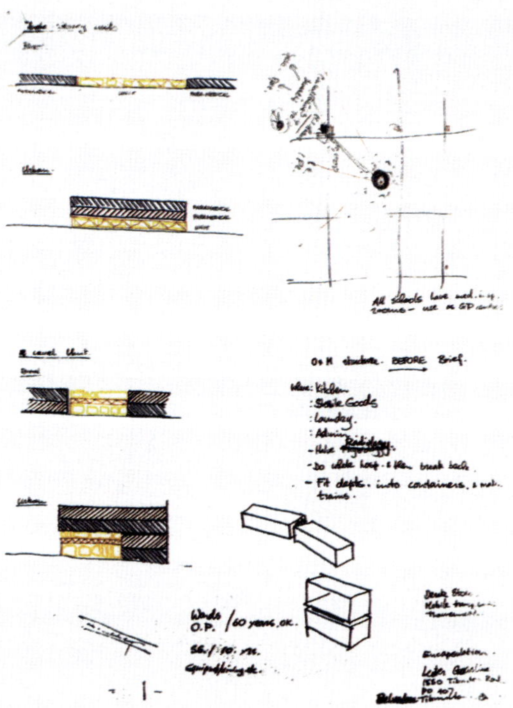

Piano+Rogers Architects, Project for a hospital module for ARAM, alternative solutions (soon discarded) (in order: "two and three activity zones with detached service tower"; "service floor with long bay and ephemeral activities arranged above and below"; "service floor with long bay and ephemeral activities arranged above only" and "service floor with long bay and containers arranged above").

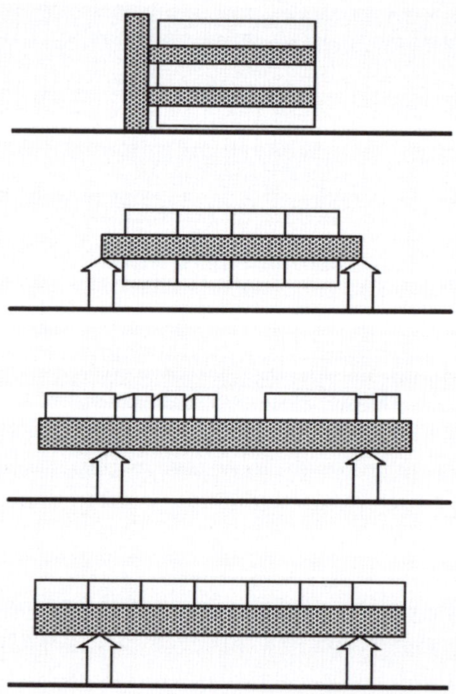

Tony Dugdale, Learning Shed (diploma project developed at the Architectural Association of London under the supervision of Cedric Price and Peter Cook), London, 1964–1965.

Renzo Piano, Industrial product advertisements selected for the "Container" research file, 1970.

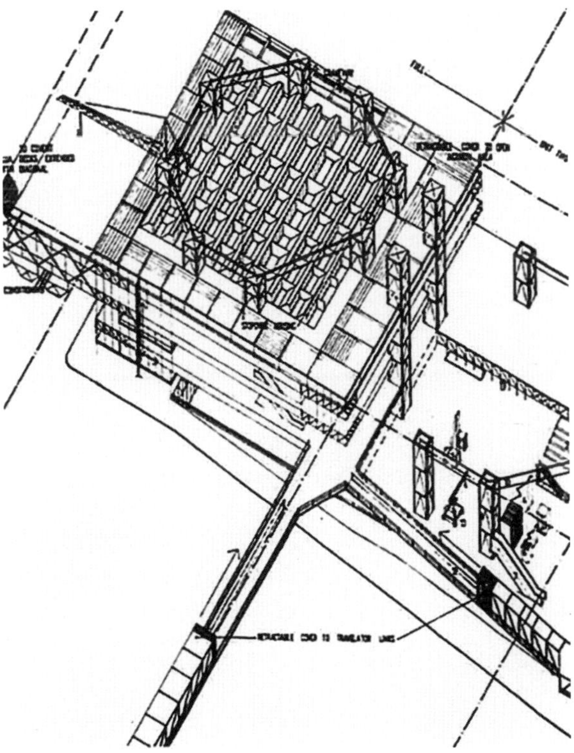

Piano+Rogers Architects, Project of a hospital module for ARAM, set in the Philadelphia suburbs, 1970–1971.

Piano+Rogers Architects, Project of a hospital module for ARAM, set in an Indian village,1970–1971.

Overleaf: Piano+Rogers Architects, Project of a hospital module for ARAM, set in the Philadelphia suburbs, section, 1970–1971.

zone de service
zone des activités
zone de service
Ullathorne st 2
Racine ave 1
EMERGENCY

ARAM
ARAM
community medicine

Richard+Su Rogers Architects, Fitzroy Street/Burleigh Street district shopping mall project, First feasibility study, section A1, Cambridge, March 1970.

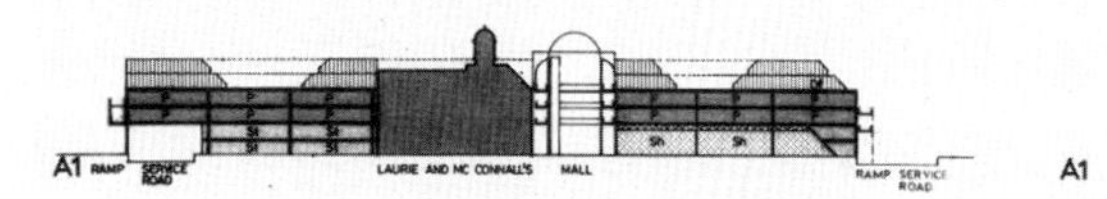

Richard+Su Rogers Architects, Fitzroyt shopping mall, First feasibility study, section A2, Cambridge, March 1970.

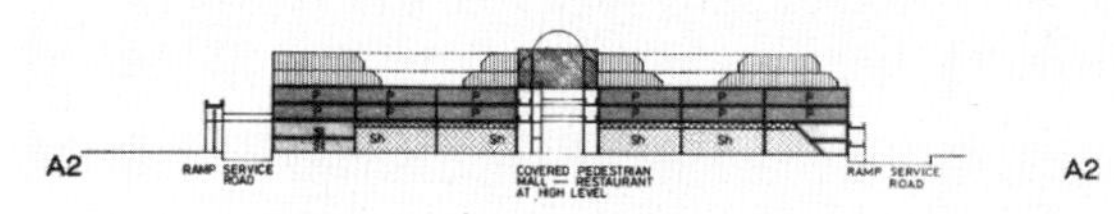

Richard+Su Rogers Architects, Fitzroy shopping mall, First feasibility study, ground floor plan, Cambridge, March 1970.

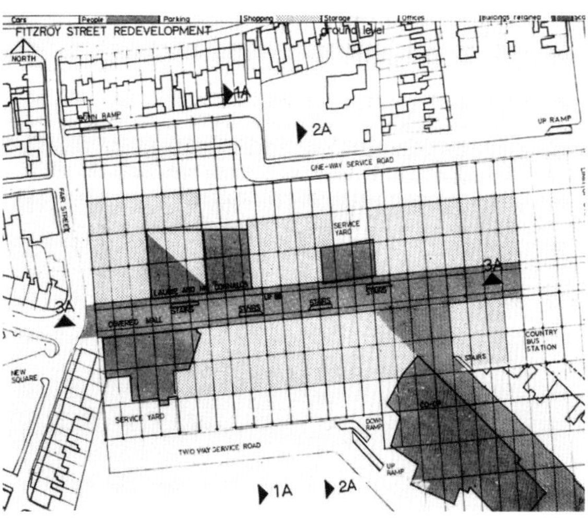

Richard+Su Rogers Architects, Fitzroy shopping mall, First feasibility study, first floor plan, Cambridge, March 1970.

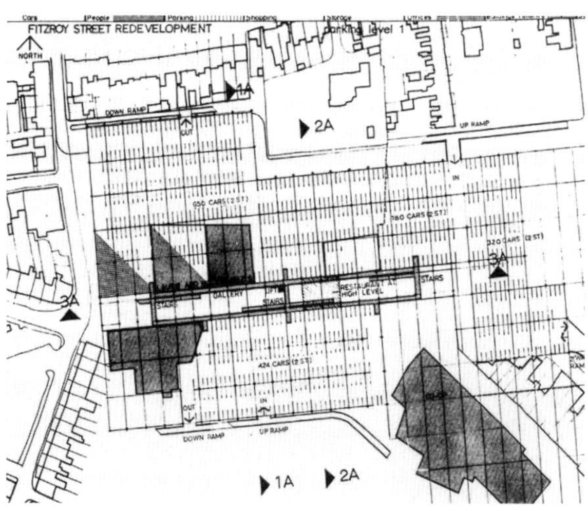

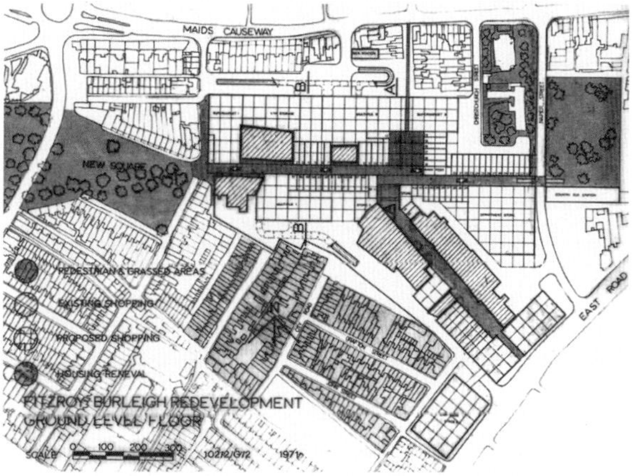

Piano+Rogers Architects, Fitzroy shopping mall, Third feasibility study, zoning, Cambridge, April 1971.

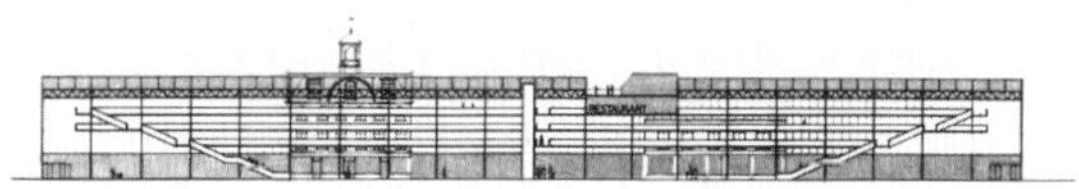

Piano+Rogers Architects, Fitzroy shopping mall, Third feasibility study, section, Cambridge, April 1971.

Piano+Rogers Architects, Fitzroy shopping mall, Third feasibility study, model, view on the passage, Cambridge, April 1971.

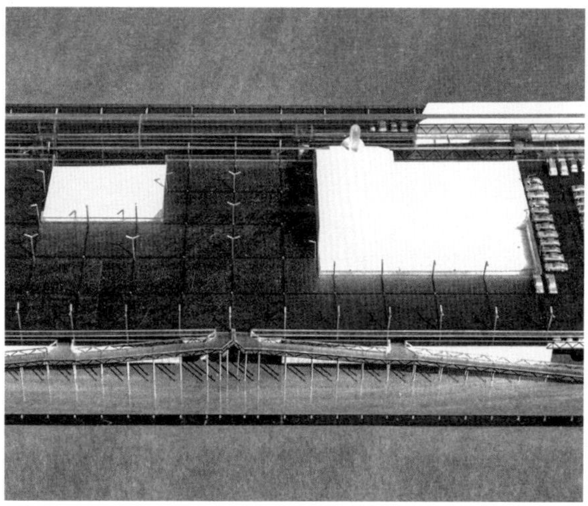

Piano+Rogers Architects, Fitzroy shopping mall, Third feasibility study, model aerial view, Cambridge, April 1971.

Piano+Rogers Architects, Fitzroy shopping mall, Third feasibility study, view of the passage (drawing by Gordon Cullen), Cambridge, April 1971.

Piano+Rogers Architects, Fitzroy shopping mall, Third feasibility study, view of the new park (drawing by Gordon Cullen), Cambridge, April 1971.

3.5

THE BURRELL GALLERY: FIRST THOUGHTS ON A TRANSLUCENT CONTAINER FOR ART

Since they were commissions initially given to Richard+Su Rogers, the ARAM hospital module and Fitzroy shopping mall projects could only represent partial opportunities to expand on the idea that Rogers and Piano had outlined with the school system. It was not until the competition for the Burrell Collection's new seat, known as well as the Burrell Gallery competition design, which Rogers and Piano decided to enter only after the latter's installation in the office at 32 Aybrook Street, that the pair could return to the ideas about the system they had initiated the previous year in order to see if they were compatible with a program, that of art conservation, which in this project they still considered an alternative to that of education, but in the end would be combined in the Centre Beaubourg competition. Drawn up entirely by Piano+Rogers Architects, the project for the new seat of the Burrell Gallery also represented the first real opportunity for Piano to combine the industrial envelopes of the practice based at 32 Aybrook Street with the special roofing modules on which he had been working since 1964. All this would make it possible to arrive not only at the first architectural application of the translucent roofing evoked the previous year with the school system, but even at the transformation of the entire envelope into a box of light.

Published in the *Royal Institute of British Architects Journal* in October 1970 with a deadline set for May 14, 1971 (then postponed to May 28), the Burrell competition invited architects registered with the Royal Institute of British Architects (RIBA) to design a new building for the art collection of the Scottish shipowner William Burrell (1861–1958), donated to the city of Glasgow in 1944 and housed in Hutton Castle, Burrell's private residence.[95] The collection consisted of over nine thousand pieces, dating from between the Middle Ages and the Renaissance and coming from Europe, China, and even Egypt, and included stained glass, doors, windows, suits of armor, pottery, and paintings by artists such as Degas and Cézanne. The site chosen by the Council for the collection's new home was a hillside bordered by ancient oaks in Pollok Park.[96]

The competition notice contained indications regarding not only the quantity and quality of the spaces but also the content and organization of the collection, the arrangement of the works and their grouping, and even an invitation to the participants to faithfully reproduce the interior decoration of three of the rooms in Hutton Castle.[97]

Instead of proposing a traditional building organized into a succession of rooms, as suggested by the notice, Piano+Rogers Architects opted for yet another variant of their industrial, prefabricated, and flexible systems.[98] Rejecting a rigid spatial organization for the artworks—"The aim has been for the Architecture not to straight-jacket the layout and viewing of the exhibits"—Piano+Rogers Architects envisaged an open setting able to offer "freedom of organisation to succeeding generations."[99] And it is precisely here that the Rogerses' shells' "freedom of choice" was applied to the museum program. With the desire to leave the organization of the museum's space to its curators and limit themselves to providing "a highly sensitive environment for the display and conservation of the collection," Rogers and Piano confirmed the role of the architect outlined in the Fitzroy project: offering users a democratic and undetermined infrastructure whose open organization they could freely self-determine.[100]

The "highly sensitive environment" took the form of a low container of an industrial character obtained by the combination of a complex metal structure with a translucent envelope that would have original lighting and spatial effects.

The structure consisted of two rows of external metal pillars supporting a colossal space frame composed of tubes and nodes as found in the kind of metal roofing in Konrad Wachsmann's and Buckminster Fuller's experiments and in the structural solutions used in the Osaka Expo pavilions. The preference for a daring metal structure over the Zip-Up series' self-supporting shells confirmed an orientation already evident in the ARAM module design.

Although Rogers was not uninterested in the possibilities of space frame built of metal—as is clear from his 1970 study of Wacksmann's *The Turning Point of Building: Structure and Design* (1961)—it was in Piano's research into prefabricated and standardized roofing that lay the origins of the roof for the Burrell Gallery.[101] From his study of Makowski's space frame, his participation in the activities of the Space Structures Research Centre in London, his reading of *Steel Space Structure*, and his research into the Mero structural system commissioned from the engineer Marano, Piano derived a structural expertise that between 1968 and 1969 had already been applied in the space frame roofs of the projects of a nursery school with two classrooms and a boat club on the Olona River, and in solutions where the space frame was transformed into a self-supporting portal structure, as in the case of the studio-workshop at Erzelli or the design for a yacht club.[102]

Against the background of experiments integrating technical systems into building envelopes carried out in the sixties, from Zanuso's hollow structures for Olivetti to Albini's partial masking of the Rinascente department store plant in Rome or the SNAM power company offices in Milan to Piano's experimental integration of envelope and technical plant in the Olivetti-Underwood factory roof in Harrisburg, Piano+Rogers Architects favored a space frame able to combine structure and plant.[103] It is likely Piano's experience in roof designs using specially fabricated pieces that lay behind the idea of developing a special Mero structure for the Burrell Gallery based on hollow tubes and spherical nodes able to ensure the passage, emission, and recovery of air. The project report has this to say on the subject: "This overall roof sandwich would be supported on a clear span tubular space deck, with conditioned air distributed through the tubes and discharged at special cast nodes."[104] The configuration of the nodes and recourse to the technique of steel casting reveals how this detail is derived from the ball joints of the space frame of Koji Kamiya's Theme Pavilion. Whether or not Happold discussed the ball joints with Rogers and Piano during the development of the Beaubourg project, there can be no doubt that this reference was due to Piano, who on his visits to the Osaka Expo to supervise the construction of his Italian Industry Pavilion took numerous photographs of the Theme Pavilion's ball joints.[105]

To put the idea of that "highly sensitive environment" into effect, Piano+Rogers Architects took the concept of a translucent and radiant surface proposed for the school system and extended it from the roof to the entire envelope. This transformation was no longer limited to the illumination of work and study areas that had interested Piano in the preceding years, but was also connected with the effects of transparency and translucency of the luminous boxes that had fascinated Rogers during his studies, from Chareau and Bijvoet's Maison de verre to Johnson's Glass House at New Canaan, as well as with the original effects of the Free University of Brussels' reflective envelope designed by Nizzoli Associati and group 1999, known to Piano.[106]

The sensitivity towards context was reflected in the search for an envelope with a reflective surface to dematerialize the building in the daytime and turn it into a luminous lantern at night.[107] "The mirror-glass walls and roof reflect the trees and sky during the day, whilst during the night the Museum will become translucent, bathing the surrounding trees in light."[108] A similar reflective device was also used in two projects by Foster Associates between 1969 and 1971, the Operations-Amenity Centre commissioned by Fred Olsen Ltd in London and the IBM Pilot Head Office in Portsmouth, on whose development Kaplický, one of the collaborators of the office at 32 Aybrook Street, worked as a draftsman.[109] In addition, the study of a container for the display and conservation of art led Rogers and Piano toward a different kind of screening and translucent element from Ludwig Mies van der Rohe's transparent envelopes and from the one designed by Foster. For the Burrell Gallery, Rogers and Piano considered a technological envelope that would filter the natural light to produce effects that could be varied to meet the curators' needs. These were the characteristics of the container that Rogers and Piano described as a "total light box." "The museum is a total light box, which offers sophisticated controls of degree, quality and character of light, according to the requirements of individual exhibits."[110]

The idea of the total light box crystallized in the use of a special multilayer panel to be applied to the whole of the envelope, on both the façade and the roof: another of those components of industrial origin, from the Zip-Up series' sandwich panels to the ARAM module's metal panels, that the Rogerses transferred to the world of construction in order to evaluate its compositional, spatial, and structural effects. The element chosen, which may have been identical to the one conceived for the Fitzroy shopping mall, was a panel, made by the German Okalux company, that consisted of a membrane of microscopic tubes inserted between two glass panels able to insulate and filter light. With the aim of defining a sophisticated and mechanized envelope and offering Burrell Gallery curators total freedom of choice, Rogers and Piano did not opt for the undifferentiated use of standard Okalux panels, but came up with a whole catalogue of them, made up of special pieces with different degrees of translucency.

The Okalux roof panel was inserted in a system composed of a low dome glazed with mirror glass and a series of mechanically operated louvers[111] derived from the polyester modules Piano conceived for controlling light, such as the roof panel for the studio-workshop at Erzelli (1969) and the sheds for Olivetti in Scarmagno and Crema created with

Zanuso. For the outer envelope, Rogers and Piano resorted instead to a module created by coupling an external panel of mirror glass, applied on both sides, with an internal panel available in the "Okalux" version but also in "solid" and "lightweight" ones and even an "optical" version able to create plays of light and luminous effects in the manner of Salvadori's artworks, with whom Piano had collaborated and Piano+Rogers Architects were trying to develop new work opportunities in December 1970.[112]

With the appearance of the "optical" version, the envelope was turned into a playful and interactive system halfway between the industrial containers conceived by Foster and the kind of fanciful technology that animated Archigram's projects. In these "optical" panels lay the models for the screens transmitting light, color and information that Piano+Rogers Architects were developing in the same weeks for the Centre Beaubourg.

The Burrell Gallery container allowed interiors to be organized around a large and undivided rectangular space in which to house the collection. At the side there was an area on two levels, containing on the ground floor a restoration workshop, the collection reserve, and technical rooms, and on the second floor a terrace opening onto the exhibition space that was divided into an area devoted to temporary exhibitions, an open-plan office, a conference room, and several accessory areas for visitors and staff.

The attention to flows of people that had generated the project for the Fitzroy shopping mall led to the conception of a spectacular movement system located between the exhibition area and the accessory area. It consisted of a large hoist set in a glass prism and a flight of stairs running the entire length of the building that harked back to the industrial airplane boarding stairs used by the Rogerses since 1966, as well as to the escalators hitched onto the Fitzroy shopping mall.[113] In its positioning as a sort of theatrical backdrop to the exhibition area and in the display of the dynamics of its mechanism and the people in motion on it, the Burrell project circulation system can no longer be described simply as a functional piece of equipment. Instead, as in the case of the envelope, it reflects Piano+Rogers Architects' emphasis on recreation, something that would inspire the Centre Beaubourg and turn its stairs, hoists, and elevators into a source of entertainment for visitors.

Delivered on May 28, 1971, Piano+Rogers Architects' proposal for the Burrell Gallery competition did not get past the first stage, even though there were two people on the jury who would have been able to grasp its innovative character: Theo Crosby, an architect close to the Archigram group and advocate at *Architectural Design* for the promotion of experimental avant-garde projects from Britain and other countries; and Philip Dowson, a collaborator with Ove Arup and founder of Arup Associates.[114]

With the ARAM module, the Fitzroy shopping mall, and the Burrell Gallery building, Piano+Rogers Architects' intention to experiment with cheap industrial containers that could be adapted to any purpose was made clear, as was their willingness to resort to special components, from the ARAM module's guyed structure to the Burrell Collection's ball joints and sophisticated reflective and screening envelope. In these designs it is also evident that the factors of functionality, flexibility and efficiency represented just one part of the values that Piano and the Rogerses intended to infuse into their projects. Piano+Rogers Architects' shells also took the political and social character of the architectural project into account in an effort to encompass the containers within "an integrated environmental plan" that would be sensitive to the context and to proceed with a domestication of functional, early machine-age technology to produce devices of an interactive, playful, and popular character.

Piano+Rogers Architects, Competition proposal for an exhibition gallery at the Burrell Art Collection (known as the Burrell Gallery), section and masterplan, spring 1971.

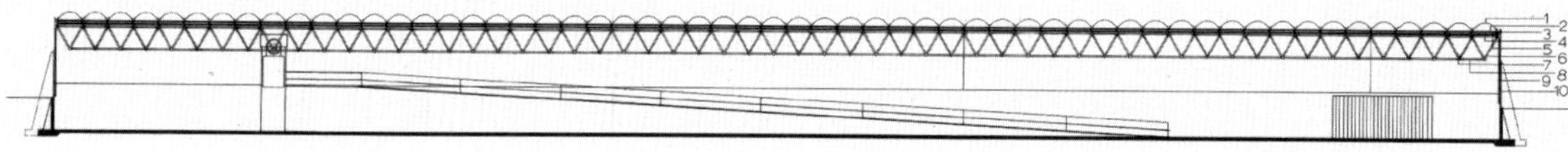

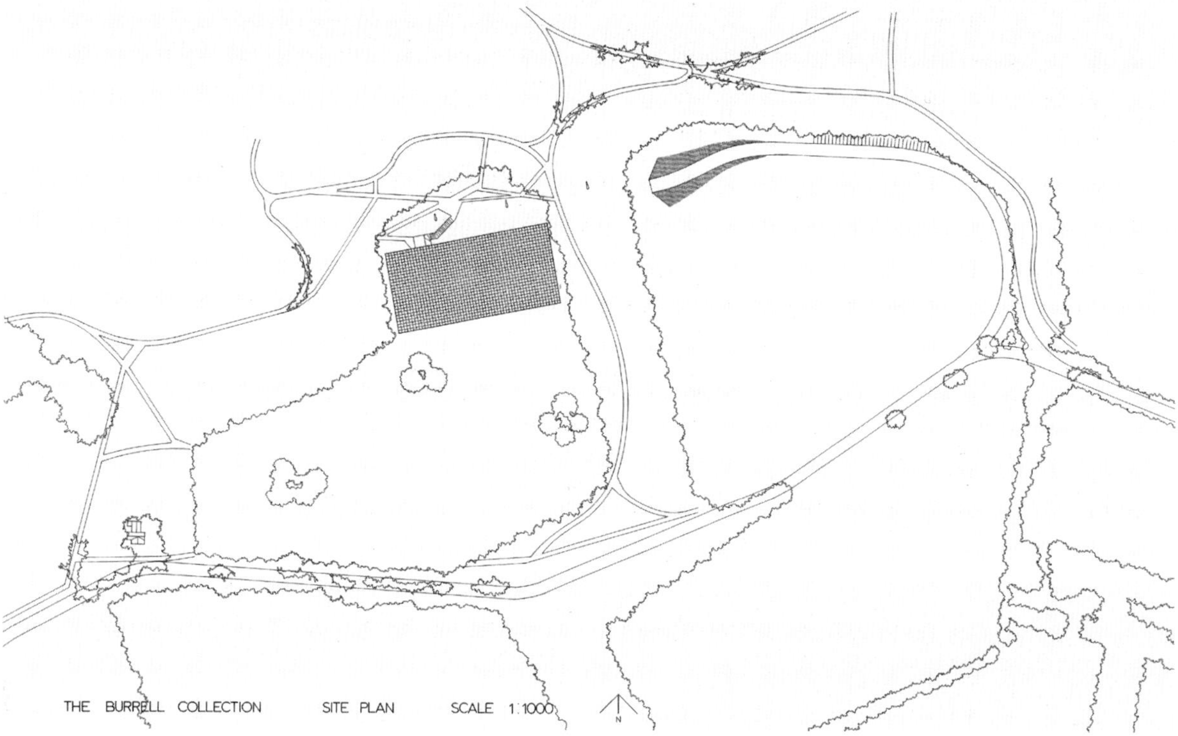

Piano+Rogers Architects, Competition proposal for the Burrell Gallery, elevation and ground floor plan, spring 1971.

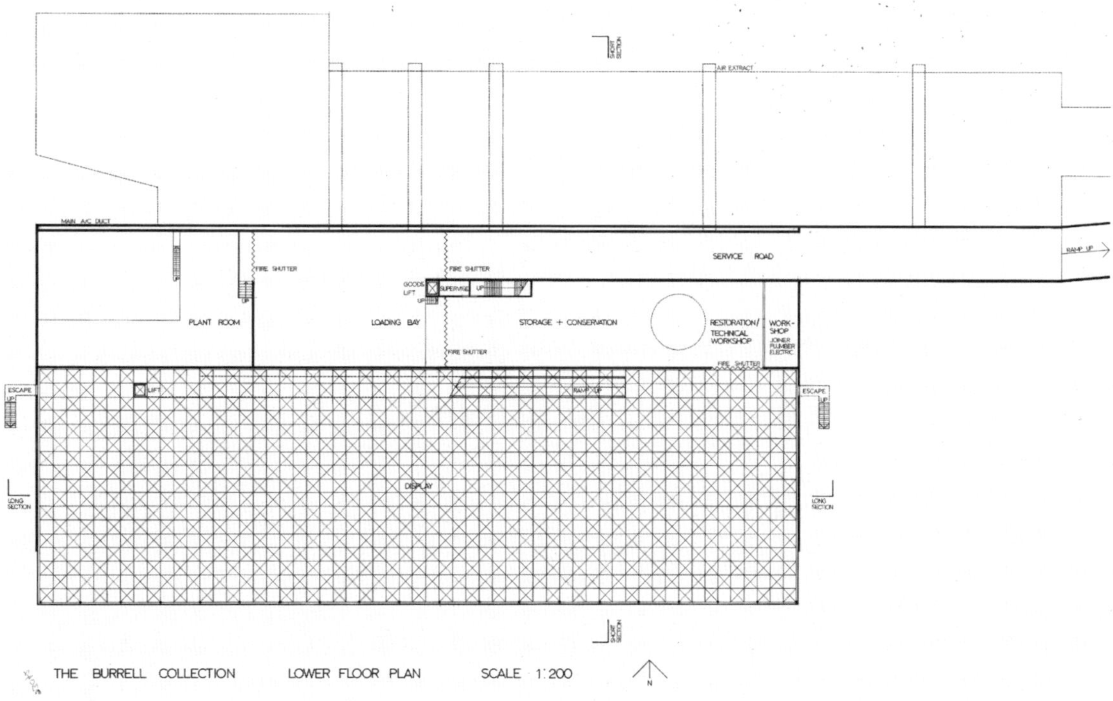

Renzo Piano Architetto, Project for a Yacht Club, sections, 1969.

Renzo Piano Architetto, Project for a Yacht Club, elevation, 1969.

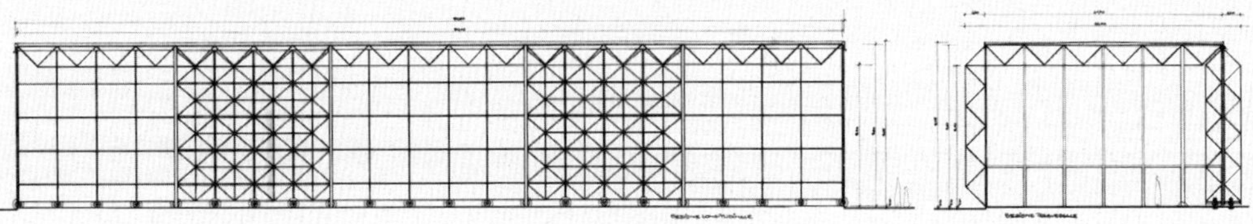

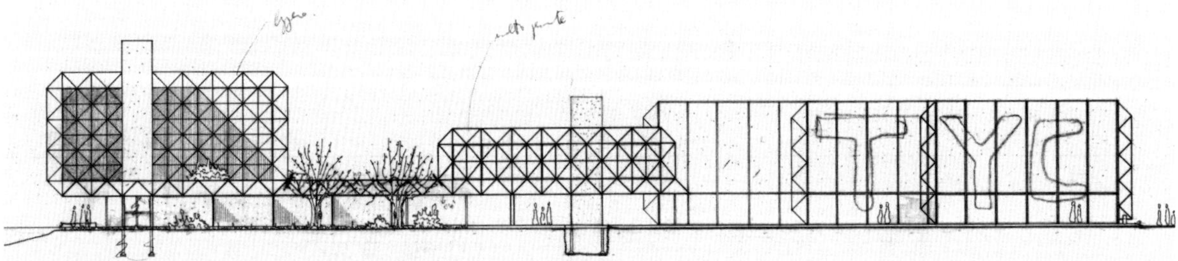

Piano+Rogers Architects, Competition proposal for the Burrell Gallery, space frame detail, 1971.

Kenzo Tange, Koji Kamiya and Yoshikatsu Tsuboi, Theme Pavilion, Osaka, space frame detail, 1969-1970.

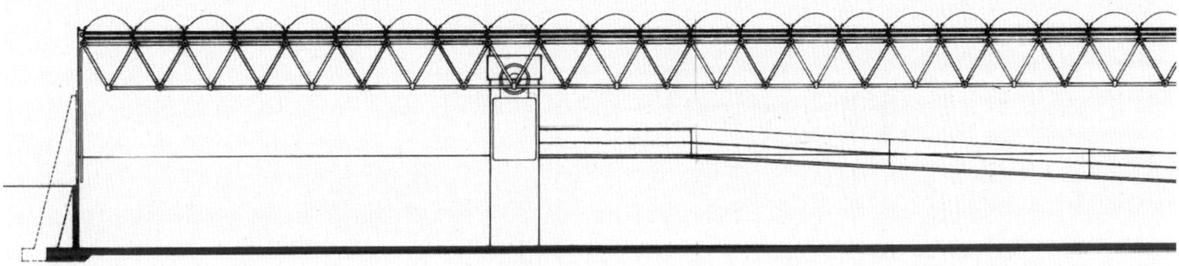

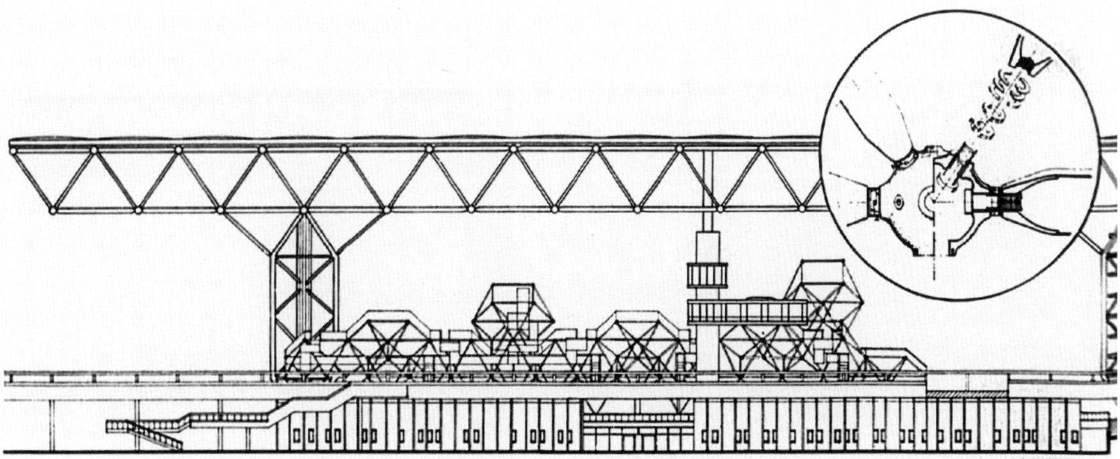

Renzo Piano, Photographs of the space frame and ball joints of the Theme Pavilion, taken during a visit to the construction site of the Italian Industry Pavilion, Osaka, 1969.

Piano+Rogers Architects, Competition proposal for the Burrell Gallery, view of Pollok park with the Okalux reflective panel envelope, Glasgow, spring 1971.

Norman Foster Associates, IBM Pilot Head Office project, view of park with translucent and reflective panel envelope, Portsmouth, 1970–1971.

1 — Su Rogers, "Environmental Planning and Its Influence on the Family," in *The Family and its Future: A Ciba Foundation Symposium* (London: CIBA Foundation, 1970), 72.

2 — Ibid.

3 — In the article published in *Domus* in 1965 the only name Rogers mentioned was that of Charles Eames. It is only in more recent interviews and monographs that Rogers made reference to the Case Study Houses and his meeting with one of their designers, the architect Craig Elwood. Richard Rogers and Ludovic Chazaszcz, "Paris 1930," *Domus*, 443 (1966), 8. For the references to Jean Prouvé, Pierre Chareau, Bernard Bijvoet, and James Stirling, see again Rogers's article in *Domus*. The first explicit reference by the Rogerses to Archigram's theories can be found in Su's contribution to a CIBA Foundation symposium in which she mentioned Archigram and the British group's Control and Choice project. The name "Peter Cook" is noted in pencil on the preparatory notes for the article. Rogers, "Environmental Planning and Its Influence on the Family," 74, 76. Su Rogers, Preparatory notes for "Environmental Planning and Its Influence on the Family," n.d. [1969], RSHPA, C01, J0002, F ARC5. As far as the approach to design based on experimentation with "Lightweight building" with "components" coming from industry is concerned, see Sheila Wheeler, "Setting Up in Practice," *Architects' Journal*, 153, no. 3 (1971), 121–62: 154.

4 — Wheeler, "Setting Up in Practice," 154.

5 — Rogers, "Environmental Planning and Its Influence on the Family," 69, 71. Richard and Su Rogers' sensitivity to the question of community against the background of environmental planning is underlined in the introduction to the report on the ARAM modular hospital-unit project conceived between 1970 and 1971. "With every increase in productive power," wrote the Rogerses, "society increases its capacity to both create and destroy. The great panaceas of religion, technology, capitalism and socialism have failed to meet the growing crisis. Radical and urgent though the problems are, habits still turn us for solutions to traditional formulae and recurring revolution. A community only holds together because a society makes sense to its members. When, as now, our institutions, industry, education, government, law and public services have become separate entities, they can no longer perform their function within the community. Every large-scale system must allow for individual ethnic groups to operate freely within it and respond to their own, locally based empirical methods." Piano+Rogers Architects, Service Module for the Association of Rural Aid in Medicine, Inc., March 1971, RSHPA, C01, J0002, n.p. [Introduction].

6 — Rogers, "Environmental Planning and Its Influence on the Family," 70.

7 — On Richard's activism, see: Bryan Appleyard, *Richard Rogers: A Biography* (London: Faber & Faber 1986); Enrique Walker, "Renzo Piano & Richard Rogers in conversation with Enrique Walker," *AA Files*, 70 (2015), 46–59: 54. On Su's activism, see Boris Hamzeian, Interview with Su Rogers, October 8, 2017, London, n.p. On the part Ruthie's played in Richard's political engagement, see Appleyard, *Richard Rogers: A Biography*, 147–52.

8 — Together with "zoning" and "flexibility," "freedom of choice" was one of the basic principles of Su's theory of environmental planning. Rogers, "Environmental Planning and Its Influence on the Family," 71, 72.

9 — The results of the course are included in a monograph published by Marco Zanuso and his assistants, Piano and Renato Lucci. Marco Zanuso, Renzo Piano, and Renato Lucci, *Elementi di Tecnologia dei materiali come introduzione allo studio del design* (Milan: Tamburini Editore, 1967). For the research into prefabrication, see the catalogue of the exhibition held at the Architectural Association School in 1969 and edited by Renzo Piano. In this connection see, too, Lorenzo Ciccarelli's monograph analyzing Piano's early career and the principal works he conceived in the sixties. Lorenzo Ciccarelli, *Renzo Piano before Renzo Piano: Masters and Beginnings* (Macerata: Quodlibet, 2017).

10 — Piano had been following Zygmunt Stanislaw Makowski's research since the mid-sixties, as attested by the presence in his library of the proceedings of the conference *Plastic in Building Structures*, held in London in June 1965 and published the following year, as well as two articles that the Polish engineer published the same year in *Architectural Design*. *Plastic in Building Structures*, conference proceedings, London, June 14–15, 1965 (Oxford: Pergamon Press, 1966); Zygmunt Stanislaw Makowski, "A Survey of Recent Three-Dimensional Structures," *Architectural Design*, no. 36 (January 1966), 10–39; Zygmunt Stanislaw Makowski, "Space Structures and the Electronic Computer," *Architectural Design*, no. 36 (January 1966), 8–9. In the spring of 1966 Piano visited Makowski in London and the Space Structure Research Centre at the University of Surrey in Guildford, of which Makowski was the director. This visit is recorded in some photographs taken by Piano on that occasion. The same year Makowski involved Piano in the First International Conference on Space Structures and included the works of the Genoese architect in the report on such experimentation in architecture published in *Art & Architecture*. Zygmunt Stanislaw Makowski, "Structural Plastic in Europe," *Art & Architecture*, no. 7 (1966), 20–30. After graduating, Piano met Jean Prouvé on a study trip to France in 1966 during which he also visited public housing projects in Marly and Pantin and two houses designed by Prouvé. In Paris Piano attended one of Prouvé's lectures in the course Art Applied to the Crafts that Prouvé taught at the Conservatoire national des arts et métiers, where he was also able to see his students' projects. The visit to the conservatory is documented in a report Piano drew up containing notes and photographs of the visit, still unpublished and kept at the Fondazione Renzo Piano in Genoa. Piano met Robert Le Ricolais in 1966 at the International Conference on Space Structures at the University of Surrey and, a few years later, decided to go to see him in Philadelphia, where he was running a research laboratory on experimental structures.
On Piano's notes and photographs of the trip to Paris and the meeting with Prouvé, see the documents found by Hamzeian in 2020 at the Fondazione Renzo Piano. See, too, Ciccarelli, *Renzo Piano before Renzo Piano.*

11 — *Kunstoffen In Dragende Konstrukties, Stichting Post-Doktoraal Onderwijs In Het Bouwen, 16/17 Oktober 1969* (Delft: TU Delft University, 1969).

12 — Renzo Piano, *Architectural Research by Renzo Piano* (London: Centre for Advanced Study of Science in Art, 1967). On Marcello Salvadori, see Emmanuel Bénézit, *Dictionary of Artists* (Paris: Gründ, 2006).

13 — Renzo Piano, *Architecture Experiment: Renzo Piano at the Architectural Association of London, June 23rd- July 5th 1969,* (London: Architectural Association, 1969).

14 — Renzo Piano, "Ricerca sulle strutture in lamiera e in poliestere rinforzato," *Domus*, no. 448 (1967), 8–22; Renzo Piano, "Nasce con le materie plastiche un nuovo modo di progettare l'architettura," *Materie plastiche ed elastometri*, no. 1 (1969), 2–20; Renzo Piano, "Renzo Piano," in *Architectural Design*, no. 3 (1970), 140–45.

15 — In relation to Piano's research and interests, see the articles annotated or simply indicated with a bookmark in his personal library (now housed at the Fondazione Renzo Piano, Genoa). Among them: Kenzo Tange, "Un piano per Tokyo," *Casabella-Continuità*, no. 258 (1961), 3–31; "I progetti di Metabolism," *Casabella*, no. 273 (March 1963), 30–38; "Il concorso per il centro di Skopje. 20 July 1965," *Casabella*, no. 307 (July 1966), 24–29; Paolo Riani, "La Città come trasformazione biologica," *Casabella*, no. 327 (June 1968), 10–19. Mike Jerome, "Whatever Happened to the Metabolism," *Architectural Design*, no. 5 (1967), 208–17.

16 — Among the sources in Piano's personal library: Guido Canella, "Vecchie e nuove ipotesi per i centri direzionali," *Casabella*, no. 275 (1963), 50–56; Francesco Tentori, "La città territorio, un esperimento didattico sul centro direzionale di Cento Celle a Roma," *Casabella*, no. 289 (1964), 50–54; Raffaella Sacchetti Bedosti and Mario Zaffagnini, "Dopo Cumbernauld. 1. New Towns e Design urbano," *Casabella*, no. 328 (1968), 6–25.

17 — These projects were brought to Piano's notice by a celebrated article written by L. M. Boschini in defense of the utopias imagined by the postwar avant-gardes. Many of the projects presented by Boschini, which included some by the Metabolism Group, would be proposed by Piano in an exhibition he staged with Marcello Salvadori at the Milan Triennale in 1968 under the title *Changing Form in Architecture*. L. M. Boschini, "Utopia come ipotesi di lavoro," *Casabella*, no. 305 (1966), 16–25. Renzo Piano, *Changing Form in Architecture*, catalogue of the exhibition at the 14th Milan Triennale curated by Renzo Piano for the Centre for Advanced Study of Science in Art, London (Milan: Edizioni della Triennale di Milano, 1968).

18 — Piano analyzed numerous designs of mobile and transportable units published in magazines. See: "Habitat mobile et extensible, étude théorique des étudiants du collège d'art de Hornsey Grande Bretagne," *L'Architecture d'Aujourd'hui*, no. 124 (1966), 96–97; Dieter Schmid, "Maison préfabriquée en matière plastique à Biberach, Allemagne," *L'Architecture d'Aujourd'hui*, no. 124 (1966), 98–101; Hausermann, Camoletti et Hoechel architectes, "Cellule préfabriquée en matière plastique," *Architecture d'aujour'dui*, no. 124 (1966), 102; Gérard Ifert and Rudolf Meyer, "Prenegozio viaggiante," *Domus*, no. 457 (1967), 24; Jean Duret, Diborodan and Dobrila Vasilevic architects, "Cellule abitative prefabbricate in accaio: una proposta per l'edilizia industrializzata," *Domus*, no. 470 (1969), 17–20; J. Vredevoogd, "La casa in viaggio," *Domus*, no. 470 (1969), 21–25; Wolfgang Doring, "Pre-fa: cellule in plastica," *Domus*, no. 467 (1968), 12–13.; Wilfred Lubiz, "La casa in viaggio," *Domus*, no. 467 (1968), 14–15; Jean Louis Lotiron and Pernette Martin-Perriand, "La casa in viaggio," *Domus*, no. 467 (1968), 16; G. R. Oliveri, "Industrializzazione dell'edilizia," *Casabella*, no. 310 (1966), 24–31. To this kind of project can be added the fitted containers of Peter Cook's Ideas Circus project, published by Piero Sartogo in *Casabella*. That Piano was familiar with this project is attested by the numerous annotations he made on the article in pencil. Carlo Pelliccia and Piero Sartogo, "Campus Design. 5. Le vie individuali all'istruzione come alternativa alle istituzioni educazionali," *Casabella*, no. 332 (1969), 11–17. Piano's readings on the subject were accompanied by research into the use of shipping containers in the design of inhabitable environments. In this connection see his collection of advertisements for containers taken from trade magazines: Renzo Piano, Untitled [Research into shipping containers], n.d. [1968–70], FRP, C photographs,

F references.

19 — Renzo Piano and Alessandro Cereda, "Alcune recenti esperienze nel campo della industrializzazione edilizia – tre architetture di Renzo Piano," *L'industria italiana per l'edilizia–LIPE*, no. 3 (1970), 95–106. That Piano derived the structural and evolutionary logic of the megastructure from the projects of the Metabolism Group seems to be confirmed by his reading of numerous articles devoted to the Japanese group, commencing with the report published in *Casabella*: "I progetti di Metabolism," *Casabella*, no. 273, entire issue.

20 — Both these features were picked out by Piano with bookmarks inserted in the respective issues in his library, now at the Fondazione Renzo Piano. "L'incontro fra antico e nuovo," *Casabella*, no. 314 (1967), 14–53; William Cowburn, ed., "Housing and the Environment," *The Architectural Review*,141, no. 11 (1967), entire issue. Among the other writings on the theme of the city and its conservation singled out by Piano it is worth mentioning the reflections on the spatial plan of the Milanese hinterland, the analysis of the Parisian banlieue and the British New Towns, as well as those on the townscape. Ernesto Nathan Rogers, "Milano. La coscienza di una metropoli," *Casabella-Continuità*, no. 256 (1961), 2–3; Virgilio Vercelloni, "Milano 1861–1961: un secolo di occasioni mancate nello sviluppo della città," *Casabella-Continuità*, no. 256 (1961), 28–41; Ian Nairn, "Stop Press (Outrage: a Monthly Anthology From All Over Britain of Townscape Problems, Outrages and Opportunities)," *The Architectural Review*, several issues (1968–69); Salvatore Tintori and Giancarlo De Carlo, "Il piano intercomunale milanese," *Casabella*, no. 282 (1963), 4–27; Aldo Rossi, "La città e la periferia," *Casabella-Continuità*, no. 253 (1961), 23–27; Giuseppe Campos Venuti, "Bologna un esempio concreto di pianificazione comprensoriale," *Casabella*, no. 269 (1962), 4–28.

21 — From the feature in issue no. 314 of *Casabella*, Piano picked out several articles: "Il problema dei valori ambientali" by Pane (14–16); "Antico e nuovo come valori" by De Fusco (pp. 17–18); "Ipotesi per la costruzione di un modello in rapporto alla sua specifica struttura temporale" by D. Borradori (37–38); "Tre considerazioni sui centri storici" by P. Marconi (43–44); and "L'economia urbana nella trasformazione del centro antico" by C. Mercogliano (46–53). Piano also cut out several of the feature's illustrations, all part of the "visual census of the Italian cultural and artificial heritage and the damage done to it," compiled by R. Bazzoni on the occasion of the exhibition *Italia da salvare*, staged on behalf of the association Italia Nostra. The first two images in the survey, of Piazza del Campo in Siena and the new districts of Rome respectively, would be selected by Piano to illustrate his theory on the "integrated design of the environment" published in *Architectural Design* in 1970. Piano also placed a bookmark on J. R. Nicholls article in the same issue: J. R. Nicholls, "In the Townscape," *Architectural Review*, 113 (1967), 335–40.

22 — The book, published in English in 1969, is an expanded and revised version of *Gaibon Kukai No Kosei* (*Exterior Space in Architecture*), brought out in 1962 by the Japanese publisher Shokokusha in Tokyo. Yoshinobu Ashihara, *Exterior Design in Architecture* (New York: Van Nostrand Reinhold, 1970).

23 — "The square, or piazza, is far more than so many square feet of open space; it is a way of life, a concept of living. Indeed, it might be said that the Italians have the smallest bedrooms but the largest living rooms of Europe. For the square, the street, and the sidewalks are their living space, their playroom, their front 'parlor.' Their tiny, ill-lit, crowded flats are primarily spots for sleep, love, meals and possessions." Ashihara, *Exterior Design in Architecture*, 16.

24 — "Only when the architect gives sufficient attention not only to the space occupied by the buildings he designs, but also to space not occupied by his buildings—that is when he pays attention to the reverse space—only when he designs the surroundings of his buildings as positive space, or only when he conceives of the whole building plot as one piece of architecture and of the parts without a roof as space, does he really begin to design exterior space." Ibid.

25 — Piano, "Renzo Piano," 140–45; Piano and Cereda, "Alcune recenti esperienze nel campo dell'industrializzazione edilizia."

26 — "The view of the centre of old Siena (1) shows how in medieval times the city centre was conceived as a whole; multifunctional and yet integrated into a marvelously complex unity. The aerial view of postwar Rome (2) shows precisely the opposite development—the structure of the city is degraded precisely because of the discrete conception of each building and the failure of the plan to make a sensible unit out of the complex as a whole." Piano, "Renzo Piano," 140.

27 — "Particularly noticeable is the way in which the streets and open spaces perform no *connecting* function but merely operate as *negative spaces*." Piano, "Renzo Piano," 140. "The finding that human settlements in the city are consolidated into monofunctional organisms, into separate blocks (housing–housing–housing, offices–offices–offices, factories-factories-factories), and that free spaces, streets and squares, are nothing more than what is left once the organisms have been removed, i.e. that they have lost their role of connective tissue in an urban framework of functionally and structurally complex organisms, leads to the assumption of functional, structural and spatial integration between the different organisms that make up the urban environment as a general aim of planning." Cereda, "Alcune recenti esperienze nel campo dell'industrializzazione edilizia," 95.

28 — Denis Clarke Hall and Partners, "School 1, Richmond," *The Architectural Review*, 139, 276–78; Stillman and East-Wickfield, "School 2, Hampstead (Stillman and East-Wickfield)," *The Architectural Review*, 139, 281–88; Erickson Massey Architects and Planners, "Ridge-top University (Simon Fraser University, British Columbia)," *The Architectural Review*, 143 (1968), 266–76; Gillespie, Kidd, and Coia, "Student centre, Hull University," *The Architectural Review*, 145 (1969), 190–92; Sheppard Robson, "Claremont Complex. Science/art Building, Newcastle University," *The Architectural Review*, 144 (1968), 170–78; Leonard Manasseh, "Communal and Residential, teachers' training college, Streatham," *The Architectural Review*, 137 (1965), 171–74; Gunnar Birkerts & Associates, "The School that Will Vanish," *The Architectural Forum*, 127, no. 4 (1967), 48–53; Joseph Rykwert, "Londra, una scuola 'lineare' (una nuova scuola media nel quartiere di Pimlico, progetto del Greater County Council)," *Domus*, no. 442 (1966), 11–14; Chiuminatto e Gambino, Ivrea, "La scuola sul colle," *Domus*, no. 441 (1966), 9–14; Costantino Corsini, Giorgio Wiskemann architetti, "Una scuola come una industria," *Domus*, no. 467 (1968), 18–19; Maurizio Sacripanti, architetto, "Prefabbricazione, Scuola elementare Feal," *Domus*, no. 486 (1970), 8–12 (annotated with underlinings and sketches); Mario Ridolfi and Volfango Frankl, "Scuola media a Terni, 1953–1960," *Casabella-Continuità*, no. 256 (1961), 32–37; Leonardo Fiori, "Dalla esperienza di Brusson agli standard per la scuola," in *Casabella-Continuità*, no. 256 (1961), 51–52 (annotated with underlinings and sketches); Emilio Mattioni, "Istituto tecnico industriale a Pordenone," *Casabella-Continuità*, no. 256 (1963), 36–38; Kammerer and Belz, "Scuola speciale a Stoccarda," *Casabella*, no. 313 (1967), 22–35 (with bookmark of Piano+Rogers Architects); Cavallotti and Schmidlin, "Scuola elementare a Monza. Via della Birona," *Architettura: cronache e storia*, 12, 720–23 (illustrations cut out); Pelliccia and Sartogo, "Campus Design, 5. Le vie individuali all'istruzione come alternativa alle istituzioni educazionali," *Casabella*, no. 332 (1969), 12–17 (Plug-In University Node, Ideas Circus projects); Giovanni Bruzzone and Marco Dasso, "Un ciclo aperto nell'edilizia scolastica," *Casabella*, no. 329 (1968), 16–27; Carlo Pelliccia and Piero Sartogo, "Campus Design, 2. Analisi ed ipotesi di sviluppo dell'istruzione superiore negli USA," *Casabella*, no. 323 (1968), 10–19; Carlo Pelliccia and Piero Sartogo, "Campus Design, 1. Il passaggio da una struttura monofunzionale ad una structtura integrata dell'educazione," *Casabella*, no. 322 (1968), 20–25; Nizzoli Associati and group 1999, "Didattica permanente. Progetto per l'università libera di Brussels," *Casabella*, no. 349 (1970), 9–12; John Andrews, "Scarborough College," *The Architectural Design*, 37, no. 4 (1967), 178–87; Cedric Price, ed., "What about Learning?" *Architectural Design*, 38, no. 5 (1968), entire issue; Jürgen Joedicke and Erwin Heinle, "École supérieure d'enseignement pédagogique et école officielle de sport de Ludwigsburg," *Bauen+Wohnen*, 20, no. 11 (1966), 412–25; "École primaire à Neckarweihingen," *Bauen+Wohnen*, 20, no. 11 (1966), 434–35; Jürgen Joedicke, "Meredith Memorial Hall Drake Universitat, Des Moines/Iowa," *Bauen+Wohnen*, 20, no. 11, (1966), 177–80; "Prolycée à Binningue près de Bâle," *Bauen+Wohnen*, 20, no. 4 (1966) 130–39; L. K., "École de classes primaires supérieures à Frauenfeld," *Bauen+Wohnen*, 21, no. 10 (1967), 373–76; "Gymnase Droste-Hülshoff à Fribourg en Brisgau," *Bauen+Wohnen*, 21, no. 10 (1967), 381–88; "Image faisant ressortir la diversité," in *Bauen+Wohnen*, 24, no. 2 (1970), 65–67; "Bâtiment des auditoriums de l'École technique supérieure de Delft," *Bauen+Wohnen*, 22, no. 5 (1968), 175–79; "École supérieure à Botby, Helsinki," *Bauen+Wohnen*, 23, no. 4 (1969), 130–31.

29 — "The problem of campus design," declared Sartogo, "is strongly oriented toward a not just functional but also emblematic integration of typically academic activities with urban and territorial ones." Both passages were underlined by Piano. Pelliccia and Sartogo, "Campus Design, 1. Il passaggio da una struttura monofunzionale ad una struttura integrata dell'educazione," 20–25: 21

30 — The projects mentioned were included in *Casabella*'s campus design feature and were picked out by Piano. Of particular interest to him was the Ideas Circus project, whose illustrations he annotated.

31 — Renzo Piano, "Architecture and Technology," *Architectural Association Quarterly*, 2, no. 3 (1970), 32–43.

32 — Piano, "Architecture and Technology," 32–33.

33 — Piano, "Architecture and Technology," 34.

34 — The interests Franchini and Piano had in common are evident in the prefabricated structure designed by Franchini for the Autogrill sull'Autostrada project in the Elements of Architecture course (1964–65), in Franchini's urban-building research project and thesis (undated but assignable to 1968–69) and in his Elements of Architecture course at the Accademia Lingustica di Belle Arti (1968–69), which involved "observation of natural phenomena and forms as an initial approach to architectural structures," "elements of plane and spatial geometry," and "indications on the static behavior of some types of structure." Gianfranco Franchini, "Elenco e documentazione dei lavori svolti," in Gianfranco Franchini, Portfolio,

[1970–71], 1–4, AGF, uncatalogued.

35 — For a closer examination of the early prototypes produced by Piano see Ciccarelli, *Renzo Piano before Renzo Piano: Masters and Beginnings.*

36 — For Piano's intervention see Renzo Piano, "Experiments and Projects with Industrialised Structures in Plastic Materials," in Robert Davies, ed., *Space Structures: A Study of Methods and Developments in Three-dimensional Construction resulting from The International Conference of Space Structures, University of Surrey, September 1966* (Oxford-Edinburgh: Blackwell, 1967), 753–64. Piano also presented his works on panels mounted in an exhibition staged on the sidelines of the conference. For Makowski's article, see Zygmunt Stanislaw Makowski, "Plastic Structures of Renzo Piano," in *Systems, Building and Design*, February 1969, 37–54.

37 — This study trip is documented by a collection of photographs at the Fondazione Renzo Piano, in the Grandi Viaggi series. FRP. Collezione Fotografie, Serie Grandi Viaggi.

38 — Piano, "Architecture and Technology"; Piano, *Architecture Experiment: Renzo Piano at the Architectural Association of London* (London: Architectural Association, 1969).

39 — As far as the meeting between Rogers and Piano is concerned, the information is contradictory. The account closest to the events comes from an unpublished interview with Rogers conducted by Alexander Fils in 1977, in which Rogers placed the meeting in the context of Piano's preparation of the exhibition *Mutazioni della forma in architettura* for the Milan Triennale of 1968 and the fact that they had an unidentified common friend. According to Bryan Appleyard, the meeting followed a letter introducing Piano to Richard+Su Rogers Architects in which the Rogerses were congratulated for the design of their offices at 32 Aybrook Street. According to Nathan Silver, Rogers and Piano were introduced to one another sometime between 1968 and 1969 by a common friend, Dr. Franklin, the Rogerses' family doctor and client for one of the houses in the Murray Mews project that Richard+Su Rogers Architects was supervising. Enrique Walker's recent interview with Rogers and Piano confirms the differences in their recollection of the encounter. In it Piano speaks of a meeting arranged by Franklin in the summer of 1969, while Rogers, although agreeing on the date of 1969, rejects Piano's reconstruction. In a series of recent interviews John Young supports the hypothesis of a meeting with Dr. Franklin, asserting that it took place in 1969, in the context of Piano's visits to the Italian Pavilion for the Osaka Expo. Appleyard, Richard *Rogers: a Biography*, 145; Silver, *The Making of Beaubourg: a Building Biography of the Centre Pompidou, Paris*, 5–6; Walker, "Renzo Piano & Richard Rogers in conversation with Enrique Walker," 48, 53. On the exhibition at the Triennale, see "Mutazioni della forma in architettura," in *Quattordicesima Triennale di Milano. Esposizione internazionale delle arti decorative e industriali moderne e dell'architettura moderna* (Milan: Arti grafiche Crespi & Occhipinti, 1968), 71–75.

40 — Richard Rogers, Letter to Alan [*sic*] and Becky Tempko [*sic*], July 28, 1970, RSHPA, C01, F General Correspondence. The letter was uncovered by Ciccarelli. See, too, Boris Hamzeian, Interview with John Young, July 25, 2017, Hayling Island.

41 — Renzo Piano, Letter to Richard Rogers, January 2, 1970, RSHPA, C01, General Correspondence, Administration Piano+Rogers Architects.

42 — The importance of setting up work groups with external consultants to carry out specific commissions was made clear by the Rogerses themselves in an article in 1971. "It is important, they believe, for architects to build up a team of consultants and thereby to be able to draw on whatever specialised knowledge any specific job requires," was the comment made in *Architects' Journal*. Wheeler, "Setting Up in Practice," 154.

43 — On Mike Davies, see Boris Hamzeian, Interview with Mike Davies, May 10, 2017, London. On Hugh Chapman, see Wheeler, "Setting Up in Practice," 129–30.

44 — "I'd like to meet you to talk about a school system that we are developing and the possibility of doing something in this sector with your office, both in Italy and in England." Renzo Piano, Letter to Richard Rogers, February 4, 1970, RSHPA, C01, General Correspondence, Administration Piano+Rogers Architects.

45 — On Franchini's stay in London, see Su and Richard Rogers, Letter to Renzo Piano, March 26, 1970, RSHPA, C01, General Correspondence, Administration Piano+Rogers Architects. "Philosophy," "Plan organisation," "Technology," "community school i.e. neighbourhood," and "urban renewal" were the project principles put forward by Rogers in March 1970 in a note that can be regarded as the first document of the project that would later go down in history under as the Centre Beaubourg in Paris. Richard Rogers, Community school, n.d. [March 1970], RSHPA, C01, General Correspondence, Administration Piano+Rogers Architects.

46 — Among the publications mentioned: Central Advisory Council for Education, *Half Our Future*, 1964; *Children and Their Primary schools 2* (1969); Alec Clegg, *The Middle School: A Symposium* (1967); Alan C. Green, *Educational Facilities with New Media* (1965). Su Rogers, untitled [bibliography of the research into the school system], n.d. [March 1970], RSHPA, C01, General Correspondence, Administration Piano+Rogers Architects.

47 — Richard and Su Rogers, Letter to Piano, March 26, 1970.

48 — Ibid.

49 — "A fully integrated deep plan as in the case of [Ehrenkrantz's] SCSD but utilizing standard components + a roof that lets in the light, i.e. Zip-Up windows on the roof or an insulating and translucent roofing material..." Richard Rogers, Schools – Renzo plan, n.d. [March 1970], RSHPA, C01, General Correspondence, Administration Piano+Rogers Architects.

50 — Rogers lost contact with Piano for around three months, until he received a letter from the Genoese architect that opened:
"I apologize for this long silence. I've moved the office from the top of the mountain, and many things have changed in the last two months: I've had very serious financial problems, owing to the difficulties of some important clients, and now I'm working a lot, very hard. I realize that I'm pretty much alone [...]." Renzo Piano, Letter to Richard Rogers, June 17, 1970, RSHPA, C01, General Correspondence, Administration Piano+Rogers Architects.

51 — Richard Rogers, Letter to Renzo Piano, June 25, 1970, RSHPA, C01, General Correspondence, Administration Piano+Rogers Architects.

52 — For the academic year 1969/70 Piano is not listed as an official tutor in the annual bulletin, but, as Ciccarelli reveals, his name does appear in the ledger of accounts and payments to the staff. It is possible that in the summer of 1970 his role was limited to tutoring in academic activities. For the following academic year, Piano is listed as a member of the "Departmental Staff" of the "Department of System Studies" in the annual bulletin and in the accounts ledger under the heading "System Staff." Ciccarelli, *Renzo Piano before Renzo Piano: Masters and Beginnings*; *Architectural Association Yearbook: session 1970–1971* (AA: London, 1970), 106; *Architectural Association Yearbook: session 1969–1970* (AA: London, 1969). Rogers had also been teaching at the Architectural Association since 1968 as a tutor in the Middle School. His name appears in the annual bulletins of the following academic years: 1968/69, 1969/70, 1970/71. In 1968/69 Rogers also gave lectures at the University of Cambridge and the Polytechnic School of London. *Architectural Association Yearbook: session 1969–1970*, 128; *Architectural Association Yearbook: session 1970–1971*, 106; *A.A. School Handbook. The Architectural Association School of Architecture, 34–6 Bedford Square, London, W.C.1* (AA: London, 1968), 90; Richard Rogers and Dolan Conway, "Three London Schools of Architecture within Ten Minutes Walking Distance of Each Other," *Architectural Design*, 39, no. 3 (1969), 129–94: 154.

53 — Rogers, Letter to Alan [*sic*] and Becky Tempko [*sic*].

54 — Rogers's stay in the United States during the fall trimester of 1970 is confirmed in a letter sent to Lalla Iverson, director of the ARAM institute. The letter is addressed to Lalla Iverson and headed "Cornell University, Department of Architecture." Rogers says he has spent the preceding weeks in the United States ("In the past few weeks I have lectured to a large number of Institutes such as Yale MIT; Cornell; Princeton; The Institute of Urban Studies, N.Y., etc."). Rogers declares that he is still involved in the studio's work in London ("Su will work on the sociological side, both press and analysis; in fact, I spoke to her the other day and the office has started work. She will be seeing CIBA, etc."). The lack of any reference to Piano would suggest that on October 31 he and Rogers had not yet finalized the terms of their collaboration. Richard Rogers, Letter to Lalla Iverson, October 31, 1970, RSHPA, C01, J0002, F ARC77583.

55 — Misha Black, Letter to the partners of Piano+Rogers Architects, September 15, 1970, RSHPA, C01, F General Correspondence; Su Rogers, Letter to Misha Black, October 12, 1970, RSHPA, C01, F General Correspondence.

56 — Rogers, Letter to Black.

57 — December 14, 1970, is the date on the first file of notes and sketches relating to the ARAM hospital module. There is no proof that Piano was personally responsible for any part of this file or had played an active part in drawing it up. As he was in the studio at 32 Aybrook Street on December 14 to convince CIBA representatives to take Rogers and Piano on as consultants for future collaborations, it is likely that Piano also took part in the discussions of the ARAM project. Preliminary sketches of the ARAM project, December 14, 1970, RSHPA, C01, J0002, F ARC77583; Minutes of meeting held at 32 Aybrook Street London W 1, December 14, 1970, RSHPA, C01, J0002, F ARC77583. The report on the ARAM project was delivered in March 1971. Piano+Rogers, Architects [*sic*], Service Module for the Association of Rural Aid in Medicine, Inc.

58 — Draft of the report "Service Module for the Association of Rural Aid in Medicine Inc.," n.d. [December 1970–February 1971], RSHPA, C01, J0002, F ARC77583.

59 — The relations between Richard+Su Rogers Architects and the CIBA chemical and pharmaceutical company originated with Su's invitation to the annual symposium *The Family and Its Future* held from March 10 to 12, 1970, by CIBA

foundation dedicated to the promotion of chemical and pharmaceutical research. Su's contribution to the event was a presentation entitled *Environmental Planning and Its Influence on the Family*.
The event turned out to be the premise for a proposal of collaboration between Richard+Su Rogers, CIBA, and ERES (Études et réalisations économiques et sociales) for a "lightweight housing project" of which a trace has survived in the record of the December 14, 1971, meeting. Minutes of meeting held at 32 Aybrook Street London W1, December 14, 1970, RSHPA, C01, J0002, F ARC77583.

60 — Minutes of meeting held at 32 Aybrook Street London W1.

61 — The first documentary record of Richard+Su Rogers Architects' participation with Piano in the Burrell competition is contained in a memorandum drawn up by Richard Rogers that can be dated to February 1971. Richard Rogers, untitled [memorandum in view of a possible participation in the Beaubourg competition], n.d. [February 1971], RSHPA, C01, J0099, F ARC73279. In Appleyard's biography of Rogers, the start of work on the Burrell competition is dated to January 1971. Appleyard, *Richard Rogers: A Biography*, 153. "Memo. Competitions. Burrell Collection," *Royal Institute of British Architects Journal,* no. 10 (1970), 487.

62 — Piano+Rogers and others, draft proposals for the redevelopment of Fitzroy and Burleigh Streets prepared by the joint consortium of Samuel Properties, Ltd. and Jesus College in association with Cambridge City Council, April 28, 1971, RSHPA, C01, JFB, F ARC4.

63 — Wheeler, "Setting Up in Practice," 151–54.

64 — The first document in the archives bearing the signature "Piano+Rogers Architects" is the report on the ARAM project dated March 1971. Piano+Rogers Architects, Service Module for the Association of Rural Aid in Medicine, Inc.

65 — "Richard and Su Rogers have amalgamated their practice with Renzo Piano, architect, Genoa, and will practice under the name of Piano & Rogers, architects, 32 Aybrook Street, London W1, and at Piazza della Vittoria 15–19, 16121, Genoa, Italy." "Announcements," *Architects' Journal* (April 7, 1971), 762.

66 — It is possible to find the names of other collaborators for the year 1971 in the credits of the projects: Richard Russell, John Doggart, Peter Southgate, and Dominique Michaelis. Kenneth Powell, *Richard Rogers. Complete Works. Volume I (Team 4, Richard+Su Rogers, Piano+Rogers, Richard Rogers Partnership)* (London: Phaidon, 1999).

67 — Boris Hamzeian, Interview with Flavio Marano, March 7, 2018, Genoa, n.p.

68 — Lalla Iverson, Notes for a research dedicated to redesign hospital for non-white communities, n.d. [1969], RSHPA [*sic*], C01, J0002, F ARC77555, 1.

69 — A note made by Iverson refers to four different sites: "(a) a sparsely settled rural area in America, the Caribbean or S. America; (b) a densely settled low-income area in W. Philadelphia; (c) a sparsely settled rural area of India: Raypur Rani in Haryana; (d) a densely settled low-income rural area in India: Barara, Haryana, India." In Piano+Rogers Architects' project the areas were reduced to two: "one low-income urban group of 100,000 in the USA and one high-density rural group of 100,000 in India." Project ARAM VII-application info, n.d., RSHPA, C01, J0002, F ARC77555, 1; Piano+Rogers Architects, Service Module for the Association of Rural Aid in Medicine, Inc., 5.

70 — Piano+Rogers Architects, Service Module for the Association of Rural Aid in Medicine, Inc., 7.

71 — Ibid.

72 — Boris Hamzeian, Interview with Anthony Dugdale, June 21, 2017, London.

73 — The Medikit was developed with Bill Busfield and Dolan Conway. Anthony Dugdale, "Medikit: Propositions," in *Architectural Design*, 39, no. 10 (1969): 566–67; Hamzeian, Interview with Dugdale. On the first design hypotheses of the ARAM project, see Preparatory sketches for the ARAM hospital module project, December 14, 1970, RSHPA, C01, J0002, F ARC77596, n.p.

74 — Ibid. See, too, Piano+Rogers Architects, Service Module for the Association of Rural Aid in Medicine, Inc., 8–9.

75 — On the Kahnian solution for the ARAM module see Piano+Rogers Architects, Service Module for the Association of Rural Aid in Medicine, Inc., 8.

76 — That these solutions' limited flexibility was the cause of their abandonment is proved by the comments included in the March 1971 report. Piano+Rogers Architects, Service Module for the Association of Rural Aid in Medicine, Inc., 8–9.

77 — Piano+Rogers Architects, Service Module for the Association of Rural Aid in Medicine, Inc., 19. Piano found images and photographs of these projects of Louis Kahn's in the article "Inurbanity in America" published in *Casabella* in 1962. Eli Buchard, "Inurbanity in America: A Parable from the United States," *Casabella*, no. 265 (1962).

78 — Piano+Rogers Architects, Service Module for the Association of Rural Aid in Medicine, Inc., 18.

79 — "Large span structure gives maximum planning flexibility." Piano+Rogers Architects, Service Module for the Association of Rural Aid in Medicine, Inc., 10.

80 — The metal floor slabs were connected to each other with special V-shaped elements, composed in their turn of tubular bars with a circular section. Ibid.

81 — Reyner Banham, *Design Quarterly 63. A Clip-On Architecture* (Minneapolis: Walker Art Center, 1965).

82 — Also involved in the project was Tony Hunt, the engineer on whom the Rogerses relied for the majority of the projects they built in the second half of the sixties.

83 — The March 1971 report followed two preliminary ones drawn up by Marco Goldschmied in March and July 1970. The project would be reworked by Piano+Rogers Architects over the course of the seventies without ever being built. Richard+Su Rogers Architects, Fitzroy Street Redevelopment-Proposal for the redevelopment of Jesus College Properties, Fitzroy Street, Cambridge, March 1970, RSHPA, C01, JFB, F ARC81086; Richard+Su Rogers Architects, Fitzroy Street Redevelopment-Proposal for the redevelopment of Jesus College Properties, Fitzroy Street, Cambridge, second report, July 1970, RSHPA, C01, JFB, F ARC81086.

84 — The document to which reference is made here is a February 1969 report commissioned by Cambridge City Council. Piano+Rogers project architects [*sic*], Fitzroy Robinson & Partners, Consultant Architects, Jones, Lang, Wootton, Chartered Surveyors, Henry Riley & Son, Quantity Surveyors, Draft proposals for the redevelopment of Fitzroy and Burleigh Streets prepared by the joint consortium of Samuel Properties Ltd and Jesus College in association with Cambridge City Council, April 28, 1971, RSHPA, C01, JFB, F ARC4, 4–5.

85 — "All movement paths, pedestrians, public transport, private cars and bicycles, should be fully developed" and "there should be traffic-free pedestrian movement within the shopping malls." Piano+Rogers project architects and others, Draft proposals for the redevelopment of Fitzroy and Burleigh Streets, 4–5. "The success of [the] Fitzroy-Burleigh area," wrote the architects, "depends on developing the framework of movement; private and public, fast and slow." Ibid.

86 — "[To] preserve the qualities of the environment it is aimed to conserve and rehabilitate the maximum number of existing buildings. Some of these buildings may, individually, have less merit than those in the conservation area, but they play an important role in preserving the continuity of a homogenous district which is one of the principal surviving areas of traditional Cambridge domestic architecture." Piano+Rogers project architects and others, Draft proposals for the redevelopment of Fitzroy and Burleigh Streets, 18.

87 — Piano+Rogers project architects and others, Draft proposals for the redevelopment of Fitzroy and Burleigh Streets, 13.

88 — "The Rogers," wrote Sheila Wheeler, "are also concerned that the buildings they design should be infinitely flexible and expandable. [...] Clients' programmes can change overnight, and a house, office or factory should be designed in such a way that it can allow for these internal changes by rapidly demountable partition systems etc., and of course expansion or contraction, or internal change, can be met much more easily by the use of lightweight, dry components." Wheeler, "Setting Up in Practice," 154.

89 — Piano+Rogers project architects and others, Draft proposals for the redevelopment of Fitzroy and Burleigh Streets, 11.

90 — "The deep plan allows for the provision of large space users in any position in the development, so that the best possible relationship of large and small shops can be achieved to the benefit of the centre as a whole. Within this framework individual occupiers, both small and large, will be able to have the maximum freedom of choice, both internal and external." Ibid.

91 — Ibid.

92 — Ibid.

93 — Although the report does not name this panel it was likely the Okalux module Piano+Rogers Architects used for the Burrell Collection and Centre Beaubourg projects. Piano+Rogers project architects and others, Draft proposals for the redevelopment of Fitzroy and Burleigh Streets, 17.

94 — "In addition, Fitzroy Street is to be enclosed by a high-level translucent covering giving all-weather protection and maximum amenity to shoppers." Ibid.

95 — The publication of the notice of the Burrell competition preceded that of the competition for the Centre Beaubourg by five months. The deadlines for submissions to the two competitions were close: May 14 for the Burrell Gallery and June 15 for the Centre Beaubourg. "Memo. Competitions. Burrell Collection," 487. While the competition for the Centre Beaubourg was open to any architect with a professional qualification recognized by the International Union of Architects, the one for the Burrell Gallery was limited to architects registered with the RIBA. Ibid. The conditions for the donation of the collection to the city were laid down in a memorandum drawn up between Burrell and the representatives of Glasgow City Council. It included indications relating to the location of the museum, the organization of the collection, and the arrangement and grouping of the

works. Alan Gordon and Peter Cannon Brookes, "Housing the Burrell Collection – a Forty-year Saga," *The International Journal of Museum Management and Curatorship*, no. 3 (1984), 19–59.

96 — Glasgow City Council's choice of site complied with the provisions of the Burrells' bequest, which called for the collection to be housed in a "smokeless zone" to avoid its being damaged by atmospheric pollution and for the building to be located in the vicinity of a large city to make it accessible to large numbers of the public. Gordon and Cannon Brookes, "Housing the Burrell Collection – a Forty-year Saga," 30.

97 — The competition notice called for a faithful reconstruction of the drawing room, hall, and dining room of Hutton Castle. On the program of the notice see Gordon and Cannon Brookes, "Housing the Burrell Collection – a Forty-year Saga," 22, 30. See, too: Thomas A. Markus, *Buildings and Power: Freedom and Control in the Origin of Modern Building Types* (London: Routledge, 1993), 211–12; Amy Bingaman, Lisa Sanders, and Rebecca Zorach, *Embodied Utopias: Gender, Social Change and the Modern Metropolis* (London-New York: Taylor & Francis, 2001), 21–22.

98 — "As with the Pompidou, [in the Burrell Collection project] we were given a very detailed and well-structured brief. It contained the disposition of all the parts composing the program. We put down this marker, saying in a way: we are not interested in where exactly the exhibition space is going to be. We are interested in giving you a very flexible space. You, the curators, decide how you want to subdivide it. All that will be known will be the structure and the surface of the space. In a way we were laying down the principles we used afterwards for Pompidou but at the same time we never really got it to a convincing design. It didn't get anywhere." "The [Beaubourg] brief was very good. It was very detailed, too. Just like the Burrell, we were not going to analyze the brief in great detail and allocate the different spaces in the building. We were very clear right from the onset that we were going to provide the floor space, almost equivalent to a football pitch, and then to provide them with a structure. We were not going to give them more than that." Hamzeian, Interview with Young.

99 — "The building offers freedom of organisation to succeeding generations. The aim has been for the Architecture not to straight-jacket the layout and viewing of the exhibits, but rather to provide a highly sensitive environment for the display and conservation of the collection. No specific layout has been proposed, as it is felt that this should be organised by a specialist team." Piano+Rogers Architects, untitled [draft of the report of the competition project for the new seat of the Burrell Collection in Glasgow], RSHPA, C01, J0005, F ARC73739, n.p.

100 — Ibid.

101 — The only three-dimensional metal structure conceived by Richard+Su Rogers Architects comparable to the one designed for the Burrell Gallery was a solution proposed for the New Ash Green Sports Centre project. Andrew Holmes recalls that during his internship at Richard+Su Rogers Architects between 1969 and 1970, Rogers was studying and annotating Konrad Wachsmann's monograph. "There was an important book at the time. John Young has it. Richard brought it from the RIBA library. *The Turning Point of Building: Structure and Design.* If you go to the RIBA library and get that copy it is written all over by Richard Rogers. It's absolutely destroyed, all written over in pencil. In all the margins, all over the book. It is the first edition of the book I remember. It is an important publication by Wachsmann." The author visited the RIBA Library on June 24, 2017, and examined the only copy present of the volume mentioned in the interview. There are no annotations in it.

102 — "Someone else who has had an influence on my development," Piano has said, "was Zygmunt Makowski. He was teaching in London, where he was carrying out research in the field of lightweight structures. He made me realize that a lightweight structure, a spatial structure, made up of pyramids or a range of geometric figures, with bars or nodes, is a training ground that obliges you to search for the essential, for lightness. This lightness requires a rigor that in the end becomes one of form as well, and so it is an excellent school."
On the relationship between Makowski and Piano, see, too, Piano, "Experiments and Projects with Industrialized Structures in Plastic Materials," in *Space Structures: A Study of Methods and Developments in Three-Dimensional Construction resulting from the International Conference on Space Structures, University of Surrey, September 23–25, 1966*, ed. R. M. Davies (Oxford-Edinburgh: Blackwell, 1967), 753–64. On the studies of the Mero System at the Renzo Piano Architetto practice see Hamzeian, Interview with Marano.

103 — The attention paid to the technical systems design for the Burrell Gallery project is confirmed by the configuration of the air intakes and vents in the form of monumental vertical elements with a rounded profile.

104 — [Piano+Rogers Architects], Burrell Collection technical solution 1971, n.d. [May 1971], RSHPA, C01, J0005, F ARC73737, n.p.

105 — It is possible that the Rogerses had been aware of this project since 1969. The Theme Pavilion nodes admired by Happold may have been discussed in the context of the collaboration between Richard+Su Rogers Architects and Structures 3 for the design of Chelsea Football Club stadium.

106 — During his years at university, Rogers produced a manuscript on the Maison de verre. This document constituted the basis for the article Rogers would publish in *Domus* in 1966. The envelope of the Maison de verre turned the building into a true "house of light." "This 'house of light,'" wrote Rogers, "is possibly the least known and the greatest of 20th century houses." Rogers and Chazaszcz, "Paris 1930," 8. According to Su Rogers, she and Richard visited the Maison de verre during a stay in Paris in the second half of the sixties. Hamzeian, Interview with Su Rogers.

107 — In a recent interview Rogers stressed the relationship that Piano+Rogers Architects intended to establish with the surroundings. "First of all, I have a vivid memory of the project's context. It was a rural setting of very special beauty. For this reason we tried not to break [*sic*] the space and to preserve the landscape, in short, the vegetation." Boris Hamzeian, Interview with Richard Rogers, May 10, 2017, London.

108 — Evidence for this includes the choice to apply a reflective silver film that was to be used for the envelope panels onto the view prepared for the competition. Piano+Rogers Architects, Burrell Collection competition 1971 [View of the building from the park], n.d. [May 1971], RSHPA, C01, J0005, F ARC73737

109 — The Burrell Gallery project presented several parallels with two Foster Associates projects built between 1969 and the spring of 1971: the Operations-Amenity Centre for Fred Olsen Ltd in London (1968–70) and the IBM Pilot Head Office in Portsmouth (1970–71). Foster put the idea of a reflective envelope into effect, in the case of the London building, with a "heat and light reflection [film] in toughened glass" and, in Portsmouth, with a panel of "bronze glass."
The similarity between Foster's designs and Piano+Rogers Architects' proposal for the Burrell Gallery is confirmed, in the case of the IBM project, by the common choice to react to a rural setting (King George Playing Field in Portsmouth and Pollok Park in Glasgow) with a low-rise glazed industrial container to dematerialize the building in the daytime by means of a mirror finish. Foster would write: "during the day the glass has a mirror-like appearance from the outside."
That Piano+Rogers Architects were familiar with these projects is proved by the friendship between Rogers and Foster and the presence of Jan Kaplický, a part-time collaborator with both offices between 1969 and 1971, as well as the creator of a series of drawings for the IBM project and the Amenity Centre. Further confirmation of the affinity between these projects comes from the common choice to represent the reflective envelope of these containers against the background of naturalistic landscapes in which cows also appear. At the time of the development of the Burrell project, construction of the IBM building was already well under way—it would be completed in the spring of 1971—and it had already been published in *Architects' Journal* in January 1971.

110 — Piano+Rogers Architects, Burrell Collection competition 1971 [report of the competition project], May 1971, RSHPA, London, C01, J0005, F ARC73737, n.p.

111 — "The roof is formed of toughened mirror-glass domes, insulated by two layers of Okalux colourless translucent capillary tube membranes, with built-in louvres supported on a space frame." Ibid.

112 — "The walls are of mirror-glass to which optical, lightweight, translucent or solid panels can be attached." Ibid.

113 — The use of stairs with a single long flight of steps in Rogers's projects was not new. After its appearance in the Yorke Mason House project (1968) in the form of a long staircase built of tubular profiles, Rogers took as his model the self-propelled boarding stairs used in airports. Rogers used this element in several versions of the Zip-Up House (1968–71) and in the Sweetheart Plastics office building in Gosport. In the Fitzroy shopping mall project in Cambridge this element was transformed into a system of escalators arranged along the full length of the building. Here the stairs were expressly designed as elements that could be reconfigured over time to meet retailers' needs. Richard+Su Rogers Architects, Proposal for the redevelopment of Jesus College properties, Fitzroy Street, Cambridge, 19, 24–25.

114 — The jury was made up of a number of architects, a representative of the City Council, and an academic. The first group consisted of Jack Coia, Theo Crosby, Philip Dowson and W. G. Howell; the Council's representative was Lord Muirshiel, chairman of the Scottish Civic Trust, who took the place of Lord Crowford (responsible for cataloguing the collection); the academic was Sir Charles Wilson, dean of the University of Glasgow. "Memo. Competitions. Burrell Collection," 487.

Piano+Rogers Architects, Project for a hospital module for ARAM (Association of Rural Aid in Medicine), model, 1970–1971 (realized by Richard Rogers Partnership in the 1980s).

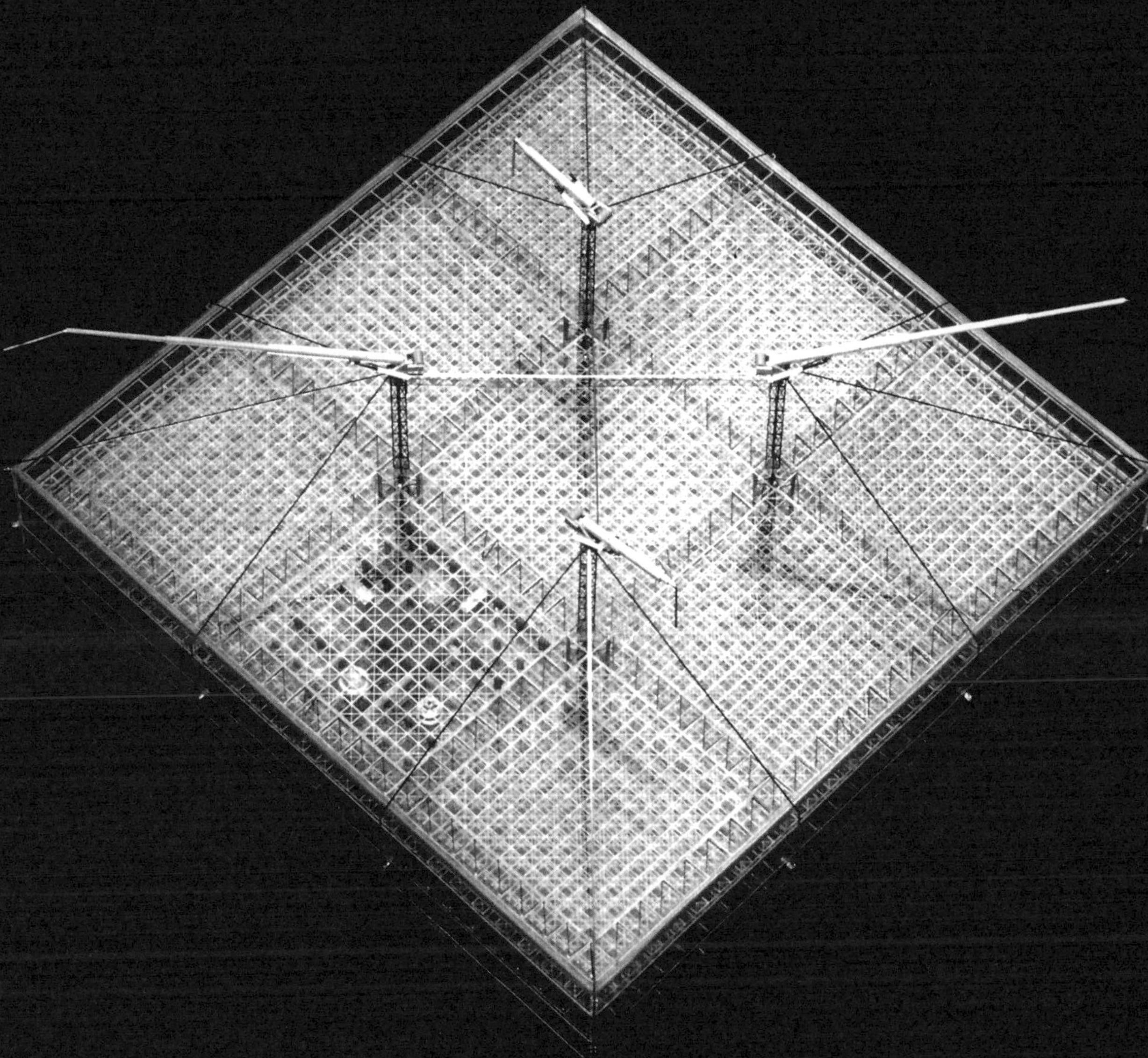

4

EARLY SKETCHES FOR THE CENTRE BEAUBOURG: A FLEXIBLE URBAN SYSTEM FOR INFORMATION

4.1

NEGOTIATIONS OVER PARTICIPATION IN THE COMPETITION, ROGERS'S HESITATION AND THE REFERENCE TO THE FREE UNIVERSITY OF BERLIN

Talks concerning Ove Arup & Partners and the Rogerses' studio at 32 Aybrook Street's collaboration on the Centre Beaubourg competition in Paris started in January 1971 when Ted Happold, unaware of the partnership Richard Rogers had recently embarked on with Renzo Piano,[1] decided to contact Rogers to see if Richard+Su Rogers Architects would be willing to take part. In all likelihood Happold's decision was based on an analysis of the competition terms and the idea of presenting a design with a metal structure that would allow the spaces of the museum the kind of flexibility on which Richard and Su Rogers had been working for years.[2] The collaboration between Richard+Su Rogers Architects and Arup's Structures 3 division engineers on Chelsea Football Club's retractable stadium roof[3] in 1969 may have led Happold to consider Rogers the ideal architect for an intrinsically dynamic kind of structure. Rogers himself must have shown interest in Happold's offer and in the chance to work with a major engineering firm again. In fact, the first meeting between Happold and Rogers may well have coincided with the writing of the article on Richard+Su Rogers Architects that appeared in the January issue of the *Architects' Journal*. As well as describing a design approach founded on the use of industrial components in the construction sector, this discussed the practice's explicit interest in projects of a certain size. "The sort of work that interests [Richard+Su Rogers Architects] the most," and "the kind of large jobs that would stretch a young practice's experience and their ingenuity to the utmost" was how the article in the *Architects' Journal* put it.[4] It was precisely to the collaboration with Structures 3 on a large-scale project such as the Centre Beaubourg that Su seemed to be alluding when she said she was convinced small practices were able to handle big projects ("Bigness would not disconcert us and I believe we could do some of the big jobs that are handed out to the big architects a lot better than they are being done now"), in part through a network of consultants able to provide specific technical expertise ("It is important, they believe, for architects to build up a team of consultants and thereby to be able to draw on whatever specialised knowledge any specific work requires").[5]

At the meeting, Rogers must have told Happold he was willing to take part in the competition and informed him of the collaboration with Piano. On January 15 Happold sent Rogers a copy of the Centre Beaubourg competition documents and arranged a meeting at 32 Aybrook Street at which Rogers, Peter Rice, and Piano would be present.[6] The involvement of Rice, at Happold's behest, can be explained by the decisive role he had played in the invention and development of the metal structures on which Structures 3 had been working since the second half of the sixties and which would prove decisive in the choice of cast steel for the Centre Beaubourg.

Of the meeting on January 21 and the discussions on participation in the competition for Paris no written records survive. Although all accounts agree that the final choice to participate in the competition was the result of a series of meetings held over a lengthy period of time, it is possible to say that on January 21, Rogers, Piano, Happold, and Rice decided to submit their candidacy to the competition secretariat.[7] On January 22 Happold left for Saudi Arabia and in his absence the members of the practice at 32 Aybrook Street and Rice took steps to formalize their participation in the competition.[8]

On January 29 Rice's secretary, Sheila Bacon, sent Rogers the official competition entry form to be signed and returned to Ove Arup & Partners together with his certificate of membership in the RIBA prior to the official candidacies registration closure date on February 26.[9] The requested certificate bears the date of February 1, and the signed and completed form names Rogers alone as the architect participating in the competition and Rice as the contact for correspondence between the French competition administrators and the participating group.[10] With this documentation Ove Arup & Partners sent the receipt of payment of the competition entrance fee: paid by Happold, it was 200 French francs (£15.50).[11]

Following registration, Rice received the competition file with the program, maps, and photographs of the site and sent photocopies to Rogers. As soon as the material arrived, Richard and Su Rogers, Piano, John Young, and Marco Goldschmied met in the studio at 32 Aybrook Street to analyze the competition terms and the still-hypothetical participation of Piano+Rogers Architects. The content of these discussions was summed up by Rogers in a memorandum datable to February 1971.[12]

The memorandum reflected Rogers's concerns about involving his practice in a demanding competition at a time when his partners and collaborators were already working on a risky commission with no guarantee of recompense, the Burrell Gallery competition, as well as several other projects whose development would overlap with that of the Centre. These included the Fitzroy shopping mall, the work on the extension of the firm's own studio at 32 Aybrook Street, the community center housing project at Basildon New Ash, and a prototype of the Zip-Up House to be built at Camden Mews in London.[13] Rogers gave a series of reasons for these reservations: the considerable amount of time needed for the preparation of the plans for the competition; the lack of staff able to devote themselves full time to the project; an aversion to the sociopolitical emphasis implied in the idea of the Centre proposed by the French government; the makeup of

the jury and the method of selection; and, lastly, his identification in the terms of a series of formal quibbles that suggested the possibility of victory and construction of the project was remote.[14]
What discouraged Piano+Rogers Architects from taking up Happold's invitation was Rogers's reluctance to participate in a competition for a project that, while proposing to renew the French art scene, looked nevertheless as if it might be a dangerous step, aimed at centralization and control of popular culture.[15] Rogers discerned political and social overtones in the competition announcement that in his view were essentially false and in any case irreconcilable with the communitarian and socialist vision of architecture that had taken root at 32 Aybrook Street.[16]
Rogers gave a succinct assessment of the majority of the members of the competition jury.[17] Notwithstanding his appreciation of Jørn Utzon and Jean Prouvé, whose experiments with prefabrication he saw as a model, Rogers was critical of Oscar Niemeyer. He also expressed his views of the jury members whom he knew personally from his time at Yale, Philip Johnson and Willem Sandberg:[18] concerning the former, with whom he was still in contact at the time the memorandum was written, he feared his erratic and unpredictable attitude, while he considered the latter a "[first rate] curator."
A counterpoint to the reticence Rogers expressed in the memorandum about participating in the Beaubourg competition was provided by Su Rogers, Piano, Young, and Goldschmied, all of whose positions can be reconstructed through indirect accounts or recent interviews. Like Rogers, but for different reasons, Young regarded the competition of ideas as a planning instrument that offered no guarantees of construction, and thus to be avoided in view of the practice's financial constraints.[19]
Piano was in favor of participation, encouraged by the presence on the jury of Prouvé, whom he regarded as a "point of reference."[20] Su Rogers, who initially agreed with Richard and then was persuaded to accept Happold's offer, seems to have been an enigmatic and uncertain figure.
And it was on Su, formally still a partner in the studio at 32 Aybrook Street, but less and less involved in the life of the practice after the separation from her husband, that the choice to take part in the competition depended.[21]
The positions set out in the memorandum were not limited to pragmatic considerations with regard to participation, but also concerned matters of architecture. Just as for Cambridge, the idea emerged that the project should be conceived as a machine able to react to the flows of people and visitors moving around and through the building.
"The scheme is very exciting and relevant with complex circulation internally and interesting urban problems" and "[the] movement system [of visitors] is one of the keys, so that they see and partake in the centre," were the words Rogers used.
The idea that the project should be developed out of a complex circulation system was taken farther in the February discussions, with Rogers citing a possible model in the memorandum: Alexis Josic, Georges Candilis, Shadrach Woods and Manfred Schiedhelm's project for the Free University of Berlin. In the memorandum notes, Candilis and colleagues' Free University of Berlin project, which Piano himself had discovered in the context of his study of new approaches to the design of educational facilities, was held up as a model for its original and urban morphology: an open horizontal infrastructure that was able to evolve, made up of roads, bridges, and viaducts that could expand into the urban fabric and encompass flexible and reconfigurable volumes within its grid.
From this moment on, Rogers and Piano also drew on the functional and conceptual nature of the Free University of Berlin. In this sense Candilis's design became the model for an original and multifunctional educational facility, integrated into its context, flexible, and open to new electronic media.
Rogers and Piano were prepared to disrupt the idea of the Centre Beaubourg as a complex centered on the promotion of contemporary art and the conservation of works and turn it into a prototype of the educational centers for information accumulation

and dissemination that had fascinated Piano for years, but that at the time had found expression solely in the schematic volumes of the Sestri Ponente project.

The memorandum also contains references to the mechanics of the building. In the indication that "a coherent entity [...] must offer the widest possibility of flexibility and adaptation" and the one inserted among the arguments against participation in the competition, that "the building will be a route and flex. volume building," Rogers made clear the project's continuity with the three shells designed in the spring of 1971.[22] It is precisely a reference to the Burrell Gallery project and its "exhibition space" as a possible model for the Centre Beaubourg that confirms the affinity between these designs. "There are vast volumes. The library and the museum alone are each over 15,000 sq. m. and the temporary exhibition space [of] 4,000 sq. m. is as big as the Burrel [*sic*] exhibition space."[23] Amidst all the uncertainty, therefore, the project for the Burrell Gallery did not constitute an obstacle to participation in the Beaubourg competition, but even turned out to represent a model for the project in Paris.[24]

According to Happold and other sources, before deciding to take part in the competition other meetings were held between the architects of 32 Aybrook Street and the Structures 3 engineers.

The final decision would be taken following a vote held in the presence of both of the Rogerses, Piano, Happold, and Rice, and perhaps Young and Goldschmied as well. On this occasion, again according to these sources, participation in the Parisian competition prevailed, probably with the backing of Piano and Su Rogers, who had chosen to support Happold.[25]

The financial and organizational misgivings raised by Rogers were dispelled by Happold and Piano. In a telephone call on March 30, 1971, the man who had first suggests the whole operation, Happold, offered to meet the project's financial and organizational burdens: he would cover the cost of £250 for an "assistant" to work on the project, as well as that of making the competition model.[26] Piano himself helped to resolve Rogers's doubts by taking responsibility for finding the assistant mentioned by Happold. The person Piano chose was Franchini—a choice that represented a continuity with the experience that the latter had the previous year in the office at 32 Aybrook Street.

Having identified Candilis's Free University design as a model for the project, the decision to involve Franchini in its development eliminated any doubt that Piano and Rogers intended to use the Beaubourg competition as an opportunity to continue and conclude the discussions they had begun the year concerning over the school system, and it was precisely from the perspective of this theme that they would interpret the project, offering the Beaubourg competition jury not a museum or a library, but an advanced information and education center. Franchini agreed without hesitation to move to London to work on the project full time, on condition that his name would be included among the project's authors.[27]

Overleaf: Articles annotated by Renzo Piano belonging to his library: Carlo Pelliccia and Piero Sartogo, "Campus Design, 1. Il passaggio da una struttura monofunzionale ad una struttura integrata dell'educazione," (*Casabella*, 1968). The Free University of Berlin by Alexis Josic, Georges Candilis, Shadrach Woods and Manfred Schiedhelm.

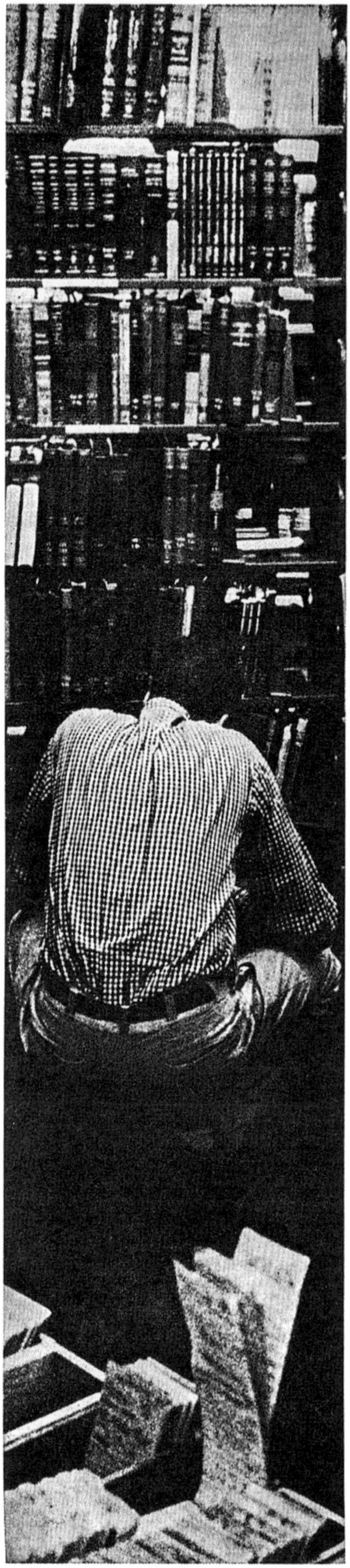

Campus design

1 Il passaggio da una struttura monofunzionale ad una struttura integrata dell'educazione

Carlo Pelliccia, Piero Sartogo

Le strutture dell'educazione riflettono ancora oggi il dualismo tra fase dell'apprendimento e fase della sua applicazione, come effetto di una educazione fortemente finalizzata a criteri di produttività tipici della civiltà industriale. Conseguentemente, la nostra vita è divisa in due periodi ben distinti: quello giovanile, spensierato, teorico all'interno del mondo accademico, e quello maturo, pratico e produttivo all'interno della società, come se momento dell'apprendimento e momento dell'applicazione non fossero un tutt'uno nel processo dell'esperienza umana.

Il campus, come luogo di vita accademica, riflette questo dualismo; negli Usa in particolare il campus tradizionale si caratterizza fisicamente come struttura chiusa verso il mondo esterno, verso la vita di tutti i giorni e, in molti casi, simboleggia ancora una minoranza di élite culturale che protegge se stessa. Anche per salvaguardare questo ideale di isolamento, la struttura originaria del campus ha via via assorbito al suo interno alcune delle funzioni tipiche della città, come la residenza, le relazioni sociali, il tempo libero. L'originaria natura monofunzionale (unicamente accademica) e la originaria legge temporale di crescita che realizza « in toto » a tempi brevi la materializzazione dei suoi programmi, si riflettono nella peculiare, unitaria adozione del linguaggio formale per cui lo stile del campus dell'Università di Yale è il neogotico, quello dell'Università della Virginia costruita da Jefferson è il palladiano, quello di Harvard il georgiano e così via.

Gli sviluppi più recenti delle comunità accademiche americane hanno però manifestato una profonda trasformazione della strut-

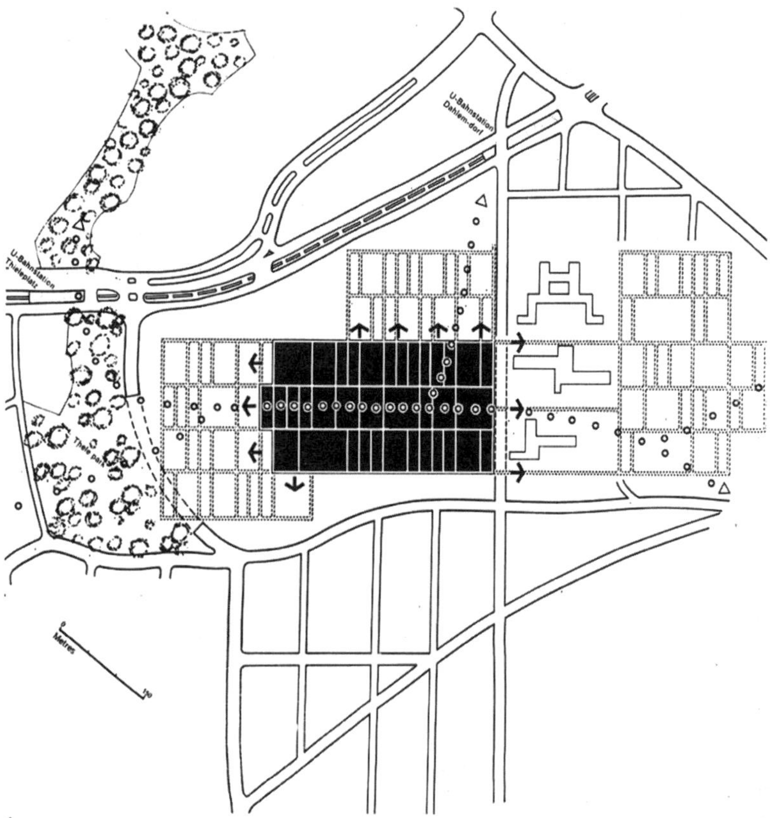

1

1 Candilis, Josic, Woods: Università libera di Berlino. Planimetria: in nero, piano di sviluppo per 3.500 studenti; a linee tratteggiate, previsione di sviluppo per 15.000 studenti. Nella Università libera di Berlino la matrice assunta è di tipo geometrico. Stabilendo gerarchie di griglie per diverse funzioni (ad esempio gerarchia dell'uso) tale sistema, rappresentato dalla sovrapposizione delle diverse griglie (matrici spaziali) persegue valori di flessibilità degli spazi e di crescita nel tempo. Il sistema è morfologicamente aperto.
2-3-4-5-6-7 Università libera di Berlino: griglia di base (2), griglia percorsi pedonali (3), griglia percorsi pedonali in rapporto agli spazi aperti (4), suddivisione per dipartimenti (5), griglia spazi aperti (6), configurazione globale (7).

tura originaria in relazione al nuovo, emergente ruolo assunto dal potere intellettuale nei confronti del potere economico e politico. In aggiunta ai tradizionali compiti educativi, alle università viene infatti oggi richiesto di soddisfare le esigenze crescenti del mondo economico e politico, costretto ad attingere in misura sempre maggiore al « brain power » del mondo intellettuale. All'università, che era una comunità singola, dedita al solo ideale degli studi, è succeduto così un agglomerato di attività multiformi e complesse che dilatano sempre di più le funzioni dell'università stessa nei confronti del suo ambiente socio-economico. Torneremo in seguito sulle cause di questa trasformazione: per il momento interessano gli effetti da essa indotti sulla struttura fisica del campus; si può dire che le università, assumendo una struttura multiforme e complessa di microcosmo della società, tendono a riprodurre nel loro configurarsi la natura processuale e fenomenologica della città.
Se, come abbiamo già detto, l'educazione assumerà un ruolo emergente unita al potere politico ed economico, logica conseguenza sarà la trasformazione del campus in struttura aperta ed integrata al tessuto urbano. In questa integrazione alla minore identità fisica della struttura del campus farà riscontro, una volta che le sue strutture saranno integrate all'ambiente urbano, una più significativa identità: quella di uno « stato mentale ».
Come la problematica attuale dell'urban design tende al recupero dell'assetto integrato della città in contrapposizione allo zoning, così la problematica del campus design è fortemente indirizzata verso una integrazione non solo funzionale ma anche emblematica delle attività prettamente accademiche con quelle urbane e territoriali. La scala di progettazione è, in molti casi, quella di una piccola città (Università della California, Santa Cruz campus: 27.500 studenti, Università dell'Illinois, Chicago Circle: 20.000 studenti, Università libera di Berlino: da 3.500 a 15.000 studenti eccetera), una città la cui comunità è sempre meno omogenea, la cui crescita nel tempo è sempre meno prevedibile, il cui controllo progettuale sfugge a tutti i livelli.
In linea generale, i modelli morfologici dei progetti sopraelencati mostrano fondamentalmente due tipi di approccio: uno che ipotizza la stabilità della forma come postulato programmatico, e l'altro che stabilizza la forma come ipotesi di arrivo.
Al primo gruppo appartengono il campus

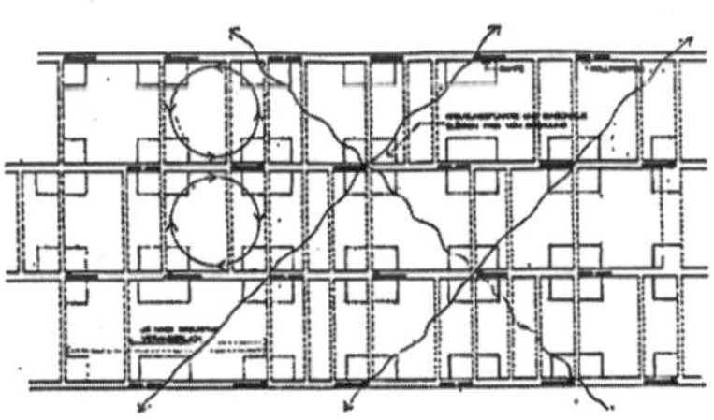

2

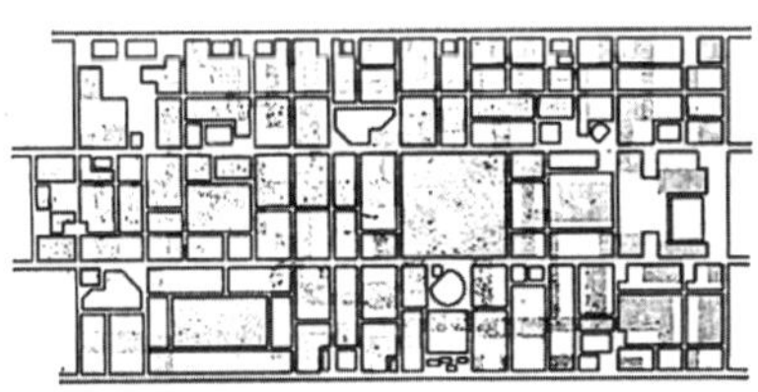

4

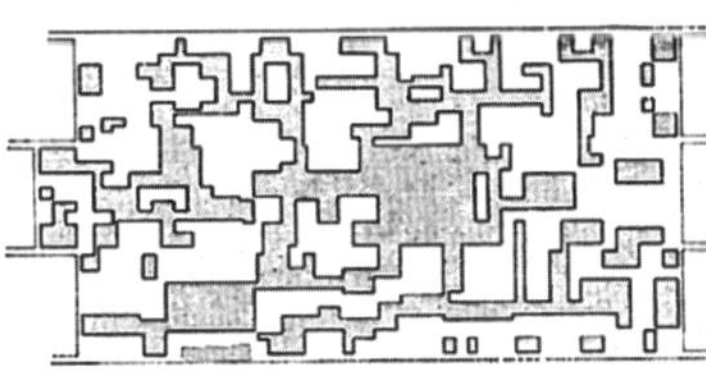

6

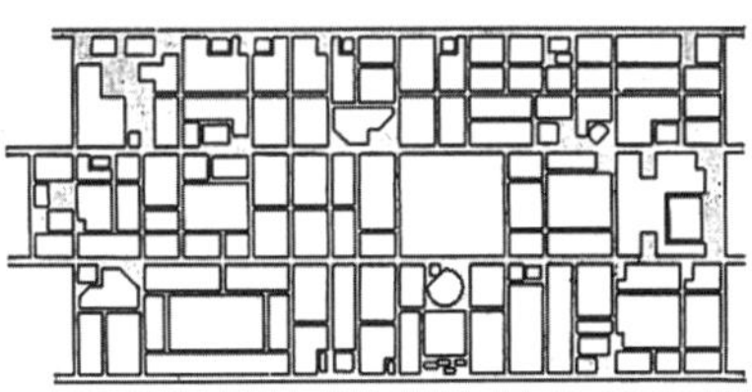

3

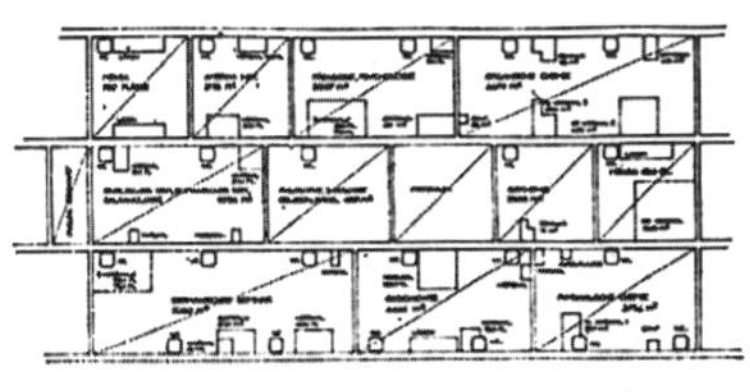

5

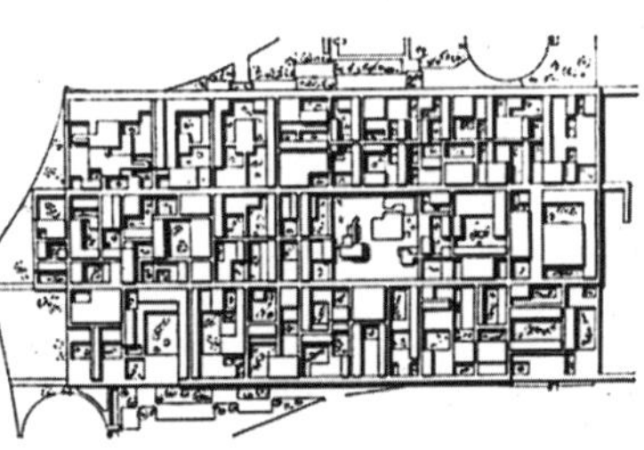

7

4.2

THE LAUNCH OF THE COMPETITION WORKS AND THE RETURN OF FRANCHINI

Between February and June 1971, while work continued on the ARAM module, Fitzroy shopping mall, and Burrell Gallery competition projects and the other commissions mentioned by Rogers in the memorandum, the architects of 32 Aybrook Street, now known as Piano+Rogers Architects, and the Structures 3 engineers set to work on the Centre Beaubourg project as well. In the absence of dated documents, it is not possible to establish the timeline with certainty. According to its authors, the project was drawn up over the course of a few weeks, just before the delivery deadline and thus in a period between the middle of May and June 15, the consignment date.

That Piano+Rogers Architects began to devote themselves to the Beaubourg competition in May is confirmed both by the rapid succession of consignments from the studio at 32 Aybrook Street between March and May—the ARAM module in March, the Fitzroy shopping mall on April 28, and the Burrell Gallery competition on May 28—and by Franchini's move to London in the second half of May.[28] While this places the crucial phase of the work in the month preceding the consignment, it is still possible that Piano, Rogers, Happold, and Franchini were already reflecting on the Beaubourg project guidelines in the months prior to that.

Some of the accounts concur in saying that the work on the plans in May in London together with Franchini had been preceded by a series of meetings in London and by a meeting at Piano+Rogers Architects studio in Genoa attended by Piano, Franchini, and Rogers,[29] who at the time was on vacation in Italy with his partner Ruthie Elias, visiting Rome, Genoa, and the Zermatt.[30]

It was during one of these meetings held in London and Genoa—perhaps right after Piano+Rogers Architects' final decision to take part in the Parisian competition with Structures 3—that the indications contained in Rogers's memorandum on the central role of the circulation system and the utilization of a flexible volume were distilled into a series of sketches that condensed the original idea for the Centre Beaubourg.[31] The document consists of two sheets from an A4-format [slightly larger than letter size] notebook with sketches drawn with an orange felt-tip pen.[32] The sheets are conserved in the RSHP (formerly Rogers Stirk Harbour + Partners) archives in London.[33]

The line of the drawing and the handwriting of the notes are recognizably Richard Rogers's.

Rogers himself acknowledged having made these drawings but did not claim to be the author of the idea contained in them.[34]

Below and overleaf: Richard Rogers, Competition proposal for the competition of the Centre of the plateau Beaubourg, (known as Centre Beaubourg) first sketches (identified by Boris Hamzeian at RSHP Archives, London, in 2017), Paris, spring 1971.

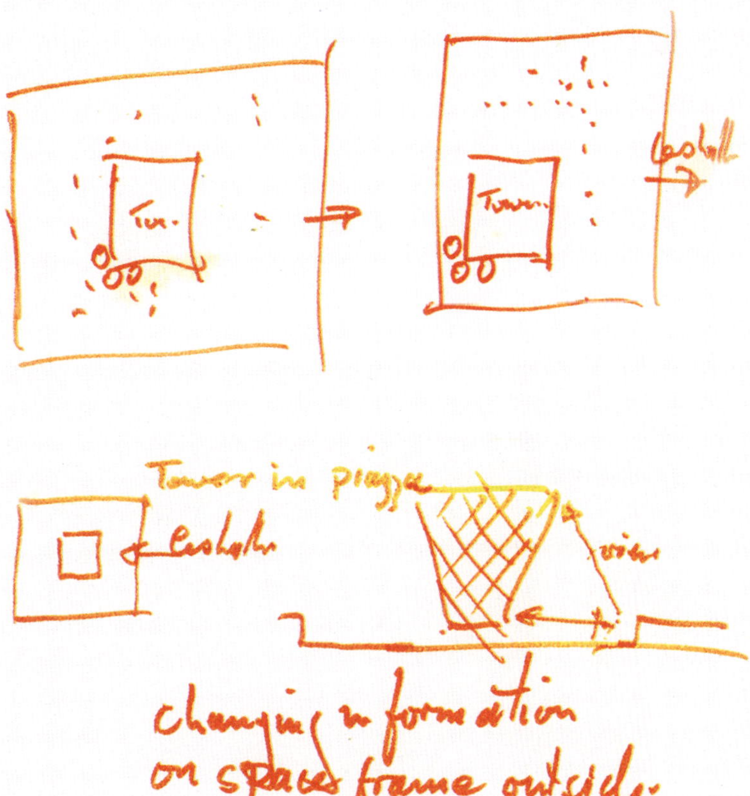

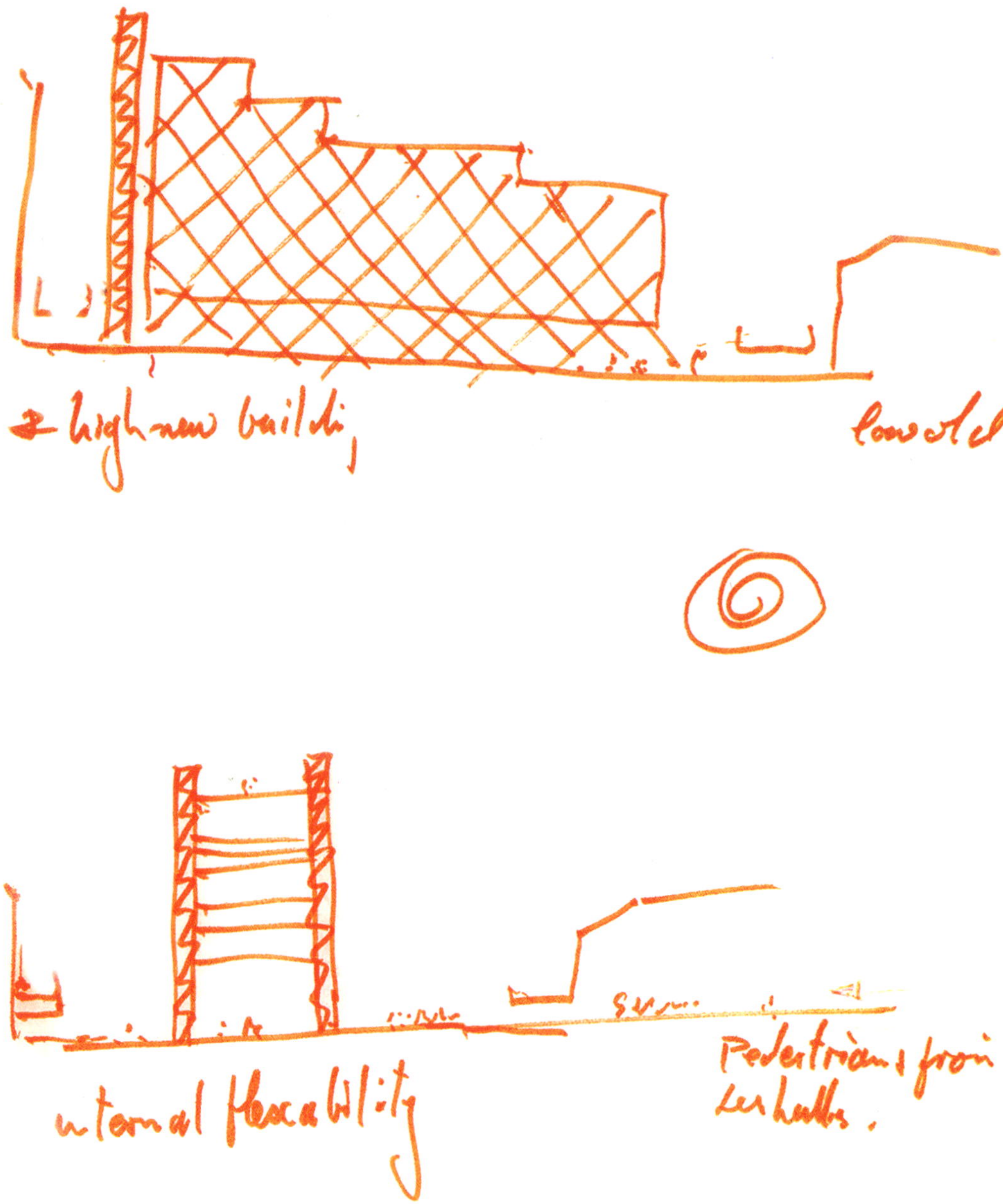
low old
internal flexibility
Pedestrians from Les halles.

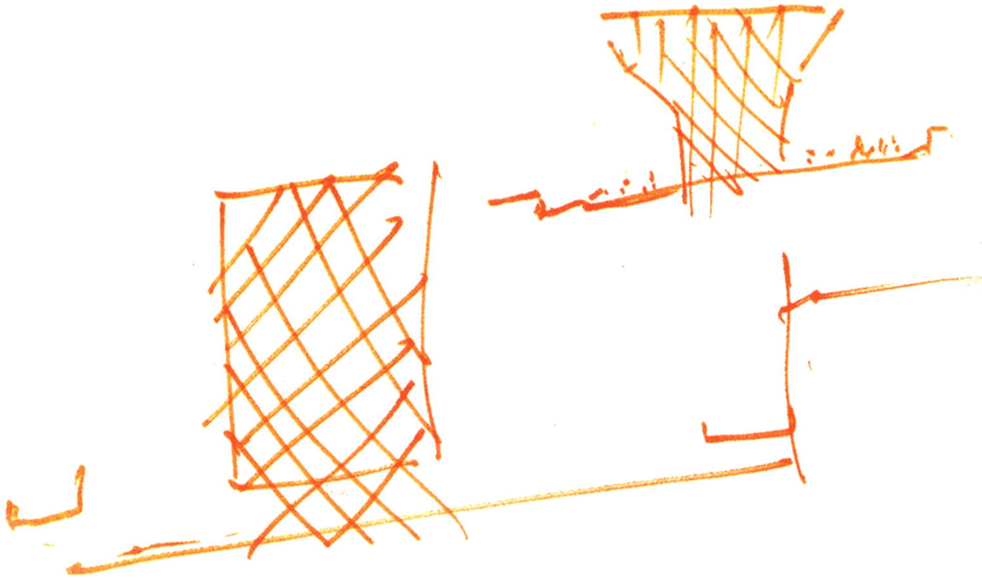

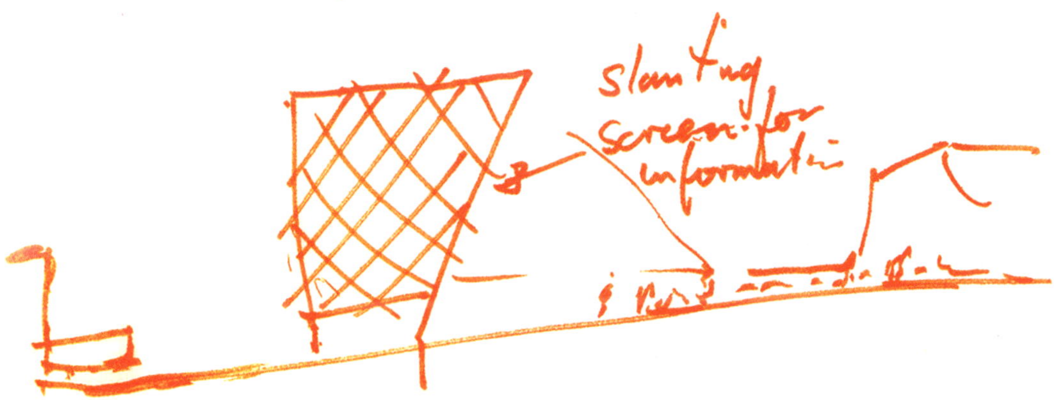
slanting
screen for
informati

4.3

A PIAZZA FOR THE PLATEAU BEAUBOURG: A MAGNET FOR THE METROPOLITAN FLOW

The radical idea summed up in the sketches was a consequence of the choice to have the Centre react to the underground Forum des Halles project and the tunnel that was going to connect it with the plateau Beaubourg. The search for a subterranean connection with the sunken city under construction at Les Halles and the compact nature of the site of the plateau Beaubourg led Piano, Rogers and Franchini to shelve the idea of a colossal piece of horizontal infrastructure conceived to insert the project into the plateau Beaubourg and extend it into the surroundings in the manner of the Free University of Berlin.

Piano, Rogers and Franchini resorted to the idea of making the building more compact in order to introduce onto the plateau Beaubourg an urban and communitarian system analogous to the square with facilities designed by Piano at Sestri Ponente or the metropolitan *passage* laid out in Cambridge by Piano and Rogers. In Beaubourg competition that idea took the form of a large open-air space that would attract and collect the metropolitan flows coming from Les Halles and become a natural continuation of them.[35]

To reinforce the relationship with Les Halles and separate it from the flow of traffic, the decision was taken to locate this great void at a level lower than its surroundings, bringing it down to the level of the tunnel. In choosing to sink the plateau Beaubourg like a sort of trough or moat, Piano+Rogers Architects again took up the concept of segregating pedestrian and vehicle traffic tried out in Cambridge and, perhaps, Sestri Ponente, and defined an original kind of public space: a place for collection of the metropolitan flow.

The configuration of its plan, its pedestrian character, and its role as a magnet and collector of flows of people coming from Les Halles likened this urban void to the public spaces of Mediterranean cities and Italian *piazze*, as confirmed by the use of the term "piazza." It is possible that the reference to the Piazza del Campo in Siena, which Piano had seen in issue no. 314 of *Casabella* and in Yoshinobu Ashihara's monograph before including it in the article he published in *Architectural Design*, had already crystallized in Rogers's sketches.[36]

In any case at the time it was not the configuration of the plan that they intended to take from this model, but its social and architectural value.[37] Ashihara had already written about this when he described the Piazza del Campo as a "plaza designed to suit any kind of gathering and festivity"—a genuine open-air work of architecture ('If one looks at the aerial photograph of the plaza, he cannot help feeling that it is truly 'architecture without a roof'").[38] Rogers could not have been indifferent to Piano's interest in the community value of Italian *piazze*. Born in Florence, Rogers had since his ado-

lescence made periodical journeys exploring Italian cities, the latest of which was the trip he made in the spring of 1971 with his partner Ruthie Elias and which may have had something to do with his reasoning about the piazza of the Centre Beaubourg. With the decision to sink the area behind a physical barrier, the piazza imagined for the Centre Beaubourg took on a subversive and dissenting value. It was transformed into an anti-acropolis in which crowds could assemble in the manner of the gatherings of the flower children, or in protest, as had happened in May '68 when French students lined up behind barricades in the Latin Quarter.
The character of this anti-acropolis remained ambiguous, however, since the fact that it was sunk below ground level meant crowds could gather there, but at the same time they could be corralled. The configuration of this original and entrenched place took the political component of the Rogerses' projects in an unprecedented direction.
The void assumed a militant connotation of protest in which a part may also have been played by Richard's partner Ruthie's interest in political activism, as demonstrated by her participation in the organization of the protest campaign in London against the Vietnam War.[39]

4.4

TOWER OR BAR? STUDIES FOR A SCENIC DEVICE

In the sketches on the two sheets from the notebook, the Centre Beaubourg looks like a multistory building set on the piazza and hollowed out at its base so as not to hamper the flow of people and allow the piazza to continue beneath it. In the absence of a structural solution able to achieve the required degree of permeability and openness of the building—still wavering in the sketches between the recourse to point-like lateral supports and the continuation of the structural grid all the way down to the ground—the desire to resort to a solution different from the traditional trilithic structure is clear in the sketches. This attempt was already evident in the Boschetto district housing Piano conceived between 1968 and 1970, where the recourse to a prestressed reinforced-concrete floor slab resting on two pairs of diaphragms in a central position was already presented as an alternative to the gravitas conferred by modernist pilotis.

The configuration of the building, sometimes a tower, sometimes a bar, and its positioning on the piazza—sometimes at the center, at others abutting onto rue du Renard—are also still undetermined, but bear witness to the search for a series of correspondences between the urban and political value of the building. The solution with the bar aligned with rue du Renard would allow the square to be configured as a single and closed space in which the models of the Italian piazza and of concert hall orchestras and stages could be identified.[40]

The solution of a tower located at the center of the square would interrupt its continuity only virtually, thanks to the complete permeability of the ground floor, and bestow a powerful role on the public space, making it a temple and a symbolic and monumentalized expression of its internal dynamics.

The study of the building's position on the square in relation to the flows of people in these sketches already draws on the intuition regarding the playful value of circulation that had appeared in the Burrell Gallery. This idea, in Paris, was destined to take the form of a mechanical system conceived to turn the upward flow of visitors in the building into a popular spectacle.

With their pronounced height, both the bar and the tower established particular synergies with the surroundings. While the tower seemed to define a relationship of opposition to the low profiles of the historic center, the bar resulted in a more complex relationship in which a form of dialogue was added to the contrast between the "new high building" and the "low old," transposed in architecture in the configuration of sloping terraces to bring it down to the height of the roofs of Paris.

Piano+Rogers Architects, Photograph of Piazza del Campo in Siena, selected for the research file "Centre Beaubourg. Piazza"), 1971.

4.5

THE RAREFACTION OF THE FRAMEWORK AND FAÇADE INTO A VERTICAL AND ICONIC "SPACE FRAME"

The lines traced on the sheets from the notebook to represent what was supposed to be the structure reflect Happold's preference for complex metal structures set in an unusual mesh with rhomboidal geometry. The configuration would change over the course of the project's development but the diagonal lines survived and can be discerned in the constructed building. The proposed solution was of a spatial structure, also called a "space frame," a rhomboidal mesh as an alternative to the traditional trilithic scheme of posts and beams. In the choice of a structure with diagonal lines the space frame also expressed a symbolic value that in its rejection of horizontal lines seemed to allude to the ideogram of movement of the building, translated here into a monumental form.

The lineage of the structural grid with a rhomboidal mesh is already evident from the sketches, revealing its roots in Richard Buckminster Fuller and Konrad Wachsmann's spatial structures based on a tetrahedral module and the original structural solutions for the Osaka Expo. This kind of space frame, the nearest example of which is the roof of Piano+Rogers Architects' Burrell Gallery, lost its value as a covering and was transformed into a structural envelope positioned vertically and conceived in synergy with the square and the vital flow moving over its surface.

It is possible to pin down the lineage of the Centre's space frame even more precisely, to Louis Kahn's Civic Tower in Philadelphia for its civic value[41] and to the "network" of Archigram's Plug-In City with its gigantic diagonal tubes containing the transport systems; while reduced to a purely structural element in the Centre, their idea of movement and their internal dynamics seem to have been transferred to the Parisian project. Alongside these conceptual influences lie concrete examples closer to Piano+Rogers Architects and Structures 3.

An example is Bush Lane House, a project developed by Arup Associates between 1969 and 1975 and already equipped in the spring of 1971 with a characteristic rhomboidal space frame that was retained in the finished building.

A similar structure was used in the Alcoa Building in San Francisco designed by Skidmore, Owings & Merrill (SOM), the office where Rogers worked in 1961 and 1962, and where he was struck in particular by the external structural solutions conceived to permit flexible and uninterrupted internal spaces.[42]

Other models might be identified in the framework of the colossal inverted pyramids conceived by Stanley Tigerman for his Urban Matrix, along with a contemporary Japanese version of the Crystal Palace, the Nagashima Tropical Garden, or the concrete framework of the residential structures that Kenzo Tange designed for Skopje: all three of these projects were picked out by Piano among the

articles in the periodicals in his library.[43]
Among other things, the use of this unusual space frame was consistent with Happold's ambition to make use of cast-steel joints, as demonstrated by the details of the Theme Pavilion and Burrell Gallery roofs. In this sense the rotation of the space frame in the form of a vertical three-dimensional lattice assumes the value of a still literal response, one that had not been studied in depth, to the question that had loomed over the Centre's structure ever since the first exchanges with Structures 3, that of how to adapt the cast joints admired in large roofs to a multistory metal framework.
The only clue to the structure's configuration is the section present on the two sheets of the notebook, probably of the bar solution: two vertical space frames positioned on the long sides of the building facing onto rue du Renard and rue Saint-Martin in which to insert continuous platforms to apply the principle of "internal flexibility" mentioned in the memorandum.
Although represented with simple lines drawn with a felt-tip pen, these platforms make clear the desire to return to the idea of an uninterrupted space proposed for the Burrell Gallery.
A multistory solution characterized by floor slabs slender enough not to be turned into structural or service floors had been proposed during the development of the ARAM module.[44]

While for that project it had been ruled out due to the impossibility of finding a truss capable of spanning the space without resorting to intermediate supports,[45] for the Beaubourg project Structures 3 must have convinced Piano+Rogers Architects of this solution's feasibility.

Overleaf Priscilla Chapman, "Design for Living. The Plug-In City by Archigram" (*Sunday Times Supplement*, 1964).

1 residential units 2 escalator tubes 3 shop supply tubes & silos 4 shop u
6 fast monorail 7 local monorail 8 craneway 9 heavy duty railway 10 r
11 fast road 12 local feeder road 13 local parking 14 local goods sorting

Left: so far there isn't a drawing to show what it would be like to walk around in Plug-In City, but this cross-section gives an idea and it is reassuring that life will still be recognisable. Note Fred's, a kayf just right of centre, and, left of centre, Big Ltd. which could be a department store. At Christmas or during the sales Big's proprietors could plug in more rooms to absorb the rush. The diagram is best read by the colour key: all yellow sections are shops. All the magenta is a shop-feed system, because there won't be any goods deliveries by lorry to clutter up the roads. Instead, food shops will be like giant cigarette machines with just a refrigerated display. You will be able to get obscure dishes, for which you now have to go to Soho, in any neighbourhood: the proprietor will dial a central depot and they will come through pneumatic tubes or along conveyor belts. The diagonal framework (green) would be the longest-lasting element in the city, and everything plugs into it. It would be self-building and self-destroying, thanks to the crane (top of diagram) on the monorail, which is shown about to plug in a room but would also carry the big tubular sections of the grid. The grid is adaptable enough to be valid for perhaps 50 years: after that time, the designers feel a whole new system would have begun to replace it. There are lifts and escalators in the grid sections so people can step out of their doors on to a bridge or street, depending on where they live, and get on the escalator to their office. Or they could take an escalator to the local monorail (Fig. 7 at the bottom of the diagram) and take that either to their stop or to the nearest station on the fast monorail, which being faster moving and quicker to respond to technological change is higher up the framework at Fig. 6. This cross-section is the best diagram for seeing what the designers call "the hierarchy of speed and change". Generally the oldest, slowest-moving and slowest-to-change elements are near the bottom of the grid, the fastest near the top. At ground level are trains (for as long as they last), local monorails and local roads. At the top are the fast monorail and the fast road (Fig. 11 at right), which is suspended from the grid so that it can be easily changed to whatever is needed when cars go out. In the long run everything can be plugged out and replaced without too much fuss, although obviously some things will change slower than others. The black colouring is housing, nine-tenths of which would be on the outside of the grid

Below: Warren Chalk's floor-plan for the house units which plug into the tower (previous page) pursues the hierarchy of change down to the fastest-changing things of all – the appliances. The units themselves could be changed whenever a new, improved one came out, but since new, improved appliances are bound to develop even faster, there is a clip-on appliance wall (Fig. 4 on the diagram) which can be snapped out and replaced with one fitted with more advanced food mixers, vibro massagers and machines like the American one which makes plastic mixing bowls meant to be thrown away after using. Kitchens and bathrooms are the next areas to become obsolete, so they are contained in a pop-out capsule (2) situated near a wide service door opening into the tower's core. The key to the diagram is: (1) Services duct; (2) Kitchen-bathroom capsule; (3) Pneumatic lift instead of a staircase; (4) Clip-on appliance wall; (5) Spring-loaded space divider; (6) Wide door for removing capsules and walls; (7) Services connection; (8) Storage unit. The dark area is soft flooring for sitting and lying on.
Foot of page: an elevation of the unit showing runners at bottom, on which units would slide into tower plug-in framework

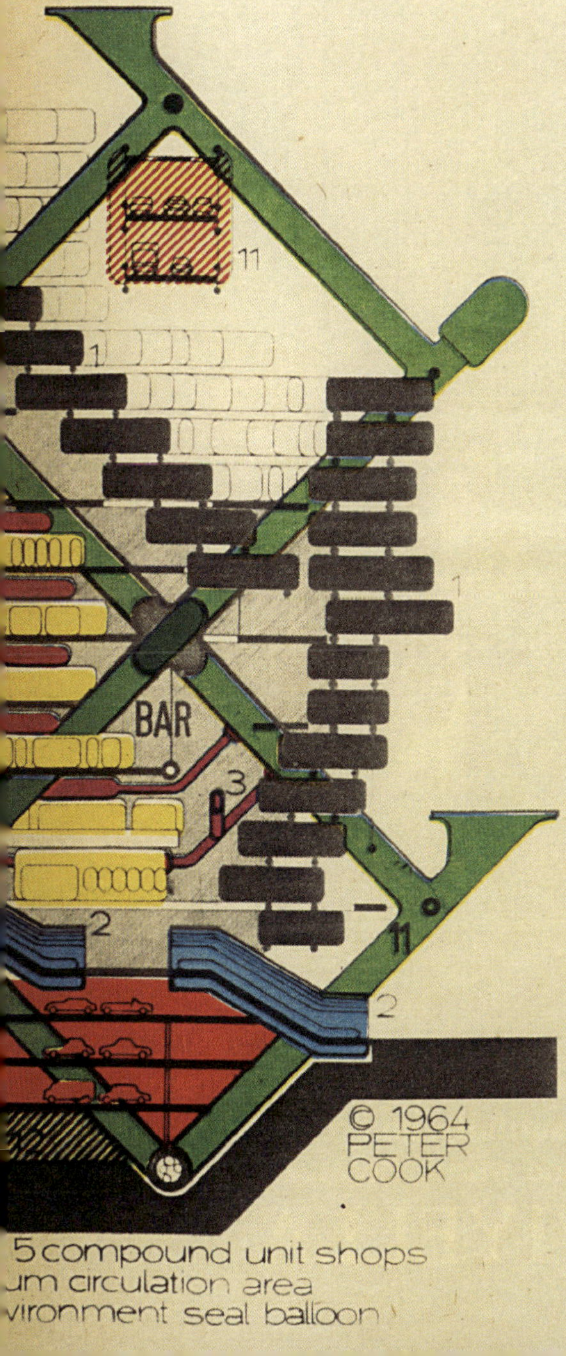

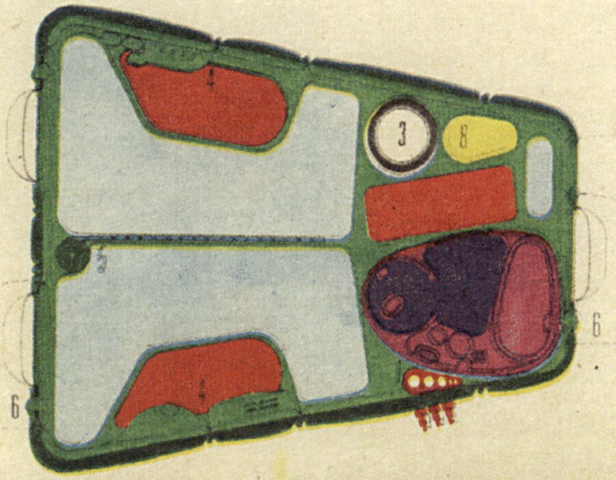

started right now and in 20 years be well on its way.

On a technical level it is set apart from other plans by its purchase on life as it will be in the future. It grasps the rate at which people and things will change and, in effect, acknowledges throw-away architecture.

But what is going to matter to people now is that this plan is so much less traumatic than others: so much so, in fact, that anyone – anyone, that is, who is not totally opposed to the future – could almost welcome the predicted millions and the opportunity to plug in with them. On an even cursory examination of the diagrams on these four pages, Plug-In City turns out not to be as heartless as it sounds. The name is more funny than frightening and the plan itself is humane, benign, even cosy – the work of well-intentioned young men who say the whole point is to have lively neighbourhoods. Chalk, Cook, Crompton and Co. find it hard to say exactly what it will be like to step out of your front door in Plug-In City, but it sounds as though it will be a mixture of a theatre (balconies, aisles and stairs) and Montmartre (passages and stairs connecting different levels): in any event, there will be lots of well-travelled, busy catwalks and streets honeycombing the grid system, all connected by the lifts and escalators. They reckon on a density of 400 people to the acre to ensure the lively neighbourhood feeling (like Mayfair's today), and while the L.C.C. do not generally allow a density of more than 135 these days advanced city planners who want to get away from the New Towns that stretch too far and too dispiritedly, are already thinking in terms of 400.

Plug-In City has two enormous advantages over cities as we know them. The first is that it is a straight line rather than a circle. What this means sinks in when you consider that London has a radius of 20 miles, that under proposals like the South-East Plan it would soon be several times that and week-end cottages wouldn't be anywhere you could get to at a weekend. Its designers see Plug-In City as a magnetic field across Europe, collecting like iron filings all the hopeless little piecemeal building that is smothering the countryside.

The second advantage /*continued overleaf*

Arup Associates, Bush Lane House at Cannon Street, London, 1969–1976.

Kenzo Tange, Skopje City Center Reconstruction Project (1963) selected by Renzo Piano from the periodicals belonging to his library (*Casabella*, 1966).

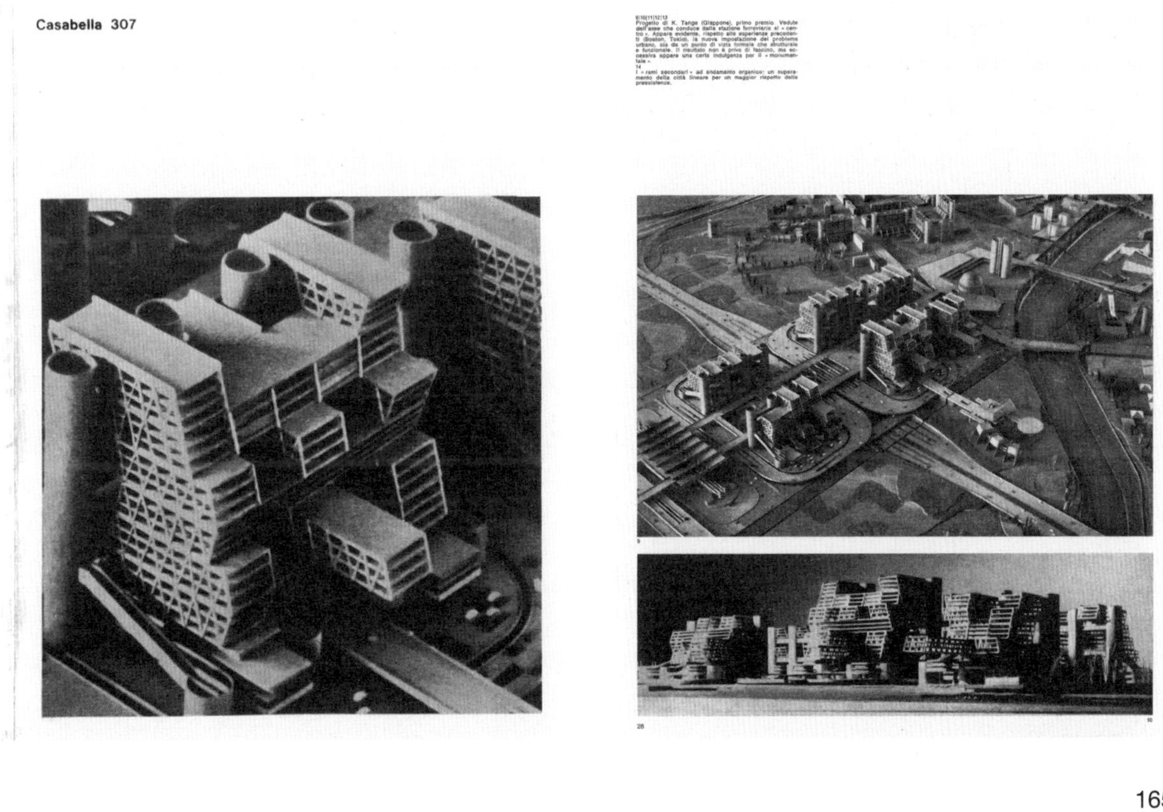

Casabella 307

9|10|11|12|13
Progetto di K. Tange (Giappone), primo premio. Vedute dell'asse che conduce dalla stazione ferroviaria al « centro ». Appare evidente, rispetto alle esperienze precedenti (Boston, Tokio), la nuova impostazione del problema urbano, sia da un punto di vista formale che strutturale e funzionale. Il risultato non è privo di fascino, ma eccessiva appare una certa indulgenza per il « monumentale ».
14
I « rami secondari » ad andamento organico: un superamento della città lineare per un maggior rispetto delle preesistenze.

4.6

THE TRANSFORMATION OF THE SPACE FRAME INTO A SCENIC DEVICE FOR TRANSMITTING INFORMATION

The Centre's platforms were equipped with a circulation system intended to collect the vital flows through the square. Although a choice between cylindrical highrise towers of Kahnian derivation and a prismatic bar abutting onto one of the short sides had not yet been made, in both cases there was a clear intention to bring the circulation system outside the building in order to turn it into a distinguishing element and a system that could be dismantled and reconfigured according to need, as with the ARAM module "service towers" and the Fitzroy shopping mall escalators. The configuration of the circulation system in the bar version also adopted the multistory solution considered and then discarded for the ARAM module. The imposing servant tower for the circulation rejected for functional reasons in the ARAM module was taken up again in the Centre and enriched with a playful and monumental component that Piano+Rogers Architects was trying out at the same time in the Burrell Gallery.

The space frame, which now took the place of a traditional façade, was not merely a structure but also supported an audiovisual system. The optical panels of light and color that Rogers and Piano were experimenting with in the Burrell Gallery project were transformed in the Centre Beaubourg into special "screens for information." Thanks to these screens Piano+Rogers Architects turned the Centre into a transmitting device, taking up the idea, in the air ever since the reference to Candilis's Free University of Berlin, of a center for the dissemination of information. The decisive passage from a façade for the creation of optical effects to an envelope conceived as a means of conveying information to people represents a cornerstone of the project. Rogers immediately made this idea his own, to such an extent that he was unwilling to renounce it even when the competition organizers tried to reduce the envelope to an artwork through the intervention of some exponents of the Op art avant-garde.

The square played a part in the conception of this viewing machine, becoming a forestage, halfway between a town hall square and a concert hall orchestra. That the building was also subject to the creation of such a broadcasting machine is confirmed by the choice to modify the volume in order to improve the visibility of the screens from the piazza. While in the bar solution structure and screens were set vertically in order to be seen from the square, in the tower solution Piano+Rogers Architects tilted the lattice fitted with the screen toward the users in the piazza. Even in the absence of a political and dissenting character from the final design submitted to the competition, the Centre Beaubourg's screens already alluded to an educational and civic intention, halfway between those of a system for the propagation of the counterculture

and a coercive machine in the Orwellian mold for the indoctrination of the masses.[46]
In the second half of the sixties such transmitting devices were iconic features of places such as Piccadilly Circus in London, Times Square in New York, and the Strip in Las Vegas, where they were used as signs and for advertising. Traces of this kind of experimental architecture could already be found in the same period. The closest architectural reference for Rogers and Piano in this regard coincided, once again, with the new structures for education put forward by Cedric Price, Piero Sartogo, and Carlo Pelliccia in *Architectural Design* and *Casabella* and centering precisely on the desire to make use of mass communication media.
These kinds of system included those Sartogo called "audiovisual aids," utilized to conceive an unprecedented form of architecture for learning. Examples are the projections and screens that Price located around the city in montages of the Atom Project or the traveling audiovisual systems that Peter Cook conceived for his Ideas Circus, the nature of which, unlike the audiovisual equipment of the celebrated Instant City, was of a device for the education of the people.
If we exclude the projects analyzed by Piano as part of his research into the theme of the school, the recourse to audiovisual instruments was at the center of numerous contributions to the debate over contemporary architecture. Robert Venturi and Denise Scott Brown included audiovisual screens in their research on American infographics for the definition of new forms of symbolic, meaningful, and communicative architecture.[47] An example is the Billboard Building for the National College Football Hall of Fame in New Brunswick, New Jersey. Venturi and Scott Brown's ideas were not so distant from Tom Wolfe's theory about the superseding of functionalism by an architecture "for visual excitement," which he called "electrographic architecture."[48]
We can also include among the experiments with audiovisual devices the LED and sound systems in the "spaces of involvement" designed by Leonardo Savioli's students at the Department of Architecture of the University of Florence, with which Piano must have been familiar given his appreciation of the Free University of Brussels project conceived by group 1999. Also within the framework of this research fall the audiovisual screens presented at the Montreal Expo in 1967[49] and then at the one in Osaka in 1970.[50] Similar plays of light, sound, and color can also be found in artworks mentioned in *Architectural Design* and *Domus*: Dan Flavin, Mario Merz, or Robert Rauschenberg's LEDs; Martial Raysse's works of Nouveau Réalisme; Robert Whitman's moving images; the plays of light and color of Martha Boto and Vittorio Vardanega and of Mario Merz; and the works of programmed art of the Gruppo T

(Giovanni Anceschi, Davide Boriani, Gianni Colombo, Gabriele Devecchi, and Grazia Varisco).[51]

In this complex lineage of avant-garde experiments connected with art, architecture, and high technology, Venturi and Scott Brown's National Football Hall of Fame Billboard Building is the one that displays a particular affinity with the audiovisual equipment imagined for the Centre Beaubourg. A museum complex devoted to American football created by combining a building of symbolic character for the exhibits, an imposing façade consisting of an electronic and interactive billboard,[52] and a public viewing space with parking lots and gardens, the National Football Hall of Fame shared with the Centre the idea of turning the museum into "architecture of communication for moving masses." Even Venturi and Scott Brown's parking lot for viewing the billboard, with its slight inclination toward the screen and its nature as a forestage, shows a parallel with the sunken square conceived for the project at plateau Beaubourg.[53]

The ideas contained in the sketches—the square entrenched in its void, the vertical space frame with a rhomboidal mesh, the flexible platforms scattered around the interiors, the display of the movement system, and the transformation of the building into a large device for broadcasting information—constitute the essential core of the project the architects and engineers were preparing to reformulate before the consignment of the project for dispatch to Paris.

Robert Venturi and Denise Scott-Brown, Competition Project for the National College Football Hall of Fame, model with audiovisual facade, New Brunswick, New Jersey, 1967.

Overleaf: Archigram (Ron Herron and Peter Cook), "Instant City in Progress," (*Architectural Design*, 1970).

the great
sky-hook

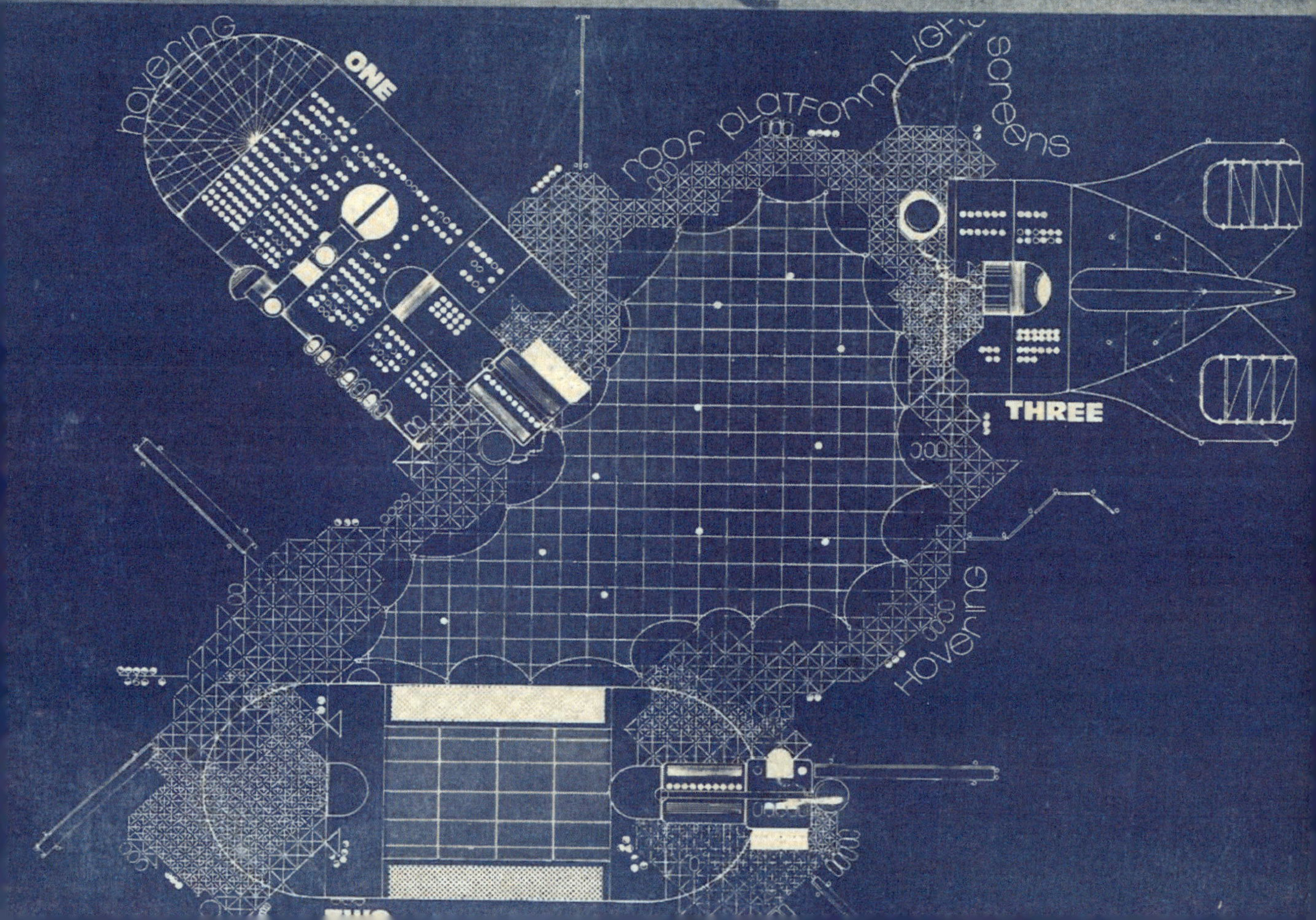
hovering
ONE
roof platform
screens
THREE
hovering

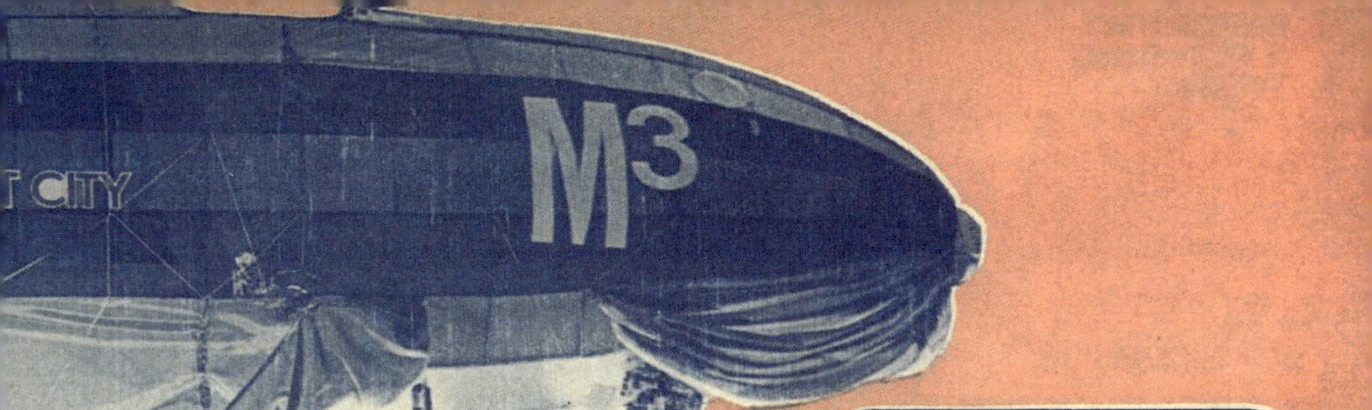

Ha Ha! are we back to heroics then? The giant, pretty, emotionally evocative object, the Blimp, the airship, the beauty-and-disaster-and-history. Back to the heroic and beautiful object? And a delightful paradox. With one hand we are building under the ground in Monte Carlo - and the surface of the ground will remain as was - on the other we are suggesting that (perhaps) a series of trucks rushing around like ants is too cumbersome and so why not service it all from the air? The Instant City could lift up its skirts and its entrails and quietly disappear. In both projects the ground just slips away; that once hot and involved discussion about crust and grain, and servicing and the event of the ground has died. In one's imagination, no more pimples on the ground. If it needs to be there all the time, it's under the surface; if it's occasional, it floats in and floats away (Just too lovely?).

In fact we are a little more pragmatic than that. All the time a primary interest was in spontaneity, and in being able to knit into any place as effectively as possible. And the interest of many around us in the airship simply suggested the possibility of a *giant skyhook*. We see it as this. A possible, available piece of mechanics its evocativeness only of secondary interest.

1 — "The [Beaubourg] competition offered an ideal opportunity to extend the relationship and we asked them if they would be interested in entering with us. The Rogerses brought along Renzo Piano, an Italian architect, with whom they were merging their practice." Ted Happold and Peter Rice, "Introduction: Centre Beaubourg Special Issue," *The Arup Journal*, no. 3 (1973), 2–3: 2.

2 — According to John Morrison, Ted Happold submitted the collaboration request for the Paris competition to several architects before contacting Rogers, and he did not exclude the possibility that Frei Otto was one of them. Boris Hamzeian, Interview with John Morrison, July 27, 2017, Bath.

3 — While collaborating on the Chelsea Football Club stadium project, Happold may also have assisted in drafting the manifesto for Richard+Su Rogers Architects, drawn up at the time of the Rogerses' collaboration with Structures 3 in 1969. Bryan Appleyard, *Richard Rogers: A Biography*, (London: Faber & Faber, 1986), 139–41. The fact that Happold turned to the Rogerses to continue the examination of an inherently dynamic structure that had begun with the stadium project contradicts the widely held view in the literature that Happold's choice was based purely on the climate of collaboration forged by the stadium experience. That Happold's decision was not solely an emotional one is supported by his pragmatism and his strategic and managerial approach to collaborations and competitions. Hamzeian, Interview with John Young, July 25, 2017, Hayling Island.

4 — Sheila Wheeler, "Setting Up in Practice," *Architects' Journal*, 153, no. 3 (1971), 121–62: 154.

5 — Ibid.

6 — Ted Happold, Letter to Richard Rogers, January 15, 1971, RSHPA, C01, J0099, F ARC84132.

7 — Happold mentioned a number of meetings prior to making the choice to take part: "A series of meetings were held to decide whether to enter, which we spent defining the answer we wanted." Happold and Rice, "Introduction: Centre Beaubourg Special Issue," 2. Rice confirmed Happold's statements. Peter Rice, *An Engineer Imagines* (London: Artemis, 1993).

8 — Happold, Letter to Rogers, January 15, 1971.

9 — Délégation pour la realization du Centre Beaubourg, *International architectural contest for the construction of the plateau Beaubourg contemporary arts center in Paris* [English version], n.d. [December 1970], AN, CNACGP, F 10.

10 — Sheila Bacon, Letter to Richard Rogers, January 29, 1971, RSHPA, C01, J0099, F ARC84132.

11 — Nathan Silver, *The Making of Beaubourg: A Building Biography of the Centre Pompidou, Paris* (Cambridge MA: MIT Press, 1994), p. 13.

12 — This date is supported by the presence in the memorandum of a preliminary analysis of the competition that Rogers must have drawn up when he first read the competition file. The date is also confirmed by the list of ongoing projects mentioned in the memorandum. The absence of any reference to the ARAM project suggests that the memorandum was written after or close to the delivery of this project in March. That it was written in February is further confirmed by the mention of May 28 rather than May 14 for the submission of dossiers for the Burrell competition—a revised delivery date announced in the February issue of the *Royal Institute of British Architects Journal* as a result of the UK Postal Workers Strike in the spring of 1971.

13 — Richard Rogers, untitled [Memorandum in view of possible participation in the Beaubourg Competition], n.d. [February 1971], RSHPA, C01, J0099, F ARC73279, 3.

14 — Rogers, untitled [Memorandum in view of possible participation in the Beaubourg Competition], 1.

15 — "It's so political [...]." In a series of handwritten notes added at the end of the memorandum, Rogers reiterated his aversion to the political emphasis implicit in the idea of centralization expressed in the announcement: "I don't like the sociopolitical overtones. Centralization is the danger." The bottom of the document has been torn off and it is not possible to read the last sentence. Rogers, untitled [Memorandum in view of possible participation in the Beaubourg Competition].

16 — The earliest evidence can be found in the unpublished interview with Rogers conducted by Alexander Fils. In 1985, Rogers's hostility was mentioned by Bryan Appleyard, too, but without any reference to Rogers's view of the competition file. "Rogers was immediately violently opposed [...]," wrote Appleyard. In 2011, Rogers reiterated in a conference his hostility to the idea implied by the announcement: "I was totally against the idea, and I fought not to get involved, and had to be dragged into it." More detailed testimony can also be found in Rogers and Piano's interview granted to *AA Files* in 2017: "Richard Rogers: My initial response was 'no way.' This was not long after the student protests of May '68 and I had absolutely no interest in what I saw as a crudely right-wing concept of a centralized cultural venue; Renzo Piano: Richard immediately said it was a very bad idea, because the French were just looking for a monumental public building that celebrated an official kind of culture." Appleyard, *Richard Rogers: A Biography*, 154; Kester Rattenbury and Samantha Hardingham, *Richard Rogers: the Pompidou Centre* (Oxon: Routledge, 2011), 61; Enrique Walker, "Renzo Piano & Richard Rogers in Conversation with Enrique Walker," *AA Files*, 70 (2015), 46–59: 49, 53.

17 — Rogers, untitled [Memorandum in view of possible participation in the Beaubourg Competition], 2.

18 — On Jean Prouvé's influence over Rogers, we can cite the words of Dugdale who, in a recent account, declared: "The ARAM Project you're showing me simply sums up all the things we said previously. They all had to do with the same ideas and everybody shared something. Where did all this come from? From all the influences we had in common, from Bucky Fuller and from the powerful influence of Cedric Price...Sometimes people don't realize how influential he was for us at the time. Richard Rogers, in particular, had other influences. He looked to Jean Prouvé and his panels..." Boris Hamzeian, Interview with Anthony Dugdale, June 21, 2017, London On Richard Rogers's assessment of the jury members, see, too: Appleyard, *Richard Rogers: A Biography*. In a recent interview Su Rogers said that she was surprised by the negative view of Philip Johnson's presence mentioned in the memorandum and in the literature. According to Su, Rogers was in contact with Johnson at the time of the competition and probably visited him during his stays in the United States between 1969 and 1971. Boris Hamzeian, Interview with Su Rogers, October 8, 2017, London.

19 — "I intended to back Richard, but my reasons were different. I hate competitions because I am interested in buildings. I always believed that if you have a direct commission, you have more chance to build it. In other words, the direct commission is intended to lead you to the building process. The competition is like gambling. It is such a huge risk. If I thought for a moment of all the hours we could put into it for that risk...I intended to be on Richard's side. I am pretty sure someone told you that we were very poor at the time." Hamzeian, Interview with Young.

20 — "Of all my teachers and masters, Jean Prouvé has always been a point of reference for me. Even before the Beaubourg competition, I went to visit him at the École des Arts et Métiers, where he taught, in Boulevard Sébastopol. As was his custom, he was asking his students to do an exercise: with a sheet of cardboard they had to build a bridge 60 cm long. It had to be capable of supporting a certain weight. When they had finished the task, he would come by and put the weight on each model. In this way he forced the students to synthesize design, material, rigidity, structural logic and the search for the essential. During the construction of the Beaubourg, old Prouvé often came to see me. His advice was never decisive: he didn't interfere; it was above all advice of a methodological kind, sometimes even of a moral and behavioral nature: he was one of those who taught me not to settle quickly, at the first result obtained." The importance of Prouvé's presence on the jury was reiterated in interviews given between 1987 and 2016. "As far as I am concerned, the presence of Jean Prouvé on the Jury was of decisive importance," said Piano in 1987, and: "For me that was really the number one argument for doing the competition. Prouvé was my absolute idol. He was untouchable. I couldn't believe that someone like Prouvé could possibly run a bad competition," he repeated in 2016. Silver, *The Making of Beaubourg: A Building Biography of the Centre Pompidou, Paris*, 27; Walker, "Renzo Piano & Richard Rogers in conversation with Enrique Walker," 50; Renzo Piano, Richard Rogers, and Antoine Picon, eds., *Du Plateau Beaubourg au Centre Pompidou* (Paris: Éditions du Centre Pompidou 1987), 11.

21 — Appleyard, *Richard Rogers: A Biography*; Boris Hamzeian, Interview with Su Rogers.

22 — Although the paragraph begins with "I don't like the following," and then presents arguments against participation, there are at least two sentences that do not follow the same train of thought: "The building will be a route and flex. Volume building," and "(the prize money is not bad)." Rogers, untitled [Memorandum in view of possible participation in the Beaubourg Competition], 3.

23 — "The program is very well documented, and volumes broken down and circulation links shown." Ibid.

24 — "The [Burrell Gallery] project wasn't successful at all. I don't know what happened exactly. It never fired up our imagination somehow. Even though it started laying down principles which then applied to the Pompidou Centre." Hamzeian, Interview with Young.

25 — The reconstructions of the decisive meeting in the literature are fragmentary and conflicting. They all agree in attributing a decisive role to Su Rogers who, in an interview, confirmed that she had supported Happold's bid. Appleyard, *Richard Rogers: A Biography*, 154; Silver, *The Making of Beaubourg*, 16; Hamzeian, Interview with Su Rogers.

26 — There is a comment written on the document by Rogers in pencil: "Su I thought you said it was 350." Su Rogers, Memo to Richard Rogers, March 30, 1971,

RSHPA, C01, J0099, F ARC73279. The document contradicts the numerous references in the literature regarding Arup's spending. Appleyard (1985) and Silver (1994) gave a figure of £300, Young in a recent interview mentioned £500. Hamzeian, Interview with Young.

27 — "Gianfranco said he could make the time available, but he imposed one condition. In case we won he wanted his name on the credits. Renzo said yes without a second thought. Nobody believed it would happen. This is the reason you see Gianfranco Franchini's name on the competition's credits. That was the deal." Hamzeian, Interview with Young.

28 — For the dates of delivery of the Fitzroy shopping mall and Burrell Gallery projects see, in the first case, the date of the report sent to the client and, in the second, the instructions in the competition notice published in the *Royal Institute of British Architects Journal*. On Franchini's transfer to London see instead Boris Hamzeian, Interview with Riccardo Franchini, June 10, 2017, Genoa.

29 — According to Silver: "Back in London, once the qualms about entering had been overcome, the preparation period had been relatively brief. [...] They managed that much in London, but then progress seemed to slow down and Rogers travelled to Genoa with Piano and Franchini and finally back to London where the scheme was completed." However, the following came out of a discussion with Young: "Boris Hamzeian:
A first phase in London, an intermediate phase in Piano's office in Genoa (Richard was there, too), and then the important conclusive phase in London. Would you agree? John Young: Yes. That's pretty correct. I never went over to Genoa. Richard went there. [...] We kicked off the project. We tossed it around in London. Then he went over to Genoa. Then, three weeks before it was due to be handed in Gianfranco Franchini came over and stayed at the London office. Renzo came over in that period, too. We basically drew the scheme up in London. So, we sent it from London." Reference is also made in the literature to meetings that were supposed to have taken place in Happold's London apartment in Gloucester Crescent. In a recent interview Young questioned this reconstruction, stating:
"I don't recall having been at a single meeting at his house in London. I can't remember what else I was working on. I might have been working on the shopping mall in Cambridge at the time. I am not quite sure what else was going on at the time but I certainly don't remember lots of meetings with Ted Happold although I think the structural drawing put at the end of the report was done by Arup." Derek Walker and Bill Addis, *Happold: The Confidence to Build* (London: Taylor & Francis, 1997); Hamzeian, Interview with Young.

30 — Appleyard, *Richard Rogers: A Biography.*

31 — The two sheets contain schematic drawings of various kinds accompanied in some cases by notes. The first sheet contains two elevations at the top, an annotated elevation in the middle and two planimetric schemes at the bottom, both annotated. The first drawing consists of a tower with a vertical profile that flares outward at the top, filled with a rhomboidal pattern and inserted in the center of the Plateau Beaubourg, lower than the surroundings, and characterized by a series of points used to indicate the crowd. In the second drawing, a variant of the first, the tower with a vertical profile is suspended from the ground by the continuation of the rhomboidal pattern and the basin extends to include the streets bordering the site, transformed into viaducts, and then stops at the height of the surrounding buildings, identified by the profile of the mansard roofs. The third drawing presents another variant in which the tower, positioned at the side of the basin and suspended through the continuation of its profile lines, assumes, on the side facing the road, a vertical profile and, on the one facing the basin, an inclined profile. On the inclined side, the building is equipped with a "slanting screen for information" to make it visible to people gathered in the basin, represented as moving points coming out of a horizontal tunnel extending under the buildings on rue Saint-Martin to connect the plateau Beaubourg and the plateau des Halles. The fourth and fifth drawings consist of two planimetric diagrams relating to the positioning of the tower in the basin according to the flow of crowds moving through the square from Les Halles. In both drawings, the tower is reduced to a square to which three circles are added to represent service towers. The second sheet contains four annotated drawings: an elevation and a schematic plan, a second elevation, and a section. The first two drawings reproduce the tower solution from the first sheet. On the right is a schematic plan entitled "tower in the square" with the square-based tower placed at the center of the basin and the reference to the flow coming from Les Halles. On the left, in the elevation, is a variant of the tower placed at the center of the basin with a flared profile on both sides; a note with the words "changing information on space frame outside" specifies the nature of the rhomboidal pattern and the content of the "slanting screens" which appeared on the previous sheet. In the elevation the building suspended in the basin through the "space frame" assumes a bar configuration characterized at the top by four terraces that slope sideways to reach the same height as the roofs of the buildings of the historical center, as is confirmed by the annotations "high new building" and "low old." The main body is combined with a narrow accessory volume whose shape and configuration seem to allude to a servant volume intended for internal circulation. The last drawing depicts a cross-section corresponding to the bar solution represented in the elevation. At the center of the "piazza," represented once again with lateral viaducts and with the users coming from the plateau des Halles ("pedestrians from Les Halles"), the building in section is represented in the form of two high lateral trusses placed at the sides of uninterrupted floors with "internal flexibility."

32 — The same orange marker was used to write the words "DWG size" in the margins of one of the competition drawings made for the preparation of the final drawing, the floor plan of the Centre. Piano+Rogers Architects, Competition for the Centre Beaubourg, floor plan 1:200, n.d. [June 1971], RSHPA, C02, J0099, F ARC 71370.

33 — The two sheets with the Centre Beaubourg sketches were found and identified by Boris Hamzeian in 2017 in a ring binder entitled "Beaubourg, services" containing fourteen documents all drawn up by the Centre Beaubourg competition *programmateurs* ("program planners") and organizers prior to the publication of the competition results. They include eleven sheets from the file *Programmation architectural et technique-rapport préliminaire-volume 2* drawn up by the *programmateurs* and dated June 20, 1971, with handwritten notes in French and a plan of the proposed layout of the Grand Palais for the staging of the competition ("rez-de-chaussée-salle A-Jury"). RSHPA, C02, J0099, F ARC84138.

34 — The attribution to Rogers is suggested by the handwriting and the choice to use English in the notes. The authorship of the paper was confirmed by Rogers and then by Young, Su, and Mike Davies. "Boris Hamzeian: Here are a series of sketches alluding to the possibility of developing a tower in the piazza. Here, on the other hand, are a series of notes on the facade in which a system of projecting information to people in the piazza is already envisioned... Richard Rogers: I don't remember precisely this series of sketches but I recognize my handwriting and I recognize the drawings. BH: So these are your drawings? RR: Yes, but it's better not to...In the sense that I don't like the idea of people saying that they are my drawings. Renzo, too, must have made a series of drawings on that occasion. You can't say that I made these drawings because between us the relationship in the project is the same as we do now (in my studio). We played ping-pong. It was intellectual ping-pong. The product at the end of the game is always the result of a debate. The drawings are very interesting, after all. Can you tell me again where they came from? BH: Sure. As I told you they are undated and uncatalogued documents. I found them among a series of invoices in one of the folders containing the Beaubourg documents." Hamzeian, Interview with Richard Rogers, May 10, 2017, London. See also: Hamzeian, Interview with Young; Hamzeian, Interview with Su Rogers; Boris Hamzeian, Interview with Mike Davies, May 10, 2017, London.

35 — The content of the sketches and the origins of the project as a device centered in urban circulation and in the proximity to Les Halles found confirmation in Rogers's interview with Enrique Walker when the former stated: "The first thing we did was to look at the site and the surrounding area. It became clear to us almost immediately that the scheme had to be structured around the provision of a new public space. In the late sixties the nearby Les Halles was still a fully functioning wholesale market. The market itself was perfectly good, but there was absolutely no space. The idea of the piazza then became fundamental to our design." Walker, "Renzo Piano & Richard Rogers in conversation with Enrique Walker," 50.

36 — This fact seems to be suggested by the presence of a sketch of the section of the site which, just west of the plateau, connects the piazza and rue Saint-Martin by means of a sloping surface. In any case, the much more accentuated inclination than that of the Piazza del Campo and the line of the drawing seem to allude to a stepped profile. Untitled [sketch of the profile of the square near rue Saint-Martin competition for the Centre Beaubourg] n.d. [spring 1971], RSHPA, C01, F ARC73279. The attribution of the sketch to the phase in which the competition project was fine-tuned is confirmed by the fact that it is drawn on the back of page 8 of Rogers's copy of the "written texts" section of the competition file.

37 — Piano not only discussed the case study of Piazza del Campo and the center of Siena in the article but also illustrated it with an aerial photo of the historical center taken by the architectural photographer and founder of *Global Architecture* magazine, Yukio Futagawa, for Yoshinobu Ashihara's publication. "The view of the centre of old Siena shows how in medieval times the city centre was conceived as a whole; multifunctional and yet integrated into a marvellously complex unity." Renzo Piano, "Renzo Piano," in *Architectural Design*, vol 40, no. 3 (1970), 140–145: 140; Yoshinobu Ashihara, *Exterior Design in Architecture* (New York: Van Nostrand Reinhold, 1970), 15.

38 — Ashihara, *Exterior Design in Architecture*, 14, 16.

39 — "She worked with the campaign against the Vietnam war by assisting draft-resisters." Appleyard, *Richard Rogers: A Biography*, 148.

40 — Ashihara describes the Piazza del Campo in Siena as a public space designed to focus attention on the city hall. "The Piazza del Campo in Siena was developed, centering on the Palazzo Pubblico, over a period of two centuries beginning around the late eleventh century; the nine sectors paved later are inclined toward the Palazzo Pubblico." Ashihara, *Exterior Design in Architecture*, 14.

41 — Between the end of his studies at the Architectural Association and his stay at Yale (1961–62) Rogers developed a keen interest in Louis Kahn's architecture, examining his works and visiting some of his buildings in America.

42 — On Rogers's internship at SOM, see Appleyard, *Richard Rogers: a Biography*, 102. The Alcoa Building is mentioned in one of the articles singled out by Piano in his library. "Awkward Expressionism," *Architectural Design*, 39, no. 12 (1969), 411.

43 — "Japan's Crystal Palace" (Nagashima Tropical Garden in Nagoya),*Architectural Forum*, 130 (December 1969), 76–83; "Urban Matrix (Stanley Tigerman Architecte)," *L'Architecture d'Aujourd'hui*, 38 (October–November 1967), n.p.; "Il concorso per il centro di Skopje" *Casabella*, no. 307 (July 1966), 24–29.

44 — In the ARAM module the solution of identical stories with slender floor slabs is a variation on the one composed of an alternation of uninterrupted floors and slabs so thick that they could be turned into structural floors for services (the solution was defined: "2 and 3 storey activity zone with separate external service towers"). Piano+Rogers Architects, Service Module for the Association of Rural Aid in Medicine, Inc., 8.

45 — "If, to reduce the overall height, a shallow floor is adopted, then a small span structural system is necessary, limiting planning flexibility and increasing on-site work of foundations and ground preparation." Ibid.

46 — The character of the audiovisual screens—not just educational and informative but also coercive—was already evident to Archigram with respect to their Instant City. "In some cases we have been concerned primarily with information. The Ideas Circus project [...] had an educational brief, and in regarding the urban scene it seems a much less simple problem than can be satisfied by a large scale device such as a mega structure. The Instant City is therefore both a collective and coercive project." "Instant City," *Architectural Design*, 39 (1969), 276–80: 278.

47 — On Robert Venturi and Denise Scott Brown's reflections on the role of infographics in architecture, see Robert Venturi and Denise Scott Brown, "A Significance for A&P Parking Lots, or Learning from Las Vegas," in *Architectural Forum*, no. 2 (1968), 36–43, 89, 91. The project for the National Football Hall of Fame, widely published in international architecture magazines between 1967 and 1969, was also covered in the magazine of reference for the architects at 32 Aybrook Street, *Architectural Design*, which presented several images in an article on Venturi and Scott Brown written by Charles Jencks. From this article we learn that the National Football Hall of Fame project would be discussed at the conference held at the Architectural Association in London on October 22, 1969, an event in which Rogers may have taken part.

48 — Tom Wolfe, "Electrographic Architecture," *Architectural Design*, 39 (1969), 379–82: 380.

49 — In one of the articles devoted to the Billboard Building, Venturi cites the example of the Czech Pavilion at the 1967 Montreal Expo as a model for experiments with audiovisual architecture. Venturi is referring to Josef Svoboda and Emil Radok's *Diapolyekran*, which consisted of 112 mobile screens creating a kinetic surface of constantly changing images. On display in the same pavilion was Radúz Činčera's projection entitled *Kinoautomat*, the first example in the world of an interactive film. Robert Venturi, "A Bill-Ding-Board Involving Movies, Relics, and Space," *Architectural Forum*, no. 4 (1968), 74–79.

50 — The experiments in electronic and interactive architecture that had appeared in Montreal became the leitmotiv of the Osaka Expo in 1970 with works such as Jacob Berend Bakema and Carlos José Maria Weeber's *Viewing Machine* for the Dutch Pavilion, the cinematic environments of Donald Brittain and Roman Kroitor, the smoke screens for an intensification of the audiovisual experience presented in the Mitsubishi Future Pavilion, the playful technological devices by the architect John Pearce called Pepsi-Cola Fun Pavilion and the Experiments in Art and Technology (EAT), the electronic systems—called "soft architecture"—composed of lights and sounds and, finally, Arata Isozaki's robots for the Theme Pavilion.

51 — Jack Burnham, *Beyond Modern Sculpture: The Effects of Science and Technology on the Sculpture of This Century* (New York: Braziller, 1968).

52 — "The giant screen has the approximate proportions of a football field. On it, 200,000 electronically programmed lights produce moving sequences of naturalistic images, words and phrases, and diagrammatic choreographies of famous football plays." Venturi, "A Bill-Ding-Board Involving Movies, Relics, and Space."

53 — "The front of our building, which is a billboard, inflects toward the big parking spaces and the stadium," wrote Venturi. "From nearby, the billboard corresponds to the largely false west facade of a Gothic cathedral, especially an Italian one like Orvieto, teeming with glittering mosaics and niched statues, whose main function is to communicate information toward the piazza," he went on. Venturi, "A Bill-Ding-Board Involving Movies, Relics, and Space." See, too, Venturi and Scott Brown, "A Significance for A&P Parking Lots, or Learning from Las Vegas."

Cannito et al. (students under the direction of Leonardo Savioli), Space of engagement (spazio di coinvolgimento) based on an infrastructure dedicated to the creation of new forms of interaction using light, color, sound and images, Department of Architecture of the University of Florence, 1968–1969.

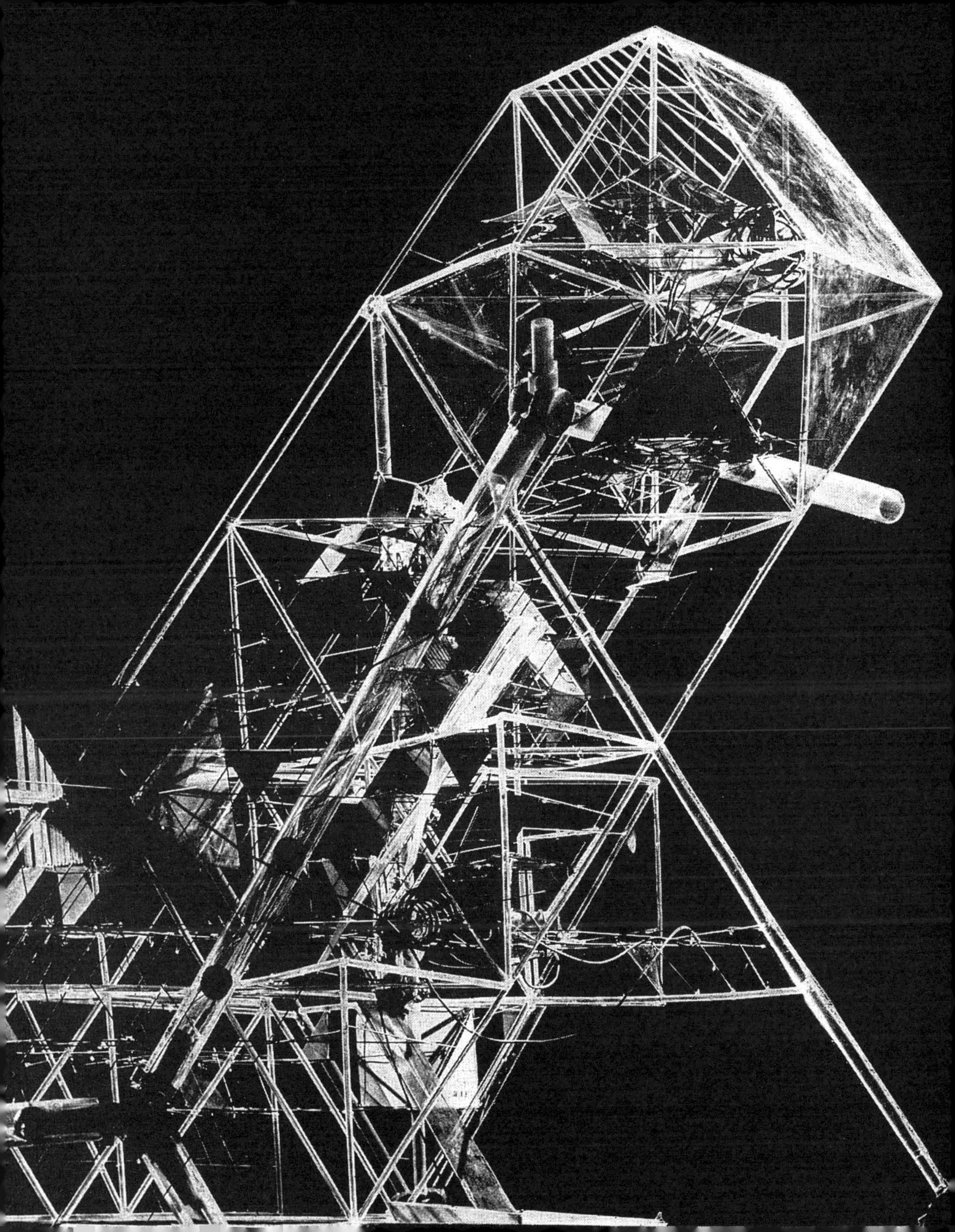

5

THE FINAL SUBMISSION: THE LIVE CENTRE OF INFORMATION

5.1

A NODE OF A GLOBAL NETWORK TO SHARE INFORMATION WITH PARIS, FRANCE AND BEYOND

The project team for the Beaubourg competition drew up the final plans in the weeks prior to the delivery date, set for June 15, 1971.
Those involved in the production of the plans were, on behalf of Piano+Rogers Architects, Richard Rogers, Renzo Piano, Gianfranco Franchini, John Young, and Marco Goldschmied, assisted by part-time collaborators Peter Flack, Jan Kaplický, and Andrew Holmes and by Gordon Bishop, Holmes's colleague at the Architectural Association.
The people from Ove Arup & Partners who contributed to the project were Ted Happold and Peter Rice, senior traffic engineer Michael Sargent, project planning engineer Peter Bolingbroke, and David Armstrong and George Innes, members of Ove Arup & Partners' "Model Workshop" team, assisted by a part-time collaborator, Peter Caller.
The ideas of a large trough to collect the crowd, an iconic structure capable of freeing up the internal spaces, and large audiovisual screens from which to project "changing information" were reworked in the conception of an avant-garde cultural center intended to provide information and which Piano+Rogers Architects defined as a "Live Centre of Information."[1] Conceived as an educational and informative broadcasting device and then as a container for artworks, the Live Centre of Information combined the idea of the traditional museum with that of an open and democratic institution, dedicated to the dissemination of information: a place in which to experiment with new forms of interactive communication between the public and the institution's cultural contents.[2] Rogers expressed this duality in a phrase that was going to become perpetually associated with the idea of the Live Centre of Information: "This centre of constantly changing information is a cross between an information-orientated, computerised Times Square and the British Museum, with the stress on two-way participation between people and activities/exhibits."[3]
In linking the electronic billboards of Times Square with the image of the British Museum, which represented one of the most traditional and conservative models in the field of museology, Piano+Rogers Architects made an ambiguous comparison that, if taken literally, could have made the Live Centre of Information both a broadcasting device and a traditional container for artworks. However, the idea his statement expressed concerning the association between broadcasting device and art container was not followed up in the actual project, which would show interest solely in the former, without considering either the museological question or the configuration of the spaces for the works of art, as happened for the Burrell Gallery.
The idea of making the Live Centre of Information a device for the transmission of information induced Rogers and Piano to go beyond the "slanting

screen of information" and propose a machine to spread information through the city, the region, and the whole world, in the manner of the radical educational centers that Piano had studied in Piero Sartogo and Carlo Pelliccia's survey.[4] "The plateau Beaubourg Information Centre will be linked up with information dispersal and collection centres, throughout France and beyond; for example, university centres, town halls, etc.," were the words used in the competition notice.

While a few decades earlier the idea of architecture for information might have been associated with the image of a radio antenna or a TV station, something that Richard Buckminster Fuller had already translated into architecture with the 4D Tower, which was at once residence, university, and radio mast connected with the rest of the globe, in the Live Centre of Information this idea crystallized into the image of a network of information centers, along the lines of the Advanced Research Projects Agency Network (ARPANET), the military data and command system that was coming into operation in the United States between 1969 and 1970.

The idea of the Live Centre of Information integrated the organizers' desire for a cultural center able "to overflow the limits of the building" through physical environments and computerized systems. It was precisely these purposes that made clear the idea that the Live Centre of Information in Paris could not be reduced to a traditional form of architecture, and thus to a single building, as the wavering between the tower and the bar in the sketches Rogers had made in the spring might have suggested.[5]

The Live Centre of Information in Paris pursued the rarefaction of architecture into a high-tech infrastructure for the rehabilitation and revitalization of historical city centers, continuing along the lines of the theory of integrated environmental planning and definitively transforming the discussions about the school system into the idea of an educational facility that had dissolved both the museum and the university, reducing itself to a mast for the transmission of the counter-information and counterculture of the street protests of 1968.

PROJET LAUREAT

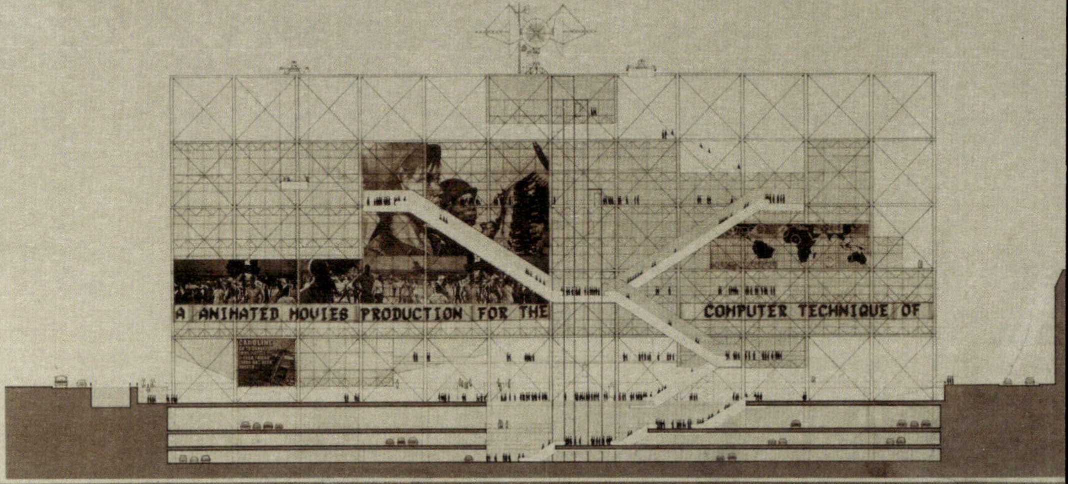

R.22.123

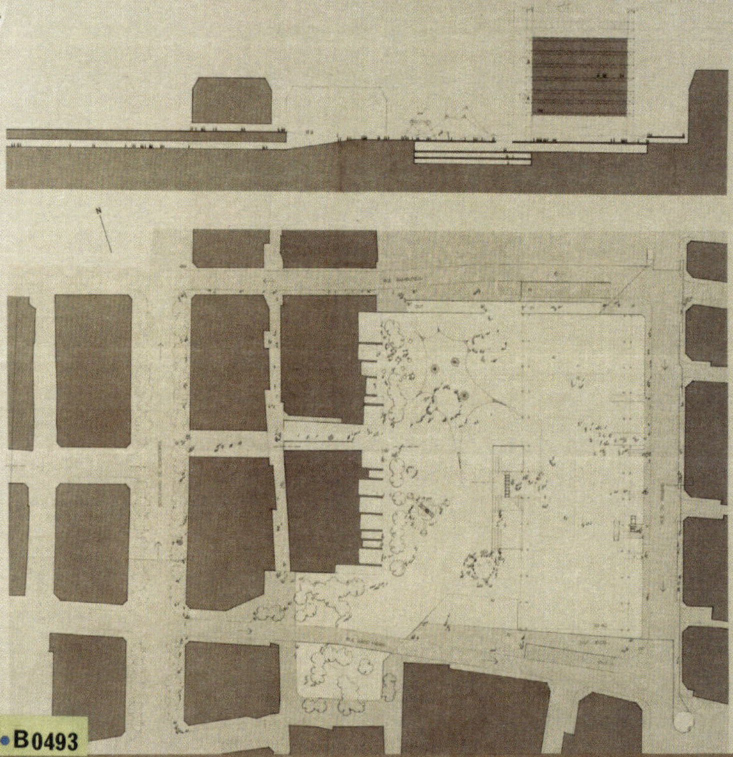

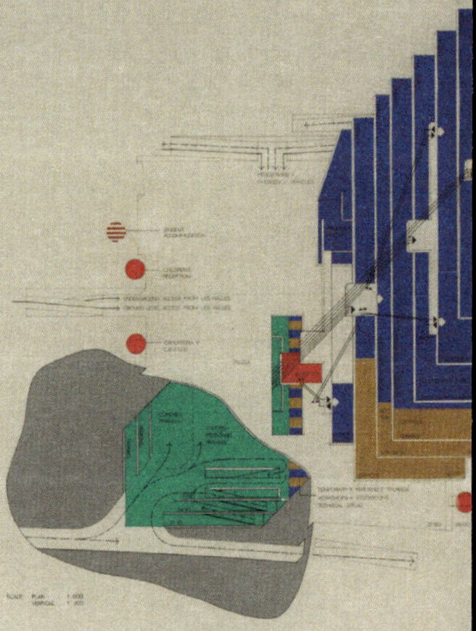

B0493

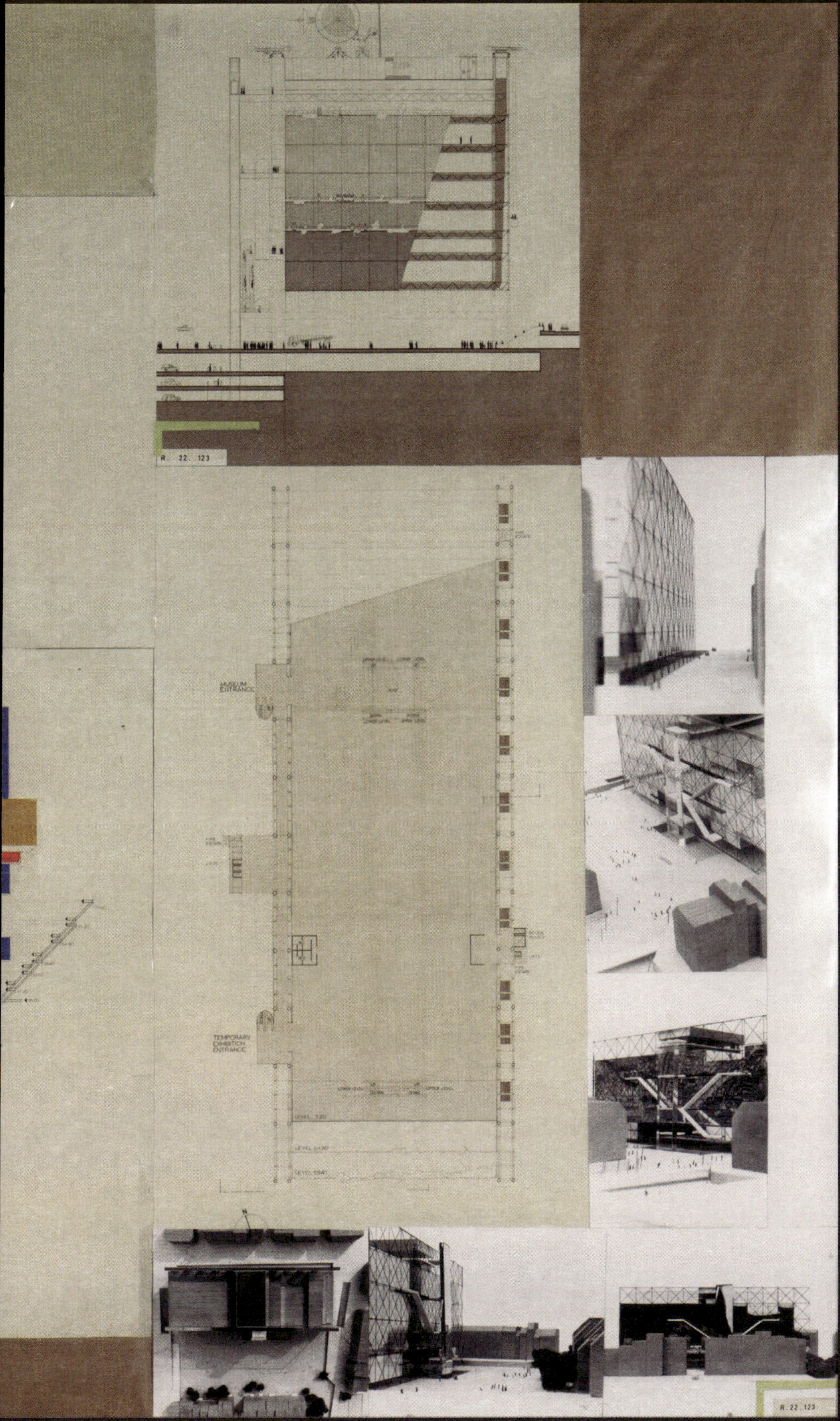

Renzo Piano, Richard Rogers, Gianfranco Franchini and Ove Arup & Partners, Competition Proposal for the Centre du plateau Beaubourg (known as Centre Beaubourg), competition panel set up at the Grand Palais, June 1971.

SUMMARY AND INTERRELATIONS OF THE CENTRE BEAUBOURG ACTIVITIES

A. Reception orientation (Red)
A1. Entrance reception
A2. Reception for children
A3. Cafeteria and canteen
A4. Restaurant

B. Main activities (Blue)
B1. Current events room
B2. Industrial design permanent gallery and documentation service
B3. Experimental Gallery of Contemporary Art
B4. Temporary exhibitions
B5. Theatres and meetings
B6. Museums
B7. Library
B8. Specialized documentation and research
B9. Temporary and permanent storage

C. Management (Green)
C1. Scientific and administrative personnel
C2. Social services
C3. Supervision and control
C4. Lodgings
C5. Workshop and storerooms
C6. Technical areas

D. Parking (Yellow)
D1. Personnel parking
D2. Visitor's parking
D3. Coaches
D4. Trucks

5.2

THE SUNKEN SQUARE AND THE MONUMENTALIZATION OF THE SUBTERRANEAN FLOWS OF PARIS

When the time came for the final formulation of the competition project, the idea of the Live Centre of Information as an infrastructure for Paris induced Piano+Rogers Architects to start again from the site study, from the indications with regard to the areas of renewal and restoration, and from the complex system of vehicular and pedestrian circulation, on the surface and below ground, of which Rogers had sensed the importance since the memorandum, and the organizers of the competition stressed in the portfolio entitled "Précision sur le programme" in April 1971.[6]

Thanks to this portfolio, in addition to the programmatic requirements and cadastral maps contained in the competition notice, Piano+Rogers Architects was able to get an idea of the pedestrian tunnel connecting Beaubourg with Les Halles and its access; of the plan for the underground route for vehicular traffic in the area, with the rue Saint-Martin road tunnel and the access ramps to the junctions of rue du Renard with rue Saint-Merri and rue Rambuteau; and of the Métro system and the stops close to the site in the east, as well as of the configuration and size of the rooms in the buildings around the edges of the plateau.

The infrastructural aspects of the site constituted the problem of the area underneath the Centre. If in the spring of 1971 these aspects had given rise to the idea of a square set below ground level, at the moment of the final formulation of the project in June they were subjected to the scrutiny of Sargent, Ove Arup and Partners' top expert on traffic and circulation. Sargent tackled the project with the aim of turning Piano+Rogers Architects' proposal of a sunken square into a something that could be integrated with the underground system of pedestrian and vehicular traffic.[7]

There is no trace in the documents of Sargent's studies and the discussions he had with his Structures 3 colleagues and Piano+Rogers Architects, just of the conclusions he reached in the "Access and Circulation" section of the competition report. From this it is evident that the idea at the root of Sargent's studies was to multiply the sunken square to create a sequence of superimposed underground platforms on which to locate the car and coaches parking facilities requested by the competition notice, freeing the surface of the plateau from the function of open-air parking lot that it still had in 1971. In his intention to turn the place into a "sunken square" and to "segregate pedestrians and vehicles," Sargent did not include access ramps to connect surface roads with the Live Centre of Information's underground parking, but envisaged direct links with the two underground tunnels of the Les Halles circuit planned along rue Saint-Merri and rue Rambuteau. In doing so, he created an entirely subterranean system to capture the movement of urban traffic toward the Live Centre of Information and divert it into the parking facility.[8]

The transformation of the sunken square into a sequence of underground platforms and the integration of this subterranean system with the road network of Les Halles became an opportunity to further possess and excavate the ground beneath the plateau Beaubourg. The aim was to make the sequence of platforms an infrastructure able to connect with Paris's underground transport system, with its networks and channels. Once brought to the surface, these flows of people, cars, fluids and grids would then be integrated into an open-air infrastructure that, not coincidentally, was to become, in its final version, a structural framework for their transformation into a scenographic and even monumental element.

With its stratification and connections, the Centre's underground infrastructure, given its nature as a machine for the circulation and collection of people and traffic, took possession of the Les Halles tunnel in order to intercept the flow from the Forum and the underground station of the RER line. The Live Centre of Information's underground infrastructure also looked to the streets, public spaces, subway stops, and buildings that were located on its perimeter and took possession of these elements in order to function as a collector of metropolitan flows. These solutions found expression in the plans submitted to the competition. Here the infrastructure of the Live Centre of Information was translated into a sequence of platforms that started in the ground beneath the plateau Beaubourg, where it eroded the stratigraphy near its perimeter so as to become integrated with the surrounding fabric. Moving upward from here, the infrastructure emerged onto the surface with a platform that revealed the underground to the city, became a piazza, and, finally, rose above the roofs of Paris with a system that was not a building but the continuation and monumental antenna of that sequence of platforms rising from under the ground.

Starting from below, the urban infrastructure of the Live Centre of Information assumed the form of three superimposed rectangular platforms located at 21.10, 24.30, and 27.50 meters ASL (above sea level) respectively. The first two, smaller in area and height, occupied only the western half of the plateau Beaubourg and housed parking facilities for cars, while the third, taller to permit the passage and parking of trucks and coaches, occupied the whole of the plateau and housed, to the east, storage areas, restoration workshops, and technical rooms which were part of the museum structure and, located on the perimeter to the west, a garage for coaches that could if necessary be extended farther west by means of additional excavation. This was a confirmation of the principle of erosion on which the underground infrastructure of the Centre was based.[9]

Continuing upward, the infrastructure became the "sunken square," an open-air platform at a level of 32.80 meters as opposed to the 35.00 meters of the surrounding streets. Conceptually it still possessed the civic value of the area that Rogers had described in terms of a piazza. This identity was reinforced by the functions Piano+Rogers Architects laid out on its surface, ranging from elements drawn from the tradition of Mediterranean piazzas ("mobile exhibitions, live theatre and music, games, stalls, meetings, parades" and "competitions")—illustrated in the technical drawings with a tensile structure derived from Frei Otto—to technological devices such as "robots, temporary structures, electronic two-way games of information, etc.," represented in the form of automata halfway between the American lunar modules that had recently landed on the Moon and the fanciful devices found in Archigram's drawings or what Arata Isozaki had just created for the Theme Pavilion in Osaka.[10] In the framework of the discussion to prepare the competition dossier the design of the sunken square was influenced by a series of references, ranging from locations such as St. Mark's Square in Venice, Piazza IV Novembre in Perugia, Piazza Grande in Arezzo, Piazza del Campo in Siena, place de Vosges in Paris, and Hyde Park in London to a set of playgrounds found in British and French architecture magazines and the interiors of some of the Osaka Expo pavilions.[11]

The sunken square could no longer be assimilated to the piazza of Rogers's sketches. Transformed into the visible surface of a subterranean collector of metropolitan flows, the sunken square extended beyond the limits of the plateau Beaubourg to connect with the city. To the south it reached as far as the plateau La Reynie ("an extension of the square"), which was turned into a sunken park at the same level as the sunken square, separated from it only by rue Saint-Merri, which, transformed into a viaduct, ran across it in elevation. To the east, along the site perimeter, the sunken square wedged itself under rue du Renard and, in the space created under the street, housed the CCI and a number of "event rooms," as well as a series of pedestrian access routes that ensured continuity with the Marais. To the west the sunken square was connected to Les Halles by the pedestrian tunnel, for which Piano+Rogers Architects designed an access with two monumental downward sloping ramps (the tunnel was about 30 meters below sea level, i.e., two meters below the sunken square) separated by a third ramp that connected the square to the historical center above, in a scenic configuration that confirmed the tunnel's role as the main channel for the circulation of visitors to the Live Centre of Information.

The sunken square extended beyond the edge of the site to the west just as it did in the east, in this case by getting rid of rue Saint-Martin for that stretch. The sunken square extended as far as the buildings on rue Saint-Martin, whose basements were transformed into stores and restaurants facing onto the square and upper floors into lodgings for students and artists.[12]

With this solution, which responded to the organizers' instructions in the competition notice, the sunken square was turned into a means for restoring and revitalizing the historical city.[13] The plan to extend the square as far as the buildings of rue Saint-Martin eliminated an arterial road but without making any provision for diversion of the traffic, a question over which architects and engineers were going to clash when fine-tuning the project.

The sunken square was also defined by the presence, at its center, of a rectangular courtyard fifty meters in length and twelve in width opening onto the subterranean platforms to reveal the circulation and activities to passersby.

On its perimeter the sunken square was equipped with a set of ramps, flights of steps, and bridges, connecting it to the level of the historical center and channeling the metropolitan flow. "[The particpants shall provide the] maximum number of pedestrian routes under the neighbourhood roads" was, not coincidentally, the formula used in the report.[14]

These connections established the sunken square

as the Live Centre of Information's main infrastructure platform; this was reinforced in the optical and visual stratagems Piano+Rogers Architects deployed to turn this space into a scenic device, strengthening its civic value. With its horizontal trough bounded by subterranean activities on its perimeter, the sunken square extended into the bowels of the city, taking possession of the buildings on rue Saint-Martin which, while still defined by the characteristics 19th-century facades, were invaded at their base by the excavation of the sunken square. The visual measures used to define this place came to determine the configuration of the sequence of elevated platforms above.

The elevated platforms were part of a structure that no longer had anything to do with a traditional building, and that could be summed up by the terms "system" or "framework" that Rogers and Piano had used in Cambridge, but for which, precisely because of its original and ambiguous nature in the case of Paris, they still called a "building," confirming the difficulty of finding a suitable definition.[15]

To avoid the sequence of elevated platforms undermining the physical and visual continuity of the sunken square, it was suspended at a height of a dozen meters, preserving the sunken square's nature as a scenic device.

"The building is lifted on piloti [*sic*], well above ground level, so that it is possible from rue du Renard to see under the building the whole of the facades of the houses on rue Saint-Martin," was the comment in the report.[16] In this way Piano+Rogers Architects raised a structure into the sky of Paris that overtopped the roofs of the buildings in the historical center by twenty or so meters.

Although this stemmed from an effort to integrate with the surroundings, the height of the "building" would be misrepresented by the project's detractors who, seeing the "building" as a monumental structure and not as a sequence of platforms, would perceive it as a disfigurement of the historical center. However, the subterranean platforms of the Live Centre of Information remained enigmatic from a structural viewpoint and were probably conceived from here on as being constructed by means of the most elementary system possible, i.e., a set of concrete pillars combined with floor slabs of the same material.

Overleaf: Renzo Piano, Richard Rogers, Gianfranco Franchini and Ove Arup & Partners, Competition proposal for the Centre Beaubourg, plan, June 1971.

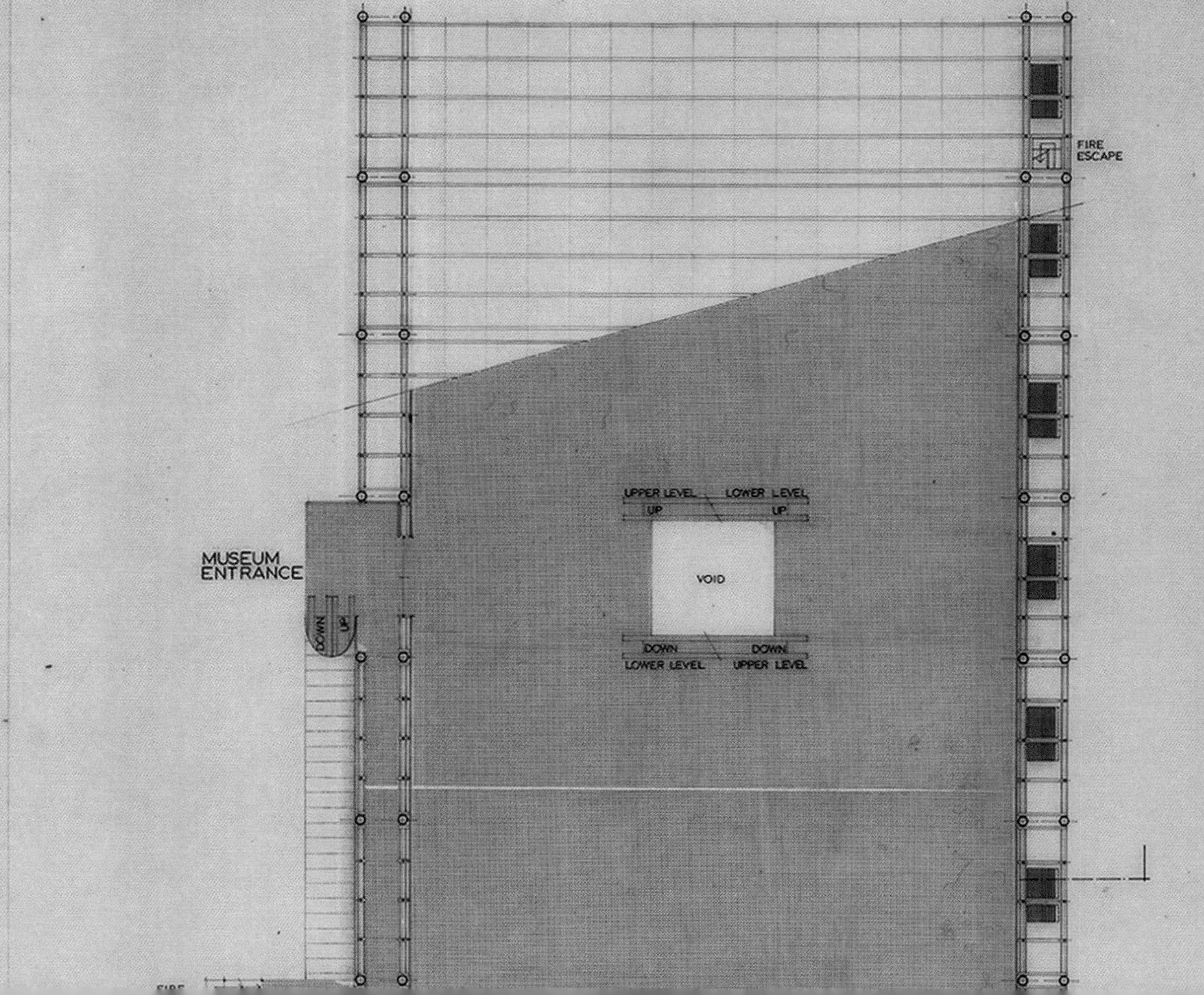
FIRE
ESCAPE
UPPER LEVEL
LOWER LEVEL
UP
UP
VOID
DOWN
DOWN
LOWER LEVEL
UPPER LEVEL
MUSEUM
ENTRANCE
DOWN
UP

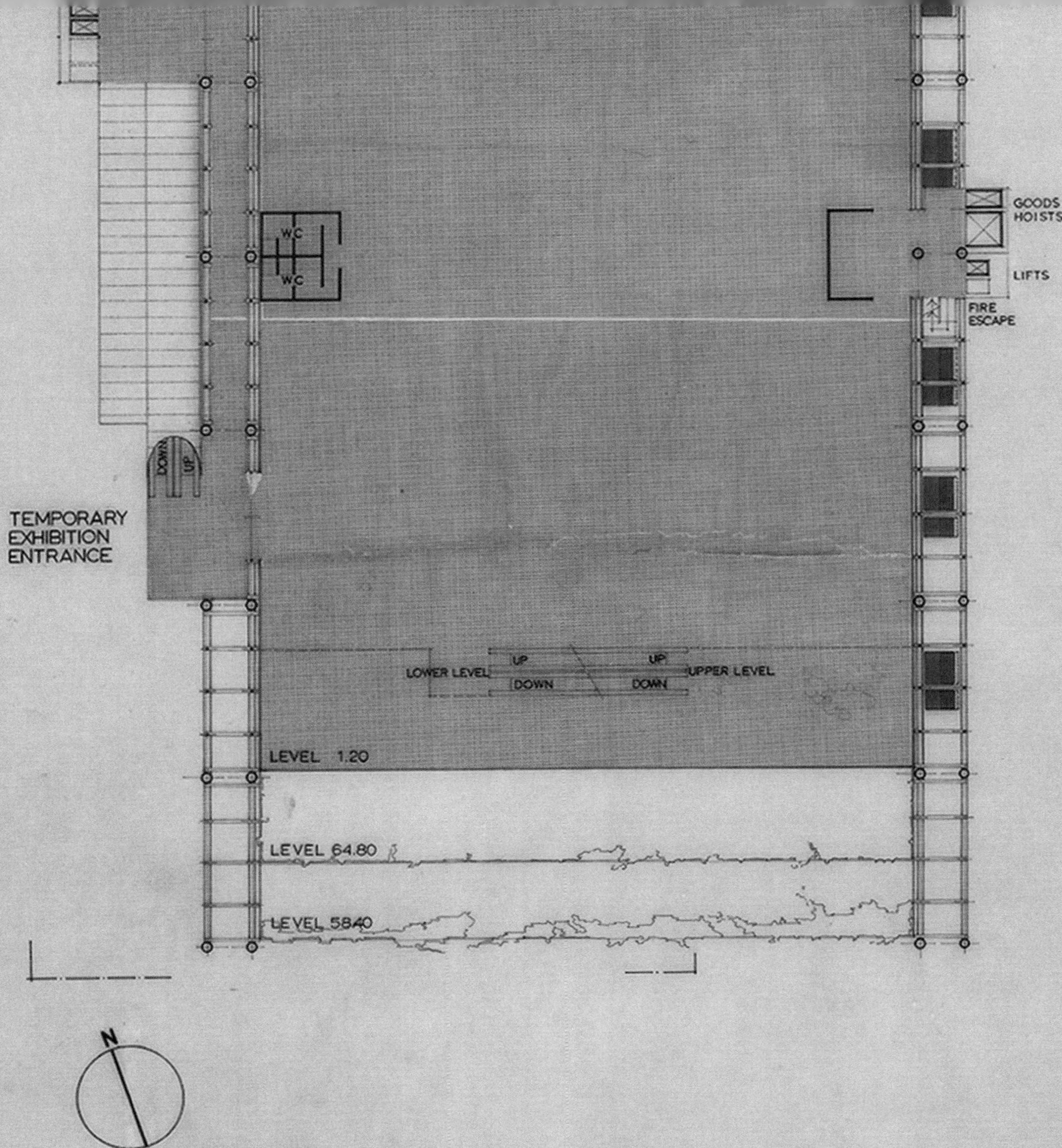
GOODS HOISTS
LIFTS
FIRE ESCAPE
WC
WC
DOWN
UP
TEMPORARY EXHIBITION ENTRANCE
LOWER LEVEL
UP
DOWN
UP
DOWN
UPPER LEVEL
LEVEL 1.20
LEVEL 64.80
LEVEL 5840
N

Renzo Piano, Richard Rogers, Gianfranco Franchini and Ove Arup & Partners, Competition proposal for the Centre Beaubourg, ground plan and section, June 1971.

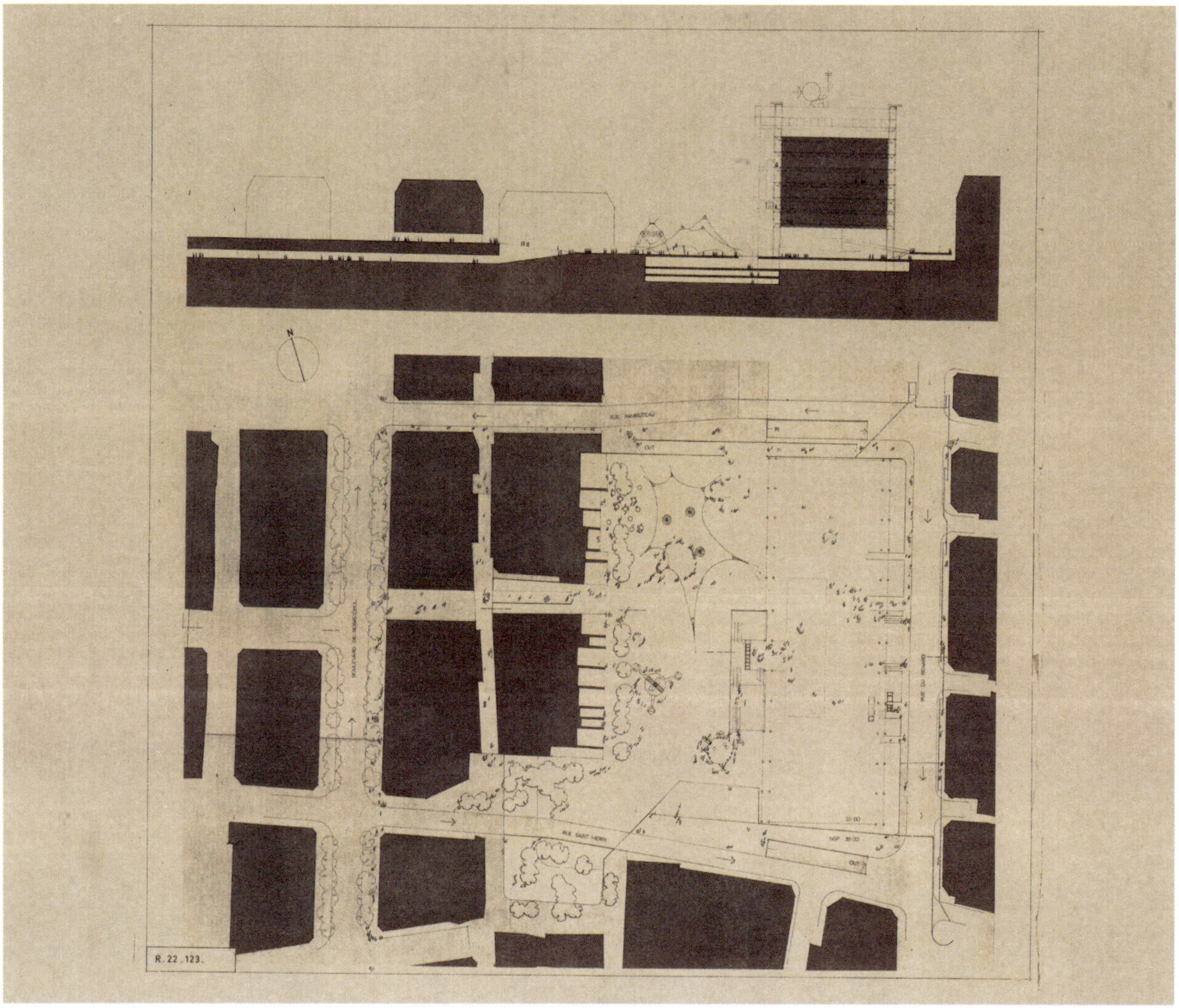

Renzo Piano, Richard Rogers, Gianfranco Franchini and Ove Arup & Partners, Competition proposal for the Centre Beaubourg, section/south elevation, June 1971.

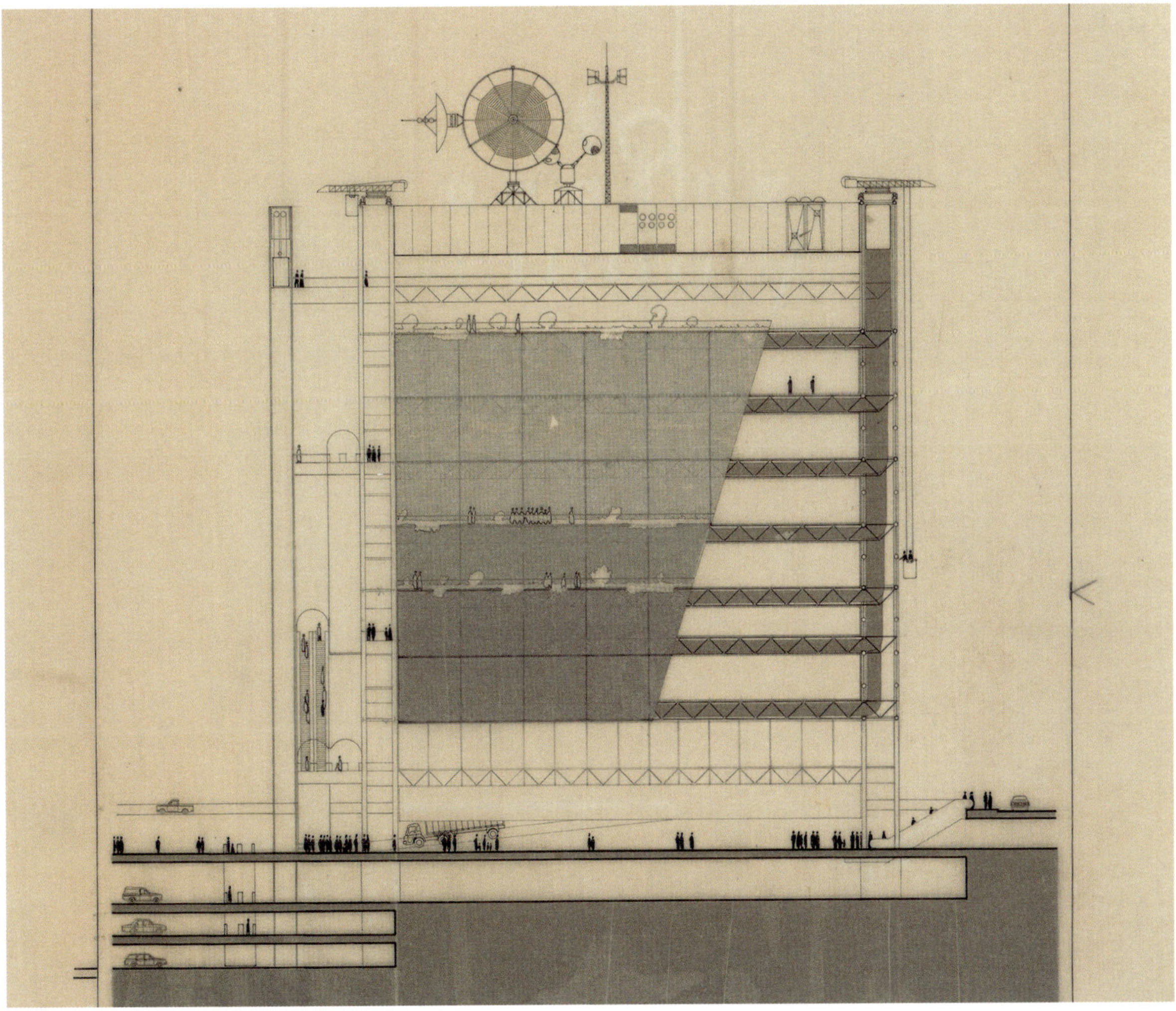

Renzo Piano, Richard Rogers, Gianfranco Franchini and Ove Arup & Partners, Competition proposal for the Centre Beaubourg, diagrams, June 1971.

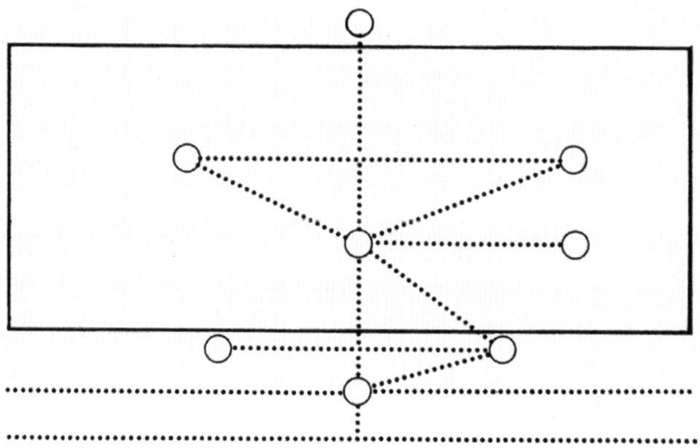

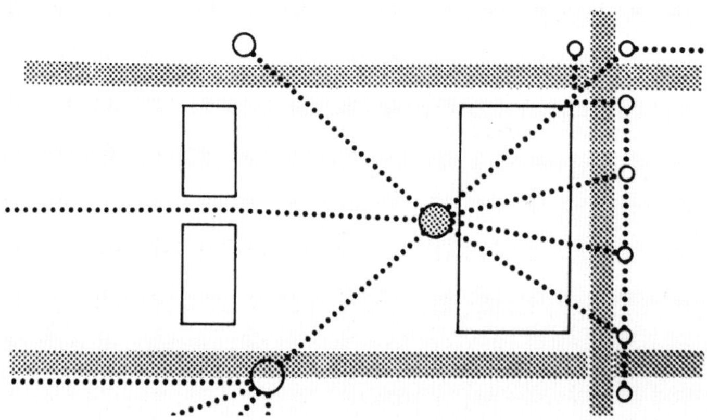

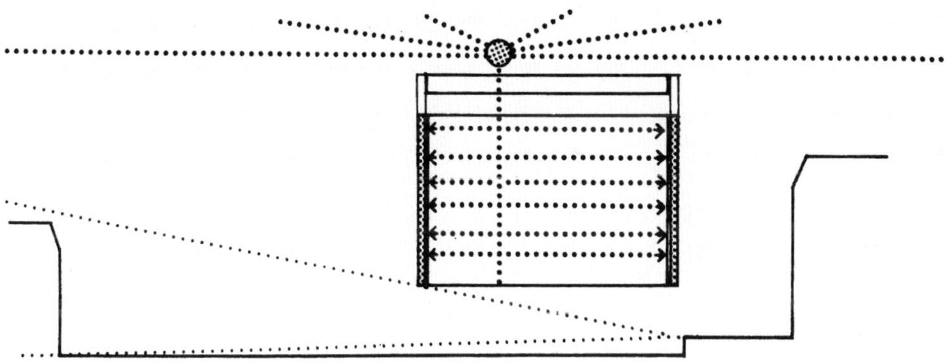

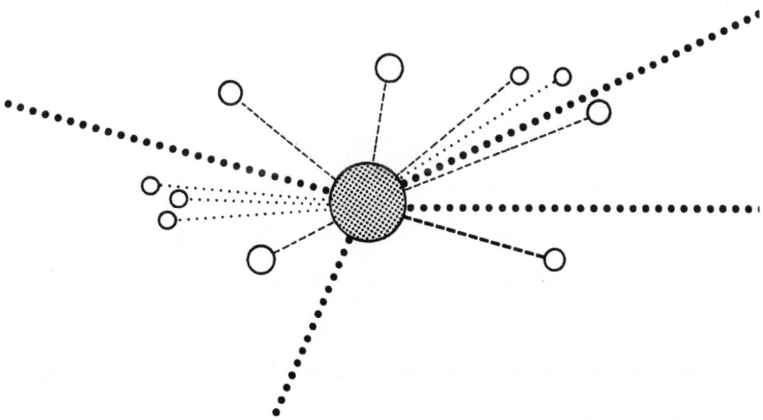

5.3

THE REDUCTION OF THE BUILDING TO A SEQUENCE OF "LARGE, FLEXIBLE UNINTERRUPTED FLOOR AREAS"

What Piano+Rogers Architects called a "building" was nothing but a sequence of platforms that, although different in size, was conceptually analogous to the stratified platforms set in the ground beneath the plateau Beaubourg and emerging onto the surface with the sunken square, which was the fundamental surface of that stratification.

The "building," i.e., the sequence of elevated platforms, could not be disconnected from the machinery of circulation flows and traffic underneath because both were conceived as flexible surfaces to house constantly changing activities. It was the competition report that confirmed the conceptual identity of these platforms when it lumped them all under the definition "free open plan." In the first section of the report Piano+Rogers Architects made the continuity of these platforms clear by declaring: "The large sunken square, including the open area under the building and the area around the edge of the square, is the horizontal continuity of the facade."[17]

The sequence of elevated platforms took to an extreme the idea of a flexible space with no vertical structural elements—a "free space"—that had been outlined in the sketches made in the spring and that in the plans for the competition assumed an architectural dimension. The hypothesis of a setting open to a theoretically infinite range of uses had been pursued in the Rogerses' shells and in Piano's projects, which in spatial terms were nothing but variations on those shells. In none of these cases had the space ever succeeded in crystallizing the image of an empty, flexible, and continuous floor because that space had always been obstructed. Sometimes what cluttered that open space was the structural framework—elementary and diffuse in the Universal Oil Products offices and the Fitzroy shopping mall, concentrated and colossal in the ARAM hospital module. At others the obstacles were formed by fixed partitions, such as the kitchen and service units of the Zip-Up House.

The Live Centre of Information brought the search for the open space to a conclusion with the invention of a sequence of unusual rectangular platforms: they were "large" ("varying between 5500–7500 sq. m.") so as to house all the functions listed in the competition notice; they were "uninterrupted" by any kind of clutter from structure to technical installations, shifting it all to the two lattices, called "3-dimensional walls," located at their ends and coinciding with their support ("totally uninterrupted floor space is achieved by limiting all vertical structure, servicing and movement to the exterior"); they were "flexible" because, freed of all clutter, they allowed any sort of occupation and division into compartments ("the building offers maximum flexibility of use"); they were completely empty and therefore reduced to simple "floor areas" or "floor

spaces." "[A] number of large, flexible uninterrupted floor areas" was the definition given in the report.[18]
The fundamental difference between the sunken square and the floor areas lay in the capacity of the floor areas to be moved up and down to vary the spaces' heights and meet their occupants' needs. That Piano+Rogers Architects was trying to come up with a setting open to the unpredictable is confirmed by the report, both through the extensive use of the word "may" to indicate the hypothetical and temporary location of certain functions—"offices may be positioned everywhere" is a typical example—and through the presentation of alternative locations for some uses.[19] "Areas needing a view, uninterrupted daylight, and/or open space, such as the roof top restaurant, with its view over Paris, experimental and temporary exhibitions, outdoor museum, children's reception area, are located either on the roof on the south end of the building, with its view toward the Seine to the north, or in the square below, all areas free of the vertical grill": this was the formula adopted in the report to convey the fact that it would be up to the organizers, not the architects, to determine how space was used in the Live Centre of Information.[20]
The idea of reconfigurability and indeterminacy was put into effect in the handling of the volume of the floor areas, which, rather than being repeated identically on each level, were reduced to a surface on the upper ones, transformed into a sequence of terraces with a stepped profile. Thus the floor areas translated the idea of flexibility into a sort of permanent building site.
Their terraced profile was also a response to the desire to blend with the surroundings by adapting to the level of Paris roofs. It was a choice, however, that would go unnoticed by public opinion.
The description of the floor areas in the report is contradicted by one of the technical drawings, the plan on a 1:200 scale of the floor areas at the 71.20 level. In this drawing the space that was supposed to be occupied by nothing but cubic meters of air features elements that go against this solution: a fixed cubicle for the bathrooms, perhaps placed there out of fear of depriving the space of an essential functional component; a square court set on the lower level, which revealed the stratification of the floor areas by means of a scenic device similar to the open courtyard on the sunken square; a series of escalators made necessary by the inability of the external circulation system to carry visitors to all levels and so betrayed the principle of excluding mechanical components from the floor areas; and, finally, a framework of braces required for stiffening the structure that Structures 3 mentioned in the report and illustrated in the axonometric projection of the 3-dimensional wall but which Piano+Rogers Architects omitted from the technical drawings.[21]

The Live Centre of Information's open floor areas have a particular genealogy. Their origins might be traced to Le Corbusier's open plan and its evolution in postwar American offices, from which the Rogerses, together with Norman Foster, took their inspiration for the Reliance Controls Building. But this would be a mistake because the floor areas of the Live Centre of Information, with an empty space and automated devices located on the sunken square but destined, as we will see, to occupy the interiors as well, were the result of certain lines of research that were taking the open plan toward new goals.

The first of these concerned the liberation of the space from any fixed division into compartments and Cartesian organization of furniture to permit an alternative and organic occupation of the space related to the German theory of *Bürolandschaft* the Rogerses had suggested applying in the Zip-Up series but had tried out only in the office at 32 Aybrook Street. The second involved the kind of fitted-out space proposed by Archigram, from which the Live Centre of Information took the idea of "freedom of choice" expressed here in the technological equipment located on the sunken square, on the terraces, and on the roof.

Despite the strength of the floor areas being their openness and adaptability, Piano+Rogers Architects had to present the organizers a configuration that could meet the program requirements. It was Franchini who worked on adapting the project to the program. From the drafting of the competition's proposal to the building's inauguration, he would be responsible for the configuration of the spaces in the Live Centre of Information. Franchini analyzed the qualitative and quantitative requirements of the competition notice, proposing a configuration that satisfied practically all of them. He illustrated the uses to which they would be put in an axonometric projection on a scale of 1:500 that represented them in terms of surfaces, producing a design that did not compete with the iconic floor plan and the idea of an open space in which everything was possible. At the level of the sunken square, access to the sequence of floor areas that Rogers and Piano called a "building" was provided by a reception center (labelled A1, according to the codification proposed by the competition's organizers), reduced to a rectangular glazed volume of moderate size to ensure the physical and visual continuity of the sunken square below the "building." The first floor area (36.00 m. ASL) was allocated to two activities for which the competition notice required direct access from the street: the multifunctional rooms for performances and meetings (B5) and the contemporary art gallery ("Galérie experimental d'art contemporain") (B3). Most of the second, third, and fourth floor areas (47.20, 53.60, and 58.40) were devoted to the library (B7), divided into three parts in compliance with the competition notice. On one side, facing south, were the offices (C1), social services (C3), and documentation and research rooms (B8), as well as apartments for the staff (C4). From the fifth to the eighth floor (64.80, 71.20, 77.60, and 84.00) space was set aside, to the north and in the center, for the museum's (B6) permanent galleries, and, to the south, the temporary galleries. The treatment of the eighth floor, with an accessible and terraced profile to the south, made it possible to configure large open-air exhibition areas for sculpture along the lines of the Sculpture Garden designed by Philip Johnson for the MoMA in New York. Above the museum and in a central position was inserted a final floor of smaller size, to be used for a panoramic restaurant (88.80). With the same dimensions but suspended above the restaurant, on the top of the "building," stood the technical volume for the air-conditioning plant.

Franchini's design for the fitting out of the floors united the idea of a system in which everything was possible—the solution that Peter Cook had defined as "the literal answer to 'anything goes'"—with the detailed and exhaustive program conceived by Lombard. The Live Centre of Information's floor areas were an offer the competition organizers couldn't refuse.

Renzo Piano, Richard Rogers, Gianfranco Franchini and Ove Arup & Partners, Competition proposal for the Centre Beaubourg, axonometry with use destination, June 1971.

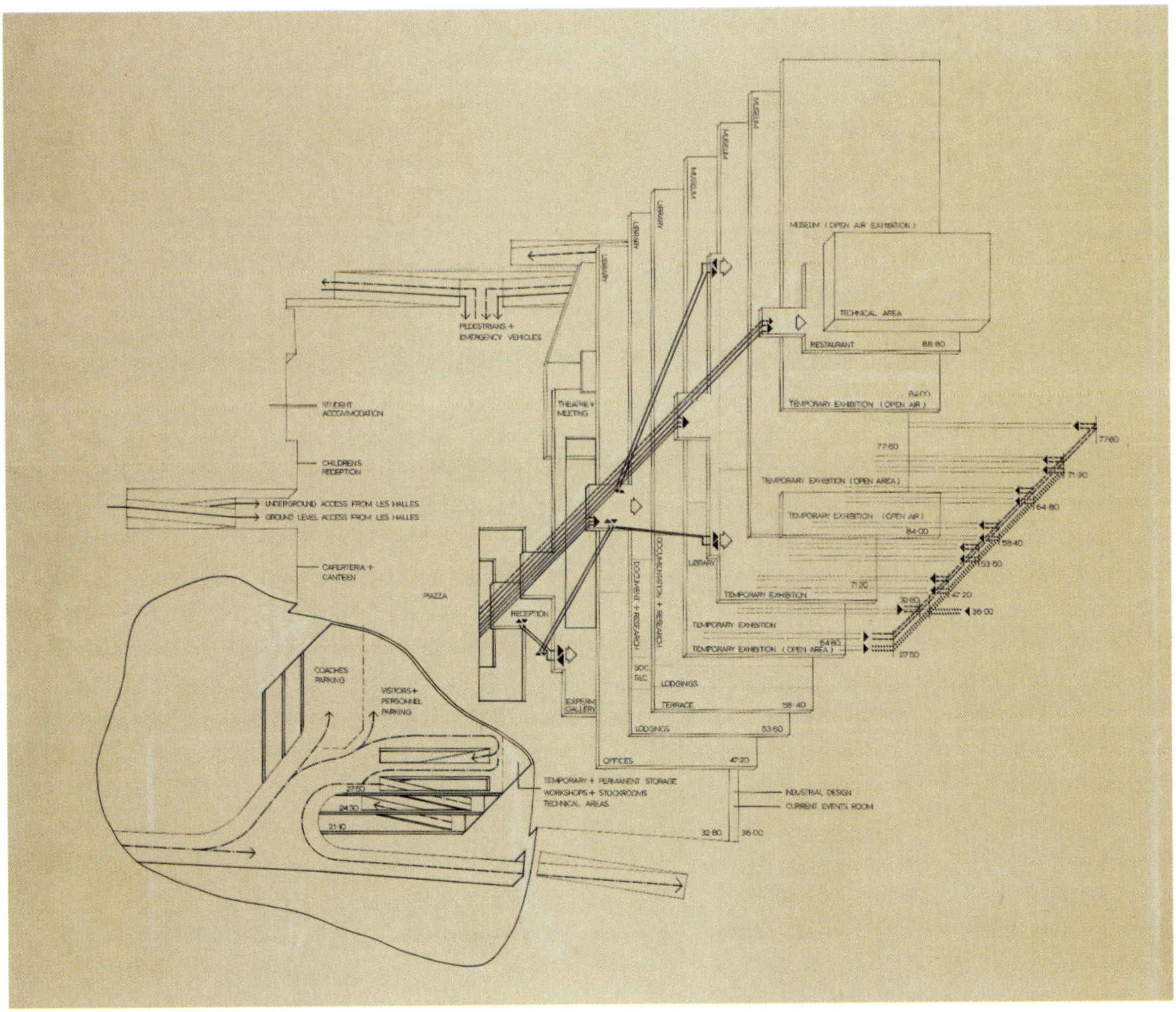

5.4

THE 3-DIMENSIONAL WALL AND THE FRICTION COLLAR: TWO INVENTIONS AT THE SERVICE OF FLEXIBILITY

The idea of "large, flexible uninterrupted floor areas" required the invention of a structure able to overcome the structural and technologic challenges implicit in the size and mobility these platforms needed. So Happold and Rice came up with a series of innovations that moved away from the space frame with diagonal lines in Rogers's sketches because this structure now had to be turned into a support for the floor areas, the technical installations, and the system for information transmission. The first of these breakthroughs consisted in a structure capable of holding a floor slab with a span of around fifty meters without intermediate supports. Happold and Rice opted for a standard, elementary truss that would be sufficiently malleable to allow periodic reconfigurations of the slabs. The solution they chose was a steel Warren truss with a length of 54.40 meters and height of 1.60. Its proportions confirm the inclination of Structures 3 for a light element perfectly in keeping with Piano's research, as well as Piano+Rogers Architects' preference for a visually unobtrusive element with as little bulk as possible in order to preserve the open space of the floor areas.

The other decisive element proposed by Happold and Rice was a joint giving the floor areas sufficient flexibility to be raised or lowered to obtain spaces of different heights. This joint would become one of the most plastic elements of the structure even once this solution of movable floors was abandoned in the fine-tuning of the project.[22] "The joint supporting the floor became the central element of the design," Rice would write years later.[23]

The joint assumed the form of a cylindrical metal collar, called a "special friction collar," designed to slide up and down the structure's vertical element and be fixed at the desired height by four wedges inserted under the collar.

Thus it was the idea of sliding the floors vertically and the invention of the friction collar that made it necessary to resort to a cylindrical column designed to be fabricated "on site from steel tubes" so this element, too, could fit into the logic of a permanent process of construction using easy-to-assemble components.

With the introduction of the friction collar and the column, the Live Centre of Information was obliged to renounce the vertical space frame with a powerful and minimalistic pattern of diagonals that Rogers had outlined in the sketches in the spring. While maintaining the nature of a three-dimensional lattice, the space frame was now transformed into a trilithic structure obtained from a combination of columns and braces.

The invention of the Warren truss, friction collar, and lattice gave rise to the solution proposed in the final plans: two three-dimensional lattices of 153.60 meters long and 64 meters high, subdivided into twelve spans of 12.80 meters and stiffened by diagonal braces, in the form of tie beams, and horizontal braces in the form of beams. Each lattice, set at a distance of 48 meters from the other, was 3.20 meters deep and consisted of two columns with a constant circular section. The structure consisted of a slender Warren truss 1.60 meters high and 54.40 long, of which the central 48 meters were free. The Warren truss had a pitch of 3.20 meters; it was placed singly on the perimeter of each span, while it was coupled in the central zones, where the stresses were greater. The structure was stiffened transversally with a second truss, this time of the Long type, of the same length as the depth of the span, 12.80 meters. On top of the set of girders was mounted a floor of slender prefabricated concrete slabs, a system of dry assembly in keeping with the principle of the Live Centre of Information's continual reconfigurability. The beams were joined to the lattice by means of an unspecified junction between the upper stringers of the Warren and Long trusses and two friction collars arranged so as to wrap around both columns of the lattice. In both its overall form and in the design of its details and the terminology adopted for some of its components, the Live Centre of Information's structure assumed particular connotations that, at times, reflected the emergence of discordant views of the structure's nature on the part of the architects and the engineers. In its overall design, the recourse to columns imparted an unprecedented vertical accentuation to the lattice that was further emphasized by the use of the term "piloti" to define the lower section of the columns precisely because it served to raise the "building" and shape a perception of the landscape that was no longer intended to dialogue with natural surroundings, as Le Corbusier had intended for his Unités d'habitations, but turned into the urban setting of the sunken square. To counter this vertical accentuation, in the competition drawings Piano+Rogers Architects extended the diagonal braces to the whole of the lattice (although in the technical drawing Structures 3 suggested using them only on some spans) to re-create on the lattice the now-iconic pattern of diagonal lines from the space frame Rogers had sketched in the spring. The desire to entrust these diagonal lines with the role of solving the aspect of the facade of the "building" was underlined by the decision to retouch the photographs of the competition model to reduce the thickness of the columns to that of the cross-bracing. The result was a structurally falsified image. Nonetheless, such a graphic solution was able to give those crosses the role of the iconic element of the lattice and to the whole structure a graphic lightness that would become fixed in the minds of Piano+Rogers Architects during the project's fine-tuning.

The vertical accentuation and the appearance of the trilithic framework in the lattice led to some terminological uncertainties. Piano+Rogers Architects were conscious of being on the brink of discovering an unusual structure that was no longer a traditional space frame but was not a generic "skeleton" or "framework" either, nor even a "grid" or "grill" because the intention was to maintain the original pattern of diagonal lines in the lattice.[24] The terminological uncertainty discernible in the competition report, where even the term "facade" appears, was resolved in the prevalence of the terms "3-dimensional load bearing wall" and "3-dimensional wall." These affirmed the spatial nature of the lattice but at the same time reactivated the idea of a wall because this system was no longer a structural skeleton. Instead, with the installations and surfaces included within it and clipped onto it, it generated the image of a wall endowed with a particular stratification: "light and semi-transparent" were the adjectives used in the report.[25]

While the technical details supplied by Structures 3 were being translated into competition drawings, the nature of the beams and the configuration of the friction collar generated a series of divergent interpretations that stemmed from the high degree of flexibility and reconfigurability of the Live Centre of Information's structure. The architects and engineers agreed on the nature of that structure as a system of easy-to-assemble components ("the structure is assembled from elements") and on the idea of the beams as a system able to move up and down or be taken apart and placed somewhere else ("the moveable parts are the floors and their supporting beams, which can be dismantled and re-positioned to create a true future flexibility").[26]

It is likely that it was precisely due to the difficulty of considering a fifty-meter-long Warren truss to be an easy-to-assemble element that Piano+Rogers Architects, in the plan and in the section on a scale of 1:200, alluded to the possibility of fabricating this element not as a monolithic piece made of bars and diagonal struts welded together, but as an assembly in which those same elements were screwed onto new, Mero System-type spherical joints similar to those studied for the Burrell Gallery. The introduction of these joints induced Piano+Rogers Architects to rethink the friction collar as well, so that, again in the only drawing of the section, it assumed a rounded profile.

Both Piano+Rogers Architects' idea of resorting to Mero joints or simply joints with rounded lines and Structures 3's invention of the friction collar confirm Happold's intention to use the Live Centre of Information as an opportunity to try out cast-steel joints. This idea, which Happold had discussed with his Structures 3 colleagues when first considering entering the competition, now caught the attention of Piano, who shared with Happold an interest in the cast details of Otto and Koji Kamiya's tensile structures and that just then, at the end of May, the Genoese architect was trying to turn into the cast ball joints of the Burrell Gallery. Although the report makes no mention of cast steel, the adjective "special" attached to the friction collar could only refer to the idea of a unique piece with an unusual geometry and mode of fabrication—it is thick in the engineers' drawings and rounded in the architects'—and so could only be made by casting steel in a mold.[27]

The idea of using cast joints, as Happold would reveal years later, was also part of the strategy adopted to respond to French regulations requiring solutions able to withstand fire for an hour and a half (later extended to two hours). From this moment on, the architects and engineers excluded the possibility of resorting to fireproof cladding because they wanted the metallic nature of every part of the structure to be evident.[28] So Happold favored cast joints thick enough to resist the transfer of heat without cladding.[29] To this he added the hypothesis of filling the structure with treated water, a technical solution that had just been put to the test for steel structures in the United States in the U.S. Steel Tower in Pittsburgh, completed in 1970, and in France with an office building for the SNCF company designed by Ernö Goldfinger and Pierre Forestier.[30] Structures 3 was also trying it out for the structure of the International Conference and Hotel Centre in Mecca (1966–74) at the same time as the Beaubourg competition was held.[31] Although the competition report suggested it would be possible to fill all the components—“tubular spaces” was the term used—with water, the technical detail of the 3-dimensional wall included in the report explored this solution for the columns alone.[32]

Renzo Piano, Richard Rogers, Gianfranco Franchini and Ove Arup & Partners, Competition proposal for the Centre Beaubourg, structural diagram, June 1971.

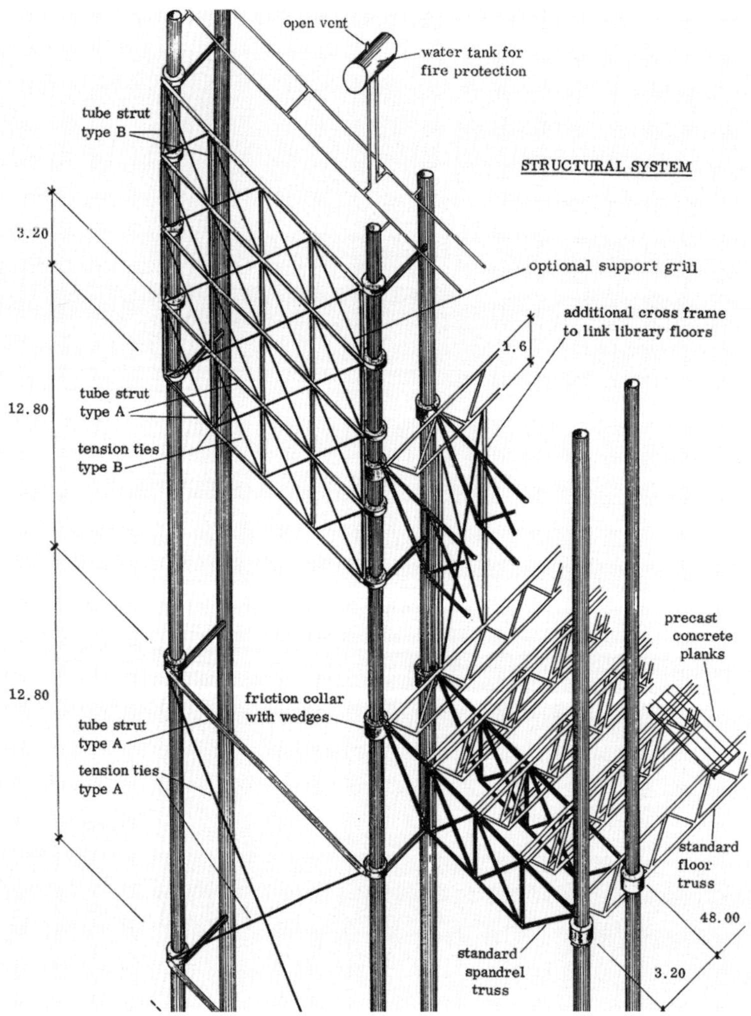

Renzo Piano, Richard Rogers, Gianfranco Franchini and Ove Arup & Partners, Competition proposal for the Centre Beaubourg, elevation on the sunken square, detail, June 1971.

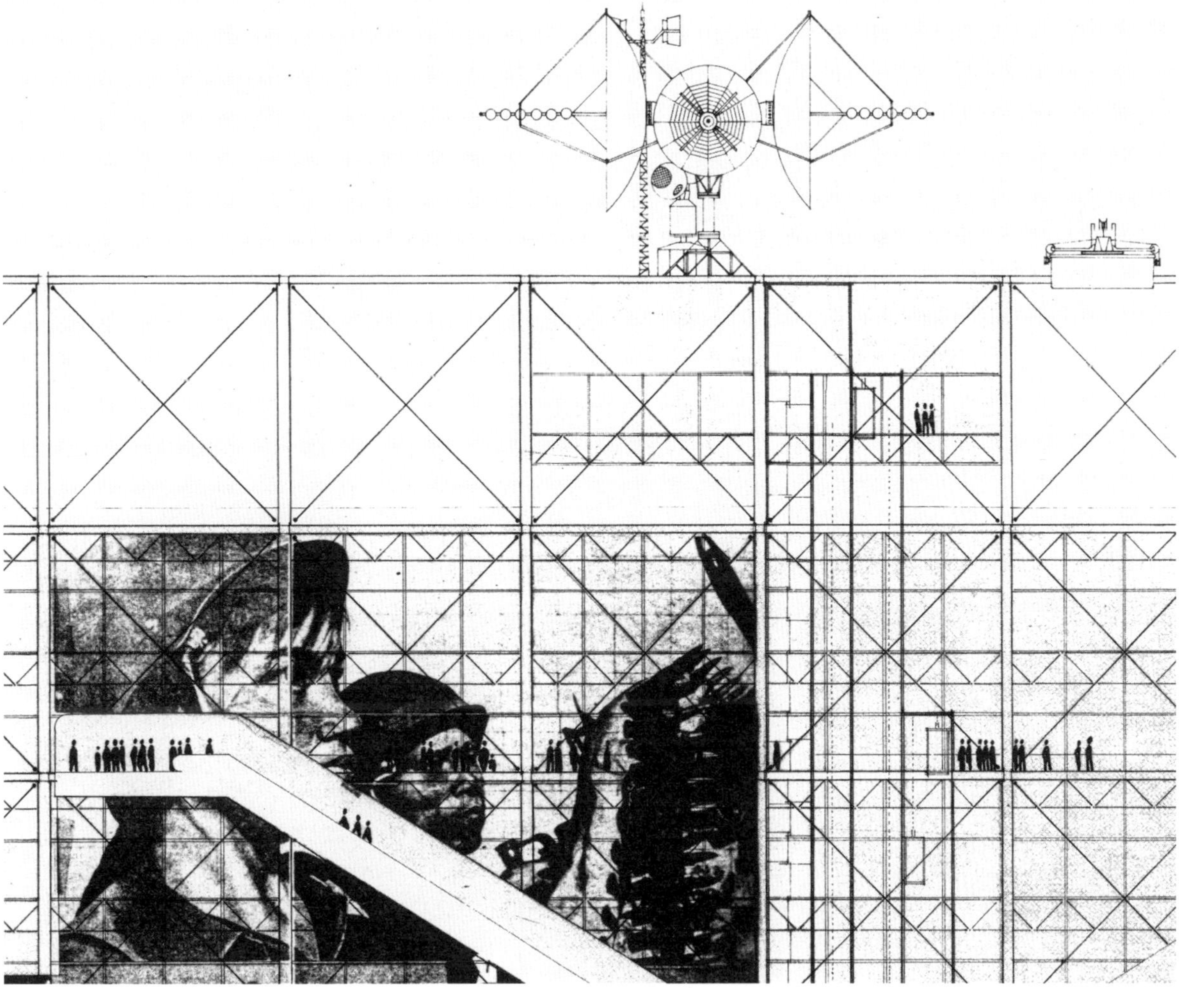

5.5

THE LAYERING OF THE 3-DIMENSIONAL WALL: A DEVICE FOR INFORMATION AND ENTERTAINMENT

In addition to holding up the floor areas and allowing them to move up and down, the 3-dimensional wall, with its depth of 3.20 meters and system of braces for fixing and support, proved to be a complex and versatile arrangement.
In the first place, precisely because of its nature as an atypical wall to which elements could be fixed, its lattices served as the support for a three-dimensional and complex layering obtained by superimposing the envelope around the floor areas and the devices for transmitting information to people outside.
Second, it housed all the technical installations, from the air-conditioning system to the mechanical circulation and even the fire escapes, guaranteeing the floor areas "true future flexibility."
Third, as suggested by the choice to extend the floor-slab beams inside it, it shared with the floor areas the nature of a live platform and for this reason was intended to house the same kind of unplanned activities as the sunken square, for the moment covered by the perfunctory definition of "temporary structures," in reference to the ephemeral devices needed to host them."[33]
Without exception, all the elements attached to the 3-dimensional wall took the form of reconfigurable industrial apparatus in keeping with the clip-on philosophy preached by Reyner Banham—something that, after the service towers of the ARAM module, now acquired a completely new dimension.
"All lifts and escalators are clipped onto the facade and can be changed";[34] "partitions may be unclipped and/or extended at will"; "a constantly changing clip-on system of information";[35] "the different clip-on parts of the building, from wall panels to electronic components";[36] "fire escapes can be freely located within the 3-dimensional grill on the outside of the building":[37] these are just some of the descriptions that confirm the transformation of the Centre's components into clip-on equipment.
As its name suggests, the 3-dimensional wall acted as a support for the envelope of the floor areas. Located on the inner face of the lattice, the envelope consisted of industrial panels available in three degrees of transparency and translucency: glass, Okalux, and an opaque sandwich unit made of reinforced plastic.[38] The choice to present these elements as a catalogue without any indication of their positioning was a further confirmation of the Archigramesque philosophy of "do-it-yourself" and "freedom of choice."
On the other hand, the decision to apply a reflective film to the envelope of the model, even though it stemmed from the need to give an impression of transparency to a model that had been constructed of wood due to time constraints, suggests that Piano+Rogers Architects was considering the possibility of cladding the envelope of the "building"

with external mirror glass panels in order to turn the Live Centre of Information into a version of the total light box of the Burrell Gallery.[39] Use of translucent and reflective film in the Live Centre of Information was ambivalent as well. It could bestow on the "building" a refined sense of enclosure and reserve that would protect the artworks during the day and reveal their presence at night thanks to the illumination of the interiors.[40] What is certain is that the mirror glass became an expression of the search for a dialogue with the surroundings, between dematerialization of the "building's" volume and reflections of the curtain of historical buildings that surrounded it. The reflective envelope was nothing but the backdrop to the layered surfaces of the 3-dimensional wall. Room was found on the outer face of the lattice for the information-transmission apparatus, in accordance with a hierarchy that made it clear that, rather than a visual and scenic device, the "building" was indeed a "live centre of information."

The slanting screen of the sketches drawn in the spring was diversified into systems that varied in their size, nature, and type of information transmitted, as well their position on the different facades of the "building." The 3-dimensional wall facing Les Halles, with a public balcony for viewing formed by the sunken square, became the preferred location for devices aimed at passersby: "art works," "television," and "electronic two-way games and information," as well as screens on which to show images and videos.[41] The 3-dimensional wall facing onto rue du Renard, in contrast, was conceived to interact with the flow of vehicles and passersby moving along the street and therefore would "have visual displays related to moving traffic."[42]

All this at the time found expression only in the competition elevation drawing of the 3-dimensional wall facing the sunken square. Notwithstanding the ample range of technological gadgets indicated in the report, Piano+Rogers Architects entrusted the image of the Informational envelope to those that were most visually representative: the screen and the LED billboard.

Among images of an educational and informative character such as those of a panel showing the movement of a satellite across a map or the computerized horizontal band for communicating news and announcements, room was found for images of an engaged and polemical nature, from the faces of Vietcong women soldiers to a throng of protesting students against the background of the American atomic bomb tests in the South Pacific and a message telling young people in revolt that one of their comrades had been picked up by the police. With the insertion of these images, Piano+Rogers Architects made these screens a support for messages that had nothing in common with of the playful character and pop lightheartedness of Archigram's

Instant City screens, nor even with the nature somewhere between decoration and advertising of the elements set on the envelope of Oscar Nitzchke's Maison de la publicité, of which Rogers and Piano were not aware at the time of their participation in the competition.

The screens of the Live Centre of Information certainly followed the path laid down by the Ideas Circus's educational screens but, unlike them, bore a militant and dissenting kind of message that was connected with condemnation of the Soviet-American arms race and the repression of the 1968 protests by French police—a message that was also addressed to the organizers of the competition, stressing the fact that the Live Centre of Information would transmit information about the people and for the people and that this information would have nothing to do with the museum exhibits in the "building."

To the broadcasting system, Piano+Rogers Architects added three elements on the roof covering that, through their design and central position, revealed their nature as symbolic devices.[43] The first and second consisted of a slender radio mast and a relay station composed of four satellite dishes oriented toward the cardinal points, to convey the idea of the Live Centre of Information as a device in remote connection with a network of information centers. The third element was nothing but a robot like the one located in the sunken square, replicated on the roof to declare the nature of the Live Centre of Information as a futuristic technological machine.

Renzo Piano, Richard Rogers, Gianfranco Franchini and Ove Arup & Partners, Photo cutout of the NASA Mission Control, Johnson Space Centre, Houston (USA), selected for the 3-dimensional wall animation, June 1971.

5.6

THE CIRCULATION SYSTEM OF BEAUBOURG: A FUNCTIONAL AND SCENIC MACHINE

Still with the aim of freeing up the floor areas, the 3-dimensional wall supported a mechanized system of circulation that collected the metropolitan flow from the sunken square and its layers of underground platforms and carried it upward to distribute it to the floor areas. Years later, Sébastien Loste would single out the idea that the Live Centre of Information was a suction pump of flows as the essence of Piano+Rogers Architects and Ove Arup & Partners' project.

The collector of flows took the form of a glass-walled elevator clipped onto the outer face of the 3-dimensional wall facing the sunken square, and was positioned in line with the seventh bay of the "building." The collector also comprised a set of escalators of varied design: on the basement levels they were uncovered, while those running from the sunken square, where they were connected to the glazed reception area located in the hollow carved out of the base of the "building," were given a rounded plastic covering. From here they climbed up the 3-dimensional wall in a tree configuration. The rounded canopy made the Live Centre of Information's escalators part of the same lineage as a series of bridges and viaducts in Canada and Europe and one in which a prominent place was held by the Starglide travelator, seen by Piano at the Osaka Expo.[44] The Live Centre of Information's circulation system assumed connotations that could no longer be ascribed solely to the idea of a piece of functional equipment at the service of flexibility, but was also open to particular scenic and spectacular effects. The fact that the system of ascent's point of departure was placed not in the sunken square but on the first subterranean platform and was given a scenic appearance by locating it at the center of the open courtyard on the sunken square celebrated the Live Centre of Information's nature as a collector of the underground metropolitan flows of Paris.

The visibility of the route of ascent also responded, through a device that for people in the square became an educational chart explaining the way it worked, to the competition notice's request for an intuitive circulation system. "For easy orientation and flexibility, all vertical movement takes place on the face of the building, so that it can clearly be seen by anyone viewing the building from the square in front," was the comment made in the report.[45] The transparency of all its parts, from the glass of the elevator to the translucent plastic shell of the escalators, turned the moving crowd and the means of its ascent into a popular spectacle, a reflection of the fact that what was being celebrated in the Live Centre of Information was not the works of art but the people.

The fact that this scenic circulation system was something other than a functional piece of equipment is confirmed by the need to combine it with secondary systems that contradicted the premises of the project. A second vertical column containing elevators and hoists for artwork was placed on the rue du Renard-facing 3-dimensional wall, into which were also set two fire escapes, a solution that, despite the presence of the screens, turned this facade into a sort of rear. While these elements were still designed in accordance with the intention of taking the equipment outside the floor areas for "true future flexibility," that intention was undermined by the insertion of two sets of escalators in those areas. The first had a pair of flights side by side and the second two flights on either side of a central court in a configuration typical of contemporary shopping malls. The reason for obstructing the floor areas with these escalators lay in the functional limits of the scenic device clipped onto the 3-dimensional wall, which, owing to its design and in spite of its size, provided access to only some of the floor areas.

Overleaf: Renzo Piano, Richard Rogers, Gianfranco Franchini and Ove Arup & Partners, Competition proposal for the Centre Beaubourg, elevation on the sunken square, June 1971.

ANIMATED
PRODUCTION
FOR
CAROLINE

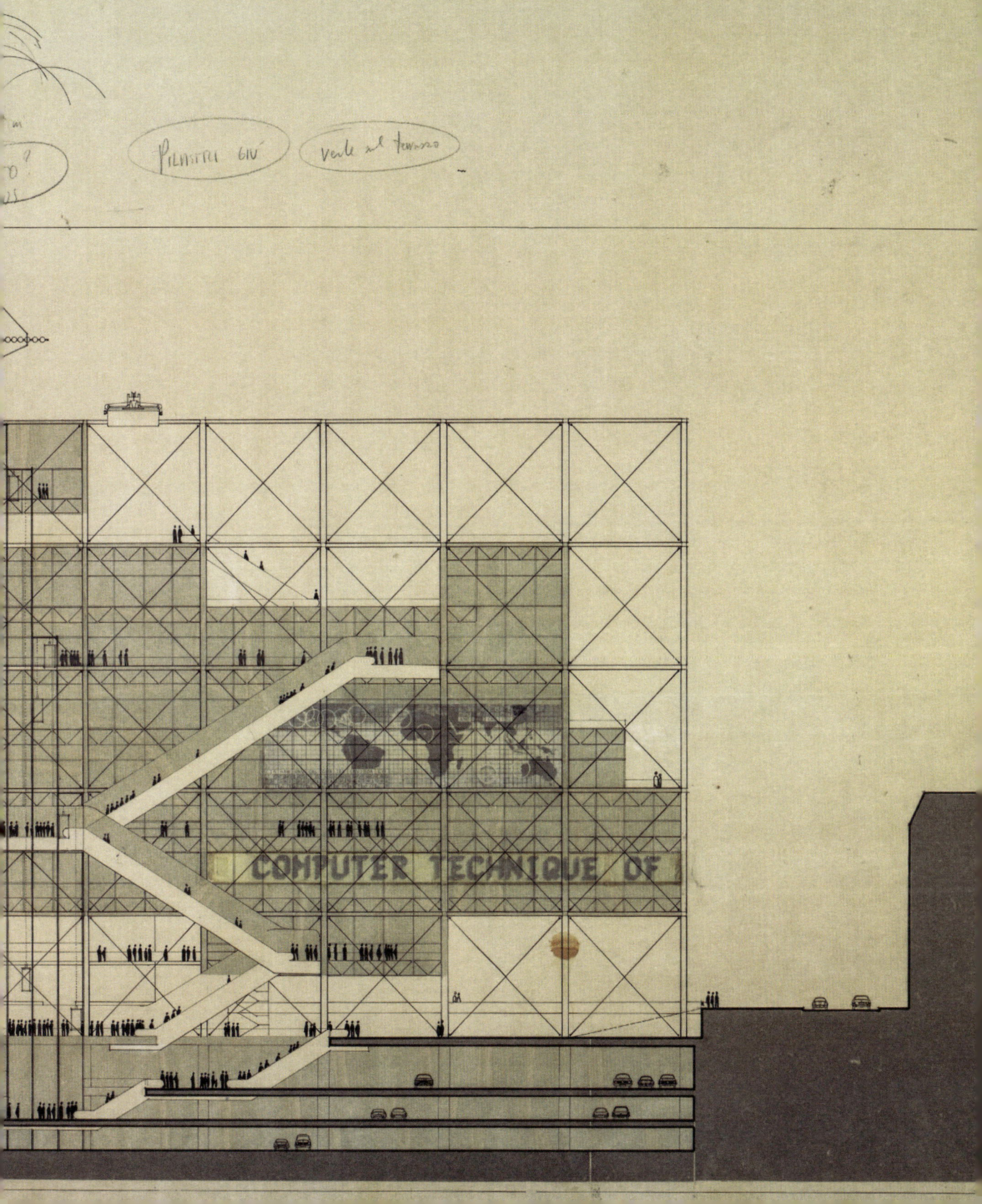
PILASTRI GIÙ
COMPUTER TECHNIQUE OF

5.7

AN AIR-CONDITIONING SYSTEM FOR ARTIFICIAL AND EVER-CHANGING MICROCLIMATES

Along with the circulation system and devices for the transmission of information, the air-conditioning system was the other element designed to be clipped onto the 3-dimensional wall.
Owing to a lack of plant engineers in Structures 3, Piano+Rogers Architects worked on its configuration at this stage without Ove Arup & Partners.[46]
With the aim of getting the air-conditioning system to conform with the desired flexibility of the Live Centre of Information, Piano+Rogers Architects designed a system whose main parts were not necessarily reconfigurable—it was the only element, in fact, that the report did not describe in terms of clip-on equipment—but that allowed the possibility of generating microclimates in the floor areas. This laid the foundations for an environment that could be subdivided by nothing but jets of air and differences of temperature, something that Rogers, drawing on Banham's ideas, would not describe in detail until several years later.[47]
The fact that, in a system where even the primary structure adhered to the logic of reconfigurability, the conditioning plant and ducts were permanent was already anticipating the idea that Rogers would have a year later when he saw the air-conditioning system as the element to which all the other components of the Live Centre of Information, even the structure, should be fastened.
The solution proposed for the competition project coincided with a "recirculated fresh-air system" based on a modular environmental unit with an area equivalent to one of the thirteen bays into which each floor area was subdivided (12.80 x 48.00 meters).
Although the type and characteristics of the system were consistent with the concept, its location proved problematic owing to the competition notice, which called for this element to be located underground—"All the technical and mechanical installations necessary to the smooth operation of the Centre will be placed in the basement."[48]
Such a location would have implied the vertical passage of the ducts at the level of the sunken square (left free thanks to the raising of the "building" on "pilotis"), compromising its visual and spatial permeability, considered by Piano+Rogers Architects to be an indispensable principle of the design. To preserve the empty space under the "building" the competition instructions were ignored in favor of a solution with rooftop installations and a cascade distribution around the perimeter.
The solution submitted to the competition consisted in a boxlike "plant room," measuring 25.60 x 48.00 meters and containing twelve independent "central station air handling units," suspended in an axial position above the roof of the "building."
The plant room was connected to a large horizontal duct with a rounded profile inserted in the 3-dimensional wall on rue du Renard, from which ran twelve

Renzo Piano, Richard Rogers, Gianfranco Franchini and Ove Arup & Partners, Competition proposal for the Centre Beaubourg, model (with air conditioning ducts), June 1971.

pairs of vertical ducts with a rectangular section (two per bay, one for the intake of air and one for its throughput). At the height of each floor slab's beams the vertical installations intercepted two horizontal duct networks concealed in the suspended ceiling and used for the distribution of conditioned air through "reheat boxes" and the intake of air through vents.[49]

In the general configuration and shaping of some of its components, the air-conditioning system reveals specific genealogies. Its overall configuration harks back to the air-conditioning system of the La Rinascente department store in Rome—a project on which Piano had worked during his internship in Franco Albini's studio.[50] The same kind of system had been used in some skyscrapers designed by Skidmore, Owings and Merrill (SOM) and in the Queen Elizabeth Hall designed by, among others, three members of the Archigram group—projects known to Rogers, in one case, thanks to his internship at SOM's San Francisco studio, and, in the other, through Banham's *The Architecture of the Well-tempered Environment*, one of Piano+Rogers Architect's reference texts at the time of the competition for the Live Centre of Information.[51]

If we look at the drawing in which the ducts can be made out behind the audiovisual wall, a more precise genealogy of the air-conditioning system is revealed, that of the experimental designs of the pop avant-garde in London. It is to this influence that we can ascribe the decision to locate the various technical plant components —probably not placed in a single volume in the early versions of the project—in an isolated central volume, as if to emphasize the unprecedented architectural character assumed by a traditionally concealed secondary element.

If we consider the configuration of the plant room as well, the derivation from the Archigram group becomes evident: a temporary "clipped-on" piece of equipment conceived as a removable or expandable capsule. Not coincidentally, Rogers gave it the appearance of his Zip-Up House, which had its own roots in Archigram.[52]

As far as the means of air circulation were concerned, the rectangular configuration of the individual ducts, the absence of any compositional stratagem with regard to the module inserted in each bay, and even the choice to conceal them from view by means of a false ceiling make it clear that at the time this element was still perceived as a technical element and therefore subject to a logic in which structure and envelope prevailed.

That the ducts were not yet seen as a predominant architectural element on rue du Renard is confirmed by the choice to apply a reflective film to the competition model that concealed the ducts inserted in the 3-dimensional wall.

What is certain is that the insertion of the ducts into the layers of the 3-dimensional wall produced an unusual image. Despite the considerable inconsistencies present in the competition plans, there can be no doubt that the structure of the 3-dimensional wall and the audiovisual panels partially covered the installations, turning them into an element only just visible in the lattice. This still uncertain image anticipated the aesthetic and decorative turn that was to lead the plant to become, over the following years, the protagonist of this front of the Centre.

Renzo Piano, Richard Rogers, Gianfranco Franchini and Ove Arup & Partners, Competition proposal for the Centre Beaubourg, section/south elevation, plant detail, June 1971

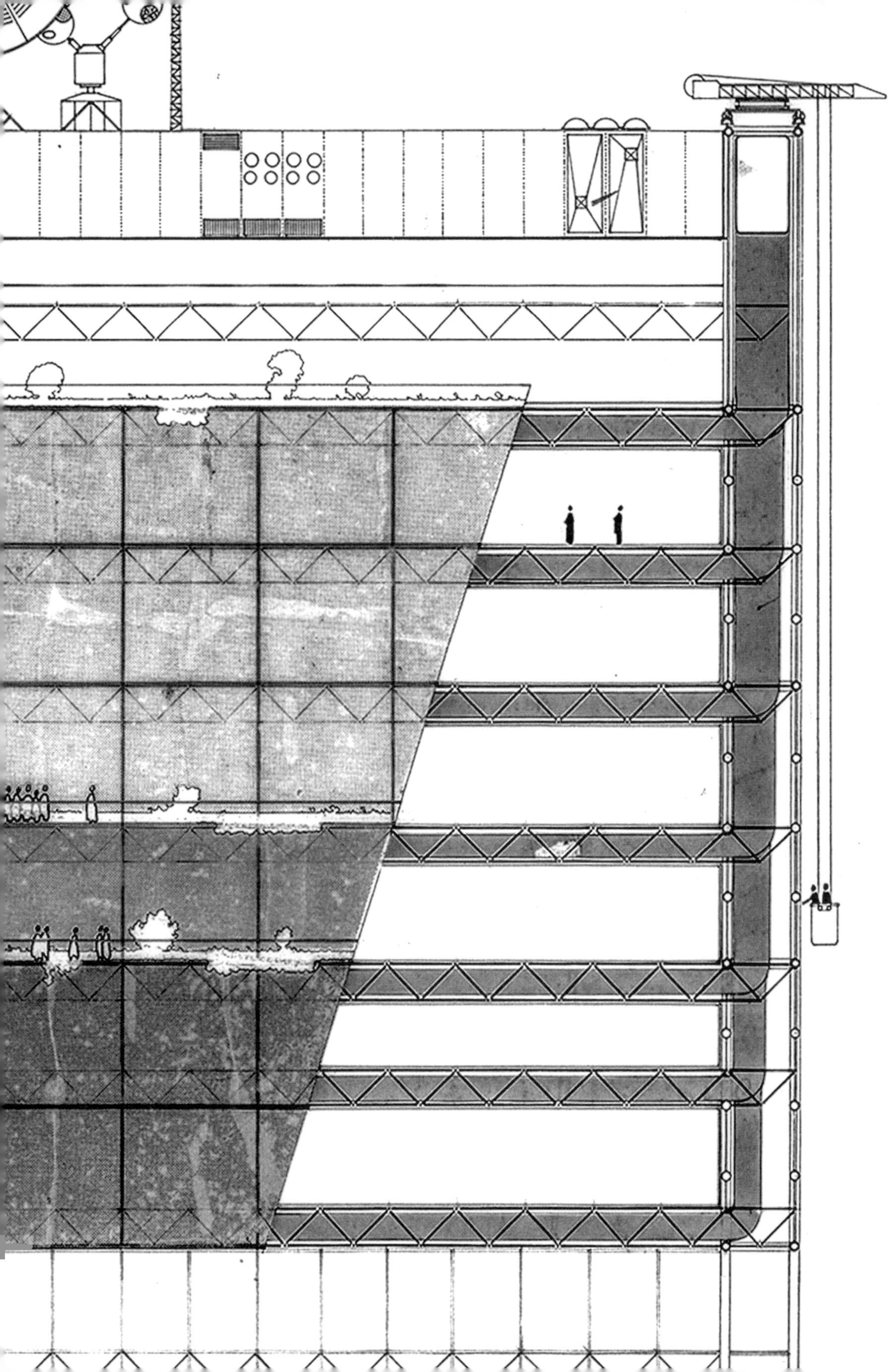

5.8

THE FINAL PLANS FOR THE COMPETITION PROJECT

To present the project to the jury in Paris, Piano+Rogers Architects and Ove Arup & Partners submitted the plans required by the competition notice, five drawings, six photographs of the model, the technical report, and the calculation of areas, to which they added a works schedule and an axonometric projection of a detail of the structure.
The drawings, made at the office at 32 Aybrook Street, constituted the principal element of the portfolio, in terms both of the space they occupied on the competition entry display panel and of the amount of work required for their production. Drawn up in the weeks prior to delivery, they were the result of a concerted effort that was divided as follows: Piano and Franchini were responsible for preparing the basis for the drawings and Young for their animation with technological installations, people, and vegetation, while Holmes, Flack, and Kaplický assisted their colleagues in the process.[53]
They were drawn in black India ink on sheets of tracing paper with a weight of 160 grams per square meter. Apart from the main façade, for which a special fixing process was used, they were given coatings of gelatin, and, once finished, reproduced on sheets of gray-ocher paper also with a weight of 160 grams, then cut to size and prepared for presentation on the competition panel (2.40 x 1.60 m), along with mounting instructions, which would be executed by the competition technicians of the Délégation in Paris.
The façade on a scale of 1:200 constituted the main drawing in terms of size, graphics, and position on the final competition panel. It represented the 3-dimensional wall facing the square, which was sectioned at the height of the open courtyard on the main circulation route, a solution that highlighted the subterranean stratification and the nature of the mechanical circulation system. The 3-dimensional wall was represented with a wireframe drawing.
A semitransparent, pale gray gelatin filter was applied to the structure to indicate the panels of the envelope. Images and texts reproduced on tracing paper were used for the audiovisual screens.[54]
Young embellished the presentation with a drawing of the satellite dishes, radio mast, and robot on the roof and of cars in the underground parking garage, and by Piano with stylized human figures that, placed among the escalators, the galleries of the 3-dimensional wall, and the terraces of the "building," proved, along with the transmitter of information, to be the protagonists of the image of the Centre.
The gelatin filter served to delineate a volume with a clear-cut and stepped but nevertheless light profile. The representation of the audiovisual screens was more complicated. Young chose some images from magazines and various sorts of manual in his library and in that of the studio at 32 Aybrook Street.

The drawing with the path of a satellite over a globe came from an atlas;[55] the image of female Vietcong soldiers was taken from *Life* or *Time*; the one with the message "Caroline, go to Canvas [*sic*] City immediately – your friend Linda has been busted," came from an article by Martin Pawley published in *Architectural Design* in November. The drawing with the words "Animated movies production for the computer technique of" may have been made by Young himself. The intention to give the images an unusual appearance of semitransparency made their attachment complicated. Young was not able to use the collage technique so much in vogue at the time: if they had been printed on ordinary paper the images would have covered the lattice, whereas if a transparent sheet had been used, it would have required adhesive tape or glue that, for different reasons, would have spoilt the image of the lattice.[56] So Young turned to Holmes who, given the experience he had gained reproducing large technical drawings during his studies at the Architectural Association, and with the aid of Bishop, reproduced the images on sheets of tracing paper of the same size as the original drawings and placed them in the correct position. In this way the desired effect was obtained, but on two layers that could be perfectly superimposed. Holmes and Bishop fixed the layers with double-sided sticky tape placed solely around the perimeter of the sheet, and thus in a position in which the traces left by the photocopier on the final sheet could be cut away. Holmes and Bishop used an ultraviolet process on a machine belonging to the Advance company of London to reproduce the two-layer drawing.

The master plan on a scale of 1:500 showed the project in the center of Paris with the Sébastopol and Les Halles districts and the extension of the square below ground. This was achieved by covering the plateau La Reynie and the cellars of the buildings on rue Saint-Martin with a sheet of white gelatin, excluding only the structural partitions, represented by dotted lines, that indicated the extension of the square into the ground underneath rue du Renard and included the Rambuteau Métro stop. The idea of the sunken square as a collector of flows was conveyed through the stylized drawing of people in an axonometric projection. Young embellished the square with a tensile structure derived from Otto and two robots that recalled Isozaki's automata for the Osaka Expo. Young was also responsible for the addition of the row of trees in front of the buildings on rue Saint-Martin and on the plateau La Reynie, arranged to form a park.

For the representation of the activities of the Centre Piano+Rogers Architects resorted to a cavalier projection on a scale of 1:500. Here the project was reduced to a superimposition of the floor areas and arrows of different kinds that confirmed the nature

of the project as a sequence of platforms.
The relationship with the area below ground was highlighted by a section with a curvilinear perimeter revealing the mechanics of the underground levels of the Live Centre of Information, emphasizing their subterranean nature with a sheet of gray gelatin.
The floor areas were colored according to the coding for the different "activities" (*ensembles fonctionels*) indicated in the competition notice, but the bright colors and the blue and yellow stripes used to indicate the programmatic heterogeneity of the floor area at level 27.50 bestowed on the diagram a pop character that would be retained in the actual construction. In the absence of a functional code, the sunken square was the only area that was simply line-drawn. This fact, while respecting the logic of the coding of uses, resulted in a distorted representation of the conceptual value of the project, with the most important of the platforms reduced to a backdrop.
Piano+Rogers Architects united in a single drawing the two 1:200-scale sections requested by the organizers. The scanty variability of composition of the sections of the "building" prompted the architects to show only a cross-section, and to combine it with the south elevation, chosen for its articulated volumes. If we exclude the layering of the platforms and the drawing of the technological devices on the roof and the crowd in motion, there are two elements to which this image draws attention: the air-conditioning system, with the dark gray shading of the horizontal and vertical ducts and the configuration of the plant in the form of a Zip-Up House; and the envelope of the south facade, where the emphasis is placed on both the sequence of terraces, through their covering with gelatins in different tones of gray, and its opaque nature, suggested by a checkered pattern different from that of the main front.[57] The idea of a blind front, moreover, was reinforced by the presence of vegetation hanging down the façade, indicated in the plan as well, but not on the main elevation. In the drawing of the structure, note the choice to present the Warren truss as an assembly of bars connected by spherical nodes of the Mero System type.
For the plan on a scale of 1:200, despite having chosen the floor area at 71.20 level, Piano+Rogers Architects conferred on the drawing such a diagrammatic nature that made it conceptually the representation of a sort of standard floor, as it is was referring to each platform of the building.
This effect was achieved by representing the floor area as an empty space, with the exception of the two sets of escalators, a service block, and a partition. The air-conditioning system was emphasized with dark gray shading.
For the construction of the model used for the photographs requested by the competition notice, Piano+Rogers Architects turned to the model-makers at Ove Arup & Partners. It is likely the model was made by Innes and Caller under the supervision of a member of Piano+Rogers Architects. Constructed in the days immediately prior to the consignment deadline, the model was on a small scale (probably 1:500) and made of composite materials; it lacked certain fundamental components, which were drawn directly on the photographs.[58]
The model represented the same area as indicated in the master plan, and consisted of a wooden base made of two different woods: one, a pale color, was used for the horizontal stratification of the square, the underground section, and the road and pedestrian surface of the area; small blocks of darker, hazel-colored wood was used for the surrounding buildings, of which only the mansard roofs were reproduced in detail. The metallic nature of the 3-dimensional wall and the transparent nature of the "building" presented a problem that the model-makers were only able to solve through special expedients. The sequence of platforms was in fact represented with small blocks of hazel-colored wood fixed onto the main facades and wrapped in a reflective film to nullify their materiality. This may have sparked the idea of trying out mirror glass on the envelopes of the entries for both the Burrell Gallery and the Centre Beaubourg competitions.
The 3-dimensional wall was left out completely—it would be represented on the photographs with

a wireframe drawing that emphasized its graphic lightness.

The equipment clipped onto the lattice was also simplified and, in some cases, added by retouching the photographs. An attempt to represent the elevator block was made both with a prism of transparent plexiglass and with the reflective film used on the main volume, showing that they were evaluating the film's optical effects. The escalators on the main facade and the system of ducts facing the rue du Renard were represented with white poster board. The audiovisual screens were omitted—added only in a photograph by means, not coincidentally, of a pattern that recalled that of the visual noise produced by a cathode-ray tube in the absence of a signal. As in the technical drawings, the model was embellished with figures of people, represented by thin silhouettes of black poster board, and with urban vegetation depicted with pieces of sponge fixed to needles but applied only on the sunken square and not on the plateau La Reynie, where only the trunks were represented.

Drawing on a certain amount of experience in photography, Holmes took the pictures in a way that concealed the model's small size and allowed the addition of missing components by retouching.

The photographs did not comply with the competition notice instructions: they were in black and white, as requested, but none of them reproduced the perspective angles mentioned in the competition notice, as for instance the bird's-eye view of the plateau Beaubourg in its surroundings. Instead, the photos chosen represented: the foreshortened front on rue du Renard taken from the junction with rue Saint-Merri; the sunken square and the 3-dimensional wall seen from the plateau La Reynie; the entire main front of the "building" taken from a distance, at the level of the Forum des Halles; and, finally, the whole of the sunken square seen from rue Rambuteau and framed, at the sides, by the "building" itself and by the buildings on rue Saint-Martin to demonstrate once more the difference between the "high new" and "low old" construction that Rogers had emphasized in his first sketches.

The competition report, presented on A4 (approximately letter-size) sheets of paper in portrait format, was made up of seven pages containing the ten sections mentioned by the organizers accompanied by four diagrams, a structural detail of the 3-dimensional wall, and a schedule of the works. Rogers and Piano drew up the sections devoted to presenting the design's main themes, from the idea of an information center to urban integration and the principle of flexibility—"the architectural and philosophical side."[59] Sargent wrote the section on the circulation and traffic systems. Rice illustrated the structure and the technical installations. The diagram of the structure can be attributed to Tony Waters, one of Structures 3's draftsmen, while the schedule was Bolingbroke's work.[60]

The report began by styling the "architectural concept of the project" as the Live Centre of Information. Information was presented as the idea that had guided the design of every part of the project. The report continued with the integration into the surroundings, presented through the system of the sunken square and the visual and scenic stratagems of the sequence of floor areas. In light of the emphasis on the project's urban nature and the idea of an infrastructure able to extend cultural activities into the neighborhood, it is no surprise that Rogers and Piano decided to leave the section "Unity of the Centre" blank. In the section "Flexibility Capacity of the Centre," Rogers and Piano showed that they had conceived a flexible system made possible by reconfigurable components and the recourse to free platforms. In "Access and Circulation" Sargent described the urban infrastructure. The report continued with an explanation of the main circulation system and its nature as an educational and easy-to-understand system for onlookers. The lack of a detailed discussion of the design's relationship with individual program activities—the subject of section seven—is telling: the Live Centre of Information was flexible and could be adapted to any eventuality. Rogers and Piano took the following section, "Inter-relationships," as an opportunity to summarize the physical and electronic relationships of the Live Centre of Information. In "Technical Concept," Structures 3 reviewed the system of emergency exits, going on to describe the air-conditioning system and the structure, highlighting the microclimatic flexibility for interiors, the assembly by components, and the recourse to the friction collar and the use of water-filled columns. The report closed with a section that limited itself to listing the range of infill panels. The crucial element of the report was the four diagrams. These were graphic illustrations of a diagrammatic and minimalistic character made up of arrows and dots and were intended to convey the essence of the Live Centre of Information as a collector of flows and urban scenic device.

The lineage of these diagrams stretches back to the representation of the Bauhaus building, Kahn's circulation schemes for Philadelphia, and even some of Alison and Peter Smithson's and James Stirling's graphic images. The diagram of a nucleus connected to perimetric nodes expressed the idea of the Centre as the hub of a network in a representation already used for the ARAM module. The second diagram shows a section of the sunken square and the "building." The visual cone traced from rue du Renard brings the rise of the "building" within the optical and scenic stratagems of the project while the arrows and dots drawn on the floor areas and around the satellite on the roof highlight the nature of the Live Centre of Information as a collector of physical and electronic flows. Also devoted to flows is the third diagram, in which the main circulation system is represented as a node designed to intercept a system of flows around the perimeter of the site. The explanation of the circulation system continued in the fourth and last diagram, where the movement of people is represented as a network against the background of the structural lattice according to a scheme that revealed the functional and scenic potential of the circulation system.

The scheme entitled "Structural System" consisted of an isometric axonometric projection of two bays of the 3-dimensional wall, representing its structural components and illustrating its articulation. Its nature as a nomogram is confirmed by the choice to detail only elements in the different parts of the "building's" structure and to include alternative solutions, as in the case of the braces, for which a second solution appears, "Type B," consisting of a 3.20-meter square frame with crosses. Conceived as a support in the bays equipped with audiovisual screens, this solution would create such a dense pattern on the structure that it made the lattice the protagonist of the front of the "building." The crucial element of Bolingbroke's schedule of works, which in essence presented a traditional procedure of construction in stages, was the decision to extend its duration to six years, as opposed to the four indicated in the competition notice.[61]

In an interview, Young suggested that Piano+Rogers Architects were not aware of this discrepancy at when the portfolio was submitted.[62] The duration of the work indicated by Structures 3 would be discussed by the jury members and Bolingbroke's schedule was removed from the competition documents.

Below and overleaf: Renzo Piano, Richard Rogers, Gianfranco Franchini and Ove Arup & Partners, Competition proposal for the Centre Beaubourg, model (view of the 3-dimensional wall and the sunken square, detail), June 1971.

5.9

THE DIFFICULTIES OF SENDING THE COMPETITION DOCUMENTS BY ROYAL MAIL

The application portfolio was signed by Piano, Rogers, Franchini, and Ove Arup & Partners, thereby giving Franchini credit as a project coauthor, as he had requested. The documents were assembled on three vertical sheets measuring 0.80 by 1.60 meters to be placed side by side on the 2.40-by-1.60-meter panel.[63]

To prevent damage to the drawings, Piano+Rogers Architects rolled them in a cardboard tube along with the other competition documents. On the evening of June 15, around 10 pm, just two hours before the dispatch deadline—submissions had to be postmarked before midnight—Goldschmied went to the Royal Mail post office on Trafalgar Square in London to send the documents to Paris. The package was rejected as being too large and Goldschmied was obliged to cut the drawings down at the post office to fit them into a tube supplied by the Royal Mail.

A few days later the tube was returned to sender because it lacked the required number of stamps. Rogers or Goldschmied—accounts differ—went to the post office to settle the bill and ask for a new dispatch with a backdated postmark.

Around June 24, the final date for the reception of competition documentation in Paris, the competition's Paris office called Piano+Rogers Architects to tell them they had not received the documents. After a few days the competition staff telephoned Piano+Rogers Architects to tell them that the tube, containing what was destined to become the Centre national d'art et de culture Georges Pompidou, had been found and readmitted to the competition.[64]

Renzo Piano, Richard Rogers, Gianfranco Franchini and Ove Arup & Partners, Competition proposal for the Centre Beaubourg, model (view of the 3-dimensional wall on the rue du Renard, June 1971.

1 — Piano+Rogers Architects and Ove Arup & Partners, Plateau Beaubourg Center Paris 1971 [competition report], July 1971 [post-competition reprint with the new authorship of Piano+Rogers Architects (formerly Renzo Piano, Richard Rogers. Gianfranco Franchini and Ove Arup & Partners)], AN, CNACGP, F 19, 1.

2 — Ibid.

3 — Ibid.

4 — Ibid.

5 — "This centre should not therefore stay isolated; its activities will necessarily overflow the limits of the building, leaving its mark on the district and spreading throughout France and other countries by means of travelling exhibitions, television broadcasts, publications, etc. The possibility of consulting from a distance reference cards programmed into the Library's computer will create a service for the diffusion of knowledge which will be well appreciated." République Française, Plateau Beaubourg Center Paris. Written texts, AN, CNACGP, F 19, 4.

6 — The author took into consideration the English version of this complementary portfolio belonged to Richard Rogers. Délégation pour la réalisation du Centre Beaubourg, Plateau Beaubourg Center. Programs and Rules of the Competition (complementary information on the texts, written documents & plans), n.d. [April 1971], RSHPA, C01, F ARC73279.

7 — Boris Hamzeian, Interview with John Young, July 25, 2017, Hayling Island.

8 — Piano+Rogers and Ove Arup, Plateau Beaubourg Center Paris 1971 [competition report], 2, 4–5.

9 — "There is space for future expansion of the coach park beneath rue Saint-Martin," was Sargent's comment in the competition report. Piano+Rogers Architects and Ove Arup & Partners, Plateau Beaubourg Center Paris 1971 [competition report], 5.

10 — Ibid.

11 — For these references, see the slides in the RSHP Archives in London and the private archives of Richard Rogers's family. RSHPA, C04, F4.

12 — "We propose closing rue Saint-Martin and removing it, opening the cellars and front doors of the neighbouring housing directly onto the sunken square, if possible, converting the houses into studios and dwellings related to the new centre. The cellars and shops above being used for cafes, restaurants, reception areas, information areas, and other commercial and cultural activities [...]." Piano+Rogers and Ove Arup, Plateau Beaubourg Center Paris 1971 [competition report], 3.

13 — In a section with the eloquent title "A District Undergoing Restoration and Renewal," the competition notice declared in this connection: "an important restoration zone includes the space which separates plateau Les Halles from the plateau Beaubourg." Délégation pour la réalisation du plateau Beaubourg, République Française, Plateau Beaubourg Center Paris. Written texts, 6.

14 — Piano+Rogers and Ove Arup, Plateau Beaubourg Center Paris 1971 [competition report], 6.

15 — Piano+Rogers and Ove Arup, Plateau Beaubourg Center Paris 1971 [competition report], 1.

16 — Piano+Rogers and Ove Arup, Plateau Beaubourg Center Paris 1971 [competition report], 2.

17 — Piano+Rogers and Ove Arup, Plateau Beaubourg Center Paris 1971 [competition report], 1.

18 — Ibid.

19 — "More highly serviced areas will tend to be located near the exterior for easier connection with vertical runs" was another formula used to illustrate the hypothetical location of the various uses of the Live Centre of Information. Piano+Rogers and Ove Arup, Plateau Beaubourg Center Paris 1971 [competition report], 3.

20 — Ibid.

21 — "Transverse stability is provided by the fire wall needed to separate the temporary from the permanent exhibition space." Piano+Rogers and Ove Arup, Plateau Beaubourg Center Paris 1971 [competition report], 7.

22 — "The idea that the floors should be able to move, which is a crazy idea, really came from us. Arup bought into it. They gave some serious thought to how they could literally do it. That's why they did that sketch. I think the idea initially came from Richard. Arup didn't say, 'this is a crazy idea. We can't do that.' They bought into the idea. They entered the conversation about how we might do it." Hamzeian, Interview with Young.

23 — Peter Rice, *An Engineer Imagines*, London: Artemis, 1993), 26.

24 — For these terms see Piano+Rogers and Ove Arup, Plateau Beaubourg Center Paris 1971 [competition report], 2, 3, 6.

25 — Piano+Rogers and Ove Arup, Plateau Beaubourg Center Paris 1971 [competition report], 2. For the use of the term "facade," see the report again on pages 1 and 2 while for the terms "3-dimensional load bearing wall" and "3-dimensional wall," see pages 1 and 3.

26 — Piano+Rogers and Ove Arup, Plateau Beaubourg Center Paris 1971 [competition report], 7.

27 — "The friction collar, yes. It was Arup's response to the architects' idea of moving floors. As for the material, I think it could be cast, yes. I think the use of cast steel could have been something in the air. I think we mentioned something about it in the competition's report. Let me check. It's interesting. It doesn't actually use the world cast. Looking at this picture I think cast steel, Boris, very likely was a theme discussed at the time. What is peculiar is that it is not mentioned in the report. To be honest I don't know how else we would have fabricated those friction collars. I am surprised we didn't actually use the word steel in the report." Hamzeian, Interview with Young.

28 — Evidence for this comes not just from the original fireproofing proposed by Structures 3, but also from the shading of the columns in the drawing of the 3-dimensional wall that suggests the use of a "raw" material.

29 — The potential of cast-steel joints from the perspective of the fireproofing of the structure for the Beaubourg competition was referred to by Ted Happold in a comment made in the nineties. "The joints would be cast—partly because castings not only also develop a patina but perform well in fire and can be made massive enough to be exposed, and partly because they could reflect 'the human hand' reasonably cheaply since the moulds could be hot wire cut from polystyrene [...]." Happold continued by mentioning the discussions about casting he held with Koji Kamiya in 1969 and declared: "I took the idea [of casting] back to use on the structure of the Beaubourg Competition." Ted Happold, "Essential Engineer. A Book Review of An Engineer Imagines by Peter Rice," *RSA Journal*, 143, no. 5456 (1995), 85.

30 — Boris Hamzeian, Interview with John Morrison, July 27, 2017, Bath.

31 — Happold, "Essential Engineer," 85.

32 — "Steel has been used throughout and this is protected against fire and corrosion by filling the tubular spaces with treated water" was the comment in the competition report. Piano+Rogers and Ove Arup, Plateau Beaubourg Center Paris 1971 [competition report], 7.

33 — Piano+Rogers and Ove Arup, Plateau Beaubourg Center Paris 1971 [competition report], 1.

34 — Piano+Rogers and Ove Arup, Plateau Beaubourg Center Paris 1971 [competition report], 3.

35 — Ibid.

36 — Ibid.

37 — Piano+Rogers and Ove Arup, Plateau Beaubourg Center Paris 1971 [competition report], 6.

38 — "Glass," "Okalux laminate [...]" and "opaque, lightweight GRP clad, sandwich panel." Piano+Rogers Architects and Ove Arup & Partners, Plateau Beaubourg Center Paris 1971 [competition report], 7.

39 — A mask with an identical mirror effect was used, in the form of a collage, on the perspective drawing of the Burrell Gallery.

40 — Hamzeian, Interview with Young.

41 — Piano+Rogers and Ove Arup, Plateau Beaubourg Center Paris 1971 [competition report], 2.

42 — Piano+Rogers and Ove Arup, Plateau Beaubourg Center Paris 1971 [competition report], 1.

43 — "How do we could symbolize on the drawings the idea of the Beaubourg Centre [as] not just a multidepartment museum but a huge head of the communication network communing with all over the world? I had the idea of putting big satellite dishes on the roof [which] seemed to be the best way to symbolize [it]." Hamzeian, Interview with Young.

44 — Consisting of a mechanical conveyer belt inserted in an elliptical shell of transparent or semitransparent acrylic material, the Dunlop Belt Division's Starglide travelator was already in use at the end of the sixties at the Los Angeles Bus Terminal and Montreal-Dorval Airport. Installed on tall steel pillars, covering a distance of two hundred meters and used by around a million visitors to the Osaka Expo every day, the Starglide was a system of pedestrian circulation and an attraction able to offer an unprecedented view of the exposition from above. Proof the architects of 32 Aybrook Street and the Structures 3 engineers were familiar with this system is provided by Piano's visit to the Osaka Expo and the publication of an article on the Starglide belt at Osaka in *Architectural Design*, and the fact that between 1969 and 1970 Ove Arup & Partners were technical consultants to the Dunlop Belt Division on a project at La Défense in Paris.
On this, see: Alistair Best, "Expo 70 Market Place and Festival," *Design Journal*, 259, no. 7 (1970), 23–28; R. Payne, "Dunlop Speedway," *The Arup Journal*, no. 4 (1970), 24–27.

45 — Piano+Rogers and Ove Arup, Plateau Beaubourg Center Paris 1971 [competition report], 5.

46 — Boris Hamzeian, Interview with Tom Barker, September 27, 2017, London/Lausanne.

47 — "[A] system designed to maintain flexibility and adaptability in space planning and usage which is considered essential in the philosophy of this building." Piano+Rogers and Ove Arup, Plateau Beaubourg Center Paris 1971 [competition report], 6.

48 — Délégation pour la réalisation du plateau Beaubourg, République Française, Plateau Beaubourg Center Paris. Written texts, 22.

49 — Piano+Rogers and Ove Arup, Plateau Beaubourg Center Paris 1971 [competition report], 6.

50 — Lorenzo Ciccarelli, *Renzo Piano before Renzo Piano: Masters and Beginnings* (Macerata: Quodlibet, 2017).

51 — On Rogers's internship at SOM San Francisco see Bryan Appleyard, *Richard Rogers: A Biography*, (London: Faber & Faber, 1986), 102.

52 — "As you said, that was meant to be a plant room and I deliberately drew it as an industrial version of the Zip-Up house. So, there was no chance of confusing it with the architecture of the museum itself." Hamzeian, Interview with Young.

53 — "To sum up the drawings there were all kinds of collaboration tasks. You know individual drawings had two or three authors each"; "I [John Young] had to do with all the details here. The details are what I added to all these drawings. Renzo and Gianfranco Franchini had more to do with the preparation of the drawings"; and "Peter Flack and Jan Kaplický helped us out in the last weeks. [...] In other words, they did something, but they did only bits and pieces." Ibid. On the role played by Andrew Holmes, see Boris Hamzeian, Interview with Andrew Holmes, June 21, 2017, London.

54 — "The drawing you like very much, the main facade toward the plazza, was done by Renzo, Gianfranco Franchini, and me. I [John Young] did the basic part of the drawing with Renzo. Then Gianfranco took over and then I did the details. I did the cleaning equipment, the satellite dishes on the roofs, and I did all the graphics, I mean the illustration. I put the Vietnamese girl soldiers, the computer techniques." Hamzeian, Interview with Young.

55 — "I found that complete map of the world in an atlas." Ibid.

56 — Hamzeian, Interview with Holmes.

57 — The opaque nature of the north and south facades of the "building" was confirmed by the competition report, where it is stated: "Transverse stability is provided [...] by infill panels at the end of the buildings [*sic*]." Piano+Rogers and Ove Arup, Plateau Beaubourg Center Paris 1971 [competition report], 7.

58 — "I [John Young] recall they were Peter, possibly Peter Gibbons and George? I've asked Lennart Grut if he can recall their names since he was at Arup at that time. [...] George Innes was definitely one of the two I worked with. I don't recall David Armstrong or Peter Caller, but the invoice you [Shunji Ishida] mention is eighteen years later than when the Beaubourg model was made. I [Shunji Ishida] have been in contact with David Armstrong. Talking with him, I found out that Peter Caller had been working [from] time to time in [the] model shop. (I had met him in 1970–1971 at [the] Arup model shop)." Boris Hamzeian, Interview with John Young and Shunji Ishida, October 2017, Lausanne/Genoa.

59 — "There is a very detailed paragraph about circulation. It goes really into depth. You can find a lot of details about routes and parking. I think that part must be Arup's contribution. The most philosophical aspects are what Richard and Renzo put together. Looking at it, if you consider the phrase right at the start about a combination between a computer-oriented Times Square and the British Museum, that's pure Richard. That sentence is purely him. I think the bulk of the text on the architectural and the philosophical side is very much Richard and Renzo while the circulation paragraph must have been written by Arup." Hamzeian, Interview with Young.

60 — "This one looks very much like Tony Waters's style of drawing. Tony was the main draughtsman, and he could draw anything. He was a wonderful Irish draughtsman." Hamzeian, Interview with Morrison. On the attribution of the calendar for the works to Peter Bolingbroke, see Hamzeian, Interview with Young.

61 — "In particular the time required for the construction should be taken into account, as it will have to be carried out over the years 1973–1974–1975" was the statement made in the competition notice. République Française, Plateau Beaubourg Center Paris. Written texts, 32.

62 — "Boris Hamzeian: The competition program demanded a four-year program, but you presented a six-year program. It was a very risky choice. Do you remember anything about it? John Young: Until you pointed it out, I had no idea we had done that. I cannot think that we would deliberately do that because something like that could have prevented us from winning the competition. I think it is something related to Arup. We certainly didn't say it can't be done in four years, it needs six. We certainly never said anything like that." Hamzeian, Interview with Young.

63 — "The registration of the projects is subject to two conditions: 1) that they are registered by mail before the 15th of June 1971, the postmark being the authority; 2) That they arrive at the competition office before Monday June 4 at 24.00 hrs., 1971." For the rules relating to the composition of the panel and the deadlines for the dispatch of the documentation see République Française, Plateau Beaubourg Center Paris. Written texts, 30.

64 — For the reconstruction of the events the author has drawn on the accounts given by Bryan Appleyard and Nathan Silver and an interview with John Young. Appleyard, *Richard Rogers: A Biography*, 156; Nathan Silver, *The Making of Beaubourg: A Building Biography of the Centre Pompidou, Paris* (Cambridge MA: MIT Press, 1994), 35–37; Hamzeian, Interview with Young.

6

THE SELECTION PROCESS : THE GRAND AND PRESTIGIOUS GESTURE AND THE ARCHITECTURAL SIMPLICITY

6.1

682 VISIONS FOR THE CENTRE BEAUBOURG

June 15, 1971, was the deadline for dispatching projects to the Centre Beaubourg competition in Paris. Over the course of the following three weeks, the Délégation pour la réalisation du plateau Beaubourg received 682 projects and put them on display in the Grand Palais, where rooms had been set aside for the selection process. Although the Centre Beaubourg didn't achieve the hoped-for record for the biggest competition in the history of architecture, the number of participants confirmed the international significance and central role that Georges Pompidou and his collaborators sought to establish for Paris and French architecture. Participants' nationalities reflected the efforts made by the Délégation to stage an international competition, with 191 French projects and 491 foreign projects from forty-six nations.[1] Among the French participants were some central figures, from established figures of the older generation to exponents of the latest tendencies: Michel Andrault, Claude Aureau, Jean Balladur, Anthony Lucien Bechu, Joseph Belmont, I. & G. Benoit et F. Mayer Architectes, André Bruyère, Christian Cacaut, Georges Candilis, François Carpentier, Paul Chemetov, Stéphane du Château, Michel Duplay, Yona Friedman, Noël Le Maresquier, Jacques Kalisz, Michel Marot, Anatole Kopp, Paul Maymont, Pierre Parat, Claude Parent, Jean Perrottet, Henry Pottier, Denis Sloan, Georges Vachon, and Jean-Paul Viguier.[2] Another of the French entrants was Ricardo Porro, whom the organizers had considered as a possible member of the jury. However, a number of architects whose participation the organizers had hoped for[3] did not take part, and neither did several for whom Georges Pompidou had publicly expressed a degree of admiration: Bernard Zehrfuss, Fernand Pouillon, and Henry Bernard. Among foreign entrants, the clear majority came from the United States, a total of 138. This reflected the interest in the American architectural scene Pompidou and his collaborators had expressed. At the same time, it demonstrated the efforts made by the Délégation and jury member Philip Johnson to persuade as many architects as possible to take part in the competition. Yet what is surprising is the fact that among these competitors there was not even one of the names that Arthur Drexler and François Mathey had settled on in their attempt to pick the leading exponents of the contemporary American debate. This is as true for established postwar figures such as Gordon Bunshaft (Skidmore, Owings & Merrill), Kevin Roche, Paul Rudolph, César Pelli, and James Speyer as for the exponents of the new avant-garde: Robert Venturi, Charles Moore, Michael Graves, Richard Meier, and Romaldo Giurgola.[4] Also absent was Marcel Breuer who, suggested by Hans Hartung, had fascinated Pompidou to such an extent that he had invited him to take part in the competition. The core of the American entrants consisted of young architects who were collaborators with or students of the big names sought by the competition organizers. To this category, looking only at the designs that stirred the jury's interest, belonged Arthur Takeuchi, a former collaborator of Ludwig Mies van der Rohe's;[5] Alexander Corazzo, a student of Walter Gropius and László Moholy-Nagy at the New Bauhaus in Chicago; Giovanni Cosco, an assistant to Venturi and Denise Scott Brown;[6] and John K. Copelin, a Yale student and follower of Vincent Scully and Louis Kahn. There were also young architects from other countries of the English-speaking world, such as Canada and the United Kingdom—although the names mentioned by the organizers a few months earlier while setting up the competition, from well-known figures such as John Leslie Martin and Denys Lasdun[7] to leading members of the younger generation such as Cedric Price, Theo Crosby, James Gowan, James Stirling, and Archigram group, were absent. If we exclude Moshe Safdie, Michael Pearson, Arthur Erickson, and Geoffrey Massey, many of the entrants came from universities. Emblematic is the example of the Architectural Association of London, whence came the projects by Nora Kohen, Will Alsop, and Julius Tabacek, in collaboration with Dennis Crompton of the Archigram group; of Rem Koolhaas and Aristides Romanos along with Elia Zenghelis;[8] and of Wolf Wolfgang Pearlman and Robert Stones. Among the foreign countries with the highest number of participants were Japan and Brazil, to which Pompidou had invited the Délégation to turn in order to find new tendencies in contemporary architecture. On the list of entrants to the competition from Japan it is worth mentioning, in addition to Kiyonori Kikutake, Kisho Kurokawa, and Kunio Maekawa, the architects Kunio Kato, Kiyoshi Kawasaki, Makoto Masuzawa, Yutaka Murata, Shin'ichi Okada, Sachio Otani, Kiyoshi Seike, Ren Suzuki, Minoru Takeyama, Youji Watanabe, and Hiroyasu Yamada.

As well as Paulo Mendes da Rocha, the Brazilians included Tito Livio Frascino, Luiz Eduardo Indio da Costa, Wilson Reis Netto, and Pedro Paulo de Melo Saraiva.[9] There were numerous Italian entrants. Despite the absence of Giancarlo De Carlo, Maurizio Sacripanti, Angelo Mangiarotti, and Carlo Scarpa, all names that had been mentioned by the organizers, there were some significant participants from Italy: Carlo Aymonino, Enrico Castiglioni, Alberto Galardi, Marcello D'Olivo, Massimiliano Fuksas, Leonardo Mosso, Eugenio Montuori, Lucio Passarelli, Dario Passi, Paolo Piccinelli, Gio Ponti, Leonardo Ricci, Alessandro Sartor, Eduardo Vittoria, and Guglielmo Ulrich.[10]

Among the other foreign entrants worth singling

out: Manfred Schiedhelm from Germany;[11] Clorindo Testa from Argentina; Stuart McIntosh and Gerd Block from Australia; Wilhelm Holzbauer and Heinz Tesar from Austria; André and Jean Polak and Charles Vendenhove from Belgium; Evgeni Zidarov from Bulgaria; Isidro Suárez from Chile; Kim Swoo Geun from South Korea; Henning Larsen from Denmark; Andrés Perea Ortega, Pablo Pintado y Riba, and Juan Daniel Fullaondo Errazu from Spain; Aulis Blomstedt from Finland; Tao Ho from Hong Kong; Aristomenis Provelenghios (mentioned by Mathey) from Greece; Rodolfo Barragán Schwarz, José Luis Benlliure López de Arana, Ernesto Gómez Gallardo Argüelles, and Francisco Serrano Cacho from Mexico;[12] Sverre Fehn from Norway; Laurens Bisscheroux and Karel Sijmons from the Netherlands; Stanisław Brukalski, Marian Fikus, and Jerzy Hryniewiecki from Poland; Rui Jervis Atouguia from Portugal; Mircea Alifanti, Ascanio Damian, Octav Doicescu, and Horia Maicu[13] from Romania; Mikhaïl Bartch, Andrey Meyerson, and Yuri Platonov from the Soviet Union; Hans-Erland Heineman and Erik Uluots from Sweden; Martin Burckhardt, Georges Brera, Justus Dahinden, and Rolf Georg Otto from Switzerland; and, finally, Eugen Kramár, Dušan Kuzma, and Jozef Lacko from Czechoslovakia.

Taken together, the proposals submitted to the Délégation constitute a unique cross-section of the tendencies in the international debate at the end of the sixties[14]. While it seems to elude immediate decipherment, this sample lends itself to a sort of classification aimed at identifying the projects complimenting the ideas contained in the competition notice.

Some entrants intended to make the Centre Beaubourg an institution open to the city and capable of establishing a relationship with the surroundings. In certain cases this idea took the form of creating pedestrian axes that would pass through the Centre, from J. L. C. Choisy et al. (31) and Andrew and Maria Zdzienicki (411) 19th-century-inspired covered *passage* to Jadav Chandra et al.'s (247) project reminiscent of an American-style shopping arcade and Dominique Ronsseray and Jean Skinazi's (17) monumental open-air *cretti*.[15] Other submissions proposed systems to make the Centre an antenna of Les Halles, such as the futuristic elevated roadways designed by Stanislas Fiszer et al. (505)[16] and by Koolhaas and Zenghelis (532) and Gérard Fénelon et al. (320), or Jean-Charles-Louis Delacour's (150) intricated underground tunnels.[17]

In yet others integration with the surroundings was represented through platforms supported by structures to create a covered and permeable setting, as in the project by Jorge Ambrosini et al. (352).[18]

The attention paid to the surroundings also led to the conception of an open-air public space as an integral part of the Centre: for James Stageberg et al. (491) it was an open space that served to ennoble the access to the building;[19] for Vsévolod Voskerenski et al. (29) a square to be used for art exhibitions; for Robert Brauer (468) a modern park in the French style; for Crompton at al. (535) an expanse of grass enlivened by reliefs and differences in level; for Maymont (297) a sunken park providing an underground cultural center with air and light;[20] for Mendes da Rocha (338) an elevated platform from which to contemplate the city;[21] for Piano, Rogers, Franchini, and Ove Arup & Partners (493), finally, a piazza for a theatrical set of images, sounds, and information.[22]

No less important was the organizers' idea of inserting into the Centre Beaubourg a space that would not just provide access to and sort visitors, but also be a place for meeting, rest, recreation, and the staging of exhibitions to offer a preview of what was on display on the upper levels of the building. From Aristomenis Proveleghios et al. (224) to Hubert Péri et al. (282) there were entrants who turned this space into a courtyard in which to locate systems of vertical movement, much like the Guggenheim Museum's helical ramps.[23]

The groups led by Erickson (466) and Safdie (308) made this public access, circulation, and recreation space a large open-air space with a profile that could be modeled with balconies and terraces.[24]

In other cases the space became a sealed and

air-conditioned environment, roofed with inflatable textile coverings by Crompton and by Henry Colomb (38) or protected with prismatic glazed envelopes by Kawasaki (529) and by Anne Astorg-Berlottier (379), with massive steel-and-glass space frames by Michael Pearson (37), by Luis Padilla Arias et al. (92), and by Hateo Hatae (503), or with Schiedhelm et al. (126) and Lewis Davis et al.'s (427) geodetic roofs.[25]

Equally interesting were the proposals that relied on unusual means to communicate information about the contents of the Centre: mural paintings for Pottier et al. (12); a mimetic and reflective envelope for Block and Sam Broudo (518); an envelope with an optical pattern generated by the design of the openings for MacDonald and Hull (331); pop billboards of a Venturian character for Cosco et al. (641); mobile and dismountable elements in the "Archigramesque" mold to be installed in various parts of Paris and its suburbs for Crompton. Piano, Rogers, Franchini, and Ove Arup & Partners and Juan Antonio Espejel Diez's (474) projects both made use of audiovisual screens.

The principle of flexibility evoked in the competition notice led to the invention of daring structures creating spaces to be reconfigured in various ways. From the heterogeneous range of solutions we can pick out: Takeuchi and Corazzo's (83) refined Miesian framework; the grids of massive concrete piers on which to hitch prefabricated and modular platforms proposed by Pierre Cabrol et al. (587), by Duplay and François-Noël Deffontaines (96), and by Kurokawa (456);[26] the three-dimensional metal frames for the insertion of prefabricated cells close to the Anglo-American concept of the "clip-on" structure designed by Pottier, by Yona Friedman and Georges Patrix (371), and by Leonardo Mosso (609);[27] the irregular structural grids that characterized Stones and Pearlman (439) and Renée Gailhoustet and Francis Gaussel's (504) projects; the spatial structures in the form of colossal shelters under which to place the Centre Beaubourg proposed by Pham Ngoc Toi et al. (137), by Hugh Stubbins et al. (181) and by Justin Lamb et al. (82);[28] the inhabitable lattices designed by Ambrosini and by Hanspeter Schmidt et al. (473);[29] and the massive Metabolist vertical structures for the attachment of containers such as those designed by Kikutake (433) or by Ricci and Daniel Branch.[30] Piano, Rogers, Franchini, and Ove Arup & Partners' proposal with its long-span trusses to permit spaces free of internal supports was another example of this kind of flexible structure.

The competition projects with a tower configuration were a response to the competition notice's declaration that the Centre Beaubourg would be free from height restrictions, as had been indicated by Pompidou. This idea generated a variety of proposals: Gabriel Tournier et al.'s (225) monumental prism, the slanting towers of Francisco Gómez Palacio et al. (155) and of Ernesto Zepeda (250); the skyscrapers with a hyperbolic profile of Claude Guilbert et al. (19), and of Terrance Waters (166); the spirals of O. Cacoub et al. (179);[31] and even the appearance of egg-shaped containers, such as those proposed by Bruyère (272) or by Voskerenski.

Although the competition notice made no reference to the fate of Victor Baltard's pavilions at Les Halles, several proposals considered the possibility of reutilizing the pavilions, as in Ponti and Ferrari's (421) wooded park to be created between the plateau des Halles and the plateau Beaubourg, or in Cler et al. (288) proposal, where six of Baltard's pavilions were remounted on the plateau Beaubourg while the Centre Beaubourg was located underground.[32]

Other projects stood out for their traditional Beaux-Arts approach to composition;[33] others still for their intention to entrust the representative character of the new Centre Beaubourg to the essential geometry of the sphere and the cube;[34] others for the organization of the Centre into cusps, into volumes generated by a centripetal design,[35] or into any other kind of composition defined by an unusual use of the curved line;[36] still others for the recourse to jagged, crystal-shaped, or even phytomorphic solutions;[37] and others, finally, for the insertion of the Centre Beaubourg into compositions of a sculptural plasticism.[38]

Different translations of the theme of the pedestrian axis in competition proposals by Chandra Jadav et al. (247) top; J. L. C. Choisy et al. (31) bottom left; Dominique Ronsseray and Jean Skinazi (17) bottom right.

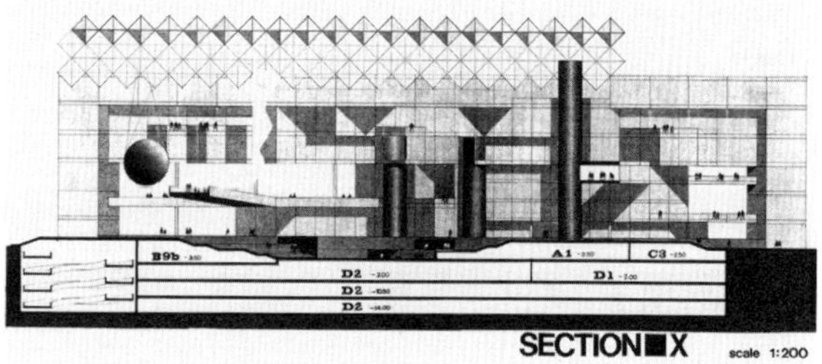

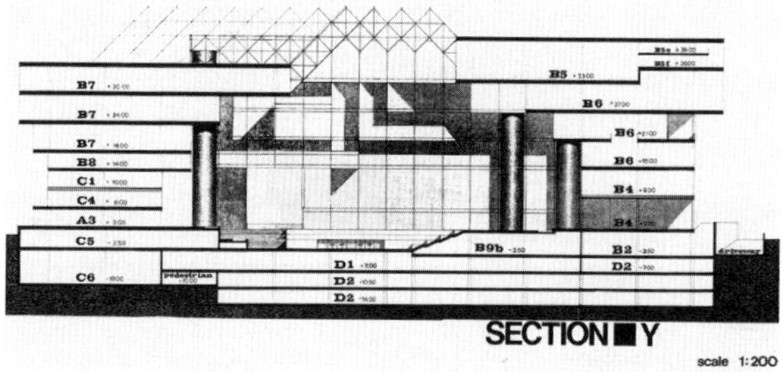

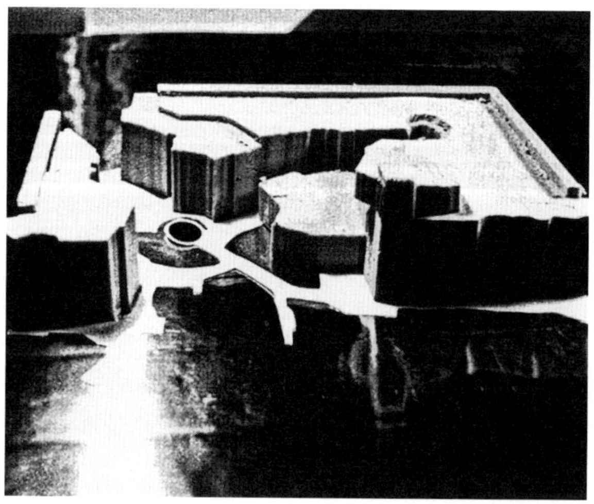

Different translations of the theme of the plateau Beaubourg connection to the plateau des Halles through underground passage by Jean-Charles Louis Delacour (150) top right, or over viaducts by Stanislas Fiszer et al. (505) bottom and Elia Zenghelis and Rem Koolhaas (532) top left.

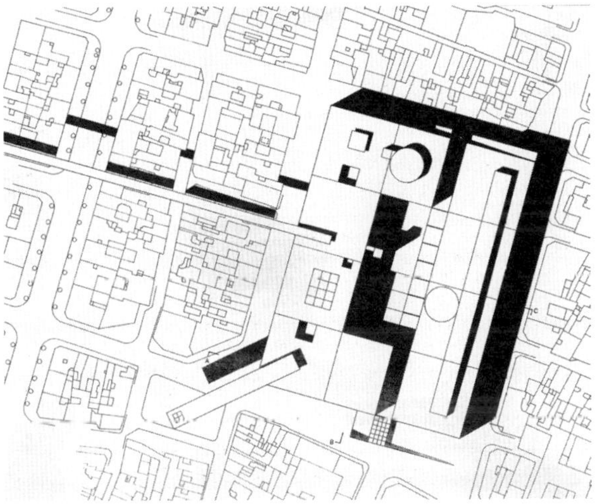

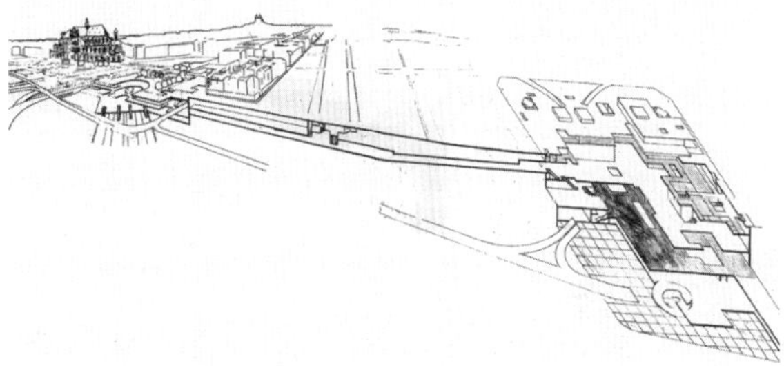

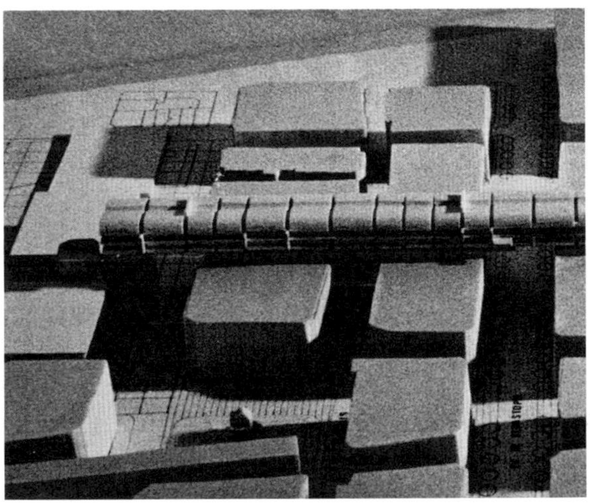

The theme of continuity of the urban fabric in the large covered piazza in the project by Jorge Ambrosini et al. (352).

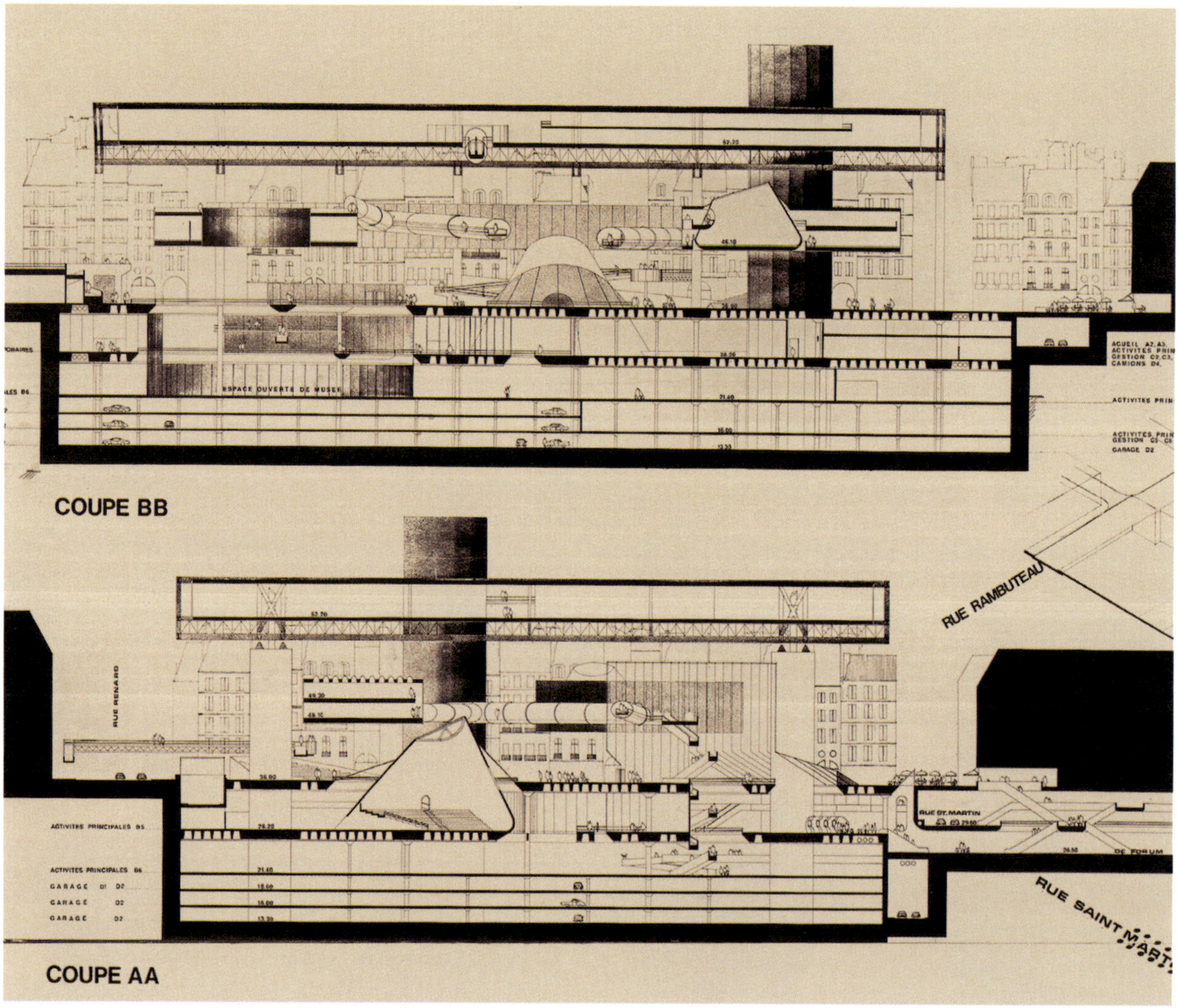

The theme of the great outdoor environment in the technological and equipped lawn by Dennis Crompton et al. (535).

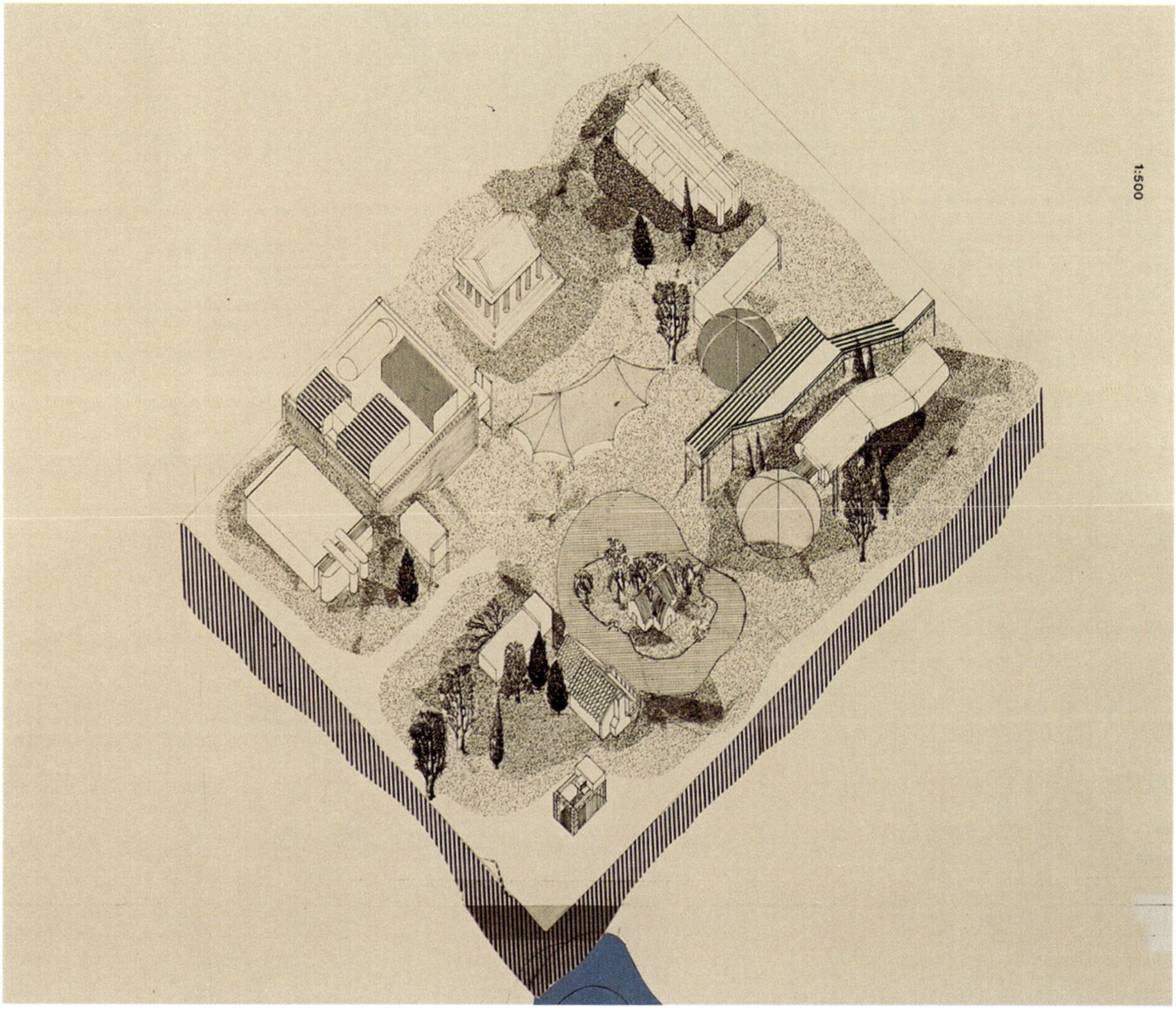

The theme of the outdoor environment in the sunken square by Paul Maymont (297).

The theme of the outdoor environment in the terrace-platform by Paulo Mendes da Rocha (338).

The theme of the outdoor environment in the piazza by Vsévolod Voskerenski et al. (29).

The theme of the outdoor environment in the piazza by Robert Brauer (469).

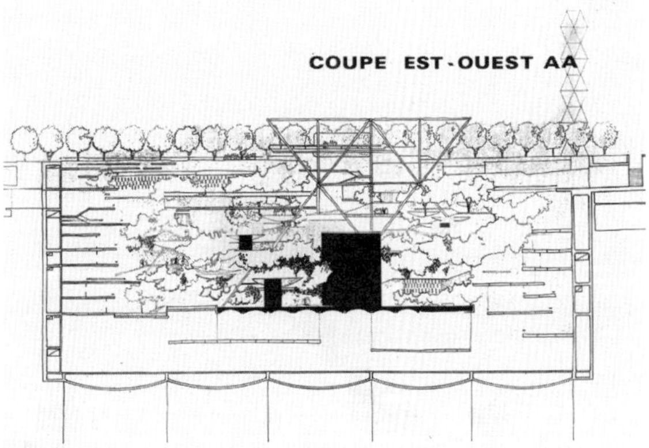

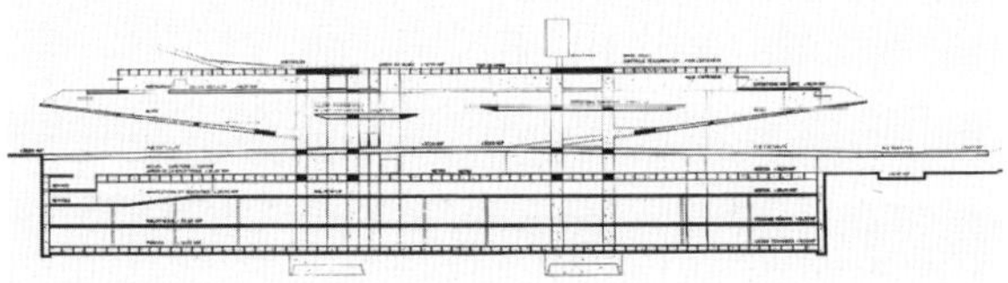

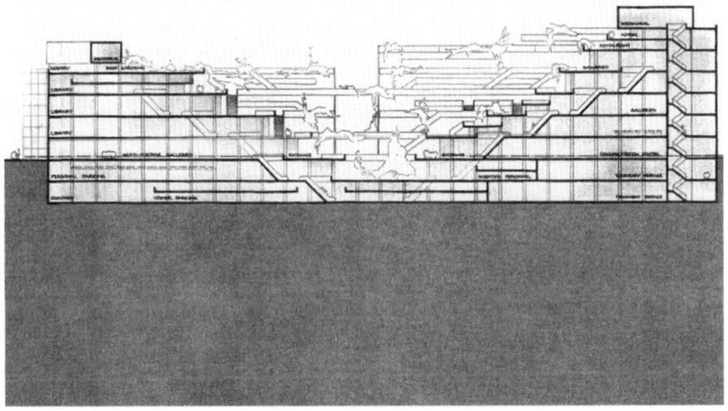

The theme of the large indoor environment dedicated to access, encounter, and information in Arthur Erickson et al.'s "crater" (466), section.

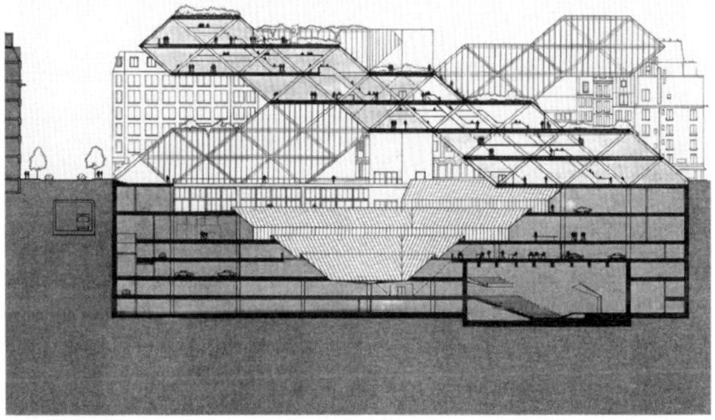

The theme of the large indoor environment dedicated to access, encounter, and information in the terrace courtyard by Moshe Safdie et al. (308), section.

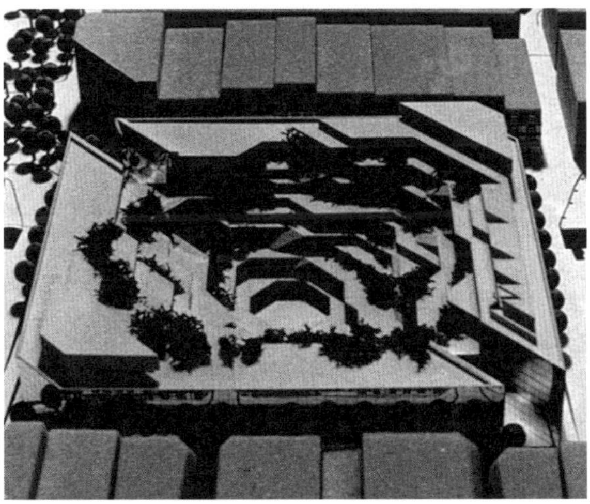

The theme of the large indoor environment dedicated to access, encounter, and information in Arthur Erickson et al.'s "crater" (466), model.

The theme of the large indoor environment dedicated to access, encounter, and information in the terrace courtyard by Moshe Safdie et al. (308), model.

The theme of the large indoor environment dedicated to access, encounter and information in the climate-controlled envelope by Luis Padilla Arias et al. (92).

The theme of the large indoor environment dedicated to access, encounter, and information in the climate-controlled envelope by Michael Pearson et al. (37).

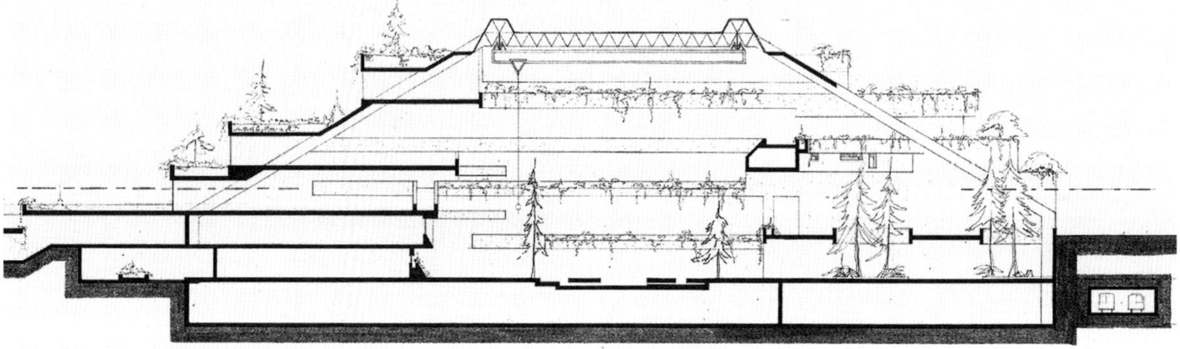

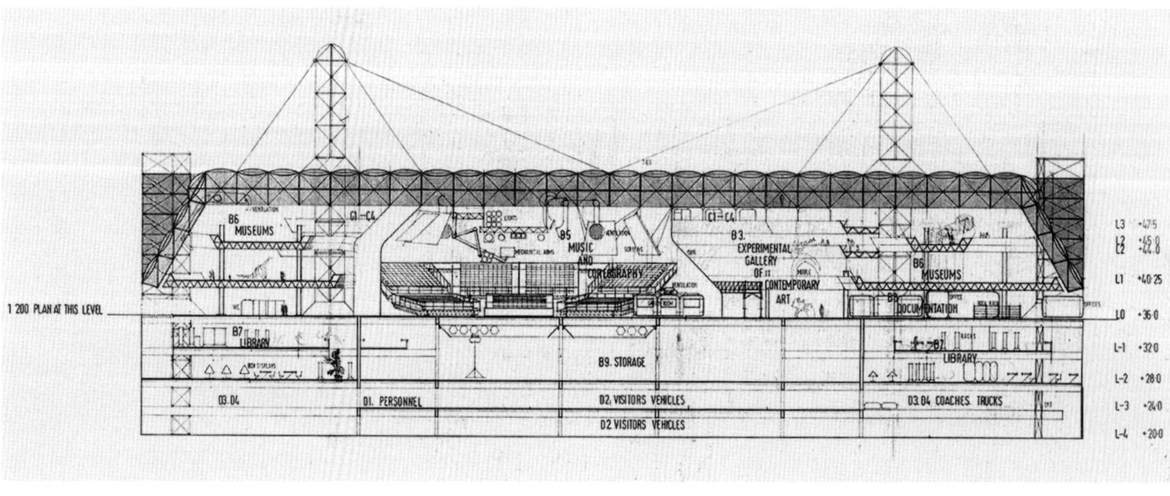

The theme of the large indoor environment dedicated to access, encounter, and information in the climate-controlled envelope by Manfred Schiedhelm et al. (126).

The theme of the large indoor environment dedicated to access, encounter, and information in the climate-controlled envelope by Lewis Davis et al. (427).

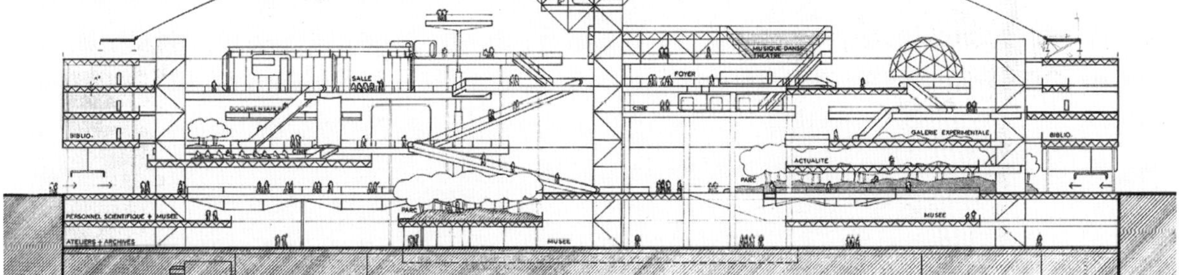

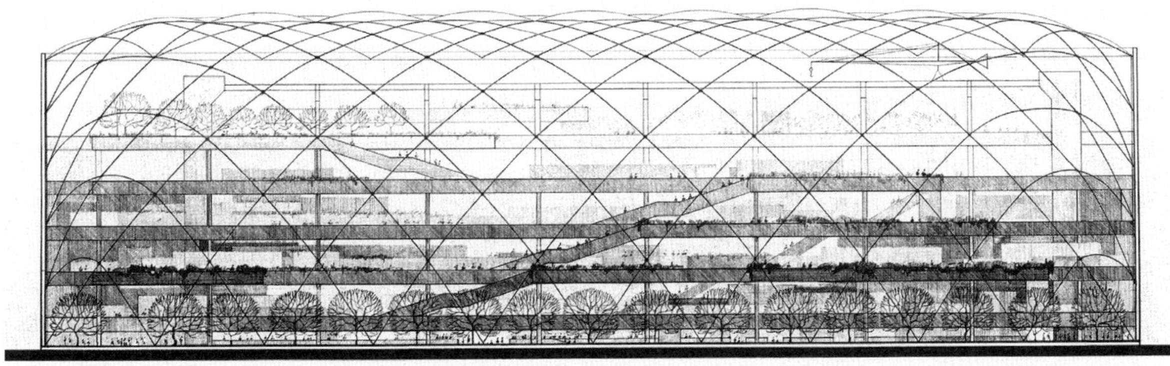

The theme of an eloquent envelope in the pop coating of the prefabricated units conceived by Henry Pottier et al. (12).

The theme of an eloquent envelope in the audiovisual panels and posters by Juan Antonio Espejel Diez (474).

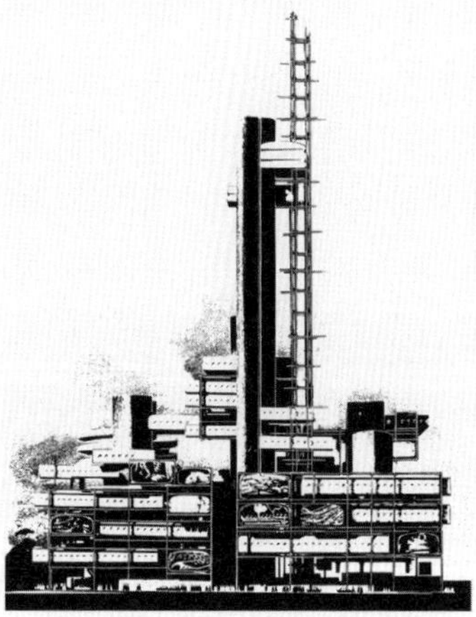

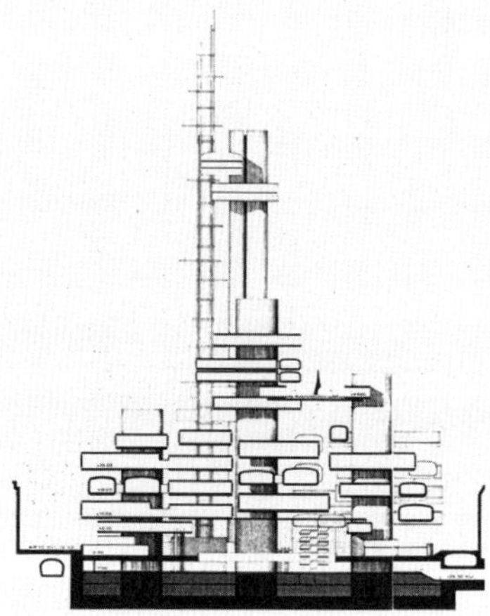

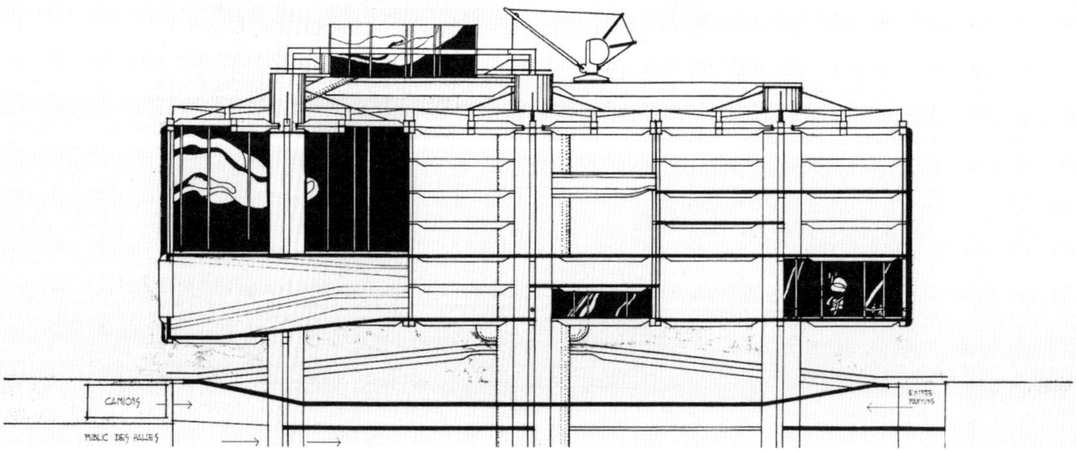

The theme of an eloquent envelope in the reflective curtain wall by Gerd Block and Sam Broudo (518).

The theme of an eloquent envelope in the pop "billboard" by Giovanni Cosco et al. (641).

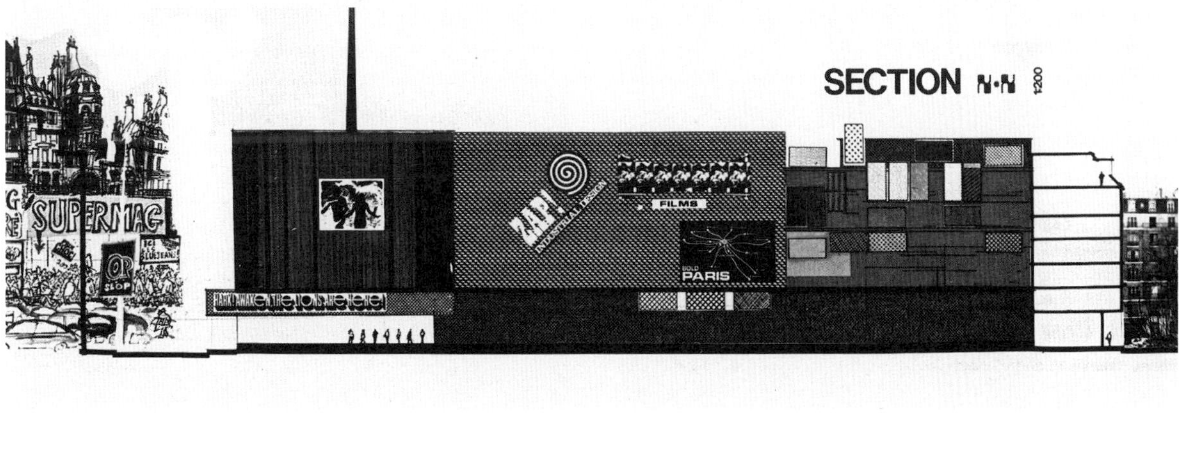

The theme of the flexible container in the Miesian box by Arthur Takeuchi and Alexander Corazzo (83).

The theme of the flexible container the three-dimensional framework for the insertion of modular units by Leonardo Mosso (609).

The theme of the continuously expanding container in the repetition of the geometrical units by Robert Stones and Wolfgang Pearlman (439).

The theme of the flexible container in the irregular structures conceived by Renée Gailhoustet and Francis Gaussel (504).

The theme of the flexible container in the colossal space frame shelter by Hugh Stubbins et al. (181).

The theme of the flexible container in the vertical megastructures by Kiyonori Kikutake et al. (433).

The theme of the flexible container in the colossal space frame shelter by Pham Ngoc Toi et al. (137).

The theme of the flexible container in the space frame by Hanspeter Schmidt et al. (473).

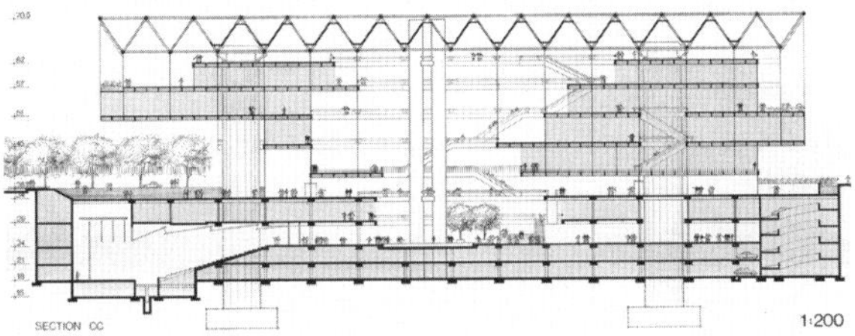

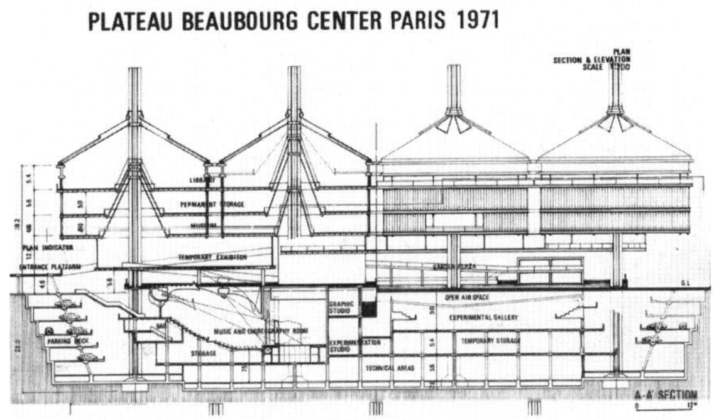

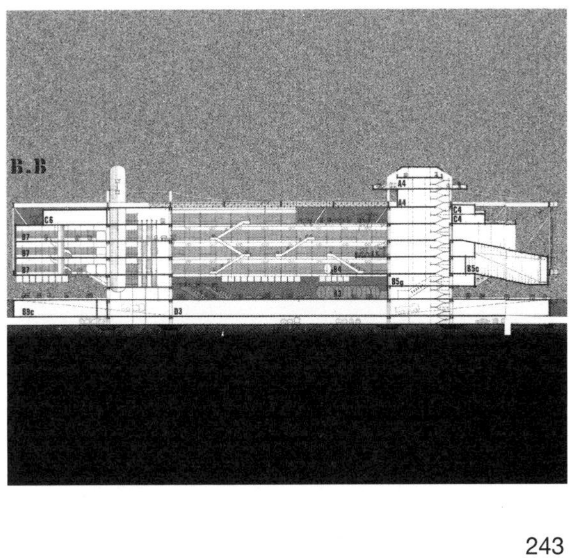

The theme of the vertical monument in the tilted volumes of Francisco Gomez Palacio et al. (155).

The theme of the vertical monument in the slender skyscraper by Claude Guilbert et al. (19).

The theme of the vertical monument in the spiral-shaped towers by O. C Cacoub et al. (179).

The theme of the vertical monument in the colossal egg by André Bruyère (272).

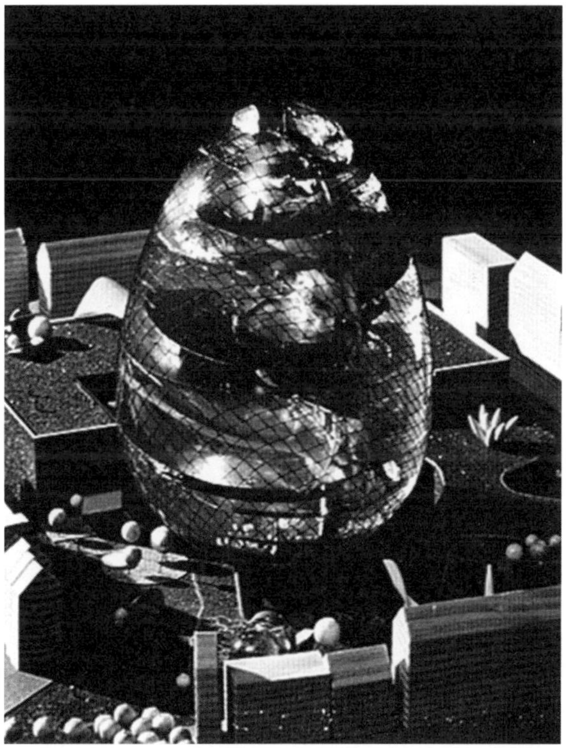

The theme of the "ggrand and prestigious architectural gesture" in the cusped volumes by Noël Le Maresquier et al. (168).

The theme of the "grand and prestigious architectural gesture" in the suspended organ by Luc Zavaroni et al. (350).

The theme of the "grand and prestigious architectural gesture" in the plastic volumes by Claude Hauserman et al. (187).

The theme of the "grand and prestigious architectural gesture" in the plastic volumes by Gérard Guillier et al. (413).

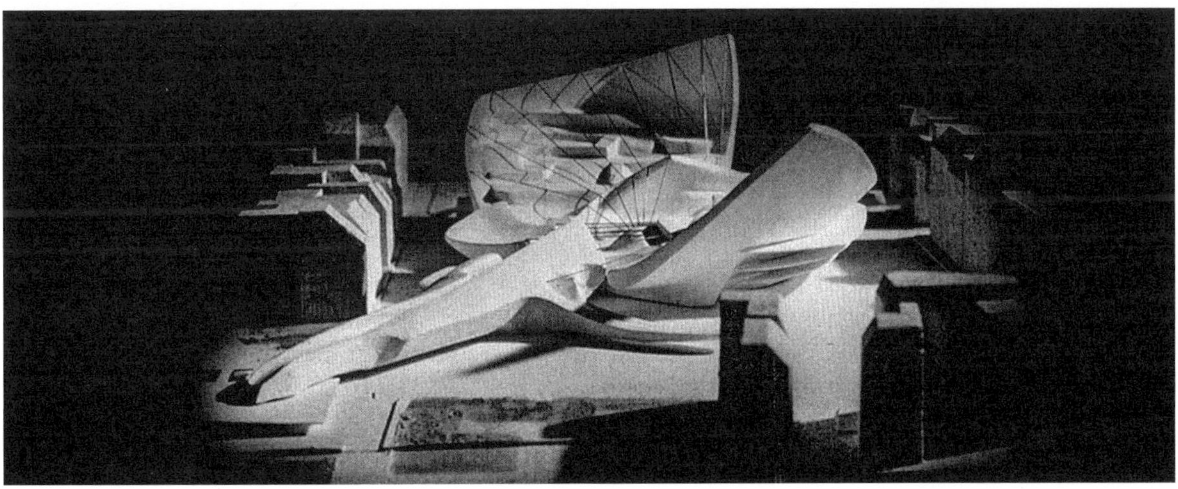

6.2

THE TECHNICAL COMMISSION'S PRELIMINARY ANALYSIS

Once the preliminary operations—from attribution of the "exhibition number" to the attachment of the plans to the display panels and the photographic reproduction of the competition drawings for projection during the selection process—had been completed, the projects were marked with their exhibition numbers, taken to the Grand Palais and put on display in an installation prepared by the architect Pierre Molins.[39] The projects numbered from 1 to 100 and 448 to 501 were put in the Grand Palais hall labeled Room B for the occasion; those from 101 to 186 and from 502 to 539 in Room C; those from 187 to 256 and from 540 to 577 in Room D; those from 257 to 344 and from 578 to 599 in Room E; those from 345 to 447 and from 600 to 641 in Room F; lastly, those numbered from 642 to 680 were displayed in Room G.[40]

Piano, Rogers, Franchini, and Ove Arup & Partners' project arrived at the Grand Palais between June 15 and 28, 1971, and was given the competition code B493. Before being put on show in Room B along with 153 other projects,[41] on June 28 the plans passed the conformity check carried out by the Technical Commission (or Board of Expert Advisors), although they drew attention to the absence of the motto that, according to the competition notice instructions, should have accompanied the identification code of the project, R22123.[42]

No mention was made of the two documents in the packet that were not required, the detail of the structure and the construction schedule, which would be presented on the panel during the selection process. They would be removed at the time of its display to the public as they were supplementary documents and, in the case of the construction schedule, presented a construction timetable necessary for the project that was essentially incompatible with that envisaged by the competition notice. Mounted on the right-hand side of the room, on the central row of panels arranged in a fretted pattern, Piano, Rogers, Franchini, and Ove Arup & Partners' project was placed between projects 491 and 495 and opposite project 496.[43]

When all the plans had been hung, members of the Technical Commission commenced their analysis of the projects, a process that would last, contrary to expectations, until the end of the first round of selection. The members of the commission were split into five groups, each headed by a "rapporteur": Didier Breton for Room B, Pierre Colboc for Room C, Paul Arnould for Room D, Gérard Struys for Room E, Alain Schmied for Room F, and Pierre Jullien for Room G.

The Technical Commission's job was to evaluate plans' conformity with the competition criteria, make a summary judgment, and propose a selection with a commented ranking.

Evident from the reports are differences in the

criteria followed by the five rapporteurs. In some cases a preference was shown for designs of a traditional modernism, while others suggested a certain attraction for sculptural and monumental modellings,[44] and yet others leaned toward projects in line with the youthful contemporary avant-gardes. This was the case for Colboc, who, out of all the projects in Room C, settled on Crompton's project[45] as "the most innovative [*frais*] of all!" The rapporteur for Room B, where Piano, Rogers, Franchini, and Ove Arup & Partners' project was on display, was Breton, employed by the Paris prefecture as an *architecte-voyer* for the Verrières-le-Buisson district.[46] Breton lamented the lack of a relationship with the surroundings in the majority of the projects: "Very often the integration into the neighborhood is not perceived as a fundamental psychological element."[47] Breton welcomed the entries that conceived Centre Beaubourg's volumes and disposition according to particular perspective views. On the other hand, he seems not to have appreciated projects that took the form of a "totally dominant, even anomalous object."[48] At the same time he hinted at his negative opinion of attempts to make the Centre the "symbol of an era," a "pure form."[49]

Breton selected twenty-five projects to which he assigned a grading from "A" to "D," accompanied by a concise assessment. Piano, Rogers, Franchini, and Ove Arup & Partners' project was not among those chosen by Breton. The projects he preferred were those of Daniel Juteau (4),[50] Sandor Majercsik (45),[51] André Brahier et al. (98),[52] Kurokawa,[53] Douglas Kelly et al. (89),[54] and Georges Brera et al. (62).[55] Breton let it be known that he had a certain preference for solutions of a horizontal character enlivened by a particular articulation of the volumes that had nothing to do with a merely gratuitous and sculptural composition, but rather one generated by the program and the logical grouping of the internal activities of the Centre, as in the case of Brera's truncated pyramids or the more articulated Majercsik's composition. In some cases Breton's idea of an integration with the surroundings translated into a partiality for designs characterized by articulated volumes and complex systems of circulation, such as Majercsik's. In other cases the importance of the surroundings led him to single out solutions that confronted the scale of the city and the view of passersby through a particular design of the façade, from the articulation of the envelope into horizontal patterns proposed by Kelly to the fragmentation of the curtain wall with terraces and hanging gardens in Brahier's project and the superimposition of modular platforms adopted by Kurokawa.

Piano, Rogers, Franchini, and Ove Arup & Partners' project was given a "C" rating. Breton emphasized the functional qualities of the partition-free floor,

but was not convinced of the degree to which the potential for flexibility had been explored, although he did appreciate the intention to develop an original structural system. Of project no. 493 he wrote: "An undifferentiated hall that permits any kind of use. The modulated façade and the detail of the structure seem to be the only elements studied in depth [in the formulation of the project]."[56]
The first two jury meetings were held on July 5 at 3:30 p.m. and July 6 at 3 p.m. in the presence of Jean Prouvé and Gaëtan Picon, who were president and vice president of the jury respectively; of the seven members, Oscar Niemeyer, Philip Johnson, Émile Aillaud, Willem Sandberg, Michel Laclotte, Herman Liaebers, and Frank Francis; and of Sébastien Loste and Robert Regard, who held the positions of jury secretary and Technical Commission president.[57] The architect Henri-Pierre Maillard also took part, even though he had only been indicated as a "reserve" jury member.
During the first meeting, the jury decided to admit to the competition the majority of the projects that, for a variety of reasons, the Technical Commission had considered not to be in conformity.
Even projects that had not met the dispatch deadline were accepted.[58] The competition minutes do not state either the identity or the number of these projects. The only ones excluded, at this stage, were two projects whose authors had not applied to enter the competition between December and February.[59] The exclusion of these two projects brought the number of projects participating to 680. For the selection of the projects it was established that each member of the jury should assign them a mark, "A, approved," "?+, uncertain, fairly favorable," "?–, uncertain, fairly unfavorable," or "N, negative judgment."[60] At the initial meetings Prouvé and other members of the jury decided to make an appeal to Pompidou for the preservation of the Baltard Pavilions.[61] The fact that this appeal was made during the competition process gives an idea of the extent to which the future of the Baltard Pavilions was proving to be a question inseparable from the Centre Beaubourg project.

It is no coincidence that Prouvé and others members of the jury made integration of the Centre with the plateau des Halles and the Baltard Pavilions two crucial criteria in the formulation of their judgments.

Pierre Molins, Project of interiors at Grand Palais for the selection process of the competition of the Center Beaubourg, Paris, spring 1971.

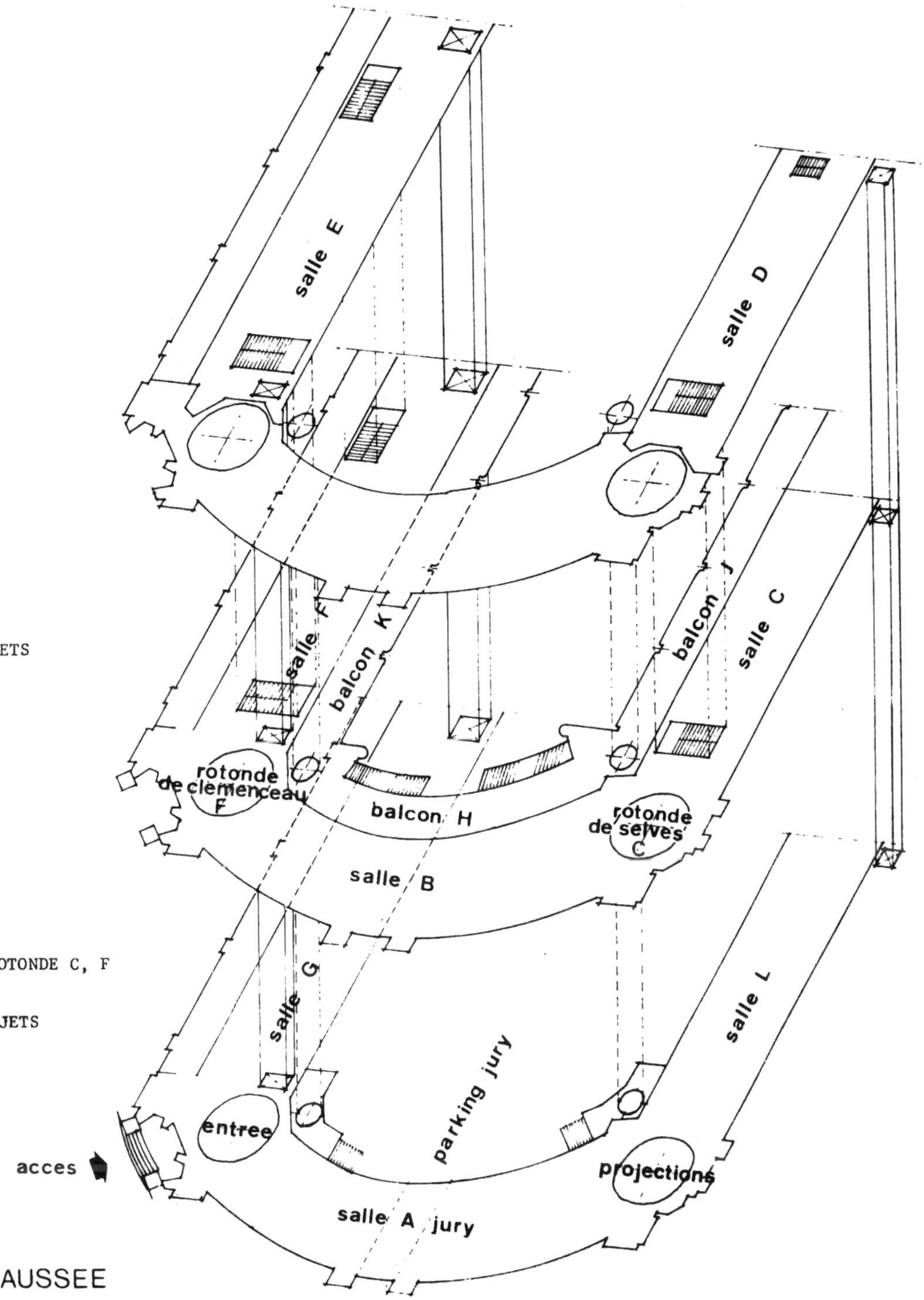

2e ETAGE
SALLES D § F
CAPACITE 218 PROJETS

1e ETAGE
SALLES F, J, B ROTONDE C, F
BALCON K, J, H
CAPACITE 519 PROJETS

REZ DE CHAUSSEE
SALLES A, G, L
CAPACITE 349 PROJETS

6.3

THE JURORS' PREFERENCES AND THE SEARCH FOR NEW CONTEMPORARY DIRECTIONS

Between July 5 and 7 the jury began evaluating projects, even though the Technical Commission was still engaged in its own evaluation, the results of which would be communicated on July 7.[62] From the official notes drawn up collectively by the members there seems to have been a propensity to favor projects with characteristics of functionality and flexibility and with particular technical and structural solutions and modes of construction, excluding projects with a markedly monumental and sculptural character. "Very rapidly, there emerged [among us] a sort of 'allergy' to what could be described as a 'grand and prestigious architectural gesture,'" would be the words used by Prouvé to recall this phase of the competition.[63]

Prouvé selected sixteen projects in which it is possible to discern his interest in factors of structure and construction. Such a preference meant including projects unrelated to the functionalist principle Prouvé alluded to during the preparation of the competition. The best example is given by his selection of Bruyère's egg, characterized by a clearly monumental, expressive, and symbolic component that were susceptible to the same criticism that he himself would make publicly at the end of the competition.[64] Piano, Rogers, Franchini, and Ove Arup & Partners' project did not belong to this kind of proposal characterized by special structures. He instead picked Schiedhelm's geodetic dome, a project that Prouvé would not succeed in getting through to the final stage but which he would mention to Pompidou at the presentation of the competition results. Another important evaluation parameter for Prouvé was the preservation and reutilization of the Baltard Pavilions, as is demonstrated by the inclusion on his list of Cler's project.

Johnson selected forty-three projects, probably because he was interested in identifying a range of proposals most representative of the contemporary debate.[65] It was also a sign of his uncertainty over which projects might best suit to the site and the content the organizers envisioned for the Centre. Piano, Rogers, Franchini, and Ove Arup & Partners' project was on Johnson's list.

The fact that it was only one among many different selected projects reflected Johnson's open quest for new directions in American architecture. In his selected projects, in fact, he recognized other contemporary influences and trajectories, be they those of Venturi in Cosco's proposal or of Kahn in Platonov et al.'s project (214)—a preference that would be confirmed in the later phases as is demonstrated by his choice to take Cosco's project through to the final stage.

The wide-ranging selection led him to pick the proposals of famous architects such as Kurokawa and Safdie. Among the projects that would make it through all the phases of selection, he also chose Erickson's open-air crater, Duplay and Deffontaines's urban fabric, and the composition of diagonally orientated prismatic volumes produced by Stageberg.

Niemeyer selected only six projects, most of which stood out for their daring structures, such as the proposals of Diez, of Piano, Rogers, Franchini, and Ove Arup & Partners, and of Mendes da Rocha, with whom Niemeyer shared a cultural affinity and an architectural style, that of Brazilian Modernism.[66] The inclusion of Platonov's project was a reflection of Niemeyer interest in the fashionable Kahnian manner.

Aillaud selected a total of twenty-three projects. He chose proposals in keeping with his formal taste and liking for the spectacular, such as Bruyère's; he also picked solutions with a crystal-shaped composition of volumes such as Stones and Pearlman's proposal; he was sensitive to the preference expressed by the competition notice and Pompidou for high-rise buildings such as Tournier's monolith and de Saraiva Melo et al.'s skyscraper with rounded corners (182).[67] The proposals picked by Aillaud did not include Erickson's crater, the very project that he would put forward when some people on the jury started to lean toward Piano, Rogers, Franchini, and Ove Arup & Partners' proposal.

The selection by jury members representing the *utilisateurs* ("users") was varied. The only exception in this sense was Sandberg, the member who, along with Johnson, seems to have exercised a certain amount of influence over the preliminary jury meetings held in the previous months.[68] Interested in the design of the space that was going to house the exhibitions put on by the Centre, Sandberg favored projects with rational and flexible settings that were on a human scale and had sophisticated lighting systems.[69] One of the projects he singled out was Erickson's crater.

Only in the later stages would Sandberg include Piano, Rogers, Franchini, and Ove Arup & Partners' project among his preferences.

Between July 7 and 8 the Technical Commission compiled a table of the jury's marks and drew up two lists of projects. The first list contained 102 projects that had received at least one "A, accepted" mark and were admitted to the next stage of selection;[70] the second comprised 117 projects that had received the evaluation just below that, "?+, uncertain, fairly favorable," from at least one member of the jury and were considered back-ups ranked with "A, accepted."[71] Piano, Rogers, Franchini, and Ove Arup & Partners' project was only given the "A, accepted" mark by Johnson and Niemeyer; Prouvé and Aillaud were uncertain ("?+, uncertain, fairly favorable" in the first case and "?" in the second, resorting to an unofficial ranking); Liebaers was hostile ("N").[72]

Put on display in Rooms A and L, the 102 projects were subjected to a new round of selection that, unlike the previous one, was the fruit of jury discussions held July 8 and 9 with all members present. The 102 projects were reduced to twenty-two by the end of the first day.[73] At this junction, Prouvé proposed refraining from any further selection from the twenty-two projects before they had been reexamined collectively in light of the views of the rapporteurs (now also referred to as "room managers"), which had not yet been taken into consideration.[74] Prouve's idea of resorting to a reexamination of all 682 proposals, a procedure he dubbed the "new selection," would allow the jury to continue its work. Meanwhile Prouvé asked the jury to select the best proposals from the twenty-two projects previously shortlisted and asked the Technical Commission and the *utilisateurs* to carry out a subsequent analysis. "[An] exhibition [in the presence] of the technicians and those *utilisateurs* of the future museum who are available (and who up until this moment have not yet given their opinion). [...] This [exhibition] could lead to a revision of our selection."[75]

Before starting on the new selection, the jury looked again at the first selection, reducing the number of projects first from twenty-two to ten[76] and then to six.[77]

The projects chosen were: Takeuchi and Corazzo; Duplay and Deffontaines; Platonov; Ambrosini; and Piano, Rogers, Franchini, and Ove Arup & Partners. The jury picked three finalists: Piano, Rogers, Franchini, and Ove Arup & Partners, Duplay and Deffontaines, and Ambrosini.[78]

The jury's choice revealed what they believed the Centre Beaubourg ought to be: a flexible work of architecture with a markedly urban character and distinguishing technical and structural traits.

At the same time, their choice also demonstrated the intention to identify three distinct and heterogeneous proposals. In Duplay and Deffontaines's project the concept of a building was negated, dissolved into a horizontal modular web that evoked the modularity of the Baltard Pavilions, although achieved by different means: those of prefabrication and contemporary construction techniques. Ambrosini's subterranean city stretched from Les Halles to the plateau Beaubourg, where it emerged as a platform that sheltered a large public square devoted to art and the neighborhood. Piano, Rogers, Franchini, and Ove Arup & Partners' project also proposed a large square but differed from the other proposals in its structural system and envelope capable of transmitting information.

Notes that can be attributed to Aillaud and refer to the meeting on July 9 allow us to follow the judges' thinking. Each of the three was given a term, referring in some cases to the jury's opinion and comments and, in others, to what may have been the name used by the members to identify the proposals. Piano, Rogers, Franchini, and Ove Arup & Partners' project was called "*l'anglais*," "the English one," perhaps because of its "Archigramesque" character or because the jury knew the origin of some of its authors. The note also quotes Johnson's comment: "Johnson: attention to the cut ('*coupure*')." This was perhaps a reference to the particular nature of the section through the Centre Beaubourg, devoid of internal supports.[79]

The term "*accord*," "agreement," attributed to Duplay and Deffontaines's project seems to be an allusion to this project having earned the broadest support among the jury members.[80] "*Le notre*," "ours," was the expression that identified Ambrosini's project, perhaps because some members thought its authors were French, or because it was supported by a group that included Aillaud.[81]

Competition jury for the realization of the Centre Beaubourg, Projects list of the competition with the preferences of each juror (excerpt featuring the appreciations of Renzo Piano, Richard Rogers, Gianfranco Franchini and Ove Arup & Partners' proposal identified with number 493), Paris, 8 July 1971.

N° Projet	J. PROUVÉ	G. PICON	E. MILLAUD	F. FRANCIS	P. JOHNSON	M. LACLOTTE	O. NIEMEYER	W. SANDBERG	H. LIEBAERS	P. MAILLARD	TOTAL
	A	A X	A	A	A X	A X	A	A	A X	A	A
	+? X	+?	+?	+?	+?	+?	+?	+?	+?	+?	+?
491	?	?	?	?	?	?	?	?	?	?	?
	-?	-?	-?	-?	-?	-?	-?	-?	-?	-?	-?
	N	N	N X	N	N	N	N	N	N	N	N
	E	E	E	E	E	E	E	E	E	E	E
	A	A	A	A	A	A	A	A	A	A	A
	+ X	+	+	+	+	+	+	+	+	+	+?
492	?	?	? X	?	?	?	?	?	?	?	?
	–	–	–	–	–	–	–	–	–	–	-?
	N	N X	N	N	N X	N X	N	N	N X	N	N
	E	E	E	E	E	E	E	E	E	E	E
	A	A	A	A	A X	A	A X	A	A	A	A
	+ X	+	+	+	+	+	+	+	+	+	+?
493	?	?	? X	?	?	?	?	?	?	?	?
	–	–	–	–	–	–	–	–	–	–	-?
	N	N X	N	N	N	N X	N	N	N X	N	N
	E	E	E	E	E	E	E	E	E	E	E
	A	A	A	A	A	A	A	A	A	A	A
	+	+	+	+	+	+	+	+	+	+	+?
494	?	?	?	?	?	?	?	?	?	?	?
	–	–	–	–	–	–	–	–	–	–	-?
	N X	N X	N X	N	N X	N X	N	N	N X	N	N
	E	E	E	E	E	E	E	E	E	E	E
	A	A	A	A	A	A	A	A	A	A	A
	+	+	+	+	+	+	+	+	+	+	+?
495	?	?	?	?	?	?	?	?	?	?	?
	–	–	–	–	–	–	–	–	–	–	-?
	N X	N X	N X	N	N X	N X	N	N	N X	N	N
	E	E	E	E	E	E	E	E	E	E	E

-8. JUIL. 1971

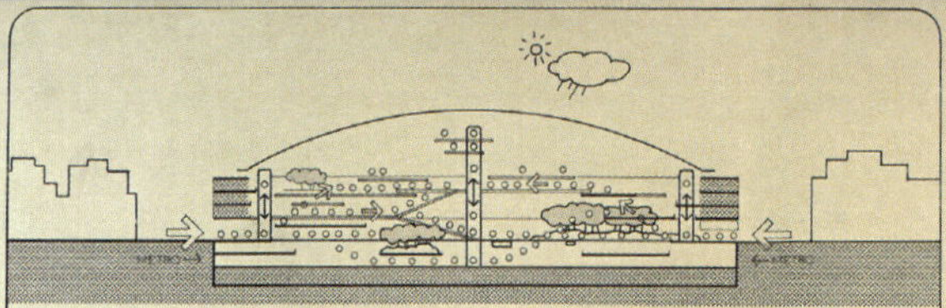

PLACE PUBLIQUE– CLIMA CONTROLE– TOUJOURS ETE– GRAND ESPACE TRAVERSABLE– PARC– OUVERT EN PERMANENCE– ENTREE GRATUITE ET DE PARTOUT– APPARTENANT A TOUS– RENCONTRE– TRAVAIL DES ARTISTES POUR LE PEUPLE ET AVEC LE PEUPLE– ACCESS DIRECTE DU METRO– PAS DE STATIONNEMENT PERMANENT POUR VOITURES PRIVEES DANS LE BATIMENT– SAUVEZ LA VILLE– STATIONNEZ HORS DE LA VILLE– RENDEZ LES TRANSPORTS EN COMMUN PLUS EFICACE.

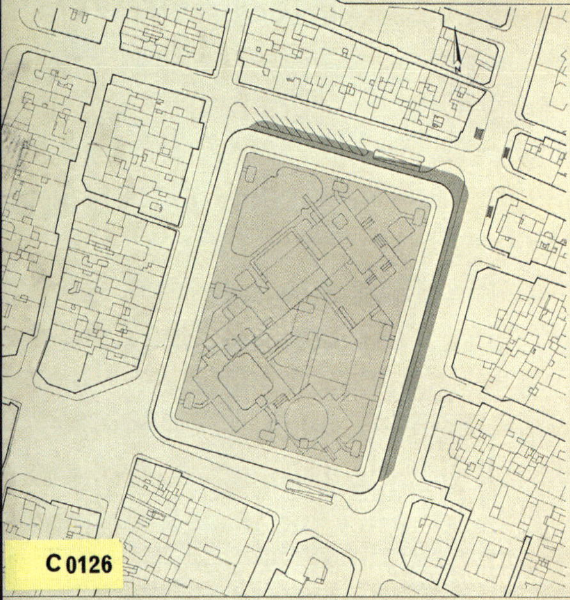

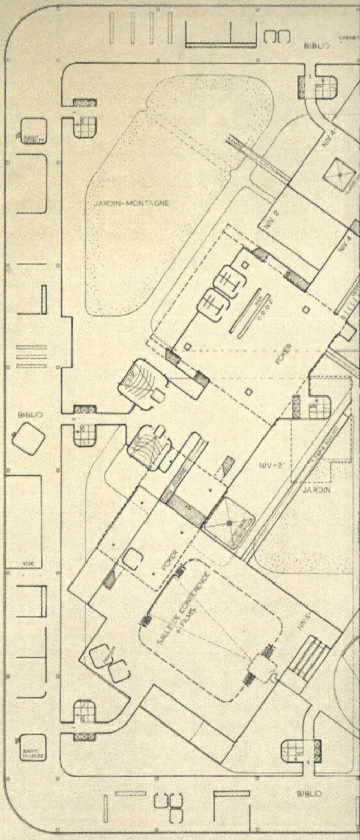

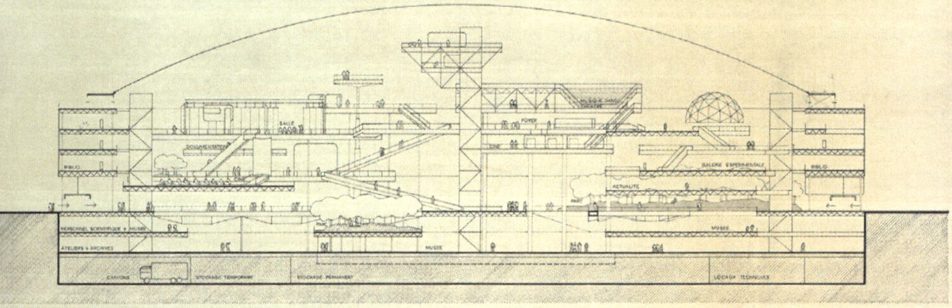

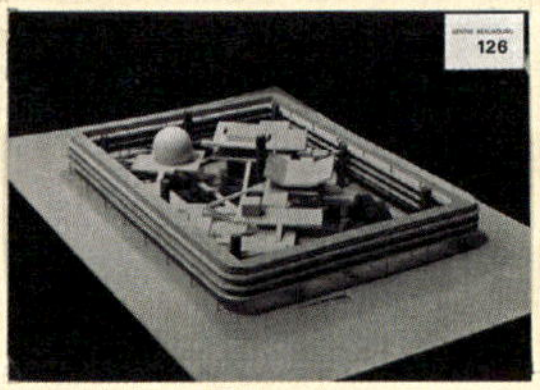

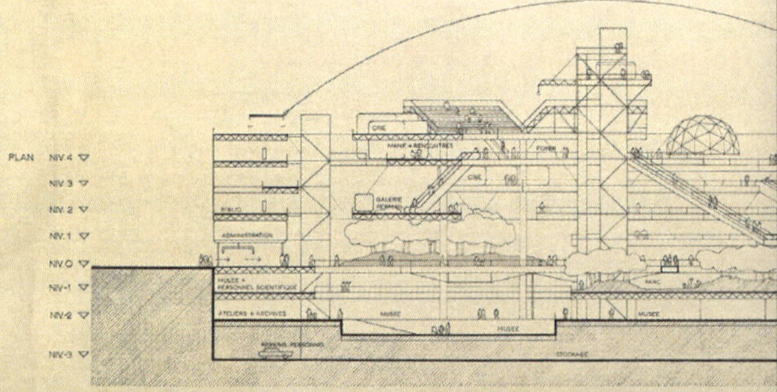

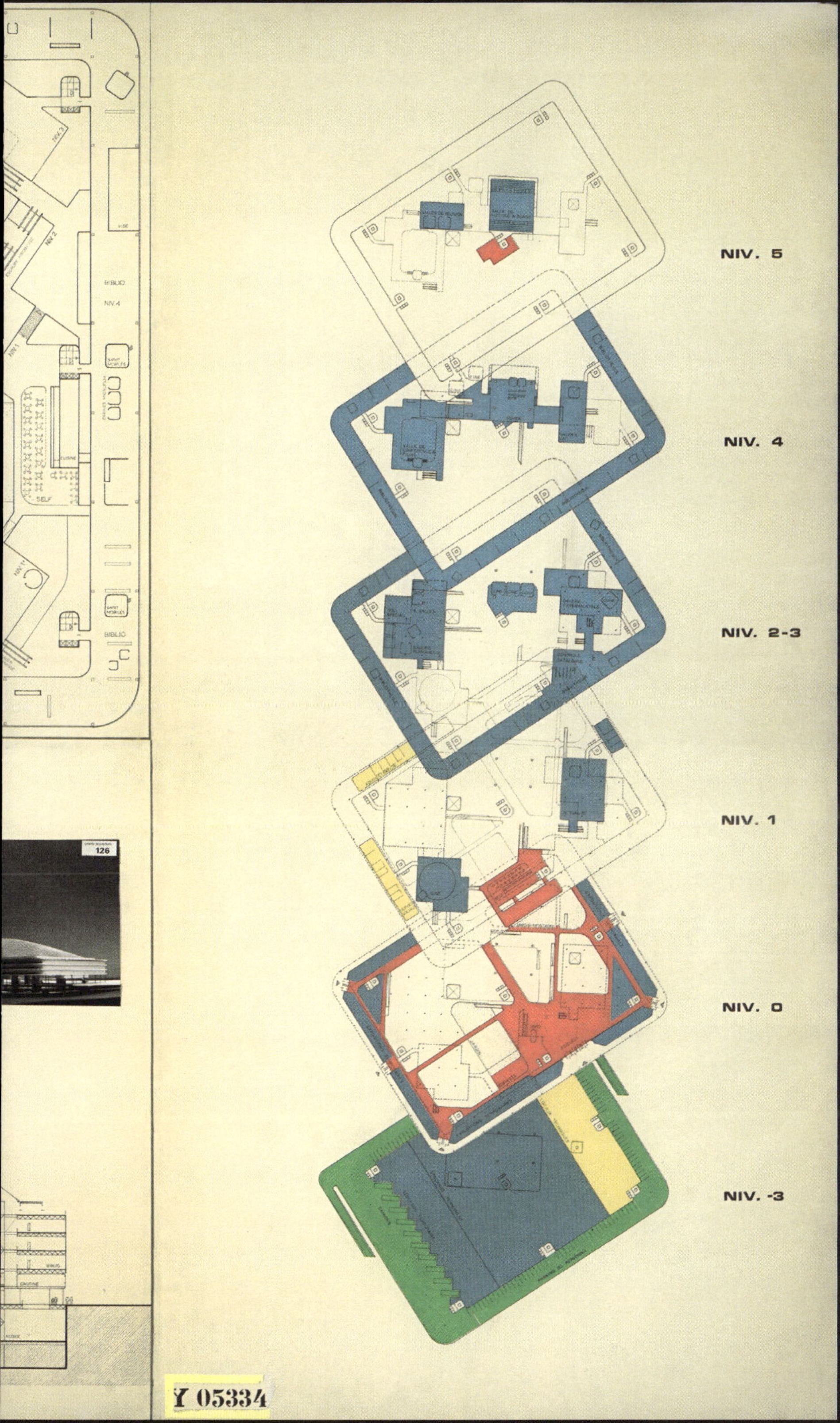

Manfred et al. (126), Project for the Centre Beaubourg competition, panel set up at the Grand Palais, Paris, June 1971.

SUMMARY AND INTERRELATIONS OF THE CENTRE BEAUBOURG ACTIVITIES

A. Reception orientation (Red)
A1. Entrance reception
A2. Reception for children
A3. Cafeteria and canteen
A4. Restaurant

B. Main activities (Blue)
B1. Current events room
B2. Industrial design permanent gallery and documentation service
B3. Experimental Gallery of Contemporary Art
B4. Temporary exhibitions
B5. Theatres and meetings
B6. Museums
B7. Library
B8. Specialized documentation and research
B9. Temporary and permanent storage

C. Management (Green)
C1. Scientific and administrative personnel
C2. Social services
C3. Supervision and control
C4. Lodgings
C5. Workshop and storerooms
C6. Technical areas

D. Parking (Yellow)
D1. Personnel parking
D2. Visitor's parking
D3. Coaches
D4. Trucks

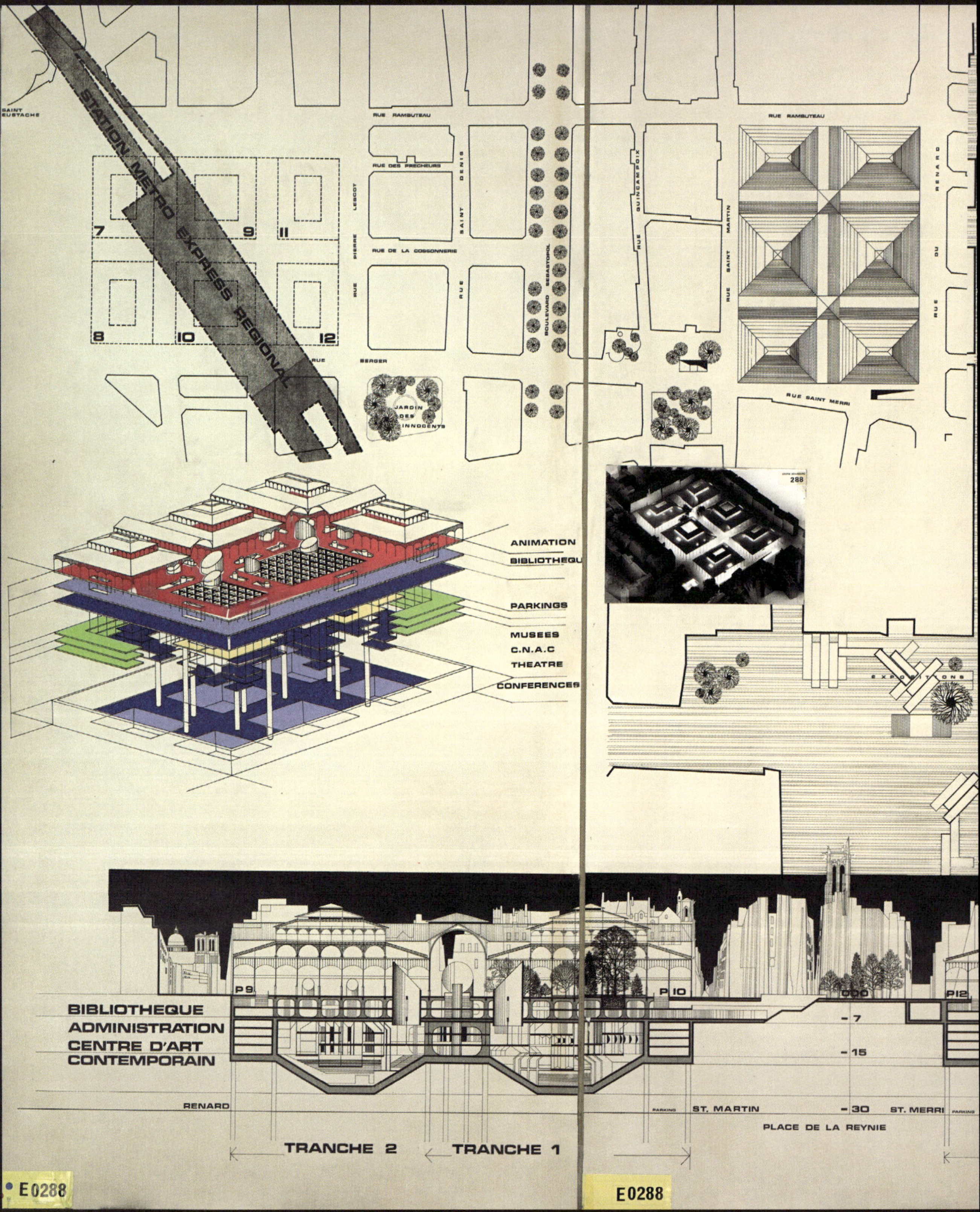
SAINT EUSTACHE
STATION METRO EXPRESS REGIONAL
7
9
11
8
10
12
RUE RAMBUTEAU
RUE DES PRECHEURS
RUE PIERRE LESCOT
RUE SAINT DENIS
RUE DE LA COSSONNERIE
RUE BERGER
JARDIN DES INNOCENTS
BOULEVARD SEBASTOPOL
RUE QUINCAMPOIX
RUE SAINT MARTIN
RUE DU RENARD
RUE SAINT MERRI
ANIMATION
BIBLIOTHEQU
PARKINGS
MUSEES
C.N.A.C
THEATRE
CONFERENCES
288
EXPOSITIONS
P9
P10
P12
BIBLIOTHEQUE
ADMINISTRATION
CENTRE D'ART
CONTEMPORAIN
000
-7
-15
-30
RENARD
PARKING
ST. MARTIN
ST. MERRI
PARKING
PLACE DE LA REYNIE
TRANCHE 2
TRANCHE 1
E0288
E0288

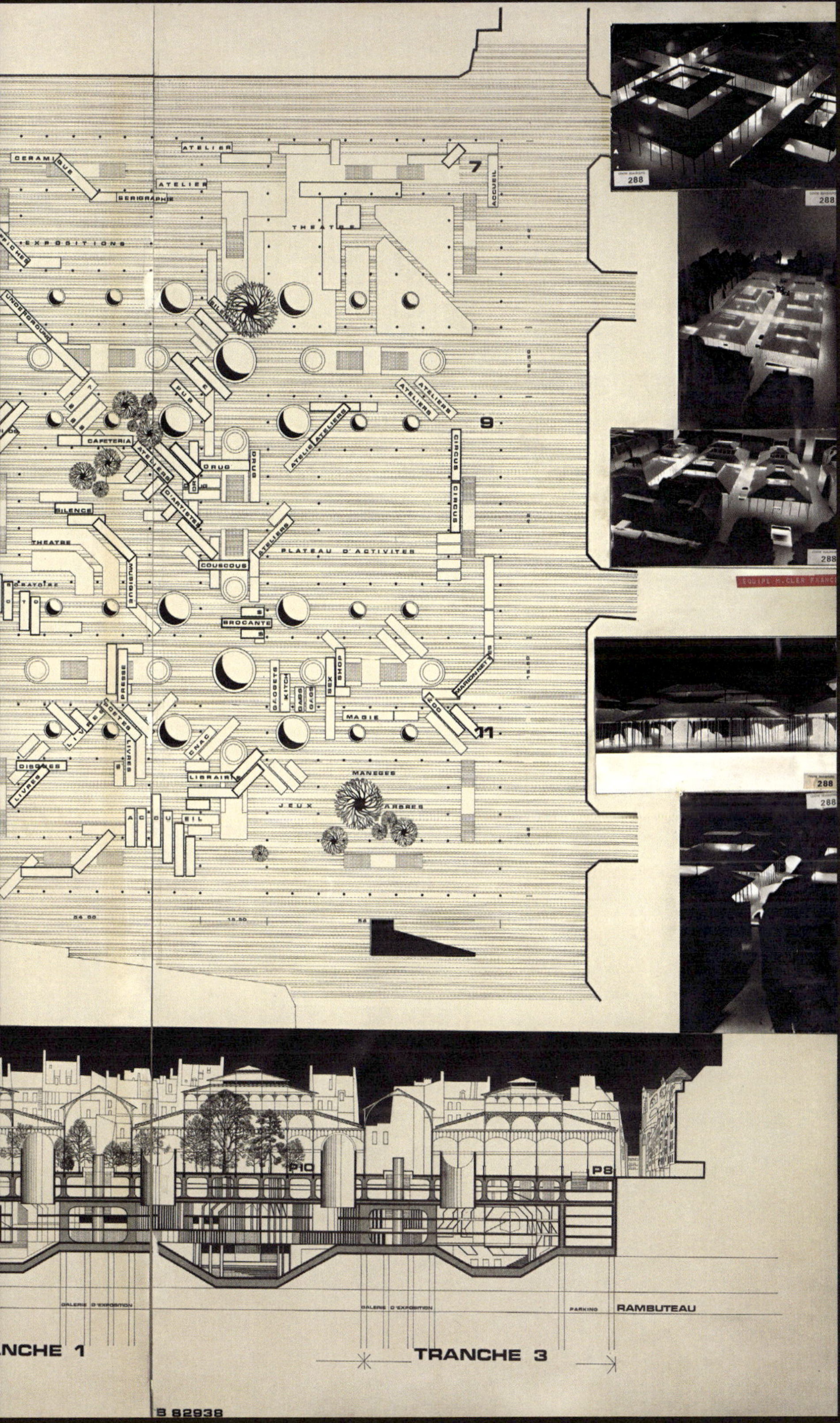

Michel Cler et al. (288), Project for the Centre Beaubourg competition, panel set up at the Grand Palais, Paris, June 1971.

SUMMARY AND INTERRELATIONS OF THE CENTRE BEAUBOURG ACTIVITIES

A. Reception orientation (Red)
A1. Entrance reception
A2. Reception for children
A3. Cafeteria and canteen
A4. Restaurant

B. Main activities (Blue)
B1. Current events room
B2. Industrial design permanent gallery and documentation service
B3. Experimental Gallery of Contemporary Art
B4. Temporary exhibitions
B5. Theatres and meetings
B6. Museums
B7. Library
B8. Specialized documentation and research
B9. Temporary and permanent storage

C. Management (Green)
C1. Scientific and administrative personnel
C2. Social services
C3. Supervision and control
C4. Lodgings
C5. Workshop and storerooms
C6. Technical areas

D. Parking (Yellow)
D1. Personnel parking
D2. Visitor's parking
D3. Coaches
D4. Trucks

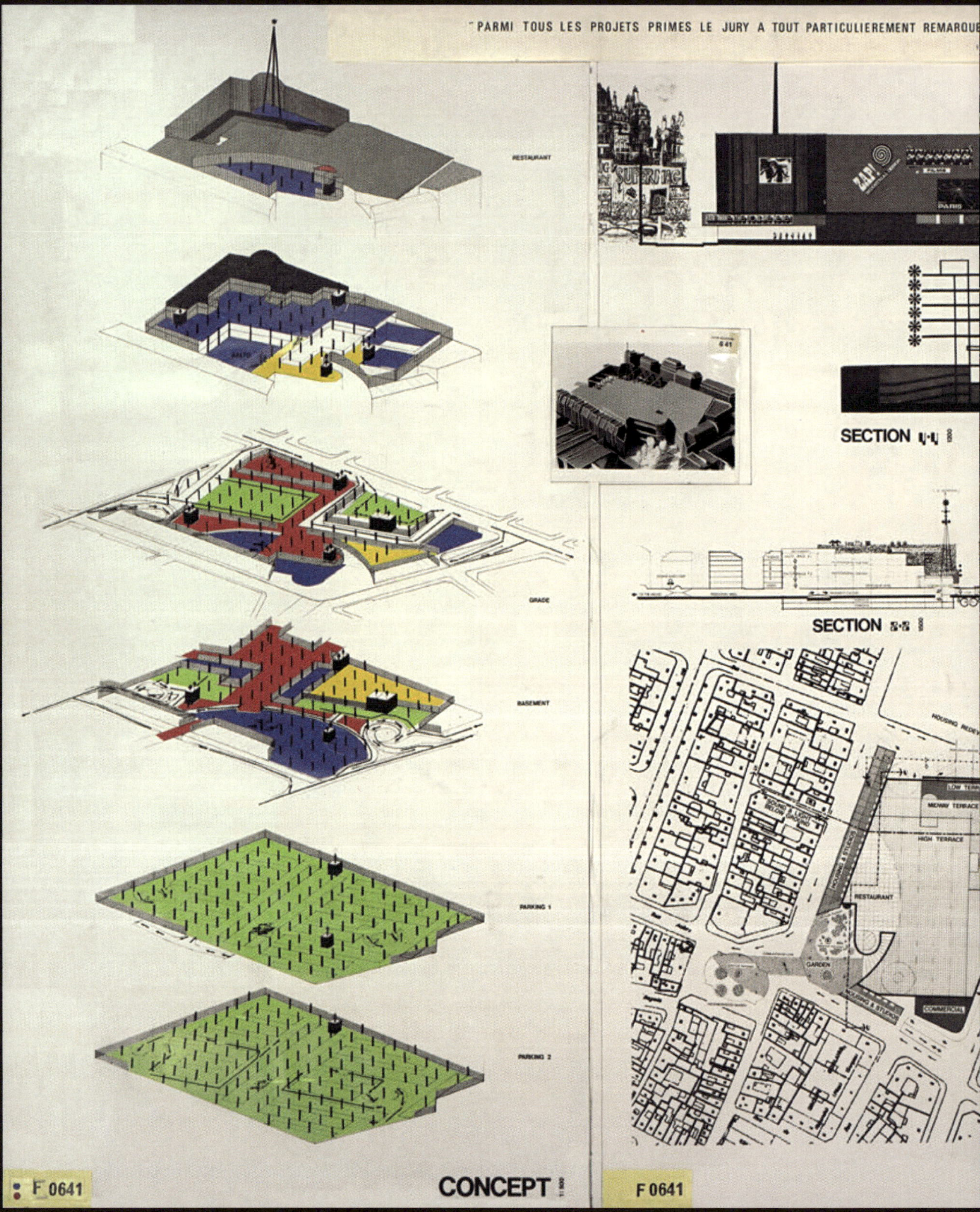

"PARMI TOUS LES PROJETS PRIMES LE JURY A TOUT PARTICULIEREMENT REMARQUE
RESTAURANT
GRADE
BASEMENT
PARKING 1
PARKING 2
SECTION
SECTION
LOW TERR
MIDWAY TERRACE
HIGH TERRACE
RESTAURANT
GARDEN
COMMERCIAL
F 0641
CONCEPT
F 0641

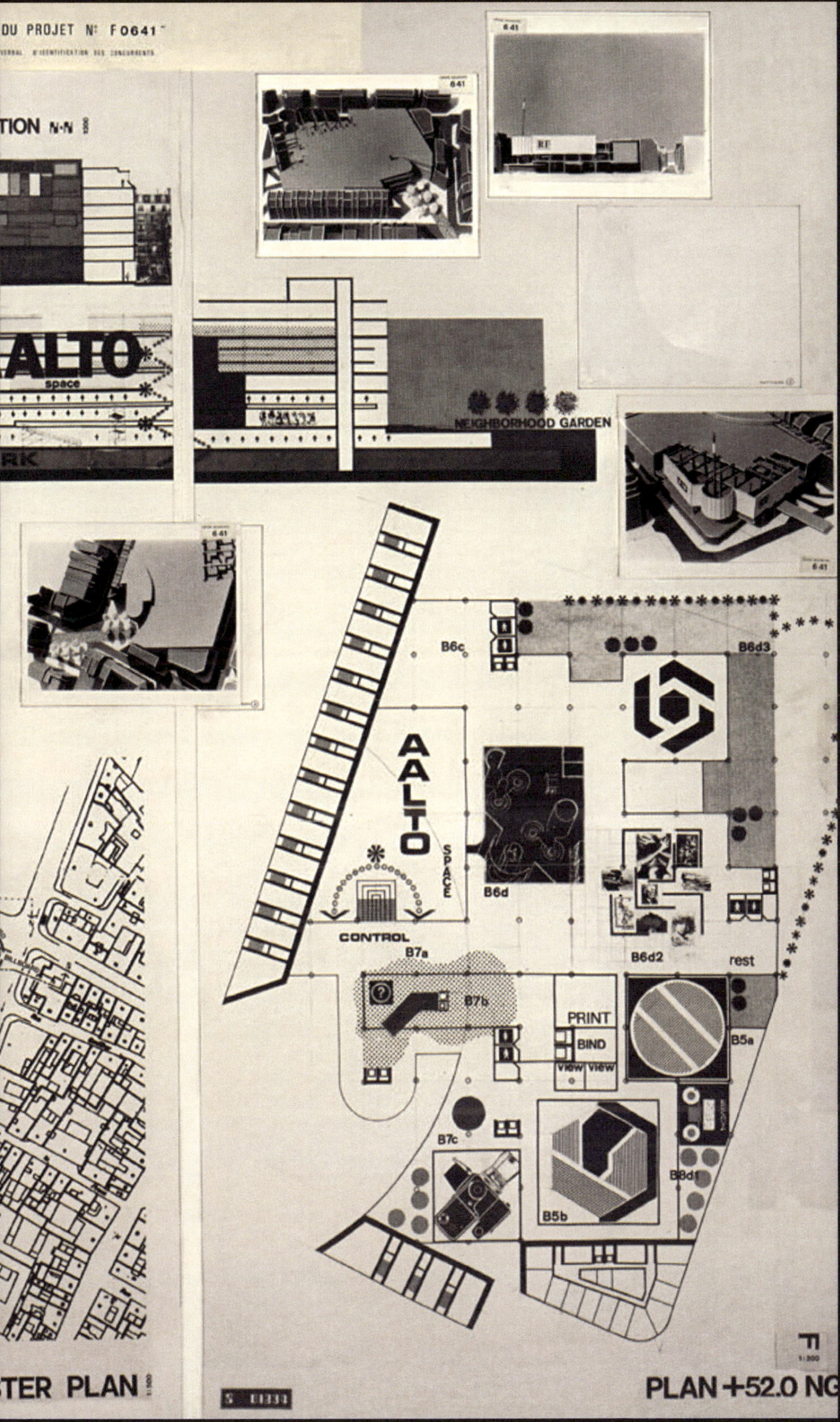

Giovanni Cosco et al. (641), Project for the Centre Beaubourg competition, panel set up at the Grand Palais, Paris, June 1971.

SUMMARY AND INTERRELATIONS OF THE CENTRE BEAUBOURG ACTIVITIES

A. Reception orientation (Red)
A1. Entrance reception
A2. Reception for children
A3. Cafeteria and canteen
A4. Restaurant

B. Main activities (Blue)
B1. Current events room
B2. Industrial design permanent gallery and documentation service
B3. Experimental Gallery of Contemporary Art
B4. Temporary exhibitions
B5. Theatres and meetings
B6. Museums
B7. Library
B8. Specialized documentation and research
B9. Temporary and permanent storage

C. Management (Green)
C1. Scientific and administrative personnel
C2. Social services
C3. Supervision and control
C4. Lodgings
C5. Workshop and storerooms
C6. Technical areas

D. Parking (Yellow)
D1. Personnel parking
D2. Visitor's parking
D3. Coaches
D4. Trucks

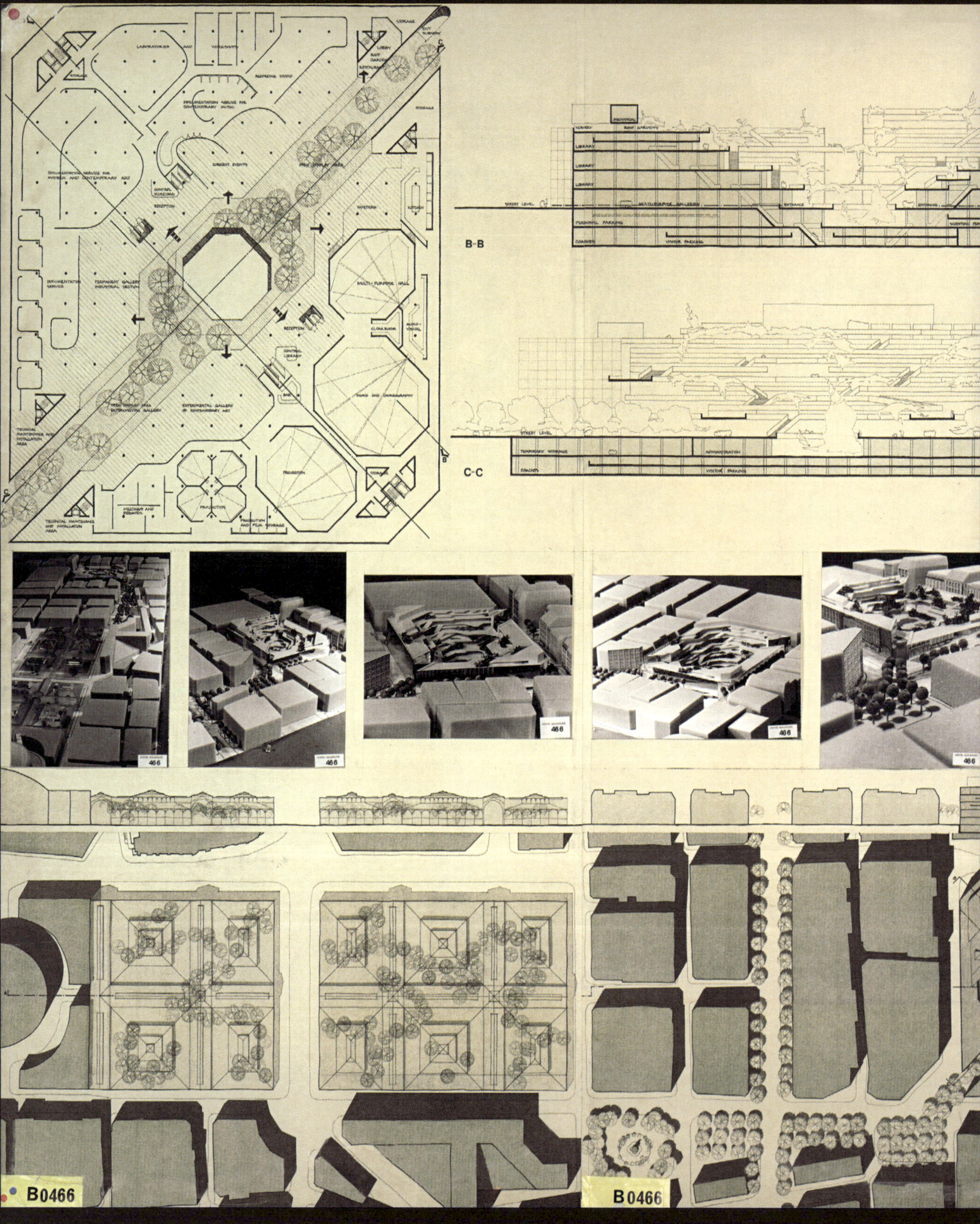

B-B
C-C
B0466
B0466

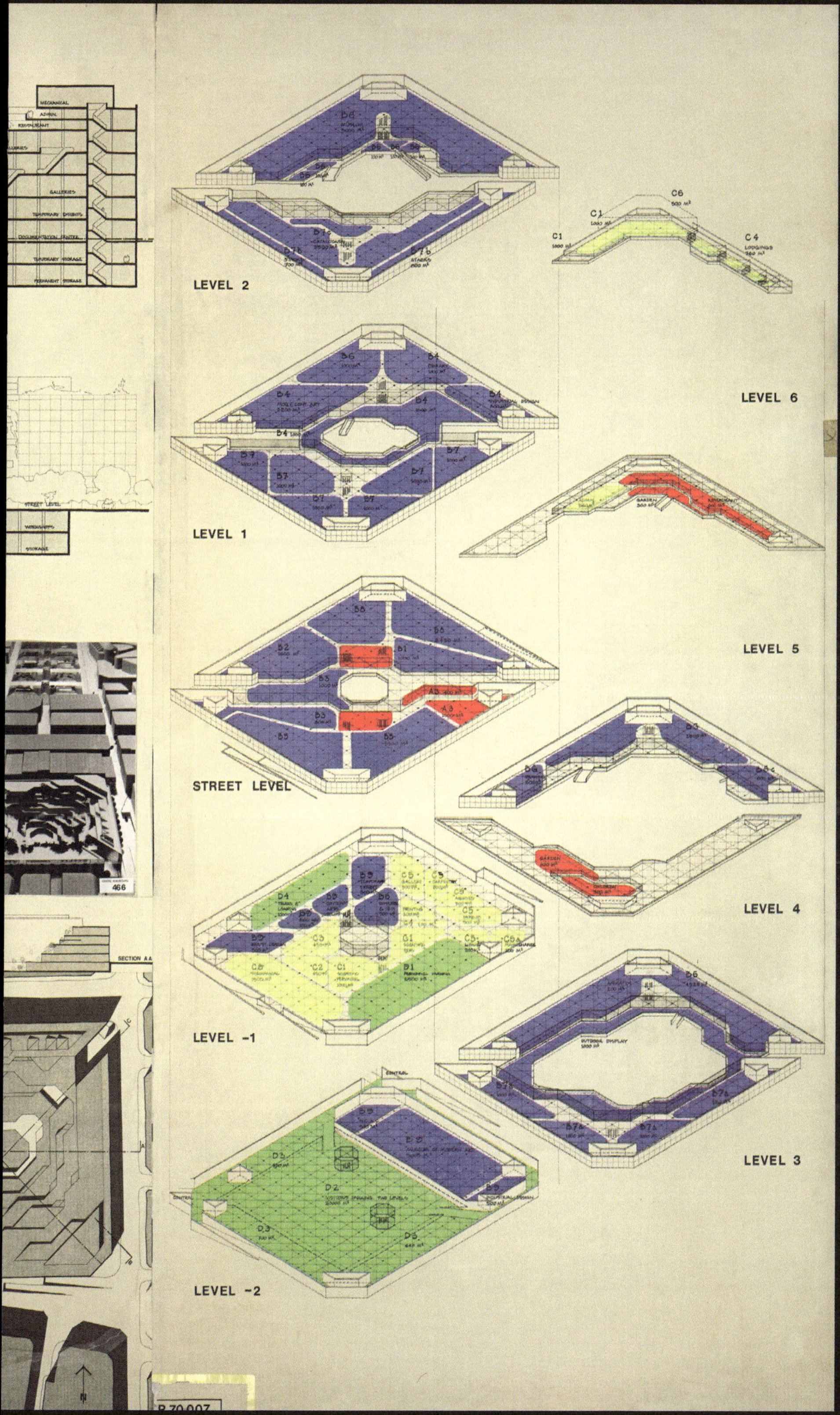

Arthur Erickson et al. (466), Project for the Centre Beaubourg competition, panel set up at the Grand Palais, Paris, June 1971.

SUMMARY AND INTERRELATIONS OF THE CENTRE BEAUBOURG ACTIVITIES

A. Reception orientation (Red)
A1. Entrance reception
A2. Reception for children
A3. Cafeteria and canteen
A4. Restaurant

B. Main activities (Blue)
B1. Current events room
B2. Industrial design permanent gallery and documentation service
B3. Experimental Gallery of Contemporary Art
B4. Temporary exhibitions
B5. Theatres and meetings
B6. Museums
B7. Library
B8. Specialized documentation and research
B9. Temporary and permanent storage

C. Management (Green)
C1. Scientific and administrative personnel
C2. Social services
C3. Supervision and control
C4. Lodgings
C5. Workshop and storerooms
C6. Technical areas

D. Parking (Yellow)
D1. Personnel parking
D2. Visitor's parking
D3. Coaches
D4. Trucks

MASTER PLAN 1:500

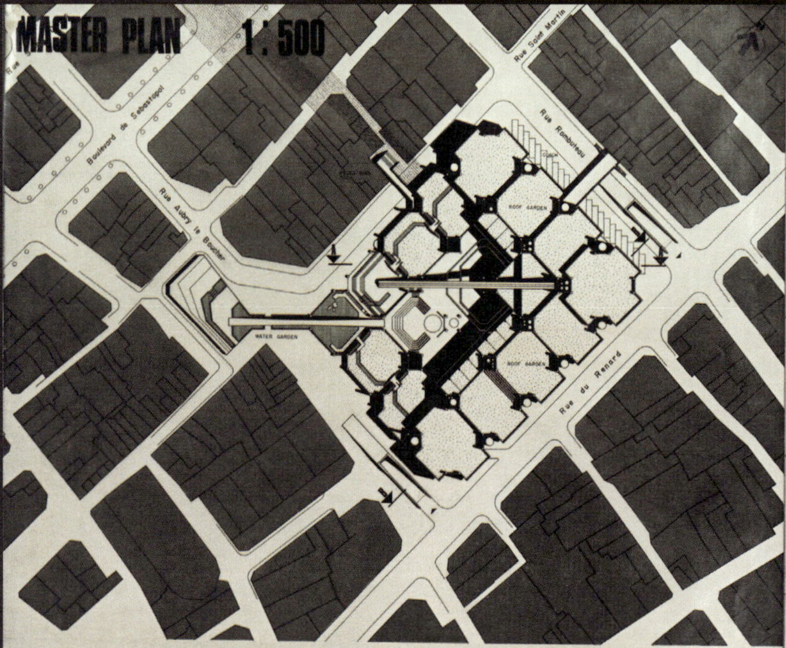

PLAN AT LEVEL +54.50 N.G.F.

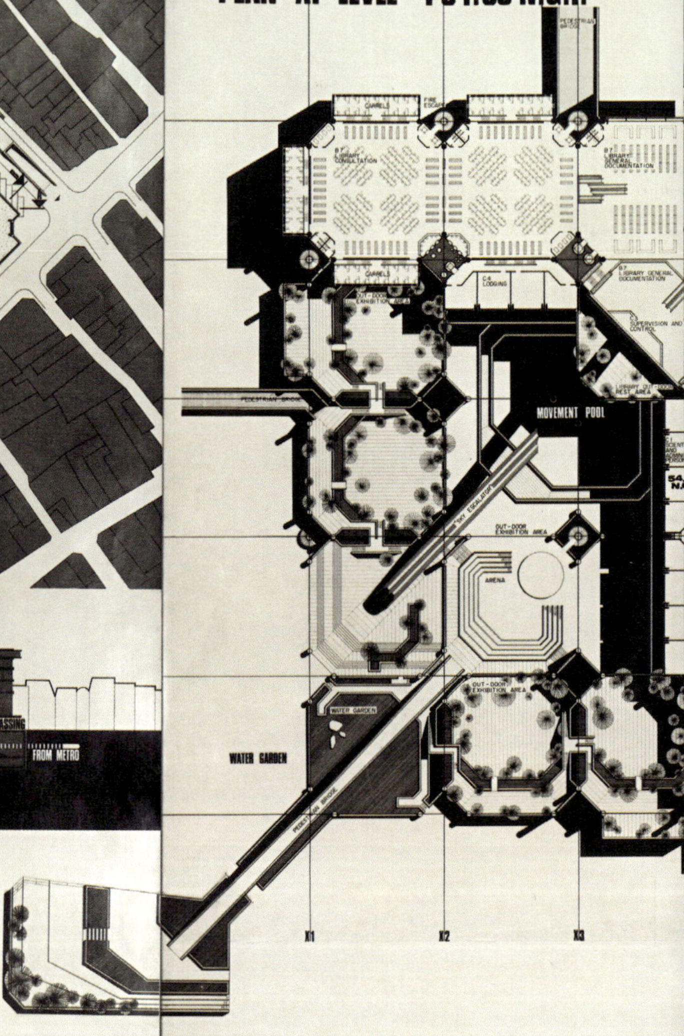

MASTER SECTION 1:500

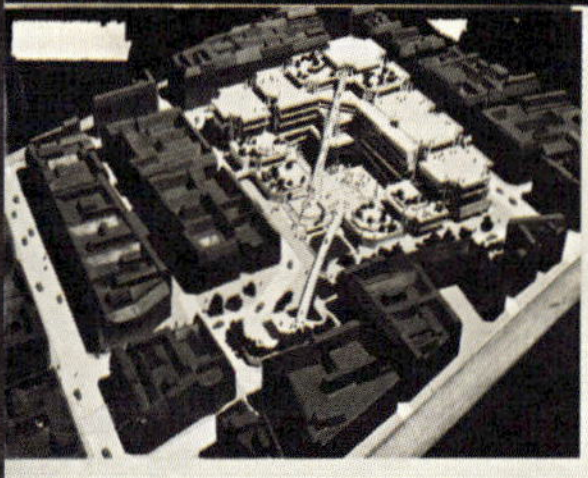

PLATEAU BEAUBOURG CENTER PARIS INTERNATIONAL CO

SECTION B-B 1:200

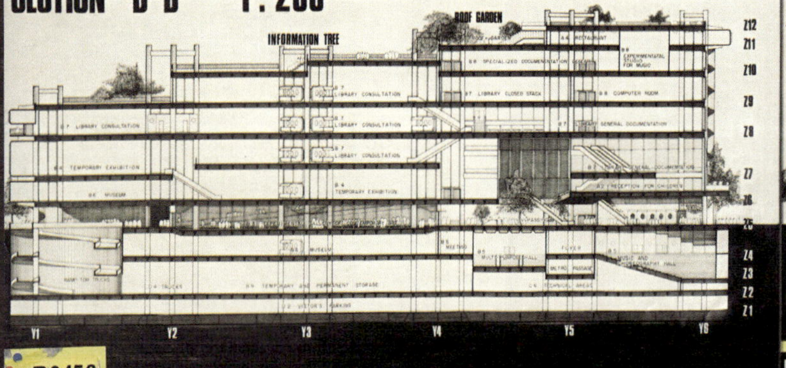

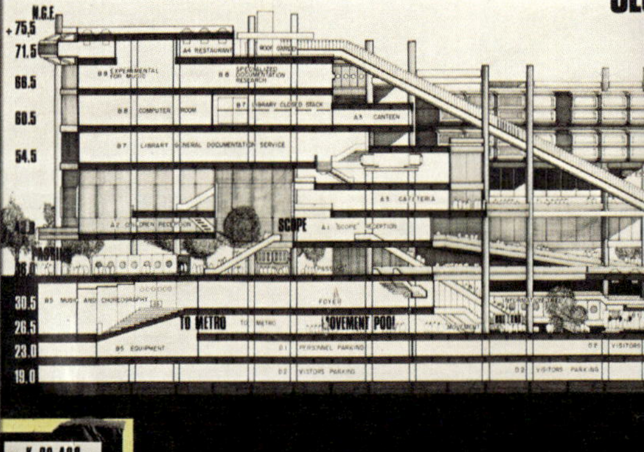

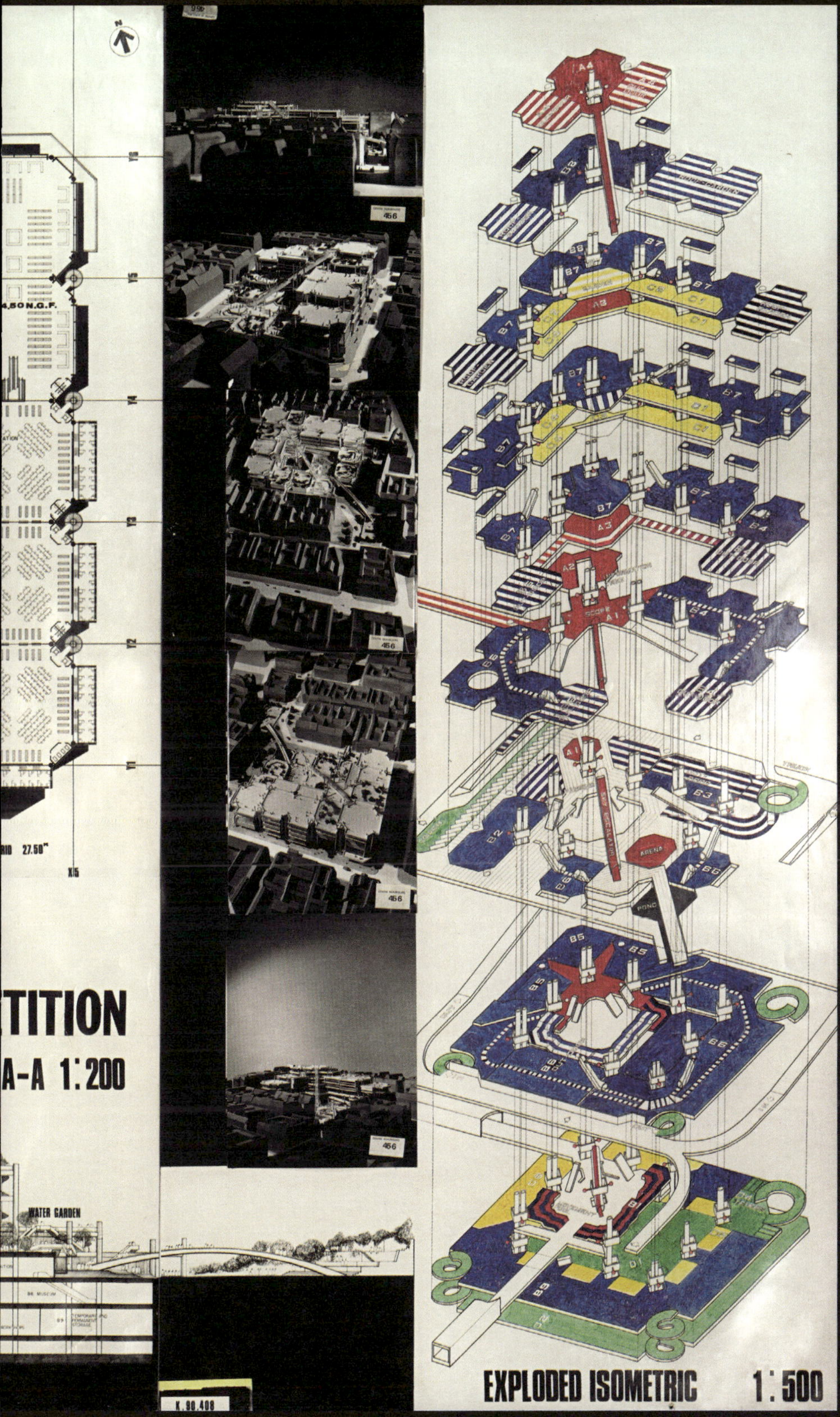

Kisho N. Kurokawa (456), Project for the Centre Beaubourg competition, panel set up at the Grand Palais, Paris, June 1971.

SUMMARY AND INTERRELATIONS OF THE CENTRE BEAUBOURG ACTIVITIES

A. Reception orientation (Red)
A1. Entrance reception
A2. Reception for children
A3. Cafeteria and canteen
A4. Restaurant

B. Main activities (Blue)
B1. Current events room
B2. Industrial design permanent gallery and documentation service
B3. Experimental Gallery of Contemporary Art
B4. Temporary exhibitions
B5. Theatres and meetings
B6. Museums
B7. Library
B8. Specialized documentation and research
B9. Temporary and permanent storage

C. Management (Green)
C1. Scientific and administrative personnel
C2. Social services
C3. Supervision and control
C4. Lodgings
C5. Workshop and storerooms
C6. Technical areas

D. Parking (Yellow)
D1. Personnel parking
D2. Visitor's parking
D3. Coaches
D4. Trucks

CENTRE DU PLATEAU BEAUBOURG PARIS

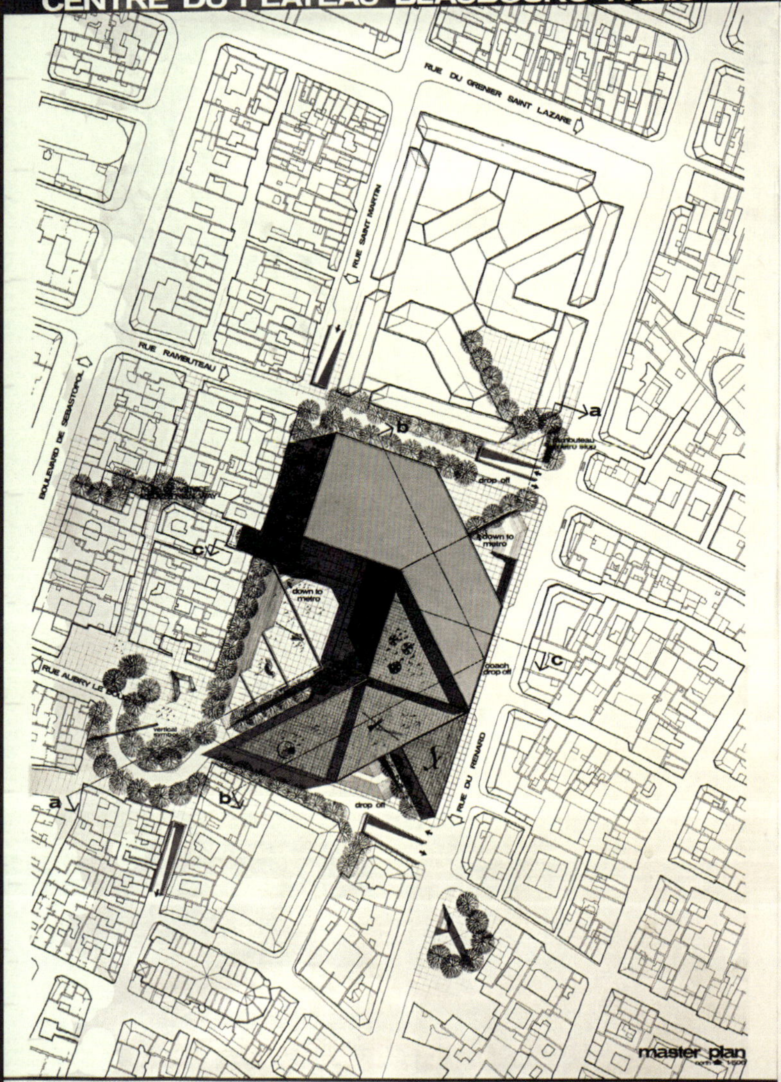

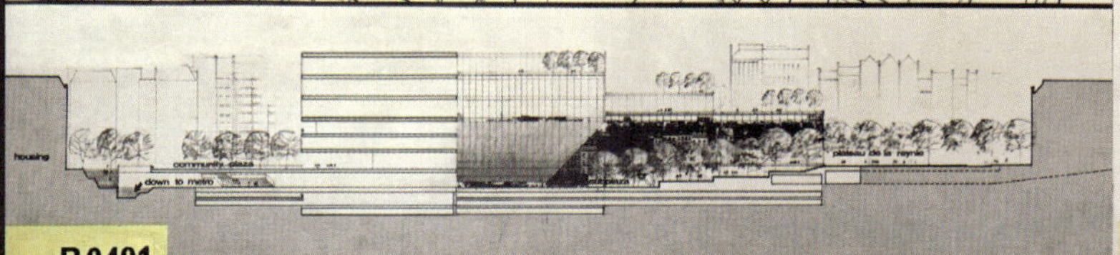

B 0491

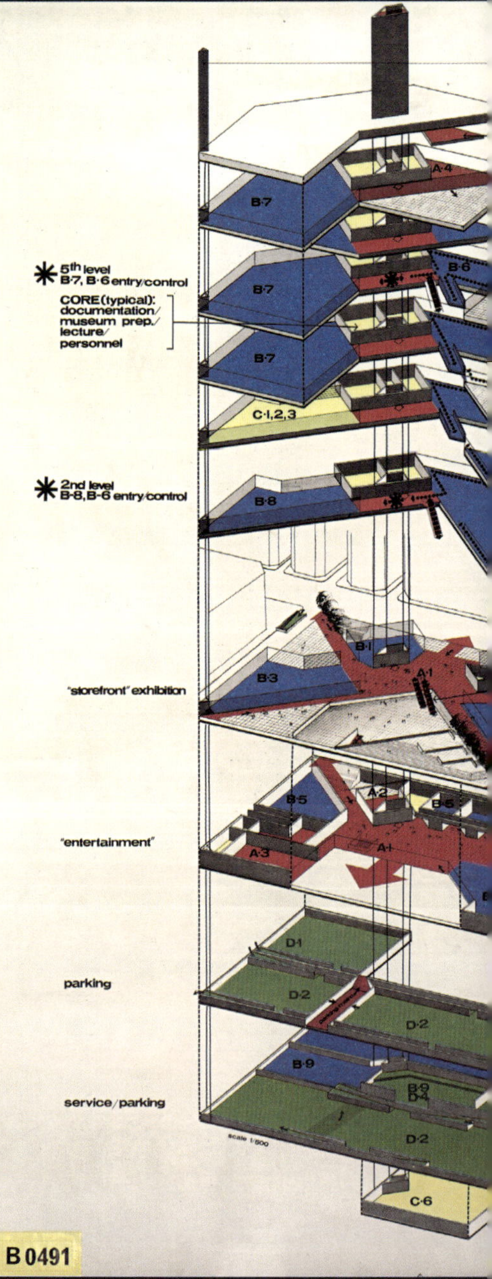

B 0491

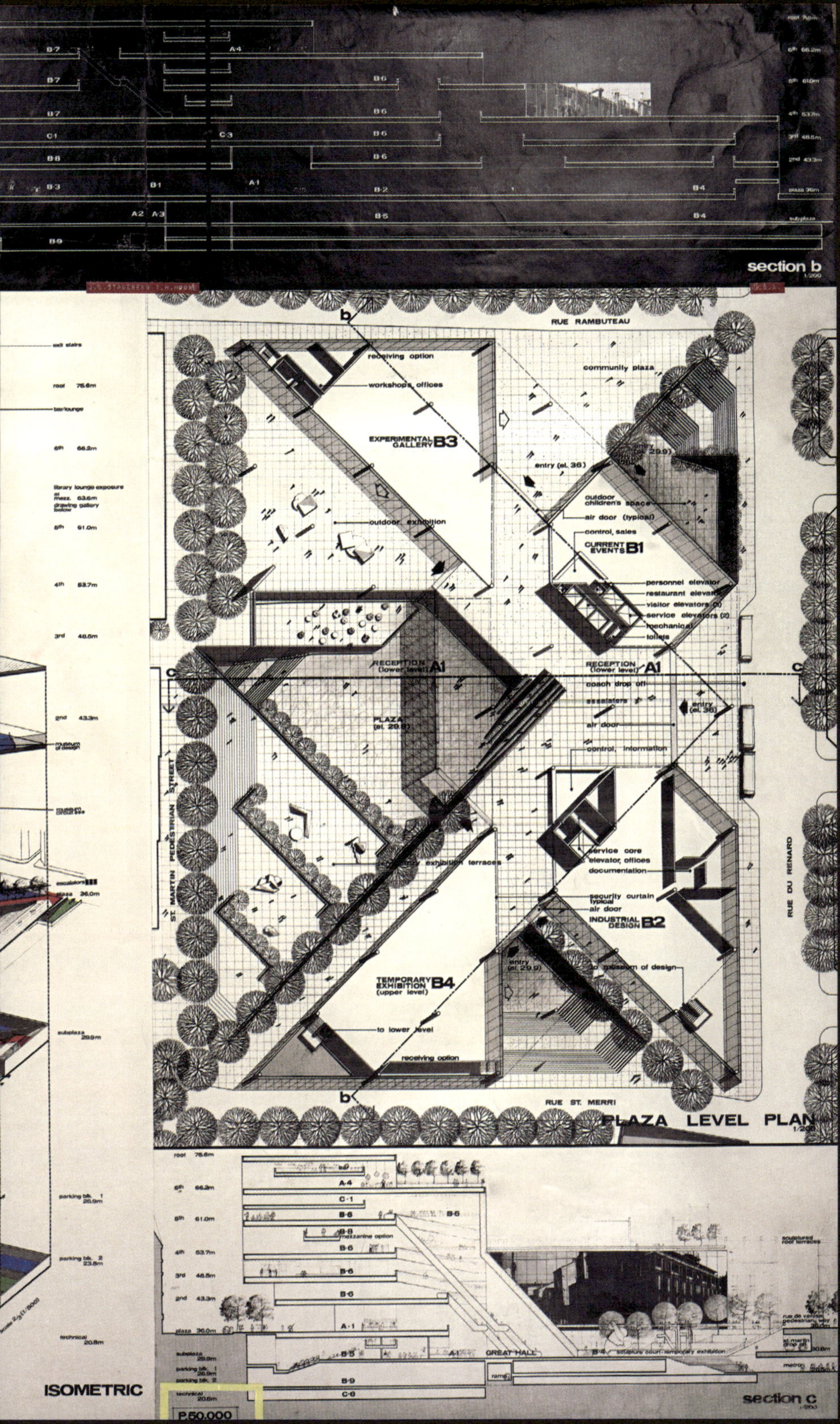

James E. Stageberg et al. (491), Project for the Centre Beaubourg competition, panel set up at the Grand Palais, Paris, June 1971.

SUMMARY AND INTERRELATIONS OF THE CENTRE BEAUBOURG ACTIVITIES

A. Reception orientation (Red)
A1. Entrance reception
A2. Reception for children
A3. Cafeteria and canteen
A4. Restaurant

B. Main activities (Blue)
B1. Current events room
B2. Industrial design permanent gallery and documentation service
B3. Experimental Gallery of Contemporary Art
B4. Temporary exhibitions
B5. Theatres and meetings
B6. Museums
B7. Library
B8. Specialized documentation and research
B9. Temporary and permanent storage

C. Management (Green)
C1. Scientific and administrative personnel
C2. Social services
C3. Supervision and control
C4. Lodgings
C5. Workshop and storerooms
C6. Technical areas

D. Parking (Yellow)
D1. Personnel parking
D2. Visitor's parking
D3. Coaches
D4. Trucks

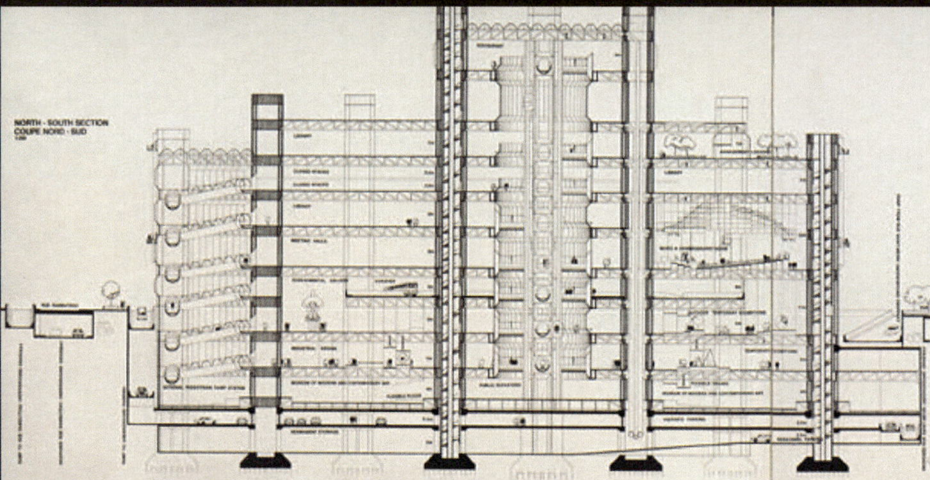

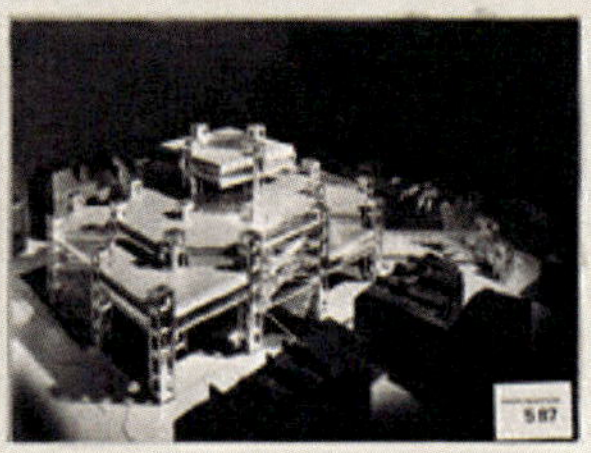

PHOTO 2

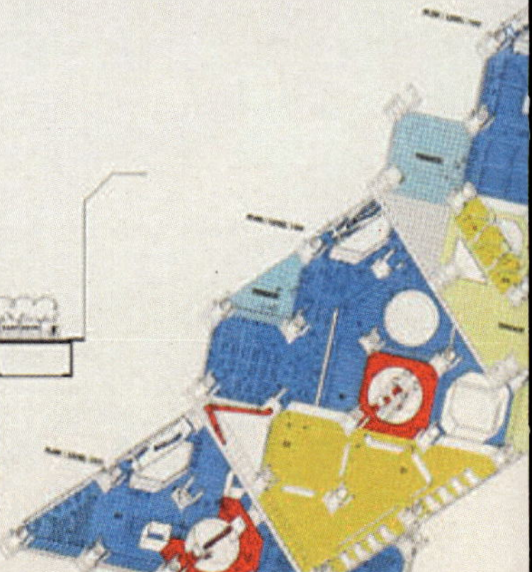

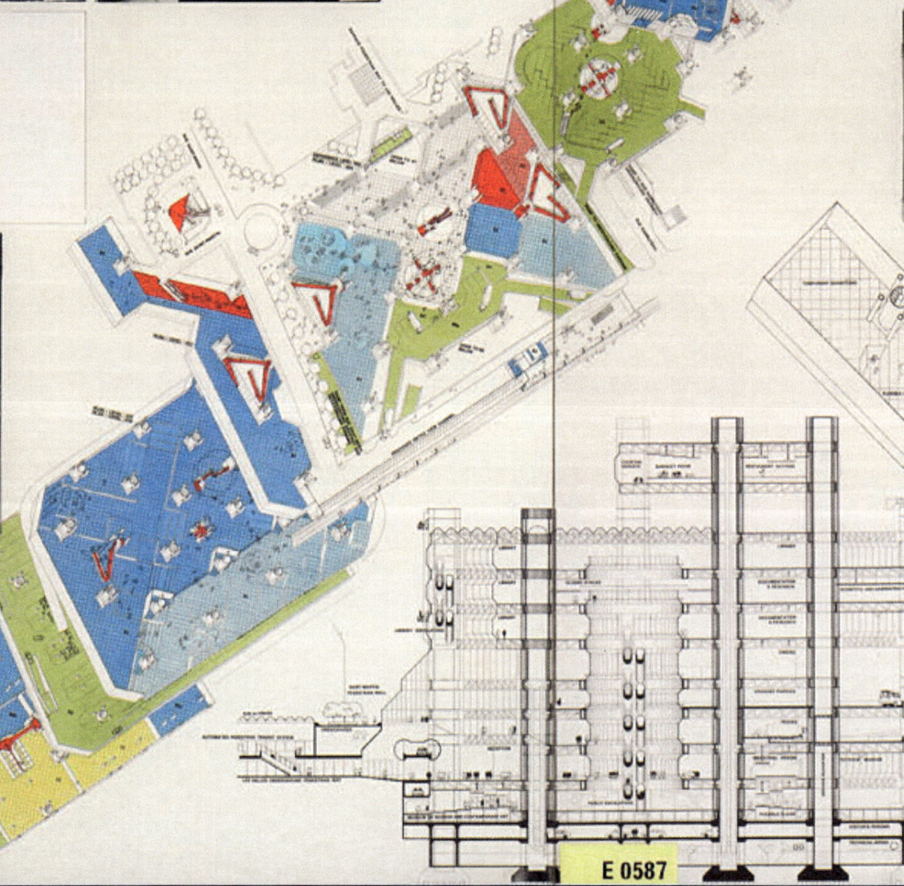

E 0587

E 0587

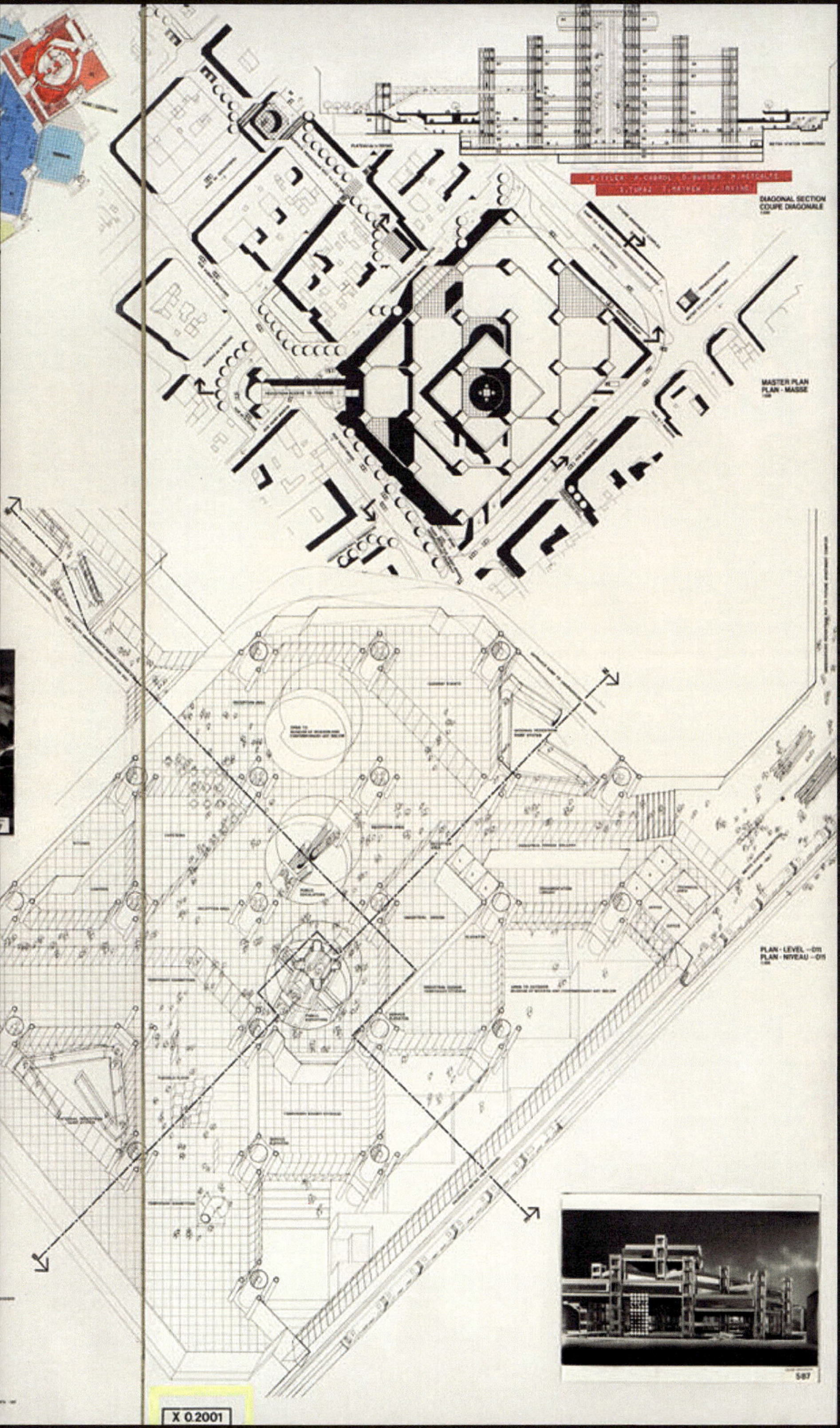

Macdonald Becket et al. (587), Project for the Centre Beaubourg competition, panel set up at the Grand Palais, Paris, June 1971.

SUMMARY AND INTERRELATIONS OF THE CENTRE BEAUBOURG ACTIVITIES

A. Reception orientation (Red)
A1. Entrance reception
A2. Reception for children
A3. Cafeteria and canteen
A4. Restaurant

B. Main activities (Blue)
B1. Current events room
B2. Industrial design permanent gallery and documentation service
B3. Experimental Gallery of Contemporary Art
B4. Temporary exhibitions
B5. Theatres and meetings
B6. Museums
B7. Library
B8. Specialized documentation and research
B9. Temporary and permanent storage

C. Management (Green)
C1. Scientific and administrative personnel
C2. Social services
C3. Supervision and control
C4. Lodgings
C5. Workshop and storerooms
C6. Technical areas

D. Parking (Yellow)
D1. Personnel parking
D2. Visitor's parking
D3. Coaches
D4. Trucks

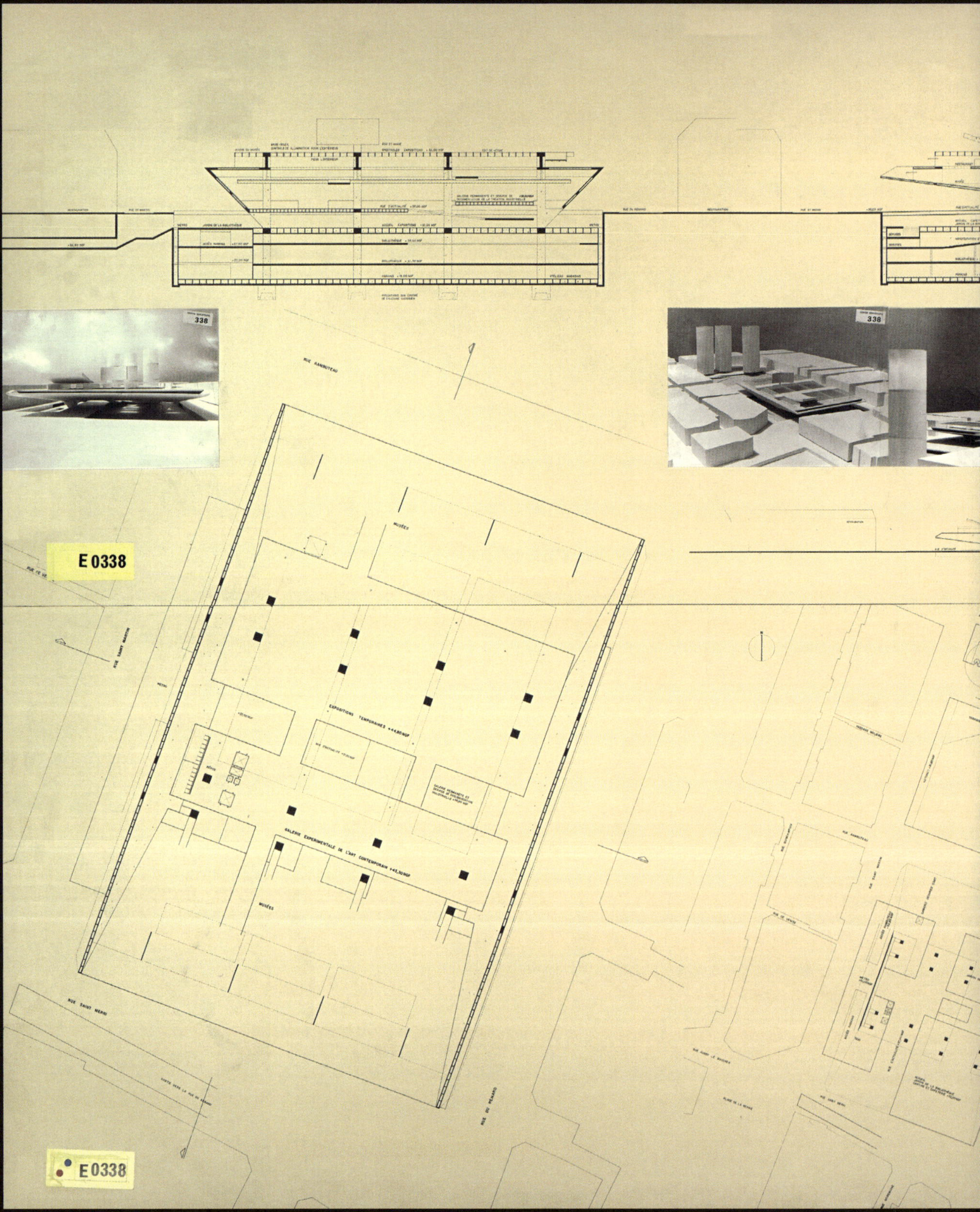

338
338
RUE RAMBUTEAU
E 0338
RUE SAINT MARTIN
MUSÉES
EXPOSITIONS TEMPORAIRES +44,80 NGF
GALERIE EXPERIMENTALE DE L'ART CONTEMPORAIN +45,30 NGF
RUE SAINT MERRI
RUE DU RENARD
E0338

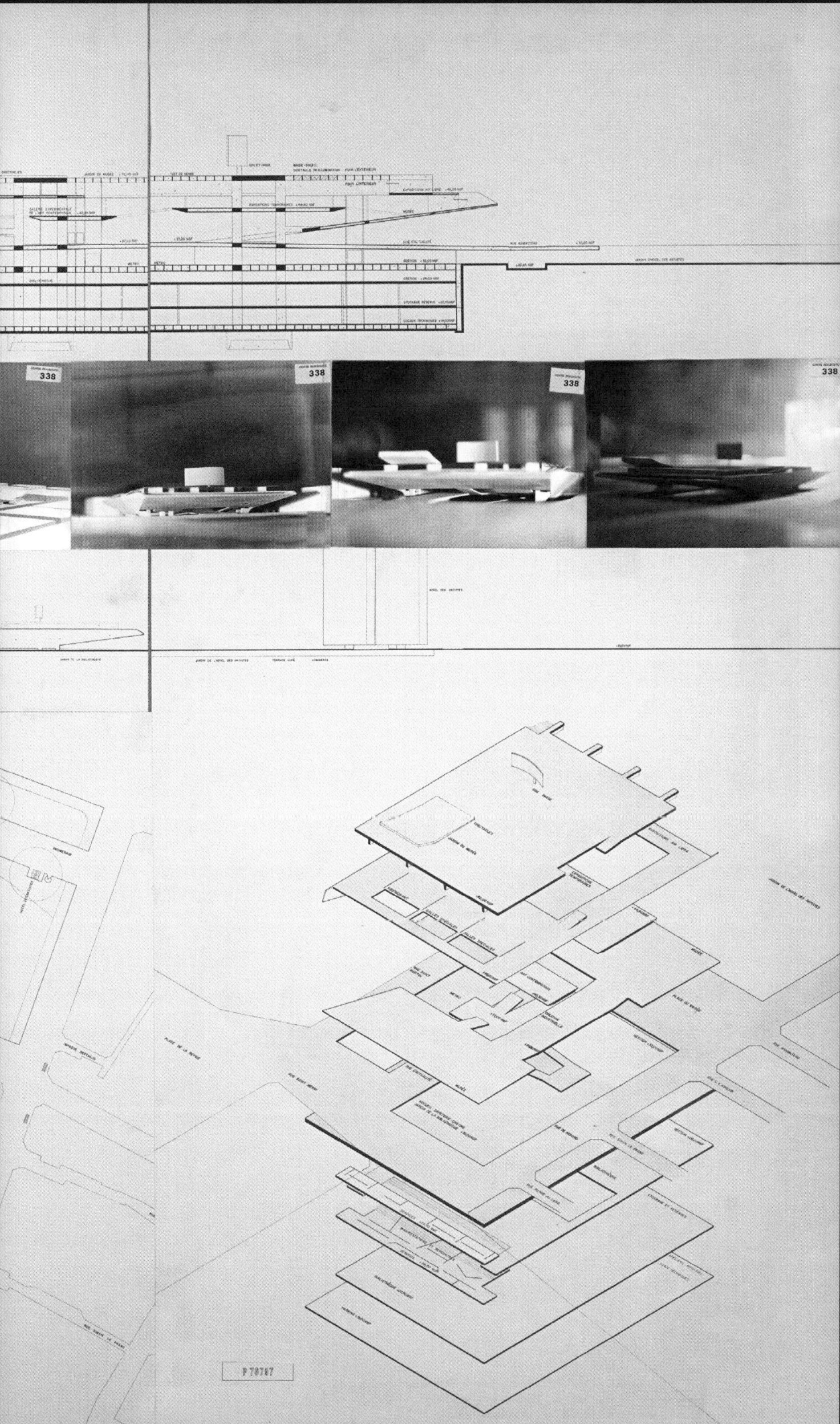

Paulo Mendes da Rocha (338), Project for the Centre Beaubourg competition, panel set up at the Grand Palais, Paris, June 1971.

SUMMARY AND INTERRELATIONS OF THE CENTRE BEAUBOURG ACTIVITIES

A. Reception orientation (Red)
A1. Entrance reception
A2. Reception for children
A3. Cafeteria and canteen
A4. Restaurant

B. Main activities (Blue)
B1. Current events room
B2. Industrial design permanent gallery and documentation service
B3. Experimental Gallery of Contemporary Art
B4. Temporary exhibitions
B5. Theatres and meetings
B6. Museums
B7. Library
B8. Specialized documentation and research
B9. Temporary and permanent storage

C. Management (Green)
C1. Scientific and administrative personnel
C2. Social services
C3. Supervision and control
C4. Lodgings
C5. Workshop and storerooms
C6. Technical areas

D. Parking (Yellow)
D1. Personnel parking
D2. Visitor's parking
D3. Coaches
D4. Trucks

Rue Rambuteau
Boulevard de Sebastopol
Rue Saint Martin
Rue du Renard
Rue Aubry le Boucher
Plateau de la Reynie
Rue de La Reynie
Rue Saint Merri
N
C

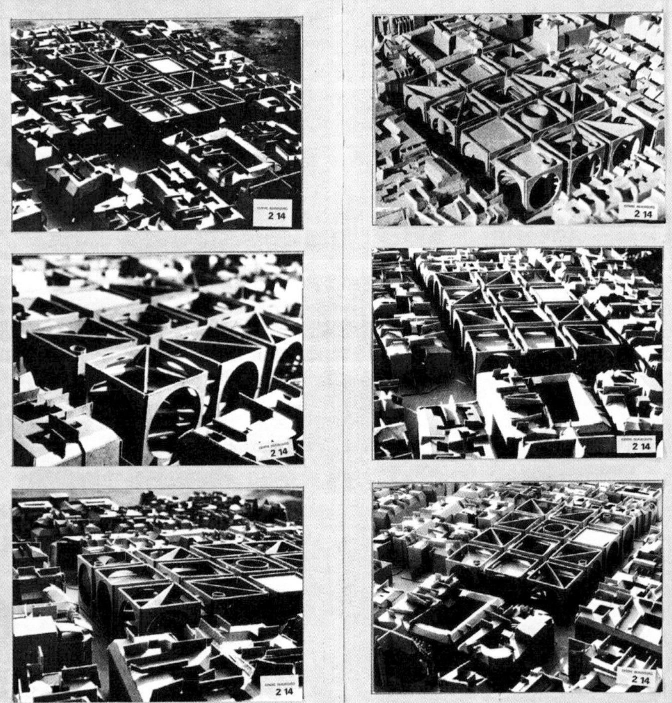

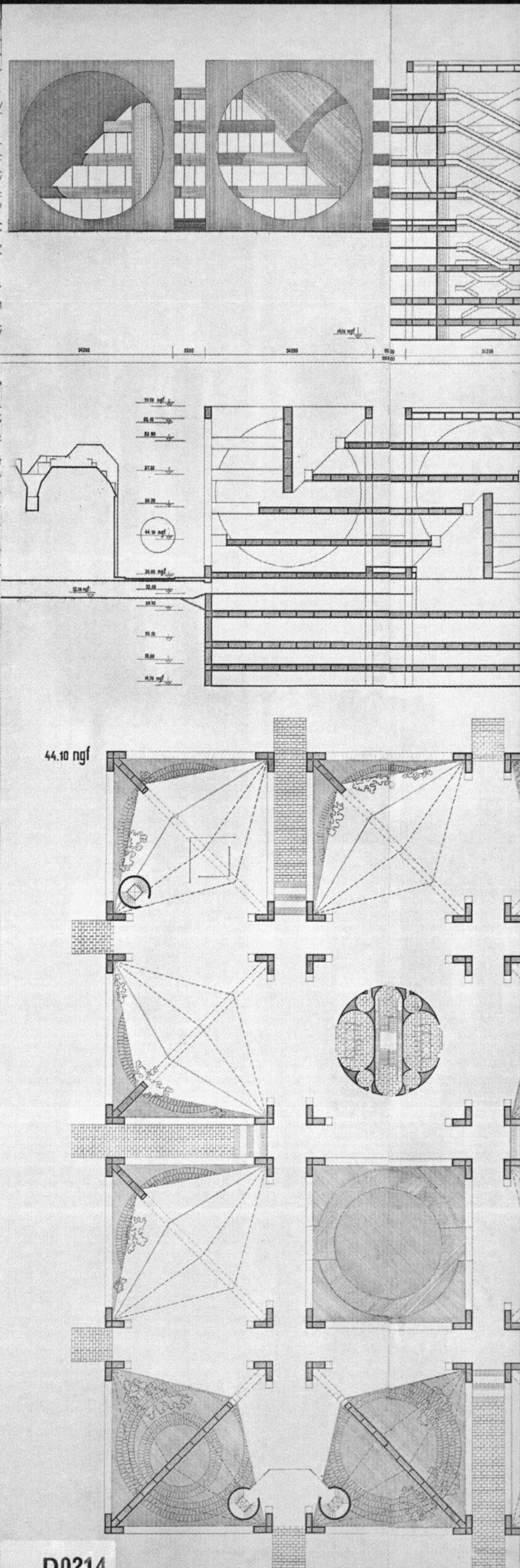

44.10 ngf

D0214

D0214

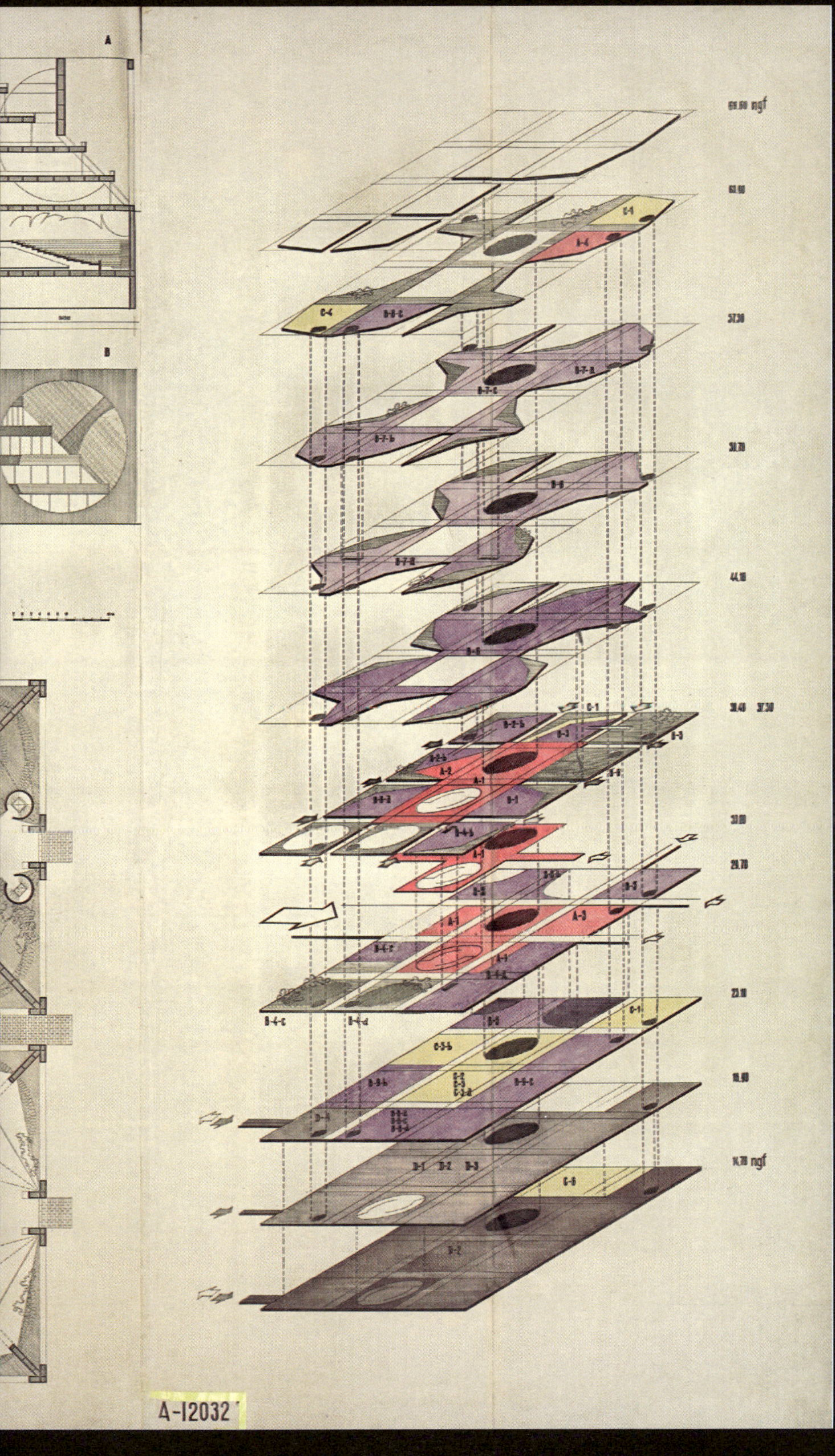

Youri Platonov et al. (214), Project for the Centre Beaubourg competition, panel set up at the Grand Palais, Paris, June 1971.

SUMMARY AND INTERRELATIONS OF THE CENTRE BEAUBOURG ACTIVITIES

A. Reception orientation (Red)
A1. Entrance reception
A2. Reception for children
A3. Cafeteria and canteen
A4. Restaurant

B. Main activities (Blue)
B1. Current events room
B2. Industrial design permanent gallery and documentation service
B3. Experimental Gallery of Contemporary Art
B4. Temporary exhibitions
B5. Theatres and meetings
B6. Museums
B7. Library
B8. Specialized documentation and research
B9. Temporary and permanent storage

C. Management (Green)
C1. Scientific and administrative personnel
C2. Social services
C3. Supervision and control
C4. Lodgings
C5. Workshop and storerooms
C6. Technical areas

D. Parking (Yellow)
D1. Personnel parking
D2. Visitor's parking
D3. Coaches
D4. Trucks

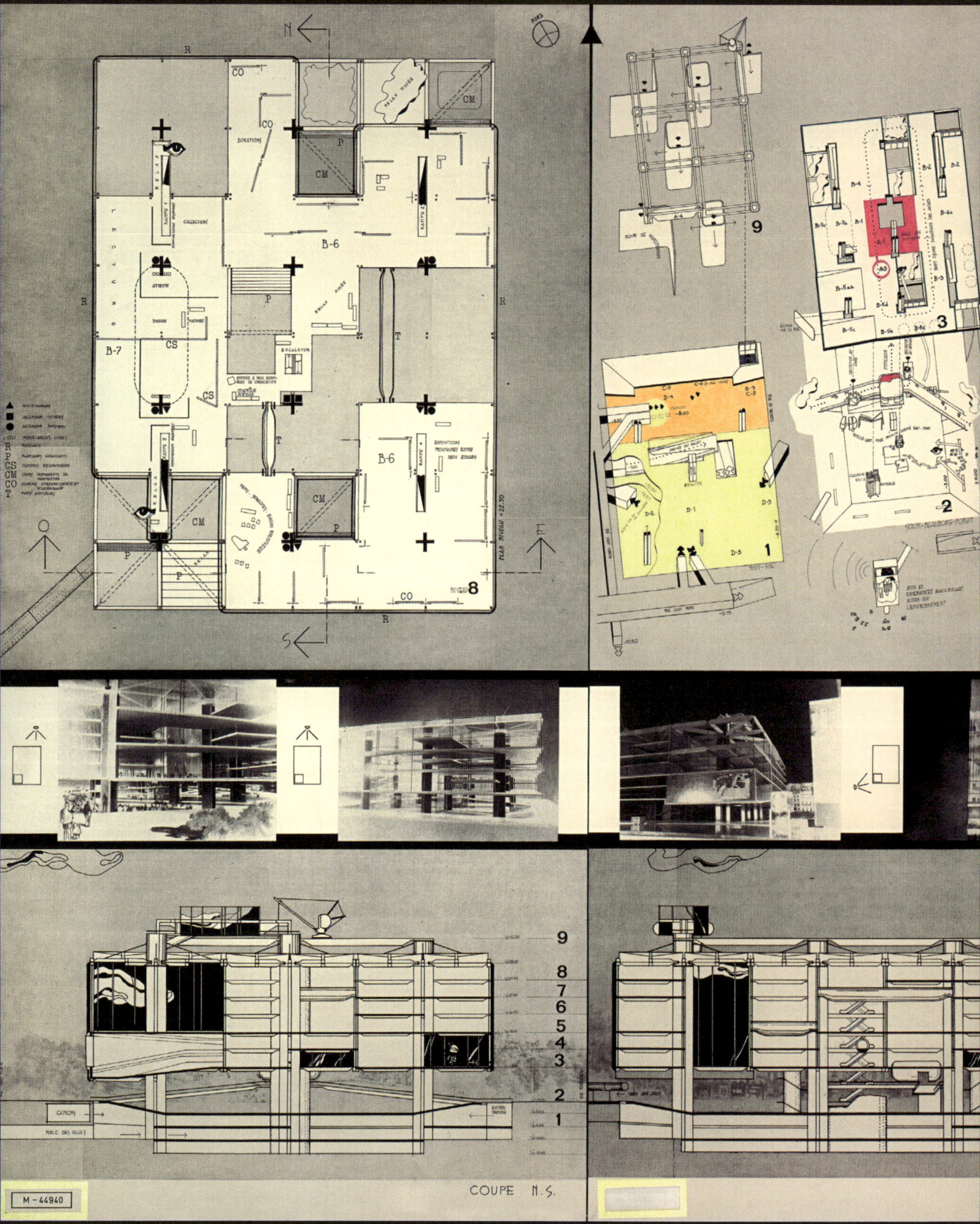

B-6
B-7
CM
CO
CS
ESCALATOR
PLAN NIVEAU +22.50
NIVEAU 8
9
3
2
1
SOUS-BEAUBOURG-FORUM
COUPE N.S.
M-44940

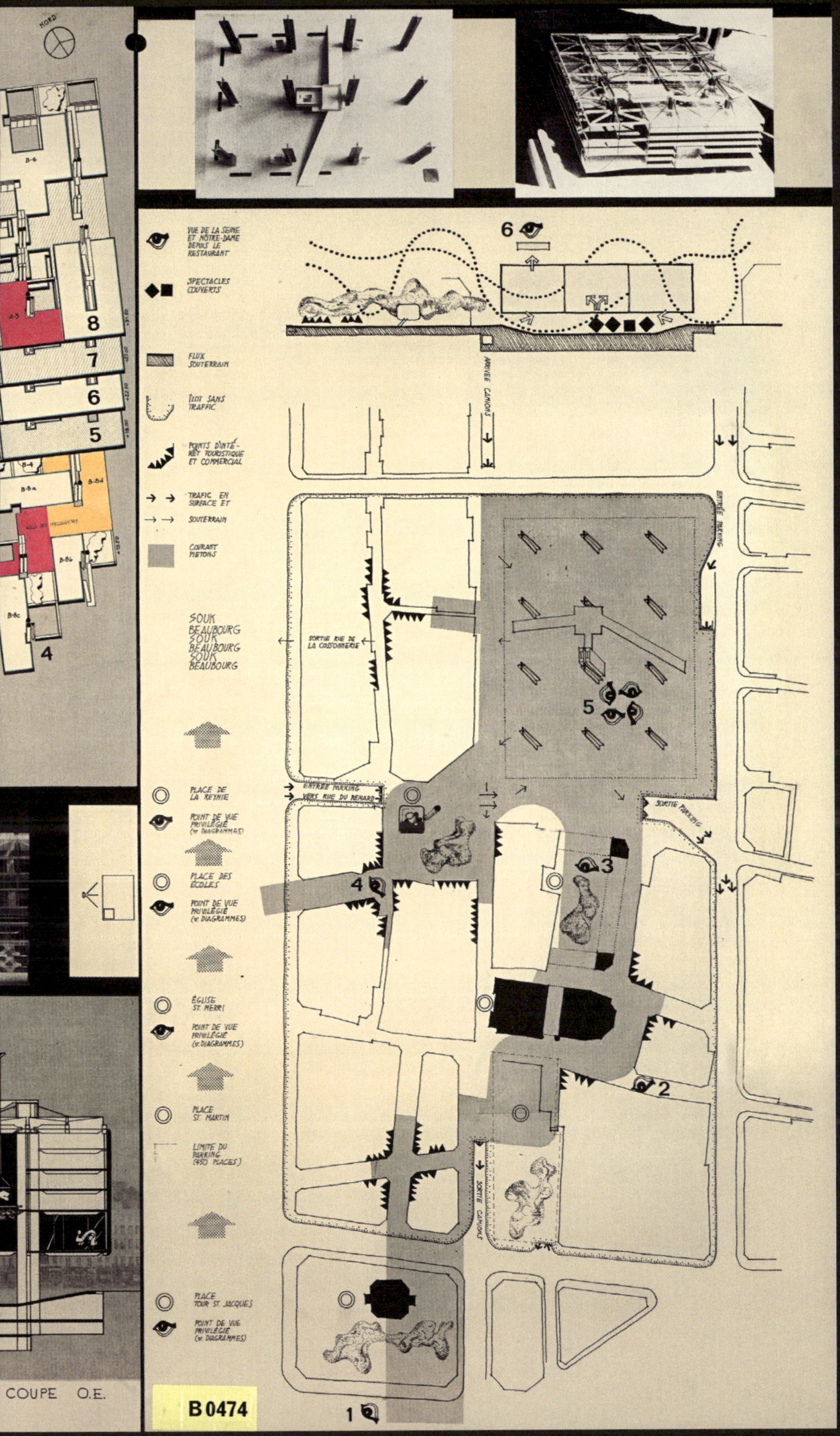

Juan Antonio Espejel Diez (474), Project for the Centre Beaubourg competition, panel set up at the Grand Palais, Paris, June 1971.

SUMMARY AND INTERRELATIONS OF THE CENTRE BEAUBOURG ACTIVITIES

A. Reception orientation (Red)
A1. Entrance reception
A2. Reception for children
A3. Cafeteria and canteen
A4. Restaurant

B. Main activities (Blue)
B1. Current events room
B2. Industrial design permanent gallery and documentation service
B3. Experimental Gallery of Contemporary Art
B4. Temporary exhibitions
B5. Theatres and meetings
B6. Museums
B7. Library
B8. Specialized documentation and research
B9. Temporary and permanent storage

C. Management (Green)
C1. Scientific and administrative personnel
C2. Social services
C3. Supervision and control
C4. Lodgings
C5. Workshop and storerooms
C6. Technical areas

D. Parking (Yellow)
D1. Personnel parking
D2. Visitor's parking
D3. Coaches
D4. Trucks

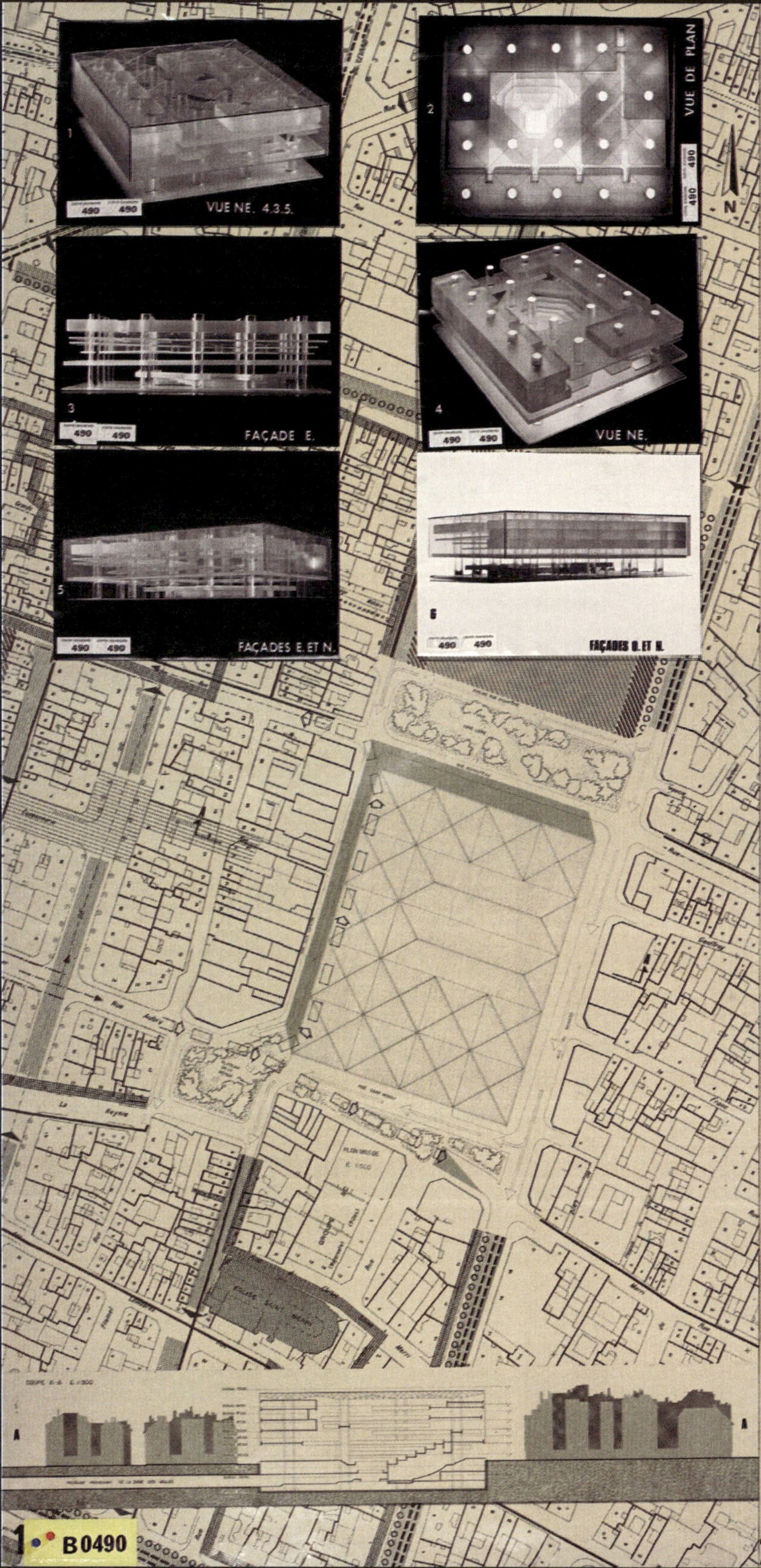

VUE NE. 4.3.5.
VUE DE PLAN
FAÇADE E.
VUE NE.
FAÇADES E. ET N.
FAÇADES O. ET N.
1
B0490

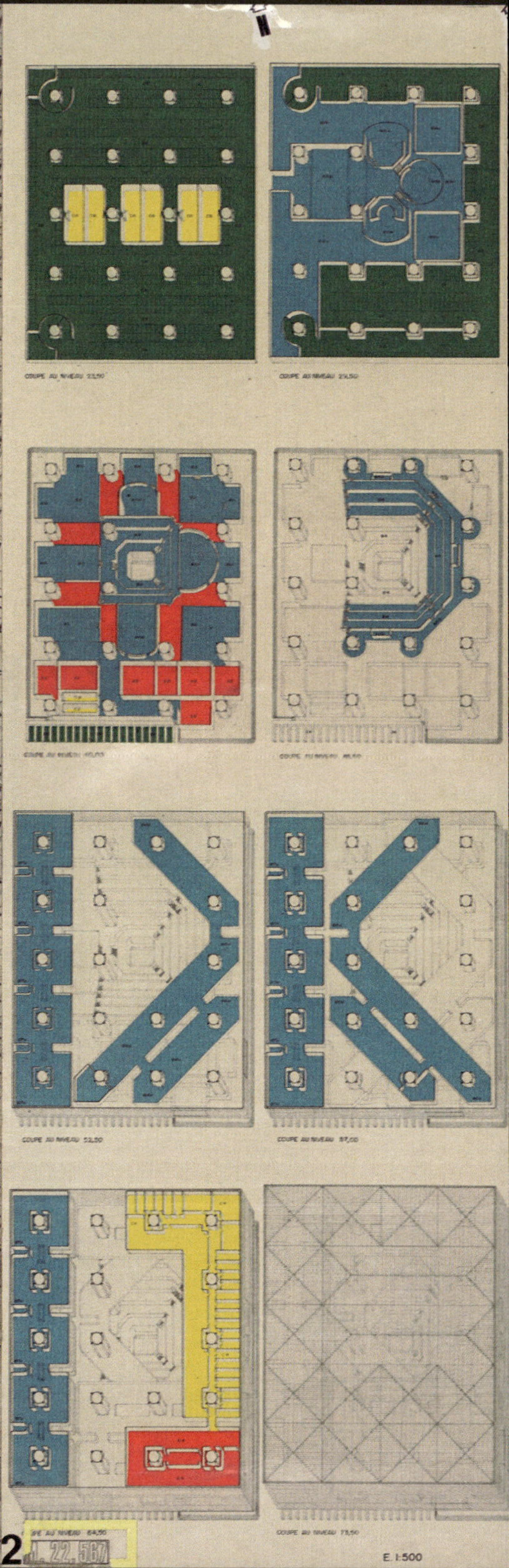

E. I:500
2

Andres Perea Ortega et al. (490), Project for the Centre Beaubourg competition, panel set up at the Grand Palais, Paris, June 1971.

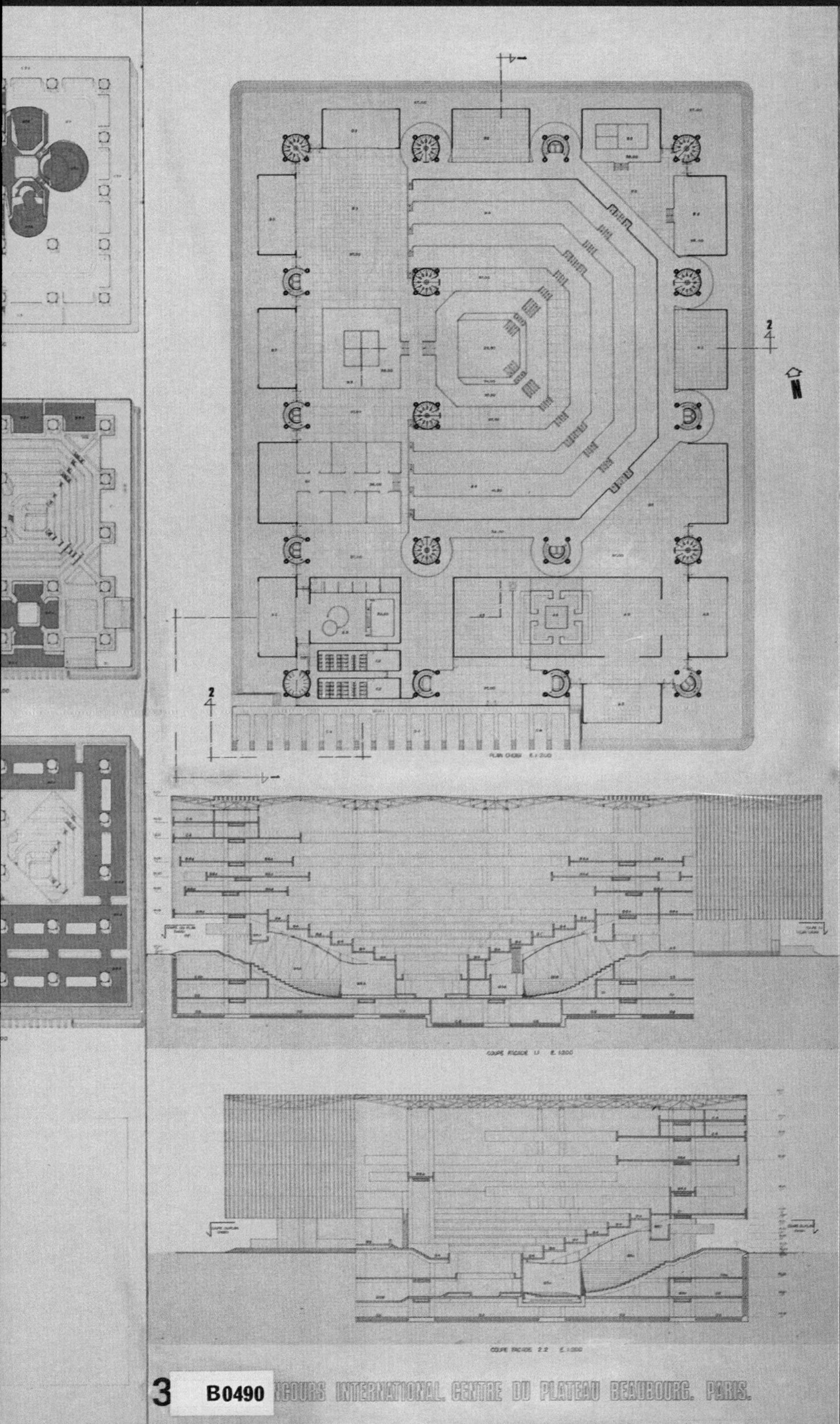

SUMMARY AND INTERRELATIONS OF THE CENTRE BEAUBOURG ACTIVITIES

A. Reception orientation (Red)
A1. Entrance reception
A2. Reception for children
A3. Cafeteria and canteen
A4. Restaurant

B. Main activities (Blue)
B1. Current events room
B2. Industrial design permanent gallery and documentation service
B3. Experimental Gallery of Contemporary Art
B4. Temporary exhibitions
B5. Theatres and meetings
B6. Museums
B7. Library
B8. Specialized documentation and research
B9. Temporary and permanent storage

C. Management (Green)
C1. Scientific and administrative personnel
C2. Social services
C3. Supervision and control
C4. Lodgings
C5. Workshop and storerooms
C6. Technical areas

D. Parking (Yellow)
D1. Personnel parking
D2. Visitor's parking
D3. Coaches
D4. Trucks

6.4

THE FIRST SELECTION BETWEEN FLEXIBLE CONTAINERS, COLOSSAL SUSPENDED PLATFORMS AND URBAN MATRICES

On Saturday, July 10, and Sunday, July 11, the jury suspended its deliberations,[82] while the Technical Commission analyzed the three shortlisted projects. The only record of the Technical Commission's work that has proved possible to track down is the *Fiche technique II* ("Specification sheet II"), a compilation of data on the areas devoted to different activities in the Centre Beaubourg.[83] In the case of Piano, Rogers, Franchini, and Ove Arup & Partners' project, the choice to make use of spaces with no partitions complicated the commission's work, which declared it "impossible" to calculate the dimensions of the majority of the areas, confirming rapporteur Breton's view of the internal spaces of the project. "Impossible to localize in the project. Everything is possible there," was the commission's comment.[84]

Equally problematic was the total area. While this could be expanded over time, both the main areas (A+B+C: 66,000 instead of 70,000 square meters) and those set aside for parking and for loading and unloading (D: 22,500 instead of 25,000 square meters) were smaller in the plans than requested in the competition notice.[85] Even at this stage the commission remarked on the decision to locate some of the Centre's activities on the ground floor and in the cellars of buildings on rue Saint-Martin, a choice that would later come to be considered problematic.

On Monday, July 12, Lombard submitted the Technical Commission's results to the jury.

From Prouvé's notebook, the only source for Lombard's report,[86] it can be deduced that Lombard presented the three projects in an order that corresponded to a grading of their merit: Piano, Rogers, Franchini, and Ove Arup & Partners; Ambrosini; Duplay and Deffontaines.

The "originality"[87] of Piano, Rogers, Franchini, and Ove Arup & Partners' project was recognized, along with the possibility of "very varied" forms of organization.[88] The Technical Commission dwelled on significant aspects of the project: the ground floor left free for "dynamic activities" and the open-air square for "external activities to get people involved"; the galleries comprised in the two 3-dimensional walls, both the service galleries facing the square for a "permanent spectacle" and those facing rue du Renard with the machinery, i.e., the ducts of the building's plant ("very imposing" was the expression used by Prouvé); the platforms that moved up and down; "the escalators," which seem to have been appreciated even though, overall, "the mechanical circulation" was judged "weak." The commission underlined the flexibility of the spaces and the conception of the technical plant and air-conditioning system. The description of the project also tackled technical questions relating to the adaptation of the project to meet the fire regulations for *immeubles de grande hauteur* ("high-rise buildings"). In this connection it is worth stressing the need for a protective treatment of the floor-slab beams to ensure they could resist fire for two hours—a question that was destined to prove complex and crucial to the development of the project. Still in relation to the project's technical aspects, the report also singled out the improvements that had to be made to the evacuation system and the decision to encapsulate the mechanical circulation in a shell and resort to elements made of plastic—a question on which it has not been possible to trace Lombard's comments. With regard to the integration of the project into its Parisian context, mention was made of the interventions planned on rue Saint-Martin to the east and underneath rue du Renard to the west, showing in the first case an appreciation of the solution and its accord with the Délégation's intentions, and in the second pointing out its nonconformity with the program.

Of Ambrosini's project, the commission appreciated the underground connection with the plateau des Halles ("level of access through Les Halles"), the configuration of the volumes on platforms and the presence of open spaces and areas of greenery ("15,000 [square meters] of terraces"). The commission criticized the part below ground level, objecting to its failure to respect the program ("respect for uses apart from beneath the ground"), the problematic insertion of the museum and the experimental gallery of contemporary art ("[exp. gallery] underground" and "underground museum [critical]") and the uncertain characteristics of the lighting ("natural light"). Problems of a technological and structural nature were also pointed out, including the depth of the excavations, the foundations ("complicated foundations [...] and below the water table) and the inadequate dimensions of the structure ("the spans of the structure should be reduced. The dimensioning of the concrete elements is very wrong").[89]

The criticism of Duplay and Deffontaines's project focused on its general grid layout, regarded as of poor quality ("poor from the architectural viewpoint"), its relationship with the urban fabric, the function of the internal courtyards, and even whether it actually met the requirements of the Centre's cultural program ("this [would do] at a pinch for a university").[90] It seems from Prouvé's notes that the project was to be excluded from the finalists: "not to keep on the shortlist."[91]

By the end of the meeting the jury was tilting toward Piano, Rogers, Franchini, and Ove Arup & Partners' proposal and decided to turn to Pompidou for his opinion of the design. The same day Robert Bordaz informed Henri Domerg of the results of the selection process and declared himself willing to send the president the documentation of the chosen project. Domerg presented it to the president in these terms: "The project that has—unofficially—been selected would have the following characteristics: a very simple quadrilateral with a glass wall as its façade. A fairly large free space would be left around it. The architecture of the monument would be in keeping with its surroundings. The interior would be particularly satisfying for the *utilisateurs*."[92] Domerg also referred to the project's origin, revealing to the president that its authors were British—"The author of the project seems to be British"—a fact that seems to confirm the idea the jury members knew their nationality.[93]

Pompidou agreed to take an unofficial look at the project's documentation and invited Domerg to inform one of his closest aides, Deputy Secretary-General Eduard Balladur, of the matter.[94]

The following day, July 13, Domerg gave the president a photographic reproduction of the competition plans, accompanied by his own presentation of the project in which he stressed the building's mechanics, the formal effects, its envelope's play of light and shade, and a number of important technical and structural aspects such as the rapidity of its construction.[95]

"The Centre will occupy about three-fifths of the total area. The width of the facade will be approximately 110 meters [*sic*]; the height will be 32 meters [*sic*]. The square in front of the building will be set two to three meters below the rest of the district. The photos give an idea of the façade. The superstructures that can be seen here, also in glass, are intended to provide access by means of escalators. The façade viewed from the plateau de la Reynie is at top left of the large drawing. Automobile traffic along rue Saint-Martin will be moved underground. The building will be constructed entirely of glass and aluminum, allowing plays of light by day and night. The interior has great functional flexibility. Its construction will be quick and easy." Domerg also made clear the jury's position and stressed that Piano, Rogers, Franchini, and Ove Arup & Partners' proposal was the one "that the Beaubourg jury was preparing to select." "The jury," continued Domerg "is almost unanimously for this project. Aillaud is the only one to have a few reservations."[96]

That evening Pompidou invited Domerg to discuss the shortlisted project over dinner.[97] Once Domerg had left, Pompidou went to the Grand Palais to look at the competition projects. He was accompanied on this visit by his wife, Claude, the very person who, on the death of her husband, would take it upon herself to ensure this work realization and defend it from its detractors. The project that the Pompidous saw at the Grand Palais seems distant from the genre of architecture which the president had favored, from the high-rise structure he had discussed with Loste to the sculptural kind of monumentality he had appreciated in Breuer's designs and the forms of biomorphic architecture he had observed in Friedensreich Hundertwasser's sketches. And yet the project in front of him was not unfamiliar. It was an example of the research into metal structures and lightweight prefabrication that Prouvé had shown Pompidou a few weeks earlier when he sent him a copy of his recent monograph, *Une architecture par l'industrie*.[98]

In the absence of documentary evidence with regard to the outcome of the visit to the Grand Palais and Pompidou's opinion of the project, it is significant that from this date until the publication of the results there would be no more official contact between the jury and the president. And it is precisely this silence that suggests Pompidou's agreement with the jury's choice.

The three finalist projects of the first collective selection: Michel Duplay and François-Noël Deffontaines (96). The urban matrix of viaducts and low volumes, zenith view.

The three finalist projects of the first collective selection: Michel Duplay and François-Noël Deffontaines (96). The urban matrix of viaducts and low volumes, south view.

The three finalist projects of the first collective selection: Jorge Ambrosini et al. (352), photo of the large covered hall created by suspending a multi-story platform, view of the covered main hall from the piazza.

The three finalist projects of the first collective selection: Jorge Ambrosini et al. (352), photo of the large covered hall created by suspending a multi-story platform, covered main hall.

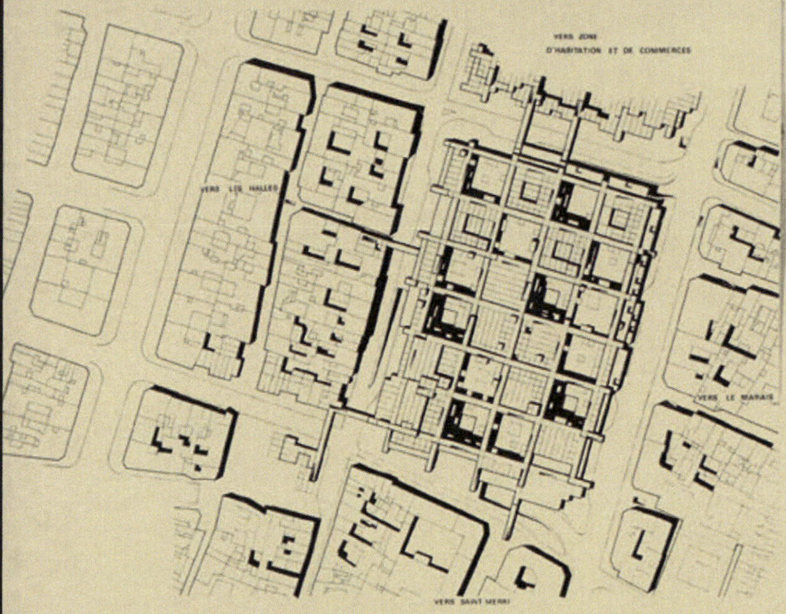

PLAN MASSE 1/500

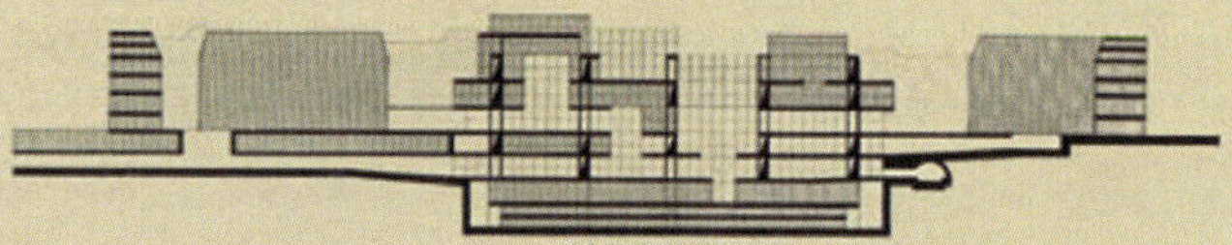

COUPE 1/500

SCHEMA AXONOMETRIQUE 1/500

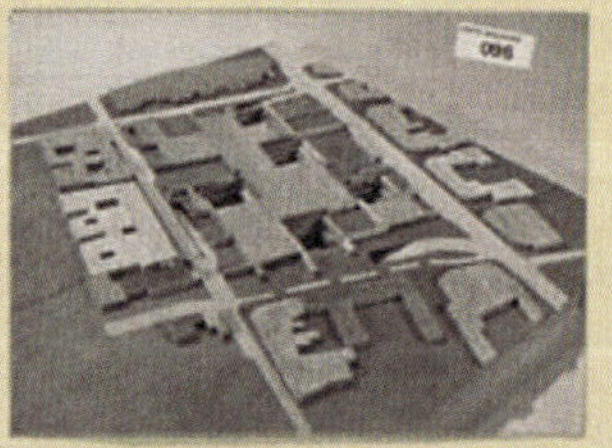

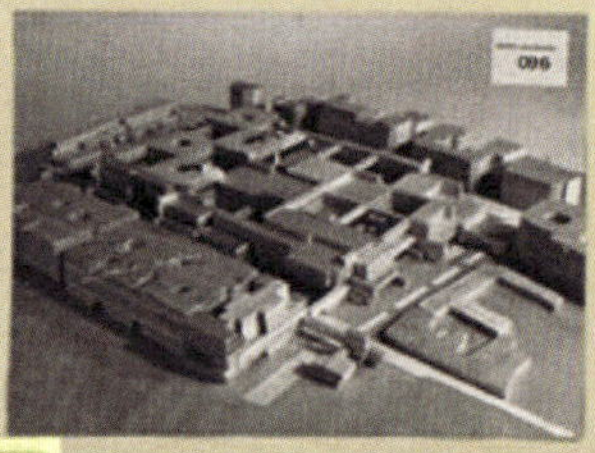

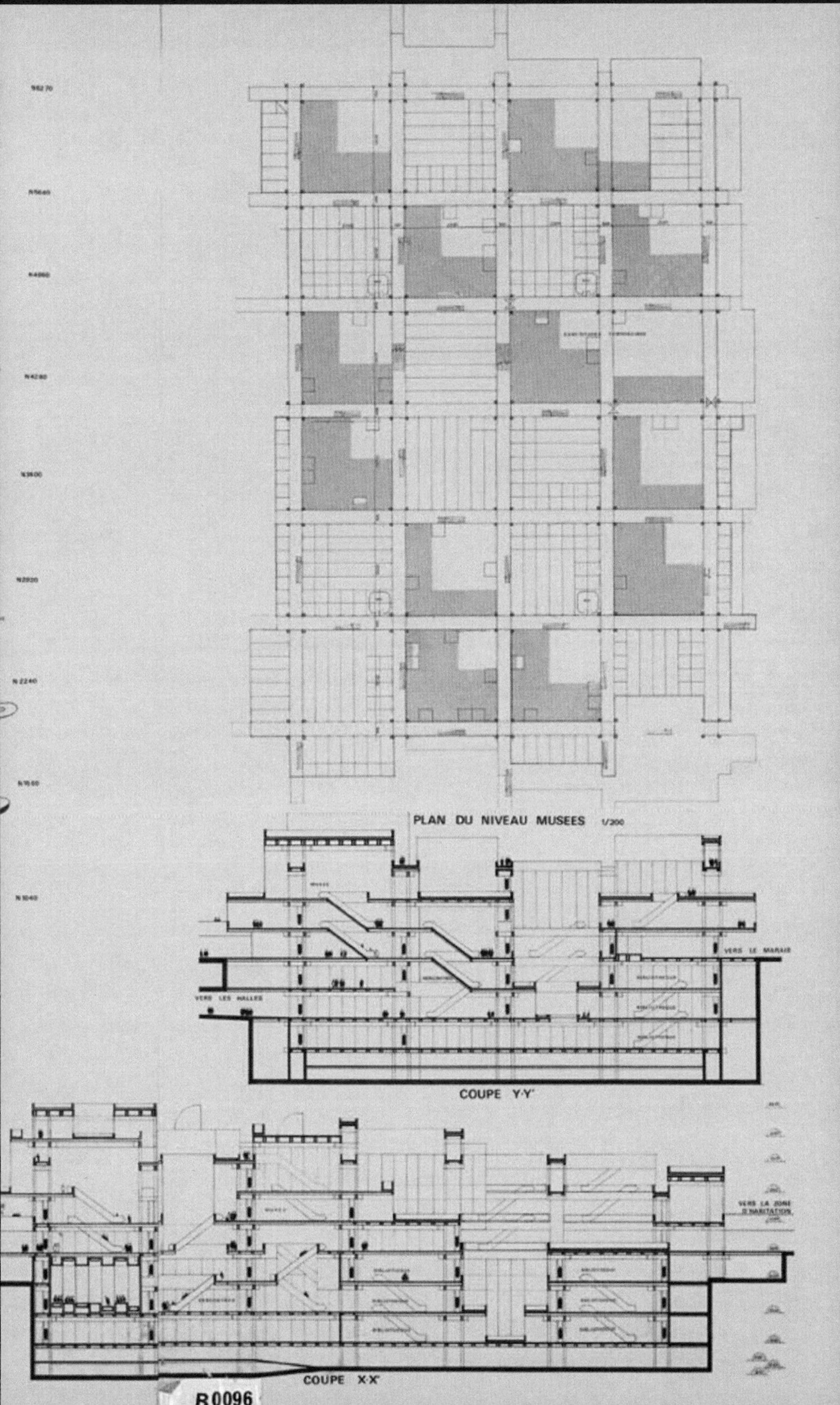

Michel Duplay and François-Noël Deffontaines (96), Project for the Centre Beaubourg competition, panel set up at the Grand Palais, Paris, June 1971.

SUMMARY AND INTERRELATIONS OF THE CENTRE BEAUBOURG ACTIVITIES

A. Reception orientation (Red)
A1. Entrance reception
A2. Reception for children
A3. Cafeteria and canteen
A4. Restaurant

B. Main activities (Blue)
B1. Current events room
B2. Industrial design permanent gallery and documentation service
B3. Experimental Gallery of Contemporary Art
B4. Temporary exhibitions
B5. Theatres and meetings
B6. Museums
B7. Library
B8. Specialized documentation and research
B9. Temporary and permanent storage

C. Management (Green)
C1. Scientific and administrative personnel
C2. Social services
C3. Supervision and control
C4. Lodgings
C5. Workshop and storerooms
C6. Technical areas

D. Parking (Yellow)
D1. Personnel parking
D2. Visitor's parking
D3. Coaches
D4. Trucks

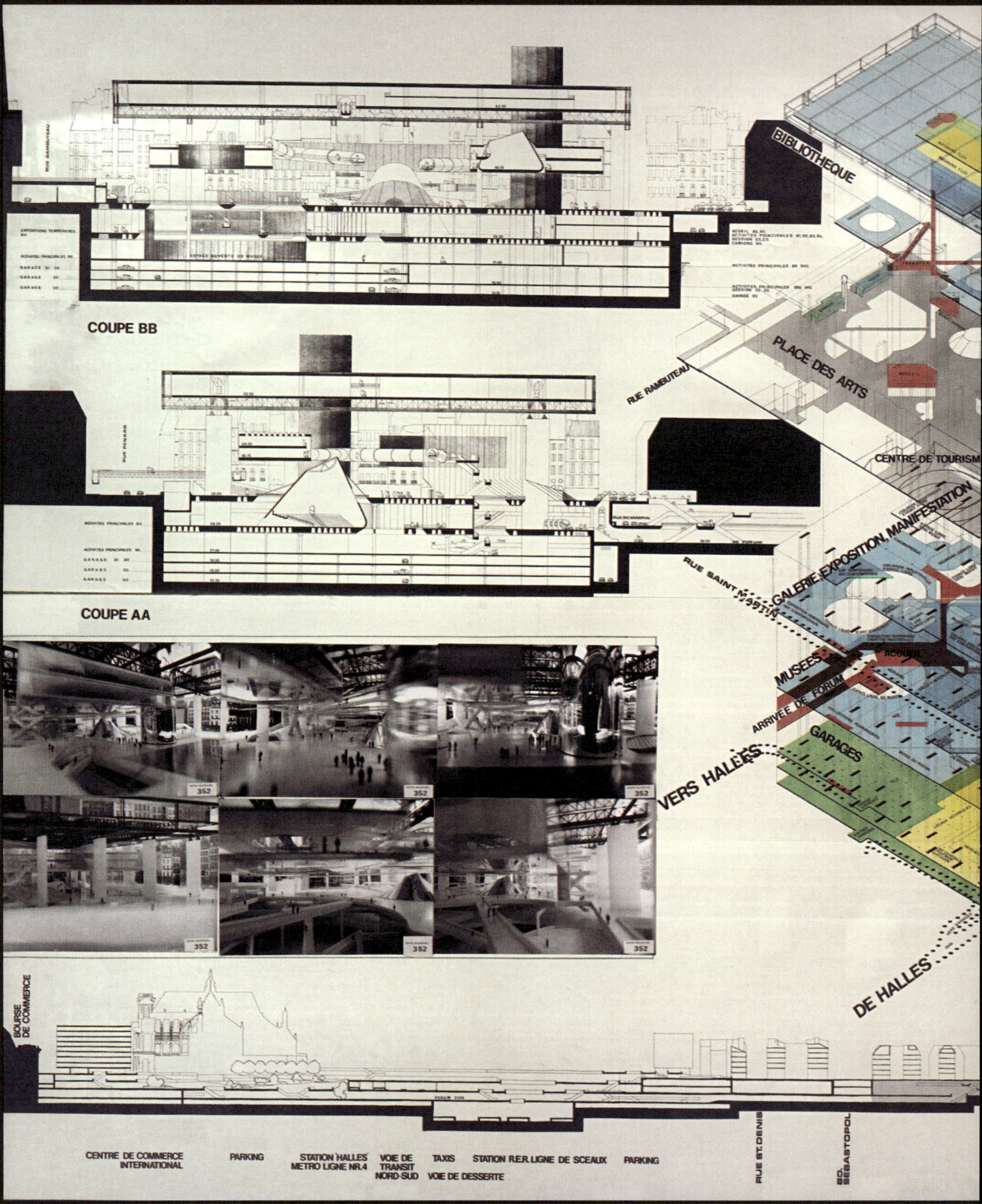
RUE RAMBUTEAU
BIBLIOTHEQUE
COUPE BB
RUE RAMBUTEAU
PLACE DES ARTS
RUE RENARD
CENTRE DE TOURISM
GALERIE EXPOSITION, MANIFESTATION
RUE SAINT MARTIN
COUPE AA
ACCUEIL
MUSEES
ARRIVEE DE FORUM
GARAGES
VERS HALLES
352
DE HALLES
BOURSE DE COMMERCE
CENTRE DE COMMERCE INTERNATIONAL
PARKING
STATION HALLES METRO LIGNE NR.4
VOIE DE TRANSIT NORD-SUD
TAXIS
VOIE DE DESSERTE
STATION R.E.R. LIGNE DE SCEAUX
PARKING
RUE ST.DENIS
BD. SEBASTOPOL

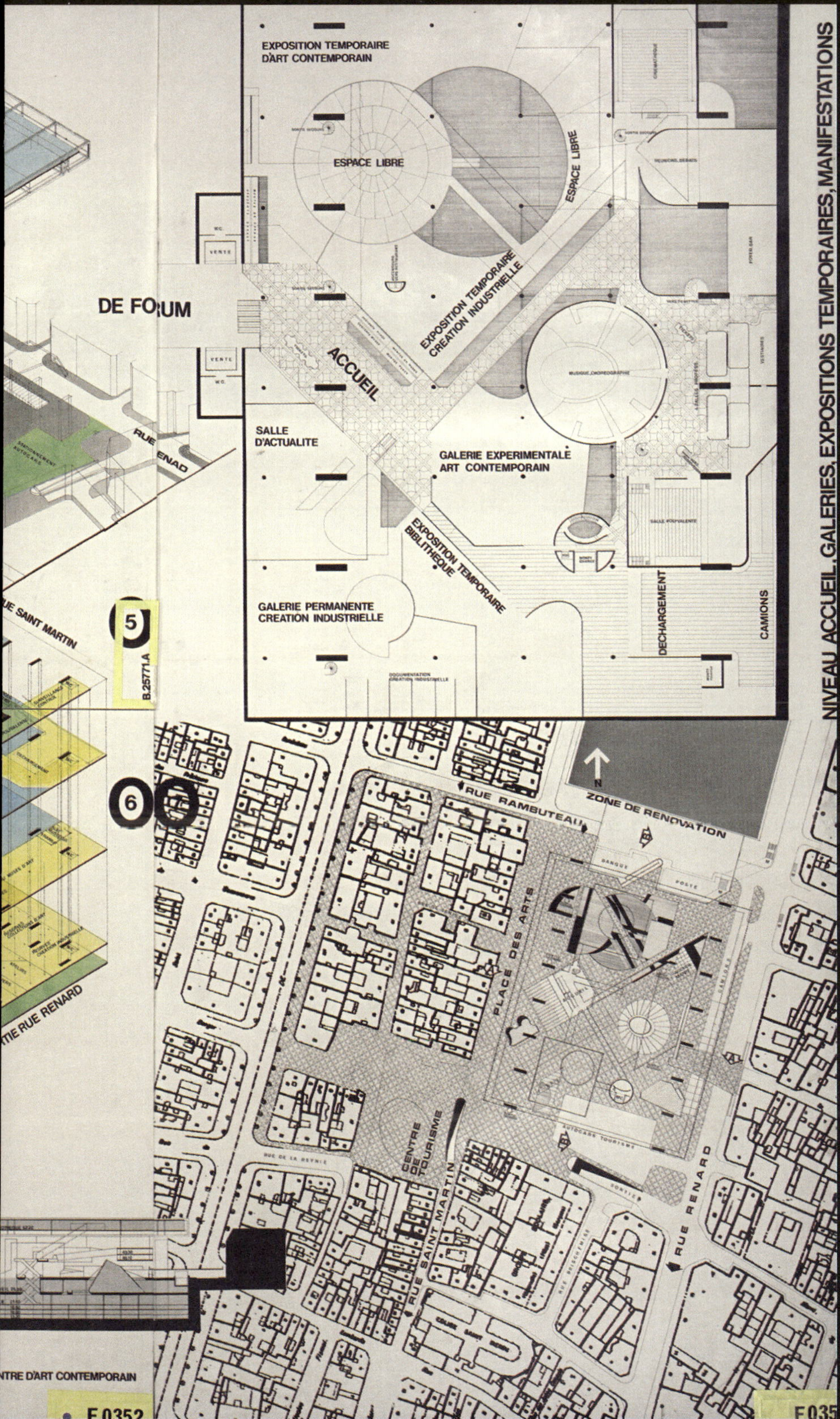

Ambrosini et al. (352), Project for the Centre Beaubourg competition, panel set up at the Grand Palais, Paris, June 1971.

SUMMARY AND INTERRELATIONS OF THE CENTRE BEAUBOURG ACTIVITIES

A. Reception orientation (Red)
A1. Entrance reception
A2. Reception for children
A3. Cafeteria and canteen
A4. Restaurant

B. Main activities (Blue)
B1. Current events room
B2. Industrial design permanent gallery and documentation service
B3. Experimental Gallery of Contemporary Art
B4. Temporary exhibitions
B5. Theatres and meetings
B6. Museums
B7. Library
B8. Specialized documentation and research
B9. Temporary and permanent storage

C. Management (Green)
C1. Scientific and administrative personnel
C2. Social services
C3. Supervision and control
C4. Lodgings
C5. Workshop and storerooms
C6. Technical areas

D. Parking (Yellow)
D1. Personnel parking
D2. Visitor's parking
D3. Coaches
D4. Trucks

6.5

THE SECOND SELECTION: TOWARD A COMPROMISE BETWEEN RECOVERING THE TRADITION OF CAST-IRON ARCHITECTURE AND THE SEARCH FOR A FLEXIBLE DEVICE

While Pompidou was making his mind up about Piano, Rogers, Franchini, and Ove Arup & Partners' project, between Monday, July 12, and Wednesday, July 14, the jury set about the new selection, passing first from forty-three projects[99] to twenty-three,[100] which were then winnowed down, by July 14, to ten. The finalists were the projects by Platonov, Bernard Dehortog et al. (223), Mendes da Rocha, the Zdzienickis, Erickson, Perea Ortega et al. (490), Stageberg, Piano, Rogers, Franchini, and Ove Arup & Partners, Cabrol, and Cosco.[101]

Only one of the three finalists chosen on July 9 appeared on the new list: Piano, Rogers, Franchini, and Ove Arup & Partners. Alongside them were three projects that the jury had picked in the first selection and five proposals dusted off during the new selection.[102]

The new selection reopened debate among jury members and led to a more complicated classification of the finalists in which Piano, Rogers, Franchini, and Ove Arup & Partners' project no longer occupied the position it had a few days earlier. In this phase of uncertainty and renegotiation the role of Johnson, Sandberg, Niemeyer, and Picon would prove decisive in reorienting the jury. While up until that moment only Aillaud had shown doubts over Piano, Rogers, Franchini, and Ove Arup & Partners' proposal, in this phase Prouvé too ceased to support the project he had previously favored but, it should be remembered, not included on his initial list.[103]

On July 14 the jury, assisted by the Technical Commission, Regard, and Loste, analyzed the shortlisted projects.[104] Each was identified by a code-name that referred, in certain cases, to the hypothetical authors and their place of origin and, in others, to an iconic feature of the project. Platonov's project was assigned the name "Kahn"; Dehortog's, "*cratère* [...]" (crater); the Zdzienickis', "*grande galérie des Halles [...] en verre*" (Les Halles grand gallery); Erickson's, "*cratère en terrasse*" (terraced crater); Perea Ortega's, "*terrasses en verre*" (glass terraces); Stageberg's, "carotte" (carrot); Cabrol's, "*modulaire*" (modular); Cosco's, "Venturi." For Piano, Rogers, Franchini, and Ove Arup & Partners's project, the epithet "*l'anglais*" was replaced by "*valise*" (suitcase), perhaps alluding to a container able to hold any kind of function or object, or perhaps to its resemblance to that shape.

The jury came to an agreement on the allotment of the prizes, orienting themselves toward three or four shortlisted projects and thirty special mentions. The former would share a prize of 250,000 francs (268,500 euros) and the latter receive an award of 10,000 each (10,700 euros).[105] For the meeting the jury chose to proceed with a preliminary vote and an individual presentation of the projects from which to select three or four finalists, to be followed first by an exchange of views with the future *utilisa-*

teurs of the Centre and then a final vote.[106]
The Technical Commission proceeded with a general presentation of the shortlisted projects, analyzing them on the basis of two criteria: land occupation and configuration of the volume of the projects with respect to their height.[107] The individual members of the jury then made their choices, selecting the following projects: Prouvé chose the proposal nicknamed *cratère en terrasse*, *valise*, *modulaire*, and Kahn; Picon, *valise*; Aillaud, *cratère en terrasse* and *valise*; Francis, *cratère du [...]*, *cratère en terrasse*, *carotte*, and *valise*; Johnson, *valise*; Laclotte, *cratère en terrasse*, *carotte*, *valise*, and Venturi; Niemeyer, Kahn and *valise*; Sandberg, *valise*; Maillard, *valise*, *modulaire*, Venturi, and the Zdienicki brothers' project; Liaebers, Kahn, *cratère en terrasse*, *terrasses en verre*, and *carotte*. Totting up the preferences resulted in the following classification: the *valise* in first place with nine votes, the *cratère en terrasse* second with five votes, the "*carotte*" and "Venturi" third with three votes, and "Kahn" and "*modulaire*" fourth with two votes.[108]
There followed an individual presentation in which the members of the jury in some cases confirmed their preferences and in others backed off from them to align themselves with one of their colleagues. The first to speak were the *utilisateurs*, followed by the architects. Picon made a broad-ranging speech to his colleagues without expressing preferences. Liaebers, focusing on the configuration of the library and circulation problems, considered all the projects "acceptable,"[109] with the sole exception of the *modulaire* project, which he thought "weakest." Sandberg, particularly attentive to the configuration of the exhibition spaces in the projects, criticized the Venturi proposal for the ridiculously low height of its interiors[110] and mentioned three projects, the *cratère*, *carotte*,[111] and *valise*, considering this last the best in terms of flexibility. "The suitcase [*valise*] offers the most flexibility" was the comment reported by Loste.[112] Francis and Laclotte went along with Sandberg's view, criticizing the Venturi and *modulaire* projects and leaning toward the projects singled out by Sandberg, but of the three preferring the *cratère*.[113]
The *utilisateurs* were followed by the architects. Niemeyer, while acknowledging the architectural quality of the Kahn project, declared his preference for the *valise*: "Niemeyer:—prefers 493 [*valise*] simplest, most rigorous;—214 [*Kahn*] project of very high architectural quality"). Given the impossibility of proposing his favored projects, as they had in the meantime been eliminated, and despite having expressed his doubts about the *valise* a few days earlier, Aillaud now admitted it had some value—"it doesn't displease him"—and chose it as his preferred project along with the *cratère*. Aillaud appreciated the internal configuration of the *valise*

but criticized its audiovisual façade. Concerning the *cratère*, Aillaud stressed the idea that its terraced configuration was intended to establish it as an urban landmark rather than a building with a distinctive structure central to the project. "Aillaud 1)—Reproaches 493 [*valise*] with [...] being the New York Times—of which the architectural element on the roof seems pointless—he does not dislike it. 2) Agreed with the internal terrace. Certainly of the city, rather [than] the image of a certain structure").[114] Prouvé was attracted to Rogers, Piano, Franchini, and Ove Arup & Partners' project, which was in line with his search for a significant work on the plane of "technical evolution" and a project that would establish a strong connection with Les Halles, but he was fascinated above all by the Venturi project. "Prouvé: There are projects that are decisive for [the future of] Les Halles. We need to try to find an architecture that does not just reflect the technical evolution of the time. We can't let ourselves lag behind. Maybe I would go for 493 [*valise*] but I attach great importance [to the] Venturi project. It is certainly the most imaginative."[115]

Johnson selected only two projects: the *valise* and the Venturi, which he dubbed "Venturi Aalto" owing to the presence in it of a fragment of the Viipuri Library designed by Alvar Aalto. His hesitation in choosing one project for the first prize sprang from his familiarity with Venturi's cultural position, which he regarded as "the most interesting direction in the world." His admiration for this "direction" in the contemporary debate and desire to identify himself with it induced Johnson to support the project, underlining its theoretical weight and the excellence of its technical report.

At the same time Johnson was aware that the project, which he recognized as having been produced at Yale University, did not have the quality of Venturi's work and was problematic precisely in its inability to translate Venturi's ideas into a design of high architectural quality. As for the *valise*, Johnson was unable to identify its authors—one of whom, Rogers, had been a student of his at Yale—but had no doubts about the conceptual and expressive force of its spatial arrangement, which he considered suited to future *utilisateurs*. The two projects became for him models of two types of modernity. In the *valise* he saw a design coherent with the avant-garde line that had permeated the 20th century, while in the "Venturi Aalto" project he sensed a contemporary and fashionable effervescence, linked to the debate in America that had emerged at Yale University out of Venturi's positions. Loste cited several times the expression used by Johnson with regard to this uncertainty, using the English word "confused" and adding its French equivalents "*confus*" and "*brouillé*." "Johnson: Venturi Aalto represents the most interesting direction in the world, but not [...]. [It has] very few constraints. Just that what it does is really mediocre. [...] [For a] Competition. Not suitable. Superb text. Clarity of thought that has been wonderfully developed p. [probably] at Yale University but [remains an intellectual and not a visual [proposal]. [...] I'm too old. [...].
No. 493 [*valise*] does not belong to Paris, it is global, a form of clean modernity. On the other hand the Venturi has very similar modalities. I am confused. I must stick with 493 [*valise*] because it makes a very strong ideological statement. It is the most suitable project for the *utilisateurs*," was Johnson's comment as reported by Loste.[116]

When Johnson started to talk about the size of the building proposed in the *valise* project, probably in response to criticisms made of it, Aillaud intervened with a reproof. It may have been Aillaud who had raised the problem of the height, given that when Johnson explained how the new building fit, in any case, into the monumental profile indicated by the churches of Paris, naming the church of Saint-Eustache, Aillaud pointed out that that example was an exception.

"Johnson: It is too big, it's true. [...] There is room in Paris for a very large building, the churches being also very large. E.g. St. Eustache. Aillaud: an example that is unique in its size. Johnson: Paris needs things that are lacking. I'm confused but vote for 493."[117]

In his uncertainty Johnson made the *valise* project his favorite again. After him Picon, the only member

of the jury not yet to have expressed his preference, made a speech in favor of the *valise* that backed and reinforced Johnson's choice.
Picon declared peremptorily that it was "the only one of the projects that has really won me over." It should not be forgotten that Picon was the person on the jury closest to Pompidou and that the president, a few months earlier, had considered him for head of the Délégation. So it is not impossible that in Picon's position in favor of Piano, Rogers, Franchini, and Ove Arup & Partners' project there was an echo of Pompidou's own thinking. Picon's preference was motivated by three characteristic elements of the project: the flexibility of the spaces, the image of "modernity" and the system of the audiovisual screens, in which he saw the potentialities of a continually changing envelope, with original chromatic effects able to attract the public to the building. "G. Picon: I vote for 493 [*valise*] alone for 3 reasons: 1) flexibility. It suits all *utilisateurs*—the 2nd reason. This project has an image.
This image pleases me personally. There is no lack of quality and modernity. The third [reason deals with the fact that] formally. [It is] not a negative. Extroverted building. It brings these colors. Durability of the screen façade. I like it. [It has the potential] to bring in the public. Practically the situation is dangerous [for the content of the screens]. But personally I see in it an attractive spirit. It is the only one of the projects that has really won me over." This is how Picon's comment was reported.[118]
Following Picon's presentation, the discussion shifted its focus to the audiovisual screens, with Aillaud challenging their significance, feasibility, and pertinence to the Centre's program, as well as their size, which he believed would have to be "gigantic." Prouvé in turn did not appreciate their informative character, seeing them as permanent artistic projections in the manner of the ones shown at the Baltard Pavilions for an exhibition devoted to Picasso in 1970. Picon associated them with Times Square, as mentioned by the architects.
Sandberg saw them as a device able to bring the contents of the museum out onto the square. "Aillaud: What are the images of Vietnamese? Prouvé: In my opinion, permanent projections. Communications screen undesirable. Picon: Times Square. Aillaud: Showing art is not so easy. Prouvé: This is also what happened with the Picasso exhibition at Les Halles."[119] From these exchanges, in other words, emerge the two possible natures of the audiovisual wall, the artistic and the informative, both of which had been investigated by Piano+Rogers Architects in their most recent projects. They had eventually come down on the side of the information screens for the project in Paris, but the competition organizers were now questioning this, something that would happen again, moreover, during the development of the project.
At a moment in which the general propensity was for the *valise*, some members of the jury reflected on the relationship that this project could establish with the architectural and urban heritage of Paris. Prouvé thought that Piano, Rogers, Franchini, and Ove Arup & Partners' building was worthy of the line of great masterpieces of French engineering of the 19th century, from the structures of the Universal Exposition of 1889 to Baltard's Les Halles, while Laclotte associated the configuration of its plan with that of the great monuments to French power in Paris: the Louvre, the Hôtel de Ville and the Palais des Tuileries. "Laclotte: Building // [oriented on a parallel] to the Hôtel de Ville, the Louvre, and the Tuileries.
Prouvé: Marking our time with a work of architecture [...]. Precedents Expo 89 and Les Halles."[120]
The debate also provided an opportunity to return to the pedestrianization of rue Saint-Martin and the transformation of its cellars. While some on the jury considered these two elements problematic, Sandberg and Prouvé were open to the possibility of a modification over the course of the project's development. "Laclotte: I remember [the issue of the renovated buildings] of rue Saint-Martin. Prouvé: It is clear that rue Saint-Martin [is a theme to revise]. Prouvé: [In the case we follow] the proposal to [integrate] the building to the east of rue Saint-Martin, it should pass [under the jurisdiction of] the City of

Paris. [In this scenario] it remains [to be clarified what would happen] to the floors [of the building] on rue Saint-Martin. Sandberg: It can be seen as a possibility. [Activities for] children could be put down below or on the roof of the building [...]."[121]
The discussion concluded with an attempt by Liebaers to undermine the credibility of the *valise*, whose internal organization he did not accept, believing it failed to respect the program. The attempt to reopen the debate was nipped in the bud by Sandberg, Picon, and Prouvé, who all now agreed on the *valise*, stressing the possibility of subsequent modifications to the project and pointing out that the competition for the Centre Beaubourg was a competition of ideas. "Liebaers: the trouble with this project is its respect of the program. Sandberg: The fact is [...] that it's a competition of ideas. Prouvé: Technical modifications can be made. Picon: [in the competition] it's a question [...] of illustrating philosophical principles."[122]
The debate also provided an opportunity to return to the question of prizes. At a time when the jury still had the idea of selecting three or four "winning projects," ranked in order of merit, it was Johnson who proved decisive again, pointing out to his colleagues the "great danger" inherent in the hypothesis of a "2nd and 3rd prize." Johnson seems to have been worried by the possibility of the Délégation subverting the final decision of the jury by choosing to entrust the execution of the work to the second or third on the list. So Johnson's choice not to award either a second or a third prize was intended to ensure the *valise* project, with which he now identified, an obstacle-free route. "Regard: A sum of 25,000,000. One or more winners—if there is a first prize or x [...] winners—[...] danger [...]. We can only award one first prize. The others: a second [and] a third prize. Johnson: [great] danger [if we give a] second and third prize. [I opt for a] first prize and 30 [mentions]."[123]
The jury proceeded with a secret vote that produced the following results: eight votes in favor of the *valise* against one vote, which can be attributed to Liaebers,[124] in favor of the *cratère*.[125]

On July 15 the Technical Commission moved to a thorough analysis of the winning project that included a calculation of the areas and compilation of the *Critères de jugement* ("Assessment Criteria") document. Checking the dimensions made clear what had already been suggested in "Specification sheet II," that the floor area of the project was smaller than called for in the program (65,500 square meters instead of 70,000). The technicians pointed out that an area equivalent to what was lacking could be found on the roof of the building (level 84 m ASL) and could be used for "all kinds of exposition, event and for [...] children."[126]
The *Critères de jugement* was a complex document of eleven pages devoted to questions ranging from urban integration to analysis of the program and technological and structural specifications. Where urban integration was concerned the technicians had emphasized the open-air piazza, the permeability of the building on the ground floor, and the pedestrian accesses to the site, expressing their appreciation of those running east-west, while criticizing those to north and south.[127] The commission thought highly of the positioning of the building with respect to the plateau Beaubourg, judging it capable of generating a "new kind perception in the city of Paris" and pointing to the plateau La Reynie as a privileged panoramic spot for the view of the Centre ("good general view").[128] It stressed the flexibility of the internal organization, appreciated in the majority of the spaces, with the exception of those devoted to "events and meetings-B5" which the *utilisateurs* imagined as a "specialized space."[129] Not coincidentally this was one of the parts that would be subjected to the greatest number of modifications over the course of the project's development.
The commission also criticized the arrangement of four of the activities in the form of independent cores difficult to connect to the rest of the Centre: the children's center-A2 (according the codification proposed by the organizers), the cafeteria, the converted cellars on rue Saint-Martin-A3, the current events room-B1, and the permanent gallery and documentation service of the CCI-B2.[130]

The commission recognized the system of mechanized circulation as the "defining idea of the project," declaring that "the originality of the public connections by means of escalators on the front part of the building is indispensable to the success of the Centre."[131] This element was also problematic owing to the decision to rely on a single point of access for the circulation to the floors[132] and the insufficient number of escalators in relation to the horizontal movement of visitors.[133] The commission also gave its view of the legibility of the spaces and the routes of circulation, saying that in the case of the exteriors it was "purely artificial through the audiovisual information on the outer façade," mentioning that this "works very well in North America"), while in that of the interiors it was practically nonexistent and judged "difficult due to the extreme standardization of the floors."[134]

Numerous observations were made on technical and structural questions.[135] The commission appreciated the originality, speed of assembly, and feasibility of the structural solution;[136] it invited the designers to analyze more thoroughly the junction of the vertical and horizontal structures and the mechanism of vertical movement of the floors;[137] and it criticized the dimensioning of the structural elements.[138] The commission also invited the designers to modify the mechanical systems, both that of the air-conditioning "extraction and recycling" system and that of the means used to transport visitors, staff, and artworks.[139] The commission stressed the need to adapt the project to meet the requirements of the fire-prevention regulations for high-rise buildings.[140]

Along with the winning project, the jury selected thirty others as worthy of mention: Choisy; Gillet et al. (39); Paul Chu Lin et al. (42); Takeuchi and Corazzo; Jean-François Seris et al. (88); Roland Morand (120); Schiedhelm; Platonov; Bernard Dehertog et al. (223); Zepeda; Safdie; Mendes da Rocha; Ambrosini; Michel Ducharme et al. (353); William Lee et al. (406); the Zdzienickis; Stones and Pearlman; Richard John Gabriel (445); Kurokawa; Erickson; Perea Ortega; Stageberg; D. C. Rowland (514); Crompton; Ken Maher et al. (539); Ralph John Thornley et al. (585); Cabrol; Cosco; Ahmet Gulgonen et al. (680)[141].

Some of the mentioned projects were on the shortlist, others were proposals discarded in the first round or even during the selection process.

So the list of these projects appears to have been the result of political and strategic choices, such as the intention to assemble a group of original proposals that would make the Beaubourg competition a manifesto of the contemporary architectural debate, or the desire to pick projects coming from as many countries as possible in order to make the competition a matter of international interest.

Among the thirty mentions, the jury singled out one in particular, that of Cosco, in recognition of the project which Johnson had identified as representing the new direction in contemporary international debate.[142]

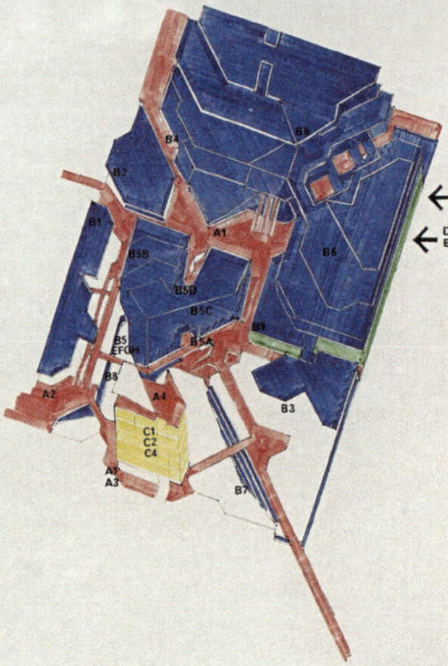

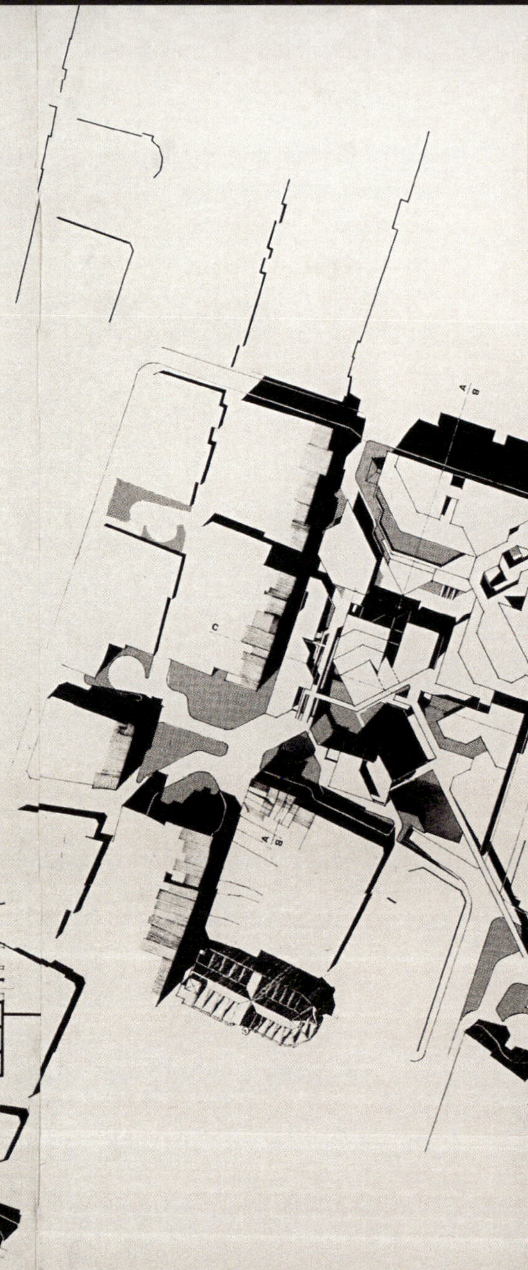

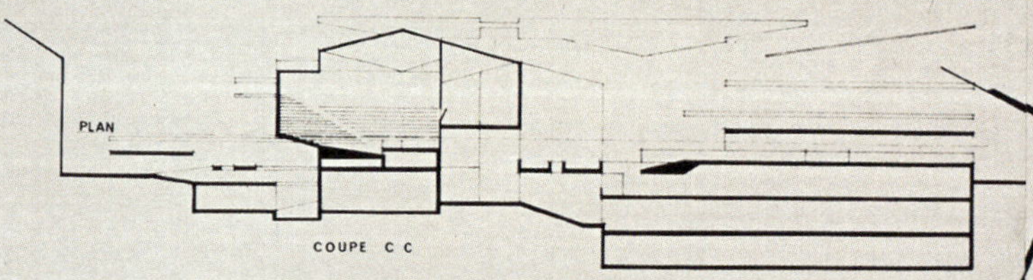

COUPE C C

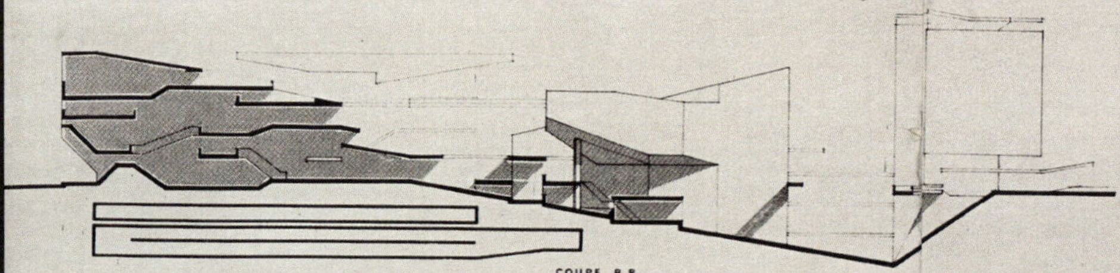

COUPE B B

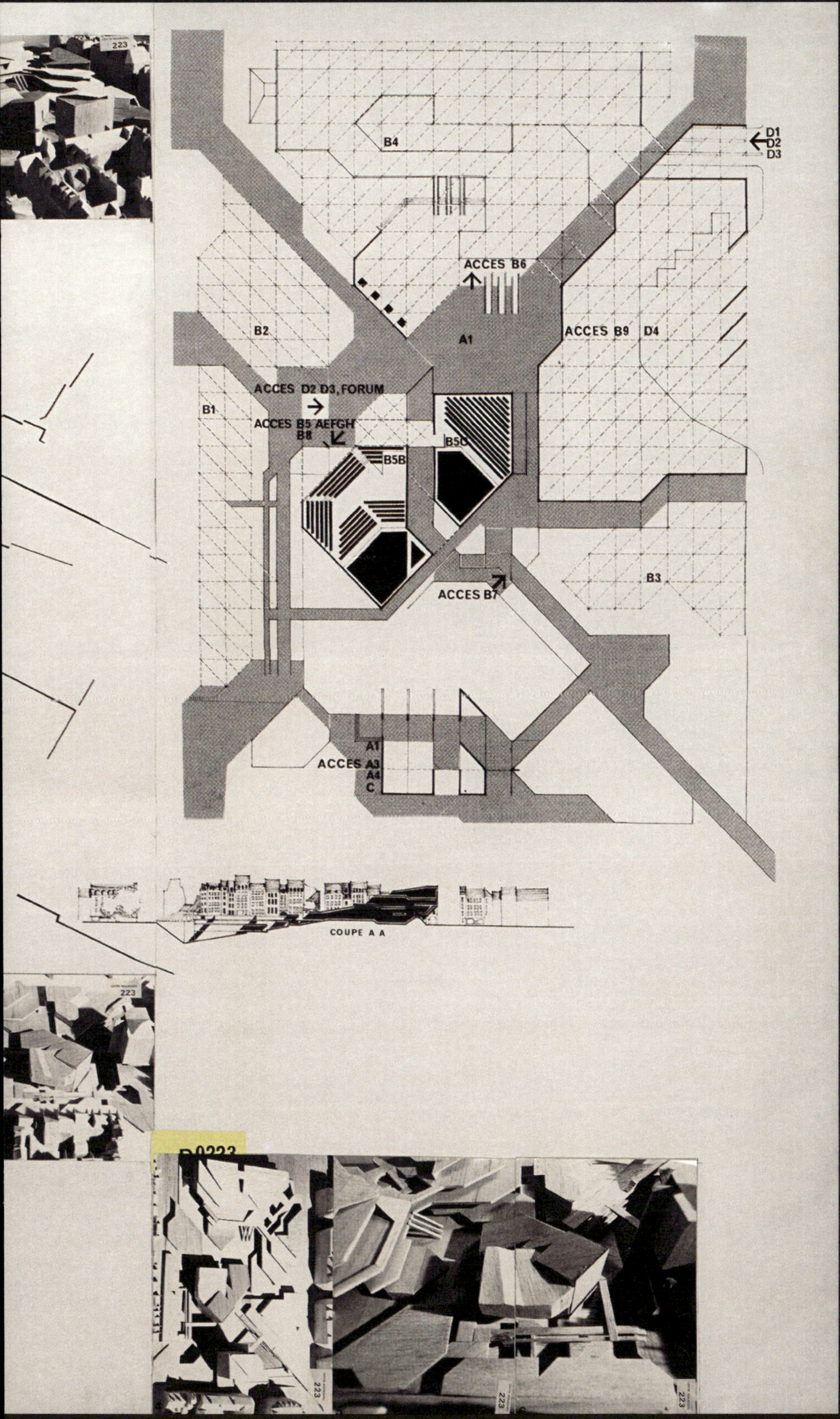

Bernard Dehertog et al. (223), Project for the Centre Beaubourg competition, panel set up at the Grand Palais, Paris, June 1971.

SUMMARY AND INTERRELATIONS OF THE CENTRE BEAUBOURG ACTIVITIES

A. Reception orientation (Red)
A1. Entrance reception
A2. Reception for children
A3. Cafeteria and canteen
A4. Restaurant

B. Main activities (Blue)
B1. Current events room
B2. Industrial design permanent gallery and documentation service
B3. Experimental Gallery of Contemporary Art
B4. Temporary exhibitions
B5. Theatres and meetings
B6. Museums
B7. Library
B8. Specialized documentation and research
B9. Temporary and permanent storage

C. Management (Green)
C1. Scientific and administrative personnel
C2. Social services
C3. Supervision and control
C4. Lodgings
C5. Workshop and storerooms
C6. Technical areas

D. Parking (Yellow)
D1. Personnel parking
D2. Visitor's parking
D3. Coaches
D4. Trucks

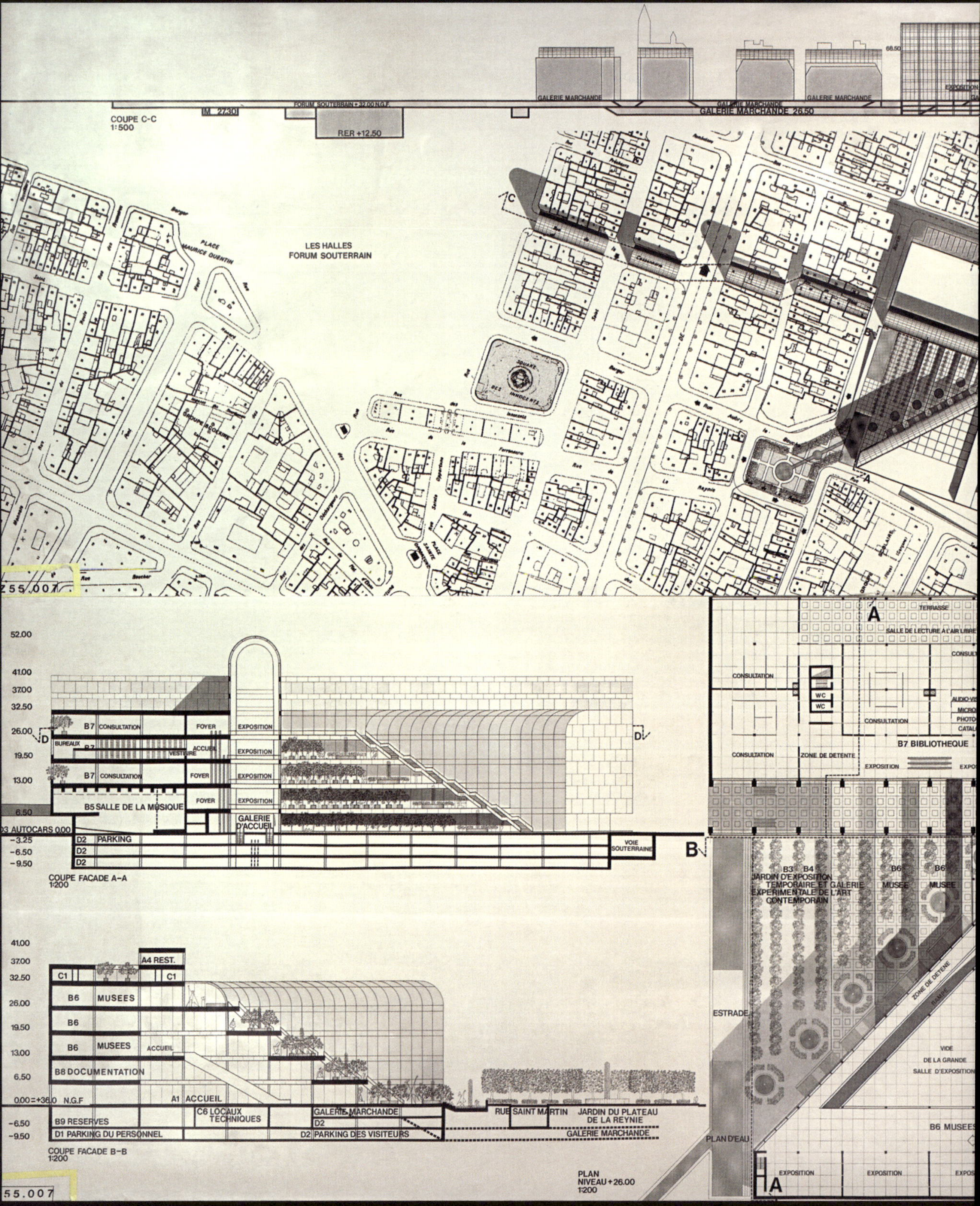
COUPE C-C
1:500
FORUM SOUTERRAIN + 32.00 N.G.F.
RER + 12.50
GALERIE MARCHANDE
GALERIE MARCHANDE 26.50
LES HALLES
FORUM SOUTERRAIN
PLACE MAURICE QUENTIN
B7 CONSULTATION
FOYER
EXPOSITION
BUREAUX
ACCUEIL
VESTIAIRE
B5 SALLE DE LA MUSIQUE
GALERIE D'ACCUEIL
AUTOCARS 0.00
D2 PARKING
VOIE SOUTERRAINE
COUPE FACADE A-A
1:200
A4 REST.
C1
B6 MUSEES
B6
B8 DOCUMENTATION
A1 ACCUEIL
0.00 = +36.0 N.G.F
B9 RESERVES
C6 LOCAUX TECHNIQUES
GALERIE MARCHANDE
D1 PARKING DU PERSONNEL
D2 PARKING DES VISITEURS
RUE SAINT MARTIN
JARDIN DU PLATEAU DE LA REYNIE
COUPE FACADE B-B
1:200
TERRASSE
SALLE DE LECTURE A L'AIR LIBRE
CONSULTATION
ZONE DE DETENTE
B7 BIBLIOTHEQUE
B3 B4 JARDIN D'EXPOSITION TEMPORAIRE ET GALERIE EXPERIMENTALE DE L'ART CONTEMPORAIN
B6 MUSEE
ESTRADE
PLAN D'EAU
VIDE DE LA GRANDE SALLE D'EXPOSITION
B6 MUSEES
PLAN
NIVEAU + 26.00
1:200

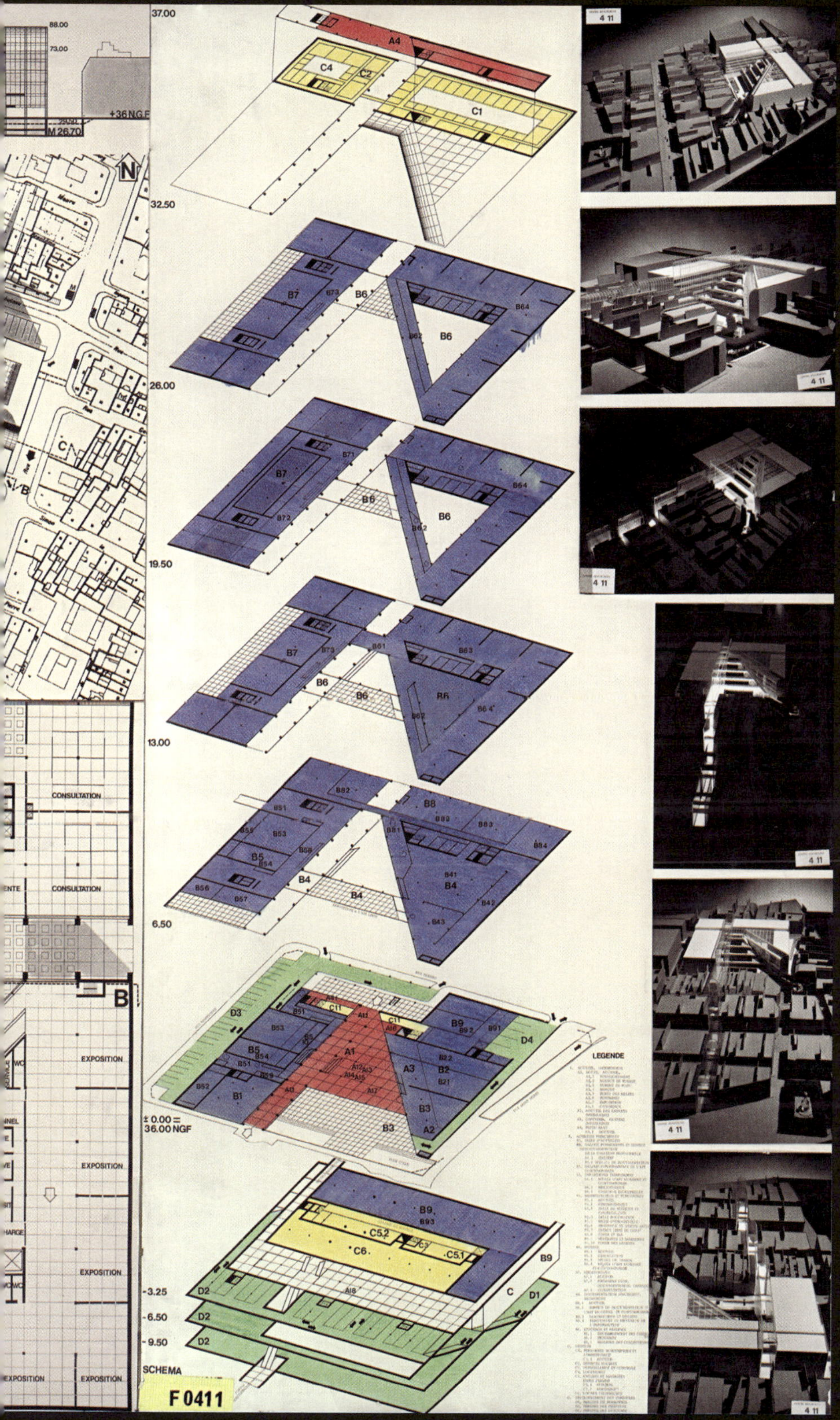

Andrew and Maria Zdzienicki (411), Project for the Centre Beaubourg competition, panel set up at the Grand Palais, Paris, June 1971.

SUMMARY AND INTERRELATIONS OF THE CENTRE BEAUBOURG ACTIVITIES

A. Reception orientation (Red)
A1. Entrance reception
A2. Reception for children
A3. Cafeteria and canteen
A4. Restaurant

B. Main activities (Blue)
B1. Current events room
B2. Industrial design permanent gallery and documentation service
B3. Experimental Gallery of Contemporary Art
B4. Temporary exhibitions
B5. Theatres and meetings
B6. Museums
B7. Library
B8. Specialized documentation and research
B9. Temporary and permanent storage

C. Management (Green)
C1. Scientific and administrative personnel
C2. Social services
C3. Supervision and control
C4. Lodgings
C5. Workshop and storerooms
C6. Technical areas

D. Parking (Yellow)
D1. Personnel parking
D2. Visitor's parking
D3. Coaches
D4. Trucks

Final meeting of the competition jury in Room A of the Grand Palais (Seated, left to right: Jean Prouvé, Philip Johnson, Sébastien Loste, Willem Sandberg, Gaëtan Picon), Paris, July 14, 1971.

Final meeting of the competition jury in Room A of the Grand Palais, (Philip Johnson describing project 493 – Renzo Piano, Richard Rogers, Gianfranco Franchini and Ove Arup & Partners), Paris, July 14, 1971.

6.6

THE AMBIGUOUS VICTORY OF ARCHITECTURAL SIMPLICITY

Prior to the publication of the final results of the selection process, Prouvé and Picon wrote to Pompidou to inform him of the results of the jury's work and to justify the choice of the winning project.[143]

Prouvé and Picon reconstructed the various stages in the selection process, offering a personal interpretation that was not free from omissions and variations with respect to the actual course of events.[144]

The letter provided an opportunity to take stock of the projects selected, which Prouvé and Picon split into four "large families."

The first two families, appreciated by the architects but considered problematic by the *utilisateurs*, consisted of horizontal buildings extending across the plateau Beaubourg, in one case with blocks crossed by broad pedestrian axes, often oriented along a NE-SW diagonal, and in the other with terraced compositions able to generate different dispositions of masses, from that of a canyon to that of large pyramids.

The third family consisted of large spatial coverings made of metal, sometimes conceived as habitable structures in which to insert the Centre Beaubourg program, at others as large shelters over plazas.

The fourth family was made up of urban grids generated by the repetition of modules composed of platforms, courtyards and viaducts—a design solution appreciated for its ease of construction, but judged unsuited to the contents of the Centre.

To these "large families" was added the design of an "inflatable structure of colossal dimensions." Its authors were not named but must have been Schiedhelm and his colleagues, whose project Prouvé and Picon had selected in the early phases of the competition.[145]

Picon and Prouvé stressed the crucial choice faced by the jury at the moment of selection between an introverted building of "reasonable" height covering the whole lot or the sort of architecture that would be capable of liberating part of the plateau Beaubourg at the cost of assuming a massive and tower-like profile that would be more difficult to integrate into its surroundings. This question, for Prouvé and Picon, was the reason for their choice of Piano, Rogers, Franchini, and Ove Arup & Partners' project. In it, in fact, they said that the jury would find a proposal able to free up the plateau Beaubourg through the layout of an open-air square and construction of a building in which, despite its imposing height, Picon and Prouvé saw, just as Laclotte had done, an affinity with one of the grand structures of the historical center of Paris, the Hôtel de Ville. The form of the latter would be echoed in the orientation and configuration of the volume and the square. Another motivation for the members of the jury was the straightforward expressiveness ("architectural simplicity") of the winning proposal in comparison with the majority of projects, whose forms were arbitrary and grandiose—in Prouvé and Picon's words: "unacceptable monumental images."[146] And the jury's choice was also driven by the appreciation of the *utilisateurs* for its internal spaces: "large free and unobstructed areas" for "dynamic and evolving uses" able to bestow on the building an intrinsic "mobility [...] that would permit over time a customization of activities as well as their adaptation to the contemporary era."[147]

The letter was also an opportunity to highlight what Prouvé and Picon held to be the characteristic elements of the project. They recognized in the mechanical system located on the façade a special means of "vertical dispersal [of people] analogous to that of a horizontal circuit"; they appreciated the audiovisual screens but, confused by the photographs of the model taken by Piano, Rogers, Franchini, and Ove Arup & Partners, misunderstood the translucent envelope, seeing it as a mirror that would reflect the historical fabric and dematerialize the building; they approved of the square, emphasizing its extension (under the Centre, beneath rue du Renard and into the basements of the buildings on rue Saint-Martin), the visual contrast with the historical center's network of narrow streets, and, finally, the sunken configuration, in which they perceived an affinity with the place des Vosges.[148]

In addition, they used the letter to Pompidou to inform the president of the need for a revision of the winning project, offering suggestions such as the proposal to turn the square into a garden and to make the plateau des Halles and the Baltard Pavilions an extension of the Centre Beaubourg.

With Picon and Prouvé's letter the *Concours pour la réalisation du Centre Beaubourg* was brought to a conclusion. Although the jury would continue to exercise an influence through the crucial contribution Prouvé, Picon, Johnson, and Sandberg made to the development of the winning project, it was already certain it had attained the objective it had been set, that of offering to the president and the people of France "a project that is not only feasible and functional, but also representative, in its formal design, of the best architectural possibilities of our time."[149]

1 — Concours international pour la réalisation du Centre Beaubourg - Rapport de Jury, n.d. [fall 1971], AN, CNACGP, F 20, 5–6.

2 — With a few exceptions, the names of the most prominent French and foreign participants in the competition were identified by the competition technicians at the end of the selection process. Liste des architectes, n.d. [July 1971], AN, CNACGP, F 18. The document produced by the competition organizers has been used as the primary reference for identification of projects.

3 — Among the architects whose participation the competition organizers invited were Jean-Louis Chanéac, Jean Deroche, Marchel Ecochard, André Gomis, Gérard Granval, Hiéronim and Alicia Listowski, Guy Rottier, Roland Simounet, Ionel Schein, Oliver Vaudou, Jean-Louis Véret, and Jean-François Zevaco. Germain Viatte et al., Propositions pour invitations, n.d. [spring 1970], AN, CNACGP, F 156.

4 — François Mathey, Architectes étrangers à inviter en dehors de ceux qui ne seraient pas retenus pour le jury, n.d. [spring 1970], AN, CNACGP, F 17. The only prominent figure from the avant-garde in the United States to take part in the competition seems to have been the Viennese-born architect Raimund Abraham (585).

5 — Franz Schulze, *Mies Van Der Rohe: A Critical Biography* (Chicago: University of Chicago Press, 1985), 285.

6 — "While I was working at the VSBA, Giovanni [Cosco] was my assistant on the general plan of the California City project (1970), published in the first edition of *Learning from Las Vegas*. He also collaborated on the translation into Italian of my essay 'Learning from Pop,' originally published in *Casabella* in 1971." Boris Hamzeian, Interview with Denise Scott Brown, February 13, 2017, Lausanne/Philadelphia.

7 — With the exception of Price, these names were mentioned by Mathey. Mathey, Architectes étrangers à inviter; Viatte et al., Propositions pour invitations.

8 — While one of the two proposals, that of Aristides Romanos, was signed by its author, the other, code no. 532, bore only the name of Elia Zenghelis. The attribution to Koolhaas is suggested both by project itself, in which we find a variation on the "platforms" Rem Koolhaas was thinking about during his years of study at the Architectural Association, and by the interview with Elia Zenghelis, who confirms that he did not personally take part in the Beaubourg competition. "Elia Zenghelis: I must tell you that I didn't participate in the competition for the Centre Pompidou; perhaps Rem did, I don't remember. You'd better contact him or OMA." Boris Hamzeian, Interview with Elia Zenghelis, May 24, 2017, Lausanne/Athens.

9 — Wilson Reis Netto was the only Brazilian on Mathey's list of architects to invite to the competition. Mathey, Architectes étrangers à inviter.

10 — Viatte et al., Propositions pour invitations; Mathey, Architectes étrangers à inviter.

11 — Frei Otto, mentioned by Mathey, was absent.

12 — Félix Candela, mentioned by Mathey, was absent.

13 — He was the architect that Jean Prouvé and François Mathey had met when sitting on the Grand prix international d'urbanisme et architecture jury in Cannes in 1969.

14 — For a complete list of the teams taking part in the Beaubourg competition and for a complete record of the names of individual participants please refer to the poster attached to this book..

15 — The anonymous project identified by the number 500 also belonged to this type.

16 — The reader is referred to the list of participants in the appendix of this volume for the full names of all the members of the teams mentioned in chapter 6.

17 — Patrick Formige et al.'s (299) proposal also belonged to this category.

18 — There were many proposals that could be included in this category. Among the ones that attracted the jury's attention were those of Hanspeter Schmidt (473); Manfred Schiedhelm et al. (126); Martin Burckhardt et al. (283); Reoven Vardi et al. (298); Michel Duplay and François-Noël Deffontaines (96); Pham Ngoc Toi et al. (137); Viktor Hufnagl et al. (357); Stanisław Brukalski et al. (568); Bohdan Paczowski et al. (243); Paulo Mendes da Rocha (338); Juan Antonio Espejel Diez (474); William Doyle et al. (246); Erik Uluots (286); Fénelon et al. (320); Viktor Sisolak et al. (447); Justin Lamb et al. (82).

19 — Georg Ladstatter et al.'s (455) project belonged to this category as well.

20 — Michel Gautier's (512) project was also in this category.

21 — To this category belonged the projects by André Wogenscky (13); Touri Cheverdiaiev et al. (25); Anatoli Poliansky et al. (129); Kyosuke Mori (362); Michel Andrault et al. (376); and Boris Roubanenko et al. (207).

22 — The project of Mendes da Rocha and the anonymous one identified by the number 578 had similar intentions.

23 — Examples from the same category were W. Chkwarikow et al. (128) and Chemetov's (293) proposals.

24 — There were numerous proposals along these lines: Posokhin et al. (120); Jean Ploquin (51); Yves Maillet et al. (56); Robert Marquis (79); Yoshiromi Tsuruoka and Sadao Izumi (85); Nabil Abdelhadi and Ezzat Sakr (94); Henry Auffret et al. (146); André Biro and Jean-Jacques Fernier (198); Richard John Gabriel (445); Henning Larsen (240); Claude and Jeanne Lefebvre (616); Élie Chagoury (393); Minoru Takeyama et al. (404).

25 — See, too, the projects by Paul Chu Lin et al. (42) and of Giovanni Tabet et al. (4).

26 — Others that can be assigned to the same category are the proposals of Jean-François Seris et al. (88); of Bohdan Paczowskiet al.; of Andres Perea Ortega et al. (490); and finally of D. C. Rowland et al. (514).

27 — See too the projects by Georgios Gerakis et al. (259), and of Ken Maher et al. (539).

28 — In this connection, see too the projects by Eduardo Liuz Paulo De Almeida Riesencampf et al. (271); Joseph Massota (345); Enrique and Nafarrate (349).

29 — See, too, V. Lebedev et al.'s (123) and John Macsai's (552) proposals.

30 — Other examples of this kind of Metabolist-derived structure are the projects by Nikolaï Oullas et al. (24); Guy Guillaume (32); Ren Suzuki et al. (432); and Paul Bessières (81).

31 — I. M. Goodovitch et al.'s (599) proposal was also based on the theme of the spiral.

32 — The anonymous project identified by code no. 169 also preserved a Baltard pavilion, inserting it in a structure intended to house the Centre's main activities.

33 — The projects by Jean Ploquin (51) and André Bonnaud (218) belonged to this category.

34 — In this connection, see the projects by Patrick Rufener (55); Giuseppe Nuovo et al. (208); Robert Montier (306); V. M. Orekhov et al. (361); Marek Krajewski et al. (454).

35 — The projects by Le Maresquier et al. (168); Léopold Vitorge (374); and Jean-Maurice Monge et al. (381) were of this kind.

36 — In this connection see the project of Jean Balladur et al. (258).

37 — The projects by André Chassin et al. (108); Luc Zavaroni et al. (350); Carlos Alvarez (390); Gérard Guiller et al.; Henri Bresler et al. (515) were of this kind.

38 — In this connection, see the projects by: Ernesto Gallardo Gómez (184); Claude Hauserman et al. (187); Andrei Meerson et al. (216); D. de Lavergne et al. (226); Massimiliano Fuksas et al. (419).

39 — From the total number of entrants—there were 1091—only 682 projects were sent to the Grand Palais. For this reason, only part of the installation prepared by Pierre Molins was utilized. The balconies and Room L were excluded. Délégation pour la réalisation du Centre Beaubourg, Galeries nationales du Grand Palais. Jugement du concours international. Planification générale, May 1971, AN, CNACGP, F 15, 15–16.

40 — For a plan of all the spaces in the Grand Palais used for the Centre Beaubourg competition, see Délégation pour la réalisation du centre Beaubourg, Planification générale, 1–8.

41 — In Room B there were projects that would attract the jury's attention during the selection process: Espejel Diez's prefabricated and modular structure; Perea Ortega's translucent box; Takeuchi and Corazzo's Miesian container; Schmidt's multistory space frame; Pottier's three-dimensional frame for the insertion of modular cells, Justin Lamb et al.'s (82) metal covering conceived as a great shelter in the manner of the Theme Pavilion at Osaka; the horizontal fabric of a metropolitan character obtained with piers and platforms of Duplay and Deffontaines and of Kurokawa; Arthur Erickson et al.'s (466) crater edged with terraces; Dominique Ronsseray and Jean Skinazi's (17) prismatic volume carved out by colossal open-air *cretti*; the translucent pyramid of an anonymous author; and, lastly, André Brahier et al.'s (98) out-of-balance towers. Although it did not stir the interest of members of the jury, Room B also housed Leonardo Ricci and Daniel Branch's (470) high-rise structure of Metabolist character and a derivation of Price's Fun Palace conceived by Michael Pearson et al. (37).

42 — Fiche technique I (Specification sheet I), June 28, 1971, AN, CNACGP, F 19.

43 — Stageberg and Jerzy Hryniewiecki et al.'s (495) proposals as well as the anonymous project identified by code no. 496 were characterized respectively by a set of prismatic volumes ranged along the diagonal axis, a composition of blocks carved out on the inside to create organic spaces similar to the work of Frederick Kiesler, and a colossal ziggurat hollowed out at the center and wrapped in an envelope of horizontal brise soleil.

44 — As in the case of Gérard Struys and his partiality for André Hryniewicki and Claude Guillemin's project (304).

45 — "535. The most innovative [*frais*] of all! It scatters the program [of the Centre] all around Paris, so that only the structures for the neighborhood and the cultural and tourist 'antennas' are kept on the plateau, centralizing the information and spreading the entertainment throughout the capital. An excellent response to the problem [posed by the project]!" Pierre Colboc, Rapport de salle [C], July 7, 1971, AN, CNACGP, F 18, 3. Colboc's sensitivity in the identification of original projects close to the themes of international debate is confirmed by his selection of Yves Adenis et al.'s (113) megastructure, Schiedhelm's geodetic dome, Pham Ngoc Toi's colossal shelter, Tarquini Martensson and Michael Tarp Jensen's (153) translucent container and Stanislas Fiszer et al.'s (505) viaduct. Ibid.

46 — Robert Bordaz, Letter to Marcel Diebolt [Prefect of Paris], May 3, 1971, AN, CNACGP, F 17.

47 — Didier Breton, Rapport de salle [B], July 7, 1971, AN, CNACGP, F 18, 2.

48 — Ibid.

49 — "Its aim is to be the symbol of an era, but this symbolism remains for the most part purely formal. It is possible to identify a large number of 'a priori' forms." Ibid.

50 — "Well-structured plan and highly sophisticated distribution of the elements, in a very classical orthogonal spirit. Modest volume in relation to the setting thanks to the deep central courtyard, the connection with the neighborhood remains external. Simple and clear façades, not lacking in movement." Breton, Rapport de salle [B], 3.

51 — "The only attempt to explain the advantage of the architecture [has been made] through an original philosophical exploration of the real questions of the program. Thanks to an excellent internalization, the much-divided volume configures more than a simple reproduction of the plot of land subdivided to an extreme. It comes close to the urban complexity of the surrounding fabric, through a process that is not imitative. It is worth noting, perhaps, a certain simplicity in the style that would merit greater depth and rigor." Breton, Rapport de salle, 4.

52 — "Particularly interesting and original disposition of masses, with great assurance in the handling of volumes. The spatial animation is sensitive, harmonious and able to adapt to the surroundings through an appropriate design of the façades." Ibid.

53 — "A very well-conducted study that follows an octagonal grid. The fundamental logic of the plan is reflected in the disposition of masses, where numerous well-balanced details complete the animation." Ibid.

54 — "The plastic organization is not lacking in severity, but it is a rigor of great beauty. Notwithstanding its monumental nature, it retains a human scale that seems to be linked to the binary rhythm of the disposition of masses. The design creates an urban square on several levels, extraordinary well-organized and able to provide the neighborhood with an area of activity and encounter like the one called for by the program."

55 — "Low volume with pyramidal walls, enlivened by multiple displacements. Beautiful clarity of the plan. The logic is reflected in the organization of the masses. Blends softly into the surroundings. Building that perfectly reflects its function." Ibid.

56 — Breton, Rapport de Salle [B], 5.

57 — Procès verbal de la réunion du Jury du Concours international pour la réalisation du Centre Beaubourg. 1er séance – 5 Juillet – 15h30, July 6, 1971, AN, CNACGP, F 18; Procès-verbal de la réunion du Jury du Concours international pour la réalisation du Centre Beaubourg. 2e séance – 6 Juillet – 15h00, July 7, 1971, AN, CNACGP, F 18.

58 — "Several projects sent prior to June 15 arrived after June 28 (between June 28 and July 2). The jury has decided to accept them, in view of the problems with transport that had occurred in that period." Procès-verbal de la réunion du Jury. 1er séance, 3.

59 — Ibid. The fact that Piano, Rogers, Franchini, and Ove Arup & Partners' project had been checked for conformity on June 28, four days after the deadline for the reception of the projects at the Grand Palais, suggests that it was one of those late to arrive and eventually allowed to take part.

60 — Procès-verbal de la réunion du Jury. 2e séance, 2.

61 — "Les Halles: the president and the majority of the members of the jury have expressed their opposition to the destruction of the Baltard Pavilions. They have decided to send a letter to the Minister of Cultural Affairs asking him to inform the President of the Republic of their point of view." Procès-verbal de la réunion du Jury. 1er séance, 3. The letter, now in the archives of Henri Domerg, runs as follows: "At the moment in which the designs for the construction of the Centre Beaubourg are being examined, the following members of the International Jury ask you, M. President, to do everything possible to preserve at least part of the Baltard Pavilions, which have been sacrificed without a precise reason. Both because they are a point of reference in the history of French architecture and a story of success that it will be hard to equal, and because, in relation to the future Centre Beaubourg, they constitute a space for activities and meetings whose disappearance threatens to compromise the very work with which you have associated your name." Jean Prouvé et al., Letter to President Georges Pompidou, July 6, 1971, AN, FHD, F 13.

62 — Procès-verbal de la réunion du Jury. 2e séance, 2.

63 — Centre Beaubourg. Notes pour la conférence de presse. Exposé de Monsieur Jean Prouvé, Président du Jury International du Concours du Centre Beaubourg, July 19, 1971, AN, CNACGP, F 19, 1.

64 — The projects chosen by Prouvé were: Jean Le Priol (16); Ronsseray and Skinazi; the anonymous project identified by code no. 54; Antony Lumsden et al. (60); Padilla Arias; Amiraly Nassor et al. (119); Schiedhelm; Balladur; Bruyère; Cler; Ladstatter; Schmidt; the anonymous project identified by code no. 500; Cabrol; Sang Wha Lee and Akira Fujita (643); the anonymous project identified by code no. 667. Liste de projets avec préférence de chaque membre du jury, July 8, 1971, AN, CNACGP, F 18.

65 — The projects selected by Philip Johnson were: Howard Stucky et al. (61); Seris; Duplay and Deffontaines; Adenis; Pham Ngoc Toi; Martensson; Platonov (214); Bernard Dehertog et al. (223); Chandra; Ernesto Zepeda (250); Jean-Pierre Vago et al. (270); Nicolas Mastrandreas et al. (300); Safdie; MacDonald and Hull; Sartor et al. (348); Hufnagl; Lee; Jean-Michel Guillaume (408); Louis Georges Noviant et al. (429); Stones and Pearlman; Gabriel; Kurokawa; Erickson; Stageberg; Piano, Rogers, Franchini, and Ove Arup & Partners; Rowland; Kim Swoo Geun (533); Kalisz and Perrottet (541); Jan Karczewski et al. (548); Brukalski; the anonymous project identified by code no. 578; Cabrol; Bianca Paleologo Imbesi (617); Benjamin Garsten Hoff et al. (620); Cosco; Brian Crumlish et al. (650); Janos Farago et al. (651); Jean Pierre Defebve and Jacques Deffet (657); William O'Dowd (661); Orlando Orraga-Yon (662); Thierry Awenengo D'Alberto (665); Alain Bourdonnais et al. (671). Ibid.

66 — Oscar Niemeyer's selection comprised the following projects: Platonov; Mendes da Rocha; Stones and Pearlman; Espejel Diez; Perea Ortega; Piano, Rogers, Franchini, and Ove Arup & Partners. Ibid.

67 — The projects selected by Emile Aillaud were: Ronsseray and Skinazi; Yves Letrosne (40); Takeuchi and Corazzo; Isabelle Béné et al. (95); Michel Lefebvre et al. (173); Saraiva Melo; Avyeris Andonyadis et al. (186); Bruyère; Burckhardt; Vardi; Jacques Lambert et al. (334); Sartor; Hufnagl; Bernard Kaleski et al. (388); Max Tournier (414); Stones and Pearlman; Stefan Imrich et al. (446); Renée Gailhoustet and Francis Gaussel (504); Block and Broudo; Kawasaki; Farago; Defebve and Deffet; Awenengo D'Alberto. Ibid.

68 — Frank Francis selected fourteen projects: Letrosne (later deleted from the list); Hazan Sener and Zulkuf Gunelli (104); Posokhin; Pierre Eibel and Gérard Huet (265); Burckhardt; Guy Laurent Lucas and Bernard André Delattre (289); Montier; Verendra Girdhar (336); Bruce Campbell Graham (343); Frank Conrad Neal and David Calder Richardson (511); William Ahern et al. (549); Hiroyashu Yamada (557); Jong-Soung Kim et al. (586); Peter Steffian et al. (598). While looking for themes such as those of the diagonal axis, the low prismatic volume with courtyards, and easy spaces to fit out, Francis did not pick the most significant examples of any of these categories. None of the projects he selected reached the final stage. Herman Liebaers chose thirteen projects: Peter Barefoot (36); Takeuchi and Corazzo; Kiyoshi Seike (86); Philippe Jaulmes and Jean-Claude Deshons (149); Lefebvre; Stubbins; Gerakis; Lee; Sisolak; Charles Du Bose and Michael Buckley (448); Stageberg; Shoichi Haryu et al. (528); E. Leucht and Denis Bruner (538). Among these projects can be found prismatic boxes set on the ground and hollowed out at the center by a courtyard, and platforms raised above the ground by imposing vertical structures to leave the square free. Michel Laclotte picked eleven projects: Alfred Bender et al. (1); Odon Dupire et al. (10); Maurice Cammas et al. (18); Stucky; Platonov; Paczowski; Jadav; Stageberg (491); Kim Swoo Geun; John Pointer et al. (610); Crumlish. The only projects indicated by Laclotte of significance for successive selections were some proposals also singled out by Johnson. It is possible that Johnson played a decisive role in the nomination of Laclotte to the jury. Although continuing to hold the role of a substitute, Henri-Pierre Maillard participated in the selection and indicated five projects: Lumsden; Pierre Forestier and Oscar Nitzchke (80); Duplay and Deffontaines; Lefebvre; and Platonov. In his case two of the projects were based on the theme of the diagonal axis and three were characterized by an infrastructure composed of *arcades* and platforms. Ibid.

69 — In their common characteristics, the projects chosen by Willem Sandberg reflect the ideas he had put forward with regard to the conception of the Israel

Museum. Willem Sandberg, "The Israel Museum in Jerusalem," *Museum*, 19, no. 1 (1966), 15–30. This idea of a museum was represented by Uluots (286), a low volume with a horizontal orientation and blind façades, illuminated from above by a shed roof and light cannons in the manner of Le Corbusier; that of Doyle, with its elementary stepped volume wrapped in a Modernist curtain wall that extended onto the roof; and, finally, two of the prismatic and translucent containers selected by Niemeyer, those of Espejel Diez and Perea Ortega.

70 — Liste de projets "A," July 8, 1971, AN, CNACGP, F 18.

71 — Liste de projets "+," July 8, 1971, AN, CNACGP, F 18.

72 — In the list of the individual members' judgments of project 493 those of Gaëtan Picon, Sandberg, Laclotte and Maillard are missing. Liste de projets avec préférence de chaque membre du jury.

73 — The list is made up of the following projects: Ronsseray and Skinazi; Letrosne; the anonymous one identified by the no. 54; Maillet; Takeuchi and Corazzo; Seris; Duplay and Deffontaines; Schiedhelm; Lefebvre; Saraiva Melo; Platonov; Jadav; Bruyère; Cler; Safdie; Mendes da Rocha; Stones and Pearlman; Erickson; Piano, Rogers, Franchini and Ove Arup & Partners; Gailhoustet and Gaussel; Jacques Lanson; Cosco. The identifying number 641 corresponding to Cosco proposal was cancelled from the list with a stroke of blue marker. Deuxième passage du jury, décision du 8 juillet 1971, projets retenus, July 8, 1971, AN, CNACGP, F 18. Between July 8 and 9 some members of the jury requested the addition of a number of projects to the shortlist. Out of these eleven projects (Brahier; Sener; Doyle; Zepeda; Uluots; Fénelon; Meyer; Espejel Diez; Perea Ortega; Suzuki; Martin-Artajo brothers), it is worth mentioning Zepeda's, picked by Johnson. Untitled text (handwritten notes on projects to be drawn to the jury's attention), July 9, 1971, AN, CNACGP, F 18.

74 — "We have made more rapid progress than I expected. It seems to me that we are not far from the result. 2) [...] to leave us before the end of our examination of the selected projects marked by the letter A. 22 [to] 100 [projects according to] Loste's statistics. Consequently, I propose devoting from half to ¾ of an hour to the completion of this operation. New selection. 3) It is clear that the [number] of the architects is diminishing 4) I'd like to go back through the exhibition rooms with you all for two reasons: a) to stop in front of the projects listed with the mark + [as well as projects indicated by the rapporteurs of the rooms]. b) for the possible identification of additional selections. This is a check of our choice - [...] excuse me." Jean Prouvé, Untitled [handwritten notes on the speech made to the jury of the Centre Beaubourg competition during the selection process], n.d. [July 8, 1971], BK, FJP, F PROU 311, n. p.

75 — Prouvé, Untitled, BK, FJP, Unidentified folder, 4.

76 — The list comprises the following projects: the anonymous one identified by the no. 54; Takeuchi and Corazzo; Duplay and Deffontaines; Platonov; Jadav; Mendes da Rocha; Stones and Pearlman; Erickson; Piano, Rogers, Franchini and Ove Arup & Partners; Cosco. Deuxième passage du jury, décision du 8 juillet 1971, projets retenus, July 8, 1971, AN, CNACGP, F 18.

77 — In the passage from ten to six projects, the jury excluded the project of Jadav; the anonymous one identified by the no. 54, described as "pyramids"; that of Erickson), referred to as "amphitheater"; and that of Mendes da Rocha. The comment relating to the elimination of this last project was particularly ambiguous—"338 [Mendes da Rocha]: Niemeyer = to eliminate"—which seems to identify Niemeyer as calling for the exclusion of the very project of which he had been the supporter up until that moment. [Emile Aillaud], Untitled [notes on a meeting of the jury of the Centre Beaubourg held in July 1971], July 9, 1971, AN, CNACGP, F 18.

78 — Deuxième passage du jury, décision du 8 juillet 1971, projets retenus, 8 July 1971, AN, CNACGP, F 18. In the first round Duplay and Deffontaines's project was selected by Johnson and Maillard. Liste de projets avec préférence de chaque membre du jury. Ambrosini's proposal was the only of the three project finalists not to have been included in either the list of selected projects or that of the projects with a positive judgment of "?+." For this reason it must be assumed that it was chosen by the jury from among the other projects between July 8 and 9.

79 — [Aillaud], Untitled [notes on a meeting of the jury of the Centre Beaubourg held in July 1971].

80 — Ibid.

81 — Ibid. The French attribution of this project may have stemmed from its authors' choice to write the captions of the competition plans in French.

82 — The decision to stop work for the weekend was made at the suggestion of Prouvé, who wrote in his notebook: "6) [...] having worked long hours, I propose that we rest on Saturday and Sunday." Prouvé, Untitled [handwritten notes on speech made to the jurors of the Centre Beaubourg competition during the selection process].

83 — Fiche technique II (projet 493) [Piano, Rogers, Franchini and Ove Arup & Partners], July 10, 1971, AN, CNACGP, F 19.

84 — "Impossible to measure the areas of the program," "impossible to locate [this space] in the project," and "difficult to locate" were the comments on the analysis of the areas of the three functional complexes "A-reception and accesses. Orientations," "B-main activities," and "management." Ibid.

85 — "Program: 70,000 m². Addition of areas of the project for a possible distribution: 66,000 m²" was the comment on the calculation of the areas for functional complexes A+B+C. "Difficult to distribute. About 22,500 m². Program 25,000 m²" was the one on the calculation of the areas for functional complex D. Ibid.

86 — Jean Prouvé, Untitled [handwritten notes on Lombard's presentation of the three finalist projects in the first selection of the Centre Beaubourg competition], BK, FJP, F PROU 311, n.p.

87 — Ibid.

88 — "493. Lombard–[...] a) renewal not in conformity (North). b) occupation of G.F. [ground floor] (good). c) r. du Renard (possible) [...] but no program. d) project on rue du Renard side—?—Valid for all projects. e) mechanical circulation access (why not!). d) almost total grouping of activities except for children's reception and self-service restaurant. Axonometric doc legible. e) dynamic activities on G.F. [ground floor] f) flexibility—[...] including machinery—even a subdivision in height—if there is [...]. g) weak mechanical distribution with multiple accesses to the upper floors—escalators very valid. h) fire safety (High Rise Buildings.) in [...]—enclosed fire escapes—evacuation needs improving—protection by steel panels 2h/ [use of] plastic!? i) panels [...] for [...] *utilisateurs*. j) up and down movement of floors—why not? k) service gallery—permanent exhibition. l) outdoor activities for people. Break? m) originality. Very varied possibilities of use n) experimental gallery on ground floor. o) heating [...] / electricity. p) deviation of [rue] Saint-Martin already planned and desired [by the Délégation]." Prouvé, Untitled [handwritten notes on Lombard's presentation of the three finalist projects], 1–3.

89 — "Lombard 352 [Ambrosini]. a) access level not [...] b) [...] c) open air d) safety e) view of street f) [...] set back g) rue Beaubourg connected? h) [rue] Saint-Martin underground i) respect for the programming less evident on floors below ground j) good accesses and in agreement with the APUR plan k) natural light l) [...] (exp. gallery) in basement m) museum in basement (critical) n) [...] of terrace. o) p) difficult foundations ([...]) and below the mean water table [...] and under pressure p) depth of spans to be decreased. Distorted dimensioning of the concrete. q) air conditioning scaffolding [...] r) greenery very important s) overhead lighting for the library t) conveyor belt." Prouvé, Untitled [handwritten notes on Lombard's presentation of the three finalist projects], 4–6. It was precisely for a university that this solution had been used, in the project for the Free University of Berlin, the very project on which Rogers had initially drawn for his design of the Centre Beaubourg. Ibid.

90 — "Lombard. 96 [Duplay and Deffontaines]. a) access b) urban fabric–dubious c) too much accommodation, inflated! d) eastern (terraces) (not to be considered) This is suited instead for a university–surely very grim architecturally e) why [spaces for] academic courses??? why?? f) You can do anything in a space like this [...]. It has to be filled or not otherwise it is fossilized g) to [...] safety [...]." Prouvé, Untitled [handwritten notes on Lombard's presentation of the three finalist projects], 7–8.

91 — Ibid.

92 — Henri Domerg, Note for the President of the Republic, July 12, 1971, AN, 574 AP, F 10.

93 — Ibid. In the note of the following day Henri Domerg returned to the subject, stating: "He [Robert Bordaz] proposes inviting some ambassadors, in particular Great Britain's if the project is of British origin."

94 — Domerg reported: "If you wish M. Bordaz will bring me some documents tomorrow to show you, including one or two photos." On the same document Georges Pompidou annotated: "Seen. Fine. Talk it over with Balladur." Ibid.

95 — Henri Domerg, Note for the President of the Republic, July 13, 1971, AN, 574 AP, F 10.

96 — Domerg, Note for the President of the Republic, July 13, 2.

97 — Madeleine Négrel, Agendas of Georges Pompidou (year 1971), IGP, n.p.

98 — Pompidou wrote in his letter of thanks to Prouvé: "Dear Sir, I thank you for sending me the volume *Une architecture pour* [*sic*] *l'industrie*. This work illustrates ideas which you care about and deals with problem that is very important in our world of today and tomorrow." Georges Pompidou, Letter to Jean Prouvé, June 1, 1971, BK, FJP, F PROU 26-28, n.p.

99 — The following projects were on the list: [in the order listed in the document] Ralph John Thornley et al. (585); Perea Ortega; Dehertog; José Paulo de Goimbra Neves (266), Hiroyasu Yamada (557); the Zdzienickis; Platonov; Rowland; Stones and Pearlman; Cosco;

Bourdonnais; Erickson; Matthias Schlaepfer (581); Fiszer et al.; Pham Ngoc Toi; Ambrosini; Piano, Rogers, Franchini and Ove Arup & Partners; Duplay and Deffontaines; Wagner Franco Facilla (195); Hufnagl; Jean-Paul Bonnemaison et al. (409); Martensson and Tarp Jensen; Mastrandreas; Jadav; Stageberg; Gabriel; Brahier; Mendes da Rocha; Lamb; Michael Louis Severin et al. (431); Suzuki; De Almeida Riesencampf; Camilo Mazuera (275), Schiedhelm; Kurokawa; Karczewski; Zepeda; Lefebvre; Cabrol; Crompton; Eibel and Huet; Cler; Paleologo Imbesi. [Robert Regard], List of projects selected on Tuesday July 13, 1971, at 9:30 am, July 13 1971, AN, CNACGP, F 18.

100 — The following projects were on the list: in the order listed in the document] Lamb; Schiedhelm; Martensson and Tarp Jensen, Platonov; Dehertog; Zepeda; Mendes da Rocha; Ambrosini; Andrew and Maria Zdzienicki; Stones and Pearlman; Gabriel; Kurokawa; Erickson; Espejel Diez; Perea Ortega; Stageberg; Piano, Rogers, Franchini and Ove Arup & Partners; Fiszer; Rowland; Thornley; Cabrol; Cosco; Bourdonnais. Ibid.

101 — With the selection of the final list of projects, the jury leaned toward a range of different architectural languages, as if wishing to find the best proposals of the various tendencies in the debate over contemporary architecture: the flexible containers and envelopes with original effects of the projects by Piano+Rogers and Ove Arup & Partners and Perea Ortega; Platonov's fashionable Kahnian composition; Cosco's Venturian collage; Mendes da Rocha's monumental concrete platform hovering in the air; the Zdzienicki brothers' original reinterpretation of the 19th-century *passage* as a device for the distribution and display of artworks; Cabrol's Metabolist megastructure obtained through a combination of plates and hollow cylinders; and the urban landmarks based on the theme of a diagonal axis and terraced building of the projects by Dehertog and Erickson.

102 — The projects by Plotonov, Erickson, and Cosco.

103 — Prouvé's uncertainty about Piano, Rogers, Franchini, and Ove Arup & Partners' project can be discerned from a list he drew up during the new selection on which there were two of the projects destined to appear among the finalists, those of Cosco and Plotonov, as well as the proposals by Jadav, Takeuchi and Corazzo, and Stones and Pearlman. The symbol adopted by Prouvé to mark these projects was not exactly the same as the one that appeared alongside Piano, Rogers, Franchini, and Ove Arup & Partners' proposal. Jean Prouvé, Untitled [list of projects identified during the two rounds of selection of the Beaubourg competition], n.d. [July 12–14, 1971], AN, CNACGP, F 18, n.p.

104 — The only documentary record of the discussion is in the notes transcribed by Sébastien Loste. Sébastien Loste, Untitled [handwritten notes of meeting on Wednesday, July 14. 4:00 pm], n.d. [July 14, 1971], AN, 640 AP, F 105. The names of those at the meeting can be deduced from photographs taken during the event.

105 — "The 1st – the next 2 or 3 (or 4) to which 250,000 F will be offered. 1-2-3. = 150-50-50. 1-2-3-4 = 100-50-50-50. 30 x 10 000." Loste, Untitled [handwritten notes of meeting on Wednesday, July 14. 4 pm], 1.

106 — In the final vote, jurors were still free to ask the representatives of the Technical Commission for their opinion.

107 — "(2 types of projects—those that do not occupy all the site—[those that] fully occupy the site)." Loste, Untitled [handwritten notes of meeting on Wednesday, July 14. 4 pm].

108 — Sébastien Loste, Vote jury Beaubourg (le 14 7 à 17h), 14 July 1971, FSL, F 105.

109 — "the nine projects: acceptable for the library." Loste, Untitled [handwritten notes from Wednesday, July 14 meeting. 4:00 pm], 2.

110 — "The Aalto 641 may offer freedom, but the height of the floors [is] only 350 centimeters. Two floors would be needed for the museum instead of one. [It] is too low." Ibid.

111 — "Sandberg. For the museum: 466 [Erickson], 491 [Stageberg] are valid." Ibid.

112 — Loste, Untitled [handwritten notes from Wednesday, July 14 meeting. 4:00 pm], 2–3.

113 — Francis aligned himself with Sandberg by criticizing Cosco's project, of which he admitted he did not understand the meaning, and leaned towards Stageberg's project, of which he appreciated both the disposition of masses and the organization of the internal activities, and the crater of Erickson of which he praised the configuration of the ground floor. Francis's preference for the latter project can be deduced from Loste's notes, which highlight Francis's favorable assessment of this project with a dot and a square bracket. Loste, Untitled [handwritten notes from Wednesday, July 14 meeting. 4:00 pm], 3. Laclotte told his colleagues of his alignment with Sandberg's ideas and expressed his appreciation for both Piano, Rogers, Franchini, and Ove Arup & Partners' project and Erickson's. Again, the fact that Laclotte's preference was for the second project was revealed by Loste's choice to underline it in his notes. Ibid.

114 — Loste, Untitled [handwritten notes from Wednesday, July 14 meeting. 4:00 pm], 4.

115 — Loste, Untitled [handwritten notes from Wednesday, July 14 meeting. 4:00 pm], 4–5.

116 — Loste, Untitled [handwritten notes from Wednesday, July 14 meeting. 4:00 pm], 5.

117 — Ibid.

118 — Loste, Untitled [handwritten notes from Wednesday, July 14 meeting. 4:00 pm], 5–6.

119 — Loste, Untitled [handwritten notes from Wednesday, July 14 meeting. 4:00 pm], 6.

120 — Ibid.

121 — Loste, Untitled [handwritten notes from Wednesday, July 14 meeting. 4:00 pm], 7.

122 — Ibid

123 — Loste, Untitled [handwritten notes from Wednesday, July 14 meeting. 4:00 pm], 8.

124 — The name "Liebaers" written in pencil on the voting card of the *cratère* suggests it was in fact Liebaers who opposed the victory of the favored project. After all, it was he who had raised his opposition to the project in the final debate. [Herman Liebaers], Untitled [card for the final vote in the competition for the construction of the Centre Beaubourg], July 14, 1971, AN, FSL, F 105. This hypothesis is supported by the fact that the project indicated in place of the *valise*, that of the *cratère*, was precisely the one Liaebers had indicated as his favorite during the discussion with his colleagues.

125 — Ibid.

126 — Centre du plateau Beaubourg, Projet n. 493, Vérifications de surfaces donnés, n.d. [July 15, 1971], AN, CNACGP, F 19.

127 — For the category "2. Urban integration" the project received an "A" grade. Centre du plateau Beaubourg, Projet n. 493, Vérifications de surfaces donnés, 1, 3.

128 — Despite this appreciation, the perception of the "building" from the different points of observation ("Perception du Centre sous les différents angles d'approche") received a mediocre grade, "B or C." Centre du plateau Beaubourg, Projet n. 493, Vérifications de surfaces donnés, 2.

129 — For activity B5, the comment "difficult to fit out" was made. For activities A2, A3, and B2 the comment was "too far from the center." Centre du plateau Beaubourg, Projet n. 493, Vérifications de surfaces donnés, 8.

130 — There were two categories related to internal programming, "3. Unity of the Centre" and "7. Program-project adaptation"), rated "A" and "B" respectively. Centre du plateau Beaubourg, Projet n. 493, Vérifications de surfaces donnés, 4, 8.

131 — Centre du plateau Beaubourg, Projet n. 493, Vérifications de surfaces donnés, 9. The two criteria of judgment relating to circulation, "5. Access and circulation" and "8. Interrelationships" received "C" and "B" ratings respectively. Centre du plateau Beaubourg, Projet n. 493, Vérifications de surfaces donnés, 6, 9.

132 — The comment on section "5. Access and circulation" was the following: "only one? any modification admissible." The rating was mediocre, "C." Centre du plateau Beaubourg, Projet n. 493, Vérifications de surfaces donnés, 6.

133 — "Horizontal movement is excessive if the number of escalators is not increased." Ibid.

134 — For the category "6. Reception and orientation of visitors" the rating was "B." Centre du plateau Beaubourg, Projet n. 493, Vérifications de surfaces donnés, 7.

135 — For technical and construction issues, the two criteria for judgment were "9. Technical concept" and "10. Construction procedures and techniques"; in both cases the project was rated "A." Centre du plateau Beaubourg, Projet n. 493, Vérifications de surfaces donnés, 10–11.

136 — "The process [of] construction [of the] superstructure" was "original." "The technique of implementation" was "good," while the "times of construction" were "rapid" and the "feasibility" was "good." Centre du plateau Beaubourg, Projet n. 493, Vérifications de surfaces donnés, 11.

137 — "Movable beam/post and floor connection technique needs study." Centre du plateau Beaubourg, Projet n. 493, Vérifications de surfaces donnés, 10.

138 — "Review the scale of horizontal and vertical superstructure." Ibid.

139 — "Review access for works... (and goods) as well as public and staff" and "review extraction and recycling." Ibid.

140 — Ibid.

141 — Jugement concours plateau Beaubourg 15 juillet 1971 19 h, July 15, 1971, AN, CNACGP, F 19.

142 — "Among all the winning projects, the jury particularly appreciated the concept of project 0641." Galbreath, East, Huffman, Weeks,

and Cosco, Plans of project no. 641 awarded at the international competition for the realization of the Centre Beaubourg (special mention), June 1971, CGP, F 13408.

143 — Jean Prouvé and Gaëtan Picon, Letter to Georges Pompidou, n.d. [July 14–18, 1971], AN, CNACGP, F 19.

144 — Picon and Prouvé described the first stage of the selection process as a procedure that would have allowed the jury to draw up a shortlist of around fifty projects, rather than three. The new selection is justified in this letter on the basis of comments made by the Technical Commission, whereas it was Prouvé who had halted the selection procedure, asking for an analysis of the three finalists and proposing a new selection. In their description of the new selection, Prouvé and Picon also spoke of a total of sixty projects chosen (instead of forty-four) and then of around thirty (instead of twenty-two), which they said coincided with the projects mentioned (in reality there were only half that number). Prouvé and Picon, Letter to Georges Pompidou, 1–2.

145 — This project was included on the list of thirty special mentions but was not among the nine projects discussed at the jury's last meeting, held on July 14, having probably been discarded the previous day when there were still twenty-two selected projects. A possible explanation for the decision to mention this particular project to the president was that Prouvé and Picon may have joined forces during the selection process with the aim of making it the winner. It is worth remembering that this project had been picked by both Prouvé and Picon during the individual selection.

146 — Prouvé and Picon, Letter to Georges Pompidou, 4–5.

147 — Prouvé and Picon, Letter to Pompidou, 5.

148 — Ibid.

149 — Ibid.

Manfred Schiedhelm et al. (126), Project for the Centre Beaubourg competition, model, June 1971.

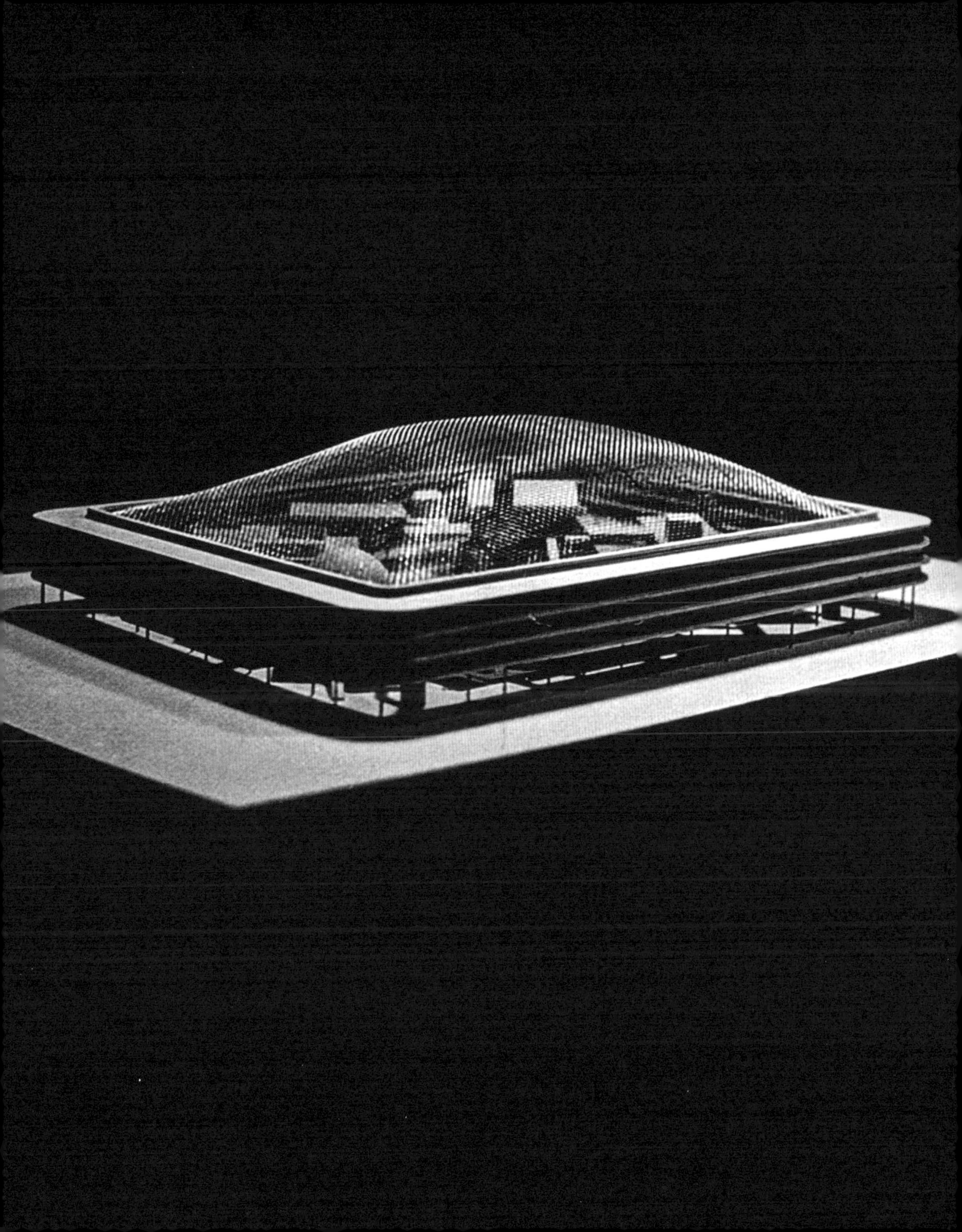

ANNEXES

<.1

BEAUBOURG: AN INFRASTRUCTURE FOR THE NEXT FIVE HUNDRED YEARS — RENZO PIANO IN DIALOGUE WITH BORIS HAMZEIAN

BH — Boris Hamzeian
RP — Renzo Piano

BH Renzo Piano, today I would like to talk to you again about one of your most cherished works, Beaubourg, known worldwide as the Centre national d'art et de culture Georges Pompidou, conceived and built in Paris by you, Richard Rogers, Gianfranco Franchini, and Ove Arup & Partners between 1971 and 1977. Since its inauguration, this work has established itself as a turning point in the history of post-World War II architecture. It challenged the visions of conservative French architecture of the time, became an emblem of the radical avant-garde of the sixties, and marked a fundamental stage in your and Rogers's research into an intrinsically flexible and prefabricated architecture. It became an engineering manifesto for the application of the cast-steel technique, and finally offered itself to Paris and Parisians as a cultural and artistic center—a "place for the people," to quote a phrase dear to both you and Rogers.
Almost fifty years after its creation, the Centre today has been subject to interventions of various kinds, from the refurbishment of the rooms destined for the collections of the Musée national d'art moderne (MNAM), to more extensive changes such as the refurbishment of the large exhibitions and events room located on the ground floor—the Forum—the changes to the Bibliothèque publique d'information (BPI) located on the upper floors, and the reconstruction of the Atelier Brancusi on the piazza in front of the building.
Today I would like to discuss with you some of the fundamental elements that characterize this project and evaluate their topicality, their evolution, and, in some cases, their betrayal.

RP Well, Beaubourg has probably managed to become everything you describe, but at the time we conceived it, it is not as if we were so far-sighted, with such a clear vision of the future. We were just young people and loved to experiment. I prefer to say bad boys. We were in our thirties, I was thirty-three and Richard, who was unquestionably the wise man of the company, was only four years older—a difference not only in age that my whole life I tried to bridge by running behind Richard.
When we came to imagine Beaubourg we did not look at the project as the demonstration of a theory but simply tried to infuse it with the themes we breathed in the air. We were in London and it was the early seventies. It was certainly not May '68, but the atmosphere in London was still deeply connected to that cultural revolution. There was a keen curiosity about everything that was happening around us, from music, art, and literature to food and love. It was a particular culture that was also a part of everyday life, with concerts to be listened to stand-

ing up with kids on your shoulders. It was a culture that some would label "with a lower-case c," but it was ours and we were in it. It was not expressed through a particular canon, it was not communicated through the tools of déjà-vu, and it was in no way institutional. I don't want to say that we didn't go to museums, but I must admit that we didn't go very much and were in any case a bit intimidated by them. The original idea of Beaubourg did not originate from a reasoning that had to do with principles or ideologies, but was nothing more than the transposition of the atmosphere of our time. The climate of rebellion that surrounded us led us to conceive of an urban machine that basically and almost instinctively aimed to subvert the effect that the places of official culture intimately conveyed to the crowd with their appearance of haughty fortresses made of stone and marble. To that image, aimed at expressing the strength and authority of knowledge, we wanted to respond with that of a joyful machine. This was our response to that official culture, a rebellious response, instinctive, even uncultured in the true sense of the word, but in any case, without contempt. Making this urban machine replaced intimidation with a different feeling that animated us, that of curiosity. What it means to do this kind of work can only be understood when it is done.
But you don't have to be a genius to make it, you just have to breathe the air of your time. Breathe your time, live things, and really live them. Seize your feelings and you will come to make things that will then turn out to be an expression of your time and indeed, as you go on your journey, you will understand why you made them and the value they will have assumed in the history of architecture, the city, and society.

BH In the Anglo-Saxon cultural revolution you speak of, was there also avant-garde architecture?

RP Of course! The London avant-garde scene at the time was dominated by the experiments of the Archigram group. When I think of the Architectural Association School, I also remember Cedric Price's lectures on a particular kind of flexible space that had led him to design the Fun Palace. I am referring to the idea of an environment that is completely modifiable and freed from all kinds of technical installations and all forms of walls and ceilings.
It is an open space but equally complex to build, which is why for Beaubourg we worked together with Ove Arup & Partners and engineers like Peter Rice. This kind of evolutionary space demanded an equally evolutionary structure and that is why for the competition we imagined a structure that could really change, with floors that could be dismantled

and reassembled to generate double levels.
And when you want to create this kind of flexible space, you have to solve the question of technical installations, from air conditioning to escalators.
To safeguard the continuity of the space, you cannot insert these elements in the middle, you have to take them outside the building, banish them to its perimeter. I don't want to trivialize too much, but the idea of the Beaubourg space was born more or less like this.

BH So, in Beaubourg, you and your former colleagues reduced architecture to an infrastructure, nothing more than a sequence of uninterrupted and inherently flexible platforms. In the course of the development, you translated this flexibility with the space you described to me, but also with devices serving that space, from technological counter-floors to audio-visual transistors to mobile furniture. Now that most of these devices for flexibility have been dismantled and removed, and that those that remain, from technical installations to escalators, seem to have lost their nature as technical elements to become iconic and monumental aspects of the building, what remains in Beaubourg of this philosophy of flexibility?

RP What you describe has happened: some devices have disappeared and others have become permanent, monumental elements. But that was not our intention. When we imagined Beaubourg, we had no intention of monumentalizing anything. Quite the opposite, in fact. Monumentalization is something we did not envisage and only discovered later.
And this makes me think of another element that was in the air when discussing the genesis of Beaubourg. I am referring to the shared desire to offer Parisians and the French a place for popular culture and education. Even more than London, Paris in 1971 was still coming to terms with the spring of '68. The idea of the *maison de la culture* (house of culture) was nothing new since at the time several such *maisons* had already been inaugurated under the impulse of their promoter, the minister of Cultural Affairs André Malraux. "Every French city, large and small, should have a house of culture where different disciplines meet, reading, knowledge with music, with art, with cinema," this was more or less Malraux's goal.
But the intrinsic relevance of Beaubourg at the time lay in the fact that until the idea of this cultural center was formulated by French president Georges Pompidou and his collaborators, no one had dared to think of a large *maison de la culture* in the heart of the historic center of Paris. Until then, the *maison de la culture* was a device for the promotion of culture in the provinces.
To return to the ideas that generated Beaubourg, not even the French government wanted to make a monument, or at least the creation of a monument was not the primary objective of all those commissioned by Pompidou to carry out the work. Fortunately, I might add.
So it was by no means conceived to be a monument. On the contrary, we conceived it to be an anti-monument. So an anti-monument that ended up being a monument. It happened, I must admit, but, today, fifty years later, the world has changed and this fact can become a premise for interesting discussion.

BH It is with this in mind that we can consider some of the elements of Beaubourg that have undergone or are about to undergo necessary transformations. Let's take one of the elements that, according to the renovation project presented by the president of the Centre Pompidou, are destined to become the subject of the Centre's next work: the technical installations. In the summer of 1971, the jury of the future Centre Pompidou saw in this element devices that could be configured according to the evolution of the microclimatic requirements of the environments, and during the fine-tuning of the project, even in spite of the warnings of some Arup engineers, these installations became, together with the steel casting structure, the significant figure of the Centre's image, helping transform it into the monument that you and Rogers opposed. What should be done with these installations today: transform them according to the new microclimatic requirements, even at the cost of going towards a miniaturization of their components, with the risk of distorting the façade's composition? Or maintain that image and those proportions at all costs by transforming those tubes into fossils, making the technology also undergo the calcification the structure underwent when the Greek temple was transformed from wood into stone?

RP First of all, you have to consider what kind of plant you are talking about. It is a system composed of a modular system of central air-handling units arranged entirely on the roof, one for each of the 12.80 meter-wide bays that make up the building. Using a system known as the dual-duct system, two pairs of ducts descend from each central unit, one for hot-air intake, one for cold-air intake and two for return air. The split inlet was designed to bring hot and cold air into the rooms to be mixed in "*boites de melange*" (mixing boxes) which released the air at the temperature required in the room.
It is a configuration that is not only technical but also ethical because it means endowing each space with the degree of flexibility that belongs to the space. It means allowing users to adapt the microclimate of each ambience virtually instantaneously. It means that crowds moving through the Centre on their way could be accommodated by different climates thanks to different adjustments of the various *boites de melange*. A flexible space for different and flexible microclimates. It is something crazy and extreme, of course, but it is just as fascinating. What is important is that we achieved it and it even worked.
The problem is that today this kind of system is energy-intensive and obsolete—it no longer meets the technical standards of and strategies for room climate control.
And it is precisely here, as you anticipate, that the question of transformation arises. I believe that it is necessary to modify this plant without it becoming a forgery. I believe that we have found a way to preserve the plant in its current configuration by modifying its operation, starting with the choice to mix the air directly in the rooftop treatment plants, before it reaches the *boites de melange*. In this way we can preserve the original air-conditioning system by operating its components, including the cooling towers. Certainly each of these components works less hard because the whole system will have to be adjusted for lower energy consumption.
The question that arises today about the transformation of the air-conditioning system is not far removed from the one faced a couple of years ago with the renovation of the escalator on the façade. It had to be completely redone because there is no escalator that can survive for fifty years, especially outdoors. But once you go to the site and observe carefully, you will realize that the decision was not to dismantle and replace but to intervene punctually with recovery and replacement. The steel arches were recovered and repainted. The glazing was replaced with elements identical in shape and geometry but with a higher performance stratigraphy and greater transparency. The same applies to the escalator machines, where current regulations require that not one but two steps be placed horizontally before the start of the actual staircase.
The alteration of the steps risked undermining the configuration of the escalators, but by working carefully and with the aim of respecting the original design, the stairs were readjusted to that design.
The example of the escalator transformation can be taken as a model for subsequent work because it outlines a strategy that could almost be described as a "mending" to the building that does not betray its form and essence. When you ride on the escalator, in fact, you discover that the essence, namely the slow discovery of the city by the crowd, has been maintained. When you ride it, you don't have to worry about the steps—you won't stumble—everything is simply a slow levitation that makes

you discover Paris through its facades, its roofs, and its horizons.
This intervention seems to me to indicate the direction in which we should proceed: transform Beaubourg without betraying the ideas that generated it, and at the same time make it work, even if its functioning does not correspond to contemporary canons given that it was conceived in the seventies.

BH Does the same apply to the asbestos removal work planned for the construction site that will start in a few years?

RP There is no doubt about it. All the opaque parts of the façade are made of materials that contain small amounts of asbestos, which for obvious reasons is now banned. The façade panels need to be replaced, and we are taking the opportunity to use a variant that is four times more thermally efficient, which further reduces the building's energy consumption.
All these transformations require patience and thought. If you don't do them hastily, if you do them with affection—because you know a building is like a child, you have to love it—then you can achieve good results. You have to live Beaubourg, observe it, visit.... I really go there. It's not a purely romantic question—well, some romanticism is involved, admittedly—but what I mean is that I visit it constantly, I see, I look, I observe.
Beaubourg needs to be transformed, but if you proceed as I have described so far, you will not encounter problematic transformations, because these will follow the spirit in which the building was conceived. It will be an evolution, a transition that will not betray Beaubourg. I believe that it will succeed because until now I think we have succeeded, perhaps not always, perhaps not for all the internal transformations, but you should know that it is not easy to manage such a complex building. Beaubourg has seen many governments and consequently many presidents and directors, some better than others...

BH Let's turn to the question of these internal transformations.
In the competition program drawn up by Sèbastien Loste and François Lombard, Mr. Piano, you and your former colleagues took a powerful and radical statement very literally. "No extension of the building is to be planned," reads the announcement. You conceived the evolutiveness of this machine not in terms of additions but of internal reconfigurations: ephemeral partitions, standardized and prefabricated furniture, and even dismountable and re-assemblable floors.
However, successive presidents and department directors over the decades have been afflicted by what one of them, Germain Viatte, described to me a few days ago as "the square meter disease," i.e., the constant desire to extend the square footage of exhibition areas at the expense of multifunctional spaces. First the plugging of the side bays on the ground floor, then the disappearance of the double-height rooms on the top floors, then the partial plugging and complete reconfiguration of that immense *cavea* for the crowd known as the Forum, where artists and creators conceived unique works and performances between 1977 and the eighties.

RP There has been the phenomenon of the race for the square meter. The Centre Pompidou went through times when the management felt the need to extend the square footage of the exhibition areas at the expense of equally important spaces. However, I want to say from the outset there was a war that Rogers and I fought, although I must admit some battles were lost. Take the ground floor, where at the time of the inauguration the idea of a large permeable void could only be maintained in the first bays to the north and south. Those bays were to remain free and, in spite of Richard's and my opinion, the choice was made to insert a cinema

to the north—a valuable element, of course, I do not dispute that—and to the south an extension of the exhibition areas dedicated to contemporary art. The defense of those voids was also lost because of the inherent difficulty of managing those kinds of spaces in the city—I don't just mean Paris, I mean in any city—be they galleries, arcades, and so on. These are environments where it is complicated to ensure cleanliness and, above all, security, and this was an issue that did not stop with those voids but was true of the whole piazza. I remember a time when the Centre authorities felt the need to fence off the entire piazza to secure it. And what about the issue of the homeless who found shelter in Beaubourg and whom we always defended on the basis of that idea you mentioned earlier, that Beaubourg should be a place for everyone, regardless of age, ethnicity, or social conditions: "A place for the people." No one could be prevented from entering; openness and even free access were radical principles and had to be preserved.
The idea of the Forum on the ground floor was equally courageous. It worked for some time thanks to the support of the first director of the MNAM, Pontus Hultén. Under Hulten's direction, the Forum hosted great works for the general public such as the *Crocodrome*, this fearsome monster on a colossal scale that children used to feed with coins to collect precious chocolates from its backside. The *Crocodrome* is simply an example to illustrate how the Forum represented a real *avant-scène* that connected the piazza and the street with the exhibitions on the upper floors of the museum.
For some time the Forum functioned as we conceived it, and I think the credit also goes to that inexplicable energy that has to do with construction sites and the act of building. It is a formidable adventure made up of solidarity and participation in the manner of a large orchestra where there are no punctual issues but a participatory creation of a choral miracle. It is an extraordinary energy that begins to dissipate when the construction site ends, and this is fatal because the project, Beaubourg in our case, is the result of that energy. The Forum went into crisis precisely when this energy ran out and so this space began to be misused until it assumed the configuration it has today.
In spite of these transformations Beaubourg can turn around any time it wants because after all it is not even a building but rather an infrastructure.
If we really want to call it a building then it is a building in possession of the structural and physical strength to withstand all these transformations.

BH I wonder if this also applies to the museum spaces. In 1977, you conceived them as flexible environments to break with the traditional museum gallery. You conceived an arrangement of semi-enclosed rooms, the "*cabannes*," and a circuit of corridors and inner squares, almost as if to recreate a metaphorical village. In 1985, Dominique Bozo, with the help of architect Gae Aulenti, preferred to return to a traditional museographic approach, bringing the idea of gallery and room back to Beaubourg. How do you judge this transformation retrospectively? Forty years after Aulenti's intervention and in the light of the evolution of contemporary art, do you think Aulenti's approach is still relevant or do you think the Centre is ready for new transfigurations of its museum device?

RP It is certainly time to move on to something else. But again, what has happened is not serious, not fatal, I mean. There is even more to the origins of this museum approach than what you mentioned. During the setting up of the exhibition, between 1974 and 1976, we and Pontus were convinced that the "*cimaises*," i.e., the walls on which the works were placed, should be suspended from the ceiling (which was perfectly capable of supporting this kind of element).
All this stemmed from the idea of suspension and levitation of the walls, which should almost touch the ground without actually touching it.
I remember Pontus always telling us: "My friends, it's OK, it's a great idea, as long as you can't see

a person's feet on the other side." It had to be a matter of a few centimeters and no more. The idea came directly from Ludwig Mies van der Rohe and his Nationalgalerie in Berlin. Mies had arranged for the entire exhibition system in the upstairs hall to make use of suspended elements. The problem is that the building's spans are so large that the temperature fluctuation between day and night elastically stretches the ceiling beams and consequently the museum's suspension system. I know this because in 2000 we had an exhibition of my work in which it was not walls but tables that were suspended. I also used the Beaubourg suspension system years later in the Paul Klee Museum in Berne, with the addition of a panic device to prevent the panels from moving.

To come back to the Beaubourg museum approach, with all the respect I have for Aulenti, whom I have always loved and who has done some extraordinary things, her intervention has somewhat plastered over the Centre's spaces. But it's not too bad because after a few decades you can remove the plaster and put everything back into question.

So you can understand the value of this work: Beaubourg lives in time. Architecture lives in time. Luciano Berio used to tell me—he was talking about music, but in some ways he also was talking about architecture—that these works live over long periods, like forests, like rivers, like mountains. Beaubourg lives for long periods. What is twenty-five years? Beaubourg is an architecture to be measured over five hundred years, or perhaps even longer.

It is an idea that was very clear to President Pompidou. When we went to Paris after the results of the competition were published, Pompidou invited us to the Elysée Palace. In front of some very strange young people in somewhat improvised clothes, Pompidou looked us in the eye and said in excellent French that we could only understand because of the simplicity of the sentence: "Do you realize, gentlemen"—he called us by name, "Monsieur Piano and Monsieur Rogers"—"that this building will have a life of five hundred years?" *Cinq-cents années* were his precise words. In fact, we looked at each other a little astonished as we had not done anything since we were students that would last more than six months or a year at most.

Beaubourg is destined to live a long time and you have plenty of time to put the plaster on it, take it off and start again. Of course, the fewer mistakes you make, the better, but it remains a work that can withstand those mistakes.

And I repeat that it is not even a Beaubourg building, it is like a bridge or an infrastructure, like the banks of a river, or like a bridge crossing the Seine, and the testimony is its structure with slabs that bear a capacity of 600 kilos per square meter to ensure that anything can happen on their surface... and anything does happen on them.

Over this long period with Richard we theorized something that was finally put into practice. It was the idea that every quarter of a century Beaubourg should stop for a moment to rethink itself. Isn't it true that in 1997–2000, i.e., almost a quarter of a century after its inauguration, Beaubourg stopped to make way for a series of transformations?

The offices moved to free up space for exhibitions, the library moved from a three-story configuration to a two-story one. So there was an internal revolution, and not a small one. And as it happens, around 2025, that is half a century after its creation, Beaubourg will stop again. This pace, this flexibility if we want to call it by a name that is dear to us, is not a technical issue. It is an ethical issue and also a cultural issue. It is the same approach that we use for hospitals, including the large hospital in Paris: an infrastructure that must be able to change over time to reflect the unforeseen and rapid evolution of medicine.

Beaubourg was designed for this kind of inherent temporality and flexibility and today it has the strength to withstand and resist any transformation. Today it is perhaps even more fascinating than the day it was inaugurated because it possesses the patina of time. In a few years it will complete half a century. I don't want to say that it doesn't need any repairs, but I must admit that the patina of time reinforces its belonging to the city, and that is exactly how two bad boys thought of it fifty years ago.

BH The urban dimension you mention is one of the most fascinating and at the same time controversial aspects of the project. When you presented the project at a press conference on July 19, 1971, to an audience irritated by the appearance of a "valise," a "barrage," a "boite métallique" (a suitcase, a dam, a metal box) in the heart of Paris, one of the strongest ideas behind your project must have escaped them: Beaubourg is a technological device for the rehabilitation of the historic center. Isn't it true that Beaubourg was born as a sunken square connected to the Halles and the Marais; a piazza that guts the underground and takes over part of it, from the cellars of the buildings in rue Saint-Martin to the underground of rue du Renard? How do you judge the fortunes of this idea?

RP It's a complex question because Richard and I were been looking for this adhesion to the city from the conception of the competition project, and I think this has to do with the influence of Italian culture. Richard and I spoke Italian until the last day, even though we worked in Paris and London. I was born in Genoa and Richard in Florence. It is not that we were two very cultivated guys but we both had an attraction for a certain humanistic dimension, a certain vision of the city and urbanity.
By the way, the term "urban" is particularly fascinating because it designates not only an inhabitant of the city but also a civilized person, a person who behaves in an urban way. Urbanity, therefore, is not only belonging to the city but is also a way of being that comes close to the concept of civilization. The partnership with Richard was born out of this common orientation. We were two different people—Richard had a different approach from mine and was undoubtedly a more cultivated person—but we had this common vision for the city and urbanity. It was from the study of the city and the research we devoted to it in the years that followed that Richard wrote books and was awarded the title of Lord while I was made a senator for life and then worked on the suburbs.
This urge for urbanity in Beaubourg resulted in the decision to allocate half the land for a piazza—a crazy idea when you consider the square footage required by the competition. Yet we were convinced that Beaubourg needed a void, that it needed a piazza. During its development, we made it slanted a bit like the Piazza del Campo in Siena.
It is clear that that Italian piazza with its particular inclination and its Italian context has nothing to do with the plateau Beaubourg, but somehow this kind of space was a constant of the European city for us. We even designed an underground tunnel from the Forum des Halles past boulevard [de] Sébastopol to bring the metropolitan crowd directly onto the piazza.
Originally, the piazza did not occupy only half of the site, it stretched over all the available land, so the building had to rise from the ground like a flying vessel or a spaceship that had landed in Paris.
It could not touch the ground because that surface had to exist entirely for the city. At the Whitney Museum I did the same thing, a vessel raised from the ground, but it is not a formalism, because what is important is to leave the ground for the city and its inhabitants.
When we won the competition, our interlocutors immediately explained to us that we were neither in Genoa nor in Florence. We were in Paris with a cold and windy climate and therefore incompatible with the kind of urban space we imagined for the plateau Beaubourg. This is true, at least in part...but this idea that the building would avoid the ground, so that at street level there would be a total opening, was not wrong. Perhaps it was a utopia, but a feasible utopia. We tried to make it happen, but in the end we were forced to enclose the void under the building with the exception of the two outermost bays, to the north and south, where this crossing space remained for a few years, until it was closed in turn to gain space.

In short, the urbanity of Beaubourg was never something added on but a component that was part of the project from the very beginning. Richard and I felt sincerely and fairly that our Beaubourg was not a gesture of disdain or disrespect for the historicity of the city, but reflected the idea that the city is a place of surprises. In all cities, the urban fabric is interrupted by works that are out of context and at the same time surprising, starting with the cathedrals, which we could define as spaceships landed in the middle of the medieval city. What I mean is that a city does not have a flat electrocardiogram, it is not homogeneous, and in this sense the fact of having created a *clairière*, a clearing, allows this object to land there.

Also part of this project of Beaubourg as an urban machine is the pedestrianization of rue Saint-Martin to further extend this piazza and give this street, too, to passers-by. The fact of pedestrianizing a street, strange as it may seem to you, was absolutely sacrilegious in 1971. When we went to the Prefect of Paris—at that time there was no mayor—he told us that our proposal was absolutely unfeasible because it would block the traffic of the whole of Paris.

Yet we did it.

The idea of this piazza also involved the use of "*pavés*," i.e. the paving typical of the historic city. Here, too, the prefect tried to dissuade us from using them. "My friends," he told us, "you are crazy. Four years ago, in 1968, the young Parisian students were shouting in the streets 'sous les pavés la plage' and throwing those *pavés* at the police." Those kids had discovered that under the *pavés* was the beach, the beach of the imagination of the youth revolution, and that's why those *pavés* had to be removed, in my opinion... Imagine if the prefect could let us install thousands of *pavés* in the heart of Paris. But do you know what we ended up putting on the piazza?

BH *Pavés*, naturally...

RP *Pavés*, indeed. Of course, we had to cement them, more or less. What I want to say to you is that this idea of urbanity touches not only on the notion of a large space or the pedestrianization of a street, but also on topical questions, even on material. In this regard there are also the large air intakes arranged on rue Saint-Martin. With these large ducts on the side of the piazza, we certainly did not intend to disrespect the urbanity of Beaubourg, on the contrary...we wanted to disclose the fact that there is something underneath the piazza, there is an underground building and these ducts are necessary to make it breathe. When we installed the vents during construction, the Prefect called us and forced us to remove them and, with the complicity of Bordaz, who was a genius, we decided to store them temporarily in a warehouse.

A few months later, we tried again and installed them again on the piazza. The call from the refect was not long in coming. "As long as I am alive," he told us, "these things will find no place in the historic center of Paris." A few months later the Prefect passed away and it was only after this sorrowful event that we were able to install the air intakes you see on the piazza.

To conclude the question, you have to understand that Beaubourg's relationship with urbanity, its being a machine for the city, was never linear, but the swinging and unpredictable result of a thousand adventures. I like to think that Beaubourg flirted with the city but it was always an unlikely if not impossible love affair of a strange vessel suspended over the ground but also an underground building. Umberto Eco, with whom I shared a beautiful friendship, wrote about Beaubourg in a passage of his *Foucault's Pendulum*, describing these vents as the way to make what he called "the underground realm of Paris" breathe.

You have to know that at the time of the competition, the client was convinced that the French would come to this grandiose Parisian *maison de la culture* from all corners of France, which is why the project had to include a huge multi-story under-

ground parking lot where parking spaces for coaches would also be included. These vehicles stopped arriving after some time and left the Centre with a huge empty space that will have to be transformed into something else.
What I want to say is that the urbanity of the Centre also reaches into the underground life of the piazza. Beaubourg is like an iceberg. If you look at the square footage, the ratio of above-ground to underground spaces is practically 1:1. The underground spaces are one of the themes at the center of the forthcoming transformation of the Centre, and the same applies to the question of the urbanity of Beaubourg, to be restored and strengthened by increasing the transparency and porosity of the ground floor.
Rethinking the urbanity of Beaubourg also means considering its immediate context. As with any monument, in the case of Beaubourg, the surrounding buildings become tourist sites for refreshments and souvenirs.

BH If the Centre Pompidou and its piazza were really an urban generator, what kind of construction site would have to be imagined in order not to lose this urbanity and this relationship with the crowd and the Parisians?

RP This is a really good topic and at the same time it is complicated to make major interventions on a building without closing it. So what always happens is that the building closes and its activities have to be relocated elsewhere. The institutions survive and the building, we could say, goes into apnea. The case of Beaubourg is very complex because being in a very dense area of the historic center, the building site can only be installed on the piazza. It is a slow construction site that will take several years and this might seem strange given that it will take almost as long as the time needed to construct the building. These are two different operations.
As I was telling you about the Forum, when the construction site of a work is finished, a special energy is released. I am thinking of the Genoa bridge where this energy also had to do with a dramatic event and generated a unique convergence in terms of both logistics and politics. I'm also thinking of the project I did at Potsdamer Platz in Berlin where this energy released by the construction site generated unique episodes such as a crane concert we did with Daniel Barenboim in 1994. This is also true of Beaubourg and the Halles building site, which since the foundation excavations have been transformed into film sets for movies—events that helped generate a real sense of anticipation in the city.
Yet as I told you, the transformation site is different from a construction site, and Beaubourg must be completely emptied in order to proceed with the rehabilitation of the interiors, and it does not even make sense to speak of access to the building because it will be empty, still there but in apnea. The effort that will have to be made is to find strategies so that everything around it does not die, and this is something I would like to propose to the municipality because it is up to the institutions to come up with a strategy for the neighborhood.

BH I would like to return one last time to the question of the works that will affect the Centre in the coming years. Born as an anti-monument to dissolve architecture into crowd infrastructure and transformed into an iconic monument loved and defended by public opinion, what is the guideline you feel you can suggest for the Centre's upcoming rehabilitation works? What does it mean, in other words, to "restore" a device born to evolve and change over time?

RP I wouldn't know how to define it, but I think I do because I am doing it somehow. As you know, my office is three hundred meters from Beaubourg and I often call myself—I am—the Quasimodo of Beaubourg because I am in it. Before COVID—now I intend to resume this habit—I always went to lunch one Sunday of the month at Beaubourg and I can claim to know every bolt of it. The transformation that Beaubourg needs must be what I have defined as mending, that is, noble, careful, artisanal work that must understand the fabric in order to repair it. The ideas that generated it and the structural skeleton that supports it have made Beaubourg alive and able to withstand time and transformations that have to do with the evolution of architecture and its materials.

It is not impossible and we human beings are the proof. When we grow old, we do not betray our physiognomy. Indeed, in some cases when we are old, we are even more beautiful, because time leaves traces of what we have been on us. One has the face one deserves and, in a way, Beaubourg also has the face it deserves because it bears the traces of time and even those of the changes it might undergo tomorrow.

If we stick to the metaphor of the human being, one could certainly resort to cosmetic surgery but I would not suggest it because it would be a betrayal of one's physiognomy. Similarly, a building should not transform itself with operations that betray its physiognomy but with metamorphoses that belong to the philosophy that generated it. This is the natural way for Beaubourg to evolve. I would never betray the *pavés* because they are part of the very essence of the building, and likewise I would betray neither the structural skeleton, nor the transparencies of the envelope, nor the air intakes that make Beaubourg breathe. On the other hand, there are things destined to change and it is logical that this should be the case in an institution, like Beaubourg, dedicated to culture in constant evolution.

This is what happened to the BPI imagined by Jean-Pierre Seguin. In the competition, he imagined a large reading room accompanied by two floors, one upper and the other lower, intended for the storage of books. While fine-tuning the project with our help, he rethought this environment as a more open place where the book shelves are accessible to readers—something revolutionary for a public library containing one million books. Since the opening, the library has changed again, starting with the area dedicated to studying and reading newspapers, the newspaper library. I do not want to say that the library is destined to disappear because I believe that books will never cease to exist, but I do believe that this institution will continue to undergo transformations that have to do with culture, which by its very nature is an immaterial, volatile, and mobile matter.

The good fortune and strength of Beaubourg to conclude is that of a building designed to be both tolerant and resistant to time and change, like a steed that bears the weight of its rider and with the same ease is capable of unseating the rider and shaking off anything that bothers it.

<.2

POMPIDOU'S FIRST DRAFT FOR THE CREATION OF A MONUMENT ON THE PLATEAU BEAUBOURG

Archives nationales,
Pierrefitte Sur-Seine, Paris,
Private archives, Collection
Henri Domerg, 574 AP,
Folder 10.

The Presidency of the Republic
Paris, 28th November 1969

[*To the attention of*]
Mr Edmond Michelet
Minister of State
Responsible for Cultural Affairs
3, rue de Valois — Paris

My dear Minister,

If the French of today can, in so many respects, compare themselves with their ancestors without blushing, they have, however, admittedly, since the beginning of the century, given too little lustre to architectural creation. And in Paris in particular, there are few examples of those monuments, witnesses of an era, which have always been the signature of the prestige of a nation.

Today we have the opportunity to fill this gap, since we have a vast space available in the heart of the capital, the site of Les Halles.

I would therefore like to see the project of constructing a prestigious building on this site, the cultural purpose of which has yet to be defined, but which we hope will be open to the present and the future and devoted in particular to contemporary art and thought.

I would like to ask you to study in depth the architectural, cultural, legal and financial aspects of such a project, to the elaboration of which I will give my personal attention.

Please accept, my dear Minister, the expression of my warmest regards.

Georges Pompidou

Handwritten note by
Georges Pompidou.

Mr. Domerg,

I have written a more precise letter than this one for the sake of the [forecoming] presentation.
I wouldn't want to write without having details about the certain availability of the plateau Beaubourg, without having seen the Prefect of Paris (if, as I believe, the land belongs to the City) and without having spoken to Mr. Giscard d'Estaing about it, because, once the thing is underway, I want it to be done quickly.
But as some people think it is lavish, I will wait until the beginning of 1970.

<.3

POMPIDOU'S SECOND DRAFT FOR THE CREATION OF A MONUMENT ON THE PLATEAU BEAUBOURG

Archives nationales,
Pierrefitte Sur-Seine, Paris,
Private archives, Collection
Henri Domerg, 574 AP,
Folder 10.

The Presidency of the Republic
Paris, 15th December 1969

[To the attention of]
Mr Edmond Michelet
Minister of State
Responsible for Cultural Affairs
3, Rue de Valois — Paris

My Dear Minister,

Following the decision taken by the Select Council on December 11 to build a monumental complex devoted to contemporary art on the site of the plateau Beaubourg, I feel I must give you some details of how I envision this project.

It seems to me that the first precaution to be taken without delay is to ask the Prefect of Paris to confirm that the City is willing to give up the land free of charge, if the State assumes all the costs of development and construction. Probably an agreement will have to be made to this effect, which should not include any imposition [by the City] regarding the [architectural] conception and internal organization of the future monument. It goes without saying that construction cannot be started without the subsequent collection of legal permits and the approval of the Paris Council, but the initial agreement only concerns the provision of the site.

At the same time as this discussion with the City, the departments [of your Ministry] will have to draft the notice of competition. I want it to be as flexible as possible. This means that the prescriptions will have to include only a few data related to the projected use of space, and it will be up to the architects to draw up their designs based on this data, without having to worry about regulations such as those related to height limits. Only at a second stage and in relation to the projects selected for their aesthetic quality and their adaptation to the needs of a modern art center, will it be possible to take a position on the height problem.

We must also make sure that the competition is accessible to all talented architects, even if they are young and lack the financial means [to participate]. The conditions for organizing the competition must therefore provide, in forms to be defined, that any architect whose project is selected will be remunerated for the work and costs incurred.

Please have financial forecasts drawn up for this purpose, so that the Minister of Economy and Finance can, for his part, release the necessary sums, considered as an exceptional supplement to your budget.

The architectural complex should include not only a large museum of painting and sculpture, but also special facilities devoted to music, records, and possibly cinema and theatrical research. It would be good if the project also included a library, or at least a collection containing all works on the arts and their most recent development.

There are two important issues on which I would appreciate your opinion.
Should foreign architects be admitted to the competition?
What should be the composition of the jury?

On this last point, in any case, it seems essential to me that a preponderant part in the jury should be reserved for some world-renowned foreign architects, as well as for the "users" of the building, such as the director of a modern art museum, a great musician, etc.

You know, my dear minister, my personal interest in this project. You have kindly confirmed to me that yours is not inferior. Since we are faced with a whole series of timelines that cannot be reduced beyond a certain extent, it is important to move quickly and start the preliminary stages and studies without delay. I am counting on you and the resources you have for this.

Please accept, my dear minister, the assurance of my highest consideration.

Georges Pompidou

<.4

RICHARD ROGERS' S MEMORANDUM FOR THE PARTICIPATION TO BEAUBOURG COMPETITION

RSHP (formerly Rogers Stirk Harbour + Partners) Archives, London, Collection C01, Projet J0099, Folder ARC73279.

Beaubourg Centre

Programme: A 20th Century, people's art, research and information centre. Libraries, Modern Arts Museum, multi-purpose halls for music, cinemas, theatres, industrial design.
Design Centre, music research, lectures, seminars.
Approx. 1,000,000 sq. ft. including 250,000 sq. ft. parking 10,000 visitors daily.
Visitors will arrive at basement and ground floors and their movement system is one of the keys, so that they see and partake in the centre.
The centre may also be sub-divided into Readers and Visitors, ie, libraries and art centres.
Flexibility and freedom of movement (A sort of University of Berlin?). "The centre will be an extension of urban fabric," page 11 [of the Competition Brief] "A coherent entity, must offer the widest possibilities of flexibility and adaptation," page 27.

Site: Central Paris, 3 blocks away from les Halles, in 5 storey, 19th Century housing and commercial area. Much of this area is being renewed.
Plot ratio: approx 4:1.
Underpasses will link this area with les Halles.
The whole area needs mixing in with the New Centre. There are complex circulation problems both in and around the centre. Horizontal and vertical - above and below ground.

Rules: Single stage – ugh! "The competition should permit the designation of the Architect to whom the final execution of the project will be given," page 27. The possibility of realising the project with the time limits 73, 74, 75 will be taken into consideration — ugh!

Completion: Despatch 16th June / Arrival 24th June

Jury: E. Aillaud, Sir Frank Francis (British Museum), Philip Johnson (strong & eratic [*sic*]), Laclotte, Niemeyer (ugh!), Picon, Prouvé (good), Sandberg (Istrate [sic: first rate] Curator), Utzon (good)

Prizes: Total 550,000 Francs / Winner 250,000 Francs / 30 indemnities of 10,000 Francs. One first prize may be awarded if "The decision of the jury does not imply any inherent right to executing..." ugh! Page 32.

Drawings: 8 pages text maximum / Master plan and section 1:500 / Exploded axonometric perspective of all levels in colour / One plan 1:200 / Two sections 1:20 / 1 model 1:500 – 6 photos off.

Comments: The scheme is very exciting and relevant with complex circulation internally and interesting urban problems.

There are vast volumes.
The Library and the Museum alone are each over 15,000 sq. m. and the temporary exhibition space 4,000 sq. m. is as big as the Burrel [*sic*] exhibition space.
The programme is very well documented and volumes broken down and circulation links shown.

Summing Up: I don't like the following.
It's so political that even without the written loopholes I don't believe there is more than a one in four chance of it ever being built (the prize money is not bad). It's very complex and will need 100 hours partners time and 300 hours others,ie, 500 hours approx. by 15th June.
This means we must start this week.
Even if Renzo, Su and I spent 50% of the next fortnight, ie, approx. 100 hours — what about Cambridge, Burrel [*sic*], Roof extension, Basildon and work getting.
I suspect the only person who could complete it is JY, say 100 hours, who is already doing Camden Mews, Cornwall, and Burrell! Dom may be willing to put in 200 hours, ie, 36 hours a week, but he can't do Burrel [*sic*] and what about his own work?
I don't like the fact that it is a single stage.
I don't much like the jury.
There is no assurance that the same jury will be appointed for the second stage of the competition.
The building will be a route and flex. Volume building.
I don't think we can do both Burrel [*sic*] and Beaubourg and I would access Burrel [*sic*] as totalling 200 hours, being half complete.
It has to be in on May 28th as against June 15th.

Richard Rogers

January 1971

Circulation: Su Rogers / John Young / Renzo Piano / Marco Goldschmied

Handwritten note
by Richard Rogers.

I don't like the socio political overtones.
Centralisation is the danger.

The rest of the note has been
torn off, probably by Richard
Rogers himself.

<.5

WINNERS' COMPETITION REPORT ON THE CENTRE BEAUBOURG

Archives nationales, Pierrefitte Sur-Seine, Paris, Public Archives, Collection Construction et aménagement du Centre National d'art et de culture Georges Pompidou, de l'établissement public du Centre Beaubourg au Cnac-Gp, 20100307, Folder 19.

1. General expose on the architectural concept with reference to the guiding principles of the centre: We recommend that the Plateau Beaubourg is developed as a "Live Centre of Information" covering Paris and beyond. It is a meeting place for the people. This centre of constantly changing information is a cross between an information-orientated, computerised Times Square and the British Museum, with the stress on two-way participation between people and activities/exhibits.

The Plateau Beaubourg information centre will be linked up with information dispersal and collection centres throughout France and beyond; for example, university centres, town halls, etc.

Information is shown in three areas: 1) Within the building, which offers a number of large, flexible, uninterrupted floor areas (varying between 5500-7500 sq.m.) housing books, fine arts, architecture, cinema and industrial design, etc; 2) On two long facades, one facing west across a sunken square and the other facing rue Saint-Martin.

A 3-dimensional loadbearing wall carries constantly changing information, news, what's on in Paris, art works, traffic situation, maps, weather and financial reports, cinema, television, robots, temporary structures, electronic two-way games and information, etc. The facade facing rue du Renard will have visual displays related to moving traffic, whilst the facade facing the sunken square will relate to pedestrians; 3) The large sunken square, including the open area under the building and the area around the edge of the square, is the horizontal continuity of the facade and will have, apart from the above-mentioned items, such things as mobile exhibitions, live theatre and music, games, stalls, meetings, parades, competitions, etc. Around the edge of the square are shops, cafes, children's reception area, current events rooms, information rooms, Design Centre, etc. These areas, many of which lie along pedestrian underpasses, act as filters and links with surrounding pedestrian environment.

2. Urban integration: In order to segregate pedestrians and vehicles, a pedestrianized sunken square has been formed 3.20 m below ground level, which links through at low level to the surrounding pedestrian routes. Rue de la Reynie is sunk to the same level, thereby forming an extension of the square. We propose closing rue Saint-Martin and removing it, opening the cellars and front doors of the neighbouring housing directly on to the sunken square, if possible converting the houses into studios and dwellings related to the new centre. The cellars and shops above being used for cafes, restaurants, reception areas, information areas and other commercial and cultural activities and thereby giving more life to the square, whilst at the same

time enlarging it, removing an unnecessary vehicular obstacle in a major pedestrian area and enhancing the scale of the square.
The building in the square has two scales. The 3-dimensional steel grill on the low long side is light, semi-transparent and higher than the neighbouring existing buildings. The much lower enclosed volume inside is broken up by the grill and the applied information coming down in scale at the south end, with stepped terraces to relate to the neighbouring buildings. The type and display of the information on rue du Renard will be related to moving vehicles and passing pedestrians, whilst that on the square will be related to more static viewing points.
The building is lifted on piloti [*sic*], well above ground level, so that it is possible from rue du Renard to see under the building the whole of the facades of the houses on rue Saint-Martin, whilst on entering the square from Les Halles direction, one is faced by the information grill.

3. Unity of the centre: See paragraphs 1, 2 and 5.

4. Flexibility capacity of the centre: The building offers maximum flexibility of use. Totally uninterrupted floor space is achieved by limiting all vertical structure, servicing and movement to the exterior. 3-dimensional walls, floors and partitions may be unclipped and/or extended at will; offices may be positioned anywhere, more highly serviced areas will tend to be located near the exterior for easier connections with vertical runs. Areas needing view, uninterrupted day-light and/or open space, such as the roof top restaurant, with its view over Paris, experimental and temporary exhibitions, outdoor museum, children's reception area, are located either on the roof on the south end of the building, with its view towards the Seine to the north, or in the square below, all areas free of the vertical grill. The roof itself is completely clear for display and community use, the restaurant being suspended over it. Three types of panels are offered for differing situations: 1) A highly insulated, lightweight, cored, solid panel; 2) A highly insulated, translucent panel, such as Okalux laminate, (hermetically sealed, insulating slab of colour less, translucent capillary tubes); 3) Glass.
All lifts and escalators are clipped on to the facade and can be changed if the intensity of use increases or the positions of the departments or their entrances are changed. The external structural grill is designed to carry a constantly changing clip-on system of information. Cranes on the roof lift and maintain the different clip-on parts of the building, from wall panels to electric components.
The square is a free open space used for congregation of people and the exhibition of things.
The building stands on piloti [*sic*], clear of the

square, so that the area underneath is protected from the weather; also temporary structures can easily be erected. Major, socially relevant, information will be found in the square, including centres for disseminating information on the latest world catastrophies [sic: catastrophes] and the collection of aid. Around the square are a variety of interchangeable smaller enclosed spaces – previously described.

5. Access and circulation: Pedestrian pass under the neighbouring roads on the way permeating through many of the "information and commercial activities" before entering the sunken square, such as under rue du Renard, where there are the current events room, industrial design permanent galleries and documentation rooms, or the sunken plateau de la Reynie, or from Les Halles under and along rue de Venise. We recommend bringing up the underpass from Les Halles so that it opens into plateau Beaubourg at the level of square 32.8 m. The removal of rue Saint-Martin helps move pedestrians in from the west side, see paragraph 2.
The car park for visitors and personnel is on three floors beneath the square. Access is by means of two entry and two exit points on the underground road system. Cars enter from the west via the underground road under the rue Aubry le Boucher and from the east via a ramp connecting the underground road with the rue Rambuteau near its junction with the rue du Renard. The exits are westwards, towards Les Halles and eastwards on to the ramp connecting with the rue Saint-Merri. Because of its large size, and to simplify management, the car park is split into two parts, with limited interconnection for vehicles. This arrangement provides access from all directions and sufficient road space for the peak traffic generation. In the short term, before the construction of the link between the underground road and rue Rambuteau, the car park will operate as a single unit with one entrance and two exits.
A separate underground coach park is proposed on one level, adjacent to a western boundary of the site, with one entry and one exit point on to the underground road system. There is space for the future expansion of the coach park beneath rue Saint-Martin. To service the centre, the square and properties fronting on the pedestrianised [sic: pedestrianized] rue Saint-Martin and to provide access for fire engines, ramps are shown connecting the square with rue Rambuteau. An enclosed service yard in the open air, with a covered loading bay, is provided under the building. In view of the heavy traffic volumes on the surrounding roads it is proposed that servicing should take place at night.

6. Reception and orientation of visitors: For easy orientation and flexibility, all vertical movement takes place on the face of the building, so that it can clearly be seen by anyone viewing the building from the square in front. The only built form which interrupts the open square is the glazed reception area under the free-standing building. The reception is vertically linked, by the escalators and lifts, down through a wide opening in the square to the parking below and up the face of the building to the different departments. Each of the major department entrances are indicated on the facade by a clearly coded system.

7. Correlation between the programme and the project from A1 to D4: See paragraph 4.

8. Interrelationships: See paragraphs 2 and 4 and diagram of activities and interrelationships.
New Proposals: 1) The closing of rue Saint-Martin, see paragraph 2 for reasons; 2) The underground pedestrian route from Les Halles enters via a ramp from the west up to the level of the sunken square; 3) The forming of the maximum number of pedestrian routes under neighbouring roads.
To do this on rue Saint-Merri, we have slightly changed its proposed depth. 4) The basic idea is of an information centre which presents information on the outside, as well as on the inside, of the building, relays it and is linked up to other centres throughout the world.

9. Technical concept: Fire escapes can be freely located within the 3-dimensional grill on the outside of the building. For security everyone passes through the reception area, each department has a single supervised entrance. Closed circuit television will be used, plus all the usual security measures. Air conditioning is proposed to normal comfort standards by a system designed to maintain the flexibility and adaptability in space planning and usage which is considered essential in the philosophy of this building. Air conditioning system, therefore, will be on a modular basis, each plan module being 48 m wide by 12.8 m of the building length.
Central station air handling units located at roof level will thus be provided to serve each of the twelve modules over six floors. Each plant will supply a treated mixture of recirculated and fresh air, via vertical main supply ducts passing within the external structural framework, to branch ducts within the false ceiling space at each floor level. Sub-division and zoning re-heat boxes or volume controllers may be readily incorporated within the ceiling space to suit final requirements. Exhaust air will be extracted through ceiling voids into vertical shafts and returned to the central plants for recirculation as required. Areas with special ventilation/cooling loads, such as television studios, restaurants and so on, will be served by separate plants. Central refrigeration plant will be located within the basement area and will provide chilled water to the various air handling units. Hot water will be taken from the district mains at basement level to serve the various heater batteries as required. The structure is assembled from elements. The permanent elements are the columns and the cross members which provide basic stability. These columns are fabricated on site from steel tubes of the same external diameter but appropriate wall thicknesses [*sic*].
The movable parts are the floors and their supporting beams, which can be dismantled and re-positioned to produce a true future flexibility. A special friction collar has been used throughout and this is protected against fire and corrosion by filling the tubular spaces with treated water. The deflection of the floor elements is controlled by ensuring that the precast concrete topping acts monolithically with the steel supporting beams. Transverse stability is provided by the fire wall needed to separate the temporary from the permanent exhibition space and by infill panels at the end of the buildings.
These infill elements are also used to reduce the spans in the heavily loaded library areas.

10. Construction procedures and techniques:
See paragraph 9 for structural materials.
Wall panels are interchangeable depending on the different activities enclosed: 1) Glass; 2) Okalux laminate hermetically sealed insulating slab of colourless translucent capillary tubes; 3) An opaque, lightweight GRP clad, sandwich panel.
Internal partitions are demountable and acoustic.

Renzo Piano
Richard Rogers
Gianfranco Franchini
Ove Arup & Partners

June 1971

Next image — Piano+Rogers Architects and Ove Arup & Partners, centre national d'art et de culture Georges Pompidou, erection of the structural skeleton, 1974.

AUTHOR'S BIOGRAPHY

Boris Hamzeian (PhD École Polytechnique Fédérale de Lausanne–EPFL, 2021) is an architect and post-doctoral fellow in History of Architecture. His research focuses on post-war avant-garde architecture and, more particularly, on the so-called "tecnomorphic architecture," namely the experiments transferring in architecture the fabrication process, methods and aesthetics of industry and technology.
He published articles on the history of the Centre national d'art et de culture Georges Pompidou in Paris (subject of his PhD thesis, 2021) and UFO group, and works by OMA and Aldo Rossi.
He is one of the curators of the exhibition *Unidentified Flying Object (UFO), performer l'architecture* held at the Frac Centre-Val de Loire.

Hamzeian is pursuing his research on the architectural and construction history of the Centre Pompidou, focusing on its modification and restoration, as deputy researcher at the architecture service (MNAM-CCI) at the Centre Pompidou, Paris. He is pursuing the study of tecnomorphic architecture with research into the origins of Archigram group, as visiting scholar of Architectural Association School of London and Princeton University School of Architecture.

His research has been funded by the Federal Commission for Scholarships for Foreign Students (CFBE, 2015-2018), the Swiss National Science Foundation (SNSF, 2018, 2022), and the Directorate General for Contemporary Creativity of the Ministry of Culture (Italy) as part of the Italian Council program (IX edition, 2020).

His PhD thesis was shortlisted for the EPFL Doctorate Award 2022 and the Doctoral Program Thesis Distinction 2022, and won two thesis prizes granted by Institut Georges Pompidou and Fondazione Ing. Lino Gentilini (in colllaboration with Università di Trento).

He is member of the scientific committee of *Archphoto 2.0* magazine, member of the Construction History Society and co-founder of False Mirror Office.

www.borishamzeian.com

From the same publisher
Unidentifying Flying Object for Contemporary Architecture: UFO's Experiments Between Political Activism and Artistic Avant-Garde, 2022 (with Beatrice Lampariello and Andrea Anselmo, eds.)

ACKNOWLEDGEMENTS

My reconstruction of the history of the Centre Pompidou originates in an encounter with Renzo, Milly, and Lia Piano and the opportunity to work first as an intern at Renzo Piano Building Worskhop and then as a researcher at the Fondazione Renzo Piano. I extend my first thanks to them and to Shunji Ishida, the pillar and custodian of the history of this institution. It is through Ishida that I was able to get in touch with dozens of key players in Beaubourg's history and record their precious memories: from Piano+Rogers Architects, Laurie Abbott, Giorgio Bianchi, Cuno Brullmann, Mike Davies, Anthony Dugdale, Riccardo Franchini (for Gianfranco Franchini's account of history), Andrew Holmes, Flavio Marano, Noriaki Okabe, Bernard Plattner, Richard and Susan Rogers, and John Young; from Ove Arup & Partners, Henry Bardsley, Tom Barker, Alan Denney, Lennart Grut, and John Morrison; from the Délégation pour la réalisation du Centre Beaubourg, Philippe Robert and Germain Viatte. Special thanks must go to Richard Rogers, for his interest in my work and for facilitating its accomplishment by all means.

No history of the Centre Pompidou is possible without the patient work of preserving and transmitting the archival heritage related to the history of this institution. Nicoletta Durante, Chiara Bennati, Giovanna Langasco (Fondazione Renzo Piano), Stephen Barrett, Simon Smithson, Karen Firmin Cooper, Aymee Thorne Clarke (RSHP), Tristram Carfrae, Jennifer Greitschus, Andy Sedgwick and Daniel Imade (ARUP), Xavier Rey, Olivier Cinqualbre, Jean-Philippe Bonilli, Nicolas Liucci, Mica Gherghescu (Centre Pompidou), Vivien Richard (Archives nationales), Olivier Sibre (Institut Georges Pompidou), Edward Bottoms (Architectural Association Archives), Arnaud Dercelles (Fondation Le Corbusier), and the institutions they represent are some of the guardians of this heritage to whom I am grateful.

The drafting of this book is inseparable from the patient and passionate guidance of Roberto Gargiani and the invaluable advice of Beatrice Lampariello, and from discussions with figures such as Giovanni Galli, Anna Rosellini, Alexandre Gady, Bruno Marchand, Christophe Van Gerreway, Dominique Rouillard, Gabriele Del Mese, Stanislaus von Moos, Éric Lapierre, Nicola Braghieri, Elena Cogato Lanza and Emanuele Piccardo.

The writing of my research on the history of the Centre Pompidou and the publication of this book are also indebted to: the Fondazione Renzo Piano, ARUP, the directorate of the Architecture section and the LTH3 Laboratory of the École Polytechnique Fédérale da Lausanne-EPFL, the Federal Commission for Scholarships for Foreign Students–CFBE, the Swiss National Science Foundation–SNSF, the Institut Georges Pompidou, the Construction History Society, and the Centre national d'art et de culture Georges Pompidou.

I would particularly like to express my gratitude to Laurent Le Bon, president of the Centre Pompidou, who has chosen to embrace the history of his institution as a cornerstone of his presidency and, on the strength of this history, is about to take on one of the greatest challenges in the architecture debate of the last half-century, that of restoring a machine which was born out of obsolescence and has become a monument.

I would like to thank Nicola Masotti, Grace Sanguineti, Benedetta Fordred, Silvia Groaz, Gloria Castellini, Olmo Martellacci, Justine Souque, Andrea Charrier, Neethu Kizhakkedom, Léa Duvauchel, Gabriele Domaine, Rosalie Dobler, Raphaël Lemerle, and my fellow False Mirror Office members Andrea Anselmo, Filippo Fanciotti, Giovanni Glorialanza—my friends—and Samuel Perier, Baptiste Mossotti and Antonin Peyratou—my Tropic of Cancer.

BIBLIOGRAPHY

This book is based on an archival and documentary historical method that has prioritized the identification and analysis of all primary sources available to researchers today.
In reconstructing the history of the Centre Pompidou, the author consulted some 53,000 pages of textual and iconographic documentation held in public archives and private institutions, as well as available audiovisual documentation.
In addition, the author conducted more than fifty hours of interviews with the key players in the realization of the center including architects, engineers, curators, and public servants.
Excluding articles, essays, and monographs written between 1969 and 1977, the bibliography of published articles, essays, and monographs on the subject was used as a secondary source.
While waiting to publish a complete version of the bibliography and a selected anthology of the critical reception of the Centre Pompidou, a selected list of titles (sorted by type, chronology, and first author's surname) devoted to the origins of the Centre Pompidou (1968–1971) and the general presentation of the work is offered here.
For a more extensive bibliography, see: Harland, Phyllis, *Beaubourg Centre, Paris: A Bibliography* (Monticello IL – USA): Vance Bibliographies, 1988); Hamzeian, Boris, Centre national d'art et de culture Georges Pompidou: Monument national e Live Centre of Information. Cronache di idea, progetto e fabbricazione, 1968–1977 (Lausanne: École Polytechnique Fédérale de Lausanne-EPFL, 2021), 597–616.

PRIMARY SOURCES

Archival documentation

Institut Georges Pompidou, Paris:
- Madeleine Négrel, Georges Pompidou's Agendas, 1959–1960;
- Madeleine Négrel, Georges Pompidou's Agendas, 1961;
- Madeleine Négrel, Georges Pompidou's Agendas, 1962;
- Madeleine Négrel, Georges Pompidou's Agendas, 1963;
- Madeleine Négrel, Georges Pompidou's Agendas, 1965;
- Madeleine Négrel, Georges Pompidou's Agendas, 1966;
- Madeleine Négrel, Georges Pompidou's Agendas, 1968;
- Madeleine Négrel, Georges Pompidou's Agendas, 1969;
- Madeleine Négrel, Georges Pompidou's Agendas, 1970;
- Madeleine Négrel Georges Pompidou's Agendas, 1971;
- Interview with Henri Domerg, 1994.

Archives nationales, Pierrefitte-sur-Seine, Paris:
Public archives
- Collection *Construction et aménagement du Centre national d'art et de culture Georges Pompidou, de l'Établissement public du Centre Beaubourg au Cnac-Gp*, 20100307, folders 1, 4, 5, 7, 8, 10, 13, 15, 17, 18, 19, 20, 21, 22, 41, 43, 47, 49, 56, 57, 60, 61, 63, 70, 71, 74, 75, 76, 77, 78, 81, 86, 95, 96, 97, 128, 129, 152, 156, 158, 160, 161, 212, 213, 214, 215, 216, 218, 219, 220, 221, 222, 236, 238, 257, 258, 259, 260, 261, 266, 267, 269, 303, 304, 305, 306, 307, 308, 309, 310, 311, 312, 313, 365, 368, 421;
- Collection Direction générale des arts et des lettres (1959–1969), DGAL, folders F21NC1333, F218294, F218267, F218265, F218307.

Private archives
- Collection *Henri Domerg*, 574 AP, folders 8, 10, 12, 13, 18, 23, 40;
- Collection *Eugène Claudius-Petit*, 538 AP, folder 79;
- Collection *Sébastien Loste*, 640 AP, folders 100, 105.

Fondation Le Corbusier, Paris:
- Folders I3-18-1, G3-6-155, I3-18-96.

RSHP (formerly Rogers Stirk Harbour + Partners) Archives, London / Richard Rogers family private archives, London:
- Project J0002, folders ARC77583, ARC5, ARC77583, ARC77555, ARC77596;
- Project J00099, folders ARC31, ARC32, ARC71370, ARC73279, ARC77586, ARC83928, ARC83931, ARC83932, ARC83935, ARC83972, ARC83973, ARC83977, ARC84125, ARC84126, ARC84127, ARC84128, ARC84132, ARC84135, ARC84136, ARC84138, ARC84156, ARC84157, ARC89159, ARC84160, ARC84162, ARC84163, ARC84164, ARC88900, General Correspondence, photographs series 1, 2, 3, 4, 5, 6;
- Project JFB, folders ARC4, ARC81086;
- Project J0005, folders ARC73739, ARC73737.

Centre national d'art et de culture Georges Pompidou:
- Bibliothèque Kandinsky Collection *Jean Prouvé*, PROU, folders 25, 27, 28, 53, 68, 309, 310, 311, 311 BIS;
- Pole Archives, series APH 13408, APH 13409.

Arup Archives, London:
- Project 4123, folders 1, 25, 26, 32, 33, 37, 40, 55, 73, 74, 75, 76, 78, 84, 85, 86, 95, 96, 109, 110, 111, 160, 166, 182, 193, 211, 214, 234, 236, 238, 248, 249, 254, 264, 266, 269, 270, 288, 310, 332, 353, 354, 355, 364, 365, 367, 369, 370, 389, 399, 411, 421, Special 1.

Fondazione Renzo Piano, Genoa:
- Collection *Centre Beaubourg 1971–1977*, BE1 (drawings), folders E202-206, E058, rp7101_006, rp7101_007, rp7101_0010, rp7101_013, rp7101_014, Be 1035, Be 1036, Be 1037, Be 1038, Be 1039, Be 1040, Be 1041, Be 1042, Be 1047, Be 1056, Be 1062, Be 1079
- Other Collections (drawings), *Peniche* (PH 001, tubes 1 and 2), *Oil Stations*;
- Collection *Centre Beaubourg 1971–1977*, BE1 (photographs), folders "modelli mezzanini e struttura," "modelli struttura gialla," "modelli forum," "modelli con struttura gialla e galleria," "modelli as built," "modelli gerberette e impianti coding," "people," "reference," Be1-182, Be1-298, Be1-297, Be1-318, Be1-487, Be1-493, Be1-494 /
- Other Collections (photographs), *Genova 1970*, *Container, Scuola Materna a due aule*, *Yacht Club* (69YTC), *Quartiere Boschetto*;
- Private Collection *Renzo Piano*, Serie Grandi Viaggi;
- Library Renzo Piano Architetto.

Interviews

For Piano+Rogers Architects: Mike Davies (May 10, 2017), Richard Rogers (May 10, 2017), Andrew Holmes (June 21, 2017), Anthony Dugdale (June 23 2017), John Young (July 25, 2017, October 2017), Shunji Ishida (August 2017, October 2017, February 2018, May 2019, January 2020, September 2021, May 2022, June 2022, September 2022), Cuno Brullman (September 27, 2017, May 10, 2021), Susan Rogers (October 9, 2017), Flavio Marano (March 7, 2018), Riccardo Franchini (June 10, 2018), Renzo Piano (January 12, 2019, June 15, 2021, November 6, 2021, April 14, 2022), Bernard Plattner (May 1, 2021), Laurie Abbott (May 6, 2021), Noriaki Okabe (June 20, 2021), Henry Bardsley (December 16, 2021, September 6, 2022).

For Ove Arup & Partners: Lennart Grut (July 5, 2017, October 9, 2017, May 1, 2018, April 29, 2021); John Morrison (July 27, 2017); Tom Barker (September 27, 2017, May 30, 2018), Alan Denney (May 2021).

For the Delegation for the realisation of the Beaubourg Centre: Germain Viatte (January 2022).

Other participants in Beaubourg competition: Denise Scott Brown (February 13, 2017), Elia Zenghelis (May 24, 2017).

SECONDARY SOURCES

Articles

Badani, Daniel, Lyons, Eric, and Michel Weill, "UIA competitions. Centre Beaubourg," *UIA: revue de l'Union internationale des architectes*, no. 12 (1971), 2–33.

"Concours Beaubourg," *Architecture, mouvement, continuité–AMC*, vol. 23, no. 11 (1971), 1–28.

"Concours international du plateau Beaubourg," *L'Architecture d'Aujourd'hui*, no. 157 (1971), 6–18.

"Piano+Rogers=Beaubourg," *Domus*, no. 503 (1971), 1–7.

Établissement publique du Centre Beaubourg/Centre national d'art et de culture Georges Pompidou, "Centre du plateau Beaubourg: concours international d'idées," *Techniques et Architecture*, vol. 34, no. 3 (1972), 35–82.

Piano, Renzo, Richard Rogers et al., "Centre Beaubourg Paris: The Award-winning Scheme by Piano and Rogers," *Architectural Association Quarterly*, vol. 4, no. 1 (1972), 36–41.

"Le Centre Beaubourg," *Paris Projet*, vol. 7 (1972), pp. 6–61

Happold, Ted, Peter Rice et al., "Centre Beaubourg Special Issue," *The Arup Journal*, no. 3 (1973), 2–10.

Piano, Renzo and Richard Rogers, "Centre Culturel du plateau Beaubourg. Interview à Richard Rogers et Renzo Piano," *L'Architecture d'Aujourd'hui*, no. 168 (1973), 34–43.

Doniat, Gustave, "Beaubourg: un cœur nouveau pour le Paris de demain," *Construction moderne*, vol. 5, no. 9–12 (1974), 17–25.

"The Pompidou Centre," *The Architectural Review*, vol. 161, no. 963 (1977), 270–294.

Demoraine, Helene and Francois Barré (eds), "Le CNAC. Georges Pompidou," *L'Architecture d'Aujourd'hui*, no. 189 (1977), 40–80.

"Centre Pompidou," *Architectural Design*, vol. 47, no. 2 (1977), 86–151.

Bub, Jochen et al., "Frankreichs Centre national d'art et de culture Georges Pompidou in Paris," *Bauwelt*, vol. 68, no. 11 (1977), 316–334.

"Centre national d'art et de culture Georges Pompidou, Parigi," *Domus*, vol. 566 (1977), 1–37.

Futagawa, Yukio, "Centre Beaubourg. Piano+Rogers," *G. A. Global Architecture*, no. 44 (1977), 1–40.

Prouvé, Jean, "La permanence d'un choix," *L'Architecture d'Aujourd'hui*, no. 189 (1977), 48–49.

Happold, Ted, "Essential Engineer: A Book Review of An Engineer Imagines by Peter Rice," in *RSA Journal*, vol. 143, no. 5456 (1995), 85–86.

Holden, Susan, "Megastructures and Monuments: the Dilemma of Finding a Permanent Image of Change, the Plateau Beaubourg Competition, 1970–71," *Fabrications: The Journal of the Society of Architectural Historians Australia and New Zealand*, vol. 21, no. 2 (2012), 82–111.

Holden, Susan, "Possible Pompidous," *AA files*, vol. 70 (2015), 33–47.

Piano, Renzo, Rogers, Richard, and Enrique Walker, "Renzo Piano & Richard Rogers in Conversation with Enrique Walker," *AA Files*, no. 70 (2015), 46–59.

Books' chapters

Dini, Massimo, "Il centro culturale Georges Pompidou," in *Renzo Piano: projets et architectures 1964-1983* (Milan, Paris: Electa, Moniteur, 1983), 126–155.

Piano, Renzo, and Franck Renevier, "Le Centre culturel Georges-Pompidou 1971–1977, Paris," in *Chantier ouvert au public* (Paris: Arthaud, 1985), 47–71.

Piano, Renzo, "Il Centre Georges Pompidou e l'istituto musicale IRCAM 1971–1977," in *Dialoghi di cantiere* (Rome: Edizioni Laterza, 1986), 30–73.

Appleyard, Bryan, "3. Ciao vecchio" and "4. Steel Cuckoo," in *Richard Rogers: A Biography* (London: Faber & Faber, 1986), 105–219.

Rice, Peter, "Beaubourg," in *An Engineer Imagines* (London: Artemis, 1993), 25–46.

Rogers, Richard and Richard Burdett, "Centre Georges-Pompidou, Parigi, 1971–1977," in *Richard Rogers Partnership: opere e progetti* (Milan: Electa, 1995), 162–178.

Piano, Renzo, "Centro nazionale d'arte e di cultura Georges Pompidou," in *Giornale Di Bordo* (Florence: Passigli, 1997), 28–39.

Walker, Derek and Bill Addis, "Beaubourg," in *Happold: The Confidence to Build* (London: Taylor & Francis, 1997), 50–54.

Bordaz, Robert, "Du Centre Pompidou à Houston et Bari," in *Entretiens. Robert Bordaz, Renzo Piano* (Paris: Éditions Cercle d'Art, 1997), 11–51.

Dal Co, Francesco, "Beaubourg," in *Renzo Piano* (Milan: Electa, 2014), 15–115.

Rogers, Richard, "Centre Georges Pompidou," in *A Place for all People* (Canongate: Edinburgh, 2017), 108–153.

Books

Rival, Ned (ed.), *Déjà Paris demain: "Beaubourg-les Halles." Un dossier de Lintas-Paris* (Paris: La Table ronde, 1974).

Mollard, Claude, *L'enjeu du Centre Georges Pompidou* (Paris: Union générale d'éditions, 1976).

Bordaz, Robert, *Le Centre Pompidou: une nouvelle culture* (Paris: Ramsay, 1977).

Pierre Cabanne, *Le pouvoir culturel sous la Ve République* (Paris: Olivier Orban, 1981).

Hommage au président Georges Pompidou, un homme de culture (Paris: Artcurial, 1987).

Seguin, Jean-Pierre, *Comment est née la BPI: Invention de la médiathèque* (Paris: Centre Georges Pompidou, 1987).

Piano, Renzo, Rogers, Richard and Antoine Picon (ed.), *Du Plateau Beaubourg au Centre Pompidou* (Paris: Éditions du Centre Pompidou, 1987).

Silver, Nathan, *The Making of Beaubourg: A Building Biography of the Centre Pompidou, Paris* (Cambridge, Mass.: MIT Press, 1994).

Tétart, Philippe (ed.), *Georges Pompidou, homme de culture* (Paris: Éditions du Centre Pompidou, 1995).

Dufrêne, Bernadette, *La Création de Beaubourg* (Grenoble: Presses Universitaires de Grenoble, 2000).

Dufrêne, Bernadette, *Centre Pompidou: trente ans d'histoire* (Paris: Éditions du Centre Pompidou, 2007).

Fleury, Laurent, *Le cas Beaubourg: Mécénat d'état et démocratisation de la culture* (Paris: A. Colin, 2007).

Viatte, Germain, *Le Centre Pompidou: les années Beaubourg* (Paris: Gallimard, 2007).

Rattenbury, Kester and Samantha Hardingham, *Supercrit 3. Richard Rogers. The Pompidou Centre* (Oxon, New York: Routledge, 2012).

Dal Co, Francesco, *Centre Pompidou: Renzo Piano, Richard Rogers, and the Making of a Modern Monument* (New York: Yale University Press, 2016).

Ciccarelli, Lorenzo, *De Beaubourg à Pompidou I. Les architectes (1968–1971)* (Paris: Éditions B2, 2016).

Jankovic, Nikola, *De Beaubourg à Pompidou II. Le chantier (1971–1977)* (Paris: Éditions B2, 2016).

Pinto, Louis et al., *De Beaubourg à Pompidou III. La machine (1977–2017)* (Paris: Éditions B2, 2016).

Piano, Lia (ed.), *Centre Pompidou* (Genoa: Fondazione Renzo Piano, 2017).

Pompidou, Alain and Cesar Armand, *Pour l'amour de l'art. Une autre histoire des Pompidou* (Paris: Plon, 2017).

Theses and dissertations

Holden, Susan, "The 'Beaubourg Moment': Movement and the Temporality of Architecture," Brisbane, University of Queensland, 2012.
Branda, Ewan, "The Architecture of Information at Plateau Beaubourg," University of California, UCLA, Los Angeles, 2012.

Hamzeian, Boris, "Centre national d'art et de culture Georges Pompidou: Monument national e Live Centre of Information. Cronache di idea, progetto e fabbricazione, 1968–1977," École Polytechnique Fédérale de Lausanne-EPFL, Lausanne, 2021.

Other published works on the centre pompidou by Boris Hamzeian

Hamzeian, Boris, "The '3-dimensional Wall' of the Centre Pompidou. Genesis and Evolution of a Polyvalent Device," in Mascarenhas-Mateus, João et al. (eds.), *History of Construction Cultures: Proceedings of the 7th International Congress on Construction History (7ICCH 2021), 12–16 July 2021, Lisbon, Portugal* (Brussels: CRC–Taylor & Francis, 2021), vol. 1, 632–639.

Hamzeian, Boris, "The Evolution of the Cast Node of the Pompidou Centre: From the 'Friction Collar' to the 'Gerberette'," in Wouters, Ine et al. (eds.), *Building knowledge, Constructing History: Proceedings of the 6th International Congress on Construction History (6ICCH 2018), July 9–13, 2018, Brussels, Belgium* (Brussels: CRC–Taylor & Francis, 2018), vol. 2, 715–723.

Hamzeian, Boris, "The Evolution of the Pompidou Centre's Air Conditioning System. Toward a New Figure of Architecture," in Campbell, James et al. (eds.), *Studies in the History of services and construction. The proceedings of the fifth conference of the Construction History Society* (Cambridge: Construction History Society, 2018), 57–70.

IMAGE SOURCES AND CREDITS

Académie d'architecture/Cité de l'architecture & du patrimoine/ Archives d'architecture contempo-raine, Collection 258 AA (Louis Arretche), anonymous: p. 49.

Académie d'architecture/Cité de l'architecture & du patrimoine/ Archives d'architecture contemporaine, Collection 266 AA (Henry Bernard), ©ADAGP Paris 2022 (Henry Bernard), anonymous: p. 19.

Archiv für Architektur und Ingenieurbau – SAAI ©Frei Otto: p. 77.

Archives nationales, Pierrefitte-sur-Seine, Paris, Collection 19950353 (BPI): p. 37.

Archives nationales, Pierrefitte-sur-Seine, Paris, 20060200/1 (Bibliothèque des Halles): pp. 40–43.

Archives nationales, Pierrefitte-sur-Seine, Paris, Collection 20100307 (Centre Pompidou) ©Délégation pour la réalisation du Centre Beaubourg/Centre Pompidou: pp. 30–31, 51, 251, 255.

Archives nationales, Pierrefitte-sur-Seine, Paris, Collection AP 604 (Sébastien Loste): pp. 20–21.

Archivio 9999 (courtesy Elettra Fiumi): pp. 94–95.

Archivio Gianfranco Franchini (courtesy Riccardo Franchini): p. 103.

ARUP Archives ©Arup: p. 76, 200.

ARUP Archives ©Arup Associates: p. 164.

Photo ©Pierre Berdoy: p. 28.

Bibliothèque Kandinsky, Collection PROU (Prouvé) ©*Paris Demain. La ville en question, une proposition pour Paris* (press clipping): pp. 56–59.

Bibliothèque Kandinsky, Collection PROU (Prouvé), anonymous: p. 63.

Canadian Centre of Architecture CCA (gift of May Cutler) ©anonymous: p. 38.

Centre Pompidou, MNAM-CCI, anonymous: p. 19.

Centre Pompidou, MNAM-CCI ©ADAGP Paris 2022 (Yaacov Agam): p. 29.

Centre Pompidou, MNAM-CCI ©Renzo Piano, Richard Rogers (courtesy Fondazione Renzo Piano/Richard Rogers Estates): pp. 180–181.

Centre Pompidou, Pole Archives, Collection *Concours Centre Beaubourg*, Herrmann et Kraemer: pp. 232–247, 256–277, 281–285, 292–295, 305.

Centre Pompidou, Pole Archives, Collection *Concours Centre Beaubourg*, anonymous: pp. 296–297.

Anthony Dugdale Archives (courtesy Anthony Dugdale): p. 117.

Fondation Le Corbusier ©ADAGP Paris 2022 (Le Corbusier): p. 36.

Fondazione Renzo Piano, Projects/Photo Archives ©Renzo Piano Architetto: pp. 89, 102, 107.

Fondazione Renzo Piano, Photo Archives, anonymous: p. 111.

Fondazione Renzo Piano, Projects/Photo Archives ©Renzo Piano, Richard Rogers: pp. 205, 211, 219–221, 223.

Fondazione Renzo Piano, Renzo Piano Private Archive ©Photographer Renzo Piano: pp. 92–93, 134–135.

Fondazione Renzo Piano, Renzo Piano Private Archive, ©Photographer Renzo Piano (unknown press clipping): p. 117.

Fondazione Renzo Piano, Renzo Piano Architetto Library ©*Architectural Design* (press clipping): pp. 133, 170–171.

Fondazione Renzo Piano, Renzo Piano Architetto Library ©*Casabella* (press clipping): pp. 96–101, 150–151, 165, 175.

Fondazione Renzo Piano, Renzo Piano Architetto Library ©*Architectural Association Quarterly* (press clipping): p. 101.

Fondazione Renzo Piano, Renzo Piano Architetto Library ©*Sunday Times Supplements* (press clipping): pp. 162–163.

Solomon R. Guggenheim Museum, New York, ©Nicholas Ceglia: p. 39.

Boris Hamzeian Private Archives ©*Paris Projet* (press clipping): pp. 22–25.

Hundertwasser Archives ©Hundertwasser: pp. 64–65.

Norman Foster Foundation ©Foster Associates: p. 137.

RSHP Archives, anonymous (courtesy Fondazione Renzo Piano/Richard Rogers Estates): pp. 13, 328–329.

RSHP Archives ©Renzo Piano, Richard Rogers (courtesy Fondazione Renzo Piano/Richard Rogers Estates): pp. 116, 118–125, 130–133, 136, 153–155, 159, 186–191, 195, 201, 208–209.

RSHP Archives ©Richard Rogers Partnership (courtesy RSHP): 143.

RSHP Archives ©Richard+Su Rogers Architects (Richard Rogers, Susan Rogers): pp. 76, 88, 90–91.

Photo ©Tim Street Porter: p. 77.

Scala Archives (Whitney Museum of American Art), Jerry L. Thompson ©Scala: p. 49.

University of Pennsylvania Stuart Weitzman School of Design, Architectural Archives, Collection Venturi-Scott Brown: p. 169.

All the images of the projects participating in the Beaubourg competition are reproduced in the book in accordance with the concession of reproduction rights granted by the rights holders to the Délégation pour la réalisation du Centre Beaubourg (now Centre national d'art et de culture Georges Pompidou) in accordance with the in accordance with the regulation of the Concours pour la réalisation du Centre du plateau Beaubourg. For a list of rights holders, see the participants records in the poster attached to this volume.

ABBREVIATIONS

Archives

AGF: Private Archives of the family of Gianfranco Franchini, Genoa

AN: Archives nationales, Pierrefitte-Sur-Seine, Paris
Public archives
- BDH: Collection *Culture; Direction de l'architecture; Sous-direction création architecturale, constructions publiques; Division des constructions publiques; Bureau bâtiments civils (1969–1969), Projet de Bibliothèque des Halles,* 20060200
- CNACGP: Collection *Construction et aménagement du Centre national d'art et de culture Georges Pompidou, de l'établissement public du Centre Beaubourg au Cnac-Gp,* 20100307
- DGAL: Collection *Direction Générale des Arts et des Lettres (1959–1969)*
- FBPI: Collection *Bibliothèque publique d'information,* 19950353
- FPRGP: Collection *Présidence de la République Georges Pompidou,* 5 AG 2

Private archives
- FAP: Collection *Alain Pompidou,* 555 AP
- FECP: Collection *Eugene Claudius-Petit,* 538 AP
- FHD: Collection *Henri Domerg,* 574 AP
- PM AP: Collection *Premier Ministre ; Secrétariat général du Gouvernement; Directeur (1963–1994),* 19950486

AA: ARUP Archives, London
- 4123: Collection *Centre Pompidou of Paris*

BK: Bibliothèque Kandinsky/Centre national d'art et de culture Georges Pompidou, Paris
- FJP: Collection *Jean Prouve,* PROU
- FCP: Collection *Centre Georges Pompidou 1969–1973, concours d'architecture, presse, cartons,* F BVG TOF CGP

FLC: Fondation Le Corbusier, Paris

FRP: Fondazione Renzo Piano, Genoa
- BE01: Collection *Centre Pompidou di Parigi, 1971–1977*

IGP: Institut Georges Pompidou, Paris

RSHPA: Private Archives RSHP (formerly Rogers, Stirk, Harbour + Partners) Archives, London/ Private Archives of the family of Richard Rogers, London
- J0002: Collection *Mobile Hospital Module for the Association for Rural Aid in Medicine–ARAM*
- J0099: Collection *Centre Pompidou of Paris*
- JFB: Collection *Fitzroy Street/ Burleigh Street shopping center in Cambridge*

COLOPHON

PA: Pole Archives/Centre national d'art et de culture Georges Pompidou, Paris
– APH: Collection *Plans du concours international pour la réalisation du "Centre Beaubourg,"* 2016W035

Bibliographic abbreviation

F: Folder/Box

C: Collection

s. d.: Undated Document

s. a. : Unauthored Document

s. p. : Unpaged Document

The Live Centre of Information
From Pompidou to Beaubourg
1968–1971

Publisher:
Actar Publishers,
New York, Barcelona
www.actar.com

Graphic design:
Artiva® Design
Daniele De Batté
Davide Sossi
www.artiva.it

Editorial consultant:
Tadzio Koelb

Proofreading/copy editing:
Jack Pownell (index and preface)
Consultants (introduction, chapters, annexes)

Translations from Italian:
Christopher Huw Evans

Printing and binding:
Arlequin & Pierrot SL

Distribution:
Actar D, Inc. New York, Barcelona
– New York
440 Park Avenue South, 17th Fl
New York, NY 10016, USA
T +1 212 966 2207
salesnewyork@actar-d.com
– Barcelona
Roca i Battle 2-4
08023 Barcelona, SP
T +34 933 282 183
eurosales@actar-d.com

ISBN 978-1-63840-055-4

Library of Congress Control No.:
2022943652

Printed in Barcelona.

Published in November 2022.

The book is based on the EPFL PhD thesis (No. 7821), Centre national d'art et de culture Georges Pompidou: Monument national e Live Centre of Information Cronache di idea, progetto e fabbricazione, 1968–1977, defended at the École Polytechnique Fédérale de Lausanne–EPFL in October 2021 under the direction of Roberto Gargiani and funded by the Federal Commission for Scholarships for Foreign Students (CFBE) and the Swiss National Science Foundation (SNSF).

The research project was awarded with Institut Georges Pompidou Thesis special prize 2022, Fondazione Ing. Lino Gentilini 2022.

The research project was shortlisted for EPFL Doctorate Award 2022 and Doctoral Program Thesis Distinction 2022.

The publishing project is funded by École Polytechnique Fédérale de Lausanne–EPFL, Fondazione Renzo Piano, ARUP and Institut Georges Pompidou.

In partnership with Centre national d'art et de culture Georges Pompidou.

Centre Pompidou

EPFL

Schweizerische Eidgenossenschaft
Confédération suisse
Confederazione Svizzera
Confederaziun svizra

Swiss National Science Foundation

FONDAZIONE RENZO PIANO

ARUP

INSTITUT GEORGES POMPIDOU